REVIEW

OF

RESEARCH

CONTRIBUTORS

JERE CONFREY
LINDA DARLING-HAMMOND
LISA HUDSON
MAGDALENE LAMPERT
JUDITH WARREN LITTLE
JOHN MADDAUS
NEL NODDINGS
JEANNIE OAKES
PENELOPE L. PETERSON
RALPH T. PUTNAM
BRIAN ROWAN

IN EDUCATION

16   1990

COURTNEY B. CAZDEN
EDITOR
HARVARD UNIVERSITY
GRADUATE SCHOOL OF EDUCATION

PUBLISHED BY THE
AMERICAN EDUCATIONAL RESEARCH ASSOCIATION
1230 Seventeenth Street, NW
Washington, DC 20036-3078

*This volume is dedicated,
with special appreciation and affection,
to the memory of Marianne Amarel,
a member of the Editorial Board
for* Review of Research in Education,
Volumes 13–16.

Contents

I.
KNOWLEDGE AND LEARNING

Chapter 1

A Review of the Research on Student Conceptions in Mathematics, Science, and Programming

JERE CONFREY
Cornell University

Since the time of Piaget, researchers have been keenly interested in how students view the concepts of science, mathematics, and, more recently, programming. In their annual review of research in science education, Shymansky and Kyle (1988) mention nearly 100 studies on student conceptions since 1984; Pfundt and Duit (1985, 1988) have amassed a bibliography of 1,500 citations in science education alone. Review articles (Driver & Easley, 1978; Driver & Erickson, 1983; Eylon & Linn, 1988; Fisher & Lipson, 1983; Wittrock, 1977) report similarly high levels of activity. In mathematics A. Graeber and M. Johnson (personal communication, May 1989) report collecting over 600 articles on student misconceptions, and in biology Mintzes and Arnaudin (1984) report on 68 studies. Reviews on probability (Hawkins & Kapadia, 1984), statistics (Well, Pollatsek, Konold, & Hardiman, 1984), and programming (Pea, Soloway, & Spohrer, 1987) confirm the evidence of vigorous research activity. At two international conferences at Cornell University (Helm & Novak, 1983; Novak, 1987), researchers gathered from many countries to report on studies in this area. Given the sheer numbers of studies, an exhaustive review of student conceptions literature is prohibitive; however, these studies show evidence of reemerging themes, issues, and findings that provide a framework for this article.

To bound this endeavor, I will use the following selection procedure: (a) Research will be selected from mathematics (including statistics and probability), science, and programming; (b) research will focus on concept-specific studies and thus will exclude research on problem solving, novice/expert studies, and Piagetian stage research; and (c) within the

This work is funded under a grant from the National Science Foundation, No. MDR-8652-160.

concept-specific studies, the selected research will have employed alternative methodologies to short-answer, paper-and-pencil tests that report only on the performance level of students.

Although these decisions will eliminate from the review a variety of provocative and influential reports on learning, it allows for a review of a reasonably coherent body of literature. These selection procedures can be argued for on the grounds that all the research included is founded on the assumption that students enter instruction with firmly held beliefs and explanations for phenomena and relationships, and these beliefs are subject matter-specific and can be identified and confirmed only through methods that encourage children to be expressive and predictive.

WHAT ARE STUDENT CONCEPTIONS AND WHY STUDY THEM?

Osborne and Wittrock (1983) summarized the position of researchers on student conceptions succinctly in their statement that "children develop ideas about their world, develop meanings for words used in science [mathematics and programming], and develop strategies to obtain explanations for how and why things behave as they do" (p. 491). These categories of children's beliefs, theories, meanings, and explanations will form the basis of the use of the term *student conceptions.* Other researchers use other terms for these constellations of beliefs, including the following: children's science (Osborne & Freyberg, 1985), children's arithmetic (Ginsburg, 1977), mathematics of the tribe (Steffe, 1988), preconceptions (Ausubel, Novak, & Hanesian, 1978), naive theories (Resnick, 1983), conceptual primitives (Clement, 1982), private concepts (Sutton, 1980), and alternative frameworks (Driver, 1981). When those conceptions are deemed to be in conflict with the accepted meanings in science, math, or programming, the term *misconceptions* (Nesher, 1987; Perkins & Simmons, 1988) is used. (See Abimbola, 1988, for an interesting discussion of the significance of the different terms.)

Researchers' interest in student conceptions has been provoked by numerous studies indicating that (a) before formal study, persons have firmly held, descriptive, and explanatory systems for scientific and logico-mathematical phenomena, that is, systems of belief; (b) these systems of belief differ from what is incorporated into the standard curriculum; (c) certain constellations of these belief systems show remarkable consistency across ages, abilities, and nationalities; (d) these belief systems are resistant to change through traditional instruction (Champagne, Gunstone, & Klopfer, 1983; Osborne & Wittrock, 1983).

Because of these findings, researchers in these traditions are united in (a) their rejection of the tabula rasa assumption that students enter instruction with no preconceptions about a topic before it is taught, and (b) their belief that these naive ideas cannot easily be ignored or replaced through direct instruction or lecture (Gilbert, Osborne, & Fensham, 1982).

The framework for the review will consist of a proposed distinction among and discussion of three traditions of research on student conceptions and student learning, implications of this research for teaching, and suggestions for new directions for the research.

THREE FRAMEWORKS: PIAGETIAN GENETIC EPISTEMOLOGY, THE PHILOSOPHY OF SCIENCE, AND SYSTEMATIC ERRORS

The foundation for research on student conceptions comprises three major traditions, and each has its own epistemological assumptions. These are Piagetian studies in the tradition of genetic epistemology (Piaget, 1970); applications of the philosophy of science in the tradition of conceptual change (Kuhn, 1970; Lakatos, 1976; Lakatos & Musgrave, 1970; Popper, 1959, 1962; Toulmin, 1972); and research on systematic errors (Davis, 1980; Perkins & Simmons, 1988; VanLehn, 1982, 1983). Research in the first two areas tends to be on student conceptions in science and mathematics, whereas research in the third area focuses on mathematics and computer programming. As a way of distinguishing these three areas, I will refer to the first as Piagetian approaches to student conceptions, the second as philosophical approaches to students' alternative conceptions, and the third as information processing approaches to student misconceptions or systematic errors. These three categories are not exhaustive, nor are they mutually exclusive; they do, however, provide an organizing framework for this broad base of research and can be helpful in interpreting the commonalities, controversies, and inconsistencies within it.

Piagetian Studies of Student Conceptions: Research in the Tradition of Genetic Epistemology

Genetic epistemology is the study of the development (or genesis) of particular concepts over time in children. Considering the history of curriculum reform in the post-Sputnik era helps us to understand the role that Piaget and this Piagetian approach to research on student conceptions have played in the last three decades, particularly in the United States. In 1960, Bruner published *The Process of Education,* a report of the Woods Hole conference where a prestigious group of physicists, psychologists, educators, biologists, chemists, and mathematicians convened to devise a plan for overhauling and updating the curriculum in science and mathematics. In this report, Bruner emphasized the importance of structure in "fitting concepts together and aiding transfer," reviewed the Piagetian stage theory, and introduced the idea of a spiral curriculum.

Common Misinterpretations of Piaget's Genetic Epistemology

Stages as limitations. Bruner's discussion of stage theory (pp. 34–46) reveals the tendency for individuals who advocated structuring the curriculum in forms consistent with the structure of the discipline (as defined by practicing mathematicians, scientists, etc.) to misinterpret Piaget's genetic epistemology. Rather than interpreting Piaget's position as providing evidence that young children's conceptions may differ qualitatively from those of the experts, they interpreted Piaget as suggesting that certain ideas cannot be learned. For instance, Bruner characterizes the preoperational stage as a time of establishing relationships between experience and action but principally as a stage that lacks reversibility. Bruner concludes,

> Because of this fundamental lack the child cannot understand certain fundamental ideas that lie at the basis of mathematics and physics. . . . It goes without saying that teachers are limited in transmitting concepts to a child at this stage, even in a highly intuitive manner. (p. 35)

In other sections of the book, however, Bruner seems sympathetic to the qualitatively different views of children. He describes the concrete operational stage as operating either directly through manipulation of objects or internally through representations. He emphasizes that operations must be internalized and reversible, unlike simple actions or goal-directed behavior. He discussed internalized structures as the way the child represents the world. Bruner then claims "It is into the language of these internal structures that one must translate ideas if the child is to grasp them" (p. 37).

Stages as the basis for acceleration. In his discussion of the other stages, Bruner shows evidence of another tendency of American readers of Piaget: to interpret the research on stages as implying that one should attempt to accelerate children's progress toward the abstraction of formal operations. The stage of formal operations is based on the child's ability to operate on hypothetical propositions, to deduce, predict, and check. Bruner states, "What is most important for teaching basic concepts is *that the child be helped to pass progressively from concrete thinking to the utilization of more conceptually adequate modes of thought*" (p. 38, emphasis added). He followed this with a statement that turned out to be a major issue of debate at the conference:

> But the intellectual development of the child is no clockwork sequence of events; it also responds to influences from the environment, notably the school environment. Thus instruction in scientific ideas, even at the elementary level, need not follow slavishly the natural course of cognitive development in the child. It can also lead intellectual development by

providing challenging but usable opportunities for the child to forge ahead in his development. (p. 39)

Inhelder was in Woods Hole as a representative of the Piagetian school and responded to this position with a concern that was to prove prophetically accurate: that researchers in the United States would focus on trying to accelerate the child's progress rather than on "seeing what goes on when a child passes to a new level of understanding." Piaget and Inhelder did not deny that learning environments could be more or less conducive to aid the intellectual development of the child; however, as Piaget put it, for him the question was not how *fast* we can help intelligence to grow but how *far* we can help it to grow (in Duckworth, 1987, p. 38). Duckworth reports on a conversation she had with Inhelder:

Physicists and psychologists, including Bruner, generally reproached the Genevan researchers for the observational passivity. In effect, they said, "You've done nothing but document the child's unaided development, you don't intervene. Surely each of the notions you have studied is composed of other simpler notions. Surely it is sufficient to decompose each of the complex notions into its simpler parts, to teach the simpler parts and to aid the construction of the whole notion in this way." The parallels with physics are clear. The world of physics is infinitely manipulable. If one knows the constituent mechanisms, one can unmake and remake a process in innumerable ways, taking it apart and putting it together as one wishes. In contrast, the biologists, on the whole, understood Inhelder's point that a child's thinking was not as manipulable as a physical phenomenon . . . a child's thinking responded with the integrity of a biological organism and not like the separate components of a physical mechanism." (p. 34)

Duckworth then reported that, of all the physicists, Friedman best understood this claim. He and others then created the Elementary Science Study, the program she claims is "most consistent with the work of Piaget and Inhelder in psychology" (p. 34). What we witness in this exchange was to have a dramatic influence on research on student conceptions in the United States. The new curricula emphasized the "structure of knowledge" of the disciplines and, in doing so, sought to weave these organizing concepts into the curriculum from the early elementary grades and on. Less attention was given to the claim that children may have their own idiographic ways of understanding these ideas and that these ways might differ or conflict with the views held by scientists and mathematicians. The result in many cases was that the curriculum became formally more current and sophisticated, but the child's world was neglected in the process. The lesson in Piaget that was ignored was his biological view of human development: that, through the process of maturation *as defined in relation to* experiences in the environment and culture, a child develops certain perspectives and beliefs that are functionally adaptive, and these perspectives and beliefs may or may not correspond well with the views of disciplinary experts.

Positive Influences of Piaget's Genetic Epistemology

The impact of the curriculum reform of the sixties on student conceptions was by no means solely detrimental: It focused on concepts (as opposed to rote procedures) and it encouraged subject-area experts to develop a keen interest in educational issues. Both of these outcomes were necessary in providing the context in which student conceptions research was to thrive. Furthermore, the Piagetian perspective required a radical shift from the behaviorism that then dominated the American educational programs, and this shift included increased awareness of the importance of students' direct physical interactions with objects, that is, the use of manipulatives. It can be argued that these reforms were exactly what was needed for developing more constructivist views of classrooms that were to recognize the schism between the formal account provided by experts and the physical, intuitive, and pragmatic world of the child.

Emphasis on students' conceptions. To understand that the Piagetian stage research provided a framework for the focus on student conceptions, one needs to recognize that Piaget's stage research constituted a macrostructure that examined such fundamental topics as space, time, causality, conservation, and object permanence. By identifying the broad, stable changes in structure, Piaget hoped to allow for the development of other studies that focused on the microgenesis (or development) of specific concepts held by students. Researchers who recognized these possibilities in the Piagetian tradition established a vital tradition of task-oriented research on student conceptions (Davis, 1975, 1976, 1980; Duckworth, 1987; Easley, 1977; Ginsburg, 1976; Hawkins, 1974).

Children's views of knowledge. Duckworth (1987) provided a careful analysis of the Woods Hole controversy in a chapter entitled "Either We're Too Early and They Can't Learn It or We're Too Late and They Know It Already: The Dilemma of 'Applying Piaget.'" She then articulated the basis for curriculum development (or for research) on student conceptions. In trying to explain why some people pursue an idea deeply, whereas others are satisfied with superficial explanations, she draws attention to the view of knowledge as a lens by which certain qualities of our experience gain clarity. She acknowledges that "all the rest of the world passes us by unless we think of thinking about it in that way" (p. 40). Providing examples from the Genevan work, she identified certain qualities that distinguished merely completing a task from understanding: (a) the child has a theory so that, when it conflicts with his or her expectations, he or she can revise it; and (b) three types of knowledge interplay—

perceptual knowledge (the way things look over time), action knowledge (the way I have done things before), and conceptual knowledge (the name I give things, the way it has been represented, that is, an idea, word, or formula). To explore the children's theories and their knowledge in these three modes, Duckworth (1987, p. 42) quotes from Blanchet (1977): "A good experimental situation must permit the child to establish plans to reach a distant goal, while leaving him wide freedom to follow his own routing" (p. 37).

Learners' need for time. A commitment to allowing the child (or teacher) enough freedom and time to explore an idea has become a basic tenet of work in the tradition of genetic epistemology. For instance, Duckworth (1987, chap. 6) and Bamberger and Duckworth (1982) report on their work with teachers, which lasted over a year, on phases of the moon. In summarizing the needs of learners to explore phenomena more fully, Duckworth (1987) wrote,

Teachers are often, and understandably, impatient for their students to develop clear and adequate ideas. But putting ideas in relation to each other is not a simple job. It *is* confusing; and that confusion *does* take time. All of us need time for our confusion if we are to build the breadth and depth that give significance to our knowledge. (p. 82)

Other research in this tradition includes the work of Papert (1980) on Logo, Franz and Papert (1988) on time, and Lampert (1986) on multiplication.

Karmiloff-Smith and Inhelder (1975) described an early example of the Piagetian genetic epistemology approach in their article, "If You Want To Get Ahead, Get a Theory." In an experiment in which 65 children ages 4 years, 6 months and 9 years, 5 months were asked to balance a variety of blocks across a narrow bar so that they did not fall, the researchers were to conduct "experiments on children's spontaneous organizing activity in goal-oriented tasks . . . [where] . . . the focus is not on success or failure, per se, but on the interplay between action sequences and children's theories in action, i.e., the implicit ideas or changing modes of representation underlying the sequences" (p. 196). They distinguished two kinds of approaches: action-response (judged as success or failure to balance) and theory-response (judged as collaboration or refutation of the theory). Those children who developed a theory such as "the geometric center is the point of balance" were unlikely to give it up. In cases where the blocks were unevenly weighted, these children were likely to label the task impossible. When they were encouraged to try it with their eyes closed, they could balance them, but when they opened their eyes, they denied the legitimacy of their solution and moved the blocks to the geometric center. In many cases, they performed less well than did their younger counterparts. The authors explored three possible strategies for assisting them in changing their theories: (a) the use of counterexamples, (b) changes in general cognitive competence, such as differentiating length and weight in their possible impact on balance, and (c) integration of proprioceptive information (e.g., information from physical sensations) gained by tactics such as placing their finger over the spot of contact (like a nail), or holding the block at opposite ends to sense the distribution of weight and deriving a sense of the multiple forces from this experience.

This research is particularly relevant to our discussion of student conceptions, because it represents the movement of Piagetian researchers away from the more fixed stages of macrolevel structures toward an exploration of the psychogenesis of ideas both within and across stages, although still using the stages as frames for viewing the data, but in a dynamic developmental context. Furthermore, this shift indicates the presaging of (a) the role of students' theories in learning, (b) the initial decrease in the flexibility of students' ideas accompanying the development of a theoretical position that later may lead to integration of information previously considered disparate (e.g., the proprioceptive information), and (c) the progressive development of these theories in response to counterexamples. As stated by Karmiloff-Smith and Inhelder:

Our observations indicate that children hold on to their initial theory for as long as they can. Even where they finally do take counter-examples into consideration, they first prefer to create a new theory, quite independent of the first one, before finally attempting to unify all events under a single, broader theory. (p. 209)

Critical barriers to learning. Hawkins and his colleagues at the Mountain View Center in Boulder, Colorado, have devoted considerable effort to the exploration of student conceptions in science (Hawkins, 1974, 1978). In 1982, Hawkins, Apelman, Colton, and Flexner published a report on the phenomena they called "critical barriers to learning." They provided the following operational definition:

First, critical barriers are conceptual obstacles which confine and inhibit scientific understanding. Second, they are critical, and so differ from other conceptual difficulties, because: a) they involve preconceptions, which the learner retrieves from past experiences, that are incompatible with scientific understanding; b) they are widespread among adults as well as children, among the academically able but scientifically naive as well as those less well educated; c) they involve not simply difficulty in acquiring scientific fact but in assimilated conceptual frames for ordering and retrieving important facts; d) they are not narrow in their application but, when once surmounted, prove key to the comprehension of a range of phenomena. To surmount a critical barrier is not merely to overcome one obstacle but to open up new pathways to scientific understanding; e) Another hallmark of the class is that when a distinct breakthrough does occur, there is often strong affect, a true joy in discovery. (p. c-1)

Hawkins et al. believe that these critical barriers need to be distinguished from other learning difficulties, which include disruptions in students' lives outside of school, poorly planned teaching, or overly quick or confusing instruction. They claim that "certain kinds of conceptual difficulties which students experience are indeed intrinsic to the growth of scientific understanding" (p. c-22). Examples of critical barriers explored by this team include size and scale, heat and temperature, and light and color.

Listening to students. Easley and Driver also are pioneers in research on student conceptions. In *On Clinical Studies in Mathematics Education,* Easley (1977) offered examples of clinical interview studies and explained that their methodological validity depended on assumptions different from those of more traditional psychometric statistical studies. When a clinical researcher focused on the elaboration of a single case, Easley argued, a different form of generalizability resulted than from studies with large samples: "Clinical researchers feel that they can generalize from a study of a single case to some other individual cases because they have seen a given phenomenon in one situation in sufficient detail and know its essential workings to be able to recognize it when they encounter it in another situation" (p. 2). One Piagetian study Easley reviewed in some detail was on the relationship between conservation of volume and the operation of multiplication. He investigated the relationship between the use of mathematical ideas as descriptions of mental phenomena and how such a use intertwines epistemology, psychology, philosophy, and history. He concluded this section by writing,

There seems to be no escaping the implications . . . that teachers would have to understand rather well the process of cognitive development and listen to and observe children carefully so as to grasp with reasonable accuracy what kind of mental operations they are bringing to bear on a given task. (p. 21)

This statement captures a fundamental commitment of these researchers to the belief that teaching is most effectively improved when the teacher learns to listen to students' thoughts and to interpret students' actions and thoughts from their perspective as children.

Driver and Easley (1978) distinguish between nomothetic and ideographic studies to focus on the idea of modeling the child's world. Nomothetic studies assess the correspondence between student's views and the accepted scientific views; in contrast, ideographic studies are those in which "the pupils' conceptualizations are explored and analyzed in their own terms without assessment against an externally defined system" (p. 63).

In mathematics, Davis and Ginsburg (Davis, 1976), working collaboratively on the Madison Project, also were learning to articulate students' perspectives. Put simply, researchers in the genetic epistemology tradition learned to listen to students. Largely as a result of work by earlier psychologists, such as Piaget (1970, 1973a) and Brownell (in Weaver & Kilpatrick, 1972), these researchers sought to describe how concepts and tasks appear to students, rather than compare students' performance against a set of preconceived categories. Value is placed on the process of solving a problem, not just its outcome. As stated by Erlwanger (1975), "If children develop their knowledge of mathematics largely through their own activity as they learn mathematics in a particular environment, then evaluation should be an attempt to discover *from their point of view* just what they have learned and understood" (p. 166, emphasis added).

To look at the ideas from a student's point of view, these researchers chose to use flexible interviews and to study individuals or small groups. What they discovered was stated bluntly in an early issue of *Children's Mathematical Behavior,* wherein Davis (1975) wrote, *"The fact that what was mathematically necessary for the solution of the equation: $3/x = 6/3x + 1$ differed considerably from what was cognitively necessary, and the details of how they differed, constitute the main value of the 15-minute interview for us, if not for Henry"* (pp. 8–9, emphasis in the original).

Intuitive mathematicians versus blank slates. Davis (1976) and Ginsburg (1976) collaborated on early work at Cornell University, reported in the same issue of *Children's Mathematical Behavior.* Ginsburg (1975) introduced another theme of great significance in conceptions research. He wrote of the young child as an "intuitive mathematician" (p. 63). Rejecting the tabula rasa view of the child, he suggested that "through spontaneous interaction with the environment, he develops various techniques—perceptual skills, patterns of thought, concepts, counting methods—for coping with the quantitative problems" (p. 63). In *Children's Arithmetic* (1977), he offers five observations about errors:

1. Errors result from organized strategies and rules . . .
2. Faulty rules underlying errors have sensible origins . . .
3. Too often children see arithmetic as an activity isolated from their ordinary concerns . . .
4. Children demonstrate a gap between informal and formal knowledge . . .
5. Children often possess unsuspected strengths. (p. 129)

Early work on student conceptions undertaken in the Piagetian tradition was devoted to legitimizing small, intensive studies on how students viewed particular concepts. It emphasized the importance of exploring errors rather than suppressing them. It recognized the significance of examining the psychogenesis of concepts rather than the meanings given to concepts by disciplinary experts. It also raised questions about the interplay of formal schooling and everyday experience.

Constructivism. Also in the Piagetian tradition, we witness the development of an approach to children's learning known as constructivism (Confrey, 1985; Easley, 1977; Hunting, 1986; von Glasersfeld, 1984b). The roots of constructivism are many: Steffe and Cobb (1983) trace their roots through structuralism (Brownell, 1945) and operationalism (Bridgman, 1927). Nik Azis Nik Pa (1986) compares these schools. Steffe's work with students focused on early number (Steffe, von Glasersfeld, Richards, & Cobb, 1983) and, more recently, on the development of multiplication in relation to the concept of counting and the evolution of increasingly complex schemes about units (Steffe, 1988; Steffe & Cobb, 1988).

Methodologically, constructivist research demands extensive interactions with students over months and years and the detailed analysis of videotapes. Its focus is on building a model of the details of the students' views, abilities, beliefs, and inclinations about certain mathematical ideas (Cobb & Steffe, 1983). Steffe (1988) refers to these descriptions as "the mathematics of children" (p. 122). Steffe (n. d.) wrote,

Individuals who believe that mathematics is the way it is rather than the way human beings make it to be might reject my work out of hand because they may not believe that mathematics of children is legitimate mathematics. I find this to be particularly unsettling, because in my way of thinking, the mathematical knowledge of the other should be taken as relative to one's own frame of reference. It can be known through interpreting the language and the actions of the others—by forming a conceptual model. These models are understood as springing from the conceptual operations that are available to the knower. They are nothing other than a constellation of available conceptual operations that are formed in organizing or making sense of experiential encounters with children. Such models constitute mathematics of children even though they are not taken to characterize how mathematical the knowledge of children really is. They are taken as fit rather than a match (Von Glasersfeld, 1983). (p. 13)

A central construct in the work of Steffe is that of a *scheme,* which Piaget defined as that which is repeatable and generalizable in an action. This idea of a scheme provides the vehicle for examining the local development of a concept, because its size and plasticity allow for a more flexible evolution than is connoted by the term *mental structures.*

Essential to the constructivist view is the recognition that "the essential way of knowing the real world is not directly through our senses, but first and foremost through our material or mental actions" (Sinclair, 1987). Thus, the parts of the scheme are not situations that exist independently from the child, but are only recognized in relation to the child's current forms of operation and action. Steffe proposes an elaborate model of functional and metamorphic accommodation, which he uses to elaborate on the process of reflective abstraction. Schemes thus function as the mental activity that can be acted on and transformed into knowledge through reflection and abstraction.

The Piagetian framework makes certain fundamental assumptions about the learner as an epistemological being. Von Glasersfeld stresses the importance of examining epistemology (the study of knowledge), rather than ontology (the study of the nature of being). He rejects the possibility of the position that knowing is ascertaining the accuracy of the correspondence between our knowledge and the external world on the grounds that a claim of certainty about the accuracy of the correspondence would itself be a product of human knowing and thus fail to test the correspondence objectively (a classic argument dating back to the skeptics). Accepting that we are trapped in our own human ways of knowing, he suggests that we seek "fit" rather than "match" in our conceptual structures, as a key fits a lock (1984a). By using this metaphor, he is suggesting that we need to determine if our concepts seem practically viable, rather than objectively true. Therefore he argues that biological adaptation is more appropriate than correspondence for examining learning. In a discussion of Piaget's concept of cognitive adaptation, he argued for this use of viability:

I have elsewhere discussed the misleading connotation of "adaptation" and suggested the term "viability" would be more adequate. From the organism's point of view, on the biological level as on the cognitive one, the environment is no more and no less than the sum of constraints within which the organism can operate. The organism's activities and operations are successful when they are not impeded or foiled by constraints, i.e., when they are *viable.* Hence it is only when actions or operations fail that one can speak of "contact" with the environment, not when they succeed. (1982, p. 615)

Explaining further, he adds a quote by Piaget, "D'autre part, l'objet se laisse faire" (Piaget, Inhelder, Garcia, & Voneche, 1977, p. 64) and comments

To say that the object—and here this refers to the "ontic" object . . . —permits the operations the subject carries out is an elegant way of saying that, in a given context, the object, the environment, the "reality" in which the acting subject is embedded, does not hinder or prevent the subject's actions, and it is this absence of obstacle or constraint that makes the action viable. (1982, pp. 615–616)

Von Glasersfeld expresses in these excerpts a key perspective on apparent errors or deviations. He emphasizes that it is through discrepancy, perturbation, or encounters with the unexpected that we can envision the qualities of our constructs; these key moments in our activities of reflection are opportunities to glimpse our own constructs. However, he also warns us that our "problems," that is, our perceptions of deviance, may not coincide (and probably will not coincide) with those of children. Thus if we want to investigate their conceptions, we need to seek out their problems, not to impose ours.

Another example of research that evolved within the Piagetian tradition can be seen in the work of Kamii on early number. In *Young Children Re-invent Arithmetic: Implications of Piaget's Theory,* Kamii (1985) described her work with Clark redefining the activities of a first grade classroom in arithmetic to be constructivist in its approaches. Kamii's discussion of Piaget's contrast between *empirical abstraction* (e.g., the abstraction of color from objects) and *reflective abstraction* (e.g., the abstraction necessary to create number) expresses her constructivist position. She wrote that Piaget defined empirical abstraction as learning to focus on a certain property while ignoring others. She then indicates the crucial interplay between these two kinds of abstraction. She describes reflective abstraction as follows:

Reflective abstraction, in contrast, involves the construction of relationships between/ among objects. Relationships . . . do not have an existence in external reality. The similarity or difference between one chip and another does not exist in one chip or the other, nor anywhere else in external reality. This relationship exists only in the minds of those who can create it between the objects. The term *constructive* abstraction might be easier to understand than reflective abstraction to indicate that this abstraction is a veritable construction by the mind rather than a focus on something that already exists in objects. (p. 9)

Summary

Piagetian work on student conceptions examined the development of student understanding of particular mathematical and scientific concepts over time. Piaget's (1970) fundamental assumption is that knowledge is a process, not a state. Hence knowledge needs to be examined in relation to its developmental associations (its local ecology of ideas). Therefore Piaget studied conceptions, not misconceptions. Second, he recognized the interplay between subject and object and declared, "Intelligence . . . organizes the world by organizing itself" (Piaget, 1973b, cited in von Glasersfeld, 1982, p. 613). To summarize the influences of genetic epistemology on research on student conceptions:

1. Researchers focus on the development of microstructures, in contrast to stage research, which focuses on macrostructures.

2. In looking at the development of particular concepts, researchers seek to examine through tasks how a child acts, perceives, and operates.

3. Mental operations (i.e., an internalized action which is reversible, involves an invariant, and exists within a structure of operations) form the basic roots of conceptual development.

4. These mental operations are embedded in schemes (sequences of actions), which become active when a certain situation is encountered.

5. The construction, refinement, and internalization of these schemes occur within a theory-building approach complete with experimentation.

6. Reflective abstraction is assumed to be the process by which the schemes are stabilized.

As Piaget stated in 1964 at a conference in the United States, "The accent must be on auto-regulation, on active assimilation—the accent must be on the activity of the subject. Failing this there is no possible didactic or pedagogy which significantly transforms the subject" (Ripple & Rockcastle, 1964, p. i).

Studies of Students' Alternative Conceptions: Research in the Philosophy of Science Tradition

Developments in the last century in the philosophy of science considerably influenced views of teaching of science and to a lesser degree, mathematics. Many of these were inspired by the work of Kuhn and his predecessors and colleagues. Kuhn's revisionary account of the history of science and his discussion of the sociology of schooling and its impact on the work of the scientist spurred avid interest in considering how the development of disciplinary knowledge might inform us about the development of an individual's knowledge.

When Kuhn published *The Structure of Scientific Revolutions* in 1970, he made widely accessible the claim and evidence that science does not proceed by a simple progressive accretion of scientific fact. He wrote of the dilemma facing historians of science, who can no longer view their discipline as one that "chronicles both [the] successive increments and the obstacles that have inhibited their accumulation" (Kuhn, 1970, p. 2). Kuhn continues:

Simultaneously, these same historians confront growing difficulties in distinguishing the "scientific" component of past observation and belief from what their predecessors had readily labeled "error" and "superstition." The more carefully they study, say, Aristotelian dynamics, phlogistic chemistry, or caloric thermodynamics, the more certain they feel that those once current views of nature were, as a whole, neither less scientific nor more the product of human idiosyncrasy than those current today. If these out-of-date beliefs are to be called myths, then myths can be produced by the same sorts of methods and held for the same sorts of reasons that now lead to scientific knowledge. If, on the other hand, they are to be called science, then science has included bodies of belief quite incompatible with the ones we hold today. Given these alternatives, the historian must choose the latter. Out-of-date theories are not in principle unscientific because they have been discarded. That choice, however, makes it difficult to see scientific development as a process of accretion. (pp. 2–3)

As an alternative to "progress through accretion," Kuhn introduced the idea of a *paradigm:* theoretical and methodological commitments shared by practicing members of a scientific community. During periods when a paradigm is thriving, the members practice normal science (puzzle solving). "And when . . . the profession can no longer evade anomalies that subvert the existing tradition of scientific practice—then begin the extraordinary investigations that lead the profession at least to a new set of commitments, a new basis for the practice of science" (p. 6). He named these "tradition-shattering" episodes *scientific revolutions.* His work spurred the attention of many science educators to the nature of scientific thought.

Kuhn's position had evolved from an exciting revision of the views of scientific thought, which can be traced to Popper (1959, 1962). Popper rejected the verification principle of the logical positivist, denying the possibility of restricting scientific inquiry to that which was observably verifiable. However, he inserted in its place the requirement that scientific ideas must be refutable—that is, they cannot be verified, but they can be rejected. Thus, he argued that one did not prove theories; their acceptance rested on a failure to discredit or refute them.

Elaborating on this theme, Lakatos (1970) further argued for a model of a "research programme" (akin to Kuhn's paradigm), which placed an irrefutable core at its center, surrounded by a protective belt of less essential theoretical positions, and finally terminating in an external boundary of empirical fact. He classified research programs as progressive, if they were gaining in explanatory potential, or degenerating, if outstanding problems were accumulating. Both philosophers of science took the position that observations are theory-laden and hence rejected a simple inductive model of "the scientific method."

In *Human Understanding* (1972), Toulmin proposed to replace Kuhn's revolutionary view of science, where paradigms overthrew previous paradigms in relatively dramatic changes, with an evolutionary view. He argued for examining the periods and conditions of change in order to examine the rationality behind a theoretical position: "Questions of 'rationality' are concerned, precisely, not with the particular intellectual doctrines that a man—or professional group—adopts at any given time, but rather with *the conditions on which, and the manner in which, he is prepared to criticize and change those doctrines as time goes on*" (p. 84, emphasis in original). Based on Toulmin's work, the conditions under which conceptual frameworks are altered became known as "conceptual change."

This work in the philosophy of science by Kuhn, Lakatos, Toulmin, and others (see Phillips, 1983) spurred the imagination of science educators, who formed an intellectual tradition in which they could interpret work that was being undertaken under the heading of preconceptions (Ausubel, 1968; Novak, 1985) and misconceptions (Clement, 1981). The attractiveness of the philosophy of science to science educators was based in part on three converging factors: (a) It allowed these researchers to critique the underlying inductive conception of science, which permeated the textbooks in the form of "the scientific method"; (b) it rejected theoretically neutral observations and, hence, could support the position that students enter instruction with firmly held beliefs or preconceptions; and (c) it strongly supported the claim that student conceptions relied on a configuration of beliefs, commitments, and expectations and thus to alter these preconceptions and misconceptions would require intellectual transformations akin to those that accompanied transitions in paradigms, a weak view of "ontogeny recapitulates phylogeny."

Early Work on Preconceptions and Misconceptions

Although I have placed the work of Ausubel under the framework of philosophy of science, it did not derive from it. In fact, the work of Ausubel (1963, 1968) and his protégés (e.g., Novak, 1985) predates the popularization of the conceptual change approaches by at least a decade. However, the merging of these two perspectives marked the beginning of the most active period of research on misconceptions and alternative conceptions; hence I have joined these perspectives in my discussion.

As explained in Novak and Gowin (1984), Ausubel distinguished between *meaningful* and *rote* learning. Rejecting the verbatim repetition of definitions and the algorithmic reproduction of procedures of rote learning, he specified the conditions for meaningful learning: appropriate materials, the disposition of the student to relate old and new ideas, and preconceptions, which allow the student to act on this disposition. He saw cognitive structure as hierarchically organized, an idea he elaborated on in his use of the terms *subsumption,* the use of general concepts to acquire and organize new concepts; *progressive differentiation,* in which new linkages are formed between related concepts; and *integrative reconciliation,* in which relating previously discrete concepts resolves conflicts in meanings.

The importance of this work comes from its emphasis on examining "what a student already knows." Because the framework in which Ausubel worked depended largely on the logical operations of differentiation and integration, it fit particularly well into the research on biological sciences, where concepts and terminology are structurally and functionally interrelated. Using this Ausubelian framework, Novak and his students (Fisher & Lipson, 1983; Novak, 1985) developed the technique of concept mapping as a way of visualizing relationships among propositions. Others use propositional skeletons (West, Fensham, & Garrard, 1985) or semantic maps. These tools drew students' attention to an overview of a field of study and led to the inclusion of metacognitive perspective in the work on student conceptions.

Clement's work (1981) provides a classic introduction to approaches to research on misconceptions in the early phase. In this work (conducted considerably earlier than its publication date), Clement and his colleagues administered four word problems to a sample of 150 freshman engineers, two of which required particular numerical results, and two of which were general equation problems of the "students and professors" type. (Students were asked to write an algebra equation for the statement: At a certain university, there are six times as many students as professors.) Their performance on writing equations for particular problems was over 90%; on the two generalized equation problems, it fell to 63% and 27%, respectively.

Clement systematically demonstrated the compulsion of the errors by placing a warning with the problems. He comments on their apparent simplicity with the statement, "The data reveal a class of problems which should be trivial for a scientifically literate person, but which are solved incorrectly by large numbers of science-oriented students" (p. 17). In other work on this same class of problems, he demonstrates the pervasiveness of the "misconception," because similar error patterns are found across different symbol systems: equations, tables, word sentences, and pictures.

Clement also demonstrates a characteristic trend in this research when he creates two explanations of the source of the errors: a word-matching strategy and a static comparison strategy. He hypothesizes that these strategies can be used to interpret the statements students make as they think aloud the solutions to problems during interviews. He contrasts those strategies with an "operative approach," in which a student "views the equation as an active operation on a variable quantity" (p. 21).

Nowhere in the paper does Clement define explicitly the term *misconception*. He uses various alternative phrases: "conceptual stumbling block" (p. 29), "inconsistent semi-autonomous schemes," and "cognitive processes responsible for errors in problem solving" (p. 16), whose referent may be "misconceptions," but the relationship is never offered explicitly.

In sum, the early phase of misconceptions research established certain parameters and themes. The dominant perspective was that, in learning certain key concepts in the curriculum, students were transforming in an active way what was told to them, and those transformations often led to serious misconceptions. Misconceptions were documented to be surprising, pervasive, and resilient. Connections between misconceptions, language, and informal knowledge were proposed.

The maturing of conceptions research quickened as the work on students' preconceptions and misconceptions was interpreted within a more explicit epistemological framework. It was postulated that students held "mini theories": configurations of beliefs that were likened to the broad theoretical commitments held by communities of scientists. Individual beliefs were set within an overall framework of beliefs about science, its content and conduct, and the certainty of its conclusions. Conflicts between the informal use of language and formal scientific usage were seen as a source of confusion and misinterpretation for students. As in the philosophy of science, a key transformation of the field of science and mathematics education began to gain acceptance. Similar to historians' rejection of the progress of science by accretion, science and mathematics educators began to reject the idea that learning proceeds by the accumulation of facts or rules. The dominant paradigm in classroom teaching of science had been to assume that new information would be assimilated nonproblematically and that concepts were basically collections of shared attributes. During this period, researchers began to make statements similar to the following:

- There is a parallel between how theory influences observation and how preconceptions influence future learning (Novak, 1977b).
- Students possess well-established beliefs when entering instruction, and those beliefs are more akin to minitheories than to propositional knowledge (Claxton, 1987; Osborne, 1984).
- To change individual conceptual frameworks, one would have to challenge the overall conception of science held by many students and teachers (Confrey, 1980; Driver & Bell, 1986).

These perspectives led to an interest in conceptual change research and eventually to conceptual change curriculum development.

To discuss this rich set of work, I am proposing a set of themes that represent the conceptions research in science. My summary of this work will rely on reviews by Driver and Erickson (1983), Driver and Easley (1978), Gilbert and Watts (1983), Gilbert et al. (1982), Champagne et al. (1983), Osborne and Wittrock (1983), Pope and Gilbert (1983), Helm and Novak (1983), Novak (1987), Eylon and Linn (1988), and the book, *Cognitive Structure and Conceptual Change* (West & Pines, 1985). Samples of the research in science education on these topics follow. For a more complete listing, see Eylon and Linn (1988, Table 1, pp. 254–255).

Preconceptions. Researchers in science were often motivated to examine students' conceptions because it was believed that an understanding of a student's prior knowledge determined the appropriate starting point for instruction (Ausubel, 1968; Bruner, 1960; Novak, 1977a, 1977b). As Hawkins et al. (1982) wrote,

In some contrast with studies which have the . . . aim of paying attention to what students don't know . . . our purpose is always, at least in principle, to find out conjecturally, and more firmly where possible, what students *do* know, and then how this knowledge can be raised by them to the level of consciousness—retrieved for their own use in further learning. (p. C-3)

The focus on preconceptions represented a basic rejection of a tabula rasa approach to learning. The assumption was that students connect new ideas to existing ideas, and that the existing knowledge thus serves as both a filter and a catalyst to the acquisition of new ideas. To understand what students will learn, one must first determine what they currently believe.

Some of the earliest work on student conceptions was undertaken in physics (Clement, 1982; McCloskey, Caramazza, & Green, 1980; McDermott, Rosequist, Popp, & van Zee, 1983; Minstrell, 1982). In this area, researchers report that students hold naive conceptions of force such as "a force is a push or a pull" (Minstrell & Stimpson, 1986), or that "continuing motion implies a continued force in the direction of the movement" (Clement, 1982). Other areas of preconceptions in physics include torque (Barowy & Lochhead, 1980), simple circuits (Fredette and Lochhead, 1980), curvilinear motion (McCloskey et al., 1980), and position, velocity, and acceleration (McDermott et al., 1983).

Conceptual structure. A second theme stresses the structure of relationships among concepts. Pines (1985) describes the meaning of cognitive structure:

Cognitive means "of the mind; having the power to know, recognize and conceive; concerning personally acquired knowledge," so cognitive structure concerns the individual's ideas, meanings, concepts, cognitions and so on. *Structure* refers to the form, the arrangement of elements or parts of anything, the manner or organization; the emphasis here is not on the elements, although they are important to a structure, but on the way those elements are bound together. (p. 101)

The importance of structure derives from the interrelationship among concepts. Often, concepts (e.g., force, mass, and acceleration; rate, time, and distance) are intricately interwoven into related concepts. Hawkins et al. suggest that such a tight weave is characteristic of scientific knowledge, as opposed to common sense knowledge, and warns that it leads to a kind of instructional paradox. They wrote,

To understand any one concept, a node in the network logically connected to other nodes, it is necessary to understand many others as well. This logical tightness of scientific ideas, their mutual interdependence, suggests immediately a paradox: they cannot be learned: not in isolation from each other; not all at once, hence not at all. Such a paradoxical conclusion only states, in extreme form, the origin of many of the student difficulties. (pp. c15–c16, emphasis in the original)

For some, methods of creating conceptual maps, semantic networks, and so forth, are important to provide a more holistic and relational perspective on concepts (Novak, 1985; Pines, 1985). Others emphasize the need to not only understand what is known, but to examine how it is organized (West et al., 1985). Still others emphasize an instructional validity for the methods, finding them useful tools to promote consideration of alternative organizations and to reveal misconceptions (Champagne, Gunstone, & Klopfer, 1985). White (1985) proposed nine dimensions of cognitive structure to explain the variation among students: extent, precision, internal consistency, accord with reality or generally accepted truth, variety of types of element, variety of topics, shape, ratio of internal to external dimensions, and availability. Pines (1985) expressed the importance of variation as he described "these bundles of meaningful relations we call concepts [which] are, on the one hand, capable of change, and, on the other hand, can never be acquired in any finalistic fashion. Any new relations will affect, to some extent, the total framework of relations" (p. 110).

For Pines (1985), this allows a definition of a misconception within conceptual structures as viewed across time and circumstance. He wrote,

> Certain conceptual relations that are acquired may be inappropriate within a certain context. We term such relations as "misconceptions." A misconception does not exist independently, but is contingent upon a certain existing conceptual framework. As conceptual frameworks change, what was deemed a misconception may no longer be a misconception; conversely, what is a central conceptual relationship in one framework may be a profound misconception within another framework. The history of science is replete with such examples. (p. 110)

Conceptual change. An alternative but complementary position to the examination of cognitive structure is a focus on conditions under which students will choose to modify, reject, or extend their conceptions. Researchers in this tradition, often building from the work of Toulmin on the evolution of conceptual systems, argue that concepts are similar to theories and paradigms; the preconceptions will act as a filter for new concepts, and the new concepts must not only be shown to explain or predict the phenomenon, but they must be regarded as providing an acceptable solution within the current framework (Confrey, 1980; Johansson, Marton, & Svensson, 1985; Strike & Posner, 1985).

Working in the area of Newtonian and Einsteinian physics, Posner, Strike, Hewson, and Gertzog (1982) borrow and refine the Piagetian terms *assimilation* and *accommodation.* They use accommodation to describe the times when a student may need to replace or reorganize his or her existing conceptions and argue for the conditions under which this is likely to occur. They require that a student be dissatisfied with an existing conception and find a new conception intelligible, plausible, and fruitful. They further indicate that accommodation is facilitated when anomalies exist within their current belief system; when analogies and metaphors assist the student in accepting a new conception and make it more intelligible; and when their epistemological, metaphysical, and other beliefs support such a change. Hewson (1981) elaborates on this position by discussing how conceptions can be in competition with each other and how, in such cases of conflict, a student will raise or lower the status of one conception relative to another.

Formal versus informal knowledge. The importance of examining not only *what* is taught in schools but also *how* it is taught can be demonstrated by research on informal learning contexts. Ginsburg (1977), in *Children's Arithmetic,* wrote specifically of the differences: "One of the most significant difficulties in children's arithmetic is the gap between informal and formal knowledge. The phenomenon is widespread: many children have trouble with written work but can cope with the same kind of problem in an informal manner" (pp. 179–180). Ginsburg reminds us of the importance of reducing the gap between formal knowledge, "seen as a meaningless game," and informal arithmetic, which "has already proved of some utility" (p. 181).

Champagne et al. (1985) explicitly discuss this gap, specifying potential sources of imprecision in students' interpretation of propositions. These include the presence of informal meanings for technical terms, errors in determining the scale of measurement (either as inappropriately large or small), and attempts to formulate general rules for concepts (e.g., motion) from their experience.

The terms *informal* and *formal* need to be analyzed into their components and possible referents. To date, the following interpretations of the distinctions seem plausible, and often their use does not distinguish among them:

1. Formal refers to that which is taught in an organized, structured educational institution where certain constraints and conditions operate that differ from outside life; informal is that which is not taught in such an institution.

2. Formal refers to a system of interrelated definitions and proofs, experiments and arguments; informal refers to more tentative intuitive conjectures.

3. Formal refers to written methods; informal refers to mental strategies.

4. Formal refers to the abstraction of a procedure from its context, where the procedure is specified and justified independently; informal refers to routines that are carried out mechanically, by habit or tradition, to complete an activity required on a daily basis.

5. Formal refers to knowledge one accepts as legitimate because it has been demonstrated by experts; informal refers to knowledge one has generated or learned through one's personal actions.

The appeal of the formal/informal distinction in researching students' conceptions is great; it captures an expression frequently uttered by students in which they distinguish between what is required or expected in school and what is required or expected in daily life apart from school. However, if one accepts the first definition, then any distinction attributed to the formal and informal cannot be altered by institutionalized schooling. This is a conclusion most researchers would be reluctant to draw.

Two areas of research in which the contrast between formal and informal knowledge is great are in biology and statistics. In biology, we find numerous examples of beliefs of young children that can be attributed to their egocentric view of the world and are charmingly reminiscent of the myths of other cultures. In a review of research on student conceptions in biology, Mintzes and Arnaudin (1984) present findings on children's animistic concepts of life; their portrayal of death as temporary and personified; their restrictions of categories of plant and animal; their versions of anatomy and physiology; and their views of reproduction, genetics, evolution, and growth. Many of these demonstrate explicitly that in spite of formal instruction, these informal ideas persist.

Knowledge of statistics is frequently populated by a mixture of intuition and formal procedures. Most students demonstrate an intuitive understanding of a mean, but when circumstances call for a weighted mean, over half continue to rely on the simple mean (Pollatsek, Lima, & Well 1981). Demonstrating the parochial character of informal knowledge (perhaps another version of egocentricity), Tversky and Kahneman (1971) found that many students believe that a small sample will be representative of a large sample. They have named this (incorrect) belief the "Law of Small Numbers," in contrast with the (correct) "Law of Large Numbers." The belief that small samples are representative leads students to predict that, in a population of equal numbers of boys and girls, a birth order of BGBGBG is more likely than BGBBBB with an n of six (Kahneman & Tversky, 1972).

Sense data versus theory. Science educators are particularly interested in how students relate their sensorial experiences to their formal knowledge. Many researchers have documented the isolation between these forms of knowledge. Other studies have suggested that misconceptions result from the lack of isomorphism between students' theoretical perspective and sensory inputs originating in the real world. The work of Nussbaum and Novak (1976) shows how the connection between theory and sensory input is not simply keen observation. In astronomy, they documented children's views of the earth and identified an egocentric view in which the children predicted that, because objects drop down on their side of the earth, they must drop "down" (which they described as "away from the earth") on the opposite side of the earth as well. Another belief they documented was that the earth is flat like a pancake.

The complexity of the relationship between theory and data is illustrated in the review article by Driver and Erickson (1983). They commence with a quote from Einstein and Infeld and then state their position on this relationship:

> Science is not just a collection of laws, a catalogue of unrelated facts. It is a creation of the human mind, with its freely invented ideas and concepts. Physical theories try to form a picture of reality and to establish its connection with the wide world of sense impressions. (Einstein & Infeld, 1938, p. 294)

> A fundamental distinction can be made in science or in any field of empirical enquiry between two general kinds of activities. On the one hand there is the cataloguing of sense impressions, the experience of the phenomena; on the other there are our attempts as humans to impose some regularity on experience by creating our models or theoretical entities. (p. 37)

As a result of the assumption of this dichotomy, the authors propose the following definition of a conceptual framework: "By the construct 'conceptual framework,' we shall mean the mental organization imposed by an individual on sensory inputs as indicated by regularities in an individual's responses to particular problem settings" (p. 39).

This passage captures one of the most interesting issues within the misconceptions tradition in science education: the relationship between ontological claims (claims about reality) and epistemological claims (claims about knowledge). In the passage, the term *sense impressions* is used first in the Einstein quote and then by Driver and Erickson. In their definition, they shift to the use of *sensory inputs*. Inputs, a mechanical, computer-based metaphor, often is assumed to imply that an external world imposes certain signals on individuals; these are chaotic and can be interpretable by the individual only through the means of mental organization. Thus it appears that the authors differentiate sensory inputs as originating externally, and mental organization as personally constructed.

If this characterization is correct, then Driver and Erickson might conclude that somehow one can assess the accuracy of students' mental organizations (internal) in relation to these sensory inputs (external). The assertion that one can assess the accuracy of an internal representation in relation to an external stimulus has been criticized since the time of the skeptics, because any such assessment would necessarily be another internal act of comparison and would fail to overcome the internal/external gap (von Glasersfeld, 1984a). Another, more obvious, example of such a distinction was stated by Fisher and Lipson (1983), who write, "We are more or less constantly engaged in assessing the 'goodness of fit' between our mental models and the world around us" (p. 1).

The passage from Driver and Erickson (1983) is ambiguous and therefore allows an alternative interpretation, wherein sensory impressions and conceptual frameworks would both be firmly placed within the individual (albeit influenced by social and cultural forces). Hence impressions are not regarded as external signals, but internal experiences of them. Then the relationships one wishes to examine are the interactions and relationships between perceptions (organized frameworks of sensations) and other conceptual tools (language, symbols, and theories). Thus, the issue of ontology (what is reality?) is minimized, and the relationship among systems of knowledge (of which sensory impressions is simply one of many) is emphasized. Pines (1985) seems to take this position:

Sensation—the raw data from the sense organs—on its own, without perceptual organization, is devoid of meaning. Organized sensation—namely, perception—enables the awareness and mental recording of objects and events. In human beings, such perception is facilitated by language—words or sentences, and thus experience is conceptually and propositionally punctuated into meaningful distinctions, relations, and complexes of such relations that transform "raw sensation" into perception. (p. 103)

If we take the position that knowledge consists of a coordination of internal representations, rather than as a more and more accurate portrayal of "the way things really are," then one is left with one more issue in the definition of conceptual frameworks offered by Driver and Easley (1978). They refer to conceptual frameworks as mental organization, as indicated by regularities in an individual's responses to a particular problem setting. What is left unanswered is the question, Whose perception of regularities are they referring to? If the answer is an *observer's* perception of regularities, then a conceptual framework is not necessarily the individual student's own ways of organizing experience, but the observer's model of the student's responses. If the model refers to the observer's own framework, then we are left with the possibility that a conceptual framework may be invisible to, or inapplicable for, the student operating within it. The answer to the question, Who is the observer?, is perhaps not as important as the recognition that a phrase such as "regularities in responses" implies a hidden observer who needs identification.

Nonetheless, it is clear that in science one must give careful attention to the role of *sense impressions.* Students often consider sensory impressions as noncontroversial, given, objective, dependable, and the bedrock on which theories are inductively inferred. The phrase "to make sense of it" is evidence of the security provided to us by translating abstract phenomena into sensory forms. The chicken and the egg relationship between conceptual frameworks and selected and recorded evidence is a serious epistemological issue, which, as this research makes evident, must be explicitly included in our science curricula.

Language. The role of language in the construction and maintenance of misconceptions has received considerable attention in misconceptions research in science education. Some researchers have focused specifically on defining and labeling concepts in relation to the structure of a discipline (Ashlock, 1987). In this case, the naming of a significant set of relationships indicates its value within the discipline. Pines (1985) described the important function of language: "A word is like a conceptual handle, enabling one to hold on to the concept and manipulate it" (p. 108).

Other work has been devoted to describing the relationships between the use of scientific terms (e.g., force, energy, heat) in daily life and the precise definitions these terms have within their discipline. Solomon (1983) expressed this relationship well:

Meanings which are in daily use *cannot be obliterated* by science lessons, however convincingly presented. Even when the concepts and theories of science have been learnt, the older meanings, and loose explications of the life-world, will still linger on. . . . This implies that our students will acquire, through their instruction in science, a second domain of knowledge which is radically different from the first but coexistent with it. Under these circumstances we shall want to know if they are aware of these two competing sets of meanings and, more importantly, how they decide which one to use during problem-solving exercises. (p. 129, emphasis in original)

Within this tradition it is frequently emphasized that the role of language in the construction of understanding extends beyond labeling and communication of propositional knowledge into the social construction of knowledge (Skemp, 1971; Vygotsky, 1978). Scientific language is examined in the larger cultural and social context (also described by Wittgenstein as "language games") in which scientific meanings are established (Confrey, 1981; Head & Sutton, 1985).

Sutton (1980) distinguished denotative meanings in science (rigorous definitions) from connotative meanings in everyday experience (a framework of associations and implications). He suggested that science often proceeds by redefining and making precise everyday terms, and that scientific terms are also incorporated into a culture through metaphoric extensions of their meanings. Hewson (1985) provided an example of such cultural-scientific mingling in her study of the conceptions of heat held by the Sotho group in southern Africa. Other studies indicate a confusion among the terms *heat, cold,* and *temperature.* Linn and Songer (1987) report that many students claim "they are basically the same," or that "temperature is all degrees and heat is above warm."

Analogy. More recently, researchers in science education have concentrated not only on students' formal ways of tackling difficult problems, but on students' use of informal but powerful analogies and models in their attempts to understand scientific conceptual systems (Gentner, 1980; Norman & Rumelhart, 1975). These analogies can both promote and hinder conceptual development as witnessed in the use of analogies such as flow in electrical circuits. Clement (1981) explored the analogical relations that doctoral students and professors in technical fields invoked in trying to solve a problem concerning the stretch of a spring. He found that *"spontaneous analogies have been observed to play a significant role in the solutions of a number of scientifically trained subjects"* (p. 1, emphasis in original). In addition to documenting the use of analogy, he also explored the processes of generating and extending analogies.

Clement (1987) studied 59 analogies generated by 16 freshman engineering majors in 24 problem-solving episodes. Half of these episodes were anthropomorphic, referring to their own body actions. Many were erroneous from the perspective of expert physicists. Occasionally, the students generated a sequence of analogies or formed a generalization based on an analogy, and used these occasions to suggest that analogies are an effective source of conceptual change. From this, Clement concluded that students are able to exhibit creative solution strategies of an analogical form, which encourages conceptual change.

Historical perspectives. Researchers in this tradition have often found the historical development of a concept to be a rich source for (a) describing potential misconceptions, (b) demonstrating at least one developmental sequence that leads to the current concepts, and (c) providing a variety of problems that provoke consideration of alternative frameworks (Clement, 1983; Lybeck, 1985; Lybeck, Stromdahl, & Tullberg, 1985; Marton, 1978).

Research on the history of the concept under consideration provides access to the milieu that often assisted people in that field in the development of the concept. For example, Confrey (1980) examined the history of the calculus and suggested seven different conceptions of number that mathematicians held. She documented that, according to Boyer (1949), it was the combination of (a) the outstanding problem in the sciences to describe growth and change, (b) the reimportation of algebra from the Middle East, and (c) the awkwardness of the theory of ratios, which created a setting in which the fundamental concepts of calculus were developed. In examining this history, it became apparent that most students were being introduced to calculus without an understanding that the application of discrete methods to continuous quantities led to disturbing paradoxes.

Without this understanding, students were baffled and therefore resistant to the complexities of limits.

Epistemology. These researchers have debated three levels of epistemological questions: (a) the epistemological underpinnings of each discipline (e.g., physics, biology), (b) the epistemological basis that guides students as they learn science, and (c) the epistemological basis for the conduct of research on misconceptions.

Disciplinary epistemology is characterized by a rejection of empiricist/positivist traditions in which science is conceived of as inductive generalizations of observations. Building from current work in the philosophy of science (Lakatos, 1976; Lakatos & Musgrave, 1970; Toulmin, 1972), science is characterized as theory-laden throughout, from its observations to its theories. The progress of scientific theories is explained in terms of meta-level considerations such as parsimony, elegance, explanatory power, and increasing acceptance by scientists. It is emphasized that the development of scientific ideas will not necessarily parallel the proof. Misconceptions research suggests that, educationally, the development of ideas may be fertile ground for providing educational researchers with insights into the nature of learning. (See Strike & Posner, 1985, for an excellent discussion of empiricist commitments.) Much of this work has been the basis for the development of constructivist theories of knowledge in science, and such a reexamination of researchers' own conceptions of science and mathematics must precede any examination of students' conceptions.

In *epistemology of students,* the implications of "the child as scientist" that result from such a reconceptualization have been highly endorsed by the community (Osborne & Freyberg, 1985). Building from the work of Kelly, a constructivist, Gilbert, Watts, and Osborne have promoted the view that what needs to be investigated is "children's science," as opposed to "adult science." The emphasis here is on the hypothesis that a child may not be "seeing" the same set of events as a teacher, researcher, or expert. It suggests that many times a child's response is labeled erroneous too quickly and that if one were to imagine how the child was making sense of the situation, then one would find the errors to be reasoned and supportable.

In more recent work, researchers have not only documented that students are acting reasonably, but they have begun to describe the basis for students' epistemological beliefs. In mathematics, Confrey (1980) argued that students see mathematics as external, unchanging, and noncontroversial. Schoenfeld (1985) suggested that students are "naive empiricists" and that formal procedures often are not used in problem-solving circumstances requiring discovery rather than proof. DiSessa (1983) hypothesized the existence of phenomenological primitives, which compete in problematic situations and create a significant fragmentation in what students know.

In a fascinating review of the research on probability, Hawkins and Kapadia (1984) describe four conceptions of probability: a priori, frequentist, subjective and intuitive, and formal. The authors explicitly reject the view that only formal probability can be legitimately taught, and argue instead that "subjective probability is an area which is often neglected in classroom-oriented research, although it may be a fundamental precursor for the formal probability taught in schools" (p. 350). They criticize the research of Piaget and Inhelder (1975) for its formalist standards, preferring instead the work of Fischbein (1975), with its emphasis on social mediation. In an interesting application of disciplinary epistemology, they apply the idea of standard error to the idea of misconceptions and argue that perhaps researchers should seek precision (the lessening of inconsistency in student responses over time) rather than accuracy (the convergence of student concepts with expert opinion).

Science educators have taught students to consider epistemological issues through techniques such as the application of Gowin's Vee (Gowin, 1987), as they struggle with the question of how to overcome the oversimplification of philosophy of science implied by "the scientific method." Gowin uses vee diagrams to map events by showing the two components (conceptual and methodological) that are linked to the focal event (hence the vee). Together with Novak's conceptual maps, these tools aid students in learning and provide teachers with alternatives to the dominant modes of evaluation of learning that currently exist.

In *research epistemology*, examining the epistemologies underlying the content and the student methods led to vigorous debates about the conduct and claims of the research itself. This debate was manifested in part in the discussions on what terminology to use for misconceptions, alternative conceptions, or child science (Abimbola, 1988) and on how structured the interviews needed to be (Steffe & Cobb, 1983). Some argued that the conceptual change approach was in conflict with the Piagetian stages (Gilbert & Watts, 1983), and others argued that it was compatible (Steffe, 1988).

Metacognition. Within the science and math education community, some have emphasized the metacognitive elements of knowing. Researchers have been concerned not only with a student's beliefs, but with the student's awareness of that belief system. Captured succinctly by Novak and Gowin's phrase, *Learning How To Learn* (1984), the research in this area often documents how difficult it is for students to describe their beliefs, their methods, or their processes for solving problems. Whimbey and Lochhead (1984) developed methods to increase students' awareness of their own knowledge in their methods of paired-problem solving.

Multiple representations. Researchers have become increasingly aware that many of the students' misconceptions have evolved from the narrowness of their means of representing phenomena. For example, in representing real world phenomena, students often rely solely on representing functions as a graph, a table, or an algebraic equation, with little facility in moving among these representations or in seeking convergence in meaning. One misconception that results from this occurs when students assume that a graph of position (y) and time (x) is identical to the physical path of an object (McDermott et al., 1983; Schuster, 1981). With the development of effective computer technology, researchers emphasized that students can access graphical portrayals rapidly; these graphs can then be manipulated dynamically (Dugdale, 1986–1987) or connected to measurement tools (Barclay, 1986). Others advocate skepticism, indicating that these representations, like any others, need interpretation and cannot be assumed to be viewed in the ways intended by designers (Goldenberg, 1987). Regardless of the apparent complexities of multiple representations, its advocates in physics (DiSessa & Wiser, 1987), statistics (Rubin, Rosebery, & Bruce, 1988), and mathematics (Confrey & Smith, 1988; Kaput, 1986) see this as the basis for deeper conceptualizations.

Cultural and social dimensions. A small segment of this literature is concerned explicitly with the cultural and social dimensions of misconceptions. As reported earlier, Hewson (1985) explored the conceptions of heat held by natives of Sotha and found interesting relationships between their cultural and cognitive beliefs and those of formal science. In another study (Hewson, 1986), she found relationships between cognition and ethnography in examining tasks on floating and sinking. Ogunniyi (1987) researched the interaction between the traditional and scientific view of cosmology and also showed interactions between traditional culture and scientific instruction. In other cross-cultural work, researchers have studied the use of arithmetic and measurement in Third World workplaces and found significant discrepancies between the formal and informal performances of the workers (Carraher, Carraher, & Schliemann, 1985; Lave, 1977).

This research challenges the Western tradition of assuming that cognition can be examined relatively independently of culture, and it has gained widespread interest in the alternative conceptions community due to its immediate implications for the informal and formal aspects of schooling. The extent to which it will actually encourage researchers and curriculum designers to reconceptualize the legitimacy of relying solely on formal scientific or mathematical approaches to their disciplines will be evident as the interest in this research area increases.

Summary

Alternative conceptions research has documented students' beliefs indicating that they enter instruction with conceptual configurations that are culturally embedded; are tied into the use of language; are connected to other concepts; have historical precursors; and are embedded in a cycle of expectation, prediction, and confirmation or rejection. For students as for scientists, it appears that the course of learning is not a simple process of accretion, but involves progressive consideration of alternative perspectives and the resolution of anomalies. The philosophy of science provides a rich resource for these investigations.

Studies on Systematic Errors: Research in the Information-Processing Tradition

The third framework for research on student conceptions has a long history in errors research. This research has connections with behaviorism in the United States, although in Germany the connections are closer to Gestalt theory, and in the Soviet Union to curriculum revision (Radatz, 1979). The emphasis in this area is on errors in procedural knowledge and, as a result, the approach is dominant in the area of mathematics and programming. The selection of procedural knowledge as the focus leads the researchers to select topics in which calculations or production of programs is constrained by the rules of the system, to select information-processing models of cognition, and to employ large-scale diagnostic tests.

Procedural misconceptions in mathematics. Radatz proposes a categorization of errors and relates them to an information-processing approach. He wrote, "Various causes of errors that cut across mathematical content topics can be identified by examining the mechanisms used in obtaining, processing, retaining and reproducing the information in mathematical tasks" (p. 164). The categories he identifies include (a) errors due to processing iconic representations; (b) errors due to deficient mastery of prerequisite skills, facts, and concepts; (c) errors due to incorrect associations or rigidity of thinking leading to inadequate flexibility in decoding and encoding new information and the inhibition of processing new information; and (d) errors due to the application of irrelevant rules or strategies.

Newman (1977) developed an alternative classification of errors, reviewed and reported in Clements (1980). Newman suggested that errors occur in the interaction between the question and the person attempting it and that, in the process of problem solving, the sources of errors include (in order from lower or earlier stages to higher or later ones) reading, comprehension, transformation (selection of appropriate model), process, and encoding. Other general sources include carelessness and motivation.

In testing and developing this hierarchical framework, Clements reports that Newman found 47% of her population of low-achievers (grade 6) made errors prior to the process stage (of which 12% were at the transformation stage). Clements found in an average fifth, sixth, and seventh grade group, fewer errors were made at the two lower levels; one-quarter of the errors were at the transformation stage. Clements interprets this data to emphasize that failure in the early stages of problem solving can lead to selection of incorrect processes later.

Errors are like misconceptions in that they result from nonrandom applications of rules based on certain beliefs. They are unlike misconceptions (as defined in the previous framework) in that they typically are not well-connected into a theoretical position, or the theoretical connections lack articulation by the researcher. For example, when a student cancels the x in the algebraic expression $(x + 3)/ (x + 5)$ to get 3/5, it is described as an error. Systematic errors are defined as errorful rules that produce a pattern of incorrect responses. However, many researchers in the information-processing tradition use the terms *error* and *misconception* interchangeably. For example, Nesher (1987) uses misconceptions to mean these systematic errors and describes them as "a line of thinking that causes a series of errors all resulting from an incorrect underlying premise, rather than sporadic, unconnected and non-systematic errors" (p. 35).

In the widely known work on Buggy undertaken by Brown and VanLehn (1980), the terminology of slips, systematic errors, and bugs is introduced. In a 1982 paper, VanLehn offers definitions of each: A slip is an "unintentional, careless mistake in that a little extra care apparently makes them disappear" (p. 6); a systematic error is "a testable prediction about what new problems a student will get wrong" (p. 6); and a bug is defined as follows:

Once we look beyond what kinds of exercises the student misses and look at the actual answers given, we find in many cases that these answers can be precisely predicted by computing the answers to the given problems using a procedure which is a small perturbation in the fine structure of the correct procedure. Such perturbations serve as a precise description of the errors. We call them "bugs." (p. 7)

In this same article, VanLehn continues to explain how the bugs are used within a larger framework, which he calls "Repair Theory." VanLehn wrote,

Repair Theory is based on the insight that when a student gets stuck while executing his possibly incomplete subtraction procedure, he is unlikely to just quit as a computer does when it can't execute the next step in a procedure. Instead the student will do a small amount of problem solving, just enough to get "unstuck" and complete the subtraction problem. The local problem solving strategies are called "repairs" despite the fact that they rarely succeed in rectifying the broken procedure[;] . . . they result in a buggy solution. (p. 9)

Buggy is exemplary of the early work on systematic errors in that its treatment of errors relies heavily on inductive reasoning. Errors are collected and categorized according to their procedural similarities. The choice of procedurally based categories (as opposed to other features of subtraction, for example, its ties to addition, its roots in human activity, its connections to informal language such as "take away") constitutes a key decision by researchers regarding their approach to the study of subtraction. Subtraction becomes identified with the rule for carrying out the procedure. This reliance on a procedural, rule-governed view of mathematical knowledge is somewhat characteristic of the work in this framework and, in the case of Buggy, the authors are surprisingly candid about their decisions:

The initial task chosen for investigation is ordinary multidigit subtraction. Its main advantage, from a psychological point of view, is that it is a virtually meaningless procedure. Most elementary school students have only a dim conception of the underlying semantics of subtraction, which are rooted in the base ten representation of numbers. When compared to the procedures they use to operate vending machines or play games, subtraction is as dry, formal and disconnected from everyday interests as the nonsense syllables used in early psychological investigations were different from real words. This isolation is the bane of teachers but a boon to the psychologist. It allows one to study a skill without bringing in a world's worth of associations. (VanLehn, 1983, p. 201)

Other work on systematic errors shares the characteristics of a strong reliance on procedural competence as a claim for knowledge. Three factors may account for this:

1. The topics of study in this area are often ones in which calculation (Resnick et al., 1989) or symbolic manipulation (Davis, 1980; Matz, 1979) is at issue, and these topics are frequently treated procedurally—not only as individually rule governed, but as constrained within a system of interdependent rules. Thus, epistemologically, validity relies heavily on consistency.

2. By selecting the information-processing paradigm as the guiding metaphor, the researchers tend to speak of knowledge as bits of information and of the mind as a processor of programs (procedures), wherein the issue is typically one of how that information is stored, processed, or retrieved (Cobb, 1987; Fisher et al., 1983).

3. This research typically employs methods of large-scale diagnostic testing followed by clinical interviews to aid in interpretation. Improving diagnostic tools frequently is an explicit goal of the work.

Work by Davis (1980) on the concept of frames illustrates the tie between the procedural focus and the information-processing metaphor. He distinguishes two kinds of mathematical ideas: "*thought processes* that are essentially sequential and consist of 'more primitive' steps" (p. 169), and *frames,* "a specific information-representation structure that a person can build up in his or her memory and can subsequently retrieve from memory when it is needed" (p. 170). After giving some examples of frames, including the Buggy work, the work of Matz (1979) in algebra, and the "students and professors" work (Clement, 1982; Kaput & Sims-Knight, 1983; Rosnick & Clement, 1980), he offers a set of characteristics of frames. Some of these are as follows:

- They serve as "assimilation schemas" for organizing input data.
- Their inner workings are revealed by the errors they produce.
- They were "correct" in a more limited setting.
- They demand certain input information and will not function correctly unless all of this input information is provided.
- They are persistent.
- Their creation and operation follow orderly rules.
- Their retrieval may be cued by brief, explicit, specific cues.

In their report entitled, "The Conceptualization of Mathematics Learning as a Foundation of Improved Measurement," Davis and McKnight (1979) offered the most elaborate example of using a procedural, information-processing approach to systematic errors. In this work, explicitly concerned with devising diagnostic measurement tools more sophisticated than simple counts of correct and incorrect answers, the authors propose a structure for algebraic understanding that includes procedures, sub- and super-procedures, visually moderated sequences, integrated sequence, frames, assimilation, heuristics, and metalanguage.

Dissatisfaction with an overreliance on procedural knowledge has more recently encouraged systematic error researchers to seek a more conceptual basis for errors. As Resnick et al. (1989) expressed in their research on decimal fractions, researchers are attempting to extend the work of "buggy algorithms" (which they characterize as lacking reference to conceptual content or meaning) to

investigate whether children's efforts to make conceptual sense of new mathematics instruction in terms of their already available knowledge may sometimes lead them to make systematic errors. In particular, we explore the possibility that children overgeneralize concepts from a familiar domain of mathematics in order to interpret a new domain. (p. 9)

Building from the rules that Sackur-Grisvard and Leonard (1985) found in fourth and fifth grade French classes, Resnick et al. attempted to explain the rules in terms of previous knowledge and overgeneralization.

Sackur-Grisvard and Leonard suggested that students' tendency to predict that the number with the most decimal places is larger (found in 25 to 40% of fourth and fifth graders) was connected with students' correct belief that the more places a whole number has, the larger it is; they called this a "whole number influence." They further predicted that the rule that "the more decimal places, the smaller the number" (found in <6% of fourth and fifth graders) was due to the (correct) belief that, because tenths > hundredths > thousandths, and so on, the value of the decimal decreases with increasing length. Finally, some children (incorrectly) predicted that the whole number rule applies except when there are zeros to the right of the decimal point (i.e., 3.02), and that these numbers are necessarily the smallest, depending on how many zeros there are. Resnick et al. predicted that an inadequate whole number place value concept generated this error.

This more conceptual work, as contrasted to approaches that generate only an inductive generalization or rule for prediction, actually attempts to specify the relationship between the rule and other mathematical ideas. Researchers can construct measurement items that validate their predictions, and the explanatory potential of this approach exceeds that of previous work. Resnick et al.'s conclusions exhibit similarities to the work on student conceptions in science education, in that these researchers see errors as a necessary part of instructional process. They concluded,

Errorful rules, on this view, are intrinsic to all learning—at least as a temporary phenomenon—because they are the natural result of children's efforts to interpret what they are told and to go beyond the cases actually presented. Several analyses . . . have shown that these errorful rules are intelligent constructions based on what is more often incomplete than incorrect knowledge. Errorful rules . . . are best regarded as useful diagnostic tools for instructors, who can often use the children's systematic errors to detect the nature of children's understanding of a mathematical topic . . . [and to document] errors and the conceptual understanding that underlies them. (p. 26)

Systematic error researchers such as Resnick et al. have advanced beyond inductive empiricism in that they express their concern for understanding that is deeper than procedural. They do not, however, expressly define what they mean by conceptual understanding. In this particular work, it appears that *conceptual sense* means relating an idea to previous knowledge. However, it can be argued that the previous knowledge they select is itself procedural knowledge—knowledge of how fractions and whole numbers behave. Is there any other way of understanding decimals than as symbolic representations? Labinowicz (1989), operating in the Piagetian framework of genetic epistemology, examined how students come to understand place value in general first and then are able to apply it to decimals.

An interesting quality of research on systematic errors is that it continues to evolve toward the other two frameworks, but is inhibited in doing so by its epistemological naïveté. An example is Nesher's concept of a "Learning System" (Nesher, 1987). Building on the work of Popper on refutation, Nesher makes a strong case for the importance of errors as a source of insight for students. She claims, "We need our beacons in the form of errors, that mark for us the constraints and limitations of our knowledge" (p. 37). The question that continually remains unexamined is the one that creates the need for a model of learning—an essential inadequacy in this work. The question again is, erroneous from whose perspective? In the systematic errors work, the errors are seen from the perspective of the expert. How is the student to come to recognize these as "erroneous"? In fact, this is exactly the question that caused philosophers of science to reject Popper's position; students cannot see their solution as erroneous until they have constructed a new problem and a new solution. Doing this usually means revising their previous belief so that number of digits is not the defining characteristic of magnitude, but a combination of place and value is the determinant. It is these changes that Piaget suggests occur through reflective abstraction and accommodation, and that philosophers of science explain through an evolutionary or revolutionary combination of sociological and psychological juggling of methodological, epistemological, linguistic, and other complex forms.

Nesher's (1987) solution is to propose a Learning System with two components: knowledge and exemplification. Knowledge is "an articulation of the unit of knowledge to be taught based upon expert knowledge" (p. 37); exemplification is "an illustrative domain, homomorphic to the knowledge component" (p. 37), but intuitively familiar. She writes, "The selection of the exemplification component should ensure that the relations and the operations among the objects be amenable to complete correspondence with the knowledge component to be taught" (p. 38). Her example is to use the folding of a piece of paper and pin pricking of the outline of a figure as an exemplification component for the knowledge component of reflection of a figure on a plane about a given axis.

The elegance of her proposal lies in her acknowledgement of a child's need for quick, convincing, and familiar feedback. This is reminiscent of the careful design of experiments conducted by Douady (1986) and colleagues to explore similarity. They created a group project on jigsaw puzzles in which each member was assigned to enlarge individual pieces and then test their solutions by "refitting" the pieces. The researchers looked for evidence of additive versus multiplicative strategies (Hart, 1988) and for particular transformations that appeared easier or harder. Success or failure was determined by the group.

What remains unaddressed in this framework is the question of what makes a mathematician or scientist claim that one system is homomorphic with another. In Nesher's example of an exemplification system, the child was asked to predict the location of a stick figure after reflection about a given axis. Then the student was to fold the paper and create a copy of the figure with pinpricks to check his or her results. This activity was labeled "discovery from the child's point of view."

Epistemologically, this is a weak form of discovery. The child was assigned a predictive task and then discovered whether he or she made the "right" prediction. The teacher operationalized reflection as the action of folding. Little is known about whether the child would later confuse translations and reflections, because the framework excluded any other transformations. Nor could one ascertain whether the student would recognize reflections as they occurred in mirrors or water. Furthermore, the child did not invent the procedure and thus could have carried out the task without insight. Thus, the situation is declared homomorphic, although to the child the lack of continuity in the lines or the transference of shape (but not color) might lead the child to see the task as isolated or irrelevant.

Researchers in the information-processing tradition of systematic errors tend to hold the position that mathematical or scientific structures exist independently of the viewer; hence these structures' existence is imperative and they await discovery. They seldom consider seriously the possibility that another interpretation of the structures is possible and thus that one can view evidence of student errors only as deviations from their own or from the dominant perspective. The question of what it is that will bring a child to see the exemplification as homomorphic is neglected in the discussion. Nesher (1987) ultimately turns the authority for truth and correctness over to the mathematician:

Clearly the child cannot reach conclusions about the truths of mathematics with such rigorous methods as those applied by pure mathematicians. While mathematicians can demonstrate the truth of a given sentence by proving its coherence within the entire mathematical system, young children cannot. (p. 38)

Not all work in the systematic error tradition is limited to considering primarily procedural knowledge. Davis and Vinner (1986) describe research on students' misconceptions about limits, which proceeds from a different origin. Rejecting the "empty vessel theory," they offer a view of naive conceptualizations as prior knowledge that may conflict with the new ideas the teacher hopes to teach. They indicate their epistemological interest by using situations in which a student may hold two competing ideas and will "retrieve" the erroneous response rather than the new one. They studied this one summer in a lab school by examining students' understanding of the limit of sequences after the students had demonstrated competence with the material during the school year. They also knew that the original introduction to limits of sequences had been done through informal examples, construction of sequences, use of geometric representation, and, finally, formal definition. This work was based on the idea of a *concept image,* a term used to refer to the configuration of mental pictures of concepts, examples, pictures, applications, and so forth, which enrich and compete with the formal definition. Nonetheless, Davis and Vinner found that significant errors resurfaced, and identified five sources of errors:

1. Language. Limits are bounds, as in speed limits, and are seen as mathematical bounds; hence only monotonic increasing sequences are allowed.

2. Assembling mathematical representations from premathematical fragments. Mathematical ideas have their basis in premathematical experiences, which can be confusing.

3. Mathematical ideas are built gradually. A partial representation can overwhelm others.

4. Specific examples can dominate. Monotonic sequences are the most common in instruction.

5. Students misinterpret their own experience. What applies in one case (algebraic transformation) will apply in another.

They drew an interesting conclusion from this experience: "It was clear that misconceptions were part of the students' ideas about limits" (p. 301). From the perspective of conceptual change or the Piagetian theorists, this conclusion would come as no surprise. In fact, these researchers would see it as an opportunity for further research. Davis and Vinner, however, show evidence of their commitment to the framework of systematic errors as they added that, if retrieval is the issue, then they needed to focus students' attention on the "crux of the matter" and "to provide a more explicit confrontation between a student's correct ideas and his or her incorrect ideas" (p. 301).

Misconceptions in programming. Much of the research on students' conceptions of programming fits within the third framework on systematic errors in that the errors are described, but learning is not considered to be adaptation. Little attention is given to the students' alternative model, only to their deviation from the approach of experts. Furthermore, this literature is easily assimilated into the research on systematic errors in that as the student learns to work with the computer, the researchers assume that their mind acts as its own processor, storage, and retrieval system.

A significant contrast between the research on programming and the research on systematic errors in mathematics is the state of evolution of programming languages and their relative novelty. The mathematics that dominates the school curriculum is relatively uniform and stable. In contrast, programming has multiple instances of alternative strategies for accomplishing programming tasks. In studying programming, researchers have the leeway to imagine and even propose changes in the languages to "fit" more appropriately with the users' cognitive tendencies. Soloway, Bonar, and Ehrlich (1983) demonstrate this in a study of Pascal programming. They found that most people in the general population prefer to have the computer read a value before processing (the read/process approach), rather than solve a basic averaging problem using a process/read method. They found that most people in the general population get higher performance and fewer errors when they use Pascal-L (which facilitates the read/process approach) than when they use Pascal (which is most compatible with the process/read method). However, experienced programmers appear to be accustomed to the process/read approach, and they demonstrate equally strong performance with either version of Pascal.

A second difference between research on programming and systematic errors research is its close ties to problem-solving strategies. Plans and strategies are typically basic constructs in programming investigations. For example, Soloway and Ehrlich (1984) propose that two types of knowledge are basic to expert programming: programming plans and rules of programming discourse. They liken programming plans to the notion of a scheme, where a scheme is defined as generic knowledge structures that guide the comprehender's interpretation, inferences, expectations, and attention. This use of schema is similar to that of Davis's frames. They found that expert programmers do rely on these plans, and their performance drops dramatically when the assumptions typical of plans or rules of discourse were violated.

In a review of the research on programming bugs, Pea et al. (1987) describe three types of bugs: programming language-independent conceptual bugs, knowledge unavailability bugs, and knowledge retrieval bugs. The transition to formal programming also requires recognition of the limitations of the computer, which students often have difficulties accepting. Evidence is provided that students tend (a) to lack precision in their instructions; (b) to expect the computer to carry out commands concurrently rather than sequentially; and (c) to attribute intentionality to the computer or assume that it will respond to their egocentric but inexplicit intentions. These last three bugs are subsumed under the "superbug," wherein a student imagines that an intelligent and interpretive mind resides in the computer.

Hancock, Perkins, and Simmons (n.d.) report on a study of children's programming difficulties in learning Logo (ages 8-12) and Basic (ages 10-16). They found that the students (a) often avoided challenging questions by declining to accept the problem; (b) exhibited a slippage in their goals when their programs produced unintended results; (c) were bounded by their templates for subroutines; (d) had difficulties transferring if there were even minimal changes in context; (e) could not effectively employ hand-executed methods of checking; and (f) could not monitor the flow of control or use primitives. Interestingly enough, these difficulties led to their introduction of critical components of the programming process: goal formation, planning, coding, checking, testing, diagnosing, and repairing. Like the work on systematic errors, the literature on programming misconceptions does not typically specify a model for learning. However, in certain ways, these critical components suggest a potential view of learning as problem solving.

Perkins and Simmons (1988) offer a comprehensive treatment of misconceptions under the framework of systematic errors. They identify four levels (or frames) of knowledge and suggest that "misunderstandings can in part be explained by a shallow repertoire in the noncontent frames and that appropriately designed education can do much to foster understanding by addressing all the frames and their interactions" (p. 306). The four levels are

- The content frame: the facts, definitions, and algorithms along with the metacognitive facility for monitoring their use.
- The problem-solving frame: the domain specific and general problem-solving strategies, beliefs, and autoregulative processes.
- The epistemic frame: domain specific and general validation strategies, explanations, and evidence.
- The inquiry frame: domain specific and general strategies for challenging, critiquing, and extending work.

Using these four levels, Perkins and Simmons describe how three patterns of misunderstandings might occur. They suggest naive concepts might result from lack of content knowledge or from preferring one concept over another (rigidity over springiness in describing a table). In addition to the content frame, they describe how the epistemic and the inquiry frame could contribute to the persistence of beliefs. Ritual patterns emerge in students who have a high degree of technical and formal knowledge when their formal knowledge exists in isolation from their intuitive knowledge. Their content frame and problem solving appear relatively sophisticated in verbal or formulae-rich areas, but their epistemic and inquiry frames lack development. Using these frames, the authors also discuss Gordian concepts wherein expert knowledge appears erroneous in hindsight, and where the four frames weave together to conceal the deficiencies. In discussing applications of their approach, Perkins and Simmons deny the necessity of a learning theory and argue that a mix of

direct instruction, personal discovery, and proceduralization will be sufficient to ensure learning, provided teaching involves all four frames.

Summary

The third framework of this review approaches misconceptions as systematic errors. Like the researchers on misconceptions in science education, systematic errors researchers see these difficulties as unavoidable
and necessary in the development of knowledge. Unlike researchers in the
other two traditions, they do not consider them epistemologically legitimate, but rather developmentally primitive. Research in this area is
largely concerned with diagnosing errors and remedying them through
exposure and rejection. No learning theory is seen as necessary to account
for these errors, beyond the recognition that the errors represent
overgeneralizations on the part of the students. The research on programming was categorized within the systematic error framework due to its
ties to the information-processing perspective and the tendency of researchers in this area to describe error patterns as atheoretical phenomena. An exception to this was discussed in the article by Perkins and
Simmons, where multiple frames were postulated to account for the
misunderstandings.

IMPLICATIONS FOR TEACHING

The work on student conceptions is heavily oriented toward examining
student learning through methods that take place outside the classroom in
interview settings. Although many researchers attempt to relate their
studies to classroom processes through observation or examination of
materials, the links remain relatively distant and tentative. As Romberg
and Carpenter (1986) state,

> We currently know a great deal more about how children learn mathematics [or science, pro-
> gramming, probability, statistics] than we know about how to apply this knowledge to math-
> ematics instruction. Research is clearly needed to explore how knowledge of children's
> learning of mathematics . . . can be applied to instruction. The learning research provides a
> starting point for designing instruction. It also provides extremely powerful tools for evalu-
> ating the effects of instruction. This may be the most significant implication that current
> cognitive research . . . has for research on instruction. (p. 859)

Research on teaching in ways that are informed by the work on student
conceptions is increasingly evident. However, the impact of the research
on student conceptions on research on teaching will vary depending on
the framework in which the work is interpreted. Gilbert and Watts (1983)
warn of this:

Work conducted with the classical view of concept will regard misconceptions as simply "wrong." An extreme response might be to merely ignore any evidence of misunderstanding on the part of the student and to "start from scratch" following a tabula rasa view of teaching (see Gilbert, Osborne, & Fensham, 1982). There might be some temptation to merely repeat earlier teaching sequences, perhaps under the illusion that simple repetition or precisely formed phrases are sufficient to engender formal understanding. (p. 83)

They go on to suggest that a more appropriate view of concepts might be that of "concept formation," because it leads toward a relational view of concepts. However, they prefer a conceptual development perspective, by which they mean "proposals that accept the existence, and value to their users, of alternative frameworks and seek to educate by the expansion of applicability of those frameworks or seek to modify them towards the consensus view of formal science" (p. 83).

Within the community of those researching student conceptions, there are increasingly more studies of how one might use the rich database of research to improve instruction. Nussbaum and Novick (1982) designed an instructional strategy for eliciting student conceptions that they hope will lead to cognitive restructuring. They suggest that a teacher should (a) create a situation that requires students to invoke their conceptual frameworks; (b) ask them to describe their framework verbally and pictorially; (c) assist them in stating their ideas clearly, avoiding evaluation; (d) have students debate the pros and cons; and (e) support the most highly generalizable solution.

Rowell and Dawson (1979) point out three possible forms of resolution when students have conflicting concepts: One alternative may seem more logical; an analogous situation may make one concept more attractive; or neither alternative may seem appropriate and a new unifying idea is constructed. Hewson's (1981) analysis of conceptual change indicates that change is relatively difficult to obtain unless one is dissatisfied with his or her present belief and sees an alternative framework as intelligible, plausible, and fruitful. Smith and Lott (1983) conducted research on practicing teachers and found that teaching teachers to teach for conceptual change was indeed difficult. They found that students often were uncertain about which empirical generalizations were important, that communication often involved sources of ambiguity, that framing of essential issues was lacking, and that instruction often addressed the wrong preconception.

A number of French researchers use the term *didactical theory* for their work on classroom instruction (Brousseau, 1986; Vergnaud, 1982). Balacheff (1987) summarized this approach by introducing the epistemological framework of the research, which consisted of hypothesizing that students must actively interpret and make sense of experience, and that problems are the origin of knowledge. Given this, they assume that teaching is the process of socializing the students' conceptions, because mathematics is a social construction. They conduct research in cooperation with classroom teachers, and they design instructional activities to elicit student conceptions through the formulation of problems, to require students to act on and validate their constructions, and to lead toward institutionalization of the curriculum through public discourse and resolution. They then study the effectiveness of the materials and methods in this ecologically valid setting.

Other instructional strategies include scheme change theory and ideational confrontation (Champagne et al., 1983). Both of these approaches require dialectic exchange in the articulation and revision of conceptions. Watts and Gilbert (1983) suggest that three processes seem to be present in successful interventions:

- Explication: performance of a task or concept analysis to lead to the articulation of a conception.
- Expectation: verbalization of a prediction based on the conception.
- Exploration: testing models and comparing results, given the conceptions.

Minstrell (1982) and Pope (1985) state the need for a classroom environment that invites and encourages open discourse and trust. Minstrell argues for a free-speaking context with encouragement for articulation, a variety of first-hand experiences with objects at all grades, and encouragement to seek the simplest rational solution. Pope adds the dimension of affect to the discussion, warning that if conceptual change is rushed or forces students to abandon their beliefs prematurely, it may cause anxiety, fear, or threat. She encourages the use of Kelly's Fixed Role Therapy, wherein a person is encouraged to see his or her current constructs as hypotheses and to express an openness and willingness to change. Pope also recognizes the importance of holding an approach to teacher education that is compatible with the epistemological and psychological assumptions of student conceptions and reviews work in this framework.

The concern expressed earlier by Romberg and Carpenter (1986) must be addressed if we are to create large-scale change in teachers' practices. However, a sweeping statement declaring the absence of research on teaching in these three frameworks ignores the detailed and extensive studies by researchers such as Kamii (1985), Easley (1977), and Duckworth (1987). Though these studies have often involved small numbers of participants, they provide a rich resource of knowledge on the kinds of intervention necessary to create lasting changes and on the ways teachers can contribute to this process.

DISCUSSION AND CONCLUSIONS:
SUGGESTED DIRECTIONS FOR RESEARCH

The field of student conceptions is healthy and, in Lakatosian terms, represents a progressive research program. A review of the research indicates that the field remains vigorous and attractive for researchers and teachers alike. Unlike much educational research, its roots lie in disciplinary competence. By focusing on particular concepts, researchers have demonstrated that cognitive development needs to be informed by the microgenesis of particular concepts and by constellations of concepts, as well as by broader stage theory and by theories of thinking and learning. Although this review called for more integration of teaching and learning perspectives, it also warned that such a movement must be well informed by exemplary (e.g., interview-based) research on learning. Otherwise, researchers risk losing the quality and specificity of their conceptual analyses in the complexity of classroom interactions.

An overly narrow focus on disciplinary content also has limitations. Researchers exhibit a tendency to read and reference the literature within their field and subfield (e.g., science, chemistry). Therefore their work could benefit from a more careful consideration of cross-disciplinary, cross-field contrasts. One of the most striking aspects of this review is the tendency for researchers to use their disciplinary commitments as a lens for viewing the phenomena of cognitive development itself in a recursive way. Thus researchers of conceptions about programming view the mind as an information-processing machine; educators in biology stress adaptation and development; physicists and chemists analyze into components; and those interested in probability view misconceptions as systematic errors. Though these interactions between content and cognition are appropriate if one views the mind as both a lens (as it frames our experience) and as a phenomenon (which is itself an experience), more specific comparisons across disciplines would produce worthwhile cross-fertilization.

Cross-fertilization is argued for on the grounds that the different academic disciplines introduce approaches and distinctions in the literature that will promote the long-term viability of the field of conceptions research. For instance, there is a value in considering how the issues of planning and goal specification, discussed in the programming literature, and prediction, from the probability literature, might be useful for research in science and mathematics education.

The review also suggests the value of careful consideration of the contrasts and similarities among the three frameworks for research: genetic epistemology, alternative conceptions, and systematic errors. The research on systematic errors deserves praise for its immediate relevance to and attractiveness for classroom teachers, but it also needs to reconsider its treatment of learning and its premature assimilation of alternative perspectives to formalist views. This weakness is attributed in part to its failure to consider sociopsychological perspectives and environmental factors.

The research on alternative conceptions can be lauded for its attention to the role of everyday experience and language in the development of conceptions and its clear emphasis on exploring students' idiographic methods. In this tradition, as in the others, there is a significant subgroup whose attention to documenting failures and labeling them erroneous becomes redundant and stifling to the development of the field; as the field matures, more attention to criticism and rigor is warranted. However, the continued vitality of this research seems largely dependent on two factors: the continued exploration of how these conceptions evolve and are affected within classroom interactions, and the complementary sense of community developed within this research community. It was also argued that this community could benefit from a more sympathetic and broader reading of the Piagetian literature, particularly on operations and their basis in human action. Taken alone, beliefs have a rather static quality, which often hides their ties to actions and situations. The work on analogy (Clement, 1981, 1987; Clement & Brown, 1984) could be productive in this direction.

Finally, researchers in the Piagetian tradition are encouraged to seek the broader perspective evident in the work on systematic errors by anchoring their work in the larger field of literature and by addressing some of the issues identified in the section on alternative conceptions. However, this should not lessen the importance of their detailed consideration of the processes of the child or alter their commitment to reconsidering the parameters of appropriate mathematics or scientific content, which is the strength of this work. In mathematics, more consideration of genuine problems is suggested, so that the definitions of operations extend beyond Piaget's logical operations into the variety of human actions we witness and participate in in the world.

The review also suggests a few issues for future examination. In all areas, more attention needs to be paid to the issue of memory and reflective abstraction. Although a "storage container" view of memory has proven useful, it has not explained convincingly why certain conceptions are so persistent and how reconstruction, not retrieval, is undertaken. Differences in the form of memories (theoretical, analogical, iconic, and phenomenological) must be clarified. Work on phenomenology and constitutionalism by Marton (1981) and Marton and Neuman (1988) may prove useful in this area.

Second, the contextual quality of tasks can be criticized for its narrowness and its tendency to replicate the formal and detached quality of schooling; this was especially apparent in the work in mathematics, probability, and programming. Modeling real-world phenomena and a stronger use of context are encouraged (see de Lange Jzn, 1987; Rogoff & Lave, 1984; Van Den Brink, 1984). In doing so, I suggest that the view of cognition needs to include more social dimensions (Wertsch, 1985), both in terms of the view of subject matter embedded in the work and in the examination of classrooms.

Finally, researchers are encouraged to undertake research on teacher education in a more sophisticated manner, without recreating the immature myopia of early research on misconceptions. It seems contradictory for researchers to expect that the frameworks they have developed for looking at student conceptions will necessarily be sufficient for looking at teachers, and yet this appears to be a common perception. In conducting research on teachers, it is hoped that time documenting failures can be minimized; instead, the emphasis should be on descriptive studies of interventions designed for the greatest possibility of success.

REFERENCES

Abimbola, O. (1988). The problem of terminology in the study of student conceptions in science education. *Science Education, 72*(2), 175–184.

Ashlock, R. (1987). Use of informal language when introducing concepts. *Focus on Learning Problems in Mathematics, 9*(3), 31–37.

Ausubel, D. P. (1963). *The psychology of meaningful verbal learning.* New York: Grune and Stratton.

Ausubel, D. P. (1968). *Educational psychology: A cognitive view.* New York: Holt, Rinehart and Winston.

Ausubel, D. P., Novak, J. D., & Hanesian, H. (1978). *Educational psychology: A cognitive view* (2nd ed.). New York: Holt, Rinehart and Winston.

Balacheff, N. (1987, April). *Towards a "problematique" for research on mathematics teaching.* Major address of the research presession of the 65th annual meeting of the National Council of Teachers of Mathematics, Annaheim, CA.

Bamberger, J., & Duckworth, E. (1982). *Analysis of data from an experiment in teacher development.* Washington, DC: National Institute of Education.

Barclay, W. (1986, June). *Graphing misconceptions and possible remedies using microcomputer-based labs.* Paper presented at the National Educational Computing Conference, San Diego, CA.

Barowy, W., & Lochhead, J. (1980). Abstract reasoning in rotational physics. *AAPT Announcer, 10*(2), 74.

Blanchet, A. (1977). The construction and balancing of mobiles, methodological problems. *Archives de Psychologie, 45,* 29–52.

Boyer, C. B. (1949). *The history of the calculus and its conceptual development.* New York: Dover.

Bridgman, P. W. (1927). *The logic of modern physics.* New York: Macmillan.

Brousseau, G. (1986). *Basic theory and methods in the didactics of mathematics.* Proceedings of the Second Conference on Systematic Cooperation Between Theory and Practice in Mathematics Education, Enschede, The Netherlands.

Brown, J. S., & VanLehn, K. (1980). Repair theory: A generative theory of bugs in procedural skills. *Cognitive Science, 4,* 379–426.

Brownell, W. A. (1945). When is arithmetic meaningful? *Journal of Educational Research, 38,* 481–498.

Bruner, J. S. (1960). *The process of education.* Cambridge, MA: Harvard University Press.

Carraher, T., Carraher, D., & Schliemann, A. (1985). Mathematics in the streets and schools. *British Journal of Developmental Psychology, 3,* 21–29.

Champagne, A. B., Gunstone, R. F., & Klopfer, L. E. (1983). Naive knowledge and science learning. *Research in Science and Technological Education, 1*(2), 173–183.

Champagne, A. B., Gunstone, R. F., & Klopfer, L. E. (1985). Instructional consequences of students' knowledge about physical phenomena. In L. West & A. L. Pines (Eds.), *Cognitive structure and conceptual change* (pp. 61–90). New York: Academic Press.

Claxton, G. (1987, April). *Minitheories: A modular approach to learning applied to science.* Paper presented at the annual meeting of the American Educational Research Association, Washington, DC.

Clement, J. (1981). Analogy generation in scientific problem solving. *Proceedings of the Third Annual Meeting of the Cognitive Science Society* (Vol. 3, pp. 137–140). Hillsdale, NJ: Lawrence Erlbaum.

Clement, J. (1982). Students' preconceptions in introductory mechanics. *American Journal of Physics, 50*(1), 66–71.

Clement, J. (1983). Students' alternative conceptions in mechanics: A coherent system of preconceptions. In H. Helm & J. Novak (Eds.), *Proceedings of the International Seminar: Misconceptions in Science and Mathematics* (pp. 310–315). Ithaca, NY: Cornell University, Department of Education.

Clement, J. (1987). Overcoming students' misconceptions in physics: The role of anchoring intuitions and analogical reasoning. In J. D. Novak (Ed.), *Proceedings of the Second International Seminar: Misconceptions and Educational Strategies in Science and Mathematics* (pp. 84–97). Ithaca, NY: Cornell University, Department of Education.

Clement, J., & Brown, D. (1984). *Using analogical reasoning to deal with "deep" misconceptions in physics* (Report from the Cognitive Processes Research Group). Amherst: University of Massachusetts.

Clements, M. A. (1980). Analyzing children's errors on written mathematical tasks. *Educational Studies in Mathematics, 11,* 1–21.

Cobb, P. (1987). Information-processing psychology and mathematics education—A constructivist perspective. *Journal of Mathematical Behavior, 6*(1), 3–40.

Cobb, P., & Steffe, L. (1983, March). The constructivist researcher as teacher and model builder. *Journal of Research in Mathematics, 14*(2), 83–94.

Confrey, J. (1980). *Conceptual change, number concepts and the introduction to calculus.* Unpublished doctoral dissertation, Cornell University, Ithaca, NY.

Confrey, J. (1981). Concepts, processes, and mathematics instruction. *For the Learning of Mathematics, 2*(1), 8–12.

Confrey, J. (1985). Towards a framework for constructivist instruction. In *Proceedings of the Ninth International Conference of the International Group for the Psychology of Mathematics Education* (pp. 477–483). Noordwijkerhout, The Netherlands: Leen Streefland, State University of Utrecht.

Confrey, J., & Smith, E. (1988, October). *Student centered design for educational software.* Paper presented at the conference on Technology in Collegiate Mathematics, Ohio State University, Columbus, OH.

Davis, R. (1975). Cognitive processes involved in solving simple algebraic equations. *Journal of Children's Mathematical Behavior, 1*(3), 7–35.

Davis, R. (1976). The children's mathematics project: An overview of the Syracuse/Illinois component. *Journal of Children's Mathematical Behavior, 1* (Suppl. 1), 32–59.

Davis, R. (1980). The postulation of certain specific, explicit, commonly-shared frames. *Journal of Children's Mathematical Behavior, 3*(1), 167–200.

Davis, R., & McKnight, C. (1979). *The conceptualization of mathematics learning as a foundation of improved measurement* (Development Rep. No. 4). Urbana, IL: University of Illinois, Curriculum Laboratory.

Davis, R., & Vinner, S. (1986). The notion of limit: Some seemingly unavoidable misconception stages. *Journal of Mathematical Behavior, 5,* 281–303.

de Lange Jzn, J. (1987). *Mathematics: Insight and meaning.* Utrecht, The Netherlands: Rijksuniversiteit Utrecht.

DiSessa, A. (1983). Phenomenology and the evolution of intuition. In D. Gentner & A. L. Stevens (Eds.), *Mental models.* Hillsdale, NJ: Erlbaum.

DiSessa, A., & Wiser, M. (1987, April). *Current research problems in novice qualitative physics reasoning.* Paper presented at the annual meeting of the American Educational Research Association, Washington, DC.

Douady, A. (1986). *Research on students' conceptions of proportion.* Seminar presented to the Department of Education, Cornell University, Ithaca, NY.

Driver, R. H. (1981). Pupils' alternative frameworks in science. *European Journal of Science Education, 3*(1), 93–101.

Driver, R., & Bell, B. (1986). Students' thinking and the learning of science: A constructivist view. *School Science Review, 67,* 443–456.

Driver, R., & Easley, J. (1978). Pupils and paradigms: A review of literature related to concept development in adolescent science students. *Studies in Science Education, 5,* 61–84.

Driver, R., & Erickson, G. (1983). Theories-in-action: Some theoretical and empirical issues in the study of students' conceptual frameworks in science. *Studies in Science Education, 10,* 37–60.

Duckworth, E. (1987). *"The having of wonderful ideas" and other essays on teaching and learning.* New York: Columbia University, Teachers College.

Dugdale, S. (1986–87). Pathfinder: A microcomputer experience in interpreting graphs. *Journal of Educational Technology Systems, 15*(3), 259–280.

Easley, J. A. (1977). *On clinical studies in mathematics education.* Columbus, OH: Ohio State University, Information Reference Center for Science, Mathematics, and Environmental Education.

Einstein, A., & Infeld, L. (1938). *The evolution of physics.* Cambridge: Cambridge University Press.

Erlwanger, S. (1975). Case studies of children's conceptions of mathematics— Part 1. *Journal of Children's Mathematical Behavior, 1*(3), 157–268.

Eylon, B., & Linn, M. (1988). Learning and instruction: An examination of four research perspectives in science education. *Review of Educational Research, 58*(3), 251–301.

Fischbein, E. (1975). *The intuitive sources of probabilistic thinking.* Dordrecht, Holland: Reidels.

Fisher, K. M., & Lipson, J. I. (1983). Ten rules of thumb: Information processing interpretations of error research in learning. In H. Helm & J. Novak (Eds.), _Proceedings of the International Seminar: Misconceptions in Science and Mathematics_ (pp. 150–152). Ithaca, NY: Cornell University.

Franz, G., & Papert, S. (1988). Computer as material: Messing about with time. _Teacher's College Record, 89_(3), 408–417.

Fredette, N., & Lochhead, J. (1980). Student conceptions of simple circuits. _Physics Teacher, 18,_ 194–198.

Gentner, D. (1980). _The structure of analogical models in science_ (BBN Rep. No. 4451). Washington, DC: Office of Naval Research.

Gilbert, J. K., Osborne, R. J., & Fensham, P. J. (1982). Children's science and its consequences for teaching. _Science Education, 66_(4), 623–633.

Gilbert, J. K., & Watts, D. M. (1983). Concepts, misconceptions and alternative conceptions: Changing perspectives in science education. _Studies in Science Education, 10,_ 61–98.

Ginsburg, H. (1975). Young children's informal knowledge of mathematics. _Journal of Children's Mathematical Behavior, 1_(3), 63–156.

Ginsburg, H. (1976). Children's mathematics project: An overview of the Cornell component. _Journal of Children's Mathematical Behavior, 1_(Suppl. 1), 7–31.

Ginsburg, H. (1977). _Children's arithmetic: How they learn it and how you teach it._ Austin, TX: Pro-Ed.

Goldenberg, E. P. (1987). Believing is seeing: How preconceptions influence the perception of graphs. In J. Bergeron, N. Herscovics, & C. Kieran (Eds.), _Proceedings of the Eleventh International Conference of the International Group for the Psychology of Mathematics Education_ (Vol. 1, pp. 197–203). Montreal, Canada.

Gowin, D. B. (1987). _Educating._ Ithaca, NY: Cornell University Press.

Hancock, C., Perkins D., & Simmons, R. (n.d.). _Children's programming difficulties—An exploratory study._ Unpublished manuscript.

Hart, K. (1988). Ratio and proportion. In J. Hiebert & M. Behr (Eds.), _Number concepts and operations in the middle grades._ Reston, VA: National Council of Teachers of Mathematics.

Hawkins, A., & Kapadia, R. (1984). Children's conceptions of probability—A psychological and pedagogical review. _Educational Studies in Mathematics, 15,_ 349–377.

Hawkins, D. (1974). _The informed vision: Essays on learning and human nature._ New York: Agathon Press.

Hawkins, D. (1978). Critical barriers to science learning. _Outlook, 29,_ 3–23.

Hawkins, D., Apelman, M., Colton, R., & Flexner, A. (1982). _A report of research on critical barriers to the learning and understanding of elementary science._ Washington, DC: National Science Foundation.

Head, J., & Sutton, C. (1985). Understanding and commitment. In L. West & A. Pines (Eds.), _Cognitive structure and conceptual change_ (pp. 91–100). New York: Academic Press.

Helm, H., & Novak, J. D. (Eds.). (1983, June). _Proceedings of the International Seminar: Misconceptions in Science and Mathematics._ Ithaca, NY: Cornell University, Department of Education.

Hewson, M. G. (1985). The role of intellectual environment in the origin of conceptions: An exploratory study. In L. West & A. Pines (Eds.), _Cognitive structure and conceptual change_ (pp. 153–162). New York: Academic Press.

Hewson, P. W. (1981). A conceptual change approach to learning science. *European Journal of Science Education, 3*(4), 383–396.

Hunting, R. (1986). Rachel's schemes for constructing fraction knowledge. *Educational Studies in Mathematics, 17*(1), 49–66.

Johansson, B., Marton, F., & Svensson, L. (1985). An approach to describing learning as change between qualitatively different conceptions. In L. West & A. Pines (Eds.), *Cognitive structure and conceptual change* (pp. 233–258). New York: Academic Press.

Kahneman, D., & Tversky, A. (1972). Subjective probability: A judgment of representativeness. *Cognitive Psychology, 3*, 430–454.

Kamii, C. K. (1985). *Young children reinvent arithmetic: Implications of Piaget's theory.* New York: Columbia University, Teachers College Press.

Kaput, J. (1986). Information technology and mathematics: Opening new representational windows. *Journal of Mathematical Behavior, 5*, 187–207.

Kaput, J., & Sims-Knight, J. (1983). Errors in translations to algebraic equations: Roots and implications. *Focus on Learning Problems in Mathematics, 5*(3 & 4), 63–78.

Karmiloff-Smith, A., & Inhelder, B. (1975). If you want to get ahead, get a theory. *Cognition, 3*(3), 195–212.

Kuhn, T. (1970). *The structure of scientific revolutions.* Chicago, IL: University of Chicago Press.

Labinowicz, E. (1989, March). *Children's use of tens as numerical building blocks.* Paper presented at the annual meeting of the American Educational Research Association, San Francisco, CA.

Lakatos, I. (1970). Falsification and methodology of scientific research programmes. In I. Lakatos & A. Musgrave (Eds.), *Criticism and the growth of knowledge* (pp. 91–196). Cambridge, England: Cambridge University Press.

Lakatos, I. (1976). *Proof and refutations: The logic of mathematical discovery.* Cambridge, England: Cambridge University Press.

Lakatos, I., & Musgrave, A. (1970). *Criticism and the growth of knowledge.* Cambridge, England: Cambridge University Press.

Lampert, M. (1986). Teaching multiplication. *Journal of Mathematical Behavior, 5*(3), 241–280.

Lave, J. (1977). Tailor-made experiments and evaluating the intellectual consequences of apprenticeship training. *Quarterly Newsletter of the Institute for Comparative Human Development, 1*(2), 1–3.

Linn, M., & Songer, N. (1987). *Teaching a post-positivist understanding of science: Incorporating technology into the curriculum.* Berkeley, CA: University of California, Computer as Lab Partner Project.

Lybeck, L. (1985, May). *Research into science and mathematics education at Goteborg.* Paper presented at the Nordic Conference on Science and Technology Education: The Challenge of the Future (pp. 125–162). Copenhagen: Royal Danish School of Educational Studies, Nordic Center of INCE and UNESCO.

Lybeck, L., Stromdahl, H., & Tullberg, A. (1985, May). *Students' conceptions of amount of substance and its S1 unit/mol—A subject didactic study.* Paper presented at the Nordic Conference on Science and Technology Education: The Challenge of the Future. Copenhagen: Royal Danish School of Educational Studies, Nordic Center of INCE and UNESCO.

Marton, F. (1978). *Describing conceptions of the world around us.* Goteborg: University of Goteborg, Institute of Education.

Marton, F. (1981). Phenomenography—Describing conceptions of the world around us. *Instructional Science, 10,* 177–200.

Marton, F., & Neuman, D. (1988, July-August). *Constructivism versus constitutionalism. Some implications for the first mathematics education.* Paper presented at the Sixth International Congress on Mathematical Education, Budapest, Hungary.

Matz, M. (1979, April). Underlying mechanisms of bugs in algebraic solutions. Paper presented at the annual meeting of the American Educational Research Association, San Francisco, CA.

McCloskey, M., Caramazza, A., & Green, B. (1980). Curvilinear motion in the absence of external forces: Naive beliefs about motion of objects. *Science, 210,* 1139–1141.

McDermott, L., Rosequist, M., Popp, B., & van Zee, E. (1983, April). *Identifying and overcoming student conceptual difficulties in physics: Student difficulties in connecting graphs, concepts, and physical phenomena.* Paper presented at the annual meeting of the American Educational Research Association, Montreal, Canada.

Minstrell, J. (1982). Explaining the "at rest" condition of an object. *Physics Teacher, 20,* 10–14.

Minstrell, J., & Stimpson, V. C. (1986). *Instruction for understanding: A cognitive process framework* (Final Report). Mercer Island, WA: Mercer Island School District.

Mintzes, J. J., & Arnaudin, M. W. (1984). *Children's biology: A review of research on conceptual development in the life sciences.* Wilmington, NC: University of North Carolina, Department of Biological Sciences.

Nesher, P. (1987). Towards an instructional theory: The role of students' misconceptions. *For the Learning of Mathematics, 7*(3), 33–40.

Newman, M. (1977). An analysis of sixth-grade pupils' errors on written mathematical tasks. In M. Clemes & J. Foyster (Eds.), *Research in Mathematics Education in Australia* (Vol. 1, pp. 239–258).

Norman, D., & Rumelhart, D. (1975). *Explorations in cognition.* San Francisco, CA: W. H. Freeman.

Novak, J. D. (1977a). An alternative to Piagetian psychology for science and mathematics education. *Science Education, 61*(4), 453–477.

Novak, J. D. (1977b). *A theory of education.* Ithaca, NY: Cornell University Press.

Novak, J. D. (1985). Metalearning and metaknowledge strategies to help students learn how to learn. In L. West & A. Pines (Eds.), *Cognitive structure and conceptual change* (pp. 189–207). New York: Academic Press.

Novak, J. D. (Ed.). (1987). *Proceedings of the second international seminar: Misconceptions and educational strategies in science and mathematics—Vols. 1, 2, 3.* Ithaca, NY: Cornell University, Department of Education.

Novak, J. D., & Gowin, D. B. (1984). *Learning how to learn.* Cambridge, England: Cambridge University Press.

Nussbaum, J., & Novak, J. (1976). An assessment of children's concepts of the earth utilizing structured interviews. *Science Education, 60*(4), 535–550.

Nussbaum, J., & Novick, S. (1982). Alternative frameworks, conceptual conflict and accommodation: Toward a principled teaching strategy. *Instructional Science, 11,* 183–200.

Ogunniyi, M. B. (1987). Conceptions of traditional cosmological ideas among literate and nonliterate Nigerians. *Journal of Research in Science Teaching, 24*(2), 107–117.

Osborne, R. (1984). Children's dynamics. *Physics Teacher, 7,* 504-508.
Osborne, R., & Freyberg, P. (1985). *Learning in science: The implications of children's science.* Portsmouth, NH: Heinemann.
Osborne, R. J., & Wittrock, M. C. (1983). Learning science: A generative process. *Science Education, 67*(4), 498-508.
Pa, N. A. N. (1986). Meaning in arithmetic from four different perspectives. *For the Learning of Mathematics, 6*(1), 11-16.
Papert, S. (1980). *Mindstorms.* New York: Basic Books.
Pea, R. D., Soloway, E., & Spohrer, J. C. (1987). The buggy path to the development of programming expertise. *Focus on Learning Problems in Mathematics, 9*(1), 5-30.
Perkins, D. N., & Simmons, R. (1988). Patterns of misunderstanding: An integrative model for science, math, and programming. *Review of Educational Research, 58*(3), 303-326.
Pfundt, H., & Duit, R. (1985). *Bibliography: Students' alternative frameworks and science education.* Kiel, Federal Republic of Germany: Institute for Science Education.
Pfundt, H., & Duit, R. (1988). *Bibliography: Students' alternative frameworks and science education.* Kiel, Federal Republic of Germany: Institute for Science Education.
Phillips, D. (1983). After the wake: Postpositivistic educational thought. *Educational Researcher, 12*(5), 4-12.
Piaget, J. (1970). *Genetic epistemology.* New York: Norton.
Piaget, J. (1973a). *The child and reality: Problems of genetic psychology.* New York: Grossman.
Piaget, J. (1973b). *La construction du reél chez l'enfant* (5th ed.). Neuchâtel: Delachaux et Niestlé.
Piaget, J., & Inhelder, B. (1975). *The origin of the idea of chance in children.* London: Routledge and Kegan Paul.
Piaget, J., Inhelder, B., Garcia, K., & Voneche, J. (1977). *Epistemologie genetique et equilibration.* Neuchâtel: Delachaux et Niestlé.
Pines (Eds.), A. L. (1985). Towards a taxonomy of conceptual relations. In L. West & A. L. Pines (Eds.), *Cognitive structure and conceptual change* (pp. 101-116). New York: Academic Press.
Pollatsek, A., Lima, S., & Well, A. D. (1981). Concept or computation: Students' understanding of the mean. *Educational Studies in Mathematics, 12,* 191-204.
Pope, M. (1985, August). *Constructivist goggles: Implications for process in teaching and learning.* Paper presented at the British Educational Research Association conference, Sheffield, England.
Pope, M., & Gilbert, J. (1983). Personal experience and the construction of knowledge in science. *Science Education, 67*(2), 173-203.
Popper, K. (1959). *The logic of scientific discovery.* London, England: Hutchinson.
Popper, K. (1962). *Conjectures and refutations.* London, England: Routledge and Kegan Paul.
Posner, G. J., Strike, K. A., Hewson, P. W., & Gertzog, W. A. (1982). Accommodation of a scientific conception: Toward a theory of conceptual change. *Science Education, 66*(2), 211-227.
Radatz, H. (1979). Error analysis in mathematics education. *Journal for Research in Mathematics Education, 10*(3), 163-172.
Resnick, L. (1983). Mathematics and science learning: A new conception. *Science, 220,* 477-478.

Resnick, L., Nesher, P., Leonard, F., Magone, M., Omanson, S., & Peled, I. (1989). Conceptual bases of arithmetic errors: The case of decimal fractions. *Journal for Research in Mathematics Education, 20*(1), 8–27.

Ripple, R., & Rockcastle, V. (1964). *Piaget rediscovered: A report of the conference on cognitive studies and curriculum development.* Ithaca, NY: Cornell University, Department of Education.

Rogoff, B., & Lave, J. (1984). *Everyday cognition.* Cambridge, MA: Harvard University Press.

Romberg, T., & Carpenter, T. (1986). Research on teaching and learning mathematics: Two disciplines of scientific inquiry. In M. C. Wittrock (Ed.), *Handbook for research on teaching* (pp. 850–873). New York: Macmillan.

Rosnick, P., & Clement, J. (1980). Learning without understanding: The effect of tutoring strategies on algebra misconceptions. *Journal of Mathematical Behavior, 3*(1), 3–27.

Rowell, J., & Dawson, C. (1979). Cognitive conflict: Its nature and use in the teaching of science. *Research in Science Education, 9,* 169–175.

Rubin, A., Rosebery, A. S., & Bruce, B. (1988). *ELASTIC and reasoning under uncertainty* (Final Report). Cambridge, MA: BBN Laboratories.

Sackur-Grisvard, C., & Leonard, F. (1985). Intermediate cognitive organization in the process of learning a mathematical concept: The order of positive decimal numbers. *Cognition and Instruction, 2,* 157–174.

Schoenfeld, A. (1985). *Mathematical problem solving.* New York: Academic Press.

Schuster, D. (1981, January). *Qualitative physics problems.* Paper presented at the national meeting of the American Association of Physics Teachers, New York.

Shymansky, J. A., & Kyle, W. C. (1988). Summary of research in science education in 1986. *Science Education, 72*(Special issue), 249–402.

Sinclair, H. (1987, July). Constructivism and the psychology of mathematics. In *Proceedings of the 11th International Conference of the International Group for the Psychology of Mathematics Education* (pp. 28–41). Montreal, Canada.

Skemp, R. (1971, April). *Mathematics as an activity of our intelligence.* Paper presented at the annual conference of the Research Council for Diagnostic and Prescriptive Mathematics, Vancouver, Canada.

Smith, E. L., & Lott, G. W. (1983). *Ways of going wrong in teaching for conceptual change: Report on the Conceptual Change Project.* East Lansing, MI: Michigan State University, Institute for Research on Teaching.

Solomon, J. (1983). Messy, contradictory, and obstinately persistent: A study of children's out-of-school ideas about energy. *School Science Review, 65*(231), 225–229.

Soloway, E., Bonar, J., & Ehrlich, K. (1983). Cognitive strategies and looping constructs: An empirical study. *Research Contributions—Communications of the ACM, 26*(11), 853–860.

Soloway, E., & Ehrlich, K. (1984). Empirical studies of programming knowledge. *IEEE Transactions on Software Engineering, SE-10*(5), 595–609.

Steffe. L. P. (n.d.). *Children's construction of meaning for arithmetical words—A curriculum problem.* Athens, GA: University of Georgia, Department of Mathematics Education.

Steffe, L. P. (1988). Children's construction of number sequences and multiplying schemes. In M. Behr & J. Hiebert (Eds.), *Number concepts and operations in the middle grades* (Research Agenda for Mathematics Education, pp. 119–141). Reston, VA: National Council of Teachers of Mathematics.

Steffe, L. P., & Cobb, P. (1988). *Construction of arithmetical meanings and strategies.* New York: Springer-Verlag.

Steffe, L., & Cobb, P. (1983). Early multiplication and division. In J. Bergeron, N. Herscovics, & C. Kieran (Eds.), *Proceedings of the annual meeting of the Psychology of Mathematics Education—North American Chapter* (Vol. 1, pp. 284–291). Montreal, Canada.

Steffe, L. P., von Glasersfeld, E., Richards, J., & Cobb, P. (1983). *Children's counting types—Philosophy, theory and application.* Westport, CT: Praeger.

Strike, K., & Posner, G. (1985). A conceptual change view of learning and understanding. In L. West & A. L. Pines (Eds.), *Cognitive structure and conceptual change* (pp. 211–232). New York: Academic Press.

Sutton, C. (1980). Science, language and meaning. *School Science Review, 62,* 47–56.

Toulmin, S. (1972). *Human understanding.* Princeton, NJ: Princeton University Press.

Tversky, A., & Kahneman, D. (1971). The belief in the law of small numbers. *Psychological Bulletin, 76,* 105–110.

Van Den Brink, F. J. (1984). Numbers in conceptual frameworks. *Educational Studies in Mathematics, 15,* 239–257.

VanLehn, K. (1982). Bugs are not enough: Empirical study of bugs, impasses and repairs in procedural skills. *Journal of Mathematical Behavior, 3*(2), 3–71.

VanLehn, K. (1983). On the representation of procedures in repair theory. In H. Ginsburg (Ed.), *The development of mathematical thinking* (pp. 201–253). New York: Academic Press.

Vergnaud, G. (1982). Cognitive and developmental psychology and research in mathematics education: Some theoretical and methodological issues. *For the Learning of Mathematics, 3*(2), 31–41.

von Glasersfeld, E. (1982). An interpretation of Piaget's constructivism. In *Revue internationale de philosophie* (142–143). France: Ministere de L'Education Nationale.

von Glasersfeld, E. (1983). On the concept of interpretation. *Poetics, 12,* 207–218.

von Glasersfeld, E. (1984a). An introduction to radical constructivism. In P. Watzlawick (Ed.), *The invented reality* (pp. 17–40). New York: Norton.

von Glasersfeld, E. (1984b, June). *Reconstructing the concept of knowledge.* (Paper presented at the Seminar on Constructivism). Geneva: Archive Jean Piaget.

Vygotsky, L. S. (1978). *Mind in society.* Cambridge, MA: Harvard University Press.

Watts, D. M., & Gilbert, J. K. (1983). Enigmas in school science: Students' conceptions for scientifically associated words. *Research in Science and Technological Education, 1*(2), 161–171.

Weaver, J., & Kilpatrick, J. (1972). The place of meaning in mathematics instruction: Selected theoretical papers of William A. Brownell. *Studies in Mathematics, 21*(special issue).

Well, A. D., Pollatsek, A., Konold, C. E., & Hardiman, P. (1984, August). *Statistical reasoning in novices.* Paper prepared for the Conference on Thinking, Harvard University, Cambridge, MA. (ERIC Document Reproduction Service No. ED 258 792)

West, L. H. T., & Pines, A. L. (1985). *Cognitive structure and conceptual change.* New York: Academic Press.

West, L., Fensham, P., & Garrard, J. (1985). Describing the cognitive structures of learners following instruction in chemistry. In L. West & A. L. Pines (Eds.),

Cognitive structure and conceptual change (pp. 29–48). New York: Academic Press.

Whimbey, A., & Lochhead, J. (1984). *Beyond problem solving and comprehension: An exploration of quantitative reasoning.* Philadelphia, PA: Franklin Institute Press.

White, R. (1985). Interview protocols and dimensions of cognitive structure. In L. West & A. L. Pines (Eds.), *Cognitive structure and conceptual change* (pp. 51–59). New York: Academic Press.

Wittrock, M. C. (1977). Learning as a generative process. In M. C. Wittrock (Ed.), *Learning and instruction* (pp. 621–631). Berkeley, CA: McCutchan.

Chapter 2

Alternative Perspectives
on Knowing Mathematics
in Elementary Schools

RALPH T. PUTNAM
MAGDALENE LAMPERT
PENELOPE L. PETERSON
Michigan State University

From all sides are coming calls for changes in the amount and quality of mathematics instruction in American schools (National Commission on Excellence in Education, 1983; National Council of Teachers of Mathematics, 1980; National Research Council, 1989). Critics of current practice posit that the mathematical achievement and understanding of U.S. students lag behind that of their peers in other industrialized countries (McKnight et al., 1987; National Commission on Excellence in Education, 1983; National Science Board Commission on Pre-College Education in Mathematics Science and Technology, 1983). Mathematics educators and researchers argue that current mathematics instruction in elementary and secondary schools focuses too much on efficient computation and not enough on mathematical understanding, problem solving, and reasoning. Leaders in business and industry are claiming that public education must change to teach to the new kinds of mathematical skills and problem-solving abilities that will be important for the worker of the future (see, e.g., Bernstein, 1988). Accompanying these criticisms of current practice are calls for reform, for making lasting and fundamental

Work on this chapter was sponsored in part by the Center for the Learning and Teaching of Elementary Subjects, Institute for Research on Teaching, Michigan State University. The Center is funded primarily by the Office of Educational Research and Improvement, U.S. Department of Education. The opinions expressed in this publication do not necessarily reflect the position or endorsement of the Office or Department (Cooperative Agreement No. G0098C0226). An earlier version of this chapter was published as a report (Elementary Subjects Center No. 11) of the Center for the Learning and Teaching of Elementary Subjects. Ralph Putnam, as a Spencer Fellow of the National Academy of Education, received partial funding for his efforts.

changes in mathematics curriculum and instruction in public schools. New guidelines and standards for mathematics curriculum, instruction, and assessment have been proposed by the NCTM (1989), and some states, most notably California (California State Department of Education, 1987), have developed or are developing new guidelines aimed at the reform of mathematics curriculum and educational practice.

Two sets of beliefs about why the learning of mathematics is important motivate current reform efforts. These beliefs parallel traditional but differing goals of schooling. First is the belief that mathematics provides essential tools and ways of thinking in our society, including those needed for a successful labor force and for an informed citizenry. Second is the belief that mathematics is important for self-fulfillment and appreciation of one of humanity's great cultural achievements.

One major argument for the reform of mathematics curriculum and instruction is that with advances in technology and information systems, the needs of the labor force in our society have changed, but the learning and teaching of mathematics in our nation's schools have not shifted correspondingly to meet these needs. To be competitive in the global economy, our country needs a well-prepared, productive work force. And our current instructional system is not providing students with the kind of mathematics they need to be productive. The ready availability of calculators and computers, along with their increasing role in the workplace, has raised serious questions about what kinds of mathematical knowledge and skills should be considered basic. In the past, an important goal of elementary school was to help a large number of students become proficient in arithmetic calculation; these skills were considered basic for a skilled labor force whose jobs largely involved carrying out repetitive and routine tasks. But with most of the repetitive production-oriented tasks being taken over by automation and by cheap labor in less developed countries, the demands on the American work force have shifted dramatically. To be productive in the workplace and to be informed citizens in our information-oriented society requires more sophisticated mathematical skills and knowledge, particularly the ability to communicate with mathematical systems and to solve a variety of complex problems.

The second argument is essentially that mathematics should be learned and used, not for any direct utilitarian purpose, but because it is a great achievement of human thinking that should be appreciated and shared with others. Knowing mathematics is an important part of what it means to be an educated person. This set of arguments is less visible than the more utilitarian one in the rhetoric of the current reform, but it is important for at least two reasons. First, much of what we value in the elementary school curriculum is justified, at least in part, by appeal to self-fulfillment and appreciation of cultural achievement. The obvious examples are history, literature, art, and music, but all subjects are valued, to some extent, because of their cultural significance. The second reason is that gaining a broad appreciation for mathematics and learning the more general ways of reasoning within it are essential to the powerful and flexible mathematical thinking and problem solving demanded by today's information-oriented society.

Resnick and Resnick (1977; see also, Resnick, 1987a) make a similar argument by pointing out the traditional tension between two traditions of schooling and literacy: A *low-literacy* tradition for training the masses to produce a competent work force has existed in parallel with a *high-literacy* tradition for an intellectual elite. Resnick and Resnick argue that the powerful and flexible thinking and reasoning that have always been the goal of education in the elite educational systems have become the basic educational goals for the masses. The challenge today is to come up with ways to work toward these difficult goals, traditionally reserved for the elite, with all students in public schools.

These and other arguments for what mathematics instruction should be like in our elementary schools raise a host of difficult questions. What kinds of mathematical knowledge will help students to become productive and informed citizens and to appreciate the beauty and power of mathematics? What does it mean to understand mathematics? What sorts of experiences with mathematics should students be having in elementary schools? In this chapter we consider various research perspectives that may help us think about some of these issues. In particular, we pose for ourselves the question, What does it mean to know and understand mathematics in powerful and useful ways? In addressing this question, we turn to three research communities or traditions that have addressed in diverse ways the question of what it means to know and understand mathematics. First we consider the views of researchers and scholars, primarily psychologists, who focus on what it means to know and understand mathematics from the perspective of the *individual knower.* Then we consider perspectives from the *discipline of mathematics.* Finally, we consider views from the perspective of *classroom practice,* in particular the ways in which researchers studying the teaching and learning of mathematics in elementary school classrooms have conceptualized mathematical knowledge.

Although each of these research traditions focuses on an aspect of the teaching and learning of mathematics that should not be ignored, they seem to exist as distinct research traditions or communities, though admittedly with fuzzy and overlapping boundaries. Researchers within these traditions have worked with different goals, assumptions, and questions, and have not considered fully the issues, concerns, and perspectives of the other traditions. When we began this effort to consider multiple perspectives on knowing and understanding mathematics, we hoped to summarize the perspectives on this issue within each of the three research traditions and then to synthesize these perspectives into some grander vision of what it should mean to understand and know mathematics in elementary schools. But as we worked, we realized the enormity and complexity of the task we had set for ourselves. Thus what we have done in three separate sections of the chapter is to consider important perspectives and issues within each of the three domains. But we are a long way from presenting a synthesis of these perspectives. Rather, we are left with a host of questions, issues, and concerns that we think will be important for all of us to consider as we respond to and participate in this current movement to reshape American mathematics education. We hope that by presenting these various perspectives in a single chapter, we will emphasize the need for researchers within the various traditions who are concerned with mathematics education to seriously consider perspectives and issues raised within the other traditions. We see the integration of these significant but diverse perspectives as being an important task for the entire community of researchers, scholars, and teachers interested in mathematics education.

In each of three major sections of this chapter, we thus consider various perspectives on knowing and understanding mathematics within one of the three research traditions: psychology, the discipline of mathematics, and research on classroom practice. But to provide a context for thinking about these perspectives, we first consider in a bit more detail current efforts to reform American mathematics education. In particular, we examine one important set of recommendations for school mathematics, the *Curriculum and Evaluation Standards for School Mathematics,* recently proposed by the National Council of Teachers of Mathematics [NCTM] (1989). At the heart of this document and most other calls for reform (NCTM, 1980; National Research Council, 1989) is the view that the current elementary school mathematics curriculum overemphasizes efficient computational arithmetic skill at the expense of understanding and problem solving. Most researchers and mathematics educators agree that there is more to mathematics than computational proficiency. But beyond this agreement are diverse views about what it means to know, understand, and learn mathematics. It is some of these diverse views we examine in the rest of the chapter.

A STATEMENT OF GOALS: NCTM CURRICULUM STANDARDS

The *Curriculum and Evaluation Standards for School Mathematics* (NCTM, 1989) represents the latest in a series of statements by the mathematics education community about what mathematics should be taught in public schools. The document is NCTM's response to the numerous calls for reform in mathematics education (National Commission on Excellence in Education, 1983; National Science Board Commission, 1983; Romberg, 1984). The *Standards* offer a vision of school mathematics that is consistent with earlier statements by NCTM and other professional organizations about ideal curriculum and instruction in mathematics (National Council of Supervisors of Mathematics, 1977; NCTM, 1980). However, NCTM has gone beyond these organizations to actually set *standards* of reform. Unlike countries in which a national curriculum exists in mathematics (e.g., Japan, United Kingdom, China), the United States has no such national curriculum or even national "vision." The NCTM *Standards* represent an attempt to develop such a vision at the national level. The recommendations are also consistent with the current efforts of the National Research Council's Mathematics Sciences Education Board (National Research Council, 1989) to rethink school mathematics from the ground up.

The NCTM (1989) *Standards* call for major changes in (a) the content of school mathematics, and (b) the nature of mathematics instruction and underlying view of mathematics learning. According to NCTM, the elementary mathematics curriculum should be broadened beyond its traditional focus on arithmetic computation to include more emphasis on conceptual understanding and on currently underrepresented mathematical domains such as geometry, measurement, and statistics. The justifications offered for these changes are largely utilitarian, focusing on the need for transformation in the kinds of mathematics that students will need in a technological, information-oriented society. The *Standards* authors argue that shifting from an industrial-based to an information-based society "has transformed both the aspects of mathematics that need to be transmitted to students and the concepts and procedures they must master if they are to be self-fulfilled, productive citizens in the next century" (p. 3).

Technology, in the form of computers and calculators, has fostered significant changes in the content of mathematics and its applications to other disciplines, just as it has caused radical changes in the workplace. Because of the growing use of computers, with their ability to manipulate huge amounts of information, quantitative approaches and techniques have become increasingly important in many disciplines. The mathematical concepts and models underlying many of these approaches, however, are not necessarily those that are emphasized in the traditional school curriculum. In addition, technology has changed the discipline of mathematics itself, by facilitating calculations and graphing, and by changing the nature of problems that mathematicians address. The traditional school curriculum has not been modified to reflect these important changes.

The nature of classroom instruction should move away from the traditionally prevalent model of teacher as teller and students as passive recipients of mathematical knowledge to an emphasis on learning mathematics through problem solving, discussion, and other practices consistent with the notion that students need to be actively involved. As justification, the *Standards* authors offer some changing features of mathematics and views on mathematical knowledge. They posit a changing view about the nature of mathematical knowledge, in particular, the view that "'knowing' mathematics is 'doing' mathematics" (NCTM, 1989, p. 7). Rather than viewing mathematics learning as the mastery of concepts and procedures, the *Standards* authors assert that such "informational knowledge" has value only to "the extent to which it is useful in the course of some purposeful activity" (p. 7). Thus, instruction should always emphasize the acquisition of and use of knowledge in the context of purposeful activity, such as problem solving, in contrast to the traditional view of mathematics teaching in which computational facts and algorithms are learned first as prerequisite skills to be applied later in the solving of problems.

In this context, NCTM (1989) offers four general social goals for education in the area of mathematics:

1. *Mathematically literate workers.* The technologically demanding workplace of today and the future will require mathematical understanding and the ability to formulate and solve complex problems, often with others. "Businesses no longer seek workers with strong backs, clever hands, and 'shopkeeper' arithmetic skills" (p. 3).

2. *Lifelong learning.* Most workers will change jobs frequently, and so need flexibility and problem-solving ability to enable them to "explore, create, accommodate to changed conditions, and actively create new knowledge over the course of their lives" (p. 4).

3. *Opportunity for all.* Because mathematics has become "a critical filter for employment and full participation in our society" (p. 4), it must be made accessible to all students, not just white males, the group that currently studies the most advanced mathematics.

4. *An informed electorate.* Because of the increasingly technical and complex nature of current issues, participation by citizens requires technical knowledge and understanding, especially skills in reading and interpreting complex information.

These social goals require that students become *mathematically literate,* a key phrase used by the *Standards* authors to describe desired outcomes of schooling. Mathematical literacy "denotes an individual's abilities to explore, conjecture, and reason logically, as well as the ability to use a variety of mathematical methods effectively to solve nonroutine problems" (NCTM, 1989, p. 5). The authors of *Everybody Counts* (Na-

tional Research Council, 1989) argue that "without the ability to understand basic mathematical ideas, one cannot fully comprehend modern
writing such as that which appears in the daily newspapers" (p. 7). They
go on to emphasize that mathematical literacy includes much more than
familiarity with numbers and arithmetic: "To cope confidently with the
demands of today's society, one must be able to grasp the implications of
many mathematical concepts—for example, chance, logic, and graphs—
that permeate daily news and routine decisions" (pp. 7–8). This view contrasts sharply with the implicit traditional view of computational skills in
arithmetic as forming the core of the basic skills needed to function effectively in the workplace and society.

The *Standards* (NCTM, 1989) authors articulate further the notion of
mathematical literacy by proposing five general goals for students:

- Learning to value mathematics—understanding its evolution and its
  role in society and the sciences.
- Becoming confident of one's own ability—coming to trust one's own
  mathematical thinking and having the ability to make sense of situations and solve problems.
- Becoming a mathematical problem solver—which is essential to becoming a productive citizen and which requires experience in solving a
  variety of extended and nonroutine problems.
- Learning to communicate mathematically—learning the signs, symbols, and terms of mathematics.
- Learning to reason mathematically—making conjectures, gathering evidence, and building mathematical arguments.

These goals reflect a shift away from the traditional practice of summarizing desired mathematical outcomes as knowledge of *skills, concepts,*
and *applications* (Fey, 1982; Trafton, 1980) to an emphasis on broader
dispositions, attitudes, and *beliefs* about the nature of mathematical
knowledge and about one's own mathematical thinking. The traditional
skills, concepts, and applications are subsumed under the more general
goals for problem solving and communication. Throughout the *Standards*
document, the authors deemphasize the view that knowledge consists of
distinct parts that should be treated separately. Rather, they emphasize
providing students with experiences through which they can build rich
connections among the various kinds of knowledge.

The curriculum standards themselves are presented as sets of standards
for elementary school (Grades K–4), middle-school (Grades 5–8), and
high school (Grades 9–12). Each set contains general standards common
to all grade levels, as well as more specific content standards for each
level. In terms of mathematical content, these standards reflect major
shifts from the content and emphasis of current mathematics curricula.

Most significant is a reduced emphasis on arithmetic computation, especially mastery of complex paper-and-pencil algorithms, with a shift in focus to meaning and appropriate use of operations, judging the reasonableness of results, and choice of appropriate procedures. Along with this shift is an emphasis on problem solving, including use of word problems with a variety of structures, everyday problems, strategies for solving problems, and open-ended problems that take more than a few minutes to solve. Mathematical topics that are considered increasingly important— but seriously underrepresented in current curricula—include geometry and measurement; probability and statistics; and patterns, relationships, and functions. For later elementary grades, algebra is included, with less focus on manipulation of symbols and memorization of rules and more focus on informal investigation and understanding of variables, expressions, and equations.

The NCTM *Standards,* and the current mathematics reform movement in general, are in some ways reminiscent of the last major reform effort in mathematics education—the "modern mathematics" of the post-Sputnik era of the 1960s (Fey, 1982; Wooten, 1965). The two reform movements have been fueled, in part, by fears of the United States losing its competitive edge in worldwide economic and scientific competition. Last time we worried about being outpaced by the Russians; this time we worry about keeping up with the Japanese. Both reform movements have called for major changes in the content of the school mathematics curriculum— expanding it beyond the traditional, almost exclusive, emphasis on mastering efficient computational skills to include more of other important aspects of mathematics. But there are some important features of the current reform movement that distinguish it from the earlier reform effort and improve its chances for success. Whereas modern mathematics was shaped by an emphasis on the formal and abstract mathematics of set theory, the NCTM *Standards* and other reform documents place more emphasis on problem solving and the links of mathematics to various situations. Current reformers also are attending more to psychological research on learning and research on classroom teaching and teacher education than did the shapers of the modern mathematics movement. The hope is that the current reform effort will be more successful than its predecessor.

The *Standards* document presents a vision of what mathematics instruction might be like. Although many of its recommendations could be supported by existing or future research, the *Standards* is not a research document. Many of the recommendations in it express assumptions and views shared by many members of the mathematics education community that have not been (or in some cases could not be) addressed by research. In the remainder of this chapter, we consider research and scholarship that can inform our thinking about recommendations like those in the NCTM *Standards,* organizing our discussion around groups of scholars focusing on the individual knower, on the discipline of mathematics, and on classroom practice.

FOCUS ON THE INDIVIDUAL KNOWER: COGNITIVE PSYCHOLOGY[1]

In considering the individual learner and knower of mathematics, we focus on cognitive perspectives that have come to dominate mainstream American psychology. The research and views we consider here include both those of psychologists using mathematics as a site for inquiry about basic issues in learning and those of researchers primarily interested in the learning of mathematics who draw on the perspectives and tools of cognitive psychology.

The dramatic shift in mainstream American psychology from its associationist and behaviorist traditions to the study of cognition has important implications for thinking about learning and teaching in schools (Calfee, 1981; Resnick, 1985; Shuell, 1986). Whereas behaviorist psychologists insisted that observable behavior was the only legitimate object of scientific study, cognitive psychologists treat "thinking processes as concrete phenomena that can be studied scientifically" (Resnick, 1985, p. 128). They continue to ground their work in observing the behavior of individuals, but use these observations as evidence for positing various cognitive structures and processes believed to produce the behavior. In thinking about learning, cognitive theorists consider learning to be changes in the knowledge or cognitive processes that produce behavior, in contrast to the behaviorist position that the learning is a change in the behavior itself (Shuell, 1986). Associationists (e.g., Thorndike, 1922) were willing to hypothesize cognitive events but built their theories of learning and knowledge around the notion of stimulus-response bonds as the building blocks of knowledge. This reductionist approach produced a view of knowledge as collections of bonds, which were combined to produce more complex forms of knowledge. Current cognitive theorists, in contrast, place much more emphasis on the structure of and relationships among various kinds of knowledge, not on knowledge as collections of discrete bits.

One important result of this shift in focus has been increased attention to and tools for studying difficult issues in learning and knowing, such as the nature of understanding and complex forms of knowledge. Whereas much psychological research on learning in the past focused on studies of isolated learning tasks such as nonsense syllables, many cognitive psychologists have turned to school-relevant domains, such as reading and mathematics, as the domains of inquiry about learning. Mathematics has served as an important site for much of this research for a variety of reasons: Mathematics' foundational role in many other disciplines makes it a prime target for understanding basic processes in thinking and knowing; much of mathematical knowledge lends itself to specification in the precise forms needed for the computational models that form the basis of cognitive science; and mathematics (or at least arithmetic) is considered an important basic skill in the school curriculum.

Another important result of this shift in focus toward cognitive processes and complex forms of knowledge has been the development of methods to examine and describe patterns of thought and knowledge, often at fine levels of detail. Methods that cognitive psychologists have used to examine what individuals do and think about as they carry out various tasks include recording reaction times or eye movements or having individuals "think aloud." Cognitive researchers use these data as a basis for hypothesizing in detail the knowledge and thought processes believed to underlie individuals' performance.

The computer has served both as metaphor and tool in the building of these theories of the knowledge and processes hypothesized to underlie performance. A basic assumption for many cognitive psychologists is that the human mind, like the computer, is essentially a processor of information. The mind receives information from the environment through the senses and processes and transforms that information. This function is similar to that performed by computers, which also process information through complex structures. The power of the computer metaphor for human thought is in its leading to precise hypotheses about how information is represented and processed in the mind. It is in building these precise hypotheses that the computer also serves as an important research tool for cognitive scientists. Some cognitive researchers write computer programs that are fine-grained simulations of human thinking. The writing of these programs promotes a certain rigor in the description of cognition.

> When computer programs behave as humans do—making similar mistakes, pausing at similar points, expressing confusion over the same issues—it is reasonable to assume that the internal processes of the human and the computer are similar, and researchers can treat the program's visible processes as a theory of the invisible processes of humans. (Resnick, 1985, p. 129).

Trying to characterize human thought in the form of computer programs has given rise to a variety of constructs for representing and describing hypothesized knowledge in people's minds (e.g., production systems, semantic networks, and schemata).

Even when they do not specify hypothesized knowledge structures in the form of computer programs, virtually all cognitive theorists share the fundamental assumption that an individual's knowledge structures and mental representations of the world play a central role in perceiving, comprehending, and acting (Shuell, 1986). An individual's perception of the environment and his or her actions are mediated through his or her cognitive structures, which are actively constructed and modified through the individual's interaction with the environment. This mediation through cognitive structures provides a basic, though overly simplified, definition of knowledge in cognitive theories: Knowledge *is* the cognitive structures of the individual knower. To know and understand mathematics from this perspective means having acquired or constructed appropriate knowledge structures.

But the story is more complicated than that. From this basic view of knowledge there has emerged a host of more specific views of what it means to know and understand mathematics. We will structure our discussion of these views around five themes. Because the themes are so highly interrelated, the order in which we discuss them is somewhat arbitrary; it will be impossible to discuss any one of the themes without bringing in aspects of the other four.

The first theme is understanding as representation, in particular the view that understanding mathematics means having internalized powerful symbols and systems for representing mathematical ideas and being able to move fluently within and between them. Because issues of representation are so fundamental to cognitive psychology and mathematics, we will also discuss representation in more general terms, foreshadowing several issues addressed later in the paper.

The second theme is understanding as knowledge structures. A large portion of research in cognitive science has been directed at describing the knowledge, in the form of cognitive structures and processes, hypothesized to underlie competent performance on various mathematical tasks. This approach builds directly on the basic view of understanding as an individual having constructed or acquired appropriate knowledge structures.

In discussing the knowledge structure of individuals, some researchers have emphasized a third theme, understanding as connections among types of knowledge. Of particular interest are connections between conceptual and procedural knowledge and between knowledge of the formal, symbolic mathematics taught in school and the rich base of informal knowledge children develop in out-of-school settings.

Researchers emphasizing the fourth theme, learning as the active construction of knowledge, have highlighted the nature of the process by which knowledge structures have been constructed or acquired by individuals. Learning mathematics with understanding from this perspective means actively reorganizing one's cognitive structures and integrating new information with existing structures.

The fifth theme, understanding as situated cognition, represents a growing movement within cognitive science to question the fundamental view of thinking and knowing underlying current cognitive theories. Rather than viewing knowledge and thinking as existing within the mind of the individual, cognition is considered to be interactively situated in physical and social contexts.

Understanding as Representation

Because the notion of representation is fundamental to both cognitive psychology and mathematics, various forms of representation are central to cognitive research on mathematics knowing and learning. One could say that cognitive psychology is about hypothesizing the sorts of mental representations that individuals have and use. At the same time, "the idea of representation is continuous with mathematics itself" (Kaput, 1987a, p. 25). Virtually all of mathematics concerns the representation of ideas, structures, or information in ways that permit powerful problem solving and manipulation of information. Thus, when one is considering the nature of knowing and learning mathematics from the perspective of cognitive psychology, issues of representation are unavoidable. In part because of its pervasiveness in this work and its role in fundamental assumptions, *representation* is a slippery term, like the term *concept*, that is used in a variety of related ways and defies precise definition (Kaput, 1985).

Kaput (1985, 1987a, 1987b), in considering the various roles of representation in learning, knowing, and doing mathematics, as well as the role of representation in posing psychological models of these phenomena, has suggested as important the following broad interacting types of representation: (a) *cognitive representation,* the representation of information or knowledge in the mind of the individual; (b) *explanatory representation,* the models that psychologists pose to describe hypothesized mental structures and events; (c) *mathematical representation,* the representation of one mathematical structure by another; and (d) *external symbolic representation,* the material forms used to express abstract mathematical ideas. As defined by Kaput (1985), following Palmer (1977), each of these forms of representation involves a *represented world* (the thing being represented), a *representing world* (the thing doing the representing), and *correspondences* between selected aspects of these two worlds.

Cognitive and *explanatory* representation are at the heart of cognitive psychology. The goal of cognitive psychologists is to construct models (explanatory representations) of what they hypothesize to be the ways information or knowledge is stored and acted upon within the minds of individuals (cognitive representations). Although psychologists often fall into using language that suggests that their models of cognition are descriptions of structures that actually exist inside the minds of individuals, it is important to remember that all psychologists' models are theories about cognitive structures and events that are, in principle, unobservable. In addition, the basic assumption in most cognitive psychology that individuals build cognitive representations of an external world runs into an epistemological dilemma: Because the external world can be known only through these same cognitive representations, there is no way of knowing what is "really" out there to be represented. In other words, it is impossible to assess the match between the representing world and the represented world (see Kaput, 1987b; von Glasersfeld, 1987).

Most researchers taking a cognitive approach in studying the knowing and learning of mathematics, however, ignore this basic philosophical dilemma by making the working assumption that it is useful to analyze and build models (representations) of the information structures and processes underlying the knowing and doing of mathematics. As we argued earlier, the (often implicit) view of what it means for an individual to know mathematics from this perspective is for that individual to have acquired or constructed the appropriate cognitive structures or representations. We consider cognitive researchers' attempts to characterize these knowledge structures in our subsequent discussion of the themes, *understanding as knowledge structures* and *understanding as connections among types of knowledge.*

Regarding *mathematical representations,* Kaput (1987a) argues that much of mathematics involves the representation of one mathematical structure by another and determining what is preserved and what is lost in the mapping between the structures. An example at a level relevant for thinking about elementary schooling is that much of algebra can be seen as representing in a general way many more particular arithmetic relationships. Kaput argues that mathematical structures are treated as abstractions or idealizations that are formally independent of the material symbols used to represent them. For example, there is a sense in which the number 3 is assumed to exist, independent of whether the number is represented by the word *three,* by the numeral *3,* or by three dots, for example, •••.

But because mathematical entities and structures are abstract, they must be expressed in some material form, and that is the role played by *external symbolic representations.* We need symbolic representations both to support our personal thinking about mathematical ideas and to communicate with others about them (Kaput, 1987b). The representations that can be used to support thinking and communicating about mathematics include not only the formal symbol systems of mathematics, such as the base-10 notational system and the Cartesian coordinate system, but more informal systems of representation as well. For example, Lesh, Post, and Behr (1987) consider the following kinds of representation systems to be important: (a) experience-based scripts, (b) manipulable models, (c) pictures or diagrams, (d) spoken languages, and (e) written symbols. All of these representation systems can be thought of as powerful tools that are developed as part of a culture and that become incorporated into the cognitive systems of individuals (Stigler & Baranes, 1988). Representation systems thus play roles similar to those of natural language in supporting personal thought and public communication. Like natural language, these symbol systems have a dual existence: There is a sense in which they exist as personal constructions in the mind of the individual and a sense in which they exist external to the individual as a product of the discourse or cultural community. One way of thinking about the goals of schooling in mathematics is for the learner to construct or internalize the shared symbol systems of mathematics.

This leads to another important set of issues about the role of representations in learning and knowing mathematics: the relationship between the *external* representation of a mathematical idea and its *internal* representation in the mind of the knower. Especially in thinking about how individuals come to know mathematics, many psychologists and mathematics educators have focused on how external representations of mathematical ideas influence the form taken by the internal cognitive representations the individual constructs or acquires (Greeno, 1987a; Hiebert & Carpenter, in press; Nesher, 1989; Schoenfeld, 1986). Thinking about this relationship from a pedagogical perspective gives rise to a host of issues, such as the degree of isomorphism, or match, between a particular external representation and the mathematical construct it is meant to represent, the accessibility or salience of particular representations for learners, and the motivational characteristics of various representations. This thinking has also given rise to the term *instructional representations* to refer to the external ways in which teachers or curriculum materials represent mathematical ideas (Ball, 1988; Greeno, 1987a; Wilson, 1988).

Some researchers have emphasized the importance of being able both to move flexibly within particular representation systems and to make translations across representation systems (Janvier, 1987). Lesh et al. (1987) argued that

part of what we mean when we say that a student "understands" an idea like "1/3" is that (1) he or she can recognize the idea embedded in a variety of qualitatively different representational systems, (2) he or she can flexibly manipulate the idea within given representational systems, and (3) he or she can accurately translate the idea from one system to another. (p. 36)

Lesh et al. offered the following example of a student moving fluently among various representations while solving a problem:

The Million Dollar Problem: Imagine that you are watching: "The A Team" on television. In the first scene, you see a crook running out of a bank carrying a bag over his shoulder, and you are told that he has stolen one million dollars in small bills. Could this really have been the case?

One student who solved this problem began by using sheets of typewriter paper to represent several dollar bills. Then, he used a box of typewriter paper to find how many $1 bills such a box would hold—thinking about how large (i.e., volume) a box would be needed to hold one million $1 bills. Next, however, holding the box of typewriter paper reminded him to think about *weight* rather than *volume.* So, he switched his representation from using a box of typewriter paper to using a book of about the same weight. By lifting a stack of books, he soon concluded that, if each bill was worth no more than $10, then such a bag would be far too large and heavy for a single person to carry. (p. 39)

The basic argument here is that learners acquire as personal cognitive tools the powerful ways of representing mathematical ideas that are used in our culture. From the perspective of cognitive psychology, this means that the individual has constructed or acquired particular internal cognitive representations or knowledge structures.

Understanding as Knowledge Structures

We have argued that a basic view of what it means to know from the perspective of cognitive psychology is for an individual to have acquired appropriate knowledge structures. From this perspective, thinking and knowing take place within the mind of the individual; interaction with the environment is always mediated through the individual's cognitive representations of the outside world. The knowledge and cognitive processes thought to reside in the mind of the individual cannot be directly observed, but it is possible to hypothesize what they might be like in terms of the information they contain and how that information might be structured. Working from these assumptions, cognitive psychologists have put considerable effort into describing, sometimes in the form of computer programs, knowledge structures and processes they hypothesize to underlie competent performance on various mathematical tasks (Greeno, 1987b; Resnick, 1985).

Greeno (1987b) has referred to this general program of research as the *knowledge structure program.* The intent is to make explicit knowledge that is often implicit, but that is required for competent mathematical performance. Knowing mathematics from this perspective means having in place the knowledge and cognitive processes needed to carry out various mathematical tasks. An important role of this research is to specify in detail what that knowledge is, especially the knowledge that is implicit.

This implicit knowledge made explicit can be viewed as revealing the knowledge underlying understanding in the domain. The resulting models might even be used to couch objectives of instruction in terms of desired cognitive structures instead of behavioral outcomes (Greeno, 1980, 1987a).

In building models of the knowledge underlying mathematical performance, cognitive researchers have relied on two kinds of analysis: (a) detailed analysis of students performing mathematical tasks, both correctly and incorrectly, and (b) detailed analysis of the mathematical content involved in the task. The work has revealed important aspects of knowledge that had formerly remained implicit and the complexity of knowledge required to perform seemingly simple tasks. The research has also resulted in rich descriptions of how children solve problems in various mathematical domains taught in school. These include descriptions of the kinds of errors or incorrect applications students make, but also the various correct or appropriate procedures children use and invent to solve various tasks. Some of the work specifies typical developmental sequences in which students progress through various strategies or procedures in a domain (e.g., Carpenter & Moser, 1984; Fuson, 1982).

Domains that have been studied from the perspective of the knowledge structure program include addition and subtraction (e.g., Carpenter & Moser, 1984; Riley, Greeno, & Heller, 1983; Vergnaud, 1982), rational numbers and fractions (e.g., Behr, Lesh, Post, & Silver, 1983), and decimal fractions (e.g., Resnick et al., 1989). In addition to these topics, many researchers have focused on the knowledge and skill involved in problem solving, both in general and in specific domains. Rather than attempt a comprehensive review of research in these domains, we will offer here a few significant examples that illustrate important implications for thinking about learning and knowing mathematics in elementary schools. We begin with the knowledge structures hypothesized to underlie competent solving of addition and subtraction word problems. We then turn to computational skills in arithmetic and, finally, to problem solving.

Schemata for Word Problems

A number of cognitive researchers have directed their efforts at describing the knowledge underlying tasks involving addition and subtraction of whole numbers (see, e.g., Carpenter, Moser, & Romberg, 1982). In part this emphasis has been due to the relative simplicity of the domain; although detailed analyses have shown that addition and subtraction are much more complex than they seem at first glance, they are not as complex as other domains in school mathematics, such as rational numbers or multiplication and division. The work has also merged with research examining the development of children's knowledge and skill in counting and counting-based strategies for adding and subtracting (Fuson, 1988; Steffe, von Glasersfeld, Richards, & Cobb, 1983), resulting in a rich body of research on addition and subtraction. Researchers studying addition and subtraction word problems have emphasized the structure of such problems and have drawn heavily on schema and related constructs arising from cognitive research on reading comprehension (Anderson, 1984; Mandler, 1984). Word problems are viewed from this perspective as a special kind of text to be comprehended.

Reading research has pointed to the powerful influence of prior knowledge on the comprehension of text (Anderson, 1984; Mandler, 1984). In contrast to earlier views, cognitive scientists generally agree that comprehension is not a matter of somehow absorbing or recording information inherent in written or spoken language. Because all written and spoken language is in some sense incomplete, the reader draws heavily on his or her prior knowledge and expectations in building a representation of the situation described by the text. Schema theory (Anderson, 1984; Mandler, 1984) holds that schemata are forms of knowledge that play a critical role in this constructive comprehension process. Schemata are prototypical versions of situations or events that are stored in long-term memory and built up over many experiences with those situations. Schemata provide a framework within which to interpret text; comprehension is impossible without an appropriate schema. An example of how the schemata that a reader brings to text can affect comprehension is offered in a study (Anderson, Reynolds, Schallert, & Goetz, 1977) in which music students interpreted the following passage as describing an evening of playing music together, whereas physical education students interpreted it as being about playing cards.

Every Saturday night, four good friends get together. When Jerry, Mike, and Pat arrived, Karen was sitting in her living room writing some notes. She quickly gathered the cards and stood up to greet her friends at the door. They followed her into the living-room, but as usual they couldn't agree on exactly what to play. Jerry eventually took a stand and set things up. Finally, they began to play. Karen's recorder filled the room with soft and pleasant music. Early in the evening, Mike noticed Pat's hand and the many diamonds. As the night progressed, the tempo of play increased. Finally, a lull in the activities occurred. Taking advantage of this, Jerry pondered the arrangement in front of him. Mike interrupted Jerry's reverie and said, "Let's hear the score." They listened carefully and commented on their performance. When the comments were all heard, exhausted but happy, Karen's friends went home. (p. 372)

Some researchers have taken the view that the comprehension of mathematics word problems, as a special kind of text, similarly requires the reader to bring to bear appropriate knowledge about quantities and relationships among quantities in the form of schemata (Briars & Larkin,

1984; Kintsch & Greeno, 1985; Mayer, 1982; Riley et al., 1983). For example, being able to solve the following word problem requires recognizing the relationships among the known and unknown quantities involved; it is not enough to have learned associations between particular words and operations (e.g., *altogether* means to add):

Jim had 10 marbles. Bob gave him some more marbles. Then Jim had 13 marbles altogether. How many marbles did Bob give to Jim?

To support this view, cognitive researchers have used the strategy of building computer models that make explicit the tacit knowledge involved in understanding and solving addition and subtraction word problems (Briars & Larkin, 1984; Riley et al., 1983). This research is clearly an example of the general strategy of describing the knowledge structures hypothesized to underlie mathematical performance. As Greeno (1987a) put it,

A cognitive model of understanding and solving problems simulates the process of understanding by constructing representations based on the words in problem texts. The representations contain information that students appear to gather from the texts and use in their solutions. The process can be characterized as the recognition of patterns of information. (p. 63)

The models developed by Riley et al. (1983) and by Briars and Larkin (1984) were built by drawing upon extensive empirical research describing the strategies children use to solve simple addition and subtraction problems and carefully analyzing the kinds of word problems that require addition and subtraction (Carpenter & Moser, 1984; Nesher, 1982; Vergnaud, 1982). These analyses have shown that there are important patterns of relationships among quantities in addition and subtraction word problems that are not typically addressed in instruction. Most characterizations of these relationships are based on the three patterns in Table 1. Successful solvers of such problems have knowledge of these patterns, but the knowledge is tacit.

Building the computer models requires representing this implicit knowledge explicitly, making it available for examination. For example, the model developed by Riley et al. (1983) uses the schema represented in Figure 1 to solve Problem 2 in Table 1. When encountering Problem 2, the computer model places the information from the problem into the various slots of the schema. It then uses a series of rules for operating on these organized quantities to produce the missing element, the answer to the problem. Riley et al. built a series of such models that, with the increasing structure and amount of information that can be represented,

TABLE 1
Types of Addition and Subtraction Word Problems

Type		Problem
Change	There is an event in which an initial quantity is increased or decreased	1. "Connie had 5 marbles. Jim gave 8 more marbles. How many marbles does Connie have altogether?"[a]
		2. "Joe had 8 marbles. Then he gave 5 marbles to Tom. How many marbles does Joe have now?"[b]
Combine	There are two individual quantities that are not changed but thought of in combination	3. "Connie has 5 red marbles and 8 blue marbles. How many marbles does she have?"[a]
		4. "Connie has 13 marbles. Five are red and the rest are blue. How many blue marbles does Connie have?"[a]
Compare	There are two individual quantities to be compared	5. "Connie has 13 marbles. Jim has 5 marbles. How many more marbles does Connie have than Jim?"[a]
		6. "Jim has 5 marbles. He has 8 fewer marbles than Connie. How many marbles does Connie have?"[a]

[a]Problems taken from Carpenter and Moser, 1983, p. 160.
[b]Problem taken from Riley, Greeno, and Heller, 1983.

parallels the development in children of the ability to solve these kinds of problems. A model developed by Briars and Larkin (1984) to solve the same kinds of problems makes less use of the explicit schematic representations, building more of the knowledge of patterns into rules for operating on the quantities in the problem. The key feature of both models, though, is that a crucial aspect of solving these word problems is recognizing the patterns of quantities in the problems. In essence, recognizing these patterns is what it means from this perspective to understand the problem. It is not enough to have knowledge of simple correspondences between individual words such as *altogether, gave,* or *less,* and mathematical operations such as addition and subtraction. Rather, it is having available schemata for grasping the relationships among the entire set of quantities involved that permits understanding and solution of the problem. For thinking about mathematics in elementary schools, this research provides a detailed characterization of knowledge hypothesized to be important for solving textbook word problems. Also implicit in this work is

FIGURE 1.
Schema for Change Situation

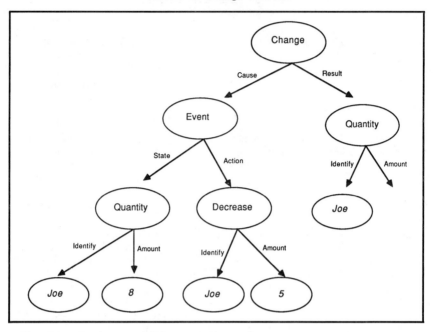

Note. From "Development of Children's Problem-Solving Ability in Arithmetic" by M. S. Riley, J. G. Greeno, and J. I. Heller in *The Development of Mathematical Thinking*, 1983, edited by H. P. Ginsburg (p. 167), New York: Academic Press. Adapted by permission.

the assumption that the schemata that provide frameworks for solving these word problems would also provide the problem solver with frameworks for thinking about problems not encountered in written form, for example, figuring out how many marbles have been won or lost in an actual marble game. The instructional implications that follow from these descriptions of existing school tasks are not automatic. One way of using these descriptions is as a set of instructional objectives described in cognitive rather than behavioral terms. Thus, given the instructional goal of being able to solve these sorts of problems, this research can be viewed as describing the knowledge that students need to acquire. Another possibility is to design instructional representations that make explicit the implicit knowledge revealed by these analyses (Greeno, 1987a). In research described later in this paper, Carpenter, Fennema, and Peterson (1987) have considered the knowledge of problem structures and children's solution strategies resulting from this work to be important knowledge for teachers to have in helping children learn addition and subtraction.

Computational Skill

Another domain that has been the object of cognitive scientists' analyses is computational skill in arithmetic. Although its central role is being questioned in most current calls for reform, computation pervades the traditional elementary school mathematics curriculum. In the high school curriculum there is a parallel focus on symbol manipulation skills in algebra. Cognitive researchers have worked to develop models of the knowledge structures underlying these ubiquitous skills and to explain the errors students make. One motivation for this research has been to use computation as a site for exploring more general issues about how people learn and know procedures (e.g., Brown & Burton, 1978). Another motivation has been to understand better the nature of computational skill and its role in knowing and understanding mathematics.

Researchers in mathematics education have long documented the kinds of errors students make in computational tasks (Ashlock, 1982; Buswell, 1926). Tools from cognitive science for representing procedural knowledge, such as production systems (Newell & Simon, 1972), have enabled cognitive researchers to conjecture with greater precision about the knowledge underlying computational skill and to develop models to explain why students make various kinds of errors. The best known example of this work deals with students carrying out the traditional subtraction algorithm involving regrouping, or borrowing. By analyzing the errors made in the subtraction algorithm as carried out by hundreds of students, Brown and Burton (1978) developed a computer model of the procedural knowledge underlying correct and erroneous computational performance. Their model considered students' computational errors as resulting from faulty rules. Like bugs in computer programs, these buggy algorithms resulted in incorrect but rule-governed performance. Thus, students' errors were seen to result not from a lack of knowledge, but from the application of faulty knowledge in the form of incorrect procedural rules. Sleeman (1982) and Matz (1982) have offered similar accounts of errors in algebra.

At one level, these analyses of computational errors simply specify in great detail student performance in the form of correct and faulty rules. But they also represent a view of procedural knowledge as consisting of organized sets of rules, both correct and incorrect, that individuals have learned. To know mathematics from this perspective is to have acquired procedural rules for manipulating the written symbols of arithmetic. But where do children learn these incorrect procedures that are obviously not directly taught in school? Brown and VanLehn (1980; see also VanLehn, 1983) argue that children infer or invent these faulty procedures from the partial procedural knowledge they have when they reach points at which they do not know what to do next in carrying out a procedure, for example, when confronted with the need to subtract a larger digit from a smaller one. What is significant about this characterization of knowledge is that it deals almost solely with features of the written symbols of arithmetic, rather than the quantities represented by those symbols or principles governing those quantities (Resnick, 1982). The fact that these theories explain so well the computational errors that students actually make suggests that students' computational knowledge acquired under current instructional conditions may indeed be organized primarily around visual cues and the physical arrangement of symbols, not around the underlying quantities to which the symbols refer (Davis, 1984; Resnick, 1982). The view of mathematical knowledge suggested here is one of structured procedural rules that operate on written symbols.

Problem Solving

Problem solving is a part of the mathematics curriculum that has been a long-standing concern for mathematics educators and has been the focus of research on knowledge structures. Most calls for reform place the ability to solve problems at the center of desired outcomes of schooling (NCTM, 1989; National Research Council, 1989). Problem solving has also been held up as a desirable means of learning mathematics, but our focus here will be on cognitive research that examines the ways individuals solve problems and that seeks to characterize the knowledge structures underlying successful problem solving—hence our inclusion of problem solving as part of the more general theme of the importance of knowledge structures. But problem solving, like representation, permeates most discussions of mathematics knowing and learning, and so will reappear throughout the paper. In particular, we later consider problem solving from the perspective of the discipline of mathematics. Here, however, our focus is on attempts by cognitive researchers to characterize the knowledge structures and processes underlying successful problem solving.

Most current theories of problem solving are based on an information-processing model of human thinking and draw heavily on early work in this tradition (e.g., Newell & Simon, 1972; Simon, 1978). Because much of this early work was directed at describing general processes of problem solving, it focused on tasks that minimized the role of an individual's knowledge in the problem-solving process (Simon, 1978). So researchers used puzzle-like tasks, such as the Tower of Hanoi, which involves moving a set of concentric disks on pegs according to certain rules, or the familiar missionaries and cannibals problem, which involves moving an equal number of missionaries and cannibals across a river in a boat with the constraint that missionaries can never be outnumbered by cannibals. These tasks require mostly knowledge that could be provided when presenting the problem. The problems were also highly structured in that permissible moves were carefully specified, and the goal of the problem was clearly defined.

Central to Newell and Simon's (1972) theory of problem solving is the mental representation of the problem that the individual problem solver creates in working memory. This *problem space* contains the individual's mental representation of the information in the problem and permissible moves to be used in solving it. In constructing this problem space, the problem solver draws upon both the problem as presented and knowledge represented in long-term memory that can be brought to bear in solving the problem. The notion of problem space brings into sharp focus the assumption in this research that thinking and knowing take place in the mind: In solving a problem, the problem solver is viewed as manipulating representations or symbols in the mind. To the extent that objects in the external environment come into play, it is the representations of these objects that the problem solver manipulates. It is this assumption of knowing and thinking being completely internal to the individual mind that is being questioned by researchers who are emphasizing the situated nature of cognition.

When focusing on structured, knowledge-lean tasks, Newell and Simon (1972) emphasized a model of problem solving as a search through the permissible moves represented in the individual's problem space. This resulted in a focus on the general strategies or heuristics that individuals use for conducting these searches in the solving of various problems. An example of such a general strategy is means-ends analysis, in which the problem solver considers the desired goal state (e.g., getting all the missionaries and cannibals to the other side of the river) and considers possible moves that will bring the representation of the problem in the problem space closer to that goal (e.g., getting one more cannibal to the other side). This sort of means-ends analysis is a general strategy that will work in a variety of contexts.

From this perspective the important knowledge to have for good mathematical thinking and problem solving was a repertoire of general processes or strategies. Clearly a person also had to have mathematical knowledge for these general strategies to operate on, but the emphasis was on the general processes. This emphasis on general strategies and processes was consistent with and supported the many attempts to train students in general strategies for problem solving, critical thinking, and other forms of "higher-order" thinking (for reviews, see Chipman, Segal, & Glaser, 1985; Nickerson, Perkins, & Smith, 1985; Resnick, 1987a; Segal, Chipman, & Glaser, 1985). In mathematics, most attempts to teach general problem-solving strategies stem from Pólya's (1957) classic characterization of the problem-solving process as involving heuristics such as finding simpler problems, using diagrams, and considering special cases. These sorts of general rules of thumb pervade many programs for teaching problem solving and the treatment of problem solving in elementary school mathematics textbooks. (We discuss in more detail Pólya's views about the role of heuristics when we consider problem solving from the perspective of mathematics.)

But researchers began to question the power of general strategies as central for problem solving and understanding. As Schoenfeld (1985, 1987) has pointed out, although heuristics like those proposed by Pólya are good descriptions of what successful problem solvers do, they are not detailed enough to be prescriptive—to help others learn to carry them out. Thus attempts to teach these heuristics generally have not been successful. In addition, as researchers extended the general information-processing model to study problem solving in information-rich domains such as physics and mathematics, the importance of specific knowledge available in long-term memory came to the fore (Chi, Glaser, & Rees, 1982; Glaser, 1984; Resnick, 1987a). The use of general strategies like means-ends analysis did not distinguish the performance of expert problem solvers in these domains from that of novices. Rather, it was the experts' rich store of organized accessible knowledge and ways of representing problems that characterized their successful performance.

One important role played by this domain-specific knowledge is in how the problem solver represents a problem to be solved. For example, in one study (Larkin, McDermott, Simon, & Simon, 1980), physics novices (undergraduates who had completed a single physics course) tended to solve problems by selecting as quickly as possible formulas and equations into which values in the problem could be placed and calculated. In contrast, experts (graduate students in physics) worked to build a representation of the entire problem, usually structured around general constructs and principles in physics. Only then did the experts move to formulas and equations, often after they had virtually solved the problem by using more qualitative representations.

Further evidence that experts construct different mental representations of problems than do novices is offered by studies in which experts and novices classify various sorts of problems. For example, when Chi, Feltovich, and Glaser (1981) had individuals sort physics textbook problems, novices sorted the problems on the basis of surface features, such as the kinds of objects involved in the problem (e.g., levers, pulleys, or balance beams) or similarities in the diagrams presented with the problem. Experts classified the problems according to the physics principles that were needed to solve the problems (e.g., conservation of energy), suggesting that they had ways of representing problems that were not readily available to the novices. Silver (1979) similarly found that those who were unsuccessful at solving mathematics word problems were more likely to rely on surface features when categorizing word problems than were those who were successful, who relied on similarities in underlying mathematical structure.

Thus, researchers studying problem solving came to focus on the domain-specific knowledge that the problem solver has available and how that knowledge is organized (Glaser, 1984). In mathematics, this focus was reflected in the research we discussed earlier on schemata for solving addition and subtraction word problems and in the argument that successful problem solving involves being fluent with a repertoire of representation systems that can be used in problem solving (Kaput, 1988; Lesh et al., 1987). Both of these views of understanding and problem solving emphasize the importance of having the appropriately structured domain-specific knowledge over knowledge of general processes or strategies. Similarly, as an alternative to the general heuristics suggested by Pólya (1957), Schoenfeld (1985, 1987) focused on specifying the strategies used by successful problem solvers at a level of detail that included more of the mathematics knowledge involved. For example, Schoenfeld found that heuristics such as "examine special cases" actually comprised more specific strategies, such as, "If there is an integer parameter n in a problem statement, consider the values $n = 1, 2, 3, 4, \ldots$. You may see a pattern that suggests an answer, and the calculations themselves may suggest the mechanism for an inductive proof that the answer is correct" (Schoenfeld, 1987, p. 19). Schoenfeld (1985) found that instruction in his own problem-solving course for undergraduate students based on these detailed strategies helped students solve both problems like those used during instruction and new problems. He also emphasized the importance of metacognitive knowledge and beliefs about mathematics for successful problem solving.

Debate over the relationship between problem-solving and thinking skills, on the one hand, and domain-specific knowledge on the other, continues (e.g., Glaser, 1984; Perkins & Salomon, 1989; Resnick, 1987a). Any resolution of the debate probably will involve some balance between the two (Perkins & Salomon, 1989). What is common to all these views of problem solving is that they attribute success in problem solving essentially to the problem solver having acquired appropriate knowledge in the form of general strategies or organized domain-specific knowledge.

Summary of Knowledge Structures

We have offered three examples of domains in which cognitive researchers have described in some detail the knowledge hypothesized to underlie mathematical performance: addition and subtraction word problems, arithmetic computation, and problem solving. These and other similar analyses have resulted in a rich understanding of some domains in the existing mathematics curriculum. Inherent in these analyses is the assumption that we can understand knowledge, thinking, and understanding in mathematics by specifying knowledge structures underlying competent performance. For solving addition and subtraction word problems, these knowledge structures included schema-based knowledge of the quantitative structures in the situations described by the story problems. For computation, procedural rules that operate on the written symbols of arithmetic have been hypothesized to account for students' computational knowledge acquired under current instructional conditions. For problem solving, researchers have emphasized different kinds of knowledge as important at various times, including knowledge of general strategies and heuristics, organized and rich domain-specific knowledge of mathematics, and metacognitive knowledge. In all these cases, knowing mathematics means having acquired appropriate knowledge structures.

The knowledge structure program has focused primarily on describing the *what* of knowing mathematics: What is the knowledge that underlies competent mathematical performance? The lens through which cognitive researchers view this question is a powerful one that can reveal hitherto unexamined aspects of mathematical knowledge. At the same time, this research program is built on a fairly narrow view of what it means to know mathematics. Most of the tasks subjected to this cognitive analysis have been taken from the traditional school mathematics curriculum and thus are descriptions of how individuals understand and perform mathematics under current instructional practices. The research does not address the issue of whether these traditional school tasks are worthwhile.

Research in the knowledge structure program has resulted, for the most part, in theories about how people think and what their knowledge might be like, not about how to best help individuals acquire that knowledge. As Greeno (1987a) put it,

Cognitive theory provides hypotheses about the knowledge and skill of successful student problem solvers and the ways in which their knowledge and skill differ from those of less successful ones. . . . Although cognitive models can describe more or less accurately the knowledge and skill we want students to acquire, the experiences that will help students acquire that knowledge and skill constitutes a separate issue. (pp. 69–70)

These researchers have examined the performance of both competent and novice individuals, but in this program of research they generally have not looked at changes in knowledge as students learn or develop expertise in a domain.

Understanding as Connections Among Types of Knowledge

In describing the kinds of knowledge that constitute or underlie under-standing of mathematics, many researchers emphasize connections among various kinds of knowledge. In part, this emphasis is a reaction to behaviorist and associationist learning theories and school curricula that present mathematical knowledge as collections of relatively isolated con-cepts, rules, and procedures to be learned. Mathematics educators have long expressed concern over the learning of the symbols and procedures of mathematics as rote learning, devoid of understanding (Buswell, 1926; Davis, 1986). Most mathematics educators and researchers agree that it is possible to learn many of the symbols of mathematics and procedures for computing and manipulating those symbols without also learning much accompanying understanding of the quantities or mathematical entities represented by the symbols and without acquiring the knowledge needed to use the skills when needed. There is less agreement about the kinds of links or connections that need to be established in the mind of the learner to constitute the desired understanding. Some researchers have empha-sized the distinction between *procedural* and *conceptual* knowledge of mathematics, and have sought to characterize the relationship between them in various ways. Others have called for more connections between the formal, symbolic mathematics learned in school and the rich base of informal knowledge children develop in out-of-school settings.

Conceptual and Procedural Knowledge

Some cognitive psychologists distinguish between knowledge and un-derstanding of concepts of mathematics on the one hand, and knowledge of the procedures of mathematics on the other (Hiebert, 1986; Nesher, 1986). Researchers vary, of course, in their definitions of these kinds of knowledge. Hiebert and Lefevre (1986) defined *conceptual knowledge* as "knowledge that is rich in relationships. It can be thought of as a con-nected web of knowledge, a network in which the linking relationships are as prominent as the discrete pieces of information" (pp. 3–4). From this perspective, terms like *understanding* or *meaningful learning* essentially refer to knowledge that is highly interconnected through relationships at various levels of abstraction.

Procedural knowledge, according to Hiebert and Lefevre (1986), con-sists of knowledge of (a) the formal symbol system of mathematics and (b) "rules, algorithms, or procedures used to solve mathematical tasks" (p. 6). The first part is knowledge of the conventional forms in which mathemat-ical ideas are expressed, including, for example, the ability to recognize that $5 + 6 = 11$ is an acceptable form, whereas $5 + = 6$ is not. The sec-ond part of procedural knowledge consists of instructions for completing various tasks. These procedures may operate primarily on standard written symbols, as is the case for the algorithms for multiplication and division, or they may operate on concrete objects or other objects that are not the standard symbols.

Elementary school mathematics instruction typically emphasizes the learning of procedures applied to standard written symbols in ways that leave them unconnected to conceptual knowledge. Students thus learn the procedures and symbols as meaningless marks on paper. From Hiebert and Lefevre's perspective, written mathematical symbols take on their conventional mathematical meanings by being linked to conceptual knowledge of ideas encountered through experience. For example, if the idea of change as in Problem 1 in Table 1 is linked to "+," that symbol takes on meaning. Hiebert and Lefevre (1986) argued that "if students connect the symbols with conceptually based referents, the symbols acquire meaning and become powerful tools for recording and communicating mathematical events" (p. 20).

Nesher (1986) argued that conceptual knowledge should be thought of as the control structure for procedural, or algorithmic, knowledge. A person can carry out procedures without much conscious thought by relying on physical feedback as long as things are going well. When something goes awry, however, the learned procedures may not work, and the person must mentally step back and take stock of the situation. This is where conceptual understanding plays a role. An important consequence of this view of conceptual knowledge as control structure is that it cannot exist without at least some procedural knowledge. Because the conceptual knowledge is, in essence, knowledge *about* the procedures, it can be developed only by reflecting, in part, on the procedures themselves, which must therefore be learned before, or at least in tandem with, the conceptual knowledge. Nesher gives the example of trying to help college students learn the concept of *arithmetic mean* in an introductory statistics class and needing to have students compute some means before being able to talk about the concept of mean with any meaning. Nesher pointed out that there is little solid evidence for the belief that solid conceptual knowledge of a topic will produce correct procedures as a natural consequence. Indeed, in at least some cases, procedural knowledge must form the basis for conceptual understanding.

Gelman and her colleagues (Gelman & Meck, 1983, 1986; Greeno, Riley, & Gelman, 1984) offer another hypothesis about the relationship between conceptual and procedural knowledge in the domain of young children's counting. They argue that conceptual competence consists of implicit knowledge of principles that constrain but do not determine procedural performance. These principles are much like the principles of grammar that constrain the utterances we make; we use these principles without being aware of them. Conceptual competence for counting includes principles such as one-to-one correspondence and the cardinality principle (that the last number recited is also the number of objects in the counted set). Knowledge of these principles provides guidance and constraints for the procedures to be used in a particular counting situation. Every counting task is a bit different, and a child that is able to count appropriately in a wide variety of settings evidences an understanding of basic principles underlying counting, rather than the learning of a single counting procedure.

Greeno et al. (1984) hypothesized that the actual procedure of counting in a particular situation is generated on the basis of the principles that constitute conceptual competence, with procedural competence providing a set of tools for transforming the principles of conceptual competence into procedures, and utilizational competence providing knowledge of the mappings of these procedures to situations. There are several points from this work that are important for our consideration of the relationship between conceptual and procedural knowledge. First, knowledge of the principles that form conceptual competence is implicitly rather than explicitly known. Second, successful performance in a variety of settings can be taken as evidence for an implicit understanding of the underlying principles. Third, having knowledge of correct principles does not guarantee being able to carry out procedures correctly or to generate appropriate procedures in new situations; the procedural or utilizational competence needed to generate the procedure in a particular situation may not be available. Finally, conceptual knowledge serves to constrain performance but not to determine it completely, an idea similar to Nesher's (1986) control structure. A similar idea is that conceptual knowledge serves as a set of critics for procedures generated (Resnick, 1982; VanLehn, 1983).

Formal and Informal Knowledge

Some researchers have emphasized the importance of having connections between knowledge of the formal, symbolic mathematics taught in school and the informal, intuitive knowledge of mathematics gained from everyday experience. Ginsburg (1977) and Resnick (1986, 1987b) have argued that a major reason for the difficulty students have in learning the formal symbolic mathematics taught in school is that this formal knowledge does not get linked to their rich informal knowledge base derived from working with quantities in everyday situations. Many children appear to view school mathematics as a collection of arbitrary rules and procedures performed on meaningless symbols, in spite of the fact that they may have developed rather sophisticated concepts and strategies for solving quantitative problems encountered out of school. The informal strategies that both children and adults construct often reveal understanding of the kind of mathematical principles that Greeno et al. (1984) referred to as conceptual competence, but students do not seem to draw upon this competence in learning and doing the procedures of school mathematics.

An example of competent informal strategies developed outside of school is offered by a series of studies of Brazilian children without much formal schooling (Carraher, Carraher, & Schliemann, 1983). Working as street vendors, these children developed considerable proficiency at mental arithmetic strategies for figuring prices for customers, as illustrated in the following:

How much is one coconut? *Thirty-five.* I'd like 10. How much is that? [Pause] *Three will be 105; with three more, that will be 210.* [Pause] *I need four more . . .* [Pause] *315 . . . I think it is 350.*

This child solved, by using repeated addition, a problem that most schooled adults would solve by using multiplication. The child used the memorized price of three coconuts to reduce the number of additions required, demonstrating implicit understanding of the important principle of additive composition—the idea that numbers can be additively broken apart and recombined (Resnick, 1986). The children studied by Carraher et al. (1983) could solve a variety of other problems dealing with figuring prices by using various invented mental arithmetic strategies. When presented with the same problems in written form, however, the children tried unsuccessfully to apply the algorithms they had learned in their short stays at school. They seemed unaware that they could apply the informal strategies they used every day to these "school" tasks.

When school tasks are set in a way to encourage it, children can use their informally invented strategies to solve problems that they could not solve using the algorithms taught in school (Carpenter & Moser, 1983; Ginsburg, 1977). Many of these informal strategies are built on the extensive use of counting and additive relationships, as in the Brazilian example. But traditional school instruction does not seem to help students connect this informal competence to the formal symbols and symbol rules that are the focus of instruction.

Researchers calling for the building of better connections between informal mathematical knowledge and formal school knowledge of mathematics generally base their arguments on two assumptions about the nature of mathematical understanding. First, children's informal knowledge can serve as a powerful base on which to build more formal knowledge of mathematics. The informal knowledge that seems to be rooted in basic principles such as additive composition can provide meaningful referents for the symbols of formal arithmetic. Thus the informal knowledge can bring meaning to the formal mathematics. Second, by linking students' knowledge of formal school arithmetic to their informal knowledge based in experience, students will be in a better position to apply their more formal knowledge to solving problems encountered in out-of-school settings. Another way to consider these connections between formal and informal knowledge is as the need for transfer in both of these directions (Pea, 1988). Both of these arguments are closely related to the constructivist perspective, with its emphasis on the meaningful learning of mathematics taking place through modifying and building on existing knowledge and ways of thinking.

Learning as Active Construction of Knowledge

Central to virtually all cognitive theories is the assumption that individuals interpret their environments through existing cognitive structures built up through adaptation to the environment (Resnick, 1983; Shuell, 1986). This constructivist perspective has had a profound influence on how many mathematics educators think about understanding and learning mathematics (Kilpatrick, 1987), especially the idea that for instruction to foster learning with meaning or understanding, it must somehow attend to and build on children's existing knowledge.

The active view of the learner in cognitive psychology contrasts with earlier behaviorist and associationist perspectives, in which a student's knowledge could be viewed as a sort of cumulative record of his or her experiences. Although the learner was considered to be active in behaviorist theories, it was in a different sense of active than in current cognitive perspectives. Behaviorists argued that learning takes place only when the individual overtly responds to environmental stimuli; an individual learns only those behaviors that are actually carried out and reinforced (Skinner, 1986). Indeed, this sort of active response provides the foundation for theories of operant conditioning. From this behaviorist perspective, an individual's learning is determined by the responses he or she makes to environmental stimuli; thus learning can be made more efficient by carefully structuring those environmental stimuli so that the learner makes responses that are gradually shaped toward the target behavior. The most efficient learning is errorless learning, with the learner's responses becoming increasingly refined.

When cognitive theorists refer to the learner as being active, they mean something quite different from overt responding. They mean that the learner plays an active role in interpreting and structuring environmental stimuli. Rather than passively receiving and recording incoming information, the learner actively interprets and imposes meaning through the lenses of his or her existing knowledge structures, working to make sense of the world. At the same time, learning or development takes place, not by the simple reception of information from the environment, but through the modification and building up of the individual's knowledge structures.

An important result of this shift in perspective has been a blurring by cognitively oriented researchers of the distinction between learning and cognitive development. When learning was considered to be acquisition or absorption of knowledge, development of fundamental cognitive structures, such as those supporting basic logical and quantitative thinking (Piaget, 1983), could be considered a separate domain of inquiry. With learning viewed as the learner's active integration of new information with existing knowledge, the line between learning and development can no longer be drawn clearly. Neither can a clear line be drawn between "natural" mathematical thinking and the use of cognitive tools available in the environment. It is important to note that analyses of how children develop or acquire mathematical knowledge and skill in specific domains (e.g., the development of children's early conceptions of number and counting—Carpenter & Moser, 1983; Fuson, 1988; Gelman & Gallistel, 1978; Steffe et al., 1983) are studies of how children's conceptions and skills develop in current cultural and instructional environments. Although the various sequences of acquiring mathematical knowledge derived from this research are sometimes assumed to be natural, they are actually the result of experience in particular environments.

Research on children's mathematical knowledge and skill provides ample evidence that they do, indeed, construct or invent new knowledge on the basis of what they already know (Resnick, 1985). Our first example comes from research on children's use of various counting strategies to solve simple addition and subtraction problems. Researchers have found that children use a variety of counting strategies to solve problems of the form $a + b = ?$, where a and b are whole numbers between 1 and 10 (Carpenter & Moser, 1983; Fuson, 1988). Of particular interest here are the ALL strategy and the MIN strategy. In using the ALL (or counting all) strategy, the child first counts to a, then counts b more units to arrive at the sum. For example, to add $3 + 6 = ?$, the child would count, "1, 2, 3," and then, "4, 5, 6, 7, 8, 9." The counting could be done with objects, with fingers, or mentally. The more efficient MIN (or counting on from larger) strategy involves beginning with the larger of the two addends and counting on for the smaller addend. To add $3 + 6 = ?$, the child would count, "6," then "7, 8, 9." Many children come to use the MIN strategy even though it is not usually taught directly (Carpenter & Moser, 1983; Fuson, 1982). In a carefully controlled study, Groen and Resnick (1977) found that a number of kindergarten children whose instruction focused exclusively on the ALL strategy invented and used the MIN strategy to solve addition problems.

Use of the MIN strategy is an example of an appropriate, or correct, invention based on existing knowledge and instruction. The buggy algorithms for subtraction we described earlier provide examples of the invention of incorrect procedures. Brown and VanLehn (1980; see also VanLehn, 1983) posit in their repair theory that the errors students make in carrying out the computational procedures are the result of inappropriately invented or repaired procedures. When a student reaches a point in carrying out the procedure at which he or she does not know what to do next, a repair or patch is made, often resulting in a computational error. These repairs can be thought of as on-the-spot, invented procedures based on the student's existing knowledge. As we pointed out earlier, Resnick (1982) has argued that the repairs children make are quite reasonable inventions if only knowledge of the syntax, or surface features, of the symbols is taken into account. For example, children usually end up putting digits in each column of the answer and "borrow" marks at the top of the problem. The repairs are not reasonable, however, if one takes the meaning, or semantics, of the symbols into account. Children making these errors violate such principles as the maintaining of the quantities represented by each number in the problem. So it seems that children are making reasonable inventions; they are just failing to base these inventions on the appropriate knowledge.

Thus, it is clear that children do not simply absorb mathematical knowledge as it is presented, but impose their existing frameworks of knowledge to incorporate and invent new knowledge. Virtually all cognitive researchers and mathematics educators ascribe to this constructive view of learning and knowledge. Some theorists and researchers take a stronger position on the constructed nature of knowledge and learning (e.g., Steffe & Cobb, 1988; von Glasersfeld, 1987). Because these radical constructivists form an important voice in the mathematics education community, we consider their views here in some detail.

Radical Constructivism

Radical constructivists emphasize the epistemological assumption that the world external to the individual cannot be known in any ultimate sense, but that all knowledge is a cognitive construction of the individual. Von Glasersfeld (1989) has identified two principles of constructivism as a theory of knowledge: "(a) knowledge is not passively received but actively built up by the cognizing subject; and (b) the function of cognition is adaptive and serves the organization of the experiential world, not the discovery of ontological reality" (p. 162). It is the first principle that most cognitively oriented psychologists and mathematics educators embrace when they argue that knowledge is actively constructed (Kilpatrick, 1987). It is adherence to the second principle that sets apart the radical constructivists. This second principle rejects the realist or empiricist assumption that the world can be known in any objective or ultimate way. Rather, physical reality can only constrain the cognitive constructions that individuals make. As von Glasersfeld (1988) put it, "Knowledge cannot aim at 'truth' in the traditional sense but concerns the construction of paths of action and thinking that an unfathomable 'reality' leaves open for us to tread" (p. 2). Sinclair (1988), writing from a Piagetian perspective, similarly argued that, "At all levels the subject constructs 'theories' (in action or thought) to make sense of his experience; as long as these theories work the subject will abide by them" (p. 29). But these personal theories will always be only approximations to reality; external reality will always possess properties unknown to the individual (Piaget, 1980; von Glasersfeld, 1988). Thus, knowledge and meaning are ultimately personal and, to some extent, idiosyncratic.

For radical constructivists, then, mathematical knowledge is exclusively a cognitive construction of the individual; there is no mathematical reality "out there" to be learned or discovered. Rather, mathematical knowledge consists of "coordinated schemes of action and operation" (Steffe, 1988), ways of understanding and acting that have been built up by the individual. We experience a sense of "out thereness" of mathematical knowledge only because we impose our own conceptual organization on the world (Cobb, 1986). Note that this view of meaning differs from Hiebert's view, discussed earlier, that understanding of symbols resulted from the learner's simply connecting or linking the symbol to external referents, implying that the meaning resided essentially in the connections between symbols and physical objects.

Because mathematical knowledge exists only as constructed by the individual, it cannot be transmitted or instilled through communication (Cobb, 1988b; von Glasersfeld, 1988). In fact, communication itself is not a process of transmitting meaning, but of sending a set of instructions from which the recipient constructs a meaning. There is no meaning inherent in words, actions, or objects independent of an interpreter (Cobb, 1988b). Thus, a view of instruction as the transmission of knowledge is not acceptable to the radical constructivists: "the seemingly obvious assumption that the goal of instruction is to transmit knowledge to students stands in flat contradiction to the contention that students construct knowledge for themselves by restructuring their internal cognitive structures" (Cobb, 1988b, p. 87). Teachers cannot use language to "tell" or transmit knowledge to students, but "here and there to constrain and thus to guide the cognitive construction of the student" (von Glasersfeld, 1988).

As a result of this basic perspective, radical constructivist researchers in mathematics education have focused on describing and analyzing the mathematics of children (Steffe, 1988)—the meanings children place on their mathematical actions and the strategies that they have constructed through interaction with their home and school environments (see, e.g., Steffe & Cobb, 1988). As we pointed out earlier, it is important to note that these environments are not inherently more natural than others. By focusing on knowledge as individual construction, constructivists create for themselves the difficult problem of explaining how people come to know and agree upon the same skills and understandings that constitute mathematics. How is it that "children come to know in a short time basic principles (in mathematics, but also in other scientific disciplines) which it took humanity thousands of years to construct?" (Sinclair, 1988, p. 1).

Increasingly, constructivists have dealt with this issue by focusing on the social nature of human interaction and its role in the individual construction of knowledge. Sinclair (1988), for example, pointed out that Piaget, especially in his later writings (e.g., Piaget & Garcia, 1983), emphasized the role of society, with its accumulation of knowledge, on the individual's construction of knowledge. The objects with which children interact are defined largely by society. Adults in general, and teachers in particular, present children with real objects or with objects of thought in a certain way that makes it possible for them to rediscover or reinvent what it took their society a long time to elaborate.

When Piaget, in his writings on education, asserted that "to understand is to invent or to discover," the inventions or discoveries are new to the child, but seen from the adult's point of view, they are re-creations. Our children do not have to *invent* the wheel: they can begin to conceptualize the intricate properties of wheels as they exist in our society. (Sinclair, 1988, p. 7)

Thus, teachers play an important role in presenting objects of thought to children. This presentation, along with the endogenous process of abstraction, accounts for the learning of society's accumulated knowledge, but the presentation often is not optimal for the child's active construction of meaning (Sinclair, 1988).

Cobb (1988a) similarly argued that constructivists need to draw on an anthropological perspective to avoid the "lonely voyage" metaphor of cognitive construction. From this perspective, "cultural knowledge (including mathematics) is continually recreated through the coordinated actions of the members of a community" (Cobb, 1988a, p. 13). This emergent meaning becomes part of the shared world view of the participants. "It is beyond justification and has emerged as a *mathematical truth* for the classroom community" (p. 13). This taken for grantedness explains, Cobb argued, the tendency to think of mathematics as having an existence external to the knower. Mathematical concepts seem so "true" and "solid" because they have become so taken for granted and agreed upon by a wide community. These meanings are so shared that they are taken for mathematical truth. They are like part of the bedrock or ultimate schemas by which we think.

Implications of Learning as Active Construction

Whether one accepts the fundamental epistemological assumptions of the radical constructivists or simply holds the more widely accepted view of learning as a constructive process, the basic tenet that learners are active in structuring and inventing their knowledge has important implications in thinking about what it means to know and learn mathematics. The learner's existing knowledge shapes in fundamental ways what will be learned. Understanding mathematics means having altered one's own cognitive structures or ways of thinking in powerful ways, not simply having acquired mathematical knowledge presented by others. If learning cannot be assumed to be a process of absorption or direct transfer of knowledge into the mind of the learner, then one cannot assume that what is presented through curriculum or instruction is what students will learn (Norman, 1980). Instruction can no longer be viewed as a matter of simply laying out, however carefully, the knowledge and skill to be acquired. As Resnick (1983) argued, we need to broaden our definition of instruction beyond the direct presentation of information or modeling of procedures for students to include *"anything that is done in order to help someone else acquire a new capability"* (p. 5), or, as Sinclair (1988) put it, to make more optimal children's efforts to "re-discover or re-invent" (p. 7) mathematical objects of thought.

But although the constructivist research agenda has highlighted the importance of attending to how children know and think about various mathematical ideas and procedures, it does not offer direct pedagogical prescriptions. In general, constructivist researchers have sought to understand the development or construction of mathematical knowledge that takes place through an individual's more or less natural interactions with the environment. It is not readily apparent, however, how this perspective should be applied to teaching and instruction. As Sinclair (1988) pointed out,

Piagetian [i.e., constructivist] studies were not designed to discover in what kind of situations (either in or out of school) certain structures and procedures of action and thought are built up. The subtle, but powerful interaction between the societal presentation of objects which allows a great number of children nowadays to master scientific concepts only geniuses could construct in the past cries out for detailed study. (p. 9)

Just as the cognitive scientists' models of knowledge hypothesized to underlie competent mathematical performance do not tell us much about the acquisition of that knowledge, constructivist models of children's developing competence do not tell us much about how this development might be constrained or guided through powerful instructional experiences.

Understanding as Situated Cognition

Underlying the perspectives from cognitive psychology we have considered thus far is the fundamental assumption that knowledge and thinking take place within the mind of the individual. Describing what it means to know and understand mathematics then becomes the task of describing the structures of knowledge hypothesized to exist in the individual's mind. The radical constructivists have emphasized the personal nature of the meanings that individuals construct through interaction with others and the environment, but the locus of those meanings clearly lies within the mind of the individual. A number of cognitive researchers are questioning this fundamental assumption of thinking and knowing (Brown, Collins, & Duguid, 1989; Greeno, 1989; Resnick, 1987b), arguing instead that these events should be considered more as an interaction or relation between an individual and physical and social situations.

The move to this new perspective has been fueled, in large part, by the integration of anthropological and cultural perspectives into cognitive science. In particular, studies of people dealing with quantitative problems in various out-of-school settings have revealed how solutions are constructed through interaction with the situation, rather than by applying more abstract knowledge and skills to the situation (Carraher et al., 1983; Lave, 1988; Lave, Murtaugh, & de La Rocha, 1984; Scribner, 1984). For example, Scribner (1984) found that dairy workers filling orders for cases of milk used their experience with various configurations of partially filled cases, rather than relying on school-like arithmetic procedures. As Greeno (1989) observed about their performance, "rather than assuming that there are cognitive structures and procedures that the workers applied, it seems more appropriate to say that they had acquired a capability for interacting effectively with objects in the situation" (p. 135). Rather than thinking being viewed exclusively as the manipulation of symbols and cognitive representations, it might better be considered an interaction with objects and structures of situations.

According to the situated cognition perspective, knowledge and thinking are inextricably intertwined with the physical and social situations in which they occur. Brown et al. (1989) argued that, like language, all knowledge indexes, or refers to, the world and thus derives its meaning from the situations and activity in which it is produced. Just as the meaning of a word is fundamentally dependent on the context in which it is used and can never be explicated completely in a dictionary definition, all knowledge depends on the contexts in which it is used.

A concept, for example, will continually evolve with each new occasion of use, because new situations, negotiations, and activities inevitably recast it in a new, more densely textured form. So a concept, like the meaning of a word, is always under construction. This would also appear to be true of apparently well-defined, abstract technical concepts. Even these are not wholly definable and defy categorical description; part of their meaning is always inherited from the context of use. (Brown et al., 1989, p. 33)

Emerging from this perspective as a way of thinking about conceptual knowledge is the notion that understanding could mean having a usable set of tools (Brown et al., 1989; Perkins, 1986; Stigler & Baranes, 1988). Both tools and knowledge "can only be fully understood through use, and using them entails both changing the user's view of the world and adopting the belief system of the culture in which they are used" (Brown et al., 1989, p. 33). One can acquire relatively inert knowledge of tools without actually using them, but to be able to use tools effectively requires experience with them in the ways they are ultimately to be used. For example, a person could acquire the division algorithm in the sense of being able to compute $1128 \div 36$ but not be able to use that tool appropriately when confronted with the problem of figuring out how many buses, each holding 36 people, would be needed to transport 1128 people. Indeed, only 23% of the sample of 13-year-olds taking the 1982 National Assessment of Educational Progress correctly solved such a problem, with 29% of students incorrectly choosing "31 remainder 12" as the answer (Carpenter, Lindquist, Matthews, & Silver, 1983). From this perspective, knowledge of how to use tools like division appropriately is acquired through actual use of those tools in a variety of situations. For some (Brown et al., 1989; Collins, Brown, & Newman, 1989), this need to acquire cognitive tools through richly embedded practice suggests that apprenticeship is an appropriate metaphor for instruction because of its emphasis on learning in the context of authentic activity (Brown et al., 1989).

In terms of what it means to know and understand mathematics, this perspective suggests that the nature of a person's knowledge of mathematics is inextricably tied to the situations in which that knowledge was acquired. This contrasts with a long-standing tradition in education of trying to separate the desired goals or outcomes of education with its means or methods (Porter, Schmidt, Floden, & Freeman, 1986; Tyler, 1949). It also suggests that meaningful knowledge of mathematics cannot be crystallized and made entirely explicit. Important aspects of knowing mathematics will inherently remain implicit and intertwined with situations in which it is used. This suggests fundamental limits to efforts to specify knowledge and understanding by explicating in as much detail as possible its components and subskills (e.g., Gagné, Briggs, & Wagner, 1988).

Focus on the Individual Knower: Summary

Cognitive psychologists studying the knowing and learning of mathematics have tried to understand the nature of knowledge underlying mathematical performance and how this knowledge is constructed or acquired. In considering the views of what it might mean to know and understand mathematics from within this research tradition, we highlighted five themes. First is the importance of representation in knowing mathematics, including the relationship between external representations of mathematical ideas and internal cognitive representations, and the view of understanding as the ability to move flexibly among various representations of mathematical ideas. Second is the attempt to explicate knowledge structures hypothesized to underlie various kinds of mathematical performance, drawn primarily from tasks in the existing school curriculum, such as problem solving and computation. Third is the view of understanding as entailing connections among various kinds of knowledge, such as links between conceptual and procedural knowledge and between informal knowledge of mathematics acquired in out-of-school settings and the more formal mathematics learned in school. Fourth is the view of the learner as an active constructor of mathematical knowledge. The cognitive structures that constitute mathematical knowledge must somehow be constructed by the learner through interaction with the physical and social environment. Fifth, understanding as situated cognition, deals with the recent questioning within cognitive science of the assumption that knowledge is best thought of as a construction or structure inside the mind of the individual. Some researchers are arguing that knowledge must be viewed more as situated in social and physical contexts. Thus, to learn mathematics in meaningful and useful ways, it becomes important to participate in mathematical activity, not simply to acquire explicitly described skills and procedures of mathematics. This idea is consonant with the emphasis in the reform documents on doing mathematics rather than simply acquiring the skills and concepts that constitute the "written record" of mathematics (NCTM, 1989; National Research Council, 1989; Romberg, 1983). But what is *doing* mathematics? What is authentic mathematical activity? How can understanding the nature of authentic mathematical activity inform our efforts to think about what mathematical activity should be like in elementary schools? To address these questions, we turn to the discipline of mathematics.

FOCUS ON MATHEMATICS: PERSPECTIVES FROM THE DISCIPLINE

Thus far we have considered the nature of mathematical knowledge and understanding from the perspective of psychologists. But psychologists have chosen to focus on a limited set of mathematical content. Their goal has been to examine what is entailed in understanding and successful performance of mathematical tasks taken for the most part from the existing school curriculum. Admittingly some psychologists have focused on important but underrepresented aspects of that curriculum, most notably problem solving, and some have considered the relationships between the mathematics learned in school and the mathematics that is or might be used in out-of-school settings. But we hope to go beyond psychology somewhat, and look at other ways of thinking about what it means to know mathematics. Scholars within the discipline of mathematics, and those engaged in philosophical and historical analyses of what mathematics is about, have attempted both to characterize mathematical knowledge and to describe the processes whereby new mathematics comes to be accepted as true. In this section, we will look at mathematical understanding from the perspective of mathematics. Our looking to the discipline for definitions of understanding arises partly from the observation that psychology has chosen to focus on limited mathematical content and partly from the assumption in major reform documents that students should be "doing mathematics" in school in order to learn mathematics (NCTM, 1989; National Research Council, 1989). This reform is seen to be necessary because school children now are learning only a very limited part of mathematics, if they are learning any at all. Much of the mathematical activity in elementary school classrooms consists of students practicing familiar teacher-prescribed procedures for adding, subtracting, multiplying, and dividing numbers until they can get the right answer most of the time—both the activity and the answers being dissociated from any sense of what either the numbers or the operations mean (NCTM, 1989; Romberg & Carpenter, 1986). In contrast, reformers believe that "doing mathematics" in the classroom ought to consist of activities such as the following: abstracting, applying, convincing, classifying, inferring, organizing, representing, inventing, generalizing, specializing, comparing, explaining, patterning, validating, proving, conjecturing, analyzing, counting, measuring, synthesizing, and ordering.[2] These are the sorts of activities that are thought to characterize the work of mathematicians.

But what do these activities have to do with coming to know mathematics? What does one need to know to engage in such activities? How does the experience of these processes relate to understanding the body of knowledge that has accrued in our culture about mathematics? By including a section in this paper on mathematical understanding from the perspective of the discipline, we do not mean to endorse the assumption that students will learn what they need to know about mathematics by doing activities in school that are like what mathematicians do. Rather, we seek to better understand the connection between mathematical practice and school learning by looking more carefully at what might be entailed in mathematics as practiced by mathematicians. Mathematical activity cannot simply be imported to the elementary school classroom without taking some care about how it is related to learning, both in terms of what a student needs to know to do it and in terms of what a student learns from doing it.

Although the reform documents have emphasized the doing of mathematics, they have not clearly distinguished between what students should do in school and what they should be able to do as a result of what they learn in school. Neither have they considered the possibility that some segments of the population might come to school more disposed to learn from doing than others. It is crucial to address these issues if we are going to provide an equitable education in mathematics across the population and evaluate the effects of educational reforms on outcomes. Do we want students to learn how to do mathematics with understanding so that we will have more mathematicians and intelligent creators of mathematical applications? Or do we want all students to appreciate what kind of knowledge mathematics is and how truth in the discipline is warranted? Or do we want students to become intelligent users of mathematical tools in the workplace and society? These goals are not unrelated or mutually exclusive, but distinguishing among them might help us better judge what constitutes good educational practice. These issues will not be resolved in this paper, but the analysis of mathematical practice that follows may shed some light on questions worth pursuing.

What Kinds of Activities Could Be Called Mathematics?

We would like to propose three categories within which to think about what it means to do mathematics, and consider both theoretical and applied activity in each of these areas. We do not wish to imply that a particular bit of mathematical work or a particular mathematician falls into one category or another, however. The three activities we have chosen to analyze are interwoven in the fabric of mathematical practice.

One of the most common associations with doing mathematics is the activity of problem solving. Mathematicians use relationships among quantities and shapes to solve all kinds of problems, and problem solving is certainly something that many people would agree students should learn in school. We will look at the various kinds of problems that might be solved using mathematics, and what one might need to know to solve them. Another, less obvious, mathematical activity is mathematizing, or building quantitative "models" of nonquantitative relationships. This activity assumes a certain view of the social and physical world, which asserts that the important elements of situations can be represented by numbers and relationships among numbers. In Western society, this view is somewhat of a given, certainly among particular segments of the population who use mathematics to formulate and solve problems and others who are consumers of their work. We don't often think of this way of thinking as something that needs to be deliberately taught. Problem solving and mathematizing are related within mathematics by the activity of problem formulating, which will be treated in both sections. The third mathematical activity we will examine is mathematical argument: How are new propositions invented in the discipline? And how is their truth established? Mathematicians make conjectures and prove or disprove them. What kind of work goes into producing a conjecture? And what are the standards of discourse by which mathematicians decide to accept a conjecture as part of the discipline's store of knowledge?

For each of these domains—problem solving, mathematizing, and mathematical argument—we need to consider whether the sorts of activity each entails constitute worthwhile goals for schooling. We also need to consider important issues within each domain. The nature of activity in each of these domains has been debated in the discipline throughout its history and continues to be controversial. Understanding these debates is a monumental task for someone who is on their periphery, at the intersection between elementary education and mathematics writ large. But they cannot be ignored if we are to look to mathematical practice for guidance on curriculum and instruction. We consider three bodies of literature in the analysis of mathematical knowledge that follows: historical descriptions of the development of the discipline, examinations of contemporary mathematical practice, and philosophical treatises on the nature of mathematical knowledge.

Mathematics as Problem Solving

At first glance, looking at mathematical understanding from the perspective of problem solving seems to be quite simple: Understanding would be knowing how to solve a mathematical problem. Assuming that the kind of solution called for is a mathematical solution (as compared with an ethical or a legal one, for example), what one would need to know to solve a problem would include heuristics or problem solving strategies, mathematical tools or conventions, and rules for justifying the appropriateness of the solution strategy. But the work of defining what kind of problem could be called a mathematical problem and what kind of solution is a mathematical solution is not quite so simple; indeed, in a recent survey of what kinds of problems contemporary mathematicians were working on, Stewart (1987) called this issue an "ideological minefield." The distinction between pure and applied mathematics divides the kinds of mathematics problems considered to be worth solving as well as the practitioners who solve them. Justifications for methods are a matter of considerable controversy, particularly as a result of the current capabilities of computational technology (P. Davis, 1988; Tymoczko, 1985). When it comes to defining what is "good" mathematics, some value most those problems whose outcome matters in some material way, like the problem of figuring out how to predict the weather or the problem of determining the most efficient scheduling algorithm for airline travel, claiming that these are the kinds of problems that lead to important new knowledge of mathematics. Others value problems whose solution adds to our accruing body of abstract knowledge about numerical and spatial relationships (Erdos, 1988; Gleick, 1987; Guillen, 1983; Hardy, 1967). An example of this kind of problem is determining a formula that will describe how far apart prime numbers (numbers whose only divisors are one and the number itself) are from one another. Work on prime numbers does not proceed in a way that is driven by any problem external to the development of mathematics itself. It is a matter of figuring out what the properties of abstract entities called *numbers* imply for patterns and relationships in the world of numbers itself.

We will look at the knowledge that one might use to solve a mathematical problem in light of both the common themes and the divergent thinking in the field about what kind of a problem is a mathematics problem, and what constitutes a mathematical solution to a problem.

Consider the following list of numbers: 1, 4, 9, 16, 25, 36, 49. They are the squares of the counting numbers: 1×1, 2×2, 3×3, and so on. Now consider the difference between each number and the one that follows it. The difference between 1 and 4 is 3, the difference between 4 and 9 is 5, the difference between 9 and 16 is 7, and so on. The differences between the squares turns out to be a list of numbers with another property: It is the list of successive odd numbers: 3, 5, 7, 9, ... Why?

If we think of a problem in general terms as something that disturbs one's state of equilibrium because it does not fit an expected pattern (Polanyi, cited in Bell, 1979), then the recognition of this unexpected regularity in the differences between successive square numbers presents us with a problem. Once the pattern is observed, there arises a curiosity about whether it will continue, and if so, why? What does one need to know to solve such a problem? If the differences between the squares are represented as follows,

$$1 + 3 = 4$$
$$1 + 3 + 5 = 9$$
$$1 + 3 + 5 + 7 = 16$$
$$1 + 3 + 5 + 7 + 9 = 25$$

it is easy to see that the number of terms in each successive addition is the square root of the sum. What does one need to know to notice this pattern? And what does one need to know to appreciate that such a pattern merits attention? One piece of useful knowledge to have here is that mathematics problems often can be tackled by representing them in alternative ways. This is a mathematical heuristic about which we will have more to say later (cf. Pólya, 1957).

The list of sums raises the question, What will the sum be in the next instance? This question was not so obvious in the earlier statement of the problem. But one must also know categories of numbers that might produce interesting results: prime, odd, and so on. What are the characteristics of prime numbers? Odd numbers? Knowing those characteristics provides some guidance in seeking to explain the pattern, but knowing that these categories exist causes us to notice the pattern in the first place. At the most basic level, one needs to know how to add a string of numbers and how to multiply one number by another to produce the pattern. These kinds of knowledge could be called mathematical tools or conventions, or more generally *resources* (Pea, 1987; Schoenfeld, 1985).

In the next line of the problem, there will be six terms and the sum will be 36. We can go on testing cases, obtaining more evidence that the sum of the first n odd numbers will be n^2. Mathematical argument can take us beyond such observations, however, to prove that this must be the case in every instance. Simply talking in terms of n and n^2 instead of restricting our argument to particular observations contributes something to the solution. So another kind of knowledge that is useful here is knowledge about generalization and symbolization, also referred to as *abstraction* (Bell, 1979; Kaput, 1987a, 1987b; Romberg, 1983). By taking a general perspective on the particular sums, looking at the elements in which an odd number of addends sums up to the square, one can see that the middle addend is also the square root of the sum. What about the elements in the list that have an even number of addends? Here, the even number that would be between the middle two terms (as 4 is between 3 and 5 in $1 + 3 + 5 + 7$) is the square root of the sum. We are well on our way now to solving the problem of why the pattern arises and whether it will continue. The introduction of a mathematical concept at this point furthers the solution: The *average* of the addends in each case is the square root of the sum. This auxiliary element was not part of the initial statement of the problem, but it enables us to further generalize the argument. Here we are using a knowledge of resources together with a knowledge of heuristics. In the odd cases, the average is the middle number; in the even cases it is the number between the two middle numbers. In all cases, the average of the addends multiplied by the number of addends yields the sum, and the average and the number of addends will always be the same, so the sum is a perfect square.

Several kinds of knowledge figured in our solution of this problem. In the sections that follow, we will treat each of these kinds of knowledge and consider how they contribute to solving various kinds of mathematics problems.

Heuristics and Mathematical Induction

In the work on the theoretical mathematics problem just described, we have been carrying out a process that Pólya (1954) called *mathematical induction.* We discovered a pattern by observation and then proved that the pattern would continue using a mathematical argument. Mathematical induction is different from the sort of induction that leads to scientific assertions because it is supplemented by logical proof. (We consider the nature of proof and its relationship to mathematical argument in a later section.) In contrast to a simple proof, however, it reveals not only the deductions that make the conclusion inevitable, but also the experiments that lead to thinking that the conclusion was plausible in the first place. Pólya calls this kind of reasoning *heuristics* and considers it to be the key to knowing how to solve a mathematical problem. He traces the study of heuristics back to Pappus, a Greek commentator on Euclid, and he credits Descartes, Leibnitz, and Balzano with building up a system that attempted to codify the sort of thinking underlying mathematical discovery. Pólya took up the task of describing the process of discovering solutions to mathematics problems in contemporary mathematics, partly in reaction to a trend in the discipline toward seeing the subject only in terms of its formal structure, without regard for the structure's emergence from human processes for coming to know it. He wanted to examine the elements of plausible reasoning or mathematical insight that lead to the discovery of mathematical assertions—in Pólya's terms, "heuristics endeavors to understand the process of solving problems, especially the mental operations typically useful in this process" (1957, p. 130).

Knowledge of heuristics is elusive, however. Pólya observed that it is hopeless to imagine that we will ever be able to ascertain a set of universal rules that will yield the solution to any problem. But he does describe procedures such as "identify the unknown," "identify the conditions on the unknown," "consider a problem with a similar unknown," "introduce suitable notation," and "identify all of the data that can be used in solving the problem." And he suggests that the best way to acquire a knowledge of heuristics is to work on solving problems with someone who knows how to use them. Recent experiments with teaching problem solving to college students attest to the importance of guided practice on problems as a key to learning to use the strategies (Schoenfeld, 1985). Although it has not been a site for research on effectiveness, there is a long tradition in mathematics of national and international problem solving contests, and preparation for these contests is most often in the form of working on problem after problem with a "coach" (e.g., Loyd, 1959).

Following his own advice for teaching heuristics, Pólya illustrates problem solving strategies by taking his readers through solutions to the sort of elementary problems with numbers as the one given earlier, but he asserts that these strategies are useful for solving practical problems as well, such as constructing a dam across a river. Recent research on teaching problem solving borrows heavily from Pólya's work, as do curriculum materials designed to help students acquire the knowledge they would need to solve mathematical problems.

To contrast with the "pure mathematics" problem considered above, we will look at an example of the sort of practical problem students might be given on which to practice Pólya's strategies:

Jennifer had been begging her mother all week for some ways to earn money. First, Jennifer cleaned the garage. Then she weeded the garden. Finally, her mother agreed to pay Jennifer $3 to wash all the inside windows in the house. Jennifer worked for over two hours, completing 30 windows before her friend, Susan, came over and offered to help her. Each of them washed ten more windows and the job was done. In order to be fair, how much money should Jennifer give Susan for the windows Susan washed? (Meyer & Sallee, 1983, p. 213)[3]

The unknown in this problem is how much money Jennifer should give Susan. The data tell us how many windows there are, how many each girl washed, and how much money there is to be distributed. "Identifying the unknown" is the first on Pólya's list of heuristics. Second is the strategy of analyzing what is known and how it might be related to the unknown but desired information. Identifying the unknown and the knowns that are related to it may seem like a fairly simple activity, but it often requires untangling relevant from irrelevant information and operating on what is given. The whole amount of money is stated straightforwardly in the problem, but we must do some calculations to find the total number of windows. To relate the known to the unknown, we must consider that the conditions on the solution are that the money should be distributed "in order to be fair." Using a mathematical concept (or what Pólya refers to as an *auxiliary element* and Schoenfeld calls a *resource*) to figure out the unknown, we could see it as a fraction of the total amount of money: Jennifer gets a fraction of the money, and she gives a fraction of the money to her friend, and the two fractions add up to the whole amount of money. How would one know to do this? By recognizing this problem as one of a type with similar unknowns, called perhaps *proportion* or *equal ratio* problems.

Here we have another kind of mathematical knowledge, which might be called knowledge of mathematical structures (Vergnaud, 1983). In these kinds of problems, what is unknown is a fraction of some quantity, and what is known is the equivalence of two fractions. The words "in order to be fair" in the context of a mathematics problem suggest that the fraction of the money each girl receives ought to be the same as the fraction of windows washed. Equivalent fractions (or a proportion) here are a tool, a resource, for shaping the problem in a way that makes it mathematically solvable. Susan washed 10 out of 50 windows, or one fifth, so she should get one fifth of the money, or 60 cents. We can call on certain tools more readily if we know that this problem is a problem that has a multiplicative structure (Vergnaud, 1983).

Another kind of knowledge that might go into a solution of this problem is knowing how to represent a situation using mathematical symbols. There is more to this process than simply mapping an element of the situation onto a symbol; it also requires the capacity to abstract the relevant qualities of elements and their relationships out of the situation. The equivalence between the fraction of windows Susan washed and the fraction of the money she should receive can be expressed in terms of a symbolic relationship: $10/50 = x/\$3.00$, where x represents what Susan should be paid for washing half of the remaining (20) windows.

Although we do not yet know what x represents, the problem is in some sense solved by establishing this relationship. Now we can find the value of x in two mechanical steps: First, cross multiply to obtain $50x = \$30$, and then divide both sides of the equation by 50 to obtain $x = \$.60$. We might also simply "figure out" that replacing x with $\$.60$ would make the ratios equal, but we would still need to prove that this insight was related logically to the conditions established in the problem.

Legitimate Transformations in Mathematical Relationships

Behind these transformations, there is another kind of mathematical knowledge, as important in solving problems as heuristics. To justify the equivalence among the three equations, it is necessary to prove that it is possible to logically deduce $ad = bc$ from the given $a/b = c/d$ for any numbers a, b, c, and d except $b = 0$ and $d = 0$. This logical argument makes the truth of the equation $x = \$.60$ an inevitable conclusion from the equivalence between the two fractions $10/50 = x/\$3.00$.

The problem of proving that this transformation in the relationship among the quantities in the problem (commonly called *cross multiplication*) is legitimate is an abstract problem whose results can be applied to any situation in which such a transformation would help to identify the unknown. It is not legitimate because of anything having to do with windows and money, but because we have precisely followed a set of mathematical laws to transform the relationships among known and unknown quantities.

There are two kinds of knowledge embedded in the use of such transformations to solve problems: knowing what actions are legitimate and knowing why they are legitimate. Among the equations that might require such justification are the following: $10/50 = 1/5$; $10/50 \times 300 = 3,000/50$; $\$3.00 = 300$ cents.

We call on knowledge of mathematical conventions, symbols, and tools, as well as knowledge about how to deduce one equation from another, in order to be able to use these in solving the problem. We never have to refer to the situation of windows, money, and girls to justify that these equations are true. They are true by virtue of their relationship in a mathematical structure. The operations that make them true (e.g., multiplying the numerator and denominator by the same number is allowed because that is multiplying by one) have no referent operations in the problem situation.

A Contrasting Approach: Instrumental Problem Solving

Thus far we have considered four interrelated kinds of knowledge involved in solving mathematical problems: knowledge of heuristics, knowledge of mathematical structures that undergird the use of those heuristics, knowledge of how to represent situations using mathematical symbols, and knowledge of transformations that can be made to those symbols (both in terms of what transformations are legitimate and why they are legitimate). In thinking about what it means to understand mathematics, one could emphasize various aspects of these kinds of knowledge. One could say that to understand mathematics is to be able to recognize those situations to which a mathematical concept can be applied to produce unknown information, as the concept of proportion helped us produce unknown information in the window washing problem. Or, from another perspective on the window washing problem, we might say that understanding mathematics means being able to explain why cross multiplication is legitimate, that is, to be able to produce a deductive argument about why the operations are legitimate given the domain of application. In these ways of thinking about understanding, problem solving entails the appropriate application of abstract strategies and constructs to situations. These perspectives have received much attention in thinking about what mathematics students should be learning in school. But there is a third way of thinking about mathematical understanding that could be illustrated by a solution to the window washing problem, less attended to by educators, but also derivable from considerations of how mathematics is practiced in the discipline. What one would need to know to solve the problem *instrumentally* is different from the knowledge outlined above, particularly in that the solution strategy is tied much more closely to the situation of the problem.

The window washing problem could be solved by estimating that the girls ought to receive something like 5¢ per window, passing out the money, finding out how much is left, passing out a little more, and so on, until you have passed out the whole amount. Or you might start by giving each girl 10¢ per window and find out you do not have enough, and then adjust downward. The solution is justified in this approach by the actuality of arriving at a state where each girl is fairly paid for the windows she has washed. Doing this in several different kinds of problems could produce the argument that the cross multiplication technique works because it always produces the same result as the trial-and-error method. Now to one who has been trained to consider deductive proof as the only legitimate foundation for mathematical conclusions, this kind of justification may seem circuitous and circumstantial, and, more important, solving the problem this way could be taken as an indication that mathematical knowledge is lacking rather than as an indication of a different kind of equally legitimate knowledge.

Historical Perspectives on Problem-Solving Knowledge

As the story is told by Kline (1980), this instrumental approach to developing new mathematics was characteristic of Hindu mathematics in the period when algebra was being invented, and their approach to the subject was radically different from the deductive approach taken by the Greeks to the same material. Kline says of the Hindus:

[They] were interested in and contributed to the arithmetical and computational activities of mathematics rather than to deductive pattern. . . . There is much good procedure and technical facility but no evidence that they considered proof at all. They had rules, but apparently no logical scruples. (p. 111)

The author of the first treatise on algebra, Al-Kwarizmi (c. 830 AD), emphasized that he wished people to know mathematics that would serve their practical ends and needs "in their affairs of inheritance and legacies, in their lawsuits, in trade and commerce, in the surveying of lands and in the digging of canals" (Solomon Gandz, cited in van der Waerden, 1985, p. 15). For the Greeks, these were not mathematical pursuits; they were thought of as problems for mechanical engineers to address by practical means, and their work did not intersect that of mathematicians. This difference between the two visions of the subject led to controversies in the discipline during the Renaissance, when both Greek and Hindu mathematics were brought into play by mathematical scholars. One issue in the debate was whether negative numbers should be allowed into mathematical analysis.[4] Pascal, a great champion of the logic of the Greeks, considered them "pure nonsense" (Kline, 1980). Argnaud, a close friend of Pascal and a renowned theologian and mathematician, disallowed negative numbers from mathematics because the idea that $1/-1 = -1/1$ contains a logical paradox: "How could a greater be to a smaller as a smaller is to a greater?" (Kline, 1980, p. 115). Yet the Hindus, and the merchants who eagerly took up their efficient use of mathematics for bookkeeping, found the negative number to be a useful concept, because negative numbers "worked" for balancing their accounts.

What is the difference between how "understanding mathematics" is conceived from the perspective of applying strategies derived from abstract propositions and how it is conceived if the process is seen as one of inventing a strategy that works according to the context in which it is applied? The former is certainly the more conventional view of how mathematical knowledge is used in practice to solve problems. But as the influence of Hindu algebra indicates, and a study of the development of the calculus would confirm, the latter view also has roots in mathematical disciplinary traditions and is present in current mathematical practice. The potential of mechanical computing power, which has enabled mathematicians to create tools that work to solve problems without knowing why they work, has brought about the replaying of old arguments about whether functional mathematics without a logical foundation is "real" mathematics (P. Davis, 1972; Grabiner, 1988; van der Waerden, 1985). For example, the approach that mathematicians use for a class of problems called *combinatorial optimization problems* is similar to the "pass out a little and reassess" strategy outlined earlier for the window washing problem. Combinatorial optimization problems are so complex that no algorithm exists to produce a logically correct solution, even with the most powerful computer[5] (cf. Stewart, 1987). Devlin (1988) considers these kinds of problems to be "an exemplary blend of the pure and the applied" and an indication that mathematics is entering a new Golden Age in which the distinctions between materially useful solutions and theoretical developments in the discipline will be less well defined.

Solving problems like these ties mathematics to the physical and social world in ways that make more theoretically inclined members of the discipline uncomfortable. However, like Devlin, Kline (1980) believes that these ties are what drives mathematical development:

How did mathematicians know where to head, and in view of their tradition of logical proof, how could they have dared merely to apply rules and assert the reliability of their conclusions? There is no question that solving physical problems supplied the goal. . . . The physical meaning of the mathematics also guided the mathematical steps and often supplied partial arguments to fill in non-mathematical steps. (p. 168)

Kline's argument does not explain, however, how it is that the development of mathematics simply out of an interest in generating new abstract knowledge later comes to be useful. This is the case with many inventions in the field of analysis, where new kinds of numbers have been created purely to extend the range of a theoretical notion, for example, complex numbers that take the form of multiples of $\sqrt{-1}$ (Guillen, 1983). At the same time, Stewart (1987) reminds us that if cryptographers did not have certain theorems of prime numbers, like Fermat's, available for use, "They would have played around on a computer, found it as an empirical rule, and no doubt used it without worrying too hard about a proof. If a proof had seemed necessary, it would have been sought and found" (p. 231).

Here we return to Pólya's notions about mathematical induction as the essence of mathematical problem solving, and also to one of the deepest controversies in current mathematical practice, that is, whether a mathematical assertion that rests on computational power, without concurrently being supported by a deductive argument, can be considered a mathematical truth (Davis, 1972; Devlin, 1988; Tymoczko, 1985). And in terms of the sort of mathematical knowledge or understanding that schools should produce, we must now ask, "Is it enough to know that it works, without knowing why it works?" And what sort of argument is acceptable in order to assert about a piece of mathematics "that it works"? These questions take us right to the edge of thinking in the discipline about what mathematics needs to be known to solve mathematical problems, but these questions are not far from the sorts of questions a teacher might wonder about when charged with producing mathematical understanding in her students. If a student solves the window washing problem by trial and error, is he or she to be considered less competent than the student who memorizes and uses the formulas? Should students be required to explain why a formula works in deductive terms, or is it enough that they know how to use it appropriately? These issues will be taken up from another perspective when we consider what it means to understand mathematics as mathematical argument.

Mathematizing, or Reducing a Situation to Its Quantitative Relationships

Mathematizing, or mathematical modeling, is the activity of representing relationships within a complex situation in such a way as to make it possible to put them into quantitative relationships with one another and thereby find out new information about the situation by solving numerical equations. For example, faced with the problem of deciding which 200 out of 1,000 highly qualified applicants should be accepted into a college's freshman class, most admissions offices make the decision by assigning numbers to the candidates' qualifications, adding up the numbers, and taking those with the highest composite scores. Or, in the realm of weather prediction, faced with the ominous consequences of a global warming trend, scientists quantify those activities that seem to be causing the trend and use relationships among these quantities to recommend emissions controls and resource development policies. Mathematical modeling requires having the knowledge to be able to decide what does *not* matter in making the model, and the disposition to accept the answers that the numerical procedure provides as a valid solution to the problem. It is this way of approaching problems that has enabled us to make such wide use of computers as problem-solving tools (Dreyfus & Dreyfus, 1986; Wiezenbaum, 1976). The computer does not mathematize, but once a mathematical model is constructed for a situation, it can quickly "crunch" all of the numbers that are fed into it and produce a solution to a complex problem.

Mathematical understanding from the perspective of mathematical modeling is knowing how to find patterns and relationships in, or impose them on, nonmathematical phenomena. It is knowing how to distill the mathematical essence out of a messy situation, and once the model is established, knowing how to define the conditions under which it is useful and appropriate. It is knowing how to identify those situations in which it is productive and appropriate to apply mathematics.

Distilling the Mathematical Essence

One of the earliest examples of formal mathematization in Western history is Eratosthenes' attempt, in about the 3rd century B.C., to determine the size of the earth[6] (Pólya, 1963/1977). By taking as a given that the earth was a sphere, he reduced the problem of finding size to the problem of finding circumference; his calculations assumed that the longest straight path around the earth would be a circle, and thus its length could be related to the mathematical idea that a circle contains 360°. His method was to establish certain quantitative relationships (between the angle of the sun's rays at given points and the distance between those points) and to reason logically from those relationships to others. He needed to adjust many realities to his formulas (like assuming that the rays of the sun at one point were sensibly parallel to those striking a nearby point because the sun is so far away), reasoning about what would affect the results of the calculation and how. His methods are similar to those used today in creating maps, and evidence suggests that such methods also were used by the Chinese circa 720 A.D. and by the Muslims circa 820 A.D. (Morrison & Morrison, 1987). By viewing reality through the lens of a theoretical mathematical structure, Eratosthenes could figure out the radius of the earth without measuring. In Pólya's words, "A mere shadow and an idea is the substance that made the pigmy a giant who spanned the earth" (1963/1977, p. 14). It was Eratosthenes' mathematical modeling of the problem that enabled him to find a solution. Assuming mathematical relationships made it unnecessary to travel around the earth to measure its girth.

As can be seen from this example, mathematization has two parts. First, it requires extracting from their context those elements of a situation deemed relevant and placing them into a quantitative relationship to one another using some mathematical construct. Mathematical transformations of this relationship are then used to establish other quantitative relationships, and the results are applied back to the situation. Eratosthenes began with the sun's inclination to the vertical at Alexandria ($7° 12'$) compared with its angle at Syrene, measured the distance between Syrene and Alexandria, and used the mathematical relationship $7° 12'$ /$360° = 1/50$ of a complete revolution of the earth to relate the Syrene-Alexander distance to the distance around the earth. Because it is mathematically true that there are $360°$ in a circle, and because the ratio *of degrees in one segment* of the sphere to the whole is equal to the ratio *between distances* in the same segment on the surface of the sphere, Eratosthenes could conclude with certainty about a phenomenon he could not observe. Dividing a circle into degrees and relating numbers in proportions are mathematical constructs he used to do this work.

Being Disposed To See Mathematics as Powerful

Descartes made his place in philosophy by expressing the hope that all physical and human relationships could be represented in the sort of clear and direct mathematical terms that Eratosthenes applied to understanding the size of the earth. He assumed that if this could be done, all matters from morals to mechanics could be decided with certainty. His program was played out during the Age of Reason, in which great strides were made in the physical sciences by quantifying the relationships between physical properties of matter. Beginning with the establishment of the heliocentric theory of planetary motion, mathematics became the basis for challenging traditional knowledge and proving that things are not always what they appear to be. With its strong ties to logic, mathematics was considered to be an unquestionably true basis on which to found knowledge in other domains. The incredible, predictive power of mathematics—for example, to establish the certain existence of the planet Jupiter before it was ever viewed by a telescope, or to point to the existence of as yet undistilled chemical substances because of their position on a numerical scale of atomic weights—gave both scientists and the public the belief that mathematics must be all powerful (cf. Judson, 1987).

Descartes thought mathematics to be a general science "beyond subject matter," and therefore to be the foundation of all knowledge:

The long chains of simple and easy reasonings by means of which geometers are accustomed to reach the conclusions of their most difficult demonstrations had led me to imagine that all things to the knowledge of which man is competent are mutually connected in the same way. (cited in Kline, 1985, p. 90)

Descartes argued that because man can comprehend mathematics, the world must be organized along mathematical lines, and even God's existence could be proven by mathematical methods. Mathematics appealed to Descartes because it was less mystical, less metaphysical, and less theological than the routes to knowledge followed by his medieval and Renaissance predecessors. Mathematics was a way of knowing that did not depend on acquiescence to authority: Man could look inside himself and decide, by logical reasoning, what was true.

In 19th century France, what Davis and Hersh (1987) call "Descartes' Dream" led to the creation of the social sciences. Auguste Comte studied Lagrange's attempt to reduce all of mechanics to mathematics, and reasoned that "if physics was built on mathematics, so was chemistry built on physics, biology on chemistry, psychology on biology, and finally his own new creation, sociology (the term is his) would be built on psychology" (Grabiner, 1988, p. 225). This notion that mathematics could be the foundation on which to build certainty about social phenomena is echoed in contemporary attempts to use social science for social problem solving. (See, e.g., Tufte, 1970. For a critique of the quantitative approach to human problem solving, see Braybrooke & Lindblom, 1963, and Wiezenbaum, 1976.) Theoreticians of social policy aim for what they call *programmatic rationality*—"to achieve substantive goals through instrumental action programs that can be proven logically or empirically, to achieve those goals" (Gans, cited in Lindblom & Cohen, 1979, p. 31). The belief underlying this quest is that the relationship between mathematics and truth in the solution of scientific and social problems will free us from tradition, prejudice, and the preponderance of power (Kaplan, cited in Lindblom & Cohen, 1979). The assumption that expressing problems in terms of mathematical relations among quantities will remove their solution from the realm of human judgment and folly pervades every aspect of our lives. We hope to use mathematics to remove gender biases from college admissions exams (Berger, 1989), for example, and to rectify the inequities in charges that physicians make for different kinds of services (Andrews, 1989).

Deciding When Mathematical Modeling Is Appropriate

What does all of this have to do with students understanding mathematics at the elementary level? Teaching students to make mathematical models obviously has enormous potential for improving both their ability to conceptualize problems and their ability to appreciate the attempts that are made to solve physical and social problems using mathematics. Appreciating the process of making mathematical models for ordinary phenomena means that students have some sense of how mathematics can be used and why it is powerful. But we might also want to consider whether there are pitfalls in engaging students in mathematizing.

Davis and Hersh (1987) observe that there are common intellectual dispositions among those who are "doing mathematics" for a living, and that these dispositions are both powerful and problematic: "Confronted with a fuzzy universe [the mathematical mind] tries to find precise statements about that which is chaotic or random" (p. 124). It is this disposition that enabled 18th century mathematicians to find the order in the solar system that supports today's explorations of the planets, but this is also the sort of disposition that "dehumanizes" human phenomena to produce statistics:

Statistics (as opposed to mere data collection) begins when one agrees to form averages. Bill weighs 168 pounds, John weighs 190 pounds, and Bobby weighs 161 pounds. Their average weight is 173 pounds. This last statement is a composition of the first three. There is a loss of meaning in passing from the first three numbers to the fourth. There is, of course, a gain in the recognition of the empirical fact of the stability of averages. It may be that one of the reasons why probability and statistics did not take off until the 17th century was precisely the refusal of people to suffer the loss of the sense of the individual. . . .

Whenever anyone writes down an equation that explicitly or implicitly alludes to an individual or a group of individuals, whether this be in economics, sociology, psychology, medicine, politics, demography, or military affairs, the possibility of dehumanization exists. Whenever we use computerization to proceed from formulas and algorithms to policy and to actions affecting humans, we stand open to good and to evil on a massive scale. *What is not often pointed out is that this dehumanization is intrinsic to the fundamental intellectual processes that are inherent in mathematics.* (Davis & Hersh, 1987, pp. 282–283)

Following on this argument, P. Davis (1988) has advocated the idea that mathematics education might take up the task of teaching students to think more critically about the application of mathematical methods to the solution of problems. He points out that the application of mathematics to the way we understand and organize the world is a *social contract* rather than the discovery of innate characteristics of situations. The idea of averages, for example, that underlies so much work in the social sciences, is an agreement to disregard certain elements of individual identity, which are not always appropriate to disregard.

The allocation of donated organs to patients in need of a transplant is an example of the sort of problem that might be solved differently using mathematization than it would be solved from a nonmathematical perspective. The quantification of life expectancy, probability of recovery, family situation, and so on, does not quite capture all that needs to be considered in who gets the next available heart transplant. On the basis of several such examples of mathematical modeling, mathematician Hofstadter (1986) concurs with Davis and Hersh's worry about the capacity of numbers to dehumanize the way we think about situations in which the problems arise, creating a kind of "number numbness" to mask the complexity of problem solutions.

For a consideration of what learning to do this kind of thinking might mean at the elementary school level, we will look again at the problem described earlier of trying to figure out how much each girl should be paid for washing windows. To "mathematize" this problem situation, one does things such as count the total number of windows and figure out how to connect the money that each girl is paid with the number of windows she has washed. The context, that is, that Janet had been "begging" her mother for money, that she had already done several other jobs, and so on is to be disregarded as mathematically irrelevant. To solve the problem conventionally, students need to learn to ignore this information. In mathematical terms, a fair distribution of the money should be proportionally related to the number of windows washed. We can apply the operations of addition and multiplication to the relationship between the windows and the money in this problem, because we assume that for the purposes of our solution, every window is equivalent to every other window; their relative size or dirtiness, and when during the job they were washed do not matter. To be able to use mathematical tools to arrive at a solution to the problem, we must attend only to how many windows there are and how many each girl washed. We know that the last 20 windows to be washed were washed by two people, each washing 10 windows. Again, using the operation of division assumes that what is divided gets divided into equal groups. So because the friend washed 10 windows, she gets 60¢. The daughter washed 30 and then 10 more, 40 altogether, so she gets $2.40. And that totals neatly to the $3.00, which the mother offered, confirming the appropriateness of our calculations.

But there are other resolutions to the problem that would not be obtained by the process of mathematization, and might be equally likely to be proposed by someone who did not immediately see this as a mathematical problem. (The alternatives that follow were indeed proposed when Lampert, 1988b, set a group of elementary school teachers thinking about the window washing problem during her Teacher Study Group on Mathematics.) Maybe the friend should not get any of the money because it was promised in a contract between the mother and daughter, in which she had no part. Maybe the mother should not give the daughter any money after all, because she and her friend were having so much fun that the window washing could hardly be considered work. Maybe the friend should pay the daughter for the privilege of participating in the window washing activity (à la Tom Sawyer whitewashing the fence). Maybe they should split the money evenly to be fair, because the friend was not really given a chance to wash half the windows from the beginning (à la the parable in the Bible about the fieldworkers who arrived at different times of the day). Maybe the mother should pay the friend something over and above the $3.00 she was planning to pay her daughter since perhaps the daughter made the agreement because she needed $3.00 for something particular that she wanted to buy. Maybe we cannot figure out what is fair, because we do not have any information about how long the job took, and we do not know whether some windows were bigger than others, or harder to reach, or dirtier. These alternative considerations emphasize the character of the kind of thinking that is involved in "doing mathematics" on a problem situation like this. Mathematics focuses on quantitative relationships, and by so focusing is able to generate new and useful information, but only by leaving something aside. Teaching students to mathematize could be done in a way that treats all of these alternatives as a distraction from really solving the problem, or it could consider the strengths and weaknesses of various approaches.

The problem in taking the mathematical activity of modeling or mathematizing as a route to thinking about what should occur in elementary curriculum and instruction is getting some distance on the assumptions that are made in our culture about the objectivity of mathematical models and the moral dispassion associated with the solutions they produce. Mathematics is a powerful tool for constructing and extending relationships among quantities, but its power is not always a positive force. In the endeavor to get learners to do the mathematics of abstracting, modeling, ordering, and classifying, we should not lose sight of the perspective on the world that these activities entail. If we think about the capacity to model situations with numerical relationships simply as an aspect of mathematical *understanding*, we are ignoring the cultural values implied in this activity (Bishop, 1988).

Mathematical Argument, or What Is True in Mathematics and Why?

In addition to solving problems and creating mathematical models, mathematicians "prove things." The distinctive content of mathematics is relationships among quantities and among shapes, and the association of quantity with qualities of shape. In mathematical argument or discourse, assertions are made about these relationships, and those assertions are proven to be true or false using logical deduction from agreed-upon assumptions. This is a simple description of a highly contested terrain, but it allows us to get into the issue of what mathematicians do when they are working to generate new mathematical knowledge.

Conventionally, the *Elements* of Euclid have been considered to represent the ideal of mathematical argument. In Euclid's geometry, numerous theorems relating characteristics of geometrical forms are generated by logical deduction from a few axioms and definitions. The theorems are assertions about relationships among shapes which can be "proven" to be true using the rules of logic and axioms and definitions and other previously proven theorems. The geometrical forms about which theorems are asserted are abstractions; that is, they are not actual triangles, squares, or circles drawn on paper or otherwise present to the senses, but they are ideas. Working on such ideas gives mathematicians the capacity to make statements about what is true of all triangles; these statements are shown to be true based on chains of logical reasoning from what we know about all triangles already. By definition, a triangle is any closed figure in a plane with three straight sides; everything else we "know" about triangles proceeds from accepting that definition and a few "self-evident" assumptions (axioms) about figures in the plane. We can know for certain within this system, for example, that the triangle that is formed by joining the midpoints of the sides of any triangle will have three angles that are the same size as the angles in the original triangle, and that its sides will be exactly half as long as the sides of the original triangle. This is true whether the triangles look like this

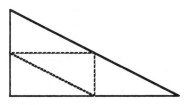

or like this

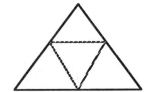

or like any other pair of triangles that meets the conditions. Proving that this assertion is true does not involve drawing and measuring lots of triangles, however. It involves making deductions from what we already know is true about angles, lines, and triangles, in the abstract. For example, we know that the line joining the midpoints of two sides is always parallel to the third side, that certain angles that are formed when a line intersects two parallel lines are equal, and so on. One way of thinking about the "goodness" of a mathematical system is to look at whether it can produce many theorems out of only a few axioms and definitions. And Euclidean geometry is often used as an example of the power of mathematical deduction because it does just that.[7] Using Euclidean geometry as the ideal of mathematical argument, we could conclude that mathematical understanding means being able to produce a deductive proof for any assertion.

What Kind of Knowledge Is Entailed in Proving?

There is a problem with thinking about Euclidean geometry as the prototype for mathematical thinking, because it emphasizes the process of proving conjectures without saying much about where the conjectures come from in the first place or what conjectures might have to do with understanding before they are proven. Once a conjecture in geometry or any other branch of mathematics is stated, its truth often seems obvious, especially to the person who stated it. It is not clear, from this perspective, what the proof of the conjecture would add in the way of understanding. This is true at the highest levels of mathematical creation, as well as at more elementary levels of mathematical argument. In mathematical practice, the quality of a conjecture has a great deal to do with whether it is formulated in such a way as to make the forthcoming proof seem uneventful:

> When a mathematician asks himself why some result should hold, the answer he seeks is some intuitive understanding. In fact, a rigorous proof means nothing to him if the result doesn't make sense intuitively. If it doesn't, he will examine the proof very critically. If the proof seems right, he will then try hard to see what is wrong with his intuition. . . . Poincare said, "When a somewhat long argument leads us to a simple and striking result, we are not satisfied until we have shown that we could have foreseen, if not the entire result, at least its principle features!" (Kline, 1980, p. 312)

A conjecture is more than a guess, and must be judged according to the quality of the evidence that supports it, even when strict logical evidence that it is true has not yet been produced. In Poincare's reflections on his own work as a mathematician, insight or intuition seems at least as important to securing mathematical understanding as logical proof (Hadamard, 1945). This phenomenon in mathematical practice is a serious challenge to the primacy of the deductive process for supporting an argument represented by the Euclidean ideal (Steiner, 1988).

Knowing How To Make Conjectures

Can we say that a learner *understands* a bit of mathematics about which he or she has made a conjecture, even if no logical proof of the conjecture can be produced? Both conjectures and theorems require what is commonly called *mathematical reasoning,* but the reasoning that leads to a theorem is much more transparent than that which leads to a conjecture, and thus much easier for the listener to evaluate. Pólya (1957) makes the distinction as follows:

We secure our mathematical knowledge by demonstrative reasoning, but we support our conjectures by plausible reasoning. . . . The difference between the two kinds of reasoning is great and manifold. Demonstrative reasoning is safe, beyond controversy, and final. Plausible reasoning is hazardous, controversial, and provisional. . . . Demonstrative reasoning has rigid standards, codified and clarified by logic (formal or demonstrative logic), which is the theory of demonstrative reasoning. The standards of plausible reasoning are fluid, and there is no theory of such reasoning that could be compared to demonstrative logic in clarity or would command comparable consensus. (p. v)

Here Pólya is saying that deductive arguments follow agreed-upon rules, and so their validity can be evaluated by others who are familiar with these classical standards. No such consensus operates, he claims, about what constitutes a legitimate argument in support of the plausibility of a conjecture.

The simplest way to make the distinction between justifying conjectures and justifying theorems is to assert that conjectures are the result of induction; that is, they are the result of observing patterns in a phenomenon, and with good reason, asserting that the pattern will continue in a way that leads to some general truth. Of course the truth of the conclusions, even those based on demonstrative reasoning, depends on the assumptions that are made, and many mathematical "truths" have required revision when the assumptions on which they were based were challenged. Assumptions can be challenged with one counterexample; it is the *mathematical* assumptions (e.g., the assumption of parallel lines in Euclidean geometry), not the universally accepted logical process, that are called into question (Lakatos, 1976). And there are no hard and fast rules for how to find the counterexample that will do the trick. So in actual mathematical practice, there is less of a distinction between induction and deduction, or between intuition and logic, than scholastic definitions would lead us to believe. Plausible reasoning produces counterexamples, counterexamples require the revision of assumptions, and the process results in the refinement of the demonstrative argument. This raises important questions for those who would have students making conjectures and producing counterexamples to challenge the assertions of other students at the level of elementary mathematics (e.g., NCTM, 1989). How are we to assess what the student understands if there are no standards in the discipline with which to judge the adequacy of "plausible reasoning"? How does one learn to have the mathematical insight that leads to good conjectures or powerful counterexamples? Is it simply a matter of being socialized to pay attention to one's own sense-making capacities? Or is mathematical insight a talent with which only a few are endowed? Or is it a matter of acquiring rich and flexible knowledge structures of the sort cognitive psychologists describe?

Freudenthal (1978) writes at length about the student who answers "I see it so" when asked how he or she has solved a mathematical problem. He, as well as Wheeler (cited in Bell, 1979) and Bell (1979), have considered versions of the problems stated earlier and the implications of their possible answers for mathematics education. Each of these writers wishes to acknowledge making a conjecture as a legitimate form of mathematical thinking for students, because it is considered with respect in the work of the discipline. They all attend to the capacity that we have to imagine a mathematical generalization from one significant example. Freudenthal (1978) calls such examples *paradigms,* using this term somewhat differently than it is commonly used. In his studies of students' attempts to convince their peers of a mathematical assertion, Balacheff (1988) considers the various ways students use examples to make an argument. He distinguishes the *crucial experiment* from the *naive experiment:* The former relies on choosing an example that does not facilitate the truth of the statement. Even more powerful is the students' use of the *generic example,* which relies on knowing enough to choose an example that cannot in any way be construed as a special case, a "good representative" of the class of objects to which the assertion is to apply (e.g., a triangle that is neither right nor equilateral as a generic example of a triangle). Balacheff considers these forms of argument to be developments toward a mathematical way of thinking about what constitutes appropriate evidence. There are two related phenomena here that raise questions about how mathematical understanding can be acquired and evaluated: One is the idiosyncratic nature of insight, and the other is the attempt to test the validity of one's insights by trying to argue their plausibility in a community of peers. These issues in mathematics education are intricately related to issues of how new mathematical knowledge is generated in the discipline, not because education is about preparing mathematicians, but because these issues go directly to the heart of what it means to know mathematics and how that knowledge is acquired (Steiner, 1988).

The Relationship Between Conjecture and Proof in Mathematics

In *Proofs and Refutations,* Lakatos (1976) portrays historical debates within mathematics about what the "proof" of a theorem represents by constructing a conversation among a group of students—fictional characters who voice the disagreements among mathematicians through the last several centuries, often using the mathematicians' own words. Lakatos's argument, which comes through in the person of the teacher, is that mathematics develops as a process of "conscious guessing" about relationships among quantities and shapes, with proof following a zig-zag path starting from conjectures and moving to the examination of premises through the use of counterexamples, or refutations. This activity of doing mathematics is different from what is recorded once it is done: "Naive conjecture and counterexamples do not appear in the fully fledged deductive structure: the zig-zag of discovery cannot be discerned in the end product" (Lakatos, 1976, p. 42). The product of mathematical activity might be justified with a deductive proof (i.e., Pólya's demonstrative reasoning), but the product does not represent the process of coming to know. Nor is knowing final or certain, even with a proof, for the assumptions on which the proof is based—the axioms accepted as self-evidently true by those who work in that branch of the discipline—continue to be open to reexamination in the mathematical community of discourse.

Mathematics has grown and changed over time, in Lakatos's view, not because the conclusions that are derived from axioms are the result of faulty logic, but because the axioms and definitions from which the logical argument begins are themselves open to revision as they are examined in the community of discourse. The need for revisions does not become obvious, however, until one engages in the process of proof and discovers the shortcomings of one's assumptions. The insufficiency of the original assumptions comes to be recognized as one tries to pursue their logical consequences: Refutations of the conclusions, often in the form of counterexamples, suggest revisions to the assumptions. Lakatos demonstrated that this zig-zag between revising conclusions and revising assumptions in the process of coming to know occurred both in the work of individual mathematicians as they exposed their work to their colleagues and over time as conclusions that had been unquestioned in the past were reconsidered.

From the standpoint of the person doing mathematics, making a conjecture (or what Lakatos calls a *conscious guess*) is taking a risk because the process of mathematical argument is social; conjecturing requires the admission that one's assumptions are open to revision, that one's insights may have been limited, that one's conclusions may have been inappropriate. Although possibly garnering recognition for inventiveness, letting other interested persons in on one's conjectures increases personal vulnerability. Lakatos asserted that to do mathematics, a scholar needed to have the courage to make guesses about what might be true in a system of mathematical relationships, and then have the modesty to examine, and let others examine, the assumptions behind those assertions. Courage and modesty are appropriate to participation in mathematical activity because truth remains tentative, even as the proof of a conjecture evolves. It is often the case that a conjecture is asserted by one individual and proven by another. In the research literature, mathematicians' names are associated both with conjectures and with proofs.

Pólya (1954) also thought courage and modesty to be essential to the activity of acquiring new mathematical knowledge. He asserted that the doer of mathematics must assume "the inductive attitude," and be willing to question both observations and generalizations, playing them off of one another in a form similar to what Lakatos called the zig-zag path from conjecture to proof and back to axioms. Pólya's emphasis on the role of induction in mathematics is intended to complement the more formalized view that mathematics is about proving theorems. Like Lakatos, he is concerned with helping students and other nonmathematicians to understand where the theorems come from in the first place, and what we really know when we have proved one.

What mathematicians do when they are creating mathematics is a relatively new focus for philosophers of mathematics. Until recently, studies of mathematical argument focused on the nature of the connection between the truth of mathematical assertions and their logical foundations, with scant attention to how the assertions came into being. What has brought the question of mathematical practice to the forefront in contemporary work are some rather profound failures on the part of the logicists and the formalists to secure the foundations of mathematical certainty by attaching it to a deductive structure (Tymoczko, 1985). The more philosophers pressed for consistency and logic in the foundations of mathematics, the more inconsistency and paradox they discovered (Kramer, 1970). And so, in the late 20th century, that *fallibilist* view of Lakatos and Pólya, with their attention to the process of generating and revising mathematical conjectures in social discourse, has gained attention.

Lakatos (1976) calls mathematics *quasiempirical* because of the way it depends on counterexamples to refine assertions, and Pólya (1954) asserts that doing mathematics requires "an inductive attitude" to discern patterns in numerical and spatial relationships. But the discourse of mathematics is distinguished from other scientific discourse because mathematics does not depend for its verity on physical evidence. Whether one is considering a conjecture or a theorem, knowing it mathematically depends on whether the assertion makes sense in an informal, intuitive way (for conjectures) or in a formal, logical way (for theorems). Mathematicians can do their work, the work of inventing and justifying mathematical assertions, without reference to empirical data, although they do use "images" drawn from experience in the world to reason about ideas (Gleick, 1987; Noddings, 1985). A common observation in several recently published popular descriptions of mathematicians at work, also found in some classical historical accounts, is that mathematicians do not need a laboratory; they have ideas while they sit or stand at their desks or at the kitchen table, or they figure things out while getting on the street car or sitting around waiting for a meal in a restaurant. In those settings, they can test the validity of their ideas as well (e.g., Cole, 1987; Gleick, 1987; Hadamard, 1945; Hoffman, 1987). This habit of working is worth noting because it is directly related to the issue of verification of beliefs. The relation between justification and certainty in mathematics is mysteriously ironic and has puzzled thinkers continuously over the centuries: How can we be certain that assertions of a mathematical sort are true when there is no physical evidence? In common sense terms, if a scientist claims that iron rusts in the presence of oxides, anyone can apply oxides to a piece of iron to observe whether the scientist is telling the truth. But what of conjectures that are put forth with considerable certainty and even used in the solution of problems when no proof has yet been produced? These questions are of interest even as we think about students "conjecturing" at the elementary level. How do we evaluate the knowledge of the student who "sees" that the difference between successive square numbers will always be successive odd numbers (as in the problem described earlier), but cannot prove the logic of this assertion? What does being able to conjecture suggest they understand? What do they need to understand to be able to do it?

Mathematical Argument as a Social Phenomenon

Beyond conjecturing, there is proof. But even in this realm, it is unclear what knowledge underlies practice. Davis and Hersh (1987) point out that the mathematician's public arguments do not match the ideal of a deductive logical argument. They assume that the interested others who are reading or hearing the argument share the concerns and values that guided its development, allowing work to proceed within a community of scholars without step-by-step deductive proofs.

In the real world of mathematics, a mathematical paper does two things. It testifies that the author has convinced himself and his friends that certain "results" are true, and it presents a part of the evidence on which this conviction is based.

It presents part, not all, because certain routine calculations are deemed unworthy of print. The reader is expected to produce them for himself. More important, certain "heuristic" reasonings, including perhaps the motivation which led in the first place to undertaking the investigation, are deemed "inessential" or "irrelevant" for purposes of publication. Knowing this unstated background motivation is what it takes to be a qualified reader of the article.

How does one acquire this background? Almost always, it is by word of mouth from some other member of the intended audience, some other person already initiated in the particular area of research in question. . . . Mathematical argument is addressed to a human audience, which possesses the background knowledge enabling it to understand the intentions of the speaker or the author. (Davis & Hersh, 1987, p. 66)

Considering the social character of mathematical knowledge—in light of the question of what constitutes "proof" in mathematical practice—raises important questions to attend to as we think about what it might mean for students to do mathematical argument at the elementary level. If we give up the idea that mathematics is about ultimate truths and see it instead as a human construction, it becomes much harder to separate disciplinary conventions from logical necessities. If we emphasize students' doing mathematics, and interpret that to mean constructing mathematical arguments in the classroom community of discourse, we also need to ask how this discourse ought to be related to more advanced work in the field and to the heritage of mathematical concepts that have been constructed and used over time.

But there is an even deeper issue here, and a fundamental irony. If, as Davis and Hersh (1987) point out, there are agreed-upon and unexamined assumptions within mathematical practice, not only about terms and symbols, but about legitimate heuristics and appropriate motivations for undertaking a problem in the first place, then what are we to make of the idea that mathematics is powerful precisely because it enables us to know things without reference to authority? If learning mathematics means becoming indoctrinated to the rules of discourse, how can learning mathematics also mean being educated to pay attention to one's own capacity for sense making? Within communities of working mathematicians, as within all such working communities, there are a host of agreed-upon assumptions: assumptions whose legitimacy is taken for granted so that they can get on with the conversation. Working mathematicians may not stop to convince themselves or anyone else that these assumptions are legitimate: Being a member of the discourse community simply implies being willing to play by the same rules by which everyone else is playing.

If one takes the view that mathematical truth is socially constructed, however, then it is difficult to also see mathematics as the subject that students can access by virtue of their own individual powers of reasoning (Cobb, 1988a). If mathematical understanding within mathematics means playing by the rules that other mathematicians play by, then how do we put together the disciplinary perspective on the subject with the perspective on understanding derived from cognitive psychology? If learning mathematical practice is a matter of being initiated into the norms, language, and heuristics used by practitioners, then how can the subject be taught at the elementary level, where most learners are unlikely to become mathematicians and few teachers have been exposed to the mathematical community of scholars?

Mathematical arguments cannot be imported whole into settings where the participants do not already understand something of what they are about. And yet we know that it is possible for elementary school children to make mathematical assertions and to produce mathematically legitimate arguments for their validity. What we need to work out is how one learns to do that in an elementary school context, how such learning might be documented and evaluated, and whether this is what ought to constitute education in doing mathematics.

Focus on Mathematics: Summary

In thinking about what it might mean to know and understand mathematics from the perspective of the discipline, we have considered three domains or categories of mathematical activity: problem solving, mathematizing, and mathematical argument. One way of viewing problem solving is as the appropriate application of abstract mathematical constructs to various problem situations. We argued that problem solving seen from this perspective entails knowledge of heuristics, of mathematical structures, of how to represent situations using mathematical symbols, and of transformations that can be made to those symbols (or more properly, to the mathematical relationships underlying the symbols). One might argue that helping students acquire these kinds of knowledge ought to constitute an important goal of elementary mathematics education. Indeed, the efforts of many of the cognitive psychologists we described earlier can be seen as attempts to explicate these kinds of knowledge so that they can better be taught. But in considering problem solving from the perspective of mathematics, we also raised the important alternative view of instrumental problem solving, inventing strategies that work out of the contexts of the problems themselves. Although this perspective on problem solving has been downplayed or ignored in the traditional school mathematics curriculum, its contrast with more deductive approaches to mathematics has been the subject of centuries-long debates within the discipline of mathematics. These debates should inform our efforts to think about what kinds of relationships between mathematical abstractions and problem situations we should consider constituting mathematical understanding appropriate in elementary schools.

In examining the activity of mathematizing, we highlighted the power of mathematical modeling for conceptualizing physical and social problems, and the pervasiveness in our society of fundamental assumptions about the "objectiveness" such modeling provides. We also pointed to some of the inherent limitations of reducing complex situations to quantitative terms. This leaves us, on the one hand, with a case for arguing that being able to think of many situations flexibly in quantitative terms should be an important outcome of mathematics education for students, and on the other hand, with questions about how much the power of mathematizing should be emphasized in relationship to its weaknesses.

Mathematical argument is an activity that is virtually nonexistent in most elementary school classrooms, where mathematics is treated as concepts and procedures to be mastered, not to be developed or questioned. But making and proving conjectures is an important part of what mathematicians do, and being able to engage in mathematical argument is an important goal in the calls for reform (e.g., the goal of "learning to reason mathematically" in the NCTM *Standards*). In discussing mathematical argument, we considered the relationship between logical deduction, which represents the traditional ideal of mathematical argument, and the process of coming up with reasonable conjectures in the first place. We argued that if one looks at the activity of mathematicians rather than just their publications (which entail the deductive kind of argument), the process of arriving at and justifying reasonable conjectures is an important one and should be considered a candidate for what it means to do mathematics in elementary schools.

FOCUS ON CLASSROOM PRACTICE

Thus far we have considered views of what it might mean to know and understand mathematics from the perspectives of cognitive psychology and mathematics. At this point we turn to perspectives emerging from a focus on the elementary school classroom. We begin by considering the assumptions, often implicit, of researchers studying classroom teaching of mathematics in the effective teaching, or process-product, approach. This research program is important in part because it builds on assumptions about the nature of mathematical knowledge and goals for schooling that are implicit in existing practice, and in part because it has had such a powerful influence on educational policy in recent years. As a contrast to process-product research, we then consider three recent cases of researchers studying mathematics teaching and learning in classrooms by attempting to change some of the fundamental assumptions about knowing and learning mathematics.

Research on Effective Teaching

Research on teaching blossomed in the early 1970s with the adoption of the process-product approach, whose proponents sought to discover stable relationships between teacher behaviors—process variables—and student achievement and attitude outcomes—product variables (Brophy & Good, 1986; Gage, 1978). Process-product researchers were motivated by dissatisfaction with laboratory-based theories of learning for informing teaching practice (Gage, 1972) and with research that "avoided looking at the actual processes of teaching in the classroom" (Dunkin & Biddle, 1974, p. 13). By focusing on what teachers do in the classroom, these researchers hoped to find behaviors and strategies for teaching that worked—that teachers could deploy to become more effective, with effectiveness for the most part defined as student achievement measured by standardized tests. Their quest was for a scientific basis for teaching, with science defined as the search for relationships among variables (Gage, 1978), and the variables being those derived from classroom teaching, not laboratory studies of learning.

The process-product research strategy was successful in producing a consistent picture of teaching that yielded achievement gains: teaching that was highly structured and directed, involved explicit explanation and modeling by the teacher, and kept students highly engaged with academic content (Brophy & Good, 1986; Rosenshine & Stevens, 1986; Shulman, 1986). But process-product research has been criticized on a number of counts, including its lack of attention to the subject matter being taught (Romberg & Carpenter, 1986; Shulman, 1986), its focus on observable behavior and resulting disregard for the cognitive activities of teachers and students (Shulman, 1986), and its inherent conservatism arising from the study of existing practice (Romberg & Carpenter, 1986). Our goal here is not to provide another critique of process-product research, but to examine its assumptions about the nature of knowledge and learning. Because this research program has had such a significant impact on educational policy, it is important to examine these assumptions, both to understand their relationships to the various perspectives we have already discussed and to inform our emerging conceptions of what knowing mathematics might mean in classrooms.

Separation of Teaching and Content

Because process-product researchers were seeking generalizable findings about teaching, they generally assumed that teaching could be usefully separated from the content being taught. This assumption was consistent with the search for general laws of learning in process-product research's parent discipline of psychology. Deciding the content of instruction was considered to be heavily values-based and to be the proper focus of curriculum experts and public debate, not of research on teaching. The goal of research on effective teaching was to answer the question, Given particular goals of instruction, what are the teacher behaviors or strategies that will foster that goal? Researchers of teaching thus were not greatly concerned with defining desirable outcomes of schooling or considering fundamental questions about what students should be learning. In searching for measures of student outcomes, they worked from existing assumptions—prevalent in the research and schooling communities—about the nature of knowledge, relying for the most part on standardized tests of student achievement.

Teaching was viewed from this perspective as a delivery system for knowledge that was specified by others. Process-product researchers carried this implicit assumption with them even when they focused on the teaching of particular subjects. Thus, when Good and Grouws (1979; Good, Grouws, & Ebmeier, 1983) studied elementary school mathematics teaching, they continued in the process-product tradition by assuming that the best indicator of effective teaching is students' achievement test scores and by focusing on instructional behaviors that were virtually free of mathematics content. The resulting recommendations, such as "focus on meaning and promoting student understanding" or "assess student comprehension" might apply as well to the teaching of history or reading as to the teaching of mathematics. These rather generic recommendations suggest that teaching is a delivery system for content that is determined by others and specified in the curriculum.

Mathematics educators have criticized process-product researchers for their failure to consider what mathematics is worth knowing and for their ready acceptance of achievement tests as the primary measure of instructional effectiveness (Romberg & Carpenter, 1986). "Residualized mean gain scores have become methodological proxies for 'what we want,' and the standardized test has become the operational definition of what is worth knowing" (Romberg & Carpenter, 1986, p. 865). But what kind of operational definition of knowing mathematics do these tests provide, and why were they so readily accepted by researchers of teaching?

Mathematics Knowledge Defined as Achievement on Standardized Tests

In searching for objective measures of student learning, process-product researchers heartily embraced standardized achievement tests. These tests were designed to be relatively impervious to minor variations in curriculum and to measure learning outcomes valued by school systems and the public. Standardized tests provided measures of learning expressed as single numbers or small sets of numbers with relatively high reliability that could be used as the outcome variables of process-product research. Having such a "clean" set of outcome measures was important for being able to describe the relationships among variables that were the focus of scientific research from this perspective. Researchers in the process-product tradition often warned that achievement tests measure only some of the important outcomes of schooling in limited ways, but that these tests are the best we have for providing relatively unbiased indicators of the effectiveness of instruction (e.g., Brophy & Good, 1986).

But many scholars have argued that standardized achievement tests represent a severely limited view of what mathematics is worth knowing (Romberg & Carpenter, 1986). There is too much emphasis on isolated computational skill. There is not enough problem solving, and what problem solving there is tends to consist of word problems that can be solved by simply applying learned algorithms. The tests do little or nothing to assess students' ability to comprehend mathematical reasoning in written communications, their ability to engage in mathematical argument, or their willingness to approach problems they encounter by drawing on quantitative tools—all outcomes that are emphasized in recent reform rhetoric (NCTM, 1989; National Research Council, 1989).

At the same time, standardized tests are not always dismissed so readily. Much of the heat generated over the sorry state of current mathematics education in the United States is fueled by pointing to students' dismal performance on standardized tests. Clearly, policymakers and the public are willing to accept test scores as an important indicator of what students are learning. But how do the assumptions about what it means to know mathematics and what mathematics is worth knowing that underlie these tests compare with those of the perspectives from psychology and mathematics that we have considered?

One point of mismatch is the tasks included in most tests. For the most part, tasks on standardized achievement tests involve isolated computation and the solving of routine word problems, resulting in a picture of knowing mathematics as knowing computational procedures and the skills needed to apply those procedures to a constrained set of problems. Our analysis of perspectives from the discipline of mathematics suggests a much broader range of tasks—tasks involving various kinds of nonroutine problem solving, the mathematization of situations and judgments about the appropriateness of mathematical models for various purposes, and the use of mathematical argument and justification.

Another point of mismatch is that the theories of testing on which standardized achievement tests are constructed assume that knowledge can be regarded as a relatively stable trait or continuum along which individuals can be ordered (Anastasi, 1976; Cronbach, 1970). Test items are considered samples from relatively homogeneous pools of potential items representing what is to be known. These simplifying assumptions are important in providing the basis for powerful mathematical models underlying test construction, but they are not necessarily consistent with other views of knowledge. The assumptions are relatively compatible with traditional views of learning as the transmission of knowledge. From that perspective it makes sense to think of measuring how much knowledge a person has acquired. But the assumptions are not so readily consistent with cognitive views of learning and knowing that emphasize the role of knowledge structures actively constructed by the individual learner. What becomes important from this perspective is not how much knowledge a person has, but how that knowledge is organized and how accessible it is in various situations. This is not to say that testing is totally incompatible with cognitive views of learning, but that most existing tests were built on assumptions of knowledge as a more static entity.

A final assumption reflected in testing that may present a more fundamental dilemma is the assumption that knowledge can be decontextualized. To believe that a written test can provide a valid picture of an individual's knowledge, one must assume that the individual "carries" that knowledge within himself or herself to the testing situation. The recent emphasis by some cognitive researchers on the situated nature of cognition raises the important question of whether it is, in principle, possible to assess a person's competence through tests that are, by their very nature, meant to measure decontextualized knowledge.

Knowledge as Separable Into Discrete Parts

Another assumption that is reflected not only in process-product research but in much of current practice in curriculum development and instruction is that knowledge can be decomposed into discrete entities. In curriculum, this assumption is reflected by the breaking up of content to be learned into sets of discrete objectives that are to be taught and tested separately. Some mathematics educators categorize knowledge into skills, concepts, and applications (Fey, 1982; Trafton, 1980). Many elementary mathematics textbooks treat two-digit subtraction with regrouping as a skill distinct from two-digit subtraction without regrouping, and contain separate lessons on skills for estimating and problem solving. This splintering of the curriculum has been fueled by a variety of sources, including the general reductionistic assumptions of psychology; associationist and behavioristic theories that consider knowledge to be collections of behaviors or bonds acquired essentially by accretion (Thorndike, 1922); instructional theories that emphasize the direct teaching of component skills that are then combined into more complex performances (Gagné et al., 1988); and the push to be as specific as possible in setting objectives for instruction (Bloom, Englehart, Furst, Hill, & Krathwohl, 1956; Tyler, 1949). This emphasis on separation of knowledge runs counter to the emphasis in cognitive views of learning and knowledge as structured and connected.

Researchers studying teaching have inherited assumptions about mathematics knowledge being decomposable and have built on them in a number of ways. For example, researchers studying mathematics teaching have viewed problem solving as a matter of learning mathematical procedures and concepts, then learning the skills or strategies that are needed to apply the procedures and concepts to problems. Good et al. (1983) measured student learning with an achievement test that separated mathematics knowledge into three subtests: knowledge, skill, and problem solving. Good et al. expressed concern over the lack of difference between their treatment and control groups on the problem-solving subtest "because we felt that if mathematics knowledge is to be applied to 'everyday' matters, students need skills in this area (e.g., to compare whether the 12 oz. or 16 oz. package is the better buy)" (p. 93). Similarly, Brophy (1988), in arguing that most of what is taught in school is amenable to the principles of active teaching, suggested that

students learning mathematics problem-solving skills need not only practice in applying procedural algorithms to well-structured problems but also modeling and explicit instruction in strategies for identifying relevant information and formulating poorly structured problems accurately, as well as strategies for analyzing, simplifying, and developing methods for solving unfamiliar problems. (p. 8)

These statements suggest the assumption that mathematical knowledge consists of fairly separable skills, concepts, and strategies that can be explicitly modeled and directly taught.

Students' Engagement as a Measure of Learning

A final assumption of some researchers in the process-product tradition is that the time a student spends actively engaged in appropriate academic tasks can serve as a proxy for the student's learning. This assumption has resulted in process-product researchers' focusing on a variety of time-related variables such as opportunity to learn, time-on-task, and academic learning time (Berliner, 1979; Rosenshine, 1979). Much of this emphasis on time spent in learning can be traced to Carroll's (1963) model of school learning, which included three variables for predicting school achievement that could be expressed in terms of time: aptitude (defined as the amount of time a student needs to learn a given task), opportunity to learn (time allowed for learning the task), and perseverance (time student is willing to spend learning the task). As operationalized by classroom researchers, these time-related variables reflect the behaviorist sense of the word *active* in learning: A student is learning if he or she is overtly responding. Thus, if a student is visibly engaged in a task, he or she can be assumed to be learning that task.

Although measures of the time students spend engaged in academic tasks have proved successful as rough predictors of student achievement, many researchers from both inside and outside the process-product tradition have criticized this emphasis on time and observable engagement (e.g., Peterson, 1988; Romberg & Carpenter, 1986) with a number of arguments:

1. A focus on time spent and opportunity to learn emphasizes efficiency, quantity, and presence or absence when both what is learned (the mathematics) and the quality (of students' thinking) may be most important.

2. Measures of time spent and opportunity to learn are behavioral measures that do not tap the cognitive processes and strategies in which the learner engages in the act of learning and which may define the essence of knowing, understanding, and problem solving in mathematics.

3. Although empirical data show a significant positive linear relationship between observed "engaged time" of the learner in low-level mathematics activities and tasks (knowledge, facts, and skill) and students' subsequent low-level mathematics achievement, empirical data do not show a linear positive relationship for higher level mathematics activities, including mathematical applications and problem solving (see, e.g., Swing, Stoiber, & Peterson, 1988).

4. Analyses based on "time spent" or on "content coverage" have led to a fragmented view of what is learned in mathematics—both the mathematical content and the aspects of mathematical knowledge, skill, and problem solving (e.g., conceptual vs. procedural knowledge)—rather than leading to an integrated view that assumes connectedness among all these aspects of knowing mathematics.

Definition of Mathematical Knowledge in Existing Classroom Practice

We have presented several assumptions underlying research on effective teaching that stand in contrast to assumptions about knowing and learning mathematics emerging from cognitive psychology and the discipline of mathematics. The assumptions of classroom researchers have been inextricably linked to existing classroom practice. This is due both to the influence of teaching effectiveness research on educational policy and practice, and to the derivation of effective teaching practices from existing classroom practice.

The tight linkage of process-product research to existing classroom practice is both a strength and a weakness. As a strength, this grounding in classroom practice helps ensure that recommendations from the research will be practical: Because the recommended teaching behaviors were derived by observing teachers, it is reasonable to assume that other teachers can carry out the behaviors as well. In addition, these studies of teaching and learning are situated not in laboratory settings, but in the classroom contexts to which researchers hope to apply them (Romberg & Carpenter, 1986). But this grounding in classroom practice is also a weakness because it makes the approach inherently conservative in seeking to improve existing instructional practices, rather than seeking more fundamental changes. Thus, Romberg and Carpenter (1986) contended that the variables of process-product research "can only make current teaching more efficient or effective, but they cannot make it radically different" (p. 865). Researchers on teaching counter with one of their original motivating concerns: concern about attempts to make mathematics teaching radically different without empirical data based on observations of classroom practice (Good, 1988). They point out the importance of seeing whether major changes will work in the classroom before calling for massive changes in practice.

As researchers have responded to the criticisms of process-product research by building new research programs to study teaching (Shulman, 1986), they have, for the most part, maintained their commitment to studying existing classroom practice. This commitment is motivated in part by the recognition that there are considerable improvements that can be made within the pervasive frameworks of teaching in existing practice, in part by understanding that more radical changes in teaching must start with a rich understanding of existing practice if they are to be realized. For example, Leinhardt (1988) has used constructs and methods from cognitive science to study the teaching and learning of mathematics by expert teachers, selecting the teachers primarily on the basis of consistent gains in student achievement. Leinhardt's analyses have revealed important teacher knowledge of mathematics subject matter and of the structures and routines for conducting good lessons, helping us to better understand expert "traditional" teaching. Although Leinhardt (1988) argued for the need to study "dramatically different teaching styles and lesson patterns," she reaffirmed the traditional criterion and kind of student learning used by researchers on teaching effectiveness as teachers who "enrich the students' concepts, concrete experiences, and extended problem-solving capabilities while not abandoning the computational aspects of arithmetic education that society seems to value" (p. 65).

Broadening Conceptions of Mathematical Knowing in Classrooms

The views of teaching and learning that seem to underlie much of current mathematics instruction in elementary school classrooms entail "teaching as telling," and learning as received knowing (Belenky, Clinchy, Goldberger, & Tarule, 1986), "where teachers supply information and show how to perform procedures, and students accept this knowledge, rather than arriving at it through their own constructive intellectual and social activity" (Greeno, 1989, p. 137). Currently, researchers are working in elementary school classrooms to explore instruction based on alternatives to these fundamental assumptions about teaching and learning (Carpenter et al., 1987; Cobb, Wood, & Yackel, in press; Lampert, 1988a). They are trying in various ways to bring alternative assumptions about knowing and learning mathematics from psychology and the discipline of mathematics into the classroom, while respecting the many constraints of classroom teaching. (Although we offer three examples of such attempts, other researchers and mathematics educators are making similar efforts to bring different views of learning to the elementary classroom—e.g., Maher, 1988; Resnick, 1989.)

Cognitively Guided Instruction

Carpenter et al. (1987; see also Carpenter, Fennema, Peterson, Chiang, & Loef, 1988) have sought to help first-grade teachers change their underlying views of learning in light of cognitive research on individual children's solving of addition and subtraction word problems. Their instructional framework, which they call *cognitively guided instruction* (CGI) is based on two major assumptions derived from cognitive studies of learning:

One is that instruction should develop understanding by stressing relationships between skills and problem solving with problem solving serving as the organizing focus of instruction. The second assumption is that instruction should build on students' existing knowledge. (Carpenter et al., 1988, p. 11)

These assumptions parallel two of the themes from cognitive psychology that we considered earlier: connections among types of knowledge and learning as active construction of knowledge. Thus, the CGI researchers' assumptions about learning and knowing mathematics are clearly grounded in psychological research on individual learners. In helping teachers apply these perspectives about individual learning to their teaching, the CGI researchers draw on research on teacher thinking (Clark & Peterson, 1986), which assumes that

classroom instruction is mediated by teachers' thinking and decisions. Thus, researchers and educators can bring about the most significant changes in classroom practice by helping teachers to make informed decisions rather than by attempting to train them to perform in a specified way. (Carpenter et al., 1988, p. 10)

Thus the route to changing instructional practice is to change teachers' knowledge, beliefs, and attitudes. In particular, Carpenter et al. (1988)

sought to provide teachers with knowledge about types of addition and subtraction problems (see Table 1) and the strategies that students typically use to solve these problems as they pass through general levels of expertise. They also urged teachers to incorporate broad instructional principles that emphasized making instruction appropriate for each student by basing instructional decisions on frequent assessment of the student's solution strategies.

Carpenter et al. (1988) found that teachers were able to learn about the research-based addition and subtraction problem types and solutions, and to use this knowledge in their instruction. CGI teachers were more likely to attend to their students' solution strategies than were control-group teachers. Students in CGI classrooms spent more time solving problems and were more successful in solving the sorts of complex addition and subtraction problems that have been the focus of the psychological research in this domain.

Constructivist Teaching of Second-Grade Mathematics

In another attempt to alter teachers' beliefs and instructional practices to reflect a particular perspective on learning, Cobb and his colleagues (Cobb et al., in press; Cobb, Yackel, & Wood, 1988) have worked with second grade teachers to alter their teaching to be consistent with a constructivist view of learning. Cobb and his colleagues (1988) began with the fundamental assumption that mathematics learning occurs as "individuals each construct *their* individual mathematical worlds by reorganizing *their* experiences in an attempt to resolve *their* problems" (p. 93). The dilemma in applying this constructivist view of learning to teaching is resolving the tension between this position and the need to meet "institutionally sanctioned goals of instruction" (p. 94), that is, for students to learn particular, accepted mathematics. To temper without entirely resolving this dilemma, Cobb and his colleagues took a second, complementary, perspective from anthropology: that mathematical knowledge is cultural knowledge, which is best fostered by "nurturing a classroom atmosphere that encourages the negotiation of meaning" (p. 102).

Cobb and his colleagues entered the classroom by way of instructional activities and materials that would facilitate teaching that was compatible with a constructivist perspective by providing rich opportunities for students to construct their own mathematical knowledge. The instructional materials were based on constructivist researchers' models of the construction of arithmetical knowledge by individual children (Steffe & Cobb, 1988; Steffe et al., 1983) and were designed to (a) make sense to children at a variety of levels simultaneously, (b) avoid an arbitrary separation of conceptual and procedural knowledge, (c) address traditional second-grade learning objectives (i.e., those measured on standardized achievement tests), and (d) facilitate sustained whole-class discussions about mathematics (Cobb et al., 1988). The materials were accompanied by a strong commitment to treat teachers, as well as students, as constructivist learners and thus avoided instructional prescriptions. Cobb and his colleagues worked closely with a second-grade teacher using the instructional materials to develop classroom management and inter-action routines that would facilitate meaningful interaction structured around the materials. Thus, like Carpenter et al. (1987), Cobb et al. began with a particular view of what it means to know and learn mathematics from the psychological perspective of the individual learner and are working with teachers to develop forms of instruction that are compatible with that view.

Bringing Mathematical Discourse and Argument
to a Fifth-Grade Classroom

In the classroom, Lampert (1988a) is also exploring alternatives to per-vasive views of knowing and learning mathematics, "in which doing mathematics means remembering and applying the correct rule when the teacher asks a question, and mathematical truth is determined when the answer is ratified by the teacher" (p. 135). But rather than taking as her primary starting point a particular view of learning from psychological re-search on the individual learner, Lampert begins with assumptions about the nature of knowledge and knowledge growth within the discipline of mathematics. She argues, following Kramer (1970), that, "in mathemat-ics, authority comes from agreeing on shared assumptions and reasoning about their consequences" (Lampert, 1988a, p. 135). Thus, according to this view, the discourse in classrooms should be more like the discourse of argument and conjecturing that takes place within the discipline of math-ematics, with a shift in authority for what constitutes valid mathematical knowledge from teacher decree to the sense making and reasoning of the individual. "Lessons will be in the form of a mathematical argument, which students accept or reject on the basis of their own reasoning" (p. 136).

As a teacher-scholar studying her own teaching of fifth-grade mathe-matics, Lampert (1988a) is developing a classroom pedagogy in which an important goal is for teachers and students to engage in mathematical ar-gument and discourse. Her research in this setting focuses on what is in-volved from the teacher's perspective in teaching mathematics with this goal and what "students' understanding look[s] like in the social context of the public school" (p. 132). Thus, although informed by psychological research, Lampert does not begin with psychological assumptions about the learning of individuals and attempt to apply them to the classroom context; rather, she uses perspectives from psychology as one lens to consider the nature of students' understanding and knowing of mathematics in classroom contexts.

Carpenter et al. (1988), Cobb et al. (1988), and Lampert (1988a) are all attempting to change fundamental assumptions about teaching and learning that are evident in most classrooms. Carpenter et al. (1988) and Cobb et al. (1988) approach this challenge by working with teachers to develop instructional strategies that are compatible with particular views of learning emerging from psychological studies of individuals learning mathematics. Carpenter et al.'s perspective draws heavily on a specific body of research—that of children's solving of addition and subtraction word problems—and emphasizes the principles from cognitive psychology of learning as an active process that builds on existing knowledge and of the importance of emphasizing connections and relationships among ideas. For Cobb et al., the key is developing instruction that is compatible with the constructivist assumption that children construct their own mathematical knowledge through interaction in social contexts. Lampert (1988a), in contrast, begins with perspectives from mathematics and classroom teaching to develop a pedagogy in which teachers and students engage in mathematical argument rather than establish mathematical truth by decree.

SUMMARY AND PARTING THOUGHTS

We began this paper with two beliefs about why it is important to learn mathematics: the role of mathematical tools and ways of thinking in today's society and workplace and appreciation of mathematics as a great cultural achievement. Both of these beliefs support the central theme of the current reform movement: that students need to be learning mathematics with understanding and in powerful ways that go beyond the emphasis on mechanical computation that pervades so much of current elementary mathematics instruction. To consider what it means to know and understand mathematics, we turned to three research traditions that have considered this issue from different perspectives: cognitive psychology, the discipline of mathematics, and research on classroom practice. Psychologists have for the most part taken as their starting point various mathematical tasks already present in the school curriculum and have attempted to explicate the knowledge needed to perform those tasks successfully. This approach has led to important understandings and questions about how knowledge of mathematics can and should be represented in the mind of the individual knower. We discussed these issues in the context of several themes that have pervaded psychological research on mathematics: the role of representations in knowing and learning mathematics, the kinds of knowledge structures hypothesized to underlie specific mathematical tasks, the importance of the connectedness of various structures of knowledge, the active construction of these knowledge structures by individual learners, and the relationships between the knowledge structures of the individual and his or her social and physical context. Turning to the discipline of mathematics led us to some views of what it means to know mathematics that go beyond the kinds of mathematical tasks studied by psychologists and to a host of questions to consider about the kinds of mathematical activity in which elementary school students should be engaging and the mathematical content with which they should be dealing. Within the discipline of mathematics, we posited three activities as views of what it means to do mathematics: mathematics as solving problems; mathematics as mathematizing, or thinking of situations in quantitative terms; and mathematics as argument, conjecture, and proof. Each of these activities plays an important role in the discipline of mathematics; the perspectives and debates about them within the discipline of mathematics ought to inform our thinking about what kinds of mathematical activity should be important in elementary schools. Finally, we considered the views of mathematics that have been assumed in much classroom-based research on mathematics teaching, views that are in many ways at odds with the perspectives from cognitive psychology and mathematics. We also described some attempts to develop new approaches to classroom mathematics instruction based on richer views of what it means to know and learn mathematics.

In considering our question of what it means to know and understand mathematics, we have presented diverse perspectives and many questions that should inform our thinking about what mathematics is worth knowing and how it might be learned in elementary schools. But we have not integrated these perspectives into a comprehensive vision or even a clear set of questions that need to be addressed. The difficulty in providing such an integration stems, in part, from these different perspectives representing fundamental issues about the nature of mathematical knowledge and learning, such as the tension between mathematical knowledge as a veridical description of an external reality versus mathematical knowledge as a human cultural construction, and the tension between socially accepted definitions of mathematical knowledge and the need for individual learners to construct their own mathematical meanings. Concentrating solely on the personal meanings of mathematics that learners construct and building on the knowledge they bring to the learning setting creates the risk of ignoring the importance of mathematical conventions, conventions that must be learned as they are used in our society if they are to serve as powerful tools for mathematical thinking and communication. Concentrating too heavily on the mathematics to be learned—on presenting conventional tools—while ignoring the role played by the individual's existing conceptions and efforts at making sense of what is learned, creates the risk that the tools will not be learned at all or that they will not be learned in ways that make them accessible to the learner when needed.

How can school practice be shaped to deal with these and other tensions that are created in considering the diverse perspectives that arise from attending to psychology, mathematics, and the classroom context? Dealing with this question is an important task to be shared by the entire community of researchers, scholars, and teachers interested in the teaching and learning of mathematics. We hope that our presentation of perspectives will facilitate the discourse on this task. Thus, rather than concluding this chapter with questions or recommendations, we close with some rather tentative suggestions about the nature of knowing mathematics and features of instruction that must be attended to in forging a school practice successful in fostering powerful mathematical understanding. We propose attending to three aspects of knowing mathematics that have emerged in various ways throughout this chapter. At one level these aspects can be thought of as the desired outcomes of a successful educational program—as the goals of instruction. But characterizing these aspects of knowing mathematics as outcomes suggests an artificial separation of outcomes from the educational process. Rather than separate process from outcomes, we present these themes as desired characteristics of the practices of teaching and learning in school. Because such practices have rarely been tried, and even more rarely studied by researchers, we have much to learn about how they might affect the outcomes of schooling.

If teaching and learning in school are to lead to genuine academic accomplishments in mathematics, it is reasonable to assert that they must be built around the corpus of "big ideas" that are fundamental to mathematics and mathematical thinking—ideas like place value, part-whole relationships, the notion that numbers related as a function will make a line on a graph. These represent knowledge that is difficult to specify explicitly and precisely and that must be constructed by the individual. These ideas and the relationships among them constitute what Vergnaud has referred to as *conceptual fields.* Although teachers can present various descriptions of these ideas to students, they cannot "tell" these ideas in all their complexity to students; rather they can create classroom activities that provide students with opportunities to construct them. The construction or development of these ideas is an ongoing process over the course of elementary schooling; the ideas are revisited and continually refined in a variety of settings. At the same time that we recognize these ideas are made meaningful through individual construction, however, we also take note of the fact that the ideas are available to us because they have been invented and recognized as important over the long history of mathematics as a discipline.

In addition to these conceptual big ideas there are conventions of mathematics that must essentially be presented to students, including many of the symbols, representations, and other tools of mathematics, for example, the labels *one, two, three,* etc. for digits, knowing that the symbol % means percent, or knowing that the x and y axes are typically used in a graph. It does not make sense to think of students "constructing" knowledge of such conventions—they have to learn and remember them as they are conventionally used or they do not play their important role in facilitating mathematical communication. Research in cognitive psychology suggests that such things will be remembered better and available when needed if they are made meaningful to the learner in the sense of relating to the learner's existing knowledge structures. The line between these conventions of mathematics that must be acquired and the big ideas that must be constructed is by no means distinct. Such pervasive concepts as place value are intricately connected to the conventions of the representation systems we use. The convention is a tool that can be used to learn and think about the concept. If the conventional representation systems for quantity with which we deal did not involve place value, place value would not constitute a fundamental mathematical concept for students to build during their elementary school years.

Besides big ideas and conventions, a third important aspect of mathematical practice in schools needs to be personal sense making. It is important for students to have the disposition of continually trying to figure things out and make sense of them. It is important for elementary classrooms to be places where thinking about ideas and making personal sense of them is valued. Both psychology and mathematics support the importance of sense making. From the perspective of cognitive psychology, students will not construct important mathematical understandings or acquire important conventions unless they actively work to integrate new information and experiences with their existing knowledge. In the discipline of mathematics, the fundamental warrant for determining what is valid mathematical knowledge is not empirical evidence or decree by authority, but whether that knowledge can be shown to derive logically from agreed-upon assumptions. It is important for classrooms to provide settings in which students' attempts to make sense of new ideas are valued and explored and their current ways of thinking are valued and examined, not ignored, and where mathematical conclusions are supported by reasoned argument rather than teachers or answer books.

In shaping classroom practice to attend to these three aspects of knowing mathematics, there are two features of instruction whose consideration is strongly supported by all three of the general perspectives we have discussed. First is the importance of talking about mathematics. In contrast to current classroom practice in which much of the activity involves students practicing procedures that have been explained or modeled by the teaching, classrooms should provide ample opportunities for students to verbalize their thinking and to converse about mathematical ideas and procedures. If we view understanding of mathematics from the perspective of cognitive psychology as the knowledge structures of the individual, but we view school as the place where individuals acquire publicly valued knowledge, then individual knowledge must be refined and revised in the social setting of the classroom. Students must learn to communicate their ideas to one another, and their teachers must learn to communicate with students in terms of mathematical arguments. Verbal discourse, as our primary mode of communication, constitutes an important means of revealing individual knowledge. If we view knowledge and thinking as inherently situated in social and physical contexts, much of what is learned about mathematics is implicit; we therefore need to communicate about and around mathematical activity to learn through participating in that activity. From the discipline of mathematics, we have seen the importance of conjecturing and defending ideas in mathematics—activities that require extended public discourse. If the teacher adopts mathematical conventions about how to justify and refine assertions, he or she will need to talk with students, challenging these with counterexamples rather than with judgments about the wrongness of their answers.

A second aspect of practice that follows from our analysis is the importance of considering the kinds of mathematical activity in classrooms. From psychology comes the notion that the kinds of activity in which learners engage is critically important in the knowledge structures they construct or acquire. Our discussion of the discipline of mathematics revealed that the traditional curriculum and much of the research in psychology has focused on rather limited aspects of mathematical activity. But what kind of mathematical activity is appropriate for elementary school classrooms? The goal of elementary school mathematics education is not for all students to become professional mathematicians, just as we do not teach reading and writing in hopes that all students will become novelists or editors, or social studies so that all students will become historians. But there is a sense in which we want all children to come to appreciate what it means to think like a mathematician. Mathematics offers powerful ways of thinking about the world, and these ways of thinking increasingly pervade our culture. It is essential that all people be able to communicate and reason about quantitative relationships as part of being a literate, participating member of our information-oriented society.

As put forth in *Everybody Counts,* "Elementary school is where children learn the mathematical skills needed for daily life" (National Research Council, 1989, p. 46). But the mathematical skills needed for daily life have changed dramatically in recent years. It is no longer enough to be proficient at the isolated arithmetic calculation that pervades current curriculum and instructional practice. Full participation in today's information-oriented society requires much more than the computational skill that has been the soul and substance of traditional elementary school mathematics. In addition to having all students appreciate what kind of knowledge they have when they know mathematics, we want to give students enough of a feeling for what the discipline is like to enable them to make informed choices about whether to pursue it in a more concentrated way. Because our education system is structured so that students may choose to virtually opt out of mathematics at the secondary level, these issues must be addressed in elementary curriculum and instruction.

Thinking about elementary classrooms as places where rich discourse about mathematics takes place, and where students can participate in the kind of mathematical activity similar to that engaged in by mathematically literate citizens, is clearly only a small step toward developing classroom environments that foster powerful forms of mathematical knowing and reasoning. As we take bigger steps toward developing such classrooms, we as an educational community of researchers, teachers, and scholars will need to think and talk about the issues, dilemmas, and problems that emerge from serious consideration of the diverse perspectives reviewed in this chapter. By discussing and describing what it means to know and understand mathematics from each of these perspectives, we attempted to make more visible the thinking going on within communities of scholars. By making this thinking more visible and accessible to others outside the community, we hoped to stimulate dialogue and reflection among scholars who represent different perspectives. Such dialogue will become more important and necessary if researchers, scholars, and educators are to respond thoughtfully and effectively to the calls for reform in the amount and quality of mathematics instruction in American classrooms.

NOTES

[1]Although this chapter was a highly collaborative effort, Putnam was primarily responsible for writing this section on the individual knower, and Lampert was primarily responsible for writing the section on the discipline of mathematics.

[2]This list is derived from documents such as the *Standards* (NCTM, 1989), *Everybody Counts* (National Research Council, 1989), California's *Mathematics Model Curriculum Guide* (California State Department of Education, 1987), national curriculum reform documents produced in Australia, and the British Cockcroft Report (Cockcroft, 1986).

[3]This problem comes from a book designed to help teachers at the upper ele-

mentary level teach problem solving. It is used here as an example of a "real" problem that someone might try to solve using mathematics, not as an example of a "school" problem. The difference between school problems and real problems is a complicated one to address. See, for example, Lave & Butler, 1987; Resnick, 1987b.

[4]"Without a logical way of thinking about negative numbers, without some conceptual model, [European] algebraists were unable to comprehend what it meant to add, subtract, multiply, and divide negative numbers. For that reason, negative numbers were not perceived as legitimate objects of algebraic study; their presence in certain algebraic equations was taken to have no greater significance than the existence of nonsense words in a language.

Not until the eighteenth century did algebraists learn how standard arithmetical operations applied to negative numbers" (Guillen, 1983, p. 63).

[5]An example of this sort of problem is the traveling salesperson problem in which the challenge is to find the shortest route among a given list of cities where each city is to be visited exactly once. For more than a few cities, the number of combinations is so large that each cannot be evaluated to find the best. Instead, mathematicians work on assessing how much better or worse one alternative is than another, which they can do by using computers to simulate different routes. Their results are of considerable interest to urban planners concerned about designing efficient public transportation and to those whose work it is to decide what would be the most efficient location for commercial airline hubs.

[6]Counting, or establishing number, is itself an act of mathematization in that it involves a disposition to attend to an abstract property of objects rather than to their particular differences. Eratosthenes' work was continuous with this way of thinking about the world, but constituted a more conscious attempt to use mathematical structures.

[7]The status of Euclidean geometry as a body of mathematical truth has changed since the invention of several non-Euclidean geometries in the 19th century. Before that development, the axioms and definitions were considered to be true abstractions from real world figures. In current thinking, they are considered as a set of agreed-upon assumptions that provide a starting point for deducing other theorems. This does not change the status of this body of knowledge as an example of an axiomatic system, however.

REFERENCES

Anastasi, A. (1976). *Psychological testing* (4th ed.). New York: Macmillan.

Anderson, R. (1984). Role of the reader's schema in comprehension, learning, and memory. In R. Anderson, J. Osborn, & R. Tierney (Eds.), *Learning to read in American schools: Basal readers and content texts* (pp. 243–257). Hillsdale, NJ: Erlbaum.

Anderson, R. C., Reynolds, R. E., Schallert, E. T., & Goetz, E. T. (1977). Frameworks for comprehending discourse. *American Educational Research Journal, 14,* 367–381.

Andrews, D. (1989, March–April). What to pay the doctor. *Harvard Magazine,* pp. 2–3.

Ashlock, R. B. (1982). *Error patterns in computation: A semi-programmed approach* (3rd ed.). Columbus, OH: Merrill.

Balacheff, N. (1987). Processes de preuve et situations de validation. *Educational Studies in Mathematics, 18,* 147–176.

Balacheff, N. (July, 1988). *The social meaning of proof.* Paper presented at the Sixth International Congress on Mathematics Education, Budapest.

Ball, D. (1988). *Knowledge and reasoning in mathematical pedagogy: Examining what prospective teachers bring to teacher education.* Unpublished doctoral dissertation, Michigan State University, East Lansing.

Behr, M. J., Lesh, R., Post, T. R., & Silver, E. A. (1983). Rational-number concepts. In R. Lesh & M. Landau (Eds.), *Acquisition of mathematics concepts and processes* (pp. 91–126). Orlando, FL: Academic Press.

Belenky, M. F., Clinchy, B. M., Goldberger, N. R., & Tarule, J. M. (1986). *Women's ways of knowing.* New York: Basic Books.

Bell, A. W. (1979). The learning of process aspects of mathematics. *Educational Studies in Mathematics, 10,* 361–387.

Berger, J. (1989, February 8). Will ruling on S.A.T. affect college admissions? *New York Times,* p. B10.

Berliner, D. C. (1979). Tempus educare. In P. L. Peterson & H. J. Walberg (Eds.), *Research on teaching: Concepts, findings, and implications* (pp. 120–135). Chicago: National Society for the Study of Education.

Bernstein, A. (1988, September). Where the jobs are is where the skills aren't. *Business Week,* pp. 104–108.

Bishop, A. J. (1988). *Mathematical enculturation: A cultural perspective on mathematics education.* Dordrecht, Holland: Kluwer.

Bloom, B., Englehart, M., Furst, E., Hill, W. S., & Krathwohl, D. (1956). *Taxonomy of educational objectives: The classification of educational goals, handbook 1: Cognitive domain.* New York: Longmans Green.

Braybrooke, D., & Lindblom, C. (1963). *A strategy of decision: Policy evaluation as a social process.* New York: Free Press.

Briars, D. J., & Larkin, J. H. (1984). An integrated model of skill in solving elementary word problems. *Cognition and Instruction, 1,* 245–296.

Brophy, J. E. (1988). Research on teacher effects: Uses and abuses. *Elementary School Journal, 89,* 1–21.

Brophy, J. E., & Good, T. L. (1986). Teacher behavior and student achievement. In M. C. Wittrock (Ed.), *Handbook of research on teaching* (3rd ed., pp. 328–375). New York: Macmillan.

Brown, J. S., & Burton, R. R. (1978). Diagnostic models for procedural bugs in basic mathematical skills. *Cognitive Science, 2,* 155–192.

Brown, J. S., Collins, A., & Duguid, P. (1989). Situated cognition and the culture of learning. *Educational Researcher, 18*(1), 32–42.

Brown, J. S., & VanLehn, K. (1980). Repair theory: A generative theory of bugs in procedural skills. *Cognitive Science, 2,* 379–426.

Buswell, G. T. (1926). *Diagnostic studies in arithmetic.* Chicago: University of Chicago Press.

Calfee, R. (1981). Cognitive psychology and educational practice. In D. C. Berliner (Ed.), *Review of research in education* (Vol. 9, pp. 3–73). Washington, DC: American Educational Research Association.

California State Department of Education. (1987). *Mathematics model curriculum guide.* Sacramento, CA: Author.

Carpenter, T. P., Fennema, E., Peterson, P. L. (1987). Cognitively guided instruction: The application of cognitive and instructional science to mathematics curriculum development. In I. Wirszup & R. Streit (Eds.), *Developments in school mathematics education around the world* (pp. 397–417). Proceedings of the University of Chicago School Mathematics Project International Conference on Mathematics Education. Reston, VA: National Council of Teachers of Mathematics.

Carpenter, T. P., Fennema, E., Peterson, P. L., Chiang, C., & Loef, M. (1988, April). *Using knowledge of children's mathematical thinking in classroom teaching: An experimental study.* Paper presented at the annual meeting of the American Educational Research Association, New Orleans.

Carpenter, T. P., Lindquist, M. M., Matthews, W., & Silver, E. A. (1983). Results of the third NAEP mathematics assessment: Secondary school. *Mathematics Teacher, 76,* 652–659.

Carpenter, T. P., & Moser, J. M. (1983). The acquisition of addition and subtraction concepts. In R. Lesh & M. Landau (Eds.), *Acquisition of mathematics concepts and processes* (pp. 7–44). Orlando, FL: Academic Press.

Carpenter, T. P., & Moser, J. M. (1984). The acquisition of addition and subtraction concepts in grades one through three. *Journal for Research in Mathematics Education, 15,* 179–202.

Carpenter, T. P., Moser, J. M., & Romberg, T. A. (Eds.). (1982). *Addition and subtraction: A cognitive perspective.* Hillsdale, NJ: Erlbaum.

Carraher, T. N., Carraher, D. W., & Schliemann, A.D. (1983). Mathematics in the streets and in schools. *British Journal of Developmental Psychology, 3,* 21–29.

Carroll, J. B. (1963). A model of school learning. *Teachers College Record, 64,* 723–733.

Chi, M. T. H., Feltovich, P. J., & Glaser, R. (1981). Categorization and representation of physics problems by experts and novices. *Cognitive Science, 5,* 121–152.

Chi, M. T. H., Glaser, R., & Rees, E. (1982). Expertise in problem solving. In R. Sternberg (Ed.), *Advances in the psychology of human intelligence* (pp. 7–75). Hillsdale, NJ: Erlbaum.

Chipman, S. F., Segal, J. W., & Glaser, R. (Eds.). (1985). *Thinking and learning skills: Vol. 2. Research and open questions.* Hillsdale, NJ: Erlbaum.

Clark, C. M., & Peterson, P. L. (1986). Teachers' thought processes. In M. C. Wittrock (Ed.), *Handbook of research on teaching* (3rd ed., pp. 255–296). New York: Macmillan.

Cobb, P. (1986). Making mathematics: Children's learning and the constructivist tradition [Review of *Young children reinvent arithmetic* and *Learning from children*]. *Harvard Educational Review, 56,* 301–306.

Cobb, P. (1988a, April). *Multiple perspectives.* Paper presented at the annual meeting of the American Educational Research Association, New Orleans.

Cobb, P. (1988b). The tension between theories of learning and instruction in mathematics education. *Educational Psychologist, 23,* 87–103.

Cobb, P., Wood, T., & Yackel, E. (in press). A constructivist approach to second grade mathematics. In E. von Glasersfeld (Ed.), *Constructivism in mathematics education.* Dordrecht, Holland: Reidel.

Cobb, P., Yackel, E., & Wood, T. (1988). Curriculum and teacher development: Psychological and anthropological perspectives. In E. Fennema, T. P. Carpenter, & S. J. Lamon (Eds.), *Integrating research on teaching and learning mathematics: Papers from the First Wisconsin Symposium for Research on Teaching and Learning Mathematics* (pp. 92–130). Madison: University of Wisconsin, Wisconsin Center for Education Research.

Cockcroft, W. H. (1986). *Mathematics counts.* London: Her Majesty's Stationery Office.

Cole, K. C. (1987, October 18). A theory of everything. *New York Times Magazine,* pp. 20–28.

Collins, A., Brown, J. S., & Newman, S. E. (1989). Cognitive apprenticeship: Teaching the craft of reading, writing and mathematics. In L. B. Resnick (Ed.), *Knowing, learning, and instruction: Essays in honor of Robert Glaser* (pp. 453–494). Hillsdale, NJ: Erlbaum.

Cronbach, L. J. (1970). *Essentials of psychological testing* (3rd ed.). New York: Harper & Row.

Davis, P. (1972). Fidelity in mathematical discourse: Is one and one really two? *American Mathematical Monthly, 79,* 252–263.

Davis, P. J. (1988). Applied mathematics as social contract. *Mathematics Magazine, 61,* 139–147.

Davis, P. J., & Hersh, R. (1987). *Descartes' dream: The world according to mathematics.* New York: Harcourt, Brace Jovanovich.

Davis, R. B. (1984). *Learning mathematics: The cognitive science approach to mathematics education.* Norwood, NJ: Ablex.

Davis, R. B. (1986). Conceptual and procedural knowledge in mathematics: A summary analysis. In J. Hiebert (Ed.), *Conceptual and procedural knowledge: The case of mathematics* (pp. 265–300). Hillsdale, NJ: Erlbaum.

Devlin, K. (1988). *Mathematics: The new golden age.* New York: Penguin.

Dreyfus, H. L., & Dreyfus, S. E. (1986). *Mind over machine.* New York: Free Press.

Dunkin, M. J., & Biddle, B. J. (1974). *The study of teaching.* New York: Holt, Rinehart & Winston.

Erdos, P. (1988, July). *Easily understood problems that are very difficult to solve.* Plenary address to the Sixth International Congress on Mathematics Education, Budapest.

Fey, J. T. (1982). Mathematics education. In H. Mitzel (Ed.), *Encyclopaedia of educational research* (Vol. 3, 5th ed., pp. 1166–1182). New York: Free Press.

Freudenthal, H. (1978). *Weeding and sowing: Preface to a science of mathematical education.* Dordrecht, Holland: Reidel.

Fuson, K. (1982). An analysis of the counting-on procedure in addition. In T. P. Carpenter, J. M. Moser, & T. A. Romberg (Eds.), *Addition and subtraction: A cognitive perspective* (pp. 67–81). Hillsdale, NJ: Erlbaum.

Fuson, K. (1988). *Children's counting and concepts of number.* New York: Springer-Verlag.

Gage, N. L. (1972). *Teacher effectiveness and teacher education.* Palo Alto, CA: Pacific Books.

Gage, N. L. (1978). *The scientific basis of the art of teaching.* New York: Teachers College Press.

Gagné, R. M., Briggs, L. J., & Wagner, W. W. (1988). *Principles of instructional design* (3rd ed.). New York: Holt, Rinehart & Winston.

Gelman, R., & Gallistel, C. R. (1978). *The child's understanding of number.* Cambridge, MA: Harvard University Press.

Gelman, R., & Meck, E. (1983). Preschoolers' counting: Principle before skill. *Cognition, 13,* 343–359.

Gelman, R., & Meck, E. (1986). The notion of principle: The case of counting. In J. Hiebert (Ed.), *Conceptual and procedural knowledge: The case of mathematics* (pp. 29–57). Hillsdale, NJ: Erlbaum.

Ginsburg, H. P. (1977). *Children's arithmetic: The learning process.* New York: Van Nostrand.

Glaser, R. (1984). Education and thinking: The role of knowledge. *American Psychologist, 39,* 93–104.

Gleick, J. (1987). *Chaos: Making a new science.* New York: Viking Penguin.

Good, T. L. (1988). Observational research . . . grounding theory in classrooms. *Educational Psychologist, 23,* 375–379.

Good, T. L., & Grouws, D. A. (1979). The Missouri mathematics effectiveness project: An experimental study in fourth-grade classrooms. *Journal of Educational Psychology, 71,* 355–362.

Good, T. L., Grouws, D. A., & Ebmeier, H. (1983). *Active mathematics teaching.* New York: Longman.

Grabiner, J. V. (1988). The centrality of mathematics in the history of western thought. *Mathematics Magazine, 61,* 220–230.

Greeno, J. G. (1980). Some examples of cognitive task analysis with instructional applications. In R. E. Snow, P. A. Federico, & W. E. Montague (Eds.), *Aptitude, learning, and instruction: Vol. 2. Cognitive process analysis of learning and problem solving* (pp. 1–21). Hillsdale, NJ: Erlbaum.

Greeno, J. G. (1987a). Instructional representations based on research about understanding. In A. H. Schoenfeld (Ed.), *Cognitive science and mathematics education* (pp. 61–88). Hillsdale, NJ: Erlbaum.

Greeno, J. G. (1987b). Mathematical cognition: Accomplishments and challenges in research. In T. A. Romberg & D. M. Stewart (Eds.), *The monitoring of school mathematics: Background papers* (pp. 3–26). Madison: University of Wisconsin, Wisconsin Center for Education Research.

Greeno, J. G. (1989). A perspective on thinking. *American Psychologist, 44,* 134–141.

Greeno, J. G., Riley, M. S., & Gelman, R. (1984). Conceptual competence and children's counting. *Cognitive Psychology, 16,* 94–134.

Groen, G. J., & Resnick, L. B. (1977). Can preschool children invent addition algorithms? *Journal of Educational Psychology, 69,* 645–652.

Guillen, M. (1983). *Bridges to infinity: The human side of mathematics.* Boston: Houghton Mifflin.

Hadamard, J. (1945). *The psychology of invention in the mathematical field.* New York: Dover.

Hardy, G. H. (1967). *A mathematician's apology.* Cambridge, England: Cambridge University Press.

Hiebert, J. (Ed.). (1986). *Conceptual and procedural knowledge: The case of mathematics.* Hillsdale, NJ: Erlbaum.

Hiebert, J., & Carpenter, T. P. (in press). Learning with understanding. In D. A. Grouws (Ed.), *Handbook of research on mathematics education.* New York: Macmillan.

Hiebert, J., & Lefevre, P. (1986). Conceptual and procedural knowledge in mathematics: An introductory analysis. In J. Hiebert (Ed.), *Conceptual and procedural knowledge: The case of mathematics* (pp. 1–27). Hillsdale, NJ: Erlbaum.

Hoffman, P. (1987, November). The man who loves only numbers. *Atlantic Monthly,* pp. 60–75.

Hofstadter, D. R. (1986). *Metamagical themas: Questing for the essence of mind and pattern.* New York: Bantam House.

Janvier, C. (Ed.). (1987). *Problems of representation in the teaching and learning of mathematics.* Hillsdale, NJ: Erlbaum.

Judson, H. F. (1987). *The search for solutions.* Baltimore, MD: Johns Hopkins University Press.

Kaput, J. J. (1985). Representation and problem solving: Methodological issues related to modeling. In E. A. Silver (Ed.), *Teaching and learning mathematical problem solving: Multiple research perspectives* (pp. 381–398). Hillsdale, NJ: Erlbaum.

Kaput, J. J. (1987a). Representation systems and mathematics. In C. Janvier (Ed.), *Problems of representation in the teaching and learning of mathematics* (pp. 19–26). Hillsdale, NJ: Erlbaum.

Kaput, J. J. (1987b). Towards a theory of symbol use in mathematics. In C. Janvier (Ed.), *Problems of representation in the teaching and learning of mathematics* (pp. 159–195). Hillsdale, NJ: Erlbaum.

Kaput, J. J. (1988, November). *Truth and meaning in representation situations: Comments on the Greeno contribution.* Remarks made at the annual meeting of the North American Chapter of the International Group for the Psychology of Mathematics Education, De Kalb, IL.

Kilpatrick, J. (1987). What constructivism might be in mathematics education. In J. C. Bergeron, N. Herscovics, & C. Kieran (Eds.), *Proceedings of the 11th International Conference for the Psychology of Mathematics Education* (Vol. 1, pp. 3–27). Montreal: International Group for the Psychology of Mathematics Education.

Kintsch, W., & Greeno, J. G. (1985). Understanding and solving word arithmetic problems. *Psychological Review, 92,* 109–129.

Kline, M. (1980). *Mathematics: The loss of certainty.* New York: Oxford University Press.

Kline, M. (1985). *Mathematics and the search for knowledge.* New York: Oxford University Press.

Kramer, E. E. (1970). *The nature and growth of modern mathematics.* Princeton, NJ: Princeton University Press.

Lakatos, I. (1976). *Proofs and refutations: The logic of mathematical discovery.* New York: University of Cambridge Press.

Lampert, M. (1988a). Connecting mathematical teaching and learning. In E. Fennema, T. P. Carpenter, & S. J. Lamon (Eds.), *Integrating research on teaching and learning mathematics: Papers from the First Wisconsin Symposium for Research on Teaching and Learning Mathematics* (pp. 132–165). Madison: University of Wisconsin, Wisconsin Center for Education Research.

Lampert, M. (1988b, April). *School/university collaboration in developing mathematical pedagogy.* Paper presented at the annual meeting of the American Educational Research Association, New Orleans.

Larkin, J. H., McDermott, H., Simon, D. P., & Simon, H. A. (1980). Expert and novice performance in solving physics problems. *Science, 208,* 1335–1342.

Lave, J. (1988). *Cognition in practice: Mind, mathematics and culture in everyday life.* New York: Cambridge University Press.

Lave, J., & Butler, M. (1987, April). *The trouble with math: A view from everyday practice.* Paper presented at the annual meeting of the American Educational Research Association, Washington, DC.

Lave, J., Murtaugh, M., & de La Rocha, O. (1984). The dialectical construction of arithmetic in grocery shopping. In B. Rogoff & J. Lave (Eds.), *Everyday cognition: Its development in social context* (pp. 67–94). Cambridge, MA: Harvard University Press.

Leinhardt, G. (1988). Expertise in instructional lessons: An example from fractions. In D. A. Grouws, T. G. Cooney, & D. Jones (Eds.), *Perspectives on research on effective mathematics teaching* (Vol. 1, pp. 47–66). Reston, VA: National Council of Teachers of Mathematics.

Lesh, R., Post, T., & Behr, M. (1987). Representations and translations among representations in mathematics learning and problem solving. In C. Janvier (Ed.), *Problems of representation in the teaching and learning of mathematics* (pp. 33–58). Hillsdale, NJ: Erlbaum.

Lindblom, C. E., & Cohen, D. K. (1979). *Usable knowledge: Social science and social problem solving.* New Haven: Yale University Press.

Loyd, S. (1959). *Mathematical puzzles* (Vol. 1). New York: Dover.

Maher, C. A. (1988). The teacher as designer, implementer, and evaluator of children's mathematical learning environments. *Journal of Mathematical Behavior, 6,* 295–303.

Mandler, J. M. (1984). *Stories, scripts, and scenes: Aspects of schema theory.* Hillsdale, NJ: Erlbaum.

Matz, M. (1982). Towards a process model for high school algebra. In D. Sleeman & J. S. Brown (Eds.), *Intelligent tutoring systems.* New York: Academic Press.

Mayer, R. E. (1982). Memory for algebra story problems. *Journal of Educational Psychology, 74,* 199–216.

McKnight, C. C., Crosswhite, F. J., Dossey, J. A., Kifer, E., Swafford, J. O., Travers, K. J., & Cooney, T. J. (1987). *The underachieving curriculum: Assessing U.S. school mathematics from an international perspective.* Champaign, IL: Stipes.

Meyer, C., & Sallee, T. (1983). *Make it simpler: A practical guide to problem solving in mathematics.* Menlo Park, CA: Addison-Wesley.

Morrison, P., & Morrison, P. (1987). *The ring of truth: An inquiry into how we know what we know.* New York: Random House.

National Commission on Excellence in Education. (1983). *A nation at risk: The imperative for educational reform.* Washington, DC: U.S. Government Printing Office.

National Council of Supervisors of Mathematics. (1977). Position paper on basic skills. *Arithmetic Teacher, 25,* 19–22.

National Council of Teachers of Mathematics. (1980). *An agenda for action: Recommendations for school mathematics of the 1980s.* Reston, VA: Author.

National Council of Teachers of Mathematics. (1989). *Curriculum and evaluation standards for school mathematics.* Reston, VA: Author.

National Research Council. (1989). *Everybody counts: A report to the nation on the future of mathematics education.* Washington, DC: National Academy Press.

National Science Board Commission on Pre-College Education in Mathematics Science and Technology. (1983). *Educating Americans for the 21st century.* Washington, DC: National Science Foundation.

Nesher, P. (1982). Levels of description in the analysis of addition and subtraction word problems. In T. P. Carpenter, J. M. Moser, & T. A. Romberg (Eds.), *Addition and subtraction: A cognitive perspective* (pp. 25–38). Hillsdale, NJ: Erlbaum.

Nesher, P. (1986). Are mathematical understanding and algorithmic performance related? *For the Learning of Mathematics, 6*(3), 2–9.

Nesher, P. (1989). Microworlds in mathematics education: A pedagogical realism. In L. B. Resnick (Ed.), *Knowing, learning, and instruction: Essays in honor of Robert Glaser* (pp. 187–215). Hillsdale, NJ: Erlbaum.

Newell, A., & Simon, H. A. (1972). *Human problem solving.* Englewood Cliffs, NJ: Prentice-Hall.

Nickerson, R. S., Perkins, D. N., & Smith, E. E. (1985). *The teaching of thinking.* Hillsdale, NJ: Erlbaum.

Noddings, N. (1985). Formal modes of knowing. In E. Eisner (Ed.), *Learning and teaching and the ways of knowing* (84th yearbook of the National Society for the Study of Education, pp. 116–132). Chicago: University of Chicago Press.

Norman, D. A. (1980). What goes on in the mind of the learner. In W. J. McKeachie (Ed.), *Learning, cognition, and college teaching. New directions for teaching and learning* (pp. 37–49). San Francisco: Jossey-Bass.

Palmer, S. E. (1977). Fundamental aspects of cognitive representation. In E. Rosch & B. B. Lloyd (Eds.), *Cognition and categorization.* Hillsdale, NJ: Erlbaum.

Pea, R. (1988). Putting knowledge to use. In R. S. Nickerson & P. P. Zodhiates (Eds.), *Technology in education: Looking toward 2020* (pp. 169–212). Hillsdale, NJ: Erlbaum.

Pea, R. D. (1987). Cognitive technologies for mathematics education. In A. H. Schoenfeld (Ed.), *Cognitive science and mathematics education* (pp. 89–122). Hillsdale, NJ: Erlbaum.

Perkins, D. N. (1986). *Knowledge as design.* Hillsdale, NJ: Erlbaum.

Perkins, D. N., & Salomon, G. (1989). Are cognitive skills context-bound? *Educational Researcher, 18*(1), 16–25.

Peterson, P. L. (1988). Teaching for higher-order thinking in mathematics: The challenge for the next decade. In D. A. Grouws & T. J. Cooney (Eds.), *Effective mathematics teaching* (pp. 2–26). Reston, VA: Erlbaum.

Piaget, J. (1980). *Les formes élémentaires de la dialectique.* Paris: Gallimard.

Piaget, J. (1983). Piaget's theory. In P. Mussen (Ed.), *Handbook of child psychology* (4th ed., Vol. 1, pp. 103–128). New York: Wiley.

Piaget, J., & Garcia, R. (1983). *Psychogenèse et histoire des sciences.* Paris: Flammarion.

Pólya, G. (1954). *Mathematics and plausible reasoning: Vol. 1. Induction and analogy in mathematics.* Princeton, NJ: Princeton University Press.

Pólya, G. (1957). *How to solve it* (2nd ed.). Princeton, NJ: Princeton University Press.

Pólya, G. (1977). *Mathematical methods in science.* Washington, DC: Mathematical Association of America. (Original work published 1963)

Porter, A. C., Schmidt, W. H., Floden, R. E., & Freeman, D. J. (1986). *Content determinants* (Research Series No. 179). East Lansing: Michigan State University, Institute for Research on Teaching.

Resnick, L. B. (1982). Syntax and semantics in learning to subtract. In T. P. Carpenter, J. M. Moser, & T. A. Romberg (Eds.), *Addition and subtraction: A cognitive perspective* (pp. 136–155). Hillsdale, NJ: Erlbaum.

Resnick, L. B. (1986). The development of mathematical intuition. In M. Perlmutter (Ed.), *Perspectives on intellectual development: The Minnesota Symposium on Child Development* (Vol. 19, pp. 159–194). Hillsdale, NJ: Erlbaum.

Resnick, L. B. (1987a). *Education and learning to think.* Washington, DC: National Academy Press.

Resnick, L. B. (1987b). Learning in school and out. *Educational Researcher, 16*(9), 13–20.

Resnick, L. B. (1989). *Developing thinking abilities in arithmetic class.* Unpublished manuscript, University of Pittsburgh, Learning Research and Development Center, Pittsburgh, PA.

Resnick, L. B., Nesher, P., Leonard, F., Magone, M., Omanson, S., & Peled, I. (1989). Conceptual bases of arithmetic errors: The case of decimal fractions. *Journal for Research in Mathematics Education, 20,* 8–27.

Resnick, L. B., & Resnick, D. P. (1977). The nature of literacy: An historical exploration. *Harvard Educational Review, 47,* 370–385.

Resnick, R. L. (1983). Toward a cognitive theory of instruction. In S. Paris, G. Olson, & H. Stevenson (Eds.), *Learning and motivation in the classroom* (pp. 5–38). Hillsdale, NJ: Erlbaum.

Resnick, R. L. (1985). Cognition and instruction: Recent theories of human competence. In B. L. Hammonds (Ed.), *Master lecture series: Vol. 4. Psychology and learning* (pp. 123–186). Washington, DC: American Psychological Association.

Riley, M. S., Greeno, J. G., & Heller, J. I. (1983). Development of children's problem-solving ability in arithmetic. In H. P. Ginsburg (Ed.), *The development of mathematical thinking* (pp. 153–196). New York: Academic Press.

Romberg, T. A. (1983). A common curriculum for mathematics. In G. D. Fenstermacher & J. I. Goodland (Eds.), *Individual differences and the common curriculum* (pp. 121–159). Chicago: National Society for the Study of Education.

Romberg, T. A. (1984). *School mathematics: Options for the 1990's. Chairman's report of a conference.* Washington, DC: U.S. Government Printing Office.

Romberg, T. A., & Carpenter, T. P. (1986). Research on teaching and learning mathematics: Two disciplines of scientific inquiry. In M. C. Wittrock (Ed.), *Handbook of research on teaching* (3rd ed., pp. 850–873). New York: Macmillan.

Rosenshine, B. V. (1979). Content, time, and direct instruction. In P. L. Peterson & H. J. Walberg (Eds.), *Research on teaching: Concepts, findings, and implications* (pp. 28–56). Chicago: National Society for the Study of Education.

Rosenshine, B., & Stevens, R. (1986). Teaching functions. In M. C. Wittrock (Ed.), *Handbook of research on teaching* (3rd ed., pp. 376–391). New York: Macmillan.

Schoenfeld, A. H. (1985). *Mathematical problem solving.* Orlando, FL: Academic Press.

Schoenfeld, A. H. (1986). On having and using geometric knowledge. In J. Hiebert (Ed.), *Conceptual and procedural knowledge: The case of mathematics* (pp. 225–264). Hillsdale, NJ: Erlbaum.

Schoenfeld, A. H. (1987). Cognitive science and mathematics education: An overview. In A. H. Schoenfeld (Ed.), *Cognitive science and mathematics education* (pp. 1–31). Hillsdale, NJ: Erlbaum.

Scribner, S. (1984). Studying working intelligence. In B. Rogoff & J. Lave (Eds.), *Everyday cognition* (pp. 9–40). Cambridge, MA: Harvard University Press.

Segal, J. W., Chipman, S. F., & Glaser, R. (Eds.). (1985). *Thinking and learning skills: Vol. 1. Relating instruction to research.* Hillsdale, NJ: Erlbaum.

Shuell, T. J. (1986). Cognitive conceptions of learning. *Review of Educational Research, 56,* 411–436.

Shulman, L. S. (1986). Paradigms and research programs in the study of teaching: A contemporary perspective. In M. C. Wittrock (Ed.), *Handbook of research on teaching* (3rd ed., pp. 3–36). New York: Macmillan.

Silver, E. A. (1979). Student perceptions of relatedness among mathematical verbal problems. *Journal for Research in Mathematics Education, 10,* 195–210.

Simon, H. (1978). Information-processing theory of human problem solving. In W. K. Estes (Ed.), *Handbook of learning and cognitive processes* (Vol. 5, pp. 271–295). Hillsdale, NJ: Erlbaum.

Sinclair, H. (1988, July). *Learning: The interactive re-creation of knowledge.* Paper presented at the Sixth International Congress on Mathematics Education, Budapest.

Skinner, B. F. (1986). Programmed instruction revisited. *Phi Delta Kappan, 68,* 103–110.

Sleeman, D. (1982). Assessing aspects of competence in basic algebra. In D. Sleeman & J. S. Brown (Eds.), *Intelligent tutoring systems* (pp. 185–199). London: Academic Press.

Steffe, L. P. (1988). *The constructivist teaching experiment: Illustrations and implications.* Unpublished manuscript.

Steffe, L. P., & Cobb, P. (1988). *Construction of mathematical meanings and strategies.* New York: Springer-Verlag.

Steffe, L., von Glasersfeld, E., Richards, J., & Cobb, P. (1983). *Children's counting types: Philosophy, theory, and application.* New York: Praeger.

Steiner, H. G. (1988). Two kinds of "elements" and the dialectic between synthetico-deductive and analytic-genetic approaches in mathematics. *For the Learning of Mathematics, 8*(3), 7–15.

Stewart, I. (1987). *The problems of mathematics.* New York: Oxford University Press.

Stigler, J. W., & Baranes, R. (1988). Culture and mathematics learning. *Review of Research in Education, 15,* 253–306.

Swing, S. R., Stoiber, K. C., & Peterson, P. L. (1988). Thinking skills versus learning time: Effects of alternative classroom-based interventions on students' mathematics problem solving. *Cognition and Instruction, 5,* 123–191.

Thorndike, E. L. (1922). *The psychology of arithmetic.* New York: Macmillan.

Trafton, P. R. (1980). Assessing the mathematics curriculum today. In M. M. Lindquist (Ed.), *Selected issues in mathematics education* (pp. 9–26). Berkeley, CA: McCutchan.

Tufte, E. R. (1970). *The quantitative analysis of social problems.* Reading, MA: Addison-Wesley.

Tyler, R. (1949). *Basic principles of curriculum and instruction.* Chicago: University of Chicago Press.

Tymoczko, T. (Ed.). (1985). *New directions in the philosophy of mathematics.* Boston: Birkhauser.

van der Waerden, B. L. (1985). *A history of algebra: From al-Khwarizmi to Emmy Noether.* Berlin: Springer-Verlag.

VanLehn, K. (1983). On the representation of procedures in repair theory. In H. P. Ginsburg (Ed.), *The development of mathematical thinking* (pp. 39–59). Hillsdale, NJ: Erlbaum.

Vergnaud, G. (1982). A classification of cognitive tasks and operations of thought involved in addition and subtraction problems. In T. P. Carpenter, J. M. Moser, & T. A. Romberg (Ed.), *Addition and subtraction: A cognitive perspective* (pp. 39–59). Hillsdale, NJ: Erlbaum.

Vergnaud, G. (1983). Multiplicative structures. In R. Lesh & M. Landau (Eds.), *Acquisition of mathematics concepts and processes* (pp. 127–174). Orlando, FL: Academic Press.

von Glasersfeld, E. (1987). Learning as a constructive activity. In C. Janvier (Ed.), *Problems of representation in the teaching and learning of mathematics* (pp. 3–17). Hillsdale, NJ: Erlbaum.

von Glasersfeld, E. (1988, July). *Environment and communication.* Paper presented at the Sixth International Congress on Mathematics Education, Budapest.

von Glasersfeld, E. (1989). Constructivism in education. In T. Husen & T. N. Postlethwaite (Eds.), *International encyclopedia of education: Supplementary Vol. 1. Research and studies* (pp. 162–163). Oxford, England: Pergamon.

Weizenbaum, J. (1976). *Computer power and human reason.* San Francisco: Freeman.

Wilson, S. M. (1988). *Understanding historical understanding: Subject matter knowledge and the teaching of history.* Unpublished doctoral dissertation, Stanford University.

Wooten, W. (1965). *SMSG: The making of a curriculum.* New Haven, CT: Yale University Press.

II.
STUDENTS AND TEACHERS
IN SCIENCE AND
MATHEMATICS EDUCATION

Chapter 3

Opportunities, Achievement, and Choice: Women and Minority Students in Science and Mathematics

JEANNIE OAKES
University of California, Los Angeles
and
The RAND Corporation

As the nation's economic base shifts increasingly toward technology, U.S. students' lack of achievement and participation in science and mathematics generates growing concern. Demographic projections show the traditional pool that supplies scientific workers is shrinking. Future workers will include growing proportions of women and minorities—groups that traditionally have not entered scientific and technological fields. These projections trigger several policy questions: How can we have enough highly trained mathematicians, scientists, and engineers in the future? How can we teach the general labor force the knowledge and skills needed for technological work? How can we attain a level of scientific literacy necessary for responsible, democratic decision making about scientific and technological matters? There are no clear-cut answers for these questions. However, many observers suggest that without substantial increases in the achievement and participation of women and minorities, the nation will not meet its scientific and technological needs.

Aligned with these human capital issues is the longstanding policy objective of a fair distribution of economic and social opportunities. As technology grows increasingly important to individual and national prosperity, women's and minorities' attainment in science and mathematics

This paper is an abridged version of *Lost Talent: The Underparticipation of Women, Minorities, and Disabled Persons in Science* (Santa Monica, CA: The RAND Corporation, 1989), work supported by the National Science Foundation (contract #87-GA-0092) and by the RAND Corporation. The author wishes to thank Lisa Oakes of the University of Texas and Martin Lipton for their assistance in the preparation of this paper, and Linda Waite of the RAND Corporation and Shirley Malcom of the American Association for the Advancement of Science, who provided helpful reviews.

will influence their ability to compete for employment, wages, and leadership positions.

Policymakers are paying more attention to the quality of mathematics and science education—as it both contributes to the underparticipation problem and as it potentially solves it. However, pinpointing the causes of underrepresentation and remedying them have proven difficult. Recent research has helped us better understand the educational "pipeline" through which all scientific personnel flow, and it has described the participation and achievement of women and minorities at critical junctures in that pipeline. Other studies have examined how women and minorities differ from white males in ways thought to be linked with attainment in scientific fields. This work suggests that three factors are critical to attainment: (a) opportunities to learn science and mathematics; (b) achievement in these subjects; and (c) the decision to pursue them. We have also learned that minorities and women lose ground on all three factors during their education. However, different groups lose ground in science and mathematics in different ways and at different points in time.

Despite these insights, our knowledge of the causes of low achievement and participation and our understanding of what policies and programs will improve them remains limited. Although interventions to increase participation among women and minorities have not been studied systematically, we have some promising clues. For example, girls and minorities typically receive less encouragement and have fewer science- and math-related opportunities both in school and out than do white males, but when they do receive encouragement and are exposed to opportunities, they respond in much the same way as white males—with interest and participation. Consequently, we may be able to increase participation with school conditions and special interventions that encourage and provide opportunities. Still, we need considerable research to determine what programs will be most successful.

This chapter summarizes what we know. The first section examines the current status and recent trends in the participation of women, blacks, and Hispanics in scientific fields. It also describes the schooling process by which students become scientists, and presents data about race and gender differences in participation in this pipeline. The next three sections describe potential influences on the learning opportunities, achievement, and choices of women and minorities that affect their pipeline participation. These include individual attributes (cognitive abilities and attitudes), schooling features, and societal factors. The paper concludes with suggestions for future policy-relevant research.

The reader will note several limitations of this review. First, some of the topics have generated a rather substantial literature, whereas others have received considerably less attention. Rather than provide a comprehensive review, I summarize major findings using selected studies as illustrative. The intent is to synthesize what is known from the best available studies, point to uncertainties, and suggest those areas about which we have little understanding. Second, the broad scope of this review (and limitations in the research) prevents detailed accounting of the experiences of different minority groups separately or consideration of gender groups separately within racial and ethnic groups. Instead, I present the experiences of blacks and Hispanics as representative of the problems underrepresented minorities face. Third, because Asians are overrepresented in science, their experiences are not considered here (although gender differences exist among Asians as well). Last, the recent growth in the number of foreign-born students in college and graduate-level science and mathematics programs is not considered.

THE PARTICIPATION OF WOMEN AND MINORITIES: CURRENT STATUS AND TRENDS

Women and non-Asian minorities are underrepresented in the science, mathematics, and technology work force. Although women's share of the professional work force had risen to 49%, in 1986 they still constituted only 15% of the employed scientists, mathematicians, and engineers. In the same year, blacks (who constitute 10% of all employed workers and 7% of professional workers) and Hispanics (5% of all employed workers and 3% of professionals) each represented about 2% of the scientific work force. The physically disabled represented approximately 2% of scientists and engineers (National Science Foundation [NSF], 1988).

During the past two decades, however, women and blacks have made progress in narrowing participation gaps. Women's current 15% share of the scientific work force grew from 9% in 1976. Blacks increased their participation in science careers by 140% between 1976 and 1984, compared with a 70% growth rate for whites (albeit the black growth rate stems from a much smaller base). Hispanic increases did not exceed those for scientists in general during this period (NSF, 1986).

Despite these gains, women and minority scientists are more often underutilized in the work force than are their white, male counterparts. Among scientifically trained women and minorities in 1986, 25% of the women, compared with 14% of the men, were employed in work unrelated to science (NSF, 1988). Although some gender disparities result from many women's late entry into the work force, gender disparities in employment are found even among recent science graduates (NSF, 1988). Among academic scientists, men are far more likely than women to hold tenure track positions, to be promoted to tenure, and to achieve full professorships. This is true even when analysts control for factors such as field of specialization, quality of graduate school attended, and years of experience beyond their doctoral degrees. Racial disparities exist also; black and Hispanic male scientists had lower rates of related employment than their white male counterparts. (National Science Board, 1987).

Salary differences exist across groups as well. Female scientists and engineers, on the average, earn less than their male counterparts. Although women scientists in general are younger than men and have fewer years of experience, women with equivalent experience also tend to earn less. Black and Hispanic scientists and engineers earn less, on average, than do whites and Asians (NSF, 1988).

Women, blacks, and Hispanics are also underrepresented among those preparing for careers in science. Although women have increased their rate of scientific preparation substantially since 1970 (NSF, 1988), much of this increase can be explained by the growing number of women obtaining college degrees in general (Berryman, 1983). Little change in degree attainment has occurred among blacks and Hispanics at any level. In 1985, blacks earned 5% of the scientific bachelor's degrees and 2% of the doctorates. Hispanics earned 3% of the bachelor's degrees, 3% of the master's degrees, and 2% of the doctorates. These percentages show little change since 1979.

Although both women and non-Asian minorities remain significantly underrepresented in scientific fields of study and work, the data suggest that women have progressed in gaining scientific preparation over the past two decades. However, two factors dampen optimism that their underrepresentation will simply take care of itself over time. First, some gains in women's participation must be attributed to their increased participation in higher education in general. Consequently, with women's overall degree attainment reaching 50%, future increases will depend more on women's switching from other fields (Berryman, 1983). Also, women continue to be at a disadvantage in obtaining comparable scientific employment and salaries. As will be discussed later, these disadvantages may discourage women from choosing scientific fields.

In contrast to positive trends for women, blacks and Hispanics have made little progress. Their lower and constant rates of participation are limited by their lower rates of degree attainment (and, as will be discussed at length in later sections, by their precollege experiences) and by lower rates of choosing scientific majors among those who do attain college degrees. Moreover, minority participation in the work force may also be constrained by factors in the job market—higher rates of unemployment, underemployment, and lower salaries among minority scientists than among whites.

All these data suggest that although women's underrepresentation is likely to continue in the near future, the gender gap in science may continue to narrow. However, little suggests a significant increase in black and Hispanic participation in the future.

The Scientific Pipeline

To understand the low participation rates of women and non-Asian minorities in scientific careers, we must first understand the educational experiences of all future scientists. We also must understand how women and minorities fare in this scientific pipeline. Fortunately, recent analyses have identified a critical sequence of precollege and college events that is prerequisite for participation in science. Other work describes how women and minorities differ from males and whites in their participation at critical points along this pipeline.

Berryman's (1983) landmark study, *Who Will Do Science?*, raised important questions about the educational pipeline and the formation of the scientific "talent pool" from which scientific professionals are drawn: When does a pool of students with scientific interests first appear in the educational pipeline? When does the pool reach its maximum size? What are the rates of migration into and out of the pool as it moves through the pipeline? What are the relationships between scientific field interests and mathematical talents at different points in the pipeline? Berryman concluded that the scientific/mathematical pool first appears in elementary school and reaches its maximum size before ninth grade. During high school more students enter the pool, but even more students leave it. Following high school the flow is almost entirely outward. Consequently, the critical period for encouraging students to enter the scientific pipeline is before high school; but, because students defect from science throughout their schooling, keeping students in the pipeline requires attention at all levels. Berryman also concluded that both talent and interests are relevant to persistence in the pipeline, but in different ways for different groups (Berryman, 1983). This analysis provides a useful framework for pulling together an array of studies to describe what leads various groups to or away from science careers.

Several studies enable us to describe critical junctures along the educational pipeline more specifically. This work supports Berryman's conclusion that both talent (i.e., achievement) and interests (i.e., choices) are crucial to students remaining in the pool of potential scientists. Also, opportunity emerges as central to persistence. Opportunity refers to the access students have to science and mathematics experiences both in and out of schools. *Opportunity, achievement,* and *choice* appear to be highly interrelated, although (as will be discussed later) we don't fully understand possible causal links among them.

Following is a description of the educational pipeline. Note that schooling experiences that lead to adult participation in science also promote scientific literacy among students who do not pursue science careers.

Elementary school. Students' early achievement in mathematics appears to relate to their interest in science and math and to the science-related experiences they have in and out of school (Armstrong, 1980). In many schools, those students with the highest achievement have enhanced opportunities to learn science and math, because they are likely to be selected for special enrichment programs or accelerated study for gifted and talented students.

Transition to secondary school. Achievement and interest in mathematics and science in elementary school may influence the opportunities children have to learn these subjects in middle schools and junior high schools. Students with high interest and high test scores often take classes that prepare them for high school mathematics courses. For example, many junior highs offer pre-algebra and algebra, and a few offer geometry for high-achieving students. In contrast, students exhibiting a lack of interest or low test scores are often assigned to remedial, review, or practical-oriented classes where they may have little exposure to topics and higher order thinking skills that will prepare them for advanced courses (e.g., algebra) in senior high school (McKnight, 1987; Oakes, 1985). These students are unlikely to become part of the scientific talent pool.

Senior high curriculum enrollment. Students' achievement and curricular choices on entering high school influence their subsequent opportunities, because these are the primary determinants of enrollment in mathematics and science courses (Alexander & Cook, 1982). Typically, high-achieving students who plan to attend college enroll in academic curricula that require them to take more courses in mathematics and science than other students and to take courses that cover advanced concepts and processes. Although requirements vary, most 4-year colleges expect students to complete courses in mathematics and science beyond the minimum necessary for high school graduation.

Lower achieving students usually enroll in vocational or general curricula that require fewer mathematics and science courses (Guthrie & Leventhal, 1985). In contrast to college-preparatory classes, nonacademic math and science courses are often nonsequential and emphasize low-level topics and skills (Oakes, 1985). Both the number and level of courses required are likely to influence achievement and future opportunities, because course taking is predictive of students' end-of-high-school scores on achievement measures and their readiness for college-level work (e.g., preparation for calculus) (Walberg, Fraser, & Welch, 1986; Welch, Anderson, & Harris, 1982).

Election of additional courses. Students who elect to take additional mathematics and science courses after they complete their college preparation requirements will have more opportunities that prepare them to major in scientific fields in college, whereas those students who complete minimum college entrance requirements are unlikely to begin college with the necessary prerequisites. Enrollment in nonrequired science and mathematics courses is related to students' interest in these subjects, their perceptions of their prospects for success, and their prior achievement (Lantz & Smith, 1981). Teachers', counselors', and parents' encouragement (usually based on these same factors) may also influence students' decisions to enroll in additional science and mathematics courses (Cicourel & Kitsuse, 1963; College Entrance Examination Board, 1986; Gross, 1988; Rosenbaum, 1976).

College attendance and choice of a science major. Attending college and choosing a science major are key to pipeline persistence. Students' selection of a science major is strongly related to their end-of-high school achievement and their completion of advanced mathematics and science courses (Ware & Lee, 1985). Mathematics preparation may be critical because many colleges require readiness for college-level calculus for admission to many science and quantitative majors (Sells, 1982). Students' confidence in their abilities and their attitudes toward math and science are also related to their choice of a major (Betz & Hackett, 1983; Ware & Lee, 1985).

Persistence in a science major. Persistence in a science major throughout the undergraduate years leads to attainment of baccalaureate degrees in quantitative fields, eligibility for graduate school, or immediate employment in science-related work. Students' persistence as science majors seems to be related to their high school achievement (as measured by the SAT), high school grades, high school class rank (Matyas, 1986), and grades earned in college (Schonberger & Holden, 1987).

Completion of graduate work. For those students pursuing the highest level of scientific work, high achievement in quantitative fields during undergraduate study, admission to graduate school, choice of a scientific graduate field of study, and persistence in graduate school lead to the attainment of the graduate degrees necessary for such work.

Although many of these pipeline junctures are obvious, they hold the key to understanding adult participation in mathematics and science. As suggested earlier, three interrelated factors appear to be important throughout, although they take on different degrees of importance at different points. Students' opportunities to learn math and science, their achievement in these subjects, and the development of attitudes and interests that lead them to choose to pursue mathematics and science study are central to progress through this pipeline and to later participation.

Where Are Women and Minorities Lost?

Understanding how and why some groups have lower adult participation rates requires that we track their progress through this pipeline, noting at what points and for what reasons members of particular groups are lost.

Using national data, Berryman (1983) found that losses among women occur primarily at the end of the precollege years and during college. Berryman traced their lower adult participation rates to two factors: First, women obtain advanced degrees at lower rates in general, and second, women fail to select quantitative college majors at rates equal to men.

Berryman found that most blacks and Hispanics leave the pipeline much earlier. Their underparticipation can be largely attributed to their lower levels of achievement in mathematics during the precollege years. However, even those blacks and Hispanics who remain in the precollege pipeline fail to choose quantitative fields of study at rates equal to whites (Berryman, 1983).

Other studies fill out these broad patterns identified by Berryman. This work permits us to better understand the opportunities, interests and attitudes, and achievement of girls and non-Asian minority children as they move through school. Doing so, we gain a clearer picture of which of these factors leads to pipeline losses among various groups and when barriers to participation emerge.

Early Schooling Experiences

Elementary school. Black and Hispanic students leave the scientific pipeline early in elementary school. White and Asian children more often exhibit higher early achievement in mathematics and science than do non-Asian minorities (Carpenter et al., 1983; Dossey, Mullis, Lindquist, & Chambers, 1988; Hueftle, Rakow, & Welch, 1983; Mullis & Jenkins, 1988). Related to their lower achievement, blacks and Hispanics are more likely than whites to be placed in low-ability and remedial classes or in special education programs (Persell, 1977; Rosenbaum, 1980), and they are less likely to be identified as able learners and placed in enriched or accelerated programs (National Center for Educational Statistics [NCES], 1985b). Consequently, as a group they are likely to have fewer opportunities than their white peers to learn science and mathematics. Despite these disparities, black elementary school students are often as enthusiastic as whites about science and math, and they often express the most positive attitudes of any group (Carpenter et al., 1983; Mullis & Jenkins, 1988).

Girls' elementary school achievement and opportunities follow a more positive course. Overall gender differences in achievement do not appear at the elementary level in either mathematics or science (Lockheed, Thorpe, Brooks-Gunn, Casserly, & McAloon, 1985; Dossey et al., 1988; Mullis & Jenkins, 1988). However, there are some early warning signals of later gender-related differences: Teachers may more frequently assign high-ability boys to top math groups than they do high-ability girls (Hallinan & Sorensøn, 1987). Elementary school-age girls show less positive attitudes toward science and science careers than do boys (Mullis & Jenkins, 1988). Finally, elementary school girls report that they have fewer science experiences (Mullis & Jenkins, 1988).

Middle school and junior high. In junior high school, the paths of many minority children continue to lead out of the pipeline. Largely because of their lower achievement during elementary school, schools more often place blacks and Hispanics in remedial mathematics programs (Persell, 1977), where they are likely to be exposed to fewer topics and skills (McKnight et al., 1987). For some, there are differences in science opportunities as well, because many junior high schools differentiate the science curricula; some schools base grouping decisions on students' mathematics achievement (Oakes, 1985). Overall, blacks and Hispanics have fewer science experiences than do whites (Hueftle et al., 1983; Kahle & Lakes, 1983). Although the differences have narrowed considerably over the past decade (Jones, 1984), the achievement gap between blacks and whites in junior high school remains, even in low-level topics and skills (Dossey et al., 1988; Hueftle et al., 1983; Mullis & Jenkins, 1988; National Assessment of Educational Progress [NAEP], 1983). As in elementary school, black students' attitudes toward science and math remain as positive as those of their white peers (Dossey et al., 1988; Mullis & Jenkins, 1988).

There are few significant gender differences in mathematics achievement at the junior high school level (Dossey et al., 1988). In the past, girls this age were more negative about math (Fennema & Sherman, 1977), but on some measures these differences have nearly disappeared (Dossey et al., 1988). However, girls remain more negative than boys about science, and they report having fewer science experiences than boys (Mullis & Jenkins, 1988).

Senior High School

Minorities and girls continue to leave the scientific pipeline in senior high school. Achievement gaps between blacks and Hispanics and whites are larger than for younger students, although here too the differences have narrowed. Nevertheless, minorities typically have fewer opportunities to learn science and mathematics. Girls exhibit more negative attitudes, pursue fewer opportunities, and by the end of high school score considerably lower than boys on measures of mathematics and science achievement.

Minority curricular enrollment and course taking. Disproportionate percentages of minorities enroll in vocational or nonacademic curriculum tracks (Ekstrom, Goertz, & Rock, 1988; West & Gross, 1986). Non-Asian minorities typically take fewer high school science and mathematics courses than do whites, partly because nonacademic track students usually lack the prerequisites to enroll in academic courses, and partly because they are nearly always required to take fewer science and mathematics courses than are college-bound students (California State Department of Education, 1984; Gamoran, 1986; Guthrie & Leventhal, 1985; Vanfossen, Jones, & Spade, 1985). However, track assignment is not the only factor in course-taking differences. Even those students in college preparatory programs at low socioeconomic status (SES) schools (those most minorities attend) typically take fewer academic classes (Rock, Braun, & Rosenbaum, 1985).

As Table 1 shows, substantially lower percentages of black and Hispanic high school students complete academic courses of study in mathematics and science (either concentrating heavily in these subjects or completing 4-year college entrance requirements). Differences are also substantial in computer science. However, these patterns may be changing. More recent data from the American College Testing (ACT) program show a substantial increase between 1978 and 1986 in the number of college-bound students taking 3 or more years of math and natural science, and that increases in courses taken by blacks and Hispanics have been among the most dramatic. However, even with these increases, minority high school students are still underrepresented in advanced courses (Bartell & Noble, 1986).

Minority achievement and attitudes. Although blacks and Hispanics continue to show attitudes comparable to their white peers about math (Dossey et al., 1988), they consistently perform below the levels of white males on measures of end-of-high-school achievement in mathematics and science (Dossey et al., 1988; Mullis & Jenkins, 1988). Achievement gaps remain among college-bound seniors as well (College Board, 1987). Furthermore, minorities' low achievement at the end of high school is undoubtedly more profound than test scores imply, because disproportionate numbers of blacks and Hispanics drop out of school (Center for Statistics, 1986a). Differences in dropout rates exacerbate differences in achievement, because those students leaving school before graduation are typically among the lowest achievers (Catterall, 1989b). However, those blacks who do remain in the precollege pipeline and take the SAT report an interest in science majors nearly equal to that of whites (Grandy, 1987).

TABLE 1
Students Exhibiting Academic Course-Taking Patterns by Socioeconomic Status and Race (percentages of students exhibiting pattern)

	SES			White	Black	Hispanic
	High	Middle	Low			
Academic math	69.1	45.7	25.1	51.5	28.1	28.9
Academic science	58.3	36.9	19.6	40.7	26.1	23.8
Computer science	17.4	12.4	8.4	13.8	10.5	8.0

Source. National Center for Educational Statistics (1985a).

Women's course-taking patterns. Gender differences at the senior high school level follow different patterns. Relatively equal numbers of high school boys and girls enroll in academic and nonacademic curricula, but girls choose to take advanced science and mathematics courses at lower rates. As Table 2 shows, girls are more likely than boys to stop taking science and math courses after completing basic college entrance requirements; boys are more likely than girls to concentrate (i.e., take additional, unrequired advanced courses) in mathematics, science, and computer science.

Although gender differences are substantially greater in science than in other subjects, the greatest discrepancies are in the physical sciences—especially physics. Mathematics discrepancies reflect differences in enrollment in the most advanced courses—trigonometry and pre-calculus (Fennema, 1984). Somewhat earlier NAEP data show that boys leave high school with pre-calculus preparation at a rate one and a half times higher than that of girls (Armstrong, 1981).

These patterns, too, may be changing. A recent study of seniors in Rhode Island found no overall gender differences in course enrollment (Rallis & Ahern, 1986), and recent ACT data show that increasing percentages of girls are completing 3 or more years of math and natural science, suggesting that they are enrolling in advanced science classes (Bartell & Noble, 1986).

Women's achievement and attitudes. By the end of senior high, boys and girls differ in achievement and attitudes. Girls achieve less in mathematics and science than boys, as evidenced by NAEP and Scholastic Achievement Test (SAT) scores (U.S. Bureau of the Census, 1987). High school girls' attitudes toward mathematics (Dossey et al., 1988) and science (Mullis & Jenkins, 1988) are more negative than those of boys. Gender differences in mathematics have decreased during the past decade

TABLE 2
Students Exhibiting Academic Course-Taking Patterns by Sex
(percentages of students exhibiting pattern)

	Males	Females
Math		
Concentrator	9.3	9.0
	(53.1)	(46.9)
4-year college-bound	34.7	38.5
	(46.8)	(52.3)
Science		
Concentrator	11.6	7.1
	(61.4)	(38.6)
4-year college-bound	26.6	28.8
	(38.6)	(61.4)
Computer science participants	13.6	11.4
	(53.8)	(46.3)

Note. The figures in parentheses represent the percentage of students within each pattern who possessed the designated characteristic (male or female). For example 53.1% of all the math concentrators were male.
Source. National Center for Educational Statistics (1985a).

(Dossey et al., 1988), but in science girls continue to express attitudes more negative than those of boys (Mullis & Jenkins, 1988).

College Experiences

College attendance. Black and Hispanic high school graduates enter college at rates lower than whites (Center for Statistics, 1986b). Furthermore, those minorities who do enroll are more likely than whites to attend 2-year rather than 4-year colleges (NCES, 1988). Those minorities in 4-year schools are more likely to be at colleges than at universities (Center for Statistics, 1986b). In addition, gaps are widening in the percentages of blacks, Hispanics, and whites completing 4-year college programs (NCES, 1988).

More women than men enter college (Center for Statistics, 1986b). However, women drop out of college earlier than men, even though equal numbers eventually complete a bachelor's degree.

Choice of science major. Blacks and Hispanics are underrepresented as college majors in science, mathematics, and engineering. Whites constitute between 78 and 85% of the science and math majors (Commission on Professionals in Science and Technology, 1986). Women choose science majors at lower rates than do men, although their enrollments have increased substantially. Of the entering freshmen in 1984, 30% of women reported they intended to major in science and mathematics, compared with 41% of men (Commission on Professionals, 1986). These gender differences appear even among equally prepared men and women (Ware & Lee, 1985). Gender differences in choice of field are less pronounced among minorities than whites. Even though their numbers are far greater, white women are consistently the least represented female group in science majors. In contrast, black women constitute a substantially larger share of black science majors than do women of other racial and ethnic groups (Commission on Professionals, 1986).

Persistence in science majors. We have few data to document the persistence of minorities in science majors during their college years. However, a comparison of the percentages of black and Hispanic freshmen choosing majors with the percentages of blacks and Hispanics attaining bachelor's degrees in these fields suggests that minorities leave science at rates higher than their white counterparts. Although these data don't tell us whether minority freshmen are switching to other fields or leaving college altogether, they do document further minority losses from the scientific pipeline.

There is conflicting evidence about gender differences in persistence in science majors. Most studies have found that men persist at higher rates than women (see, e.g., Corbett, Estler, Johnston, Ott, Robinson, & Shell, 1980; LeBold and Shell, 1980; Matyas, 1986; McNamara & Scherrei, 1982; Schonberger & Holden, 1984, 1987), whereas a few studies have found persistence rates to be equal or actually higher for women (DeBoer, 1984b; Gardner, 1976; Greenfield, Holloway, & Remus, 1982; Ware & Dill, 1986).

Some of the conflict in findings may be explained by changes in persistence rates over time. A study of engineering majors at Purdue, for example, found that in the 1960s persistence rates of women were half those of men, but since the 1970s persistence rates have been nearly equal (Jagacinski & LeBold, 1981). But more of the contradictions can be attributed to differences in sample sizes, year during which attrition was measured, and the extent of study controls for ability and experience. We can probably be most confident about recent work studying attrition among large and comparable groups of male and female students. This work suggests that equally prepared women defect from science at higher rates than men, particularly during their freshman year (Schonberger & Holden, 1987; Ware & Dill, 1986; Ware, Steckler, & Leserman, 1985).

Degree attainment and graduate study. As was detailed in the previous section, blacks and Hispanics are significantly underrepresented among those earning baccalaureate degrees in science and mathematics. These minority college graduates do not continue in graduate school at the same rates as whites, and minority graduate students in scientific fields constitute about one percentage point less of their proportion of undergraduate majors (NSF, 1988). Consequently, both the failure of blacks and Hispanics to acquire the necessary undergraduate preparation and, among those who do earn bachelor's degrees in scientific fields, the failure to pursue graduate study in these fields contribute to the underrepresentation of black and Hispanic minorities attaining graduate degrees in science. Throughout, black males experience the greatest difficulty attaining the necessary preparation for science careers.

Women, unlike minorities, are not negatively affected by overall lower rates of bachelor's and master's degree attainment generally (they earned slightly more than 50% of these degrees overall in 1986). Like minorities, however, they are constrained by lower rates of attaining scientific bachelor's degrees, by lower rates of doctoral level participation generally (they earned 36% of the doctoral degrees overall in 1986), and by lower rates of selecting scientific majors in graduate school (NCES, 1988).

Achievement, Opportunities, and Choice: Why Such Differences?

In the following sections I summarize work investigating why women and minorities fail to persist in the educational pipeline and what changes might forestall these losses.

We divide studies on participation into three categories: (a) studies of individual influences, that is, cognitive abilities and attitudes; (b) studies of schooling factors; and (c) studies of societal factors. Two of these domains—the individual and the societal—are not likely to be altered directly by education policy. However, policymakers need to understand these domains because they are linked to students' experiences at school. Moreover, it is in the nexus between student characteristics and schooling opportunities that *alterable* influences on unequal participation are likely to be found. All three domains, then, should be considered by policymakers and educators as they frame interventions to increase participation and by researchers who conduct policy-relevant studies.

Several caveats must be noted about the research as a whole. First, some questions have received a great deal of research attention, whereas others have received almost none. For example, much research seeks to identify factors related to women's participation in mathematics; less work considers influences on women's participation in science; even less examines factors related to minorities' participation in either field. Second, and related to the first caveat, many studies of minority participation have been hampered by inadequate samples that have limited researchers to aggregating data across minority groups or to looking at only one group, typically blacks. Work that has lumped several groups together may provide an inaccurate portrayal of the experiences of any one group. Little work has looked at subgroups of minorities separately, or has integrated studies of race and gender.

Third, few studies have used designs adequate for ascertaining the determinants of unequal participation. Most work focuses on documenting associations among variables thought to be related to participation. Although this work provides substantial insight into how groups differ, it contributes only clues about the causes of race- and gender-related differences. Moreover, because little of the work has been guided by theory about how gender or racial and ethnic differences are produced, much of the research reporting patterns of relationships fails to shed light on the relationships found.

Last, as detailed earlier, three interrelated factors appear to be critical for explaining the differences in the progress of various groups of students through the educational pipeline: opportunities to learn, achievement, and choices about whether to pursue study in scientific fields. Although analysts and researchers have acknowledged the importance of one or more of these dimensions, and a few have considered relationships among them (e.g., Berryman, 1983; Chipman & Thomas, 1984; Peterson & Fennema, 1985), little theoretical or empirical work has investigated how these factors work together, attempted to disentangle the relative contribution of each of these influences on participation, or established causal links among them. Because of these gaps in the literature, serious questions remain about what roles schooling opportunities play in achievement, why different groups of students achieve at different levels, or why some groups tend not to choose to take advantage of the schooling opportunities they have available to them. These issues will be revisited in the final section of this review.

POSSIBLE CAUSES AND CONSEQUENCES: COGNITIVE ABILITIES AND ATTITUDES

Group differences in individual attributes have been studied as potential contributors to race and gender-linked differences in achievement levels and persistence. These individual attributes fall roughly into two domains: cognitive and affective. Most researchers see cognitive abilities as prerequisite to students' achievement and to the learning opportunities that schools decide are appropriate for them. Most researchers hypothesize that affective factors are related most to whether students choose to pursue and persist in science study, although considerable research has also investigated whether and how affective factors and achievement are linked.

Cognitive Factors

Race and Cognitive Ability

For the past 25 years, considerable attention has centered on the intellectual capacities of economically and socially disadvantaged children. The main question that has driven this discussion is whether disadvantaged children possess the basic intellectual abilities when they enter school that are necessary for success in academic work. Most theorists have focused on whether impoverished homes stunt intellectual growth and handicap children with fundamental cognitive deficits (see, e.g., Hunt, 1969). Because most blacks and Hispanics are disadvantaged, this work is appropriate for consideration here. Other work has been related more directly to minorities, and has investigated the question of racial differences in intelligence (see, e.g., Jensen, 1969).

Most of the discussion of possible cognitive deficits has stemmed from evidence about differences in aptitude and achievement as measured by standardized tests on cognitive abilities learned at school, rather than from direct research on cognitive abilities themselves. Consequently, there is considerable evidence that blacks and Hispanics as a group do more poorly than whites on cognitive tests at school. However, little solid evidence supports theories of cognitive deficiencies of minorities as the basis of their poorer school performance, or assesses the effects of any deficiencies on achievement and persistence should they be found. It is reasonable to conclude (as many theorists have) that there is no empirical basis for the hypothesis underlying this work—that is, that racial or socioeconomic groups differ in basic cognitive processes (see reviews by Cole & Scribner, 1974; Ginsburg & Russell, 1981).

In one of the few rigorous studies that have examined the question directly, Ginsburg and Russell (1981) assessed preschool and kindergarten children's cognitive abilities thought to be associated with later math abilities and achievement—for example, early counting, enumeration (saying how many items are in a display), conservation, determining which display has more items, among others. A major outcome was that whites as a group never outperformed blacks on tasks measuring these abilities, and that those race effects that were found interacted with socioeconomic status. That is, lower socioeconomic groups performed at a lower level than middle-class children on 4 of 17 tasks. On 2 of these tasks, however, the differences disappeared in the older children (kindergarteners). Furthermore, 3 of these 4 tasks (1 of those where the difference disappeared, and the 2 others) required an understanding of *some* and *more*, two difficult verbal concepts. On 2 other tasks that required the understanding of these terms no socioeconomic differences were found.

There are several conclusions we can draw from Ginsburg and Russell (although with less confidence than if other studies had replicated this work). First and most important, the differences between blacks and whites found later in schooling cannot be attributed to early cognitive deficits. Assertions that there are genetic deficiencies which limit the cognitive abilities necessary for sophisticated mathematical understanding are countered by this study. Neither can one use impoverished environments as an explanation. Although there were socioeconomic differences on some tasks, there are many more tasks where no differences were found.

Finally, the finding that, by kindergarten, many of the group differences disappeared rules out the possibility that cognitive differences are irreversible, detrimental effects of impoverished, preschool environments.

Although it is not clear that the abilities that Ginsburg and Russell studied are linked to later mathematical ability, or that the results found in this Washington, D.C., sample generalize to the nation, this rather comprehensive study may provide the best empirical evidence available about racial differences in basic cognitive abilities before schooling.

Culture, Language, and Cognitive Style

Other work has investigated differences in cognitive style, especially the potential effects of field dependence—that is, learning that is highly influenced by the context in which knowledge and skills are imbedded—and field independence on mathematics performance. These style differences are usually seen as cultural in origin, with Mexican-Americans often depicted as prototypical of field-dependent learners. (However, women, too, are sometimes viewed as field dependent.) Some theorists have suggested that lower Hispanic achievement in mathematics might be explained by this preference for more holistic and less abstract learning conditions, conditions typically absent in mathematics classrooms (Ramirez & Castaneda, 1974; Valverde, 1984). Although few studies have explored this connection, Kagan found in his studies of Hispanic and Anglo children that field independence was related positively to mathematics performance (Kagan & Zahn, 1975; Kagan, Zahn, & Gealy, 1977).

Other work has examined the potential influence of primary language on students' mathematics and science performance. Most studies have found that language facility is related to performance, with Hispanic students, especially those students whose primary language is Spanish, achieving less well in mathematics and science (Cuevas, 1984; McCorquodale, 1983). These results must be viewed with caution, because few of these studies have controlled for the confounding effects of social class on the language-achievement relationship (Lockheed et al., 1985).

Gender and Cognitive Ability

Gender differences in cognitive ability (spatial visualization ability, in particular), their causes, and their consequences for achievement (mathematics, in particular) have been investigated more thoroughly. Because the nature and findings of these studies are complex and varied, only a brief overview of this work is given here.

Several studies have found male superiority on spatial visualization tasks (e.g., Brush, 1985; Fennema & Tatre, 1985; Maccoby & Jacklin, 1974), whereas others have found no such gender differences (Linn &

Peterson, 1985; Newcombe, Bandura, & Taylor, 1983). Recently, analysts reviewing this evidence have suggested that the findings are mixed because a variety of types of spatial abilities exist, and that gender differences exist only on some types (e.g., Linn & Peterson, 1985). The Ginsburg and Russell (1981) study considered a much wider range of cognitive abilities than just spatial visualization. In their work, preschool and kindergarten boys did not outperform girls on any of the tasks.

Another line of work has generated considerable controversy about whether those gender differences in spatial ability reflect biologically based differences or result from differences in childhood experiences and socialization of boys and girls (see Linn & Peterson, 1985, for a review). Some who hold that biological differences exist suggest that prenatal hormones may play a part, or that differences at puberty may be important (see Crockett & Peterson, 1984, for a review). At this point, however, neither the biological or environmental position is supported by unequivocal evidence. Most responsible analysts take the position that, if biological factors are involved, they are only one of many types of influences, and their effects on spatial ability may be relatively small (see review by Crockett & Peterson, 1984).

The meaning of the relationship between spatial ability and gender differences in performance has also been hotly debated. Although scholars have found a correlation between the two (for a review, see Fennema & Sherman, 1977), some researchers (e.g., Benbow & Stanley, 1982) have suggested that the relationship helps to explain gender differences in mathematics achievement. However, most researchers conclude that studies linking visualization and mathematical skills have been inconclusive at best (e.g., Fennema, 1984). Few studies have directly tested the relationship, or collected the longitudinal data necessary to establish causation. Moreover, recent meta-analyses of the existing work have concluded that the relationship itself has insufficient empirical support (Chipman, Brush, & Wilson, 1985; Linn & Peterson, 1985).

Fortunately, a recent reanalysis and synthesis of studies of gender differences over the past 20 years makes most of these debates moot. Linn and Hyde (in press) report that gender differences in math and science abilities have dwindled to almost nothing over the past 20 years. Although one sex difference remains (greater speed with which males mentally rotate figures), girls' poorer performance can be remedied with training. Most relevant for policymakers interested in increasing achievement and participation among underrepresented groups are the solid theoretical and empirical studies demonstrating that cognitive abilities can be learned (e.g., Brown & Campione, 1982; Sternberg, 1983; see Derry & Murphy, 1986, for a review) and that both girls (e.g., Connor & Serbin, 1985) and minorities (e.g., Ginsburg & Russell, 1981) can acquire them.

This work implies that, even if group differences in cognitive abilities do exist, they are not unalterable; interventions can overcome the differences in achievement.

Affective Factors

Attitude, motivation, and self-perception have been investigated as influences on the achievement and participation rates of minorities and women. Speculation about the relevance of these factors arises from work suggesting that individuals pursue areas that they value and in which they expect success (see, e.g., Chipman & Thomas, 1984). Other support for the potential importance of affective factors comes from the types of analyses described earlier suggesting that a primary reason that women are underrepresented in science is that they choose not to pursue study and careers in cognitive fields.

Among the hypothesized affective factors for women's and minorities' lower achievement and participation in quantitative fields are group differences in the following: relative interest in "people" and "things"; liking for math and science; perceived utility of science and mathematics; stereotyping of these subjects as the purview of white males; and confidence in abilities. A few of these factors have been researched extensively in relationship to women and mathematics. Less attention has been given to the role of affective factors in women's participation in science, and even less has been focused on minorities in either field. Most analyses have been correlational, many based on rather small samples. In general, then, conclusions about the influence of most affective factors remain tentative.

Interest and Liking

Considerable work suggests that girls and minorities show a greater interest in people, whereas white boys show more interest in things. These early interest patterns appear to have some connection to unequal rates of participation in quantitative fields of study (such as choice of college major) (Chipman & Thomas, 1984; Ware & Lee, 1985). Some analysts reason that, because mathematics, science, and technology are taught most often as abstract and disconnected from other people, these subjects are more appealing to white males than to women or minorities. This analysis is consistent with considerable evidence that black college-bound men (Sewell & Martin, 1976) and black college men (Hager & Elton, 1971) show proportionately more interest in service professions than in science compared to their white peers. However, virtually no evidence directly linking these preferences with participation exists, and recent analyses showing that blacks and whites taking the SAT express nearly equal interest in science majors make these earlier findings suspect.

Other evidence (and common sense) suggests that students—regardless of race or gender—who like mathematics and science are more successful in these subjects (Antonnen, 1969; Bassham, Murphy, & Murphy, 1964; Schofield, 1982), choose to take mathematics courses (Brush, 1985), and select science majors in college more frequently (Ware & Lee, 1985). Consequently, researchers have investigated race and gender differences in liking mathematics and science as possible influences on participation. Analyses of both national data and small-scale studies have found boys expressing attitudes toward math that are more positive than girls' attitudes (Sherman, 1980; Sherman & Fennema, 1977). In science, NAEP data reveal that gender differences in attitudes show up in 9-year-olds, 13-year-olds, and 17-year-olds. Moreover, 9-year-old and 13-year-old girls expressed attitudes toward science more negative in 1982 than their counterparts had 6 years earlier (Hueftle et al., 1983). NAEP data from 1986 show these negative attitudes have continued (Mullis & Jenkins, 1988). Finally, a recent study by Zimmerer and Bennett (1987) found gender differences in California eighth grade students' responses about enjoying and liking science and science-related activities. Both boys and girls were enthusiastic about doing science experiments in science class, but boys were generally more excited about this activity and other science activities both in and out of school.

Evidence about the overall relationship between liking science and achievement is consistent with the speculation that girls may do less well because they like these subjects less (Armstrong, 1980). Also, findings that college women who persist in science majors enjoy their science classes more than do women who switch (Ware & Dill, 1986) suggest that within-gender differences in liking may be linked to participation.

However, there is an important reason for skepticism about the effects of liking science on achievement and participation. Almost none of this work has attempted to establish a direction of causality between liking and achievement. Although evidence exists that girls' changes in attitudes toward math accompany and sometimes precede a change in achievement (Fennema & Sherman, 1977, 1978), we would not find it surprising if doing well in math and science were also a precursor to more positive attitudes. This is especially likely, because gender differences in liking science are less pronounced among high-achieving students (Matthews, 1980).

Also contrary to what theories about interest in people and things might suggest, black students tend to be as enthusiastic as whites about science and math, and in a number of studies (including NAEP) black students express the most positive attitudes of any group (Hueftle et al., 1983; Matthews, 1980; Zimmerer & Bennett, 1987). Moreover, black females are often more positive than their white counterparts (Dossey et al.,

1988; Zimmerer & Bennett, 1987). These studies make it doubtful that there is a direct or simple relationship between liking science and math and doing well in these subjects, because liking math and science does not appear to lead to high achievement and participation for minority students.

Perceived Utility

Some analysts suggest that even if students do not enjoy math, they will persist if they believe that it will be useful to their careers. Following this logic, we might hypothesize that one reason that women and minorities take no more than the minimum required math courses is because they do not perceive it as useful to their future career goals (e.g., Reyes, 1984). Supporting this hypothesis is evidence that students' perceptions of the usefulness of mathematics is an important predictor of future math course taking for both sexes (Armstrong, 1985; Hilton & Berglund, 1974; Pedro, Wolleat, Fennema, & Becker, 1981; Sherman, 1980; Sherman & Fennema, 1977), and persistence in college majors (Ware & Dill, 1986).

The link between perceptions of usefulness and participation is supported further by findings that boys, more than girls, see math as useful. Several studies have found this difference as early as seventh grade (Brush, 1985; Eccles et al., 1985; Fennema & Sherman, 1977; Hilton & Berglund, 1974; Wise, Steel, & MacDonald, 1979). Researchers also have linked perceptions of the usefulness of mathematics to gender differences in achievement at the middle and senior high school levels (Armstrong, 1980; Fennema & Sherman, 1977, 1978) and to women's decisions to pursue college study in these subjects (Berryman, 1983).

The few studies investigating links between perceived usefulness and minority participation are equivocal. Some studies (e.g., Matthews, 1984) find that minority students have lower expectations than whites about the future usefulness of mathematics in jobs, schooling, or everyday life. Other studies (e.g., Zimmerer & Bennett, 1987) find that minorities, more than whites, expect that science will be important in their careers. Neither finding sheds light on the relationship between perceived usefulness and minority students' achievement or participation.

Stereotyping of Math and Science

Recent studies have found that many students believe that math is more useful for males than for females (Eccles et al., 1985); that studying science is more important for boys; and that boys understand science better (Zimmerer & Bennett, 1987). Vockell and Lebonc (1981) have found this sex-stereotyping of math and science occurring as early as the primary grades. Some analysts also have suggested that those girls who see mathematics and science (particularly physical science) as masculine, and therefore not particularly relevant to their own lives, may be less motivated to do well in these fields (Stage et al., 1985). And some empirical evidence does support the hypothesis that perceptions of math as masculine relate to girls' lower rates of math course taking (Lantz & Smith, 1981; Sherman, 1980) and lower levels of achievement (Dwyer, 1974; Fennema & Sherman, 1978; Sherman, 1980). Also, girls have been found to lower their expectations for success when tasks are seen as masculine (Lenny, 1977).

Nevertheless, we need to interpret these findings cautiously. The overall amount of sex stereotyping of mathematics among girls appears to be limited (Brush, 1985; Fennema & Sherman, 1977, 1978; Zimmerer & Bennett, 1987), and the correlation between stereotyping and participation is low (Lantz & Smith, 1981). Furthermore, sex stereotyping may be changing rather rapidly, and boys and girls may not stereotype equally. Although many girls are convinced that math is open to everyone, boys more often see math as masculine and place girls in more traditional roles (Fennema & Sherman, 1977, 1978). This finding may be important, because the support of significant others appears to influence girls' participation in mathematics (Lantz & Smith, 1981). The opinions of male peers are likely to be seen as significant by school-aged girls.

Girls may be also deterred by what they see as both current and future social costs to women who aspire to mathematics and science careers (Chipman & Thomas, 1984); this concern may be particularly pronounced among Hispanic women (McCorquodale, 1983). One such cost is anticipated conflict between male-dominated careers and child raising. For example, some work suggests that women college students who remain in science-oriented majors have nontraditional views of sex-roles—they anticipate delegating more household responsibility to their future spouses (Matyas, 1986). Similarly, women science majors have been found to give a lower priority than other women to future family and personal life (Ware & Lee, 1985). These findings may also suggest that women expect that science and family may conflict later in life.

The potential importance of stereotyping and perceived role conflicts gains support from programs that have successfully used female role models to increase girls' participation in mathematics (Brody & Fox, 1980; MacDonald, 1980; Tobin & Fox, 1980). These programs attempt to compensate for the fact that girls have little exposure to women who are engaged in mathematics and science, or who successfully juggle career and home responsibilities, or who are confident about their mathematics abilities (see Stage et al., 1985, for a review). Other support comes from studies finding that exposure to female role models influenced women's choice of science majors (Matyas, 1986) and their grades in college science courses (Boli, Allen, & Payne, 1985).

Less is known about the possible effects of stereotyping science, mathematics, and technology as white domains on minority achievement and participation. Evidence reveals negative effects of stereotyping (Matthews, 1984), but research has inadequately explored this relationship.

Confidence

A long line of research suggests that children's attributions of their success to their own ability and efforts contribute to their persistence and performance in school and to their efficacy (for reviews, see Stipek & Weisz, 1981; Weiner, 1976). More specifically, children's belief in their ability appears to predict their performance on mathematics tasks (Schunk, 1981, 1982). Betz and Hackett (1983) link confidence in math ability to students' selection of science-based college majors. Others link confidence to the taking of elective college courses in mathematics and science (DeBoer, 1984a, 1984b). Parallel work has established negative links between "math anxiety" and math achievement for students from grade school to college (see Reyes, 1984, for a recent review).

Although boys and girls appear to be equally motivated to do well, girls appear to be less confident that their efforts will succeed (see, e.g., Lantz & Smith, 1981). Hudson's (1986) review reveals that girls give up more easily than boys after experiencing failure or difficulty. They appear to be especially insecure about their prospects for success on tasks they see as requiring high ability and on unfamiliar or difficult tasks. Even very able girls' expectations for success appear to be more fragile than boys. Some have used these findings to suggest that girls have less confidence in their ability to achieve in general (Hudson, 1986).

In mathematics, boys are more confident about their abilities than are equally able girls (Fennema & Sherman, 1977, 1978; Linn & Hyde, in press), and they are more confident with mathematics achievement tests (Hudson, 1986). When boys and girls have similar math performance, boys report that they expend less effort to do well in math, and they have higher expectations for further success (Eccles et al., 1985; Matthews, 1980). These sex differences in math confidence emerge in junior high school (Brush, 1985; Eccles et al., 1985; Fennema & Sherman, 1977; Fox, Brody, & Tobin, 1985), just before enrollment and achievement differences begin to appear and about the time important gender-role decisions are being made.

Evidence that girls more often attribute their failures to lack of ability and their successes to effort may compound the effects of their own levels of confidence. For example, a recent study (Ware et al., 1985) of gender differences at the college level found that male students tended to attribute their difficulties to something external—the inherent difficult nature of the course or poor instructors. Women, on the other hand, tended to blame their own perceived inadequacy. Conflicting evidence emerges from DeBoer's (1984a) study of freshmen at a small, selective liberal arts college, where no gender differences were found in attributions of success or failure to external or internal factors among a sample of students in science courses. However, selection bias in the sample may account for this contradictory finding.

Finally, girls more often tend to be subject to math anxiety (e.g., Betz, 1978; Reyes, 1984; Stage et al., 1985). As students (girls particularly) increasingly believe that high school math gets progressively harder, their math anxiety increases (Brush, 1980). Probably the most convincing evidence, however, comes from Linn and Hyde's (in press) recent synthesis. Their work shows that girls' lower levels of confidence have not diminished over the past 20 years.

Important links between confidence and girls' math achievement have been found both in analyses of national data (Armstrong, 1980) and in smaller, well-controlled studies of precollege students (Fennema & Sherman, 1977, 1978). The relationship appears to grow stronger as girls get older (Armstrong, 1980). Other studies have found that lower levels of confidence relate to girls' lower rates of mathematics course taking (Armstrong & Price, 1982; Sherman, 1980; Stage et al., 1985) and persistence in science majors at college (Ware & Dill, 1986).

As with other affective factors, we know far less about race- and ethnicity-linked differences in confidence, attributions, and anxiety in science and mathematics. Early evidence suggests that blacks have lower levels of confidence about their general ability than do whites (Wylie, 1963), and a more recent study of Hispanic community college students found them to be far less confident than their white peers (Rendon, 1983). Other work has found black males in particular far less certain about their ability to learn enough math to become a scientist, engineer, or math teacher (Matthews, 1980). However, 1982 NAEP data show black 13- and 17-year-olds to be the most favorably disposed toward science careers of any group (Hueftle et al., 1983). Recent California Assessment Program data show all eighth grade minority students indicating more often than whites that science will be important to their future careers (Zimmerer & Bennett, 1987). However, as with the patterns of liking noted earlier, these high levels of interest in science careers tell little about students' confidence that they could actually attain these goals.

The following tentative conclusions may best capture our current understanding of the role of attitudes in race and gender differences in participation. We have considerable evidence that women are more negative about science and about the role it might play in their future. Although there is little evidence that these attitudes *cause* the lower levels of achievement and participation with which they are often linked, negative attitudes may deter high-achieving girls from persisting in science and mathematics courses and career plans. In contrast, minority students generally express positive attitudes about science and mathematics, but these are not paralleled by high levels of achievement and participation. Most likely, then, is that attitudes have a conditional effect—that is, among students with low achievement and perhaps fewer learning opportunities (some women and most minorities), positive attitudes will be insufficient to promote achievement or to encourage students to seek further study of science and mathematics. Among students who achieve at high levels and who have ample opportunities to learn science and mathematics, positive attitudes are necessary to choose and persist in scientific study.

CONCLUSIONS: THE INFLUENCE OF ABILITIES AND ATTITUDES

Despite the volume of work that has been conducted on group differences in cognitive abilities and attitudes, conclusions about the associations of these differences with student achievement and participation must be cautiously drawn. Research has not established the causes of these differences or their effects on students' opportunities, achievement, or choices to pursue science.

Few differences in basic cognitive abilities or attitudes among racial and ethnic groups emerge to help explain racial differences in achievement, opportunities, and choices in science or mathematics. Perhaps the most striking findings regarding minority students are those from the NAEP, showing blacks as having the most positive attitudes of any group about science. However, their lower levels of achievement in science cast doubt on the proposition that positive attitudes lead to higher achievement or more opportunities to participate. A more plausible hypothesis is that for positive attitudes to affect minority students' behaviors, they may need to be expressed in the context of actual science experiences. For example, for blacks, interest in science projects as a child and participating in science clubs in high school have been found to relate to the choice of science as a college major (Thomas, 1984) and to making this decision before entering college (Snelling & Boruch, 1972). We know from NAEP data and other work to be considered in the following section that minorities as a group have fewer such opportunities. However, the paucity of research on minorities probably best explains our lack of understanding of the role of individual factors on black and Hispanic participation.

Although we find no important gender differences in cognitive abilities, we do find less positive attitudes among women, which provide a plausible explanation for girls achieving less well as they get older, and for why they choose not to pursue scientific fields even though they have the cognitive prerequisites. Even though the studies are largely correlational, they certainly suggest that girls like science and math less than do boys, see them as less relevant to their futures, and feel less confident about their ability to succeed in these subjects. Interventions to change girls' attitudes may increase their achievement and their willingness to pursue the opportunities that are available.

However, we must be cautious about concluding that attitudes cause gender differences in achievement and participation. In a comprehensive meta-analysis of the correlational literature linking student affect, ability, and science achievement, Steinkamp and Maehr (1983) conclude that little overall relationship exists between attitudes and achievement. They suggest that overall gender differences in attitudes, abilities, and achievement in science are quite small, and that additional variables must be found to explain the much larger gender differences in adult participation.

Taken together, the current body of research indicates that no single factor (e.g., attitudes) is likely to explain participation differences. The inconclusive findings summarized in this section highlight weaknesses in much current research. These weaknesses include an overreliance on correlations among single variables, the use of varying definitions of attitudinal variables, the difficulty of measuring attitudes, and the near absence of empirical work based on models or theories that suggest how a variety of factors (including attitudes) work together to affect differences in achievement and choices.

The most useful and revealing studies have developed models that incorporate other factors (e.g., prior achievement, schooling experiences) as well as attitudes in explaining differences in achievement. For example, Kulm's (1980) model for attitude-behavior relationships suggests that attitudes may operate differently among students of different achievement levels, or attitudes may have different effects in different learning situations or on different learning tasks. Peterson and Fennema's (1985) more recent work includes a model of gender differences in mathematics achievement that describes a chain of influence from both external factors (e.g., classroom conditions) and attitudes (including confidence, perceived usefulness, attribution for success and failure) to autonomous learning behaviors (including choosing tasks to work on, working independently, and persisting), and finally to achievement. One area where more sophisticated modeling has been used to guide empirical work indicates the potential usefulness of models: influences of attitudes on gender differences in high school mathematics course taking. This research (e.g., Eccles et al., 1985; Eccles, MacIver, & Lange, 1986) provides more clues about the role of attitudes in a complex process of decision making. In fact, in their recent review of this literature, Chipman and Thomas (1984) conclude that the research reveals that attitudes become central once achievement is controlled. That is, among males and females of equal achievement levels, differences in interest in mathematics, perceptions of its utility, and confidence are sufficient to explain students' choices.

This type of conclusion is also supported by studies of women's persistence in science majors in college. As noted earlier, Ware et al. (1985) found that, among a group of freshman college men and women who were equally predisposed toward science majors and of equally high ability, fewer women than men persisted after the first year of study. Schonberger and Holden (1987) found that, although women science majors had higher means on both SAT verbal and quantitative subtests and ranked higher in their high school graduating class, women defected from science in greater percentages than their male peers. Finally, in the High School and Beyond (HSB) sample, a greater proportion of female science majors switched to other fields, even though they had higher overall grades during their first 2 years in college than did the men (Ware & Lee, 1985). These studies suggest that, when other factors are taken into consideration, attitudes may play a critical role in high-achieving women's leaving science.

POSSIBLE CAUSES AND CONSEQUENCES: SCHOOLING EXPERIENCES

This section summarizes what we have learned about how schooling experiences differ for girls and minorities, and suggests how these differences may influence students' learning opportunities, achievement, and decisions to study science. Four features of students' experiences have been investigated: (a) students' access to educational resources, (b) their access to guidance and encouragement from school adults, (c) their access to math and science content, and (d) teacher expectations and classroom teaching strategies. Although the likely effects of schooling experiences on opportunities to learn science and mathematics are fairly straightforward, evidence documenting differences in these experiences is insufficient for establishing that they cause discrepancies in students' achievement and choices with which they are often correlated. Nevertheless, that gender- and race-linked achievement differences grow wider with years spent in school signals that school experiences may, at the least, interact with students' backgrounds and attitudes in ways that contribute to these growing discrepancies.

Access to Resources

Funding Levels

State and federal funding for public education is particularly critical for the educational opportunities of non-Asian minority students. As a group they are poorer than other students, they are less likely to have access to science and mathematics experiences outside school (e.g., enrolling in museum classes, hiring a tutor, or purchasing a home computer), and they typically have fewer educational resources in their homes (Ekstrom et al., 1988).

In 1983, 71% of blacks and 58% of Hispanics were reported to live in inner cities (American Council on Education, 1983). Related to this, the proportion of minority enrollments in large city school districts has increased dramatically in the past 15 years—in some cases doubled. By 1982, at least 15 of the largest districts' minority enrollments topped 70% (NCES, 1985b). Moreover, current projections suggest these trends will continue.

In most of these communities property wealth and personal income are low, and fewer dollars are spent on schooling (e.g., per-pupil expenditures). Lower expenditures in many urban communities have persisted even in those states where school finance reforms have attempted to equalize schooling resources (Carroll & Park, 1983). In some cases, per-pupil expenditures between neighboring high- and low-wealth districts differ by as much as a factor of 2 (see Catterall, 1989a). Unequal funding patterns mean that poor, minority children have less access than their more advantaged counterparts to well-maintained school facilities, highly qualified teachers, smaller classes, and instructional equipment and materials—important educational resources that funding dollars can buy.

Poor, minority children have been affected more negatively than others by recent changes in educational funding policies. First, the reduction of federal assistance to education since 1980, including that for compensatory programs and desegregating school districts, has reduced the resources available to poor and minority children (Levin, 1986). For example, districts that cannot be integrated because of too few white students are not eligible for desegregation funding that could be used to establish science or mathematics magnet schools. Second, changes in the way federal funds are distributed have further diminished programs and services to disadvantaged children. The Educational Consolidation and Improvement Act (ECIA) of 1981 lessened the regulation and monitoring of Chapter 1 compensatory funds with respect both to targeting aid for particular populations and ensuring comparable spending in target and nontarget schools. In addition, by clustering the Emergency School Assistance Act program aimed at assisting desegregating school districts with a number of other programs into enrollment-based, block grant funding, ECIA further reduced funds and programs for urban schools and minority children (Darling-Hammond, 1985).

At the state level, decreased public willingness to support schooling (best exemplified by the tax revolt beginning with California's Proposition 13 in 1978) led to less money for education in general. In many advantaged school districts, community groups have partly offset these reductions with foundations to raise additional funds. These, however, are not the districts where most poor, minority children live. And even though many states are currently increasing funding in conjunction with educational reforms, few urban districts have been able to recoup their losses from the previous decline.

Finally, at the local level, declining enrollments in some urban districts have decreased income further. Many urban districts are forced to cut back on facilities maintenance and purchases of textbooks and equipment. Some have closed schools altogether. Spending for science-specific resources is often the first to be curtailed, including the equipment and supplies necessary to provide science laboratory experiences, participation in museum-sponsored programs and activities, and the purchase of up-to-date science texts. These differences imply that minority students are likely to have less access to schooling resources important for providing opportunities to learn science.

Teacher Resources

Many observers also suggest that minority and poor students have less exposure to high-quality teaching because predominantly minority and poor schools are less able to attract or retain qualified and experienced teachers. For example, a report of the California Commission on the Teaching Profession (1985) argues that disproportionate numbers of poor and minority students are taught during their entire school careers by the least qualified teachers. The Commission pointed to high levels of teacher turnover, larger numbers of misassigned teachers, and classrooms staffed by those holding only emergency credentials as problems in schools serving these at risk groups. Nationally, in 1983, the proportion of teaching vacancies (including those positions that were withdrawn or for which a substitute was hired) was about three times larger in central cities than in other types of districts (NCES, 1985b).

Gaps in the distribution of teacher quality may be particularly critical in mathematics and science. There is currently widespread concern about a national shortage of qualified science and math teachers, especially in the area of physical science. In 1981, over half of the newly hired teachers in these fields were either not certified or lacked the qualifications for certification in the courses they were to teach (NCES, 1983b). As of 1984, there was a 67% decrease in the number of science and math teachers who graduated from college during the previous 12 years. At that time, some estimates indicated that as many as 30% of the teachers teaching science and math at the secondary level are unqualified or underqualified (Johnston & Aldridge, 1984). More recent data suggest that most science courses are taught by teachers who specialize in science, although perhaps not in the specific subject taught (National Science Teachers Association, 1987). Taken together, these data suggest that in inner-city schools suboptimal teaching conditions in math and science are far more likely, including cancelled courses, larger classes, teaching misassignments, and the use of substitutes.

Although there is little hard evidence to document the effects of teacher quality differences on students' achievement or choices, few disagree that teachers are an important part of the educational process. Having teachers who are well prepared and knowledgeable in the subjects that students are expected to learn is an important prerequisite (although not a guarantee) to student learning (see Darling-Hammond & Hudson, 1989). Thus, the existence of a teacher-quality gap among schools serving different student groups is, in itself, an important dimension of the distribution of opportunity to learn science and mathematics.

Science and Math Resources

Recent studies have documented differences in access to specific mathematics and science resources. Studies have reported inequities in the number of microcomputers and the ways that computer use varies for different subpopulations of children (Becker, 1983, 1986; Furr & Davis, 1984; Winkler, Shavelson, Stasz, Robyn, & Feibel, 1984). For example, in 1983 the 12,000 wealthiest schools were four times more likely to have microcomputers than the 12,000 poorest schools (Furr & Davis, 1984). Only about 40% of middle schools in low socioeconomic communities had as many as 15 microcomputers, in contrast to high socioeconomic communities, where two thirds of the middle schools had at least this number (Becker, 1986). These data echo earlier findings that schools with many students in the federal free lunch program are less likely to have computers, calculators, and resource centers (Weiss, 1978).

Fewer microcomputers are available to minority children in elementary schools. Fewer poor and minority schools have teachers who are computer specialists. These schools are more likely to use their computers for drill and practice and less likely to use them for instruction in school programming (Becker, 1983; Miura, 1987).

Differences in access to schooling resources for girls enter the picture at the within-school level. For example, in secondary schools, probably because computers are concentrated in mathematics and science courses and in computer courses with advanced mathematics prerequisites, girls use computers less frequently than do boys (Furr & Davis, 1984). Also, boys outnumber girls by three to one in their before- and after-school use of computers (Becker, 1986). In California schools, eighth grade boys reported that they use many more science instruments than girls do in class

(Zimmerer & Bennett, 1987). Most pronounced were differences in the use of physical science tools, such as power supplies and prisms. Girls more often reported using biologically oriented tools; for example, more girls reported using microscopes than did boys.

Type of College

At the college level, the level of resources also influences the quality of students' experiences. Blacks and Hispanics appear to be at a disadvantage. More minorities than whites attend 2-year colleges, fewer of them are either enrolled in 2-year degree programs or transfer to 4-year schools, and greater percentages of those attending 4-year institutions are enrolled in colleges rather than universities. These differences mean that black and Hispanic students have less access to those institutions with the greatest resources for science programs. Moreover, recent cuts in financial aid to college students have undoubtedly had a disproportionate effect on minorities, who more often have families with lower incomes.

For blacks, attendance at a historically black institution may be a factor in obtaining a science PhD. Pearson and Pearson's (1985) survey showed that of 515 black doctoral scientists who had received their degree before 1974, 87% had their undergraduate origin in black institutions. These results are echoed in Thomas's (1984) study of college juniors in the South that found that students in predominantly black 4-year colleges were more likely to major in science. However, work based on national samples has found no discrepancies in the percentages of blacks choosing science majors at predominantly black or predominantly white colleges (Baratz & Ficklen, 1983; Berryman, 1983).

Access to Guidance and Encouragement

Counselors and teachers influence student participation and achievement with their expectations, advice, and encouragement. Teachers encourage or discourage future course taking and higher achievement in their day-to-day interactions with students and, for women and minority teachers, with the role models they provide.

I just hate to see a girl get in over her head. I always try to place students at a level where I know they'll be successful. I mean, wouldn't it be frightful to spoil a beautiful record by doing poorly in a course your senior year? (A woman counselor in her 20s during the 1974–1975 school year, as quoted in Casserly, 1980)

Advice and Encouragement

Counselors and teachers can provide students with important encouragement; knowledge about course options, college entrance requirements, and career opportunities; and information about financial support for college (Chipman & Thomas, 1984; College Board, 1986). Evidence suggests that girls and minorities receive less encouragement and information about courses and careers in scientific fields.

Perhaps the most overtly different counseling practice is the continued use in many schools of vocational interest tests with sex-specific norms for counseling students about career choices and appropriate school preparation (Chipman & Thomas, 1984).

Most differences in counseling practices are subtle. Poor and minority students appear to receive limited advice about academic courses, college entrance preparation, and financial assistance (Cicourel & Kitsuse, 1963; College Board, 1986; Erickson, 1975). Recently, minority and low SES students in the HSB sample reported less access to guidance counselors. This is important, because the researchers also found that those students with the greatest access to counselors were the most likely to be put in academic tracks that required taking advanced math and science courses (Lee & Ekstrom, 1987). These data suggest, then, that the students whose families are least likely to be able to provide academic counseling also receive the least advice and assistance at school (College Board, 1986).

Schools may discourage students covertly in the form of expectations or attitudes that reflect sex stereotypes (Harway & Astin, 1977). Males traditionally (although perhaps decreasingly) have been the object of higher expectations for mathematics achievement and the recipients of greater counselor encouragement (Casserly, 1980). They tend to garner greater praise and rewards for achievement (see Stage et al., 1985, for a review). For example, in a study of engineering majors, male students more often reported that teachers and counselors encouraged them to improve technical work skills, encouraged them to try engineering, made them aware of engineering as a possible career, and informed them about courses that would help prepare for engineering (Erickson, 1981).

Other work finds that support and information can positively affect girls. For example, Casserly (1980; Casserly & Rock, 1985) found that teachers who actively encourage girls with sincere praise and support the value of math for high-pay, high-prestige careers have a positive influence on girls' attitudes toward math.

Role Models at School

Most believe that female and minority science and mathematics teachers acting as role models encourages participation among girls and minority students. This effect is fairly well documented for girls, but little either supports or refutes this belief in regard to minority students.

The evidence about the actual impact on girls of contact with teacher role models is mixed. Studies have found that female teachers and counselors can influence girls' math attitudes by providing active encouragement with their role modeling (Casserly, 1980; Casserly & Rock, 1985). Similar findings suggest that exposure to role models is related to the achievement of high-achieving women. In a study of Stanford freshmen, women with female math teachers in high school had somewhat higher SAT math scores. This was not simply an effect of superior teaching ability on the part of women math teachers, as no such effect was found for men. Moreover, nearly three times the women who had had one or more female role models in high school received A's in their college math course than those who had all male math teachers in high school. Finally, only half as many women with role models failed to complete chemistry as those with no models (Boli et al., 1985).

Role models may not be powerful enough to counteract stereotypical views of science fields. For example, Vockell and Lebonc (1981) have found that the presence or absence of female teachers makes little difference in girls' perceptions of physical science careers as masculine or feminine. However, the absence of stronger role-model effects on girls may be in part because advanced math and all science courses are more likely to be taught by men (Fox, Fennema, & Sherman, 1977; National Science Teachers Association, 1987).

Given the differences in attitudes and self-perceptions that were explored in the last section, girls and minorities may be especially sensitive to the modeling and support of important adults. With the encouragement of teachers and counselors, they may be more likely to overcome initially negative attitudes—perceptions that math and science have little future utility to them, seeing these subjects as the province of white males, or lack of confidence in their ability to be successful. With the support and encouragement of adults in schools, these attitudes may be cemented. However, neither the distribution of counseling, information, and encouragement nor their effects on various groups has been studied adequately.

Access to Science and Mathematics Knowledge

Curriculum Tracking

Growing evidence indicates that schools' judgments of students' intellectual abilities and achievement play a major role in determining what opportunities they have available to them (Guthrie & Leventhal, 1985; Lee, 1986; Oakes, 1985). As a result of these judgments, the access that different students have to mathematics and science knowledge diverges early in their school careers. In elementary schools, students who appear to be slow to catch on to mathematics are often placed in "slow" groups or remedial programs; students who learn more easily are placed in "fast" groups or high-ability classes. At the senior high level, judgments about students' ability influence decisions about curriculum track enrollment—whether students take college preparatory, general, or vocational courses of study. Curriculum track enrollment, in turn, is a critical factor in course taking (Lee, 1986; Rock, Braun, & Rosenbaum, 1984, 1985) and in the nature of curriculum content, instructional practices, and learning environments students' experience (Oakes, 1985). Data from A Study of Schooling (Goodlad, 1984) and the Second International Math Study (McKnight et al., 1987), for example, show that upper level mathematics classes focused more on mathematical concepts; low-level classes focused almost exclusively on computational skills and math facts.

Track-level differences in content and pace of instruction in elementary schools affect what and how much students actually learn. In particular, students who are not in the top classes appear to learn less because of these placements (Barr & Dreeben, 1983; Hallinan & Sorensøn, 1983; Slavin, 1986). The result is that some students leave elementary school already having had learning opportunities that prepare them for high school mathematics concepts and skills; others still lack understanding and skill in basic facts and operations.

In secondary schools, tracking also works against students in low-ability classes or non-college-preparatory groups (see, e.g., reviews by Calfee & Brown, 1979; Esposito, 1973; Findley & Bryan, 1971; Noland, 1986; Rosenbaum, 1980). National data suggest that students who are similar in background and aptitude exhibit widening achievement differences following their placements in higher and lower tracks (Alexander, Cook, & McDill, 1978; Alexander & McDill, 1976; Gamoran, 1986). The net effect appears to be cumulative, because students' track placements tend to be fixed and long term. Students placed in low-ability groups in elementary school are likely to continue in these tracks in middle schools and junior highs; typically they are placed in non-college-preparatory tracks in senior high school (Rosenbaum, 1980; Oakes, 1985). At the senior high level, recent well-controlled studies provide evidence that this effect has been attributed largely to differences in student course taking that result from tracking (Lee & Bryk, 1986).

These findings about curriculum tracking raise the possibility that in schools' efforts to accommodate ability differences, schools may actually exacerbate the differences by limiting some students' opportunities to learn these subjects. These findings are particularly relevant for minorities' opportunities and achievement, because patterns of track placement tend to favor white students.

Course Offerings

The courses high schools offer also limit opportunity. This obvious conclusion is relevant because poor and minority students are more likely than others to attend schools with fewer offerings in mathematics and science. For example, in California, the number, size, and substance of the courses in the curriculum differ: the greater the percentage of minorities, the larger the low-track program, the poorer the students, the less rigorous the college preparatory program (California State Department of Education, 1984). High School and Beyond data also show that, nationally, schools serving poor and minority populations offer fewer advanced courses and more remedial courses in academic subjects, and that they have smaller academic tracks and larger vocational programs (Ekstrom et al., 1988; NCES, 1985b).

Advanced courses in mathematics and science are less likely to be taught at predominantly poor or minority schools (Matthews, 1984). NAEP data show that at schools with substantial black populations, students take fewer mathematics courses than at schools with substantial white populations (Jones, 1984).

These patterns of course offerings are undoubtedly influenced by the lower levels of mathematics and science achievement typically found at these schools. Schools respond to those differences with programs they see as educationally appropriate. Of particular interest here is that lower track math and science courses themselves may limit students' opportunities to learn science and mathematics. As noted earlier, placement in these programs continues a cycle of restricted content, diminished outcomes, and exacerbated differences between low-track students and their counterparts in higher tracks. Moreover, such placement does not appear to overcome students' deficiencies in mathematics and science. Important, too, is that the restricted courses available to students at predominantly poor and minority schools limit the math and science opportunities of the highly able students who attend these schools. They may be denied mathematics and science opportunities for which they are prepared simply because of the school they happen to attend.

Course Taking

In an earlier section, race- and gender-related differences in science and mathematics course taking were detailed. For minorities, course-taking differences result primarily from tracking practices and course offerings. For girls, lower rates of course taking appear to be by choice, rather than because of academic deficiencies.

Considerable evidence supports the influence of lower levels of course taking on achievement. A whole body of work exploring the "differential course-taking hypothesis" has been generated, particularly with the advent of large data bases (HSB and NAEP) that have enabled analysts to test models linking students' course taking with their scores on achievement tests. Other work suggests that course taking influences choices of a quantitative major in college (Sells, 1982) and persistence in that major (Boli et al., 1985).

Early studies of sex differences in mathematics achievement consistently found male superiority (Fennema, 1984). Because these studies used random samples enrolled in secondary schools, they included a population of males and females who had taken disproportionate numbers of mathematics courses; therefore, these conclusions should be viewed with caution. Unexplained findings of sex differences are less frequent in studies after the mid-1970s, as researchers began to control for students' course-taking histories (e.g., Fennema & Sherman, 1977, 1978). The most recent well-controlled analyses suggest that sex-related achievement differences are largely explained by greater course taking by boys than by girls (Pallas & Alexander, 1983). This relationship appears to hold even when prior mathematics achievement is controlled (Wolfle & Ethington, 1986).

This evidence about course-taking effects is consistent with evidence that whereas boys perform better on tests, they do not necessarily perform better in class as measured by teachers' grades. When girls do enroll in mathematics courses, their grades are as high as boys' (Benbow & Stanley, 1980, 1982; DeWolf, 1981; Pallas & Alexander, 1983). Some might argue that this occurs because only high ability girls actually enroll in advanced mathematics courses. NAEP data showing nearly equal mean mathematics achievement scores for 13-year-old boys and girls provide evidence counter to this argument. These NAEP data suggest that it is only after different course-taking patterns are evidenced that girls and boys exhibit different mathematics ability. However, these data do not explain the disproportionate percentage of boys among seventh grade, early SAT takers who attain exceedingly high scores (Benbow & Stanley, 1982). One might speculate, however, that among this small fraction of students, the boys may have had greater encouragement and out-of-school math experiences.

Analyses of both NAEP and HSB data have found that differences in the number of high school courses taken by blacks and whites account for many of the differences between their mathematics and science achievement (Jones, 1984; Jones, Davenport, Bryson, Bekhuis, & Zwick, 1986). Similar findings for Hispanics and whites have come from analyses of the Longitudinal Study of Youth Labor Force Behavior (Moore & Smith, 1985).

But the number of courses taken is not enough to explain the full impact of course taking on either girls or minorities. Minority and white differences are also found in the level or type of courses taken (Jones, 1984; Moore & Smith, 1985). As we have seen, blacks and Hispanics are disproportionately found in low-level high school mathematics and science courses, whites in advanced courses (NCES, 1985c; Peng, Owings, & Fetters, 1981). In analyses of HSB data, differences among these groups in senior year achievement are fully explained by achievement differences in the sophomore year and by representation of these groups in different types of math courses. Whites' superior performance is explained by their higher 10th grade achievement and their disproportionately higher rates of enrollment in advanced math classes (Jones, 1985). At the postsecondary level, too, the level as well as the number of courses taken in high school is an important factor in subsequent achievement and participation, with completion of calculus predicting success and persistence in college mathematics (Peng et al., 1981; Sells, 1982).

For all students, course taking is the most powerful school-related predictor of achievement, particularly in mathematics (see, e.g., Welch et al., 1982). Science course taking has considerably smaller effects on students' science achievement test scores. However, this finding is less relevant to adult participation because mathematics achievement is far more critical in students' eligibility to pursue science-related majors in college.

Precollege course taking is key to the participation discrepancies for both minorities and women. However, for women, choices appear to be the critical factor. Until high school, girls as a group achieve in mathematics at levels equivalent to boys. Although current analyses do not permit us to know for sure, we can probably be confident that relatively equal numbers of both sexes are qualified for advanced mathematics and science course sequences as they enter high school and complete minimum college entrance requirements. However, girls who are academically qualified more often choose not to take more advanced mathematics and science course offerings. Blacks and Hispanics, in contrast, are most affected by academic deficiencies. On average, these groups fall behind early, are less likely to have opportunities that prepare them for advanced work, and less often qualify for advanced high school courses. These differences suggest that changing course-taking patterns will be far more difficult for minorities than for girls.

Teacher Expectations, Teaching Strategies, and Classroom Activities

More than simply being enrolled, what students actually experience in their science and mathematics classrooms, from the earliest grades through senior high school, will influence what they learn and whether they continue along the precollege mathematics and science pipeline. The quality of these experiences will be determined by factors including the following: what instructional goals and objectives teachers hope to accomplish; what knowledge and processes teachers make available for students to learn; what books, materials, and equipment are used to aid student learning; what classroom learning activities teachers arrange; what expectations teachers hold for their students' success; and how teachers interact with their students. These dimensions of classrooms work together to create opportunities for students to learn and the extent of different opportunities offered to various groups. Some dimensions have been researched with respect to group differences; many have not.

Evidence suggests that students' experiences are likely to differ both between classrooms and between students within the same classroom, and that these differences contribute to unequal participation for minorities and women. In the previous section, we noted one of the most critical differences, that is, that minorities are more likely to experience lower level science and mathematics content as a consequence of their placement in remedial or nonacademic classes. In this section, we consider differences in teacher expectations, teacher behaviors and classroom activities, and differences in how various groups of students respond to the opportunities that are provided.

Different Teacher Expectations

Differences in the expectations school adults hold for whites and middle-class children, and those they hold for girls, blacks, Hispanics, and poor children have been well documented (see Persell, 1977, for a review). Some expectation differences coincide with school tracking practices, with students in lower track classrooms—disproportionately minority students—typically expected to do less well (Oakes, 1985; Page, 1987). Expectations can also differ for various students within the same class. Teachers frequently have higher educational expectations for boys than for girls (Good, Sikes, & Brophy, 1973; Hilton & Berglund, 1974), and believe that boys are better than girls at math (Casserly, 1980). One study of elementary teachers found that almost half believed that boys were better than girls at math, and none believed that girls were better (Ernest, 1980). The findings of these latter studies should be viewed with caution because much discussion of higher expectations for girls has occurred during the past decade. It is possible that expressed differences in expectation have diminished.

That expectations can influence students' attainment is well known. [See, e.g., the series of studies following Rosenthal and Jacobson, 1968, and the more recent literature on effective schools (e.g., Purkey & Smith, 1983; Rowan, Bossert, & Dwyer, 1984).] When teachers differentiate expectations on the basis of race or gender, these expectations are likely to erect barriers for minorities and girls. In addition, Persell (1977) concludes from her review of the teacher expectation literature that the less powerful social positions of lower class and minority children result in their being more influenced by teacher expectations. The same hypothesis might be raised about girls.

Studies of how teacher expectations influence student outcomes have resulted in several findings. Persell (1977) offers two central differences in teaching behaviors that result from teacher expectations and influence achievement: the amount of material taught, and the number and type of teacher-pupil interactions. Brophy and Good (1974) found that teachers gave those students for whom they had high expectations more praise when students were correct and less criticism when students were wrong. Kester and Letchworth (1972) found that teachers were more friendly and encouraging with "bright" students. The studies noted in the following section suggest how these differences might affect the science- and math-related attitudes and achievement of underrepresented groups.

Differentiated Teacher Behaviors and Classroom Activities

Several studies document that minority students and girls have different classroom experiences in science and mathematics. Because minority children are disproportionately enrolled in low-level classes in these subjects, differences in teacher behaviors associated with tracking may be a factor in their lower achievement and participation. For example, teachers of high-track classes have been found to spend more time in class on instruction, and they expect their students to spend more time doing homework. Teachers in high-level classes also tend to be more enthusiastic, to present instruction more clearly, and to use ridicule and strong criticism less frequently (Oakes, 1985). These differences undoubtedly enhance the learning opportunities for students in more advanced classes. Also, NAEP data indicate that black students have fewer science experiences in their classrooms (Kahle & Lakes, 1983), as may all students attending predominantly minority schools (Kahle, Matyas, & Cho, 1985). We lack research, however, that examines the effects of these differences on student outcomes.

More research has looked at gender-related differences, and notable differences have been found in elementary and junior high mathematics and science instruction. NAEP data show that boys tend to have more experiences with science equipment and with different kinds of science instruments in elementary school science classrooms than girls, even though girls say they would like to use them (Kahle & Lakes, 1983). Other studies have found that teachers interact with boys more frequently than with girls during mathematics instruction and encourage boys more in both science and mathematics (Becker, 1981; Brophy & Good, 1974; Leinhardt, Seewald, & Engel, 1979; Sadker & Sadker, 1986). These differences have been particularly noticeable among groups of high-ability students (Eccles et al., 1986; Parsons, Kaczala, & Meece, 1982). Even when the number of interactions do not differ for boys and girls, other important distinctions may exist in the type of interactions. For example, Eccles et al. (1986) found that in the middle grades (5 through 9) girls for whom teachers had high expectations for success were subjected to more public criticisms, whereas their male counterparts received the most public affirmations. At the same time, some middle-grade teachers spent more time interacting with students for whom they had low expectations. Here, too, gender differences were found, with teachers more critical of boys of whom they expected less and giving more praise to girls. Finally, teachers at this level have been found to gravitate toward groups of boys in sex-segregated classrooms (Sadker & Sadker, 1986).

At the high school level, math teachers have also been observed to initiate more interactions with boys and provide more specific feedback to them (Stallings, 1985).

The actual effects of these gender-related differences in classroom opportunities and teacher interactions are unclear. Despite the apparent effects of teacher expectations, research has not yet firmly established that differences in teacher behaviors actually influence students' attitudes, achievement, or future enrollment in mathematics (Stage et al., 1985; Stallings, 1985). There is evidence, however, that gender differences in science attitudes and future enrollments may be lessened by some teachers. For example, in a study of biology classes taught by teachers who had previously taught girls, many of whom went on to study chemistry and to choose science-oriented majors in college, both boys and girls had very positive feelings about and experiences with biology materials. Further, girls in these classes indicated that they felt more confident and successful on NAEP items than had 17-year-old girls in general in the 1983 NAEP sample. Experience with these teachers, however, did not overcome all gender-related attitude differences: Boys still reported greater interest in science-related careers than did girls (Kahle et al., 1985). Unfortunately, other than the fact that the girls in these classes reported they had participated in biology-related classroom experiences as much as boys, we know little about what these teachers did to encourage girls.

Student Responses to Instruction

A third line of work has explored the possibility that different participation rates may be influenced by differences in the way various groups of students respond to teaching behaviors and classroom activities. If groups respond differently, and if the most commonly used instructional methods are those that elicit more positive responses from whites and boys, then unequal participation and performance might be linked to the widespread use of methods that favor this group.

Science and math teaching at all levels—and increasingly from elementary to secondary levels—is dominated by textbooks, teacher lectures, workbook exercises, and writing answers to questions (Goodlad, 1984). These strategies generally focus on presenting knowledge and skills in isolation, rather than in the context of real-life problem-solving. For example, though textbooks may do a good job of presenting the steps of the "scientific method" as a list of rules, they do less well providing students with opportunities to actually apply these models for scientific inquiry. Johnston and Aldridge (1984) suggest that the abstract character of instruction may be a fundamental problem in science and mathematics education. That is, high school science and math are taught as an introduction to the topics that the students will again encounter in college; and these courses may be so abstract that students who do not have the (abstract) reasoning skills or high interest or external motivation (family expectations) find them dull and difficult. Consequently, many students may conclude, perhaps incorrectly, that they are unable to succeed in or learn science. The result of the attempt to gear high school science courses toward college preparation is that courses are focused on abstract science and are largely devoid of practical applications, technology, or the relevance of science to society and its problems (Johnston & Aldridge, 1984).

Work cited earlier suggests that minorities and women may have a greater interest in people than in things, and that these groups may respond more positively to ideas in context (field dependence) than in isolation (field independence). This work, then, also suggests that these groups may respond more negatively than white males do to the type of math and science instruction just described. There is also direct evidence that boys benefit from conventional teaching strategies (e.g., whole class instruction and competitive reward structures), and girls and minorities benefit from strategies using cooperative and hands-on activities. For example, in an attempt to identify "girl friendly" elementary classrooms, Eccles et al. (1986) found that girls in competitive classrooms with frequent public criticism had attitudes toward mathematics less positive than boys' attitudes, whereas few or no gender differences were found in classrooms where few social comparisons were made. Peterson and Fennema (1985) found that competitive classroom activities contributed to boys' mathematics achievement, but were detrimental to girls' achievement. In contrast, cooperative activities contributed to girls' acquisition of basic math topics and skills and to their achievement on high-level math tasks. Yet these cooperative activities did not hinder boys' attitudes or achievement.

The conclusion we can draw from these analyses is that although there are no documented sex-related achievement differences in elementary school, the different effects of classroom activities may have an effect on girls' attitudes and decisions about math. Also, the competitive teaching practices employed by many junior high math teachers may increase these effects. This implies that conventional teaching strategies lead to early gender differences in attitudes which, in turn, lead to later gender-related differences in participation.

Other evidence documents that nontraditional instruction can also be more effective for minority children. Black and Hispanic children tend to succeed better in classrooms featuring cooperative, small groups (Au & Jordan, 1981; Cohen & De Avila, 1983; Slavin, 1985; Slavin & Oickle, 1981) and experience-based instruction (Cohen & De Avila, 1983). This work is consistent with recent analyses of the effectiveness of activity-based science curricula (e.g., those developed by the Elementary Science Study, Science—A Process Approach, and the Science Curriculum Improvement Study). These analyses conclude that, although all students profit from such curricula, disadvantaged students make exceptional gains in their understanding of science processes, knowledge of science content, and logical development when activity-based methods are used (Bredderman, 1983). As noted earlier, theories that black and Hispanic children favor relational learning environments (those that involve other people) and field-dependent learning tasks (those that focus on whole concepts or real situations rather than fragmented skills or abstractions) (Gilbert & Gay, 1985; Ramirez & Casteneda, 1974) may help explain why these untypical classroom approaches are more effective.

Perhaps an even more important factor in girls' and minorities' classroom opportunities is that science instruction gets pushed to the back burner of elementary schooling. Recent surveys of teachers found that on the average children in grades K–3 spend only about 1 1/2 hours a week learning science, and those in grades 4–6 spend less than 3 hours a week (Goodlad, 1984; I. Weiss, personal communication, 1987). Moreover, elementary teachers often feel uncomfortable with science. Finally, because science is not usually included on tests that measure children's basic skills, it often receives less attention than subjects that are tested. Some elementary teachers don't teach science at all. The lack of attention to science may be particularly detrimental to girls and minorities, because they have far fewer opportunities to participate in science-related activities outside school (Kahle & Lakes, 1983).

Conclusions: The Role of Schooling Experiences

Trends in adult attainments in scientific and technical fields in college and occupational choice reflect equally disturbing trends in elementary and secondary schooling experiences. Race and gender discrepancies in opportunities to learn math and science begin early and appear to increase over time in school. They become most evident in secondary school, when curriculum tracking and course selection are available to students, with women and non-Asian minorities having less access to advice and encouragement in mathematics and science, and enrolling in fewer courses and lower level courses than white males and Asians (NCES, 1985c). However, differences in secondary school course-taking patterns are preceded by more subtle differences in students' experiences in elementary classrooms.

Of course, evidence that unequal schooling experiences parallel achievement and participation differences, is, in itself, insufficient to establish that the differences in schooling experiences are their cause. And, unfortunately, little of the research described earlier examines the effects of group differences in these important classroom dimensions on students' outcomes. Clearly, differences in students' access to school resources, guidance and counseling, science and mathematics knowledge, and classroom experiences do represent critical and policy-relevant interactions of student characteristics and opportunities that may play a crucial role in achievement and decisions to pursue science.

POSSIBLE CAUSES AND CONSEQUENCES: SOCIETAL INFLUENCES

Much has been written about the very real disadvantages that poor children bring to school with them and about how these disadvantages may influence school performance. The low economic status of most blacks and Hispanics is a major consideration in understanding minority students' opportunities, achievement, and choices. In addition, both past *de jure* and remaining *de facto* discrimination may influence minority students' access to high quality schooling and jobs and may erect barriers to students' aspirations and attainments. In regard to women, growing numbers of scholars and women's advocate groups have argued that gender-related differences in societal expectations and childhood socialization create important obstacles to women's confidence, ambitions, and career attainments. For women, too, work force discrimination may work against their choosing to enter scientific fields. In this section is a brief overview of what is known about the relationship of these social and economic factors to students' schooling opportunities, achievement levels, and choices regarding science and mathematics.

Socioeconomic Factors

Family Status

A great deal of work has demonstrated the connection between students' SES and their performance on a wide range of measures of academic achievement (e.g., grades, standardized achievement and aptitude tests) and their schooling attainment. Specifically related to math and science, Welch et al.'s (1982) analysis of NAEP data found that home and community background factors accounted for 24% of the variance in the math achievement of individual 17-year-olds. Similarly, recent analyses of HSB data show students' SES (defined by parents' education levels, father's occupation, family income, and household possessions) accounts for much of the difference in mathematics achievement (Ekstrom et al., 1988). Parallels are found as well in SAT scores of college-bound students (College Board, 1985). Analyses of NAEP data also suggest that attitudes and SES are related, with children of better educated parents exhibiting more positive attitudes toward mathematics (Tsai & Walberg, 1983). Other work links minorities' and women's high school performance and postsecondary plans with their families' affluence or poverty (Chipman & Thomas, 1984; Dunteman, Wisenbaker, & Taylor, 1979).

Socioeconomic status is particularly important in understanding racial and ethnic differences in achievement and participation, because many of the poorest children in this country are black and Hispanic. Almost half of all black children live in families with incomes below the poverty line, and black family incomes have shown steady declines relative to white family incomes over the past two decades (U.S. Bureau of the Census, 1987a) along with rising black unemployment rates (Bureau of Labor Statistics, 1983). Even though employment opportunities for minorities have improved over the past three decades, minorities with jobs are most likely to be found in the lowest paying and lowest status positions within their occupations (Westcott, 1982). Hispanic children have socioeconomic disadvantages similar to blacks.

Evidence that SES may be a critical factor in race-related achievement differences can be drawn from data about Asians. Asian-American students are usually considered an anomaly among racial and ethnic minorities. They have the highest rate of participation and achievement in quantitative fields of any of the racial and ethnic subgroups of American students and are significantly overrepresented in scientific careers (Berryman, 1983; NCES, 1985b). In the HSB sample, however, the high levels of achievement and participation for Asian students are paralleled by distinct advantages in their home backgrounds. Asian-American students in the HSB sample had the best-educated parents (both fathers and mothers) of any group, participated most in out-of-school educational activities (music lessons, travel, museum experiences), and were most likely to own microcomputers. Only white families equaled Asians in ownership of other educational resources, such as books, newspapers, calculators, and so forth. Other minority groups lagged far behind on all these measures of home advantages.

Parents' education. Some analysts have posited that SES measures such as occupation and income are important primarily because they signal parent education levels, and that parent education is the most important predictor of women's and minorities' school success and participation in mathematics and science (Berryman, 1983; Malcom, George, & Matyas, 1985). For example, Berryman found that being a second-generation college student equalized the likelihood of choosing quantitative majors across groups of non-Asian minority and white college students. Moreover, she found this education effect for minority students whose parents had *any* amount of college experience (Berryman, 1983).

Parents' education has also been found to be important to women's achievement and participation in science. Women coming from more privileged backgrounds are more likely to choose scientific majors (Thomas, 1984; Ware et al., 1985), and female science majors (more than males) tend to have mothers employed in a relatively high prestige occupation (Ware & Lee, 1985). For example, a study of engineering majors at the University of Wisconsin found that among otherwise similar students, the females' fathers were more highly educated (2 to 4 years of college) than the males' fathers (high school) (Greenfield et al., 1982). Further, mother's and father's education levels have been found to relate to women's persistence in scientific majors (Ware et al., 1985).

SES and achievement. The relationship between achievement and SES may not be as clear-cut as many analyses may suggest. White's (1982) careful meta-analytic review of 200 studies reveals important insights about the SES and achievement relationship. White found, for example, that although the relationship is positive and strong (an average of 0.70) when aggregate units of analysis are used (e.g., school or district), it is considerably weaker when individual students are the unit (an average of 0.20). Also, different SES measures yield considerably different results. The relationships appear to be weakest in studies using traditional measures (e.g., education, income, occupation of head of household, and education) and strongest when more behavioral family characteristics are used (e.g., home atmosphere).

White's findings are considerably more optimistic than much work linking SES and achievement, because it points to two directions for further investigation and intervention. First, White's finding that SES is only weakly related to achievement when individual students are the unit of analysis indicates that there is a great deal of variance in the achievement of individuals within SES groups, and that not all poor children are low achievers. White's parallel finding is that, at aggregate levels (schools and districts), SES is rather strongly related to achievement. Taken together, these findings suggest that the SES and achievement relationship found at the aggregate level is likely to be influenced by more than simply the characteristics of individual students. These findings suggest that researchers attempting to explain the relationships found at the school and district level must also examine how school and district characteristics may affect this relationship. Obviously, the schooling factors described in the previous section are good candidates for such work. If found to be important, such characteristics are more likely to be altered by schooling policies and practices than are characteristics of children's families.

Second, White found that the SES variables measuring home atmosphere (e.g., parents' attitude toward education, parents' aspirations for their children, cultural and intellectual activities of families) are more strongly related to student achievement than are status variables such as occupation, income, and education. Although home environment characteristics such as parent-child interactions are not likely to be easily altered by education policy and school programs, they appear to be more tractable than income or parents' education themselves, and more easily improved than other effects of poverty, such as inadequate child health and nutrition. Therefore, White's findings provide a ray of hope for those seeking strategies for improving outcomes for poor children.

Parents' Involvement and Expectations

White's findings are consistent with other work suggesting that parents' involvement can be an important influence on student achievement and participation both at the elementary (Epstein & Becker, 1982) and secondary school levels (Fehrmann, Keith, & Reimers, 1987). This relationship has also been found in studies specifically focusing on women and minorities. For example, Ware and Lee (1985) found that women science majors more often than their male counterparts had parents who were involved in their high school academic activities. And Berryman's (1983) analyses showed that parents' education affects minorities' choice of quantitative majors through its effects on their high school performance and postsecondary education plans. These findings led Berryman to reason that parents' education is probably critical to minority participation, because parents who have been to college are more likely to expect that their child will also attend, and will put him or her on the road to college early. These parents are more likely to understand and encourage the kinds of precollege training necessary for a successful college career. Moreover, children whose parents have been to college have already had the "white collar barrier" broken and will have more career options open to them—that is, they will have been exposed to more different kinds of majors and adult careers (Berryman, 1983).

Ware et al. (1985) made similar speculations based on their findings that parents' education has a more positive relationship with persistence in science majors for women than for men. They hypothesized that highly educated parents expect their children to go to college, and they are more likely to afford educational advantages. Perhaps more important, these parents may convey to their daughters less conventional ideas about appropriate behavior for women, and may be more willing to encourage their daughters in nontraditional pursuits (Ware et al., 1985).

These hypotheses are supported by other work that explores differences in parents' expectations and the significance of parents' views on students' interests and perceptions of their own abilities. In one study, for example, white and Asian females reported far less often than other students that their parents thought that math was important to get a good job. (Much higher percentages of black females reported their parents voiced such opinions.) Although all race and gender groups reported that their parents wanted them to do well in math, white and Asian males reported in far greater proportions that their parents wanted them to take advanced math courses (Matthews, 1980). Three more recent studies strengthen the evidence about a link between parent perceptions and students' own attitudes. These studies found that even when girls' performance equals or exceeds that of boys, parents believe that girls find math more difficult and think that higher math courses are more important for boys than for girls. Despite what appear to be objective inaccuracies in these parent beliefs, they were related to students' perceptions of their own math ability, future expectations, and course-taking plans (Yee, Jacobs, & Goldsmith, 1986).

Discrimination

Many of the achievement and participation differences between minorities and whites disappear when family income and parents' education are controlled. Nevertheless, SES does not fully explain the poorer performance of minorities. For example, NAEP data show that differences in science achievement between minority and white senior high students persist even when SES, school experiences, and prior achievement are controlled (Armstrong, 1985; Walberg, Fraser, & Welch, 1986). A similar unexplained achievement difference is related to gender (Chipman & Thomas, 1984; Fennema & Carpenter, 1981; Maccoby & Jacklin, 1974; Stage et al., 1985).

Real and perceived race and sex discrimination may be relevant to these unexplained differences. For minorities, discrimination in access to education may contribute to these students' lower aspirations and efforts. That past discrimination has limited minorities' life chances is supported by important recent evidence that as minorities have gained greater access to education, their overall economic and social position has improved substantially (Smith & Welch, 1986). Consequently, educational access appears to be a key to adult accomplishments. To the extent that de facto discrimination in educational access still exists, it may continue to constrain minority achievement and participation.

For both minorities and women, past and continuing work force discrimination may also be a factor. Historically, even equally well-educated women and minorities have been unable to market their achievements in the work place with returns equal to those of white males. For example, neither women nor minorities (including high-achieving Asian-Americans) have been able to translate school attainments into commensurate employment or salary rates (U.S. Commission on Civil Rights, 1978). The more recent data on race- and gender-linked differences in unemployment, underutilization, and salaries among scientists noted previously suggests that real or perceived discrimination may exist within the scientific work force (Block, in NSF, 1988).

Although little direct evidence is available, more general theoretical work to be described in the next section suggests that the social and economic consequences of discrimination influence race and gender differences in parents' aspirations, students' attitudes, and self-perceptions. Anticipation of employment discrimination and, for women, the difficulty of combining the demands of science careers with other social and cultural expectations may play a significant role in shaping these attitudes (Chipman & Thomas, 1984). Empirical evidence documents that perceptions of job opportunities can be an important factor in the college major choices of black college men (Thomas, 1984). Moreover, attitudes such as the perceived utility of mathematics and science, and the stereotyping of these subjects as the purview of white males, flow logically from these social conditions.

Conclusions: The Influence of Societal Factors

The importance of societal factors on the attainments of women and minorities cannot be overlooked. Undoubtedly, they play a significant role in race and gender differences in achievement and decisions to pursue science. Although much literature has documented the relationship of socioeconomic factors to student achievement, opportunities, and choices, less work has explored the mechanisms through which societal factors may actually have these effects. However, recent work, although not directly related to math and science attainment, provides insight into how out-of-school factors may influence students' attitudes and behaviors that relate to their school achievement. This work allows speculation about possible interactions among societal factors and minority students' science and mathematics achievement and participation.

Psychological research, for example, supports the idea that environmental conditions influence children's beliefs about their prospects for success and about the rewards they can expect from their efforts. This work also suggests that self-perceptions and expectations can affect their school performance. Self-efficacy (closely related to confidence in ability, described earlier) depends in part on two factors: first, how responsive the environment is to an individual's attempts to gain rewards; and second, the perceptions of others about that person's efficaciousness. When individuals are placed in subordinate roles or given labels that imply inferiority or incompetence, their self-efficacy and performance are often affected negatively (Bandura, 1982). This work supports the notion that students respond to school in ways that seem reasonable to them, given the messages schools and larger society send them about their prospects for school success and the rewards they might expect from the hard work that success requires. For poor minorities and girls, the messages about science and mathematics can be discouraging.

For example, most middle-class children and their families—minority and white—expect that school success will bring real-life rewards in the form of good jobs and salaries. The promise of these rewards motivates them to work hard to succeed in school. In their homes and neighborhoods, most of these children have parents and friends who were successful at school and who expect them to do as well, and for many these expectations are echoed by the adults at school. These children have daily reminders of the economic and social payoffs that educational achievement can bring. Although these factors don't automatically make schools serving middle-class children successful (indeed many such schools have considerable difficulties), these expectations about the consequences of schooling certainly ease the schools' task.

On the other hand, many minority children in central cities have little real-life experience to support such beliefs and expectations. Some may know few adults who have achieved at school or who have translated school achievement into economic gain. On the other hand, they may know many streetwise teenagers and adults who exchange their informal knowledge and skills for success "on the street" (Valentine, 1979; Weiss, 1985). In many central city schools, for example, teachers and administrators may not be salient models for success, particularly if they don't live in the communities where they teach, or if they have little contact with children's families. Moreover, these school adults may have only modest expectations for the school success and future prospects of inner-city children. Some urban minority children have neither churches nor community organizations to support their school efforts and provide contacts with successful, educated adults. These conditions undoubtedly affect children's beliefs about what they can expect from schooling, and they make the task of schools far more difficult.

Perhaps due in part to their meager employment prospects, the lack of supportive community institutions, and their isolation from children and adults who have anything better, many poor, minority children and their parents may respond to school opportunities quite differently from those in more privileged communities. These responses may contribute to young children's lower levels of academic achievement in general; to adolescents' higher rates of truancy, inattention, misbehavior, and dropping out; and to low rates of participation in science and mathematics.

Yale psychiatrist James Comer (1985) suggests that the psychological and social distance between schooling and poor, minority children's larger environments and its potentially negative consequences for schooling was not the case for earlier generations of poor children. Unlike today's isolated, inner-city children, the families of earlier generations of poor, minority children worked and sometimes lived among the middle class—providing daily models of a better way of life:

Employment opportunities generally played a major role in enabling families to feel they were a part of the American mainstream and in motivating them to embrace its attitudes, values, and ways. As a result, children from such families had access to social networks of experience, information, and opportunities that facilitated good education and future opportunities for them. (Comer, 1985, p. 246)

These conditions create a context that education policy alone can do little to change—a context shaped by racism, poverty, unemployment, and isolation that hinder many minority children's school attainment. At the same time, as noted earlier, schooling remains the best opportunity available to poor, minority students for gaining the knowledge and skills to interrupt the predictable cycles of poverty, undereducation, unemployment, and social disintegration.

The Nexus of Race, Class, and Schooling

Although societal factors undoubtedly influence the educational attainments of minorities and women, these background characteristics do not operate independently of students' experiences in schools. The evidence about schooling differences cited in the previous section suggests that schools, too, respond to race, class, and gender in ways that exacerbate the difficulties of girls and minorities in science and mathematics. Most likely, it is the coming together of individual student characteristics, societal influences, and schooling opportunities that is most relevant to understanding and improving the participation of underrepresented groups.

Some analysts have hypothesized that both schooling opportunities and students' responses to schooling (e.g., effort and achievement) are influenced by the current social milieu that holds particular norms and expectations about different groups of students. If this is the case, schools' definitions of individual differences and decisions about what opportunities should be provided to different students may be influenced by societal as well as educational factors. For example, Reyes and Stanic (1988) suggest that societal factors influence student outcomes through their direct effects on teacher attitudes, school mathematics curricula, and students' attitudes and achievement-related positive behavior (e.g., course taking), and through their indirect effects on classroom processes and student achievement. A similar model suggested by Oakes (1987) links factors in the larger society to student outcomes through their influence on structure and climate of individual schools.

Although causal links among these hypothesized relationships have yet to be explored, evidence about the uneven distribution of schooling opportunities to women and minorities is consistent with the view that students' race, gender, and SES characteristics may affect the schooling opportunities that are available to them.

Causes and Consequences: An Optimistic Finding

Despite the wealth of studies describing differences among racial and gender groups in individual characteristics, school experiences, and societal factors, we have developed relatively little understanding of how race- and gender-related differences are produced. Nonetheless, taken together, one rather optimistic conclusion appears to be supported by this batch of diverse studies. Both in and out of school, those resources, experiences, and attitudes that encourage and support white boys in mathematics and science also appear to encourage girls, minorities, and poor students. For example, in nearly all studies, factors such as prior achievement, course taking, expectations of parents and school adults, academically oriented peers, interest in science and math, perceived future relevance of these subjects for career and life goals, and confidence in ability emerge as related to the achievement and participation for all groups of students. In other words, what produces educational attainment for white boys also works well for girls, minorities, and poor students.

Moreover, analysts who have modeled how various factors influence achievement find similar processes at work across race and gender categories. Recent studies (Wolfle, 1985; Wolfle & Ethington, 1986) have used structural equation methods to determine whether the process of attainment is similar across groups. This work is particularly important given previous research suggesting that the processes of educational attainment are different for blacks and whites (see, e.g., Kerckhoff & Campbell, 1977; Porter, 1974; Portes & Wilson, 1976), and some speculation that females may need educational experiences different from those of males.

Using data from the National Longitudinal Study (NLS) and HSB, Wolfle (1985; Wolfle & Ethington, 1986) has demonstrated that few differences exist in the factors that lead to achievement of various groups or in the relative importance of those factors. His studies find, for example, that across racial groups, SES influences ability; that ability is the best predictor of placement in an academic curriculum, with social background factors having a far more modest direct effect; and that placement in an academic track is the most important predictor of postsecondary attainment for both blacks and whites. Moreover, equal changes in either social background variables or within-school variables lead to the same outcomes for both groups. These analyses suggest strongly that the process of educational attainment is the same for both blacks and whites.

Other studies support these findings. Jones (1985) found the relationship between senior year math scores and a composite of predictors, including course taking, to be the same for all racial and gender groups. And, in a similar study, Ware and Lee (1985) found the same model to be useful for explaining achievement among HSB male and female seniors, even though the model was a slightly stronger predictor for males.

The importance of this work is that it suggests that race- and gender-related differences may be caused less by some unique needs of women or minorities than by the fact that they typically have less access to the positive factors that favor high achievement and continued participation in general. This is critical to understanding the causes of low achievement and underrepresentation and to developing interventions to increase participation.

ISSUES FOR FURTHER RESEARCH

The participation of women and minorities in science is a complex and multidimensional issue. Consequently, it is not surprising that the research to date has been uneven, both in its coverage of all the relevant dimensions of the problem and in the understanding it provides. Several analyses have described well how women differ in their mathematics achievement, attitudes, and experiences (both in and out of school), and have examined these differences at critical points in women's schooling and in their careers. However, other areas have not received as much attention. Little is known about women's achievement and participation in science, and even less is known about racial minorities' participation in math and science. Among minority groups, less is known about Hispanics and other minorities than blacks. Few researchers have investigated the impact of various intervention strategies aimed at increasing participation. Few studies explore the conditions under which particular types of strategies are likely to be effective.

The existing work provides many clues about factors that are strongly associated with various groups of students' progress, or failure to progress, through the educational pipeline. We have learned that opportunities to learn mathematics and science, achievement in these subjects, and choices about whether to pursue study in scientific fields are central to whether students participate in scientific endeavors as adults. These factors also seem to be central to the level of scientific literacy students attain. Yet many gaps remain in our understanding of what causes group differences in opportunities, achievement, and choices. Neither do we know how differences along one of these dimensions relates to the others (e.g., how the presence or absence of various learning opportunities may influence choices). These gaps result in part because little research exploring race and gender differences has been experimental or has included longitudinal data. Where longitudinal data have been available, albeit rather limited in both time span and number of relevant variables included (e.g., recent HSB data on senior high school students), analysts have been able to provide more useful data about the determinants of participation (e.g., the link between course taking and achievement).

However, part of the difficulty lies in the complexity of the problem itself. Although we have learned a great deal about associations among a wide range of variables that, on the surface at least, seem to be linked with participation for particular groups, the issue is unlikely to be unravelled by the manipulation of empirical data alone. More promising would be work that is guided more by general theory of how race- and gender-related differences in participation might be produced. Because we currently lack such work, we have no grounds for interpreting the relationships among variables that are found, for suggesting what underlying processes and conditions may create group differences, or for speculating about what processes and conditions might be altered to effectively increase participation. As a result of these limitations, analysts have had difficulty interpreting findings and deriving trustworthy policy implications from them.

Future research should fill these gaps. We need additional basic research on how individual factors (such as cognitive style and self-efficacy) may be linked to race, ethnicity, and gender. Other work might profitably focus on societal issues such as family and community socialization.

Most essential for policymakers, however, is research on how alterable features of schooling may contribute to group differences and what changes in schooling may increase the achievement and participation of underrepresented groups. In future work of this kind, however, it will be important to push beyond the limits of much prior work. We should develop research designs that permit understanding the causes and consequences of race and gender differences, and we should encourage theoretical work that places the specifics of these differences into a larger framework. Promising directions for such policy-relevant research follow.

Analyses of Status and Trends in Participation

Of highest priority are continued and expanded efforts to monitor overall trends in the status of women and minorities in science and mathematics and to translate these data into indicators that are accessible to policymakers and educators. Currently, data generated by the Census, NSF surveys, the College Board, and the Department of Education's Center for Statistics enable analysts to chart the achievement, senior high course taking, college attendance, and degree attainments of blacks, Hispanics, and women. These national data bases have been central to our current understanding of participation. Moreover, proposed expansions in NAEP and the upcoming Department of Education's National Educational Longitudinal Study of 1988 (NELS) should permit even more comprehensive monitoring. NELS, for example, will provide much needed longitudinal data that begins with students' junior high school experiences.

Critical to the usefulness of these data bases for understanding participation, however, are sample sizes that permit the disaggregation of data by the full range of racial and ethnic groups, by gender groups within racial and ethnic groups, and by social class differences among these groups. Few data sets currently permit an examination of the experiences of important racial and ethnic subpopulations; typically Hispanics include Mexican-Americans, Central Americans, Puerto Ricans, and Cubans, and the Asian category usually includes such culturally diverse groups as Chinese, Vietnamese, Japanese, and Filipinos. Moreover, recent work has suggested that race, gender, and social class are inseparable and interactive influences on children's educational experiences, achievement, and occupational attainments, and that analyses that treat racial groups, gender groups, or social class groups as homogeneous oversimplify and mislead (Grant & Sleeter, 1986). Currently, however, few national data bases permit the analyses of achievement and participation differences by social class subgroups within minority groups.

Understanding School Conditions Related to Minority Participation

A second priority is new research that focuses on filling out our understanding of how schooling conditions may relate to minority students' learning opportunities, achievement, and decisions about their future careers. Of particular interest would be studies that examine how particular features of schooling interact with students' individual characteristics (e.g., attitudes) and social background characteristics (e.g., social class) to influence achievement and participation in science and mathematics. Such research should span the range of schooling—from children's earliest schooling experiences with science and mathematics through college students' decisions to select and persist in scientific fields.

Because most minorities are precluded from participating in mathematics and science by virtue of their low achievement levels, the most urgent need is to understand how schooling factors contribute to the achievement of black and Hispanic children in the earliest grades. Although national data bases provide evidence that increases in minority achievement, particularly among the youngest children, have steadily reduced the minority and white achievement gap over the past several years, we have little understanding of what schooling conditions led to these increases and how schools can foster further increases.

At the most basic level, we need good descriptive research to document the schooling experiences of blacks and Hispanics. Other issues, however, require applied research to identify schooling strategies that will boost achievement. The following questions might guide such work:

- What mathematics and science opportunities are provided to blacks, Hispanics, and other underrepresented minority students? How qualified are their teachers? How much time is spent on science and mathematics instruction? What teaching strategies are used? What facilities and materials are used? What is the curricular emphasis (e.g., basic skills instruction, experience-based activities, etc.)? What grouping strategies are used? What language is used for instructing bilingual students?
- What are the less tangible characteristics of minority schooling in science and mathematics (e.g., teachers' expectations and encouragement, academic guidance from counselors, career information, etc.)?
- Are there school-level differences in opportunities and effects for minority students? For example, are those minority students who attend predominantly minority schools disadvantaged in their opportunities and outcomes compared with those attending predominantly white schools? Does school SES make a difference in the opportunities provided?
- How do different school and classroom resources, curricula, and learning experiences affect students' attitudes (particularly confidence in abilities, perceived usefulness, and attributions for success and failure) toward science and mathematics? their achievement? their further participation in mathematics and science?
- What are the effects of various types of supplementary and compensatory school programs on early mathematics and science achievement? For example, what are the relative effects of basic skill instruction, activity-based learning experiences, small-group work, individual tutoring, and so forth?

- What are the effects of various school and classroom experiences on the decisions of high-achieving minorities to pursue study in quantitative fields?

Understanding School Conditions Related to Women's Participation

Unlike blacks and Hispanics, girls' achievement in mathematics and science does not prevent them, as a group, from pursuing advanced study in these fields. Although girls' mathematics achievement dips below that of boys at the senior high school level and is slightly lower in science in earlier grades, achievement differences alone are insufficient to explain the large disparities in participation between male and female students. We have considerable evidence of gender differences in attitudes toward math and science and that, for the most part, women are more negative about science and the role it might play in their future. However, there is little evidence about the role these attitudes play in later achievement differences or in decisions about future careers. Work is needed to explore how attitudes may work together with other individual and societal factors to contribute to women's lower participation.

Even more important for education policy purposes, we need a better understanding of how schooling conditions may contribute to these differences or interact with them to produce differences in achievement and choices. To examine these issues, questions similar to those listed in the previous section should be explored, with the focus on the effect of various school and classroom experiences on women's attitudes, achievement, and persistence. For example, researchers might want to pursue the following questions:

- What is the nature of girls' school and classroom experiences in science and mathematics (e.g., in classroom interactions, instructional strategies, access to science equipment and computers, teachers' expectations and encouragement, academic guidance from counselors, career information, etc.) compared with boys' experiences?
- How do different school and classroom experiences relate to girls' attitudes (particularly confidence in abilities, perceived usefulness, and attributions for success and failure) toward science and mathematics? to their achievement? to their further participation in mathematics and science?
- What are the effects of various school and classroom experiences on the decisions of high-achieving girls to pursue study in quantitative fields?

Here, as with research on minority participation, studies of girls' schooling experiences and their effects should span the range of elementary and secondary schooling.

Documenting and Understanding the Effectiveness of Interventions

Research is also needed to document which special intervention programs developed by schools, universities, museums, businesses, or communities in mathematics and science have effectively increased achievement among low-achieving minorities; increased further participation among high-achieving minorities; or increased persistence in scientific choices among girls and women.

This research should look not only at the effects of programs per se, but it should also identify the effects of various program types and particular program features. For example, we need answers to the following questions:

- What activities are characteristic of the most successful programs for increasing learning opportunities? achievement? choices? What formats are employed? What staffing patterns? What durations?
- What are the effects of mentor programs? What characterizes effective relationships between students and mentors? By what age should mentoring relationships begin?
- What are the effects of providing career information? in what form? at what age?
- What are the effects of role models? How effective are contacts with professional scientists and mathematicians? contacts with minority and female role models?
- What are the effects of early college experiences for highly able students? for average or low-achieving students?
- What are the effects of single-sex intervention environments on girls?
- What programs are suitable for regular classrooms? Which are most effective as extracurricular, after-school, or summer activities?
- How might parents be effectively involved in special mathematics and science intervention programs?
- What types of financial assistance or other incentives might be feasible and effective in encouraging poor minorities and women to choose scientific fields and persist in higher education?

In examining intervention strategies, researchers also will need to consider the ages at which particular strategies are most effective and differences in effectiveness of particular strategies directed at various racial and ethnic groups and at women. This line of research is likely to be particularly useful for suggesting ways schools can adapt their regular programs to achieve more successful outcomes. Investigation of intervention strategies should not neglect those that consider large-scale alterations of various schooling structures: tracking, age grading, the separation of academic from technological and vocational education.

Integrated Research on Race, Gender, and Social Class

As noted, recent work suggests that new studies will provide greater insight into race and gender differences and will be more useful in framing policy if they integrate analyses of race, gender, and social class—that is, if they consider the combined influences of students' multiple status characteristics, or if they enable analysts to disentangle typically confounded effects such as race and social class.

This conclusion is drawn from recent studies of gender differences within racial groups that have found different patterns in these subgroups. For example, although the overall pattern is that more boys enroll in advanced high school mathematics courses than do girls, the opposite pattern has been found among black students (Matthews, 1984). Also, national data show that even though more black women than men begin college studies in science and mathematics, fewer of them earn advanced degrees (NSF, 1986). Other work suggests that lower class minorities may follow patterns different from those with middle class status (Grant & Sleeter, 1986). Such analyses suggest that students' race, gender, and social class are all important for understanding the effects of different school conditions or for framing appropriate intervention strategies for various groups. Consequently, wherever possible, future studies of factors contributing to participation should consider all of students' relevant characteristics in collecting, analyzing, and reporting data.

Explaining Underparticipation

Finally, we badly need research that moves beyond simply describing patterns of differences among various groups to correlating those differences with participation. We need work that develops and tests new theories about how these differences are produced. Such work should be directed at explaining how individual, societal, and schooling factors contribute to lower achievement and participation among blacks and Hispanics and to women's lower rates of choosing these fields. Some tentative models have been suggested (Oakes, 1987; Peterson & Fennema, 1985; Reyes & Stanic, 1988), but they remain underdeveloped and largely untested. Moreover, these models are firmly grounded in current relationships among race, class, gender, and schooling. In a recent discussion of gender-related research, Marini (in press) suggests a more far-reaching direction for new theoretical work. She recommends that future model building break out of the immediate situational circumstances that shape participation for any one group. Rather, such work should develop and test theories that link group differences to more general theories about basic social processes, such as stratification and status organizing. Such theories could lead to research on mathematics and science participation as an example of these more fundamental social processes. This research could explain more fully why and how group differences in participation develop, and could provide a far more solid basis for interventions aimed at remedying race- and gender-related discrepancies.

REFERENCES

Alexander, K. L., & Cook, M. (1982). Curricula and coursework: A surprise ending to a familiar story. *American Sociological Review, 47,* 626–640.
Alexander, K. L., Cook, M., & McDill, E. L. (1978). Curriculum tracking and educational stratification: Some further evidence. *American Sociological Review, 43,* 47–66.
Alexander, K. L., & McDill, E. L. (1976). Selection and allocation within schools: Some causes and consequences of curriculum placement. *American Sociological Review, 41,* 963–980.
American Council on Education. (1983). Demographic imperatives: Implications for educational policy. Report on the June 8, 1983, forum *The Demographics of Changing Ethnic Populations and Their Implications for Elementary-Secondary and Postsecondary Educational Policy.* Washington, DC: American Council on Education.
Antonnen, R. G. (1969). A longitudinal study in mathematics attitude. *Journal of Educational Research, 62,* 467–471.
Armstrong, J. (1981). Achievement and participation of women in mathematics. *Journal for Research in Mathematics Education, 12,* 356–372.
Armstrong, J. M. (1980). *Achievement and participation in mathematics: An overview.* Washington, DC: National Institute of Education.
Armstrong, J. M. (1985). A national assessment of participation and achievement of women in mathematics. In S. F. Chipman, L. R. Brush, & D. M. Wilson (Eds.), *Women and mathematics: Balancing the equation,* Hillsdale, NJ: Lawrence Erlbaum Associates.
Armstrong, J. M., & Price, R. A. (1982). Correlates and predictors of women's mathematics participation. *Journal for Research in Mathematics Education, 13*(2), 99–109.
Au, K. H., & Jordan, C. (1981). Teaching reading to Hawaiian children: Finding a culturally appropriate solution. In H. Trueba & K. H. Au (Eds.), *Culture and the bilingual classroom: Studies in classroom ethnography.* Rowley, MA: Newbury House.
Bandura, A. (1982). Self-efficacy mechanism in human agency. *American Psychologist, 37,* 122–147.
Baratz, J. C., & Ficklen, M. (1983). *Participation of recent black college graduates in the labor market and graduate education.* Princeton, NJ: Educational Testing Service.
Barr, R., & Dreeben, R. (1983). *How schools work.* Chicago: University of Chicago Press.
Bartell, T., & Noble, J. (1986). *Changes in course selection by high school students: The impact of national educational reform.* Paper presented at the annual meeting of the American Educational Research Association, San Francisco.
Bassham, H., Murphy, M., & Murphy, K. (1964). Attitude and achievement in arithmetic. *Arithmetic Teacher, 11,* 66–72.
Becker, H. J. (1983). *School uses of microcomputers: Reports from a national sur-*

vey. Baltimore: Johns Hopkins University, Center for the Social Organization of Schools.

Becker, H. J. (1986). *Computer survey newsletter.* Baltimore: Johns Hopkins University, Center for the Social Organization of Schools.

Becker, J. R. (1981). Differential treatment of females and males in mathematics classes. *Journal for Research in Mathematics Education, 12,* 40–53.

Benbow, C. P., & Stanley, J. C. (1980). Sex differences in mathematical ability: Fact or artifact? *Science, 210,* 1262–1264.

Benbow, C. P., & Stanley, J. C. (1982). Consequences in high school and college of differences in mathematical reasoning ability: A longitudinal perspective. *American Educational Research Journal, 19,* 598–622.

Berryman, S. E. (1983). *Who will do science?* New York: Rockefeller Foundation.

Betz, N. E. (1978). Prevalence, distribution, and correlates of math anxiety in college students. *Journal of Counseling Psychology, 25,* 441–448.

Betz, N., & Hackett, J. (1983). The relationship of self-efficacy expectations to the selection of science-based college majors. *Journal of Vocational Behavior, 23,* 329–345.

Boli, J., Allen, M. L., & Payne, A. (1985). High-ability women and men in undergraduate mathematics and chemistry courses. *American Educational Research Journal, 22,* 605–626.

Bredderman, T. (1983). Effects of activity-based elementary science on student outcomes: A quantitative synthesis. *Review of Educational Research, 53,* 499–518.

Brody, L., & Fox, L. H. (1980). An accelerative intervention program for mathematically gifted girls. In L. H. Fox & D. Tobin (Eds.), *Women and the mathematical mystique.* Baltimore: Johns Hopkins University Press.

Brophy, J. E., & Good, T. (1974). *Teacher-student relationships: Causes and consequences.* New York: Holt, Rinehart, and Winston.

Brown, A. L., & Campione, J. C. (1982). Modifying intelligence or modifying cognitive skills: More than a semantic quibble? In D. K. Detterman & R. J. Sternberg (Eds.), *How and how much can intelligence be increased?* Norwood, NJ: ABLEX.

Brush, L. R. (1985). Cognitive and affective determinants of course preference and plans. In S. F. Chipman, L. R. Brush, & D. M. Wilson (Eds.), *Women and mathematics: Balancing the equation.* Hillsdale, NJ: Lawrence Erlbaum Associates.

Bureau of Labor Statistics. (1983, November). *Employment and earning.* Washington, DC: Author.

Calfee, R. C., & Brown, R. (1979). Grouping students for instruction. In *Classroom management* (78th yearbook of the National Society for the Study of Education). Chicago: University of Chicago Press.

California Commission on the Teaching Profession. (1985). *Who will teach our children?* Sacramento: Author.

California State Department of Education. (1984). *California high school curriculum study: Paths through high school.* Sacramento: Author.

Carpenter, T. P., Matthews, W., Lindquist, M. M., & Silver, E. A. (1983). *Results from the Second Mathematics Assessment of Educational Progress.* Reston, VA: National Council of Teachers of Mathematics.

Carroll, S. J., & Park, R. E. (1983). *The search for equity in school finance.* Cambridge, MA: Ballinger.

Casserly, P. (1980). Factors affecting participation in advanced placement programs. In L. H. Fox, L. Brody, & D. Tobin (Eds.), *Women and the mathematical mystique.* Baltimore: Johns Hopkins University Press.

Casserly, P., & Rock, R. (1985). Factors related to young women's persistence and achievement in mathematics. In S. F. Chipman, L. R. Brush, & D. M. Wilson (Eds.), *Women and mathematics: Balancing the equation.* Hillsdale, NJ: Lawrence Erlbaum Associates.

Catterall, J. (1989a). Resource measures for a science and mathematics education indicators system. In R. J. Shavelson, L. McDonnell, & J. Oakes (Eds.), *Indicators for monitoring mathematics and science education: Background papers.* Santa Monica, CA: RAND.

Catterall, J. (1989b). School completion and dropout measures for mathematics and science indicator systems. In R. J. Shavelson, L. McDonnell, & J. Oakes (Eds.), *Indicators for monitoring mathematics and science education: Background papers.* Santa Monica, CA: RAND.

Center for Statistics. (1986a). *The condition of education, 1986 edition.* Washington, DC: U.S. Department of Education.

Center for Statistics, Office of Educational Research and Improvement, U.S. Department of Education. (1986b). *Digest of education statistics, 1985–86.* Washington, DC: U.S. Government Printing Office.

Chipman, S. F., Brush, L. R., & Wilson, D. M. (Eds.). (1985). *Women and mathematics: Balancing the equation.* Hillsdale, NJ: Lawrence Erlbaum Associates.

Chipman, S. F., & Thomas, V. G. (1984). *The participation of women and minorities in mathematical, scientific, and technical fields.* Washington, DC: Howard University.

Cicourel, A. V., & Kitsuse, J. I. (1963). *The educational decision makers.* Indianapolis: Bobbs-Merrill.

Cohen, E. G., & De Avila, E. (1983). *Learning to think in math and science: Improving local education for minority children* (final report of the Walter S. Johnson Foundation). Stanford, CA: Stanford University, School of Education.

Cole, M., & Scribner, S. (1974). *Culture and thought.* New York: Wiley.

College Entrance Examination Board. (1985). *National college bound seniors, 1985.* New York: Author.

College Entrance Examination Board. (1986). *Keeping the options open.* New York: Author.

College Entrance Examination Board. (1987). *Scholastic aptitude scores, 1987.* New York: Author.

Comer, J. P. (1985). Demand for excellence and the need for equity: The dynamics of collaboration. In M. Fantini & R. Sinclair (Eds.), *Education in school and non-school settings* (84th yearbook of the National Society for the Study of Education). Chicago: University of Chicago Press.

Commission on Professionals in Science and Technology. (1986). *Professional women and minorities.* Washington, DC: Author.

Connor, J. M., & Serbin, L. A. (1985). Visual-spatial skill: Is it important for mathematics? Can it be taught? In S. F. Chipman, L. R. Brush, & D. M. Wilson (Eds.), *Women and mathematics: Balancing the equation.* Hillsdale, NJ: Lawrence Erlbaum Associates.

Corbett, J. G., Estler, S., Johnston, W., Ott, M. D., Robinson, H., & Shell, G. R. (1980). *Women in engineering: An exploratory study of enrollment factors in the seventies.* (Contract No. 400-77-0004). Washington, DC: National Institute of Education.

Crockett, L. J., & Peterson, A. C. (1984). Biology: Its role in gender-related educational experiences. In E. Fennema & M. J. Ayers (Eds.), *Women and education: Equity or equality?* Berkeley, CA: McCutchan.

Cuevas, G. J. (1984). Mathematics learning in English as a second language. *Journal for Research in Mathematics Education, 15,* 134–144.

Darling-Hammond, L. (1985). *Equality and excellence: The educational status of black Americans.* New York: College Entrance Examination Board.

Darling-Hammond, L., & Hudson, L. (1989). Indicators of teacher and teaching quality. In R. J. Shavelson, L. McDonnell, & J. Oakes (Eds.), *Indicators for monitoring mathematics and science education: Background papers.* Santa Monica, CA: RAND.

DeBoer, G. (1984a). Factors related to the decision of men and women to continue taking science courses in college. *Journal of Research in Science Teaching, 21,* 325–329.

DeBoer, G. (1984b). A study of gender effects in science and mathematics coursetaking behavior among students who graduated from college in the late 1970s. *Journal of Research in Science Teaching, 21,* 95–103.

Derry, S. J., & Murphy, D. A. (1986). Designing systems that train ability: From theory to practice. *Review of Educational Research, 56,* 1–39.

DeWolf, V. A. (1981). High school mathematics preparation and sex differences in quantitative abilities. *Psychology of Women Quarterly, 5,* 555–567.

Dossey, J. A., Mullis, I. V. S., Lindquist, M. M., & Chambers, D. L. (1988). *The mathematics report card. Are we measuring up?* Princeton, NJ: Educational Testing Service.

Dunteman, G. H., Wisenbaker, J., & Taylor, M. E. (1979). *Race and sex differences in college science program participation.* Research Triangle Park, NC: Research Triangle Institute.

Dwyer, C. A. (1974). Influence of children's sex role standards on reading and arithmetic achievement. *Journal of Educational Psychology, 66,* 811–816.

Eccles, J., Adler, T. F., Futterman, R., Goff, S. B., Kaczala, C. M., Meece, J. L., & Midgley, C. (1985). In S. F. Chipman, L. R. Brush, & D. M. Wilson (Eds.), *Women and mathematics: Balancing the equation.* Hillsdale, NJ: Lawrence Erlbaum Associates.

Eccles, J., MacIver, D., & Lange, L. (1986). *Classroom practices and motivation to study math.* Paper presented at the annual meeting of the American Educational Research Association, San Francisco.

Ekstrom, R. B., Goertz, M. E., & Rock, D. (1988). *Education and American youth: The impact of the high school experience.* New York: Falmer Press.

Epstein, J. L., & Becker, H. J. (1982). Teacher practices of parent involvement: Problems and possibilities. *Teachers College Record, 83,* 103–113.

Erickson, F. (1975). Gatekeeping the melting pot. *Harvard Educational Review, 45,* 44–70.

Erickson, L. R. (1981). Women in engineering: Attitudes, motivations, and experiences. *Engineering Education, 72,* 180–182.

Ernest, J. (1980). Is mathematics a sexist discipline? In L. H. Fox, L. Brody, & D. Tobin (Eds.), *Women and the mathematical mystique.* Baltimore: Johns Hopkins University Press.

Esposito, D. (1973). Homogeneous and heterogeneous ability grouping: Principal findings and implications for evaluating and designing more effective educational environments. *Review of Educational Research, 43,* 163–179.

Fehrmann, P. G., Keith, T. Z., & Reimers, T. M. (1987). Home influence on school learning: Direct and indirect effects of parental involvement on high school grades. *Journal of Educational Research, 80,* 330–337.

Fennema, E. (1984). Girls, women, and mathematics. In E. Fennema & M. J. Ayers (Eds.), *Women and education: Equity or equality?* Berkeley, CA: McCutchan.

Fennema, E., & Carpenter, T. P. (1981). Sex-related differences in mathematics: Results from national assessment. *Mathematics Teacher, 74,* 554–559.

Fennema, E., & Sherman, J. A. (1977). Sex-related differences in mathematics achievement, spatial visualization, and affective factors. *American Educational Research Journal, 4,* 51–72.

Fennema, E., & Sherman, J. A. (1978). Sex-related differences in mathematics achievement and other factors: A further study. *Journal for Research in Mathematics Education, 9,* 189–203.

Fennema, E., & Tatre, L. (1985). The use of spatial visualization in mathematics by girls and boys. *Journal for Research in Mathematics Education, 16,* 184–206.

Findley, W., & Bryan, M. (1971). *The pros and cons of ability grouping.* Washington, DC: National Education Association.

Fox, L. H., Brody, L., & Tobin, D. (1985). The impact of early intervention programs upon course-taking and attitudes in high school. In S. F. Chipman, L. R. Brush, & D. M. Wilson (Eds.), *Women and mathematics: Balancing the equation.* Hillsdale, NJ: Lawrence Erlbaum Associates.

Fox, L. H., Fennema, E., & Sherman, J. (1977). *Women and mathematics: Research perspectives for change.* Washington, DC: National Institute of Education.

Furr, J. D., & Davis, T. M. (1984). Equity issues and microcomputers: Are educators meeting the challenge? *Journal of Educational Equity and Leadership, 4,* 93–97.

Gamoran, A. (1986). *The stratification of high school learning opportunities.* Paper presented at the annual meeting of the American Educational Research Association, San Francisco.

Gardner, R. E. (1976). Women in engineering: The impact of attitudinal differences on educational institutions. *Engineering Education, 67*(3), 233–240.

Gilbert, S. E., & Gay, G. (1985). Improving the success in school of poor black children. *Phi Delta Kappan, 66,* 133–137.

Ginsburg, H. P., & Russell, R. L. (1981). *Social class and racial influences on early thinking* (Monographs of the Society for Research in Child Development). Chicago: Society for Research in Child Development.

Good, T., Sikes, J. N., & Brophy, J. E. (1973). Effects of teacher sex and student sex on classroom interaction. *Journal of Educational Psychology, 65,* 74–87.

Goodlad, J. I. (1984). *A place called school: Prospects for the future.* New York: McGraw-Hill.

Grandy, J. (1987). *Trends in the selection of science, mathematics, or engineering as major fields of study among top-scoring SAT takers.* Princeton, NJ: Educational Testing Service.

Grant, C. A., & Sleeter, C. E. (1986). Race, class, and gender in education research: An argument for integrative analysis. *Review of Educational Research, 56*(2), 195–211.

Greenfield, L. B., Holloway, E. L., & Remus, L. (1982, November). Women students in engineering: Are they so different from men? *Journal of College Student Personnel,* 508–511.

Gross, S. (1988). *Participation and performance of women and minorities.* Rockville, MD: Montgomery County Schools.

Guthrie, L. F., & Leventhal, C. (1985). *Opportunities for scientific literacy for high school students.* Paper presented at the annual meeting of the American Educational Research Association, Chicago.

Hager, P., & Elton, C. (1971). The vocational interest of black males. *Journal of Vocational Behavior, 1,* 153–158.

Hallinan, M. T., & Sorensøn, A. B. (1983). The formation and stability of ability groups. *American Sociological Review, 48,* 838–851.

Hallinan, M. T., & Sorensøn, A. B. (1987). Ability grouping and sex differences in mathematics achievement. *Sociology of Education, 60,* 63–72.

Harway, M., & Astin, H. S. (1977). *Sex discrimination in career counseling and education.* New York: Praeger.

Hilton, T. L., & Berglund, G. W. (1974). Sex differences in mathematics achievement: A longitudinal study. *Journal of Educational Research, 67,* 231–237.

Hudson, L. (1986). *Item-level analysis of sex differences in mathematics achievement test performance.* Unpublished doctoral dissertation, Cornell University, Ithaca, NY.

Hueftle, S. J., Rakow, S. J., & Welch, W. W. (1983). *Images of science: A summary of results from the 1981–82 national assessment in science.* Minneapolis: University of Minnesota.

Hunt, J. McV. (1969). *The challenge of incompetence and poverty.* Urbana: University of Illinois Press.

Jagacinski, C. K., & LeBold, W. K. (1981). A comparison of men and women undergraduate and professional engineers. *Engineering Education, 72,* 213–220.

Jensen, A. R. (1969). How much can we boost I.Q. and scholastic achievement? *Harvard Educational Review, 39,* 1–123.

Johnston, K. L., & Aldridge, B. G. (1984, September/October). The crisis in education: What is it? How can we respond? *Journal of California Science Teachers,* 19–28.

Jones, L. V. (1984). White-black achievement differences: The narrowing gap. *American Psychologist, 39,* 1207–1213.

Jones, L. V. (1985). *The influence on mathematics test scores, by ethnicity and sex, of prior achievement and high school mathematics courses.* Paper presented at the annual meeting of the American Educational Research Association, Chicago.

Jones, L. V., Davenport, E. C., Bryson, A., Bekhuis, T., & Zwick, R. (1986). Mathematics and science test scores as related to courses taken in high school and other factors. *Journal of Educational Measurement, 23*(3), 197–208.

Kagan, S., & Zahn, G. L. (1975). Field independence and the school achievement gap between Anglo-American and Mexican-American children. *Journal of Educational Psychology, 67,* 643–650.

Kagan, S., Zahn, G. L., & Gealy, J. (1977). Competition and school achievement among Anglo-American and Mexican-American children. *Journal of Educational Psychology, 69,* 432–441.

Kahle, J. B., & Lakes, M. K. (1983). The myth of equality in science classrooms. *Journal of Research in Science Teaching, 20,* 131–140.

Kahle, J. B., Matyas, M. L., & Cho, H. H. (1985). An assessment of the impact of science experiences on the career choices of male and female biology students. *Journal of Research in Science Teaching, 22,* 385–394.

Kerckhoff, A. C., & Campbell, R. (1977). Black-white differences in the educational attainment process. *Sociology of Education, 50,* 15–27.

Kester, S., & Letchworth, G. (1972). Communication of teacher expectations and their effects on achievement and attitudes of secondary school students. *Journal of Educational Research, 66,* 51–55.

Kulm, G. (1980). Research on mathematics attitude. In R. J. Shumway (Ed.), *Research in mathematics education.* Reston, VA: National Council of Teachers of Mathematics.

Lantz, A. E., & Smith, G. P. (1981). Factors influencing the choice of nonrequired mathematics courses. *Journal of Educational Psychology, 73,* 825–837.

LeBold, W. K., & Shell, K. D. (1980). The utility of cognitive and noncognitive information in predicting engineering retention and selection of specialization. In *1980 Frontiers in Education Conference* (pp. 504–510). Houston, TX: American Society for Engineering Education.

Lee, V. E. (1986). *The effect of curriculum tracking on the social distribution of achievement in Catholic and public secondary schools.* Paper presented at the annual meeting of the American Educational Research Association, San Francisco.

Lee, V. E. & Bryk, A. S. (1986). The effects of single-sex secondary schools on student achievement and attitudes. *Journal of Educational Psychology, ,78,* 381–395.

Lee, V. E., & Ekstrom, R. B. (1987). Student access to guidance counseling in high school. *American Educational Research Journal, 24,* 287–310.

Leinhardt, G., Seewald, A. M., & Engel, M. (1979). Learning what's taught: Sex differences in instruction. *Journal of Educational Psychology, 73,* 825–837.

Lenny, E. (1977). Women's self confidence in achievement settings. *Psychological Bulletin, 84,* 1–13.

Levin, H. M. (1986). *Educational reform for disadvantaged students: An emerging crisis.* Washington, DC: National Education Association.

Linn, M., & Hyde, J. (in press). Gender, mathematics, and science. *Educational Researcher.*

Linn, M. C., & Peterson, A. C. (1985). Emergence and characterization of sex differences in spatial ability: A meta-analysis. *Child Development, 56,* 1479–1498.

Lockheed, M. E., Thorpe, M., Brooks-Gunn, J., Casserly, P., & McAloon, A. (1985). *Sex and ethnic differences in middle school mathematics, science, and computer science: What do we know?* Princeton, NJ: Educational Testing Service.

Maccoby, E. E., & Jacklin, C. N. (1974). *The psychology of sex differences.* Stanford, CA: Stanford University Press.

MacDonald, C. T. (1980). An experiment in mathematics education at the college level. In L. H. Fox, L. Brody, & D. Tobin (Eds.), *Women and the mathematical mystique.* Baltimore, MD: Johns Hopkins University Press.

Malcom, S. M., George, Y. S., & Matyas, M. L. (1985). *Summary of research studies on women and minorities in science, mathematics and technology.* Washington, DC: American Association for the Advancement of Science.

Marini, M. M. (in press). Sex and gender. In E. F. Borgatta & K. S. Cook (Eds.), *The future of sociology.* Beverly Hills, CA: Sage.

Matthews, W. (1980, December). *Adding up race and sex: A study of enrollment in high school mathematics classes.* Paper presented at the Program on Women, Northwestern University, Chicago.

Matthews, W. (1984). Influences on the learning and participation of minorities in mathematics. *Journal for Research in Mathematics Education, 15,* 84–95.

Matyas, M. L. (1986). *Persistence in science-oriented majors: Factors related to attrition among male and female students.* Paper presented at annual meeting of the American Educational Research Association, San Francisco.

McCorquodale, P. (1983). *Social influences on the participation of Mexican American women in science* (final report to the National Institution of Education). Tucson: University of Arizona.

McKnight, C., Crosswhite, F. J., Dossey, J. A., Kifer, E., Swafford, J. O., Travers, K. J., & Cooney, T. J. (1987). *The underachieving curriculum.* Champaign, IL: Stipes.

McNamara, P. P., & Scherrei, R. A. (1982). *College women pursuing careers in science, mathematics, and engineering in the 1970s.* (NSF Report No. FGK 57295). Washington, DC: National Science Foundation. (ERIC Document Reproduction Service No. ED 217-778)

Miura, I. T. (1987). *Gender and socioeconomic status differences in middle school computer interest and use.* Paper presented at the annual meeting of the American Educational Research Association.

Moore, E. G. J., & Smith, A. W. (1985). Mathematics aptitude: Effects of coursework, household language, and ethnic differences. *Urban Education, 20,* 273–294.

Mullis, I. V. S., & Jenkins, L. B. (1988). *The science report card: Elements of risk and recovery.* Princeton, NJ: Educational Testing Service.

National Assessment of Educational Progress. (1983). *The third national assessment: Results, trends, and issues.* Denver, CO: Education Commission of the States.

National Center for Educational Statistics. (1985a). *An analysis of course offerings and enrollments as related to school characteristics.* Washington, DC: U.S. Department of Education.

National Center for Educational Statistics. (1985b). *The condition of education, 1985 edition.* Washington, DC: U.S. Department of Education.

National Center for Educational Statistics. (1985c). *High school and beyond: An analysis of course-taking patterns in secondary schools as related to student characteristics.* Washington, DC: U.S. Department of Education.

National Center for Educational Statistics. (1988). *Digest of education statistics.* Washington, DC: U.S. Department of Education.

National Science Board. (1987). *Science and engineering indicators—1987.* (NSB 87-1). Washington, DC: Author.

National Science Foundation. (1986). *Women and minorities in science and engineering.* (NSF 86-301). Washington, DC: Author.

National Science Foundation. (1988). *Women and minorities in science and engineering.* (NSF 88-301). Washington, DC: Author.

National Science Teachers Association. (1987). *Survey analysis of U.S. public and private high schools.* Washington, DC: Author.

Newcombe, N., Bandura, M., & Taylor, D. G. (1983). Sex differences in spatial ability and spatial activities. *Sex Roles, 9,* 377–386.

Noland, T. K. (1986). *The effects of ability grouping: A meta-analysis of research findings.* Unpublished doctoral dissertation, University of Colorado, Boulder, CO.

Oakes, J. (1985). *Keeping track: How schools structure inequality.* New Haven, CT: Yale University Press.

Oakes, J. (1987). Tracking in secondary schools: A contextual perspective. *Educational Psychologist, 22,* 129–154.

Page, R. (1987). Lower-track classes at a college-preparatory high school: Caricatures of educational encounters. In G. Spindler (Ed.), *Interpretive ethnography of education at home and abroad.* Hillsdale, NJ: Lawrence Erlbaum Associates.

Pallas, A. M., & Alexander, K. L. (1983). Sex differences in quantitative SAT performance: New evidence on the differential coursework hypothesis. *American Educational Research Journal, 20,* 165–182.

Parsons, J. E., Kaczala, C. M., & Meece, J. L. (1982). Socialization of achievement attitudes and beliefs: Classroom influences. *Child Development, 52,* 322–339.

Pearson, W., & Pearson, L. C. (1985). Baccalaureate origins of black American scientists: A cohort analysis. *Journal of Negro Education, 54,* 24–34.

Pedro, J. D., Wolleat, P., Fennema, E., & Becker, A. D. (1981). Election of high school mathematics by females and males: Attributions and attitudes. *American Educational Research Journal, 18,* 207–218.

Peng, S. S., Owings, J. A., & Fetters, W. B. (1981). *Effective high schools: What are their attributes?* Paper presented at the annual meeting of the American Statistical Association, Cincinnati, OH.

Persell, C. H. (1977). *Education and inequality: The roots and results of stratification in America's schools.* New York: Free Press.

Peterson, L., & Fennema, E. (1985). Effective teaching, student engagement in classroom activities, and sex-related differences in learning mathematics. *American Educational Research Journal, 22,* 309–335.

Porter, J. N. (1974). Race, socialization, and mobility in educational and early occupational attainment. *American Sociological Review, 39,* 303–316.

Portes, A., & Wilson, K. L. (1976). Black-white differences in educational attainment. *American Sociological Review, 41,* 414–431.

Purkey, S. C., & Smith, M. S. (1983). Effective schools: A review. *Elementary School Journal, 83,* 427–452.

Rallis, S. F., & Ahern, S. A. (1986). *Math and science education in high schools: A question of sex equity?* Paper presented at the annual meeting of the American Educational Research Association, San Francisco.

Ramirez, M., & Casteneda, A. (1974). *Cultural democracy, biocognitive development, and education.* New York: Academic Press.

Rendon, L. L. (1983). *Mathematics education for Hispanic students in the Border College Consortium.* Laredo, TX: Border College Consortium. (ERIC Document Reproduction Service No. ED 242-451)

Reyes, L. H. (1984). Affective variables and mathematics education. *Elementary School Journal, 84,* 558–581.

Reyes, L. H., & Stanic, G. (1988). Race, sex, socioeconomic status, and mathematics. *Research in Mathematics Education, 19*(1), 26–43.

Rock, D., Braun, H. I., & Rosenbaum, P. R. (1984). *Excellence in high school education: Cross-sectional study, 1972-1980* (Final Report). Princeton, NJ: Educational Testing Service.

Rock, D., Braun, H. I., & Rosenbaum, P. R. (1985). *Excellence in high school education: Longitudinal study, 1980-1982* (Final Report). Princeton, NJ: Educational Testing Service.

Rosenbaum, J. E. (1976). *Making inequality: The hidden curriculum of high school tracking.* New York: John Wiley and Sons.

Rosenbaum, J. E. (1980). Social implications of educational grouping. In D. C.

Berliner (Ed.), *Review of research in education* (Vol. 8, pp. 361–401). Washington, DC: American Educational Research Association.

Rosenthal, R., & Jacobson, L. (1968). *Pygmalion in the classroom.* New York: Holt, Rinehart, and Winston.

Rowan, B., Bossert, S. T., & Dwyer, D. C. (1984). Research on effective schools: A cautionary note. *Educational Researcher, 12*(4), 24–31.

Sadker, M., & Sadker, D. (1986). Sexism in the classroom: From grade school to graduate school. *Phi Delta Kappan, 67,* 512–516.

Schofield, H. L. (1982). Sex, grade level, and the relationship between mathematics attitude and achievement in children. *Journal of Educational Research, 75,* 280–284.

Schonberger, A. K., & Holden, C. C. (1984, April). *Women as university students in science and technology: What helps them stick with it?* Paper presented at the annual meeting of the New England Educational Research Organization, Rockport, ME.

Schonberger, A. K., & Holden, C. C. (1987). *College women's persistence in engineering and physical science: The mechanical connection.* Paper presented at the annual meeting of the American Educational Research Association, Washington, DC.

Schunk, D. H. (1981). Modeling and attribution effects on children's achievement: A self-efficacy analysis. *Journal of Educational Psychology, 73,* 848–856.

Schunk, D. H. (1982). Effects of effort attribution feedback on children's perceived self-efficacy and achievement. *Journal of Educational Psychology, 74,* 548–556.

Sells, L. (1982). Leverage for equal opportunity through mastery of mathematics. In S. M. Humphreys (Ed.), *Women and minorities in science: Strategies for increasing participation.* Washington, DC: American Association for the Advancement of Science.

Sewell, T. E., & Martin, R. P. (1976). Racial differences in patterns of occupational choice in adolescents. *Psychology in the Schools, 13,* 326–333.

Sherman, J. A. (1980). Mathematics, spatial visualization, and related factors: Changes in girls and boys, grades 8–11. *Journal of Educational Psychology, 72,* 476–482.

Sherman, J. A., & Fennema, E. (1977). The study of mathematics by high school girls and boys: Related variables. *American Educational Research Journal, 14,* 159–168.

Slavin, R. (1985). Cooperative learning: Applying contact theory in desegregated schools. *Journal of Social Issues, 41,* 45–62.

Slavin, R. E. (1986). *Ability grouping and student achievement in elementary schools: A best evidence synthesis.* Baltimore: Johns Hopkins University, National Center for Effective Elementary Schools.

Slavin, R. E., & Oickle, E. (1981). Effects of cooperative teams on student achievement and race relations. *Sociology of Education, 55,* 174–180.

Smith, J. P., & Welch, F. R. (1986). *Closing the gap: Forty years of economic progress for blacks.* Santa Monica, CA: RAND.

Snelling, W. R., & Boruch, R. F. (1972). *Science in liberal arts colleges: A longitudinal study of 49 selective colleges.* New York: Columbia University Press.

Stage, E. K., Kreinberg, N., Eccles, J., & Rossi-Becker, J. (1985). Increasing the participation and achievement of girls and women in mathematics, science, and engineering. In S. S. Klein (Ed.), *Handbook for achieving sex equity through education.* Baltimore, MD: Johns Hopkins University Press.

Stallings, J. (1985). School, classroom, and home influences on women's decisions to enroll in advanced mathematics courses. In S. F. Chipman, L. R. Brush, & D. M. Wilson (Eds.), *Women and mathematics: Balancing the equation.* Hillsdale, NJ: Lawrence Erlbaum Associates.

Steinkamp, M. W., & Maehr, M. L. (1983). Affect, ability, and science achievement: A quantitative synthesis of correlational research. *Review of Educational Research, 53,* 369–396.

Sternberg, R. J. (1983). Criteria for intellectual skills training. *Educational Researcher, 12,* 6–12.

Stipek, D. J., & Weisz, J. R. (1981). Perceived control and academic achievement. *Review of Educational Research, 51,* 103–137.

Thomas, G. (1984). *Determinants and motivations underlying the college major choice of race and sex groups.* Baltimore: Johns Hopkins University, Center for the Social Organization of Schools.

Tobin, D., & Fox, L. H. (1980). Career interests and career education: A key to change. In L. H. Fox & D. Tobin (Eds.), *Women and the mathematical mystique.* Baltimore: Johns Hopkins University Press.

Tsai, S. L., & Walberg, H. J. (1983). Mathematics achievement and attitude productivity in junior high school. *Journal of Educational Research, 76,* 267–272.

U. S. Bureau of the Census. (1987a). America's black population: 1970–1982—A statistical view. In J. D. Williams (Ed.), *The state of black America, 1984.* New York: National Urban League.

U. S. Bureau of the Census. (1987b). *Statistical abstracts of the United States.* Washington, DC: U.S. Government Printing Office.

U. S. Commission on Civil Rights. (1978). *Social indicators of equality for minorities and women.* Washington, DC: Author.

Valentine, B. (1979). *Hustling and other hard work.* New York: Free Press.

Valverde, L. A. (1984). Underachievement and underrepresentation of Hispanics in mathematics and mathematics-related careers. *Journal for Research in Mathematics Education, 15,* 123–133.

Vanfossen, B. E., Jones, J. D., & Spade, J. Z. (1985). *Curriculum tracking: Causes and consequences.* Paper presented at the annual meeting of the American Educational Research Association, Chicago.

Vockell, E. L., & Lebonc, S. (1981). Sex-role stereotyping by high school females in science. *Journal of Research in Science Teaching, 39,* 563–574.

Walberg, H. J., Fraser, B. J., & Welch, W. W. (1986). A test of a model of educational productivity among senior high school students. *Journal of Educational Research, 79,* 133–139.

Ware, N., & Dill, D. (1986). *Persistence in science among mathematically-able male and female college students with pre-college plans for a scientific major.* Paper presented at the annual meeting of the American Educational Research Association, San Francisco.

Ware, N. C., & Lee, V. (1985). *Predictors of science major choice in a national sample of male and female college students.* Unpublished manuscript, Radcliffe College, Cambridge, MA.

Ware, N. C., Steckler, N. A., & Leserman, J. (1985). Undergraduate women: Who chooses a science major? *Journal of Higher Education, 56,* 73–84.

Weiner, B. (1976). An attributional approach for educational psychology. In L. Schulman (Ed.), *Review of research in education* (Vol. 4). New York: Plenum.

Weiss, I. (1978). *Report of the 1977 national survey of science, mathematics, and social studies education.* Research Triangle, NC: Research Triangle Institute.

Weiss, L. (1985). *Between two worlds: Black students in an urban community college.* Boston, MA: Routledge and Kegan Paul.

Welch, W. W., Anderson, R. E., & Harris, L. J. (1982). The effects of schooling of mathematics achievement. *American Educational Research Journal, 19,* 145–153.

West, J., & Gross, S. (1986). *Performance of women and minorities in mathematics: A large school system perspective.* Paper presented at the annual meeting of the American Educational Research Association, San Francisco.

Westcott, D. N. (1982, June). Blacks in the 1970s: Did they scale the job ladder? *Monthly Labor Review, 29–38.*

White, K. R. (1982). The relation between socioeconomic status and academic achievement. *Psychological Bulletin, 91*(3), 461–481.

Winkler, J. D., Shavelson, R. J., Stasz, C., Robyn, A., & Feibel, W. (1984). *How effective teachers use microcomputers for instruction.* Santa Monica, CA: RAND.

Wise, L., Steel, L., & MacDonald, C. (1979). *Origins and consequences of sex differences in high school mathematics achievement.* Washington, DC: National Institute of Education.

Wolfle, L. M. (1985). Postsecondary educational attainment among whites and blacks. *American Educational Research Journal, 22,* 501–525.

Wolfle, L. M., & Ethington, C. A. (1986). *Race and gender differences in a causal model of mathematics achievement.* Paper presented at the annual meeting of the American Educational Research Association, San Francisco.

Wylie, R. C. (1963). Children's estimates of their schoolwork ability, as a function of sex, race, and socioeconomic level. *Journal of Personality, 31,* 203–224.

Yee, D. K., Jacobs, J., & Goldsmith, R. (1986). *Sex equity in the home: Parents' influence on their children's attitudes about math.* Paper presented at the annual meeting of the American Educational Research Association, San Francisco.

Zimmerer, L. K., & Bennett, S. M. (1987). *Gender differences on the California statewide assessment of attitudes and achievement in science.* Paper presented at the annual meeting of the American Educational Research Association, Washington, DC.

Chapter 4

Precollege Science and Mathematics Teachers: Supply, Demand, and Quality

LINDA DARLING-HAMMOND and LISA HUDSON
The RAND Corporation

In recent years, a series of national commission reports have pointed to the need to improve mathematics and science teaching in our nation's schools (cf. National Commission on Excellence in Education, 1985; National Governors' Association, 1986; National Science Board [NSB], 1983). Meanwhile, public concerns about shortages of elementary and secondary school teachers, especially those qualified to teach mathematics and science, have been mounting (Carnegie Forum on Education and the Economy, 1986; Darling-Hammond, 1984; NSB, 1983; Shymansky & Aldridge, 1982). Concerns have also been raised about suboptimal adjustments that school districts may make to cope with supply problems: hiring uncertified teachers, assigning current teachers to teach outside their fields of preparation, cancelling course offerings, or expanding class sizes.

Although there is evidence that shortages of mathematics and science teachers have existed for most of the last 30 to 40 years (Kershaw & McKean, 1962; Levin, 1985), renewed attention to this problem has been occasioned by at least two aspects of the current educational reform movement. First, there is a belief that America's ability to compete in a more technological international economy depends in part on the production of a more sizable, well-trained scientific work force, as well as the general education of a more scientifically literate population (Carnegie Forum, 1986; NSB, 1983). Second, there is a growing belief that further educational improvement in American schools will depend largely on the caliber of the teaching force (cf. Carnegie Forum, 1986; Education Commission of the States, 1986; National Governors' Association, 1986). Educators and policymakers agree that if teachers are not prepared to address the needs of their students and the demands of their subjects, other reform strategies will fail.

These new reform theories point toward policies that produce an adequate supply of well-qualified mathematics and science teachers as key to improving education. This differs from many previous approaches to educational change, which sought to improve mathematics and science education by developing new curricula, mandating course requirements, or creating new programs rather than improving the schools' human capital.

If focusing policy attention on the character and capacity of the teaching force seems desirable to many, reaching consensus on the size, scope, and nature of problems to be remedied is more problematic. Until recently, few sources of data have existed that could be analyzed to confirm, refute, or characterize many of the suspected problems. Data that do exist have not always been analyzed to illuminate trends in the precollege mathematics and science teaching force. These shortcomings in data availability and analysis impede the development of sound policies that rely on information about where problems exist, the nature of the problems, and what the potential difficulties are.

Nonetheless, there is widely scattered evidence that can be gathered to depict what is currently known about the nation's teaching force, and about mathematics and science teachers in particular. We describe what we know and what we need to know about the supply of and demand for mathematics and science teachers and about their preparation for their teaching assignments. We also examine how new and existing data sets might be used to answer important questions about the interrelationships among teacher supply, demand, qualifications, and teaching practices.

THE PROBLEM IN CONTEXT

The terms *scientific illiteracy* and *innumeracy* have recently been coined to describe the findings of a growing number of studies and reports documenting the American public's ignorance of basic scientific and mathematical facts and their beliefs and attitudes about the difficulties and "irrelevance" of these fields. A recent survey by the National Science Foundation, for example, found that only 6% of Americans could be termed "scientifically literate" based on their knowledge of the process of science, their identification of scientific concepts and terms, and their understanding of the impact of science on society.

Data on trends in technical occupations support these impressions of a population that is ill-prepared to meet the needs of an increasingly technological society. While occupational need in science-related fields has increased dramatically in the past decade, fewer U.S. students have been majoring in science and mathematics fields, especially at the graduate levels (Bloch, 1986). Between 1976 and 1983, for example, science and

TABLE 1
The Scientific Labor Market: Degrees and Employment

	Computer sciences	Engineering	Life sciences	Physical sciences	Mathematics
Degrees[a]					
Bachelor's					
1975	5,033	39,388	51,741	20,778	18,181
1985	38,878	77,154	38,445	23,732	15,146
(% change)	(+672)	(+96)	(−26)	(+14)	(−17)
Master's					
1975	2,299	15,127	6,550	5,807	4,327
1985	7,101	20,926	5,059	5,796	2,882
(% change)	(+209)	(+38)	(−23)	(0)	(−33)
Doctorates					
1975	213	3,106	3,384	3,626	975
1985	248	3,221	3,432	3,403	699
(% change)	(+16)	(+4)	(+1)	(−6)	(−28)
Employment[b]					
1976	116,000	1,278,300	198,200	154,900	43,800
1986	437,200	2,243,500	340,500	264,900	103,900
(% change)	(+277)	(+76)	(+72)	(+71)	(+137)

[a]National Center for Education Statistics, 1987b, pp. 190-192.
[b]National Science Board, 1987, p. 218.

engineering jobs increased at three times the rate of national employment, while college enrollments in most science areas were declining (NSB, 1985, cited in Shavelson, McDonnell, Oakes, & Carey, 1987).

As Table 1 indicates, employment in engineering and the sciences nearly doubled between 1976 and 1986, while employment in computer science fields increased almost fourfold. But the number of degrees awarded by U.S. universities in the life sciences, physical sciences, and mathematics was stagnant or declined during these years. Furthermore, a growing number of these degrees (between 20% and 40% for each field by 1986) were awarded to foreign students, many of whom return to their home countries after graduation. Increases in engineering degrees were almost entirely accounted for by foreign students (Commission on Professionals in Science and Technology, 1987).

The picture is not much more promising when one looks at the progress of students in elementary and secondary schools. The most recent mathematics assessment from the National Assessment of Educational Progress (NAEP) found that "most students, even at age 17, do not possess the breadth and depth of mathematics proficiency needed for advanced study in secondary school mathematics" (Dossey, Mullis, Lindquist, & Chambers, 1988, p. 10). The NAEP science assessment indicated that, despite recent increases, science achievement scores in 1986 were still lower than they had been in 1970. The authors estimated that "only 7 percent of the nation's 17-year-olds have the prerequisite knowledge and skills

TABLE 2
Ratio of Expected Salaries of College Graduates To Be Hired
To Beginning Teachers' Salaries

	1972	1974	1976	1978	1980	1982	1984	1986	1987	1988
Teaching	1.00	1.00	1.00	1.00	1.00	1.00	1.00	1.00	1.00	1.00
Engineering	1.52	1.43	1.54	1.66	1.72	1.86	1.73	1.61	1.55	1.52
Accounting	1.49	1.37	1.36	1.34	1.35	1.39	1.30	1.20	1.21	1.24
Sales/marketing	1.28	1.22	1.25	1.26	1.36	1.33	1.27	1.17	1.08	1.16
Business admini- stration	1.23	1.12	1.13	1.20	1.21	1.33	1.25	1.21	1.18	1.16
Liberal arts	1.19	1.10	1.10	1.13	1.14	1.25	1.25	1.19	1.10	1.15
Chemistry	1.41	1.27	1.31	1.46	1.47	1.59	1.56	1.37	1.45	1.31
Math or statistics	1.33	1.33	1.36	1.35	1.51	1.54	1.45	1.36	1.37	1.33
Economics/finance	1.33	1.26	1.17	1.20	1.24	1.37	1.32	1.26	1.18	1.18
Computer science		1.20		1.41	1.52	1.63	1.61	1.48	1.41	1.39
Others	1.33	1.28	1.30	1.38	1.50	1.51	1.49	1.51	1.18	1.34

Source: American Federation of Teachers, 1988, p. 47.

thought to be needed to perform well in college-level science courses"
(Mullis & Jenkins, 1988, p. 6).

International achievement comparisons are even more discouraging. In
the Second International Science Study, U.S. 5th-grade students ranked
8th among 17 countries in science achievement, and U.S. 7th-grade students ranked 15th. Among 13 countries, the most advanced U.S. 12th-
graders ranked 9th in physics, 11th in chemistry, and 13th in biology
(International Association for the Evaluation of Educational Achievement, 1988). The Second International Mathematics Study presents similar results for the 8th-grade and 12th-grade students tested on
mathematical knowledge. Among 20 countries, 8th-grade American students ranked 10th in arithmetic, 12th in algebra, 16th in geometry, and
18th in measurement. Among 15 countries, American 12th-grade students ranked 12th in elementary functions/calculus, 12th in geometry
and 14th in advanced algebra (McKnight et al., 1987).

These data do not portend immediate improvements in the number of
students interested in pursuing scientific fields in college, graduate
school, and later life. Given the projected growth in demand for scientific
workers, we can anticipate that many occupations will be competing with
each other and with teaching for this dwindling supply of newly trained
entrants. Teaching is not helped by the fact that the numbers of college
graduates have been especially anemic in the standard secondary school
subject fields: mathematics, biology, chemistry, and physics. Given the
wage disparities that continue between teaching and other scientific and
technical occupations (see Table 2), the task of recruiting teachers from
this pool is not a trivial undertaking.

It appears as though a vicious cycle has been launched: As shortages of mathematics and science teachers have eroded the ability of American schools to offer adequate preparation in these subjects to large numbers of American students, the pipeline of entrants into college-level advanced study has become inadequate to meet the nation's needs for scientific personpower. As a consequence, competition for these scientifically trained graduates is keen, and the schools' needs for well-trained mathematics and science teachers to better prepare the next generation often lose out to the needs of business and industry. When this occurs, the cycle of inadequate preparation leading to inadequate numbers of able and interested potential scientists begins again. This is the worst case scenario. The extent to which such a cycle exists or can be analytically examined and portrayed is discussed next.

THE TEACHER SHORTAGE DEBATE

Despite the fact that college placement officers have reported shortages of mathematics and science teachers in most states over the last decade (Association for School, College, and University Staffing [ASCUS], 1984, 1986), and scholars have presented evidence that these shortages have existed for several decades (cf. Levin, 1985; Rumberger, 1985), there has recently been some debate about whether teacher shortages are a myth or a reality (Feistritzer, 1986; Hecker, 1986). This debate rests on characterizations of teacher supply that treat location- and field-specific variations differently, define shortages disparately, rely on different indicators, and make widely varying assumptions about human behavior and occupational trends.

Because of the confusion exhibited in these disputes, and the fundamentally different assumptions undergirding each side's arguments, we discuss them in the following section. The issues we raise are critical for understanding various perspectives on teacher supply and quality and for placing the pieces of evidence in context.

The Nature of the Argument

For several years, at least two thirds of the states have reported shortages of mathematics and science teachers, especially physics and chemistry teachers (ASCUS, 1986; Howe & Gerlovich, 1982). Other data suggest that many new mathematics and science teachers hired in recent years are not certified to teach their assigned fields (Shymansky & Aldridge, 1982; National Center for Education Statistics [NCES], 1983). Many states and districts have launched special initiatives to recruit and train teachers for these fields, sometimes offering a wide variety of incentives to candidates (Carey, Mittman, & Darling-Hammond, 1988).

Meanwhile, the NCES has published data that show negligible levels of shortage, and recent reports (Feistritzer, 1986; Hecker, 1986) have declared that there is no current, or prospective, shortage of teachers. A General Accounting Office (GAO) (1984) report concluded that there are insufficient data to establish the magnitude or severity of teacher shortages in science and mathematics. Policymakers do not know what to believe, and those who inform policymakers seem unable to muster enough evidence to resolve the dispute. Although useful sources of new data will be available soon, important conceptual issues remain.

The problem is twofold. First, there has been disagreement on what constitutes a real shortage of teachers, because there is little consensus on what measures are useful indicators of a shortage and on whether or how qualifications enter the definition of shortage. Evidence of shortages in education is usually indirect, as classrooms do not remain empty when school starts each year. The adjustments schools make when teacher supply is low often seem to render shortages invisible (National Academy of Sciences [NAS], 1987).

Second, there is little consensus on how to interpret projections, which are based on past trends in the components of teacher supply and demand that may or may not hold in the future. In particular, assumptions about the factors influencing new supply and re-entrance into the teacher market from the reserve pool have not been well tested. And until recently, data needed to provide key estimates for projection models have not been routinely gathered.

Defining Shortage

The term *shortage* is, as the NAS (1987) points out, perhaps the most abused and overused term in the teacher supply and demand literature. Although a shortage can be theoretically defined in general terms, measuring the specific factors that contribute to a shortage is difficult. As a result, incomplete or inaccurate indicators are often used to assess teacher shortages.

The standard definition of a shortage specifies that a shortage exists when too few persons with the requisite qualifications offer their services for the openings available (Rumberger, 1985). Thus, assessing the degree of mathematics and science teacher shortages requires accurate knowledge of the number of mathematics and science teacher openings, the number of individuals willing to apply for these openings, and the qualifications of those willing to apply. Because data on each of these elements—especially the latter two—typically are unavailable, indirect indicators must be used as a proxy for shortages. These indicators, in turn, are subject to limitations and disagreements about their utility for identifying the magnitude, nature, or source of labor supply problems.

To follow, we examine various indicators of potential shortages, data regarding trends in teacher supply and demand, and factors that should influence projections of mathematics and science teachers. We also examine evidence on teacher qualifications, both as it relates to questions of general preparedness and as an indicator of labor market shortfalls.

Indicators of Shortages

School districts have many alternatives to pursue if the labor market does not produce enough well-qualified teachers. They may raise the salary of positions difficult to fill or offer other inducements (recruitment bonuses, choicer assignments); they may make do with fewer candidates by enlarging class sizes, increasing the number of courses teachers must teach, or cancelling certain courses; or they may fill positions with teachers with fewer qualifications than they would seek otherwise. Districts may assign more classes to teachers currently teaching in other fields, they may hire teachers who lack one or more of the desired qualifications, or they may fill positions with short- or long-term substitute teachers until a qualified candidate can be found.

The variety of strategies available suggests the range of indicators that might be needed to ascertain whether or not a teacher shortage exists. One might look for salary hikes or the appearance of special recruitment incentives; changes in class size or teaching load; course cancellations or fewer curricular offerings; unfilled positions or vacancies of long duration; positions filled by substitute teachers or other temporary personnel; out-of-field teaching assignments; or the hiring of underqualified candidates, such as those with substandard certification or lower levels of preparation (Haggstrom, Darling-Hammond, & Grissmer, 1988).

Each of these measures has its own utility and shortcomings, because various factors could offset or engender changes in any one of them. For example, because all teachers are paid on a single salary schedule, spot shortages of teachers might not create salary hikes until they become severe. Similarly, unfilled vacancies could be a sign of poor school district planning as much as a sign of labor market shortages, whereas an absence of vacancies might be no cause for complacence if positions are filled with unqualified candidates. Out-of-field assignments of teachers could occur to prevent reductions in force during times of declining enrollments just as they appear during times of high demand and inadequate supply. Changes in class size or course offerings can result from budgetary ups and downs and state or local policies as well as labor market forces. Thus, establishing the existence and nature of a labor market shortage requires multiple indicators and enough information to interpret them correctly.

Interpretation of Shortage Data

In recent years the Association for School, College, and University Staffing (ASCUS) has provided the most timely and regular data on

TABLE 3
Relative Teacher Demand by Teaching Area and Year in Continental United States

	1986	1985	1984	1983	1982	1981	1976
Teaching fields with considerable teacher shortages (5.00-4.25)							
Mathematics	4.55	4.71	4.78	4.75	4.81	4.79	3.86
Science—physics	4.44	4.57	4.45	4.46	4.41	4.56	4.04
Science—chemistry	4.40	4.42	4.25	4.30	4.13	4.42	3.72
Bilingual education	4.27	4.12	4.04	3.83	4.13	4.10	—
Special education—multiple handicaps	4.25	3.94	3.77	3.82	3.93	4.13	—
Special education—mentally retarded	4.25	3.76	3.55	3.71	3.84	4.14	2.87
Teaching fields with some teacher shortage (4.24-3.45)							
Special education—learning disabled	4.23	3.95	3.98	4.09	4.20	4.47	4.00
Computer science	4.22	4.37	4.34	—	—	—	—
Special education—emotionally disturbed/other	4.20	4.02	3.84	4.08	3.98	4.22	3.42
Speech pathology/Audiology	4.09	4.01	3.83	3.62	3.95	4.27	3.68
Data processing	3.97	4.30	4.18	4.36	3.86	—	—
Special education—gifted	3.91	3.85	3.74	3.80	3.81	4.10	3.85
Science—earth	3.86	3.79	3.70	3.80	3.89	4.08	3.44
Science—general	3.82	3.65	3.65	—	—	—	—
Science—biology	3.65	3.58	3.40	4.10	3.66	3.98	2.97
Language—Spanish	3.64	3.43	3.18	2.77	2.68	2.95	2.47
Special education—reading	3.46	3.39	3.48	3.39	3.73	4.21	3.96

Note. 5 = greatest demand; 1 = least demand.
Source: Association for School, College and University Staffing, 1986.

teacher supply and demand by field. These data are based on opinion surveys of teacher placement officers in institutions of higher education; thus, they do not provide precise or quantifiable information on shortages. Nonetheless, the data are a useful indicator of employment opportunities for prospective teachers from those who have first-hand experience with the labor market.

From 1976 to 1986, the ASCUS surveys indicate that mathematics and science have remained in the group of teaching fields showing "some" to "considerable" teacher shortages (see Table 3). Mathematics has led the list of shortage fields in recent years, followed closely by physics and chemistry. All of these fields showed fairly substantial jumps in their shortage index between 1976 and 1981. Computer science has shown a high and stable level of shortage for the 3 years in which it has been on the list. Shortage levels are somewhat lower for earth science, general science, and biology, but they have increased slightly since 1984.

Although certainly informative, these survey data are limited due to their qualitative nature. They cannot tell us, for example, how many teachers we need to solve a teacher shortage of 4.55. Or how concerned we should be with a shortage index of 3.70. Though other sources of quanti-

TABLE 4
Unfilled Vacancies and Uncertified Teachers, 1979 and 1983

Teaching field	1979		1983	
	Vacancies (per 1,000 teachers)	Layoffs (per 1,000 teachers)	Vacancies (per 1,000 teachers)	% not certified
All fields	11,300 (4.4)	23,900 (9.4)	3,965 (1.6)	3.5
Science	900 (6.9)	1,100 (8.4)	225 (1.7)	4.1
Biology	100 (3.3)	300 (10.0)	49 (1.7)	3.8
Chemistry	NA	NA	27 (1.9)	4.1
Physics	600 (24.0)	100 (4.0)	39 (4.5)	5.6
Other sciences	200[a] (2.6)	700[a] (9.2)	111 (1.4)	4.0
Mathematics	900 (6.0)	1,100 (7.3)	263 (1.8)	4.1

[a]For 1979, data are for general science; chemistry and other sciences were not reported separately.
Source: National Center for Education Statistics, 1982; 1985, pp. 146-158.

tative data are clearly necessary to answer these questions, the remarkable consistency with which mathematics and science have placed on the surveys over a period of years strongly suggests labor market shortages that are tenacious and real rather than imaginary.

Though the desire to quantify shortages is understandable, such a goal can only be approximated and never completely met. As noted earlier, absolute shortages as indicated by unfilled positions occur rarely; a variety of adjustments to schedules, class sizes, and hiring standards are used to meet staffing exigencies (Haggstrom et al., 1988). Neither can a count of "supply" be compared to an estimate of "demand" to produce a positive or negative balance. As an NAS panel on teacher supply and demand pointed out, both supply and demand are slippery concepts; they refer to relationships (between districts' and candidates' preferences and conditions and constraints surrounding hiring), not to numbers. And these conditions may produce imbalances between the numbers of teachers hired and real demand, as well as between both of these and supply (NAS, 1987).

The NCES reports of shortages as measured by unfilled vacancies illustrate some of the problems associated with developing valid shortage indicators using quantitative data (i.e., counts of supply relative to demand). Based on data collected from school district administrators in 1979 and 1983, NCES (1982, 1985) found little evidence of shortages (see Table 4).

Reported shortages (i.e., vacancies) for 1983 were only 1.6 per thousand currently employed teachers; the figures were only slightly higher for science and mathematics teachers (1.7 and 1.8 per thousand, respectively). This does not appear to represent a crisis. Paradoxically, in 1979, when teacher layoffs were reported—and far exceeded shortages—levels of vacancies in mathematics and science were much higher.

These data, however, do not reveal a great deal about labor market shortages. First, the data do not use levels of vacancy as a benchmark for measuring success in filling positions. Because the reported data assess vacancies *as a proportion of all current teachers,* they do not reveal the extent to which new teachers were sought or found. The tabulation does not take into account varying demand or hiring rates from year to year; thus it does not reveal the degree to which current posted positions were adequately filled. Additional calculations from the 1983 data reveal that, *as a proportion of all vacancies,* 19 per thousand were not filled—a figure that suggests a level of shortage substantially greater than the reported 1.6 per thousand teachers.

A greater vacancy level also may explain why shortages appeared so much larger in 1979, when teacher surpluses and layoffs in general were thought to be widespread: If more hiring occurred during 1979, relatively higher levels of vacancies would be expected, even if labor market shortages were not comparatively more pronounced. Alternatively, the differences between the 2 years may be because NCES changed its definition of shortage between the two surveys. Finally, it is possible that levels of vacancies really were relatively higher in 1979 than in 1983. However, because there were more layoffs than vacancies for mathematics and science teachers in 1979, the explanation for this is probably not that absolute levels of shortage were greater in 1979, but that labor market volatility and geographical imbalances contributed to a greater disequilibrium between supply and demand.

There is a second problem with using vacancies as a proxy for shortages. In general, leaving vacancies unfilled is the last of the many options districts use to respond to a labor market shortage. Combining this shortage indicator with another, such as the percentage of new teachers who are uncertified, more accurately indicates shortages. Unfortunately, although NCES reported district officials' estimates of uncertified teachers by field in 1983 (see Table 4), comparable field-specific data on the certification status of newly hired teachers were not collected. Thus, although we know that districts counted 3.5% of all teachers (and 4.1% of all mathematics and science teachers) as uncertified in the field to which they were assigned, the survey did not report how many newly hired mathematics and science teachers were uncertified for their assignments.

Overall, 12.4% of newly hired teachers in 1983 were reported as not certified for the field to which they were assigned. If these were added to the

FIGURE 1.
Alternative Indicators of Shortage

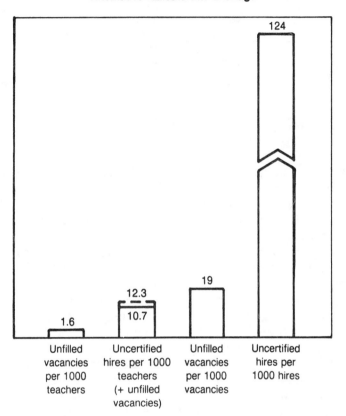

Source: Haggstrom, Darling-Hammond, and Grissmer, 1988.

counts of vacancies as evidence of shortage, the estimate of shortages would skyrocket from 19 per thousand vacancies to over 140 (see Figure 1). The estimates would undoubtedly be higher for mathematics and science, given the larger number of vacancies and uncertified teachers reported for these fields.

Data on uncertified newly hired teachers by field are available from two other sources. First, the National Science Teachers Association found in a 1981-82 survey of school principals that half of the newly employed mathematics and science teachers in that year were not certified to teach in their assigned fields (Shymansky & Aldridge, 1982). A more recent survey of 29 state departments of education by the Council of Chief State School Officers (CCSSO) found somewhat lower, but still substantial, es-

TABLE 5
Percentage of Teachers Uncertified in Subject Hired To Teach

Subject	No. new hires	No. uncertified new hires	% uncertified new hires	% uncertified teachers
Biology	1,625	90	9	6
Chemistry	574	63	13	10
Earth science	964	76	21	17
General science	1,938	184	16	18
Physics	328	60	20	15
Mathematics	6,124	478	12	8

Source: Capper, 1987.

timates of the numbers of newly hired mathematics and science teachers uncertified in 1985 (Capper, 1987). As Table 5 shows, these estimates ranged from a low of 9% for biology to highs of 20% for physics and 21% for earth science. These estimates are higher than those of the NCES but lower than those based on surveys of teachers or principals. The discrepancies undoubtedly are due in part to the particular sample of states responding to the CCSSO survey (which did not include the largest states) and to the fact that state departments have less accurate information about out-of-field teaching than do school principals or teachers themselves.

For many shortage indicators, the source of the data is important. School districts have little incentive—and a large disincentive—to collect and report information on how many teachers are assigned in fields for which they are not certified. Favorable certification data enhance a district's reputation with its clientele; moreover, the practice of assigning teachers out of field is illegal in some states. Thus, it is not surprising that teachers' own accounts of their certification status reveal much higher levels of out-of-field teaching than do district reports. For example, a 1980-81 National Education Association (NEA) survey of teachers indicated that 16% of all teachers teach some classes outside their field of preparation, and 9% spend most of their time teaching out of field (NEA, 1981). The High School and Beyond special survey supplement of 10,000 teachers indicated that, among high school teachers, 11% teach primarily outside their area of state certification and 17% have less than a college minor in the field they most frequently teach (Carroll, 1985) (see Figure 2).

These examples demonstrate that the form in which data are collected and reported affects how they are interpreted later. Although one picture of the supply and demand situation may engender complacence, a closer look may create cause for concern. In addition, reliance on untested assumptions about supply and demand trends produces different perspectives on the current situation and different prognoses for the future.

FIGURE 2.
Alternative Indicators of Misassignment

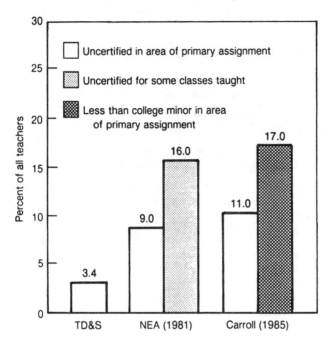

Source: Haggstrom, Darling-Hammond, and Grissmer, 1988.

TRENDS IN TEACHER SUPPLY

Throughout the 1970s and mid-1980s, the supply of newly prepared entrants into teaching declined sharply; this was especially true for mathematics and science teaching. The most regular and reliable source of information on trends in teacher supply is the data on earned degrees collected by NCES. These data show that between 1972 and 1985 the number of students graduating with 4- or 5-year bachelor's degrees in education dropped by more than half, from 194,229 to 88,161 (NCES, 1987a). Between 1971 and 1982, graduates with degrees in mathematics education dropped from 2,217 to 629; graduates with degrees in science education dropped from 891 to 558 (NCES, 1982, 1986).

Since then, increased demand along with salary hikes and recruitment incentives have boosted enrollments in mathematics and science education programs. By 1985-86, the number of degrees earned in mathematics education had rebounded to 1,259, though still well below levels of a decade earlier. Degrees in science education had climbed to 1,052 (NCES, 1988a).

FIGURE 3.
Qualifications of New Teachers for the Field They Are Currently Teaching (1981)

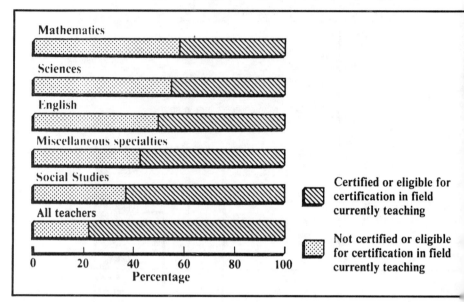

Source: Darling-Hammond, 1984.

These data are only a partial indicator of teacher supply, because they do not take account of the students who receive degrees in other fields but become certified to teach. Unfortunately, the only national source of data on this pool of potential teachers—NCES's Recent College Graduates Surveys (RCGS)—does not routinely report information by field. One analysis of these data, though, suggests that, of the 1979-80 college graduates who reported that they were certified or eligible for certification in mathematics and science, only 21% actually majored in mathematics or science education (Rumberger, 1985). This would suggest that the estimates of supply indicated by the data on degrees earned might be increased by as much as 500% to reflect the actual numbers of recent graduates prepared to teach.

Nonetheless, of this same cohort of college graduates, the RCGS data show that fewer than half of those newly hired to teach mathematics or science full time in 1981 were certified or certifiable in these fields (see Figure 3). This may be in part because demand exceeded even the more generous estimate of available supply and because many newly prepared teachers do not go on to teach. Time-series data from the RCGS show that, of a decreasing pool of graduates prepared to teach between 1978

TABLE 6
Elementary/Secondary Teaching Status of Recent Bachelor's
Degree Recipients Newly Qualified To Teach

Teaching status	1978	1981	1985
Recent bachelor's degree recipients			
newly qualified to teach	171,100	132,200	98,658
Mathematics	4,800	4,900	NA
% applying to teach	77	85	74
(Mathematics)	(78)	(73)	NA
% teaching full or part time	60	64	58
(Mathematics)	(58)	(59)	NA

Source: National Center for Education Statistics, 1983, 1985b.

and 1985, only about 60% were teaching full or part time a year after graduation (see Table 6). The proportion teaching full time was about 50% in each of these years. NCES provided specific data for mathematics teachers in 1978 and 1981 showing that these prospective teachers were less likely than others to seek a teaching job after graduation or to be teaching. Sample sizes were too small to provide similar information on science teachers.

That mathematics and science teachers might be less likely than other candidates to enter teaching after qualifying to do so is not surprising, because the wage discrepancies between teaching and other careers are much higher in these fields than others. Yet, like candidates in other fields, those in mathematics and science seem to be responding in recent years to the large wage hikes in teaching. The increased enrollments in mathematics and science education programs occurred after states and local districts began raising teacher salaries by 40% between 1981 and 1986 (Darling-Hammond & Berry, 1988).

We noted earlier that real wage hikes are one of the most useful economic indicators of a tight labor market. This appears to have been true in recent years. However, as increases in teacher salaries began to flatten out again in 1989 without closing the wage gaps with other occupations, the extent to which supply will increase to meet demand is still a major question.

TRENDS IN TEACHER DEMAND

According to the NCES projections of teacher demand, overall demand will rise through most of the coming decade as enrollments grow and teacher turnover due to retirement increases (see Table 7). If demand for mathematics and science teachers remains a constant share of overall demand during these years, we will need an estimated 20,000 teachers annually over much of the next decade (Carey et al., 1988). As a rough point of

TABLE 7
Projected Demand for New Classroom Teachers in Public Elementary and
Secondary Schools in 50 States and DC, Fall 1988–Fall 1997

| | | Demand for new teachers | | | |
| | | | Due to: | | |
Year	Total teachers	Total	Turnover	Enrollment changes	Other factors
1988	2,313	155	118	−1	38
1989	2,333	140	120	−1	21
1990	2,355	143	121	21	2
1991	2,381	149	122	32	−5
1992	2,419	161	124	35	2
1993	2,459	166	126	35	5
1994	2,500	169	128	37	4
1995	2,544	174	130	28	16
1996	2,585	174	132	22	20
1997	2,622	171	134	13	24

Source: National Center for Education Statistics, 1988b.

comparison, if we assumed, according to the estimates presented in the preceding section, that the pool of newly prepared entrants equals five times the number of mathematics and science education graduates, the current "new supply" could reach approximately 11,000 annually. Though these ballpark estimates still suggest a gap, we cannot rush to a judgment about whether shortages will exist and how large they might be.

Two important assumptions that have produced opposing views of teacher supply and shortages are assumptions about teacher turnover rates and about the size of the reserve pool of prospective teachers. Ultimately, whether the number of new entrants to teaching will be adequate in any given year or period of years is largely a function of teacher turnover, on the demand side, and on how many more entrants from the reserve pool are available to fill those positions, on the supply side. Unfortunately, we have little data to assess either of these major factors.

As Table 7 shows, teacher turnover is the single largest source of demand for new teachers. Measures of teacher turnover, however, have been inconsistent and inconsistently applied to demand projections. Until this year, NCES has used an annual turnover rate of 6%, based on a downward adjustment made to the 8% turnover rate estimated in 1969. Using this turnover rate, NCES projected the nation will need to hire about 1,080,000 new teachers between 1987 and 1992 (NCES, 1985a). However, more recent data from the Census Bureau's Current Population Surveys placed the teacher turnover rate in 1984 at slightly more than 9%. If this estimate is correct, the number of new teachers needed over this period will exceed 1,500,000. On the other hand, the most recent NCES projections use teacher turnover rates developed by the Bureau of Labor

Statistics, which estimated elementary teacher turnover in 1983-84 at 4.9%, and secondary teacher turnover at 5.6%. These estimates yield a turnover in demand to 1992 of about 1,000,000. Because attrition was at a historic low in 1983 due to a preponderance of mid-career teachers in the teaching force, this estimate is sure to increase with pending retirements (Grissmer & Kirby, 1987). These various estimates and projections reveal that there are serious problems with both the measurement of teacher turnover and the use of such measures in projection models (Haggstrom et al., 1988; NAS, 1987).

Whatever estimate one uses for overall teacher turnover, it is not appropriate to apply the same figure to mathematics and science teachers. Teachers in these areas tend to have a wider range of nonteaching job options—with most jobs paying much better than teaching—and so are more likely than teachers in other subject areas to leave teaching. For example, Murnane and Olsen (forthcoming a, forthcoming b) have found that physics and chemistry teachers in the two states they examined (Michigan and North Carolina) leave teaching sooner than other types of teachers.

Data on teacher turnover also need to distinguish between more and less permanent types of turnover (e.g., retirement vs. temporary leaves of absence). Those teachers who leave teaching only temporarily constitute one part of the reserve pool, a major component of teacher supply in any given year. The other major component of this reserve pool consists of individuals switching from other fields into teaching at mid-career or after retirement. There are no reliable sources of national data on the reentrance rates of former teachers from the reserve pool, and only a few small studies of individuals switching to education from other fields (see Darling-Hammond, Hudson, & Kirby, 1989). Most of the conclusions made about the prospects of shortage are based on untested assumptions about the propensity of those currently in other fields to enter teaching.

For example, two researchers who doubt that shortages exist or are imminent make unfounded assumptions about reserve pool availability. Feistritzer (1986) relies on the assumption that all individuals certified to teach since 1970 but not currently teaching are available members of the reserve pool. Similarly, Hecker (1986) assumes, without supporting data, that more openings and current education reforms will produce a large enough increase in the number of newly trained entrants and returnees from the reserve pool to fill the demand gap.

Although the plausibility of these assumptions may be furthered by new initiatives to increase the supply of mathematics and science teachers (see Carey et al., 1988), existing data do not support the view that many individuals in the scientific and technical labor force will leave their jobs to enter elementary or secondary school teaching. Analyses of the NSF's

Longitudinal Surveys of Scientists and Engineers, for example, show that of the 21,423 respondents employed in scientific and technical occupations in 1970, no more than 121 (about 0.5%) ever switched to jobs in precollege teaching during the course of the decade. Most of these did not stay in teaching for more than 1 or 2 years. For the 1980 sample, less than 0.2% entered precollege teaching in 1982 or 1984 (Darling-Hammond et al., 1989). As these data suggest, the incentives for individuals trained in mathematics or science-related fields to enter or remain in teaching may be more tenuous than for other fields, where wage discrepancies are smaller and alternative job opportunities fewer.

These assumptions about turnover rates and reserve pool availability are key to an assessment of whether shortages will continue. Assessments of whether current shortages are severe rest on judgments about the importance of teacher qualifications as a measure of supply. However, the definition of a qualified teacher is a source of dispute, and some measures of supply and shortage ignore teacher qualifications altogether. With changes in certification and hiring standards, the supply of teachers can be altered at will so that, based on body counts at least, supply can always equal demand. Essentially, the competing claims about teacher shortages are arguments over the degree to which qualifications are an important indicator of supply.

In the following sections, we examine the data that are available about the qualifications of mathematics and science teachers, pointing out what studies would be needed to provide a fuller picture of supply and demand and to resolve the debate over teacher shortages.

WHAT KIND OF TEACHER PREPARATION MATTERS?

In the teacher shortage debate, teacher quality typically is defined only by reference to certification status; thus, the definition varies substantially from state to state. Because certification rules also change within states (often in response to teacher shortages), the measure also lacks stability over time and—where several types of certificates are offered—may mean different things for different candidates in a single state even at one point in time. Part of the reason for such inconsistency among teacher certification policies is that there is a lack of agreement about what knowledge teachers need to teach well.

"Good teachers are born, not made." "Those who can, do; those who cannot, teach." "Anyone can teach." Implicit in each of these clichés is the belief that teaching is a simple, or at least intuitive, task that requires no special training. This belief does not distinguish between formal and informal instruction, nor does it incorporate a sophisticated notion of what effective teaching may entail. Just as a parent may be an appropriate "doctor" for tending a child's minor cuts and colds, so too a parent is an appropriate "teacher" for transmitting basic cultural knowledge. But an untrained parent may not be the most effective provider of medical care for a serious illness or injury or the most effective instructor for passing on the full depth and breadth of knowledge required of an "educated" person.

In the classroom, a teacher must understand not only the subject matter to be taught, but also how to teach that subject matter, how to modify and adapt instructional practice to individual student needs, and how to diagnose those needs. To assume that such skills and knowledge can be acquired without formal preparation is to seriously underestimate the complexity and scope of instruction. Education has multiple, and frequently changing, instructional goals. Teachers handle many clients simultaneously, with these clients typically benefitting in different ways from different types and levels of instruction. In the face of these complexities, many new and experienced teachers note the importance of methods courses that link theory to practice, internship opportunities, and adequate preparation in understanding student motivation and behavior in increasing their effectiveness in the classroom (see Darling-Hammond et al., 1989).

A growing body of research on teacher effectiveness suggests that the effectiveness of different teaching behaviors varies depending on both the goals of instruction and the types of students taught. For example, many of the *direct* instruction behaviors that seem to result in increased achievement in standardized tests of rudimentary skills are dissimilar, indeed nearly opposite, from those *indirect* teaching activities that seem to increase complex cognitive learning, problem-solving ability, and creativity (McKeachie & Kulik, 1975; Peterson, 1979; Soar, 1977; Soar & Soar, 1976). Moreover, desirable affective outcomes of education— independence, curiosity, and positive attitudes toward school, teacher, and self—seem to result from teaching behaviors that are different from those prescribed for increasing student achievement on standardized tests (Horwitz, 1979; McKeachie & Kulik, 1975; Peterson, 1979; Traub, Weiss, Fisher, Musella, & Kahn, 1973).

Effective teaching behaviors also appear to vary for students of different socioeconomic, mental, and psychological characteristics (Brophy & Evertson, 1974, 1977; Carbo, Dunn, & Dunn, 1986; Cronbach & Snow, 1977) and for different grades and subjects (Gage, 1978; McDonald & Elias, 1976). Druva and Anderson (1983), for example, found that teachers' background in science was related positively to students' science achievement, and this relationship became stronger at progressively higher grade levels. Also, it has been found that a student-structured approach to teaching and learning improves males' attitudes toward science, whereas a teacher-structured approach improves females' attitudes (Abhyankar, 1977).

In sum, accumulated research on teaching demonstrates that it is a highly complex activity requiring extensive knowledge and a wide repertoire of skills, flexibility, versatility, and commitment. One might expect that to be an effective teacher would require adequate formal preparation.

To prove this point, various teacher preparation and qualification measures have been examined for their relationship to student learning. These include teachers' years of education, recency of educational enrichment, years of teaching experience, and subject-matter knowledge (e.g., Andrews, Blackmon, & Mackey, 1980; Ayers & Qualls, 1979; Druva & Anderson, 1983; Murnane & Phillips, 1981; Penick & Yager, 1983; Summers & Wolfe, 1975). These studies have had equivocal results, primarily because of (a) an inability to specify and take into account the effects of the many variables that mediate between teacher preparation and student performance, and (b) the frequent absence of adequate student-attainment measures that reflect a wide range of content and modes of performance. Under these conditions, measures of association are likely to be weak if they appear at all; thus, we should be encouraged by any detectable relationships evident in the existing research literature.

In general, there are two basic types of knowledge that are perceived to be necessary for effective teaching: knowledge of what to teach (subject) and knowledge of how to teach (teaching methods). There is support for the assumption that a teacher with better subject knowledge is a better teacher, although the findings are not as strong or consistent as one might expect. Studies of teachers' scores on the National Teacher Examinations have found no consistent relationship between subject knowledge and performance, as measured by either student outcomes or supervisory ratings (Andrews et al., 1980; Ayers & Qualls, 1979; Quirk, Witten, & Weinberg, 1973; Summers & Wolfe, 1975). However, other measures of subject knowledge fare better. When Byrne (1983) summarized the results of 30 studies relating teachers' subject knowledge to student achievement, 17 studies showed a positive relationship. Of the 13 showing no relationship, Byrne noted that many had such little variability in the teacher knowledge measure that insignificant findings were almost inevitable.

Comparisons of teachers with degrees in education and those with subject-related degrees often have found no relation between the type of degree held and teacher performance. This may be because certification standards are such that teachers with different degrees have backgrounds that are similar (Murnane, 1985). However, Druva and Anderson (1983), in a meta-analysis of teacher characteristics and behaviors, found consistently positive relationships between student achievement in science and the teacher's background in education, biology (for biology teachers), and science. Also, Casserly (cited in Kolata, 1980) found that girls perform relatively better in mathematics when taught by teachers with a background in science, mathematics, or engineering.

It is likely that the degree of pedagogical skill may interact with subject knowledge to either bolster or reduce teacher performance. Glaser's (1983) work suggests that how one teaches mathematics or science (i.e., knowing how to teach problem solving, reasoning from evidence, checking one's procedures, and checking for understanding) is as important as what is taught. Also, in a review of findings of the National Longitudinal Study of Mathematical Abilities, Begle (1979) found that the strongest indicator of preparation as a correlate of student performance was the number of credits a teacher had taken in mathematics methods courses.

Teachers' educational level and recency of educational enrichment have also been used as proxy measures for teacher knowledge. Penick and Yager (1983) found that teachers in exemplary science programs not only had more years of education, but also more recent educational experiences than the average science teacher. Hanushek (1970) also found that the recency of voluntary educational experience is related to teacher performance. As Murnane (1985) notes, these findings suggest that it may not be only the knowledge acquired with a higher degree that is important, but also the enthusiasm for learning that leads the teacher to seek new knowledge that relates to increased student learning.

In sum, the kinds of knowledge that seem to promote learning include pedagogical as well as subject knowledge. Findings also suggest particular benefits from continuing course work or in-service training.

How Well Prepared Are Mathematics and Science Teachers?

As is true for indicators of teacher shortages, teachers' qualifications can be assessed only indirectly, because there is no absolute measure of qualification or preparation. Existing data bases provide potential indicators of teachers' preparation. Those reviewed here are certification status, college major, courses taken, and teachers' own perceptions of their qualifications. These indicators are derived from the following recent national surveys of teachers:

- High School and Beyond (HS&B): A supplemental survey of 11,000 public and private secondary school teachers drawn from High School and Beyond sample schools, conducted in 1984.
- National Survey of Science and Mathematics Education (NSSME): A survey of 1,383 elementary teachers, 1,239 secondary mathematics teachers, and 1,708 secondary science teachers in public or private schools, conducted in 1985-1986.

• National Assessment of Educational Progress (NAEP) Science Assessment: A survey of 774 3rd grade teachers, 325 7th grade science teachers, and 289 11th grade science teachers in public and private schools, conducted in 1986.

In addition, data from transcript analyses of college graduates in the Southern Regional Education Board (SREB) states provide detailed information on the course work background of the pool of teacher candidates in one region of the country (Galambos, Cornett, & Spitler, 1985).

Certification

Most state governments require that all public school teachers be certified before they teach in the classroom. In practice, individuals who do not fully meet certification requirements often are hired when qualified applicants are unavailable. This is done rather than cancel courses or increase class sizes, alternatives typically viewed as even less desirable than hiring marginally qualified teachers. Because schools usually must hire certified candidates when they are available, the proportion of uncertified teachers hired provides a measure of labor market shortages, even though it is not a standardized measure of preparation.

Certification has a number of advantages as an indicator of teacher preparation or qualification. First, it is a relatively easy measure to collect, at least in comparison to measures such as college course work and grades, which are more susceptible to errors in recall and reporting biases (or which must be obtained through the difficult and expensive procedure of transcript analysis). Also, certification standards are a richer indicator of preparation than, for example, course work counts, as they typically rely on a number of relevant domains of knowledge necessary for effective teaching (e.g., basic skills knowledge, subject knowledge, pedagogical knowledge, student teaching experience).

We have mentioned the disadvantages of certification status as an indicator, especially that certification standards are highly variable, changing across states and over time, as well as within states. In years when hiring is more difficult, states often permit hiring under "provisional" or "alternative" certification for those meeting less stringent preparation requirements (see Darling-Hammond & Berry, 1988). Also, the meaning of a particular certification status will vary substantially from one state to another, limiting cross-state comparisons. In addition, practicing teachers are usually granted full certification when standards are raised for entering teachers. This also limits comparability, because two teachers in a single state with the same certification status may have met very different preparation requirements.

TABLE 8
Percentage of Secondary Mathematics or Science Teachers Who
Are Certified for the Courses They Teach

Survey	% mathematics teachers	% science teachers
High School and Beyond[a]	91	87
National Survey of Science and Mathematics Education		
grades 7-9[b]	65	76
grades 10-12	85	91
National Assessment of Educational Progress—Science		
grade 7[c]	—	63
grade 11	—	80

[a]These data represent the percentage of teachers with mathematics or science as their primary teaching assignment who are certified for the courses they teach.
[b]These data represent the percentage of mathematics or science teachers who are certified in those fields.
[c]These data represent the percentage of students taught mathematics or science by teachers certified in those fields.
Sources: Carroll, 1985; Mullis and Jenkins, 1988; Weiss, 1987 (figures adjusted for nonresponse).

Problems in comparability are evident in data from the three national surveys that collect and report information on teacher certification (see Table 8). Although most secondary mathematics and science teachers are certified in the subjects they teach, estimates diverge across data bases and by level and field. In both fields, it appears that significantly more senior high than junior high teachers are certified. In ballpark terms, it appears that roughly 80 to 90% of high school teachers are certified for their subjects, compared to 65 to 75% of junior high school teachers. The worst case estimate appears in the NAEP science assessment, where 37% of seventh grade students are taught by teachers who are not certified in science. The best case estimate appears in the HS&B survey, which shows 91% of senior high mathematics teachers are certified.

Probably neither the worst case nor the best case estimate paints an entirely accurate picture. In the case of seventh grade science teachers, many may have received full certification in K-8 elementary education when that was the normal area of licensure. On the other hand, the high school mathematics teachers responding to the HS&B survey were those whose primary teaching assignment is mathematics. Many out-of-field teachers are probably teaching only one or two courses of the subject for which they are less well qualified. If mathematics or science was their secondary assignment area, they did not respond to this question.

It is important to note that the data in Table 8 include teachers who have regular, provisional, alternative, or in some cases emergency certification in mathematics or science. Most surveys include a separate item that asks what kind of certification the teacher has without specifying what subject area the certificate is in, thus preventing analysis of certification type by field taught. Because the definitions of certification types vary so much from state to state, comparisons would be difficult in any event. Provisional certification, for example, is equivalent to emergency certification in some states, but in others, it is equivalent to full certification for a beginning teacher (who does not become fully certified until satisfactorily completing a year or more of regular classroom teaching). In some states alternative routes lead to full certification, whereas in others they do not. Where provisional certification is separated from regular certification (e.g., the NSSME), the percentage with regular science or mathematics certification is found to be about 6% lower than that given in the table.

College Major

Aside from general measures of certification, most measures of teacher preparation focus directly or indirectly on teachers' subject knowledge. This focus on subject knowledge addresses not only the college courses prospective teachers choose to take, but also the out-of-field assignment of teachers when qualified candidates are unavailable.

One general measure of subject knowledge is a teacher's college major. This indicator is predicated on the growing belief that secondary teachers should have a major (or its equivalent) in the subject they teach. Some states have had such a requirement for many years, and many teacher education reform proposals have recommended it, with the result that other states have recently mandated this requirement.

Because of its policy relevance, we present data on this indicator here; however, it has limitations. First, teachers who did not major in a subject field may nonetheless have taken at least as many courses in the subject area as is taken by those who do receive a major. Second, a subject major (as opposed to a specialized education major) addresses only one part of the preparation question. It does not address how well prepared the teacher is to translate subject knowledge into instruction that is appropriate, informative, and interesting to students.

The one national survey that reports data on college major, the NSSME, reports both the proportion of teachers who majored in mathematics or science and the proportion who majored in mathematics or science education (see Table 9).

These data, consistent with the certification data, show a greater degree of preparation among senior high school teachers than among middle or junior high school teachers. For example, 84% of grade 10-12 science teachers majored in science or science education, compared to only 68%

TABLE 9
Percentage of Teachers with Major in Given Field

Major	Grades	
	7-9	10-12
Mathematics teachers		
Mathematics	30	52
Mathematics education	18	24
Either or both majors	48	76
Science teachers		
Science	59	76
Science education	9	8
Either or both majors	68	84

Source: Weiss, 1987.

of grade 7-9 science teachers. Also consistent with the NSSME data showing a lower proportion of mathematics than science teachers certified, mathematics teachers appear to be less likely than science teachers to have either a subject major or an education major in their field. Only 48% of grade 7-9 teachers and 76% of grade 10-12 mathematics teachers majored in mathematics or mathematics education.

College Course Work

Another measure of teachers' academic preparation is the number of courses they have taken in relevant subjects. These analyses tend to concentrate on subject courses, with only the NSSME reporting data on teachers' education courses. According to the HS&B data, secondary mathematics teachers tend to have taken fewer courses in their subject area than either science teachers or teachers in other fields (see Table 10). Science teachers appear to take the most courses in their discipline; 89% of science teachers have taken at least seven courses in their subject area. This compares to 81% of mathematics teachers and 83% of other teachers.

The NSSME provides the most detailed information on teachers' subject area and pedagogical preparation. Weiss (1987, 1988) examined these

TABLE 10
Percentage of Teachers Who Have Taken College Courses
in Their Primary Assignment Field

Primary assignment field	No. of subject-area courses			
	0	1-6	7-12	13+
Mathematics	1	18	27	54
Science	1	10	30	59
All others	2	15	22	61

Source: Carroll, 1985.

data separately for elementary teachers, grade 7-9 and 10-12 mathematics teachers, and grade 7-9 and 10-12 science teachers. In addition, transcript data on 6,000 graduates at 17 major universities in states belonging to the SREB also provide detailed course work data on prospective mathematics and science teachers (i.e., those college graduates meeting all teacher certification requirements in their state) (Galambos, 1985; Galambos et al., 1985). Although the SREB data do not necessarily reflect the course backgrounds of actual teachers, because not all of those who are eligible for teacher certification actually obtain certificates or enter teaching, they do provide insight into the nature of teacher preparation in one region of the country.

Here we discuss the course work findings from the NSSME and the SREB studies as they compare to the recommendations for certification made by the two professional teacher organizations that have developed course work standards for teachers of mathematics and science: the National Council of Teachers of Mathematics (NCTM) and the National Science Teachers Association (NSTA).

The NSTA guidelines for K-12 science teachers (see Appendix 1) are designed to form the core requirement for a national certification program. This certification is designed, among other things, to identify the most highly qualified science teachers for advancement opportunities within teaching. An important feature of the NSTA certification program is the dual certification that is being recommended for secondary teachers. This recommendation stems from the NSTA research finding that most science teachers at the secondary level have assignments in more than one area of science: 65% of physics teachers' assignments, 52% of chemistry teachers' assignments, and 37% of biology teachers' assignments are in other areas (predominantly other sciences) (Aldridge, 1986).

The NCTM established a set of revised guidelines for the preparation of mathematics teachers in 1981. The guidelines "present the minimal standards for programs for the preparation of teachers of mathematics," as well as a "minimal list of competencies that . . . teachers in mathematics should meet" (NCTM, 1981, p. v.). To provide the desired competencies, the courses listed in Appendix 2 are recommended for teachers of mathematics.

Science Teachers

The NSTA (1983) recommends that elementary teachers have a minimum of 12 semester hours of science, including one course each in biological, physical, and earth sciences, plus a science methods course. The SREB (Galambos et al., 1985) and Weiss (1987, 1988) studies found that elementary teachers (and prospective elementary teachers) do take an average of 12 science credits. However, the courses they take tend to be heavily concentrated in the biological and life sciences, with much less work in the physical and earth sciences. Thus, only 34% of all elementary teachers meet the full set of course standards. More specifically, 85% of all elementary teachers meet the biology course requirement, 72% meet the physical science standard, and only 53% meet the earth sciences standard. Further, although most elementary teachers have taken an elementary science methods class, over 10% have not had such a course.

At the middle school level, the NSTA recommends 36 semester hours in the three science areas (12 hours in each area), a science methods course, and at least 9 semester hours in mathematics and computer science. At the secondary level, the NSTA recommends a minimum of 50 semester hours in science. The SREB study reveals that prospective secondary science teachers take an average of 49.4 hours in science, roughly comparable to that recommended by the NSTA, but that only 31% of this course work is at the upper level.

Weiss (1988) examined teachers of grades 7-9. Sixty-seven percent of these teachers met the NSTA standards for the overall number of science courses, but only 22% met the standards for the number of courses in each area. Within each science area, those teaching earth science were the least well prepared. Whereas only 10% of biology teachers and 10% of physical science teachers had taken fewer than three courses in the specific science subject they teach, 52% of earth science teachers had taken fewer than three earth science courses; 22% of these teachers had taken no college courses in earth science. About 20% of the grade 7-9 science teachers lacked a science methods course, and two thirds lacked a computer programming course.

A similar pattern emerged in the secondary (grade 10-12) data. Only 56% of teachers at this level met the NSTA standard of at least 50 semester hours in the sciences (based on an assumed 3.5 semester hours per course). The NSTA standards also recommend that secondary science teachers take at least 32 semester hours in their specialization. The NSSME teachers were categorized by whether they taught a specific subject or not, rather than by their specialization. Including multiple assignments, 59% of science teachers teach biology, 33% teach chemistry, and 24% teach physics. Table 11 shows the extent to which teachers in each of these subject areas met the NSTA's specific course standards. It is clear from this table that biology teachers are more likely than physical science teachers to meet the NSTA recommendations in their specialization. Only about half of all chemistry or physics teachers have taken 32 semester hours in their subject area. In contrast, a relatively stable 82 to 84% have completed a science methods course.

TABLE 11
Percentage of Grade 10-12 Science Teachers Meeting National Science Teachers
Association Standards, by Standard and Type of Science Teacher

| NSTA standard | Type of science teacher | | | |
	Biology	Chemistry	Physics	All
50 semester hours in science	—	—	—	56
32 semester hours in science specialty	80	53	41	64
Methods course	83	84	82	83
All science course requirements plus methods course	29	31	12	26

Source: Weiss, 1988.

Mathematics Teachers

At the elementary level, the NCTM recommends a minimum of two mathematics courses for lower grade teachers, and three for upper grade teachers, all with prerequisites of 2 years of high school algebra, 1 year of geometry, and a mathematics methods course. The SREB found that prospective elementary teachers do take an average of about 2.5 mathematics courses, but that many of the courses do not meet the NCTM's prerequisites. Weiss's (1988) data also show that only 18% of elementary teachers meet the NCTM recommendations for specific courses. However, most are missing only one recommended course, usually geometry. As in science, about 90% of elementary teachers have taken a mathematics methods course.

The NCTM recommends that junior high mathematics teachers take five college mathematics courses, in separate subspecialty areas, plus a computer science course and a methods course. Weiss (1988) found that only 10% of grade 7-9 mathematics teachers meet all the NCTM standards. Eighty-three percent of mathematics teachers are lacking courses in one or more of the five mathematics areas outlined in the NCTM standards (most often in applications of mathematics). Fifty-two percent lack a computer programming course, and 14% lack a methods class.

Recommendations for high school mathematics teachers are similar, but include 10 mathematics courses. The SREB found that prospective secondary mathematics teachers take an average of about 11 courses in mathematics, with about 45% of them at the upper level.

Weiss (1988) found that only 12% of grade 10-12 mathematics teachers had taken all the NCTM-recommended courses, although about 50% either met or came close to meeting all the standards. The courses these teachers were most likely to be missing were applications of mathematics, history of mathematics, and other upper division mathematics. On the other hand, 12% of grade 10-12 mathematics teachers had taken fewer than 5 of the 10 recommended mathematics courses. Thirty-six percent had not had a computer programming course, and 15% had not had a mathematics methods course.

Summary

These data show that in terms of the overall number of courses taken, most teachers meet the NCTM and NSTA standards. However, fewer teachers are able to meet the recommendations pertaining to specific course content and level. For example, elementary science teachers appear to take too few courses in the earth sciences, whereas middle and secondary teachers rarely take the recommended number of courses in all areas of science concentration. Among middle school teachers, courses in earth science are particularly lacking, while at the upper high school level, courses in physical science are lacking. Among mathematics teachers, few teachers take as many upper level mathematics courses as the NCTM recommends, and few have the recommended courses in applications of mathematics, history of mathematics, or computer programming.

To some extent, these findings may reflect inadequacies in the courses available to prospective teachers, rather than in the choices that prospective teachers make. Few colleges, for example, offer a wide range of courses in the earth sciences; courses in mathematics history and applications are also fairly uncommon. However, these findings also indicate an underlying tension in teacher preparation. On one hand, the professional standards suggest that teacher preparation be academically rigorous, providing prospective teachers with both a broad and deep understanding of the material they teach. On the other hand, the topics that are most important for teachers to know well are those that they will be teaching within the elementary and secondary curriculum. Filling a limited college schedule with courses in calculus and analytical chemistry, for example, may seem inappropriate to the prospective elementary teacher who feels that courses in finite numbers or animal behavior, although possibly of lower level or lacking in breadth, are more relevant to areas in which he or she should be well prepared to teach.

The data on teachers' pedagogical preparation clearly show that elementary teachers are better prepared for this aspect of teaching than are middle or high school teachers. Although 90% of elementary teachers have had a science methods course and 90% have had a mathematics methods course, only 80 to 85% of middle and secondary school teachers have had such courses.

Perceptions of Qualifications

A final potential indicator of adequate preparation is whether teachers believe they are adequately prepared to teach specific subjects. We do not yet know to what extent this subjective measure is related to the more

TABLE 12
Percentage of Elementary Teachers Who Believe They Are Adequately Qualified To Teach a Subject, by Subject Area

Subject area	% believing they are adequately qualified
Mathematics	99
Life science	89
Physical science	76
Earth/space sciences	77
Social studies	96
Reading	99

Source: Weiss, 1987.

commonly used measures of teacher preparation. Biases could affect this perceptions measure in either direction. For example, if teachers are reluctant to admit that they are not prepared for their teaching position, they may overestimate the true level of preparedness. On the other hand, if teachers believe that there is always more they could know or do for their students, they may underestimate their preparedness. In either case, though, a tendency for teachers to believe they are unprepared is cause for concern, and to the degree that teachers' responses on this measure mirror those on other indicators of preparation, they help illustrate the extent to which mathematics and science teachers are adequately prepared for their teaching positions.

Data on this indicator are available from the NAEP science assessment and the NSSME. The NAEP data show that although virtually all 7th and 11th grade teachers believe they are adequately prepared to teach science (95% and 97%, respectively), only 80% of 3rd grade teachers believe they are adequately prepared (Mullis & Jenkins, 1988).

As Tables 12 and 13 show, teachers responding to the NSSME show a similar pattern of responses: The higher the grade level, the more likely teachers are to believe they are adequately prepared to teach science. Table 12 also shows that, as the data on course work would imply, elementary teachers believe they are more qualified for teaching the life sciences than the physical sciences; almost one fourth of all elementary teachers

TABLE 13
Percentage of Secondary Teachers Who Believe They Are Adequately Qualified To Teach All Their Courses

Grade	Mathematics teachers	Science teachers
7-9	91	88
10-12	95	93

Source: Weiss, 1987.

TABLE 14
Percentage of Teachers Meeting Each Preparation Standard

| | % of those teaching: | | | | | |
| | Mathematics | | | Science | | |
Preparation standard	K-6	7-9	10-12	K-6	7-9	10-12
Certified in subject (includes all forms of certification)	—	65	85	—	76	91
College major in subject area (including mathematics or science education)	—	48	76	—	68	84
Meet National Science Teachers Association/National Council of Teachers of Mathematics standards	18	10	12	34	22	26
Methods course taken	90	85	85	90	80	83
Believe prepared in subject	99	91	95	89/77[a]	88	93

[a] 89% believe they are prepared to teach biology; 76-77% believe they are qualified to teach the physical and earth sciences.
Source: Weiss, 1987, 1988.

do not believe they are adequately qualified to teach the physical and earth sciences. Elementary teachers report being less prepared to teach the physical sciences than any other academic subject, although virtually all believe they are prepared for teaching mathematics. Table 13 also shows that secondary mathematics teachers are slightly more likely to believe they are prepared for their courses than are secondary science teachers.

Comparison of Preparation Indicators

Is there any consistency in these various indicators of teachers' preparation? Yes and no. As Table 14 demonstrates, the measure of preparation one chooses to use determines how well prepared teachers appear to be. Based on teachers' own perceptions or on their pedagogical course work, most mathematics and science teachers appear to be reasonably well prepared. Based on professional standards for content courses, however, these teachers appear to be less well prepared.

The data consistently show that mathematics and science teachers in grades 7-9 are less well prepared than their counterparts in grades 10-12. It is not as easy to draw conclusions about elementary teachers' preparation relative to teachers at other levels; the nature of preparation and teaching responsibilities are different. The indicators consistently suggest, though, that they are the least well prepared and comfortable with teaching the physical and earth sciences.

The question of adequacy of teacher preparation is not easy to answer, mainly because there is no single, reliable standard for measuring preparation that is valid for all purposes. Further, the few proxy measures that are available, none of which is very satisfactory, paint different pictures. Until we are clearer on exactly what a well-prepared mathematics or science teacher should know, the best approach to examining this issue is one that is similar to the multitrait multimethod matrix approach for examining construct validity. That is, a broad range of preparation indicators should be examined and compared for different types of teachers (e.g., mathematics, science, English, foreign language). At present, there are no data bases available with which to conduct such extensive analyses. The NSSME is the only data set that provides data on a wide range of preparation indicators, but because it surveys only mathematics and science teachers, it does not permit comparative analyses of how well prepared mathematics and science teachers are compared to teachers in other subjects.

RESEARCH NEEDS

Some of the research needed to examine the quality, supply of, and demand for precollege science and mathematics teachers can rely on existing, or soon-to-be-created, data bases at NCES. Other kinds of research will require different approaches and new data collection. The research portfolio, as a whole, should inform the nation not only about the levels of teacher supply, shortage, and qualifications, but also about the nature of supply or quality problems and, hence, about the prospective success of alternative means for addressing these problems. Below we discuss the key research questions that we believe should be addressed and several avenues for research in these areas.

Research Issues

In the area of teacher supply and demand, several questions need to be addressed:

- What are the major sources of supply for precollege mathematics and science teachers? How many of the new entrants each year are recent graduates of teacher education programs, recent graduates of other bachelor's or master's degree programs, entrants from other occupational fields (e.g., mid-career switchers or retirees starting new careers), immigrants from other fields of teaching, or re-entrants into teaching who left the teaching force for some period? Understanding the supply pool for mathematics and science teachers will allow better targeting of recruitment and training initiatives.
- What routes into teaching do these different types of teachers take (e.g., traditional undergraduate teacher education programs, gradu-

ate-level programs, alternative certification programs, retraining programs)? What are the qualifications of these different pools of teachers? How well prepared do they believe they are to teach different subject areas?

- What are the turnover rates of mathematics and science teachers of different types (by teaching field; age, sex, family status; source of entry; qualifications level; salary)? Where do these teachers go when they leave teaching? How many return to teaching?
- What is the demand for mathematics and science teachers of different types, and how is it likely to change based on demographic trends and policy initiatives, such as student course requirements?
- How are teacher qualifications and teaching conditions distributed across schools, students, and courses of different types? How do these distributional differences influence teacher turnover and teaching quality?
- Where are the greatest imbalances between the supply of and demand for mathematics and science teachers, by field, level, sector, and geographic location? What are the factors that contribute to these imbalances? How do these imbalances affect the qualifications of those hired to teach mathematics or science? What policies seem to be successful in ameliorating shortages while maintaining quality?

In the area of teacher preparation, we still know little about how mathematics and science teachers are prepared; few studies provide current information, and each of these studies has certain biases (e.g., nonrepresentative samples, possibility of response bias from self-report data). Some of the issues we need to know more about are as follows:

- How does teacher preparation vary across types of teachers (by field, level, sector, source of entry, type of certification, and type of students taught)? Also, what preparation do teachers believe is most useful or necessary, and how do these perceptions relate to more objective measures of preparation and quality?
- What are the effects of different types of preparation on teacher effectiveness and retention? Especially important to examine is the degree to which teacher candidates may differ because of their (a) previous academic training, (b) selection or self-selection into preparation programs, (c) previous occupational experience, (d) pedagogical training and field experience prior to teaching, and (e) instructional support (e.g., mentoring) during the first year of teaching.
- How does teacher preparation relate to teaching practice—that is, what types of preparation encourage the teaching practices that are most desired, or most strongly related to student outcomes?
- How does in-service course work supplement initial teacher prepara-

tion? What types of additional training or preparation do mathematics and science teachers need once they are in teaching and under what circumstances? Do they receive enough of such training? How can teaching be better structured to allow teachers the time and opportunity for additional training?

Sources of Data

Many of these research questions can be answered at least in part by analyses of existing or soon-to-be created data sets. Others will require special studies and the collection of new data.

Analyses of NCES Data Bases

In addition to the extant data bases just discussed, NCES has recently revised its previous surveys of teacher demand and shortage and of public and private school teachers and administrators. The earlier surveys of teacher demand and shortage were not designed to allow field-specific estimates of new teacher supply or qualifications. The public and private school teacher and administrator surveys did not focus on supply and demand issues. However, the teacher surveys did collect useful and relevant data on teacher qualifications, assignments, and mobility, which have not yet been analyzed. Furthermore, mathematics and science teachers were oversampled for these surveys in 1985 and 1986, providing an adequate sample size for many analyses of interest. Such analyses would provide better information than is currently available on a national basis about who is teaching science and mathematics in elementary and secondary schools, and how these teachers are distributed.

The new surveys, called the Schools and Staffing Surveys (SASS), were first fielded in 1988 and will be repeated biannually starting in 1991. They provide an integrated data base that will yield a much more complete set of data on teacher supply, demand, turnover, shortage, and qualifications that can be analyzed by teaching field. The survey set links the former district-level surveys of teacher demand and shortage with surveys of schools and teachers, correcting many of their previous shortcomings, and extending their capacity for assessing issues of supply and quality.

The much larger samples of teachers, and the design of the instruments to capture field-specific aspects of teacher hiring, assignment, qualifications, and distribution, will permit analyses of what kinds of individuals, with what kinds of training and experience, are teaching what kinds of science and mathematics classes to what kinds of students. Furthermore, the surveys will allow analyses of attrition, mobility, and turnover, reasons for leaving and destinations, and re-entry from the reserve pool, along with analyses of the sources of teacher supply, extent of shortage, and school-level strategies for handling shortfalls of qualified teachers. If continued funding is available to NCES for fielding these surveys on an ongoing basis, and the proper analyses are then performed, many of the missing pieces in the supply and demand puzzle can be filled in using this data set.

Other existing data bases can be plumbed further to fill gaps in needed information about the supply and qualifications of science and mathematics teachers. The National Longitudinal Study (NLS) special teacher supplement, conducted as part of the fifth follow-up of the high school class of 1972, includes all members of the cohort sample who ever taught, plus an added sample of students who majored in mathematics or science but did not enter teaching, thus permitting examination of career paths and decisions. Analyses of these data can illuminate some questions related to teacher attrition and the reserve pool, but the sample of science and mathematics teachers is likely to be too small for many analyses of interest. Findings also will be limited to the single cohort of individuals in that sample.

The periodic SRCG also suffer from small sample sizes of science and mathematics teachers, but analyses that aggregate these teachers into one or two groups (e.g., all science teachers, all mathematics teachers) can nonetheless illuminate patterns of entry into teaching and, equally important, losses of prospective teachers to other occupations. If longitudinal follow-ups of these graduates were conducted, reserve pool behavior could be examined also.

Other Sources of Data

State personnel files are an extensive and useful source of data about the entry and exit of teachers from the state teacher labor market, and can sometimes be linked to certification files, which describe teacher preparation in at least general terms. These data can be used to examine patterns of mobility and turnover; supplemented by surveys, they can provide a basis for examining reserve pool entry and exit behavior for particular types of teachers. The RAND Corporation is currently conducting such a study using state files supplemented by surveys of new teachers in Indiana for the Indiana Department of Public Instruction.

The NSF-sponsored, 1985-86 NSSME provides a rich source of data about teacher preparation, qualifications, and assignments, and how teachers are distributed across schools and students of different types. The data set offers many possibilities for analysis of the linkages among teacher preparation, source of entry and certification status, teaching practices, and teaching conditions. Some analyses have been done already (e.g., Weiss, 1987, 1988), but more are possible.

Finally, supplements to ongoing, large-scale national surveys are a potentially fruitful source of data. For example, the NSF's longitudinal surveys of scientists and engineers have not, in the past, sampled precollege teachers. However, they would be an ideal source of information about labor force behavior and job characteristics for mathematics and science teachers, as compared to their scientifically trained peers in other occupations, if the sample were expanded. An NAS panel is considering this proposal, among others, that might render the data set more useful.

Special Studies

Several important questions are worthy of special studies. For example, as mentioned earlier, examination of what teaching practices are related to particular forms of teacher preparation is critical to an understanding of what kinds of preparation—either preservice or in-service—should be encouraged. Although this question can be examined in part by using large-scale data sets like the NAEP (using the supplemental teacher surveys for the mathematics and science assessments), more controlled and carefully designed case studies of teaching practices would provide richer data about the factors influencing teaching, including teaching conditions and assignments.

Given the proliferation of alternative certification and other nontraditional preparation programs for mathematics and science teachers, it would be useful to examine in-depth the outcomes of these programs, not only in terms of teacher supply and retention, but also in terms of teacher effectiveness. Several small-scale studies have been conducted of a few of these programs, but these have relied on record data and surveys of cross-sectional samples; none have tracked these nontraditional recruits over time, or directly examined their experiences in teaching. Equally important, none have yet compared the nature and outcomes of these programs to those of traditional teacher preparation and certification programs.

Finally, a great deal more needs to be learned about what motivates qualified individuals to go into mathematics and science teaching and what dissuades others from doing so. Obviously, the same kind of information is needed about what encourages some highly qualified individuals to remain in precollege mathematics and science teaching and what convinces others to leave. This requires information about early career choices in college as well as labor market choices thereafter at various career points. Until we know what matters most to the talented individuals we would like to attract and keep in teaching, we can do little to develop policies to achieve these goals.

APPENDIX 1
National Science Teachers Association Standards

Elementary Level
1. Minimum 12 semester hours in laboratory or field-oriented science, including courses in biological, physical, and earth sciences. Course content should be applicable to elementary classrooms.
2. Minimum 1 course in elementary science methods.
3. Field experience in teaching science to elementary students.

Middle/Junior High School Level
1. Minimum 36 semester hours of science with at least 9 hours in each of biological science, physical sciences, and earth/space science. Remaining 9 hours should be science electives.
2. Minimum 9 semester hours of mathematics and computer science.
3. A science methods course designed for the middle school level.
4. Observation and field experience with early adolescent science classes.

Secondary Level
General Standards for All Science Specializations
1. Minimum 50 semester hours in one or more sciences, plus study in mathematics, statistics, and computer applications.
2. 3-5 semester hour course in science methods and curriculum.
3. Field experiences in secondary science classrooms at more than one grade level or more than one science area.

Specialized Standards
1. Biology: minimum 32 semester hours plus 16 semester hours in other sciences.
2. Chemistry: minimum 32 semester hours plus 16 semester hours in other sciences.
3. Earth/space science: minimum 32 semester hours, specializing in one area plus 16 semester hours in other sciences.
4. General science: 8 semester hours each in biology, chemistry, physics, and earth/space science, and applications to society. 12 hours in one area, plus mathematics to at least the precalculus level.
5. Physical science: 24 semester hours in chemistry and physics and applications to society, plus 24 semester hours in earth/space science; also an introductory biology course.
6. Physics: 32 semester hours in physics plus 16 in other sciences.

APPENDIX 2
National Council of Teachers of Mathematics Guidelines

Early Elementary School
The following three courses, each of which presumes a prerequisite of 2 years of high school algebra and 1 year of geometry.
1. number systems
2. informal geometry
3. mathematics teaching methods

Upper Elementary and Middle School
The following four courses, each of which presumes a prerequisite of 2 years of high school algebra and 1 year of geometry.
1. number systems
2. informal geometry
3. topics in mathematics (including real number system, probability and statistics, coordinate geometry, and number theory)
4. mathematics methods

Junior High School
The following seven courses, each presuming a prerequisite of 3-4 years of high school math, beginning with algebra and including trigonometry.
1. calculus
2. geometry
3. computer science
4. abstract algebra
5. mathematics applications
6. probability and statistics
7. mathematics methods

Senior High School
The following 13 courses, which constitute an undergraduate major in mathematics, and which each presume a prerequisite of 3-4 years of high school math, beginning with algebra and including trigonometry.
1-3. three semesters of calculus
   4. computer science
5-6. linear and abstract algebra (one course in each)
   7. geometry
   8. probability and statistics
9-12. one course each in mathematics methods, mathematics applications, selected topics, and the history of math
  13. at least one additional math elective course

REFERENCES

Abhyankar, S.B. (1977). A comparative laboratory study of the effects of two teaching strategies on sixth grade students' attitudes and self-confidence in science (Doctoral dissertation, Florida State University, Tallahassee, 1977). *Dissertation Abstracts International, 38,* 2023A.

Aldridge, W.G. (1986). What's being taught and who's teaching it. In A.B. Champagne & L.E. Hornig (Eds.), *This year in school science 1986: The science curriculum.* Washington, DC: American Association for the Advancement of Science.

American Federation of Teachers. (1988). *Survey and analysis of salary trends, 1988.* Washington, DC: Author.

Andrews, J.W., Blackmon, C.R., & Mackey, A. (1980). Preservice performance and the National Teacher Examinations. *Phi Delta Kappan, 6*(5), 358-359.

Association for School, College, and University Staffing. (1984). *Teacher supply/demand, 1984.* Madison, WI: Author.

Association for School, College, and University Staffing. (1986, January). *Tenth annual teacher supply/demand survey.* Madison, WI: Author.

Ayers, J.B., & Qualls, G.S. (1979). Concurrent and predictive validity of the National Teacher Examinations. *Journal of Educational Research, 73*(2), 86-92.

Begle, E.G. (1979). *Critical variables in mathematics education.* Washington, DC: Mathematical Association of America and National Council of Teachers of Mathematics.

Bloch, E. (1986). Basic research and economic health: The coming challenge. *Science, 232*(4750), 595-599.

Brophy, J.E., & Evertson, C.M. (1974). *Process-product correlations in the Texas teacher effectiveness study: Final report.* Austin, TX: Research and Development Center for Teacher Education.

Brophy, J.E., & Evertson, C.M. (1977). Teacher behavior and student learning in second and third grades. In G.D. Borich (Ed.), *The appraisal of teaching: Concepts and process.* Reading, MA: Addison-Wesley.

Byrne, C.J. (1983). *Teacher knowledge and teacher effectiveness: A literature review, theoretical analysis and discussion of research strategy.* Paper presented at the meeting of the Northeastern Educational Research Association, Ellenville, NY.

Capper, J. (1987). *A study of certified teacher availability in the states.* Washington, DC: Council of Chief State School Officers.

Carbo, M., Dunn, R., & Dunn, K. (1986). *Teaching students to read through their individual learning styles.* Englewood Cliffs, NJ: Prentice-Hall.

Carey, N., Mittman, B., & Darling-Hammond, L. (1988). *Recruiting mathematics and science teachers through nontraditional programs: A survey* (N-1736-FF/CSTP). Santa Monica, CA: RAND Corporation.

Carnegie Forum on Education and the Economy. (1986). *A nation prepared: Teachers for the 21st century.* Washington, DC: Author.

Carroll, C.D. (1985). *High school and beyond tabulation: Background characteristics of high school teachers.* Washington, DC: National Center for Education Statistics.

Commission on Professionals in Science and Technology. (1987). *Professional women and minorities: A manpower resource service.* Washington, DC: Author.

Cronbach, L.J., & Snow, R.E. (1977). *Aptitudes and instructional methods: A handbook for research on interactions.* New York: Irvington.

Darling-Hammond, L. (1984). *Beyond the commission reports: The coming crisis in teaching.* Santa Monica, CA: RAND Corporation.

Darling-Hammond, L., & Berry, B. (1988). *The evolution of teacher policy* (JRE-01). Santa Monica, CA: RAND Corporation.

Darling-Hammond, L., Hudson, L., & Kirby, S.N. (1989). *Redesigning teacher education: Opening the door for new recruits to science and mathematics teaching* (R-3661-FF/CSTP). Santa Monica, CA: RAND Corporation.

Dossey, J.A., Mullis, I.V., Lindquist, M.M., & Chambers, D.L. (1988). *The mathematics report card: Are we measuring up?* Princeton, NJ: Educational Testing Service.

Druva, C.A., & Anderson, R.D. (1983). Science teacher characteristics by teacher behavior and by student outcome: A meta-analysis of research. *Journal of Research in Science Teaching, 20*(5), 467-479.

Education Commission of the States. (1986). *A survey of state school improvement efforts.* Denver, CO: Author.

Feistritzer, E. (1986). *Teacher crisis: Myth or reality?* Washington, DC: National Center for Education Information.

Gage, N.L. (1978). *The scientific basis of the art of teaching.* New York: Teachers College Press.

Galambos, E.C. (1985). *Teacher preparation: The anatomy of a college degree.* Atlanta, GA: Southern Regional Education Board.

Galambos, E.C., Cornett, L.M., & Spitler, H.D. (1985). *An analysis of transcripts of teachers and arts and sciences graduates.* Atlanta, GA: Southern Regional Education Board.

General Accounting Office. (1984). *New directions for federal programs to aid mathematics and science teaching.* Washington, DC: U.S. Government Printing Office.

Glaser, R. (1983). *Education and thinking: The role of knowledge* (Tech. Rep. PD5-6). Pittsburgh, PA: University of Pittsburgh.

Grissmer, D.W., & Kirby, S.N. (1987). *Teacher attrition: The up-hill climb to staff the nation's schools* (R-3512-CSTP). Santa Monica, CA: RAND Corporation.

Haggstrom, G.W., Darling-Hammond, L., & Grissmer, D.W. (1988). *Assessing teacher supply and demand* (R-3633-ED/CSTP). Santa Monica, CA: RAND Corporation.

Hanushek, E. (1970). *The production of education, teacher quality and efficiency.* Paper presented at Bureau of Educational Personnel Conference, Washington, DC.

Hecker, D. (1986, Winter). Teachers' job outlook: Is chicken little wrong again? *Occupational Outlook Quarterly, 13-17.*

Horwitz, R.A. (1979). Effects of the "open classroom." In H.J. Walberg (Ed.), *Educational environments and effects: Evaluation policy and productivity.* Berkeley, CA: McCutchan.

Howe, T.G., & Gerlovich, J.A. (1982). *National study of the estimated supply and demand of secondary science and mathematics teachers, 1980-1872.* Ames, IA: Iowa State University.

International Association for the Evaluation of Educational Achievement. (1988). *Science achievement in 17 countries: A preliminary report.* New York: Teachers College, Columbia University.

Kershaw, J.A., & McKean, R.N. (1962). *Teacher shortages and salary schedules.* New York: McGraw-Hill.

Kolata, G.B. (1980). Math and sex: Are girls born with less ability? *Science, 210,* 1234-1235.

Levin, H.M. (1985). Solving the shortage of mathematics and science teachers. *Educational Evaluation and Policy Analysis, 7*(4), 371-382.

McDonald, F.J., & Elias, P. (1976). *Executive summary report: Beginning teacher evaluation study, phase II.* Princeton, NJ: Educational Testing Service.

McKeachie, W.J., & Kulik, J.A. (1975). Effective college teaching. In F.N. Kerlinger (Ed.), *Review of research in education* (Vol. 3). Itasca, IL: F.E. Peacock.

McKnight, C.C., Crosswhite, F.J., Dossey, J.A., Kifer, E., Swafford, J.O., Travers, K.J., & Cooney, T.J. (1987). *The underachieving curriculum.* Champaign, IL: Stipes.

Mullis, I.V.S., & Jenkins, L.B. (1988). *The science report card: Elements of risk and recovery.* Princeton, NJ: Educational Testing Service.

Murnane, R.J. (1985, June). *Do effective teachers have common characteristics: Interpreting the quantitative research evidence.* Paper presented at the National Research Council Conference on Teacher Quality in Science and Mathematics, Washington, DC.

Murnane, R.J., & Olsen, R.J. (Forthcoming a). The effects of salary and opportunity costs on duration in teaching: Evidence from Michigan. *Review of Economics and Statistics.*

Murnane, R.J., & Olsen, R.J. (Forthcoming b). The effects of salary and opportunity costs on length of stay in teaching: Evidence from North Carolina. *Journal of Human Resources.*

Murnane, R.J., & Phillips, B.R. (1981). Learning by doing, vintgage, and selection: Three pieces of the puzzle relating teaching experience and teaching performance. *Economics of Education Review, 1*(4), 453-465.

National Academy of Sciences. (1987). *Toward understanding teacher supply and demand: Priorities for research and development.* Washington, DC: National Academy Press.

National Center for Education Statistics. (1982). *The condition of education, 1982.* Washington, DC: U.S. Government Printing Office.
National Center for Education Statistics. (1983). *The condition of education, 1983.* Washington, DC: U.S. Government Printing Office.
National Center for Education Statistics. (1985a). *Condition of education, 1985.* Washington, DC: U.S. Government Printing Office.
National Center for Education Statistics. (1985b). *Survey of recent college graduates.* Unpublished data.
National Center for Education Statistics. (1986). *Earned degrees highlights.* Washington, DC: Author.
National Center for Education Statistics. (1987a). *Condition of education, 1987.* Washington, DC: U.S. Government Printing Office.
National Center for Education Statistics. (1987b). *The digest of education statistics, 1987.* Washington, DC: Author.
National Center for Education Statistics. (1988a). *Digest of education statistics, 1988.* Washington, DC: U.S. Government Printing Office.
National Center for Education Statistics. (1988b). *Projections of education statistics to 1997-98.* Washington, DC: Author.
National Council of Teachers of Mathematics. (1981). *Guidelines for the preparation of teachers of mathematics.* Reston, VA: Author.
National Commission on Excellence in Teacher Education. (1985). *A call for change in teacher education.* Washington, DC: American Association of Colleges for Teacher Education.
National Education Association. (1981). *Status of the American public school-teacher, 1980-81.* Washington, DC: Author.
National Governors' Association. (1986). *Time for results: The governors' 1991 report on education.* Washington, DC: Author.
National Science Board, Commission on Precollege Education in Mathematics, Science, and Technology. (1983). *Educating Americans for the 21st century.* Washington, DC: Author.
National Science Board. (1987). *Science and engineering indicators, 1987.* Washington, DC: Author.
National Science Teachers Association. (1983). *Standards for the preparation and certification of teachers of science, K-12.* Washington, DC: Author.
Penick, J.E., & Yager, R.E. (1983). The search for excellence in science education. *Phi Delta Kappan, 64*(9), 621-623.
Peterson, P.L. (1979). Direct instruction reconsidered. In P.L. Peterson & H.J. Walberg (Eds.), *Research on teaching.* Berkeley, CA: McCutchan.
Quirk, T.J., Witten, B.J., & Weinberg, S.F. (1973). Review of studies of the concurrent and predictive validity of the National Teacher Examinations. *Review of Educational Research, 43,* 89-114.
Rumberger, R. (1985). The shortage of mathematics and science teachers: A review of the evidence. *Educational Evaluation and Policy Analysis, 7*(4), 355-369.
Shavelson, R., McDonnell, L., Oakes, J., & Carey, N. (1987). *Indicator systems for monitoring mathematics and science education.* Santa Monica, CA: RAND Corporation.
Shymansky, J.A., & Aldridge, W.G. (1982, November). The teacher crisis in secondary school science and mathematics. *Educational Leadership,* pp. 61-62.
Soar, R.S. (1977). An integration of findings from four studies of teacher effec-

tiveness. In G.D. Borich (Ed.), *The appraisal of teaching: Concepts and process.* Reading, MA: Addison-Wesley.

Soar, R.S., & Soar, R.M. (1976). An attempt to identify measures of teacher effectiveness from four studies. *Journal of Teacher Education, 27,* 261-267.

Summers, A.A., & Wolfe, B.L. (1975). *Equality of educational opportunity quantified: A production function approach.* Philadelphia, PA: Department of Research, Federal Reserve Bank of Philadelphia.

Traub, R., Weiss, J., Fisher, C., Musella, D., & Kahn, S. (1973). *Openness in schools: An evaluation of the Wentworth County Roman Catholic school board schools.* Toronto: Educational Evaluation Center, Ontario Institute for Studies in Education.

Weiss, I.R. (1987). *Report of the 1985-86 National Survey of Science and Mathematics Education.* Research Triangle Park, NC: Research Triangle Institute.

Weiss, I.R. (1988, April). *Course background preparation of science and mathematics teachers in the United States* (Paper prepared for the National Science Foundation, Office of Studies and Program Assessments). Chapel Hill, NC: Horizon Research.

III.
ISSUES IN THE ORGANIZATION OF PUPILS, PERSONNEL, AND SCHOOLS

Chapter 5

Parental Choice of School:
What Parents Think and Do

JOHN MADDAUS
University of Maine

Political leaders at both national and state levels, from both parties and varying ideological perspectives, have advocated parental choice plans as ways to promote competition and increase accountability in public education. After highlighting the positions of Presidents Reagan and Bush and briefly summarizing the history of parent choice plans in American education, this review examines research on parental perspectives and actions with respect to choice of school. A section on research issues highlights the connections between parental choice and the issues of excellence and equity. Following a brief discussion of research methods, two major sections are devoted to (a) criteria, frequency, and the issue of excellence and (b) family backgrounds and the issue of equity. A concluding section highlights the strengths and limitations of parental choice as a means of promoting both excellence and equity and suggests possible topics for further research.

PRESIDENTIAL PERSPECTIVES

Throughout his two terms in office, President Reagan made parental choice of school one of the key concepts around which he sought to reorient educational policy. He advocated tuition tax credits, educational vouchers, and "public schools of choice" plans (Reagan, 1985). The major parental choice initiative during his second term was a proposal (introduced in Congress as The Equity and Choice Act of 1985—H. R. 3821) to convert the Chapter 1 program for educationally disadvantaged students into a compensatory voucher program (Bennett, 1985; Pear, 1985).

Despite Congressional rejection of H. R. 3821, Reagan reaffirmed his support for the concept of choice. At a White House Workshop on Choice in Education held on January 10, 1989, just before he left office, Reagan stated,

Choice works, and it works with a vengeance. . . . Choice is the most exciting thing going on in America today. . . . We're talking about reasserting the right of American parents to play a vital—perhaps the central—part in designing the kind of education they believe their children will need. (Snider, 1989c, p. 24; see also Shanker, 1989)

Reagan's remarks were echoed by President-elect Bush, who linked the concept of choice to the achievement of the goals of educational improvement set forth in *A Nation at Risk.* After attacking the prevailing system of school assignment based on residence as "a system of self-perpetuating mediocrity," Bush (1989) added, "Too often it is our disadvantaged children who are most likely to be burdened by inadequate public education. So it is working poor and low income families who suffer most from the absence of choice in public schools" (p. 24). Significantly, in view of past Congressional opposition, both Reagan and Bush sidestepped the issues of tuition tax credits and education vouchers, focusing instead on parent choice among public schools. Two months later (Bradley, 1989), President Bush told a student group that "I've been intrigued with the concept of tuition tax credits," but "we can't afford to do that" because of the federal budget deficit. Although respecting the right of parents to choose private schools, he added that "It is the obligation of all taxpayers to support a public education system. We want it to be the best" (p. 1).

HISTORY OF CHOICE IN AMERICAN EDUCATION

Although the concept of government financial support for choice in education has been traced back to Adam Smith, Thomas Paine, and John Stuart Mill (Coons & Sugarman, 1978), the earliest modern proponent of the concept was free market economist Milton Friedman (1962, 1973; Friedman & Friedman, 1980). Friedman has argued that providing parents with a voucher with which to purchase educational services would result in a competitive market for such services. In contrast to the alleged bureaucratic monopoly exercised by public education, Friedman believes that a free market in education would result in both lower cost and improved quality. In response to criticisms that such a plan would result in serious inequities related to socioeconomic status and race, Friedman has argued that the disadvantaged would benefit most from his proposal because their schools are currently the worst.

In contrast to the unregulated vouchers advocated by Friedman, the Center for the Study of Public Policy (CSPP) (1970) and Coons and Sugarman (1978) have proposed regulated vouchers designed to ensure that disadvantaged families would have equal access to quality education under a voucher plan. Proposed regulatory features have included a ban on supplemental payments by parents, supplemental government payments for students needing compensatory services, school disclosure requirements, and independent school counseling services.

The Reagan administration was not the first to express interest in the voucher concept. In the early 1970s, the Nixon administration initiated a 5-year (1972–77) voucher demonstration based on the CSPP model, but it was unable to include the involvement of private schools that CSPP had advocated. This project was conducted in the Alum Rock Unified School District, a predominantly low income section of San Jose, California, with a Mexican-American majority. A Rand Corporation study of the Alum Rock public school voucher demonstration is still the most extensive study of parental choice of school (Bridge & Blackman, 1978; Weiler, 1974).

The Nixon administration also sought to test the unregulated voucher model advocated by Friedman in the traditionally conservative state of New Hampshire. Begun in 1973, this effort was marked by conflicts in the planning stage between federal, state, and local participants. The end came 3 years later, when the people of six towns, including the parents who would presumably benefit, voted in school district meetings against submitting proposals to seek funds for project implementation (Donaldson, 1977).

Several subsequent efforts to promote voucher and tuition tax credit plans were likewise unsuccessful. A campaign led by John Coons and Stephen Sugarman to place a voucher initiative on the June 1980 primary ballot in California failed due to significant opposition and lack of widespread support (Catterall, 1982). Meanwhile, tuition tax credit legislation for elementary and secondary education was approved by the U.S. Senate on six occasions between 1969 and 1978, only to be defeated in the House of Representatives. President Reagan proposed a tuition tax credit plan in 1982, but that too failed to receive Congressional endorsement (Catterall, 1983).

From the perspective of advocates of parental choice plans including private schools, one positive development was the U.S. Supreme Court's 1983 decision in *Mueller v. Allen* (Darling-Hammond & Kirby, 1985; McCarthy, 1983). Despite significant questions regarding support of or entanglement with religion, the Court upheld, five to four, Minnesota's education tax deduction. Originally enacted in 1955, this deduction covers direct parental expenditures for tuition, books, and transportation for children attending either private or public schools.

The idea that government should assist parents who wish to exercise choice of schools has received more widespread acceptance when the range of options available has been limited to public schools. The alternative schools movement of the late 1960s and early 1970s provided urban parents with alternatives that were based on instructional styles rather than religious faith or membership in a social elite. Some of these alternative schools were incorporated into public school systems, creating what Fantini (1973; see also Smith, Barr, & Burke, 1976) has called "public schools of choice." Magnet schools were created when the public alternative schools of Minneapolis were incorporated by court order into the school desegregation plan for that city (McMillan, 1980). Magnet schools have since become widely accepted as a primary means of achieving school desegregation (Blank, Dentler, Baltzell, & Chabotar, 1983; Massachusetts Department of Education, 1986, 1988a). Alternative schools have also been widely adopted at the secondary level as a dropout prevention program (Raywid, 1982, 1984).

In rural areas, the primary example of the parental choice concept at work has been the traditional practice of town tuitioning in Vermont, New Hampshire, and Maine. Sparsely populated towns in these states are legally responsible for providing education for resident children in grades K-12, but they may not have enough students to operate their own schools, particularly at the high school level. Instead, these towns pay tuition to enable their children to attend school in a nearby town. In Vermont and Maine, town tuitioned students also may attend nonsectarian private schools (Coons & Sugarman, 1978; Goldberg, 1988; National Governors' Association, 1986).

In 1985, the Minnesota legislature, at the urging of Governor Rudy Perpich, adopted legislation permitting high school juniors and seniors to take college courses for precollege credit and providing options for at-risk students. Two years later the state added a statewide, open enrollment plan, under which the first students began attending new schools in other districts in September 1989. As of March 1989, almost 2,800 students, or an average of approximately 6 students for each of the state's 436 school districts (Council of Chief State School Officers, 1987), had applied for open enrollment transfers (Snider, 1987, 1989a, 1989c).

Other states have also adopted parental choice plans. In 1985, Governor Richard Lamm of Colorado initiated a "second chance program" to allow students who were not successful in the schools of their own district to transfer to schools in other districts. In 1989, the Iowa and Arkansas legislatures adopted statewide, open enrollment. Governors and legislators in several other states, including urban industrial states such as Massachusetts, New Jersey, and California, are considering parental choice of public school plans in 1989. In each case, the plans ensure that existing racial desegregation efforts are maintained (National Governors' Association, 1986; Snider, 1987, 1989b, 1989c).

Thus, although opportunities for parents to choose among schools have increased significantly in the past 20 years, this change has occurred primarily with respect to choices among public schools. Furthermore, until

1985, most opportunities for choice among public schools were provided by urban school systems seeking to achieve racial desegregation or to provide alternatives for actual or potential dropouts. Only in a comparatively few instances were options provided as a means of improving schools, increasing access to quality education for the disadvantaged (other than on the basis of racial balance), or increasing parents' involvement in their children's education, all themes that President Reagan and President-elect Bush articulated in their remarks to the White House Workshop on Choice in Education.

Parental choice of school has been a controversial political issue in other countries also, although past institutional practice has given the issue some rather different twists. Most other Western democracies provide government financial support for dual systems of schools based on religious affiliation. In some countries, notably France and The Netherlands, advocates of public education have challenged public support for sectarian schools, and in the process have questioned the legitimacy of parental preferences and the social consequences of existing practice (Massachusetts Department of Education, 1988b).

The situation in the United Kingdom most closely resembles that of the United States, although there are also significant institutional differences. Like the Reagan administration, the Thatcher government supported parental choice of schools as an application of the concept of the free market to education. However, because of the weaker system of checks and balances and the greater centralization of power in the British political system, the Thatcher government was able to push its desired legislation through Parliament with greater success than the Reagan administration experienced with Congress and the states. Although the British legislation applies to both nondenominational and Catholic schools, the primary policy emphasis has been on the former. The situation thus offers a rough approximation to the Bush administration's current emphasis on the public schools. Finally, because the initial legislation applying to Scotland provided greater opportunities for parental choice than the corresponding legislation for England and Wales, published research on the subject to date has focused on the Scottish experience (Massachusetts Department of Education, 1988b; Petch, 1986; Raab & Adler, 1987).

RESEARCH ISSUES REGARDING PARENTAL CHOICE OF SCHOOL

Various policy analysts have sought to identify the major conceptual issues involving parents' exercise of choice in school enrollment. These issues frequently have focused on current policy concerns regarding excellence and equity.

With respect to excellence, Bridge (1978) lists several optimal conditions for a voucher system, one of which is that "there be widespread differences in tastes, and these differences are recognized as legitimate" (p. 507). In other words, a system of choice assumes that parents differ with respect to the goals of education, or at the very least with respect to the means of attaining those goals. Bridge assumes, however, that a consensus exists with respect to the goal of preparation for future employment, and asks whether voucher holders will "invest in education that improves their [children's] economic leverage in the labor market, or . . . buy the educational equivalents of junk food, easy to consume but lacking in substance" (p. 511).

Lines and McGuire (1984) examined the relationship between choice and the excellence reform movement catalyzed by *A Nation at Risk.* They note that consumers (parents and students), service providers (teachers and administrators), and society (represented by state and local policymakers) have had different, and at times conflicting, perspectives on educational goals. Historically, they argue, many public policies have been adopted that had the intent or at least the effect of denying parental choice. Such policies include requirements regarding attendance, curriculum, teacher certification, and tracking, among others. Recently adopted measures seeking accountability and promoting a core curriculum have continued this trend to limit choice. The issue of how school policymakers, administrators, and teachers view their jobs with respect to the choice issue, although beyond the scope of this review, certainly has important implications for parents. If schools are basically designed to be as much alike as possible, then parents choosing among such schools will be left to choose based on criteria that are beyond the responsibility and control of educators, such as neighborhood conditions and before/after school child care arrangements.

In short, an analysis of parental choice in relation to excellence focuses on the question of what parents' educational goals (or more narrowly, their criteria for selecting schools) actually are, compared to existing and potential institutional arrangements. Implicit in this question is the question of the proportion of parents who take advantage of existing choice opportunities and would take advantage of expanded opportunities should they be created in the future.

Another important cluster of concerns centers on the issue of equity. In addition to differences in tastes (cited earlier), Bridge (1978) identifies six other optimal conditions for choice plans, including (a) "individuals have incentives to shop aggressively"; (b) "individuals are well informed about market conditions"; (c) "there are many competing suppliers of the goods and services people want"; (d) "there is some excess capacity in the system so that people have true choices"; (e) "the quality of goods and services is easily measured"; and (f) "the product or service is relatively inexpensive and purchased frequently" (pp. 507–508). These conditions make demands on parents, but also on policymakers and administrators. If parents, including minority parents with low levels of education and limited family incomes, such as those living in the Alum Rock school district, do not make choices in accordance with the goal of preparation for future employment, then the problem must lie in the absence of one or more of these conditions. Based on the Alum Rock experience, Bridge concludes that such a problem exists, and that it is best explained as due to "information imperfections" involving inadequate sources of information, the difficulty of measuring educational quality, and the infrequency of educational choices.

Murnane (1984) argues that choice can result in improved student performance, at least for some students (including some low income students). He cites three conceptually distinct mechanisms that could improve student performance: (a) matching student interests and capabilities with program characteristics; (b) choosing schools as an occasion when students and their parents focus on educational goals and the means necessary to achieving them; and (c) being chosen to participate in a competitive program requiring sustained effort for continuation. The first two mechanisms depend primarily on parental actions, whereas the third involves school administrators as well as parents. Murnane also argues that the last mechanism, although potentially powerful, also implies that some students, most likely those with the greatest needs, will be left out. Choice, at least when it involves programs with selective admissions, may not be compatible with equity. Furthermore, support for choice programs may undermine support for other programs for which the primary purpose is to improve the performance of the most disadvantaged students, who in Murnane's view are least likely to benefit from parental choice programs.

Raywid (1987) also is concerned with the issue of equity, but she argues that the consequences of "public schools of choice" plans differ from those of voucher plans. She cites several possible benefits of public schools of choice plans, including higher student motivation, increased parental satisfaction, and greater autonomy for staff at both the classroom and building levels. However, she believes that vouchers would result, especially in larger cities, in a two-tiered system of schools: private schools serving the affluent, public schools serving the poor. Under such an outcome, poor students who need quality education most would be concentrated in those inner city schools least able to provide it.

Raywid's criticism of voucher plans, however, also has been leveled at programs providing parental choice of public schools. Braddock (1981) points out that although magnet schools and alternative school programs may have raised educational outcomes for some students, "little attention has been given to the educational consequences for minority students in particular who, either by choice or by luck of the draw, are excluded from participation in highly specialized school programs" (p. 156). Creaming off higher status and more able students, he suggests, may have left other students isolated without successful role models in schools in which quality education is even more difficult to provide. Chicago's Designs for Change group (Snider, 1988) studied four large urban school districts and concluded that selective admissions criteria had resulted in serious inequities in each city.

In summary, an analysis of equity concerns in relation to parental choice suggests that there are both parental and administrative actions involved in the outcomes. It is important to investigate whether there are differences among families in their awareness of choice, access to information, criteria of school selection, and frequency of participation related to race, ethnicity, or socioeconomic background. To the extent that such differences exist, they may have the net effect of increasing the gap in the quality of education now received by less advantaged children. However, it is also important to note that serious equity problems may be associated with selective admissions procedures for parental choice programs, which suggests that the actions of policymakers and school administrators should be examined also.

RESEARCH METHODS

Researchers cannot predict with certainty what would happen if parental choice of public schools were institutionalized nationwide. Opportunities now exist to study the effects of statewide plans, but to date the only published study of such a plan is a study of Minnesota's educational tax deduction (Darling-Hammond & Kirby, 1985). In addition, there are nationwide surveys (Elam, 1984; Gallup, 1986; Gallup & Clark, 1987; Williams, Hancher, & Hutner, 1983) in which parents are questioned about their current situation and about what they would do under certain choice plans. But most studies deal with choices under particular choice plans within individual communities or even with choices of individual schools. This is not necessarily a disadvantage, because even under statewide plans parental responses may differ from community to community and school to school based on local conditions.

Researchers operating within quantitative or qualitative research traditions, as well as others taking advantage of the strengths of both traditions, have explored the questions listed earlier about parental choice of schools.

In the quantitative tradition, researchers (Bridge & Blackman, 1978; Convey, 1986; Darling-Hammond & Kirby, 1985; Williams et al., 1983) have chosen survey research techniques. Researchers in the qualitative tradition (Clerico, 1983; Maddaus, 1987, 1988a, 1988b, 1988c; Slaughter

& Schneider, 1986) have relied primarily on in-depth interviews. Several researchers (Gerritz, 1988; Gratiot, 1980; Nault & Uchitelle, 1982; Nelson, 1988; Petch, 1986) have used both highly structured and more open-ended questioning techniques.

Surveys are an efficient way to gather quantifiable data from relatively large numbers of subjects (in this case, parents). Qualitative researchers' use of open-ended questions with follow-up probes provides parents with opportunities to express their own perspectives, thus allowing the researchers to go beyond their initial conceptualizations of the issues. Studies in both research traditions have contributed significantly to our understanding of this complex issue.

PARENTS' CRITERIA IN SELECTING SCHOOLS

Those who advocate parental choice as a means of promoting excellence in education assume that, given more opportunities, parents will (a) make choices based on academic quality (or other criteria involving some recognizable conception of excellence); and (b) act on their preferences in large enough numbers to significantly influence how schools are operated. Although there can be legitimate differences of opinion over how much is enough with respect to the importance of academic quality and the proportion of parents using that criterion, the existing research does shed some light on both issues.

Numerous studies have surveyed parents about the criteria they use in selecting schools for their children, and a fairly lengthy list of such criteria has been identified. These include the following: academic quality (teacher attitudes and competence, curriculum, administrative leadership, academic standards, instructional methods, etc.), school atmosphere (climate, discipline, values, etc.), school size, class size (individual attention), parental involvement, extracurricular activities, physical condition of the building, safety, location (distance from home, transportation arrangements), student characteristics (race/ethnicity, socioeconomic status), neighborhood characteristics, financial cost, before- and after-school child care arrangements, preschool enrollment, religious instruction, religious training and commitment of staff, prior enrollment by family members or friends, parental employment on school staff, and child's preferences.

Several studies report that academic quality was the reason parents cited most frequently when asked about their school choices. Nault and Uchitelle (1982) studied the choices of parents living in optional attendance zones in the public school system of a suburban community they identify only as "Collegeville." They report that parents choosing the most important items from a list of 15 possible criteria selected "general atmosphere of school," "principal's philosophy of education and attitude toward children," "child's teacher's personal teaching style and classroom skills," and "overall curriculum and academic program" most often. These parents also identified "convenience of transportation," "physical facilities," "similarity of children's background," and "overall achievement levels" as the least important considerations. Nault and Uchitelle suggest that although advocates of parental choice "should draw comfort from this investigation," "we stress again the atypical characteristics of the parent populations," consisting primarily of highly educated parents. However, the low ranking of overall achievement levels seems inconsistent with the emphasis on academic quality, unless there was little difference among schools in the community in this respect.

Studies of magnet schools (Blank et al., 1983; Rossell, 1985) have noted that distinctive curricular options or instructional approaches have been the primary attractions of magnet school programs. In a review of the literature on magnet schools, Rossell notes that higher status whites who are most supportive of integration and therefore most likely to send their children to schools in minority neighborhoods can be attracted by gifted and talented programs, by programs that are child centered, and by programs that stress hands-on science, second language experience, or other types of academic enrichment. She also notes that popular, white principals and teachers and low pupil-teacher ratios also help to attract white students to inner city schools.

Several studies focusing on private school enrollment (Convey, 1986; Gratiot, 1980; Nelson, 1988) have reported that academic quality has become the most important reason for choosing a private school. Convey reports that among parents surveyed with children in Catholic schools, 48.8% of Catholic parents cited academic program as the most important reason for their decisions, compared to 29.4% citing any one of three possible religious factors. For non-Catholic parents, academic program emerged even more strongly, being cited by 66.3% of those surveyed, as against 14.0% who cited discipline. Maddaus (1988a) found that Catholic parents who transferred their children from Catholic to public schools cited stronger, more diverse, and better funded academic programs in public schools as the primary reason for the change, followed by the rising cost of Catholic school tuition. What remains unclear, however, is what proportion of private school parents would switch to public schools if they perceived that public schools had improved their academic standards, and what would bring about such a change in perception.

Both Convey and Nelson argue that there has been a significant shift in the attitudes of Catholic school parents, citing earlier studies (Greeley & Rossi, 1966; Kraushaar, 1972) indicating that religious factors were once paramount, and many Catholic parents automatically enrolled their children in parish schools. Several studies (Clerico, 1983; Convey, 1986;

Gratiot, 1980; Nelson, 1988; Slaughter & Schneider, 1986) also suggest that the image of the religious (more specifically Catholic) school as a neighborhood institution is no longer accurate for many of today's religious schools. They found many children attending schools outside their neighborhoods and little evidence that school location was a significant consideration for parents. Convey, for example, found location of school seventh in importance among eight factors considered by parents of children enrolled in Catholic schools.

Williams et al. (1983) and Darling-Hammond and Kirby (1985) obtained similar results when they asked parents to identify the important factors influencing current school enrollment. In both studies, academic quality was cited most frequently when private school parents and public school parents who considered other schools at the time of enrollment were asked to identify the (single) most important factor in their decisions. The next most frequent responses of private school parents to this question were religious or moral values and discipline standards, whereas public school parents who made choices ranked finances a distant second and transportation/convenience third. Responses to a question seeking *very* important factors (and allowing multiple, positive responses) were similar. In both studies, academic standards, teaching staff, and discipline topped the list for both groups of parents, whereas moral and religious values were higher for private school parents and financial costs for public school parents. Location/convenience ranks in the bottom half for both groups in both studies, along with child's desire and the rather ambiguous desegregation and backgrounds of students (these last two items will be discussed in relation to equity).

Although these findings are interesting, they are overshadowed in some respects because the largest category of parents in both studies consisted of public school parents who did *not* consider other schools at the time of current enrollment. When asked for the most important factor in their children's enrollment, the factors they cited most often were assignment to a school (in the Darling-Hammond and Kirby study, this apparently was included under the ambiguous heading "situational factors") and transportation/convenience.

Unlike most of the studies cited, but consistent with findings of the last two studies regarding "nonactive" public school parents, Bridge and Blackman (1978) found that the primary consideration in school choice for most Alum Rock families was location. In response to a question asking why parents chose certain schools for their children, over 70% of the parents surveyed cited location, whereas only 32% cited program features, 30% cited family/friends/prior enrollment, 18% cited school quality, and 18% cited staff.

The finding that location was the primary factor in school choice for most parents is supported by several other types of evidence. During the development phase of the voucher demonstration, parents' main desire was to ensure the right of their children to attend their neighborhood school (Weiler, 1974). Only 11.2% of parents in the 1st year and approximately 20% of parents in succeeding years took advantage of the interschool transfer options that the demonstration made available to them. Finally, 60 to 80% of the parents surveyed, depending on the year and program status, agreed with the statement that location was the single most important factor for most parents in enrolling their children in school, with no consistent trend developing over time (Bridge & Blackman, 1978). Unfortunately, none of these data were analyzed according to socioeconomic or racial/ethnic subgroups.

Interpreting the significance of location is complicated by the fact that the plan that emerged from the development stage of the Alum Rock demonstration provided an alternative to interschool transfers: minischools within each voucher school (Weiler, 1974). This alternative may have reduced the number of interschool transfers, because these minischools offered parents options within their own neighborhood schools that to a large degree duplicated the options available at other voucher schools. In short, the major differences at Alum Rock were within schools rather than among them. Regrettably, the questionnaires used by Bridge and Blackman did not distinguish between these two choices, making it impossible to interpret the extent to which parents made choices among minischools based on program characteristics.

In contrast to such educationally relevant criteria as curriculum content and classroom organization, Bridge and Blackman describe location as a "simplistic and educationally irrelevant" consideration, and add (in a footnote) that although such factors "are extremely important to a parent who is comparing various alternative schools . . . , no theory of learning that we know of would say that school location per se has an impact on learning" (p. 45). In a separate article, Bridge (1978) attributes the high proportion of parents citing location as their primary consideration to "information imperfections" especially pronounced among low-income families, apparently assuming that location would be a less important factor among middle-class parents. He concludes that "until effective policies to overcome information imperfections have been developed in experimental programs" (p. 523), choice plans in education should not be implemented.

One important clue to understanding the importance of location for public school parents who do not choose among schools at the time of enrollment is the finding of three studies (Darling-Hammond & Kirby, 1985; Williams et al., 1983; Wimpelberg, 1982) that between 50% and 60% of public school parents say that they considered public schools in making decisions about housing. This is more than twice the number of public school parents who say they consider other schools at the time of enrollment. Furthermore, Williams et al. note that 18% of public school parents say that what public schools their children would attend was the most important factor in their choice of housing. As will be discussed in more detail later, all three studies found substantial differences among socioeconomic and racial/ethnic subgroups.

Maddaus (1987, 1988a, 1988b, 1988c) found that most of the parents he interviewed in five lower to upper middle-income neighborhoods of Syracuse, New York, were very conscious of the characteristics of the neighborhoods in which they lived and in which particular schools were located. But unlike Bridge and Blackman, he argues that this concern about location was based on the parents' educational and child-rearing goals. Parents with the same goals but living in different neighborhoods had different enrollment options and thus different concerns about schools. Academic considerations predominated only in choices among schools that met their standards in certain other respects. The concerns of many parents were primarily moral but also to some extent social: These focused on the beliefs, attitudes, and values that children learned at home and through neighborhood activities but also in large part from their classmates at school. These parents believed they were responsible for ensuring that their children would grow to be self-sufficient, productive, contributing adults. They seemed to realize intuitively what Green (1988) has stated so clearly: "Moral education is best conducted in a world in which both the costs of virtue and the benefits of evil are slight" (p. 132). They saw it as their responsibility to manage their children's lives in such a way that they grow up in the kind of community environment that Green envisions. To the extent that their financial resources allowed, these parents chose to live in neighborhoods in which they believe that other families, as well as the schools and other institutions engaged in child-rearing activities, share their child-rearing values. Every parent interviewed in the lowest income neighborhood volunteered that they would like to move out of that neighborhood, either to a better neighborhood, to a suburb, or to the country. As one low-income parent put it, "The city's no place to raise decent kids any more. You can do it, but it's harder" (p. 118).

Although real estate agents in some communities have taken advantage of parents' interests in public schools to market houses, choice of school as a factor in housing choice may be limited in its effects on educational excellence. Maddaus (1987, 1988a) notes that some parents make tacit assumptions about school quality. In the words of one middle-income parent, "Certain kinds of community foster certain kinds of school. The better the socio-economic conditions of an area, the better the schools"

(p. 180). These parents may not investigate the schools in their new neighborhoods carefully, and a few did not even know which schools their children were actually supposed to attend until they went to register them. Despite such minimal investigation of schools, however, many parents believe that their housing choice carries with it a school choice and thus resist efforts to assign their children to schools other than the ones they believe they have chosen.

Petch (1986) interviewed Scottish families about their reasons for rejecting the district school (i.e., the school of assignment based on residence) and choosing a different school at the time of initial primary school enrollment. Some parents sought to "overcome catchment area boundaries which place them closer to a non-district school" (p. 26). "Parents are, in effect, redrawing the boundaries to reflect patterns of individual convenience and of more rational distribution" (p. 46). For other parents, "a major emphasis was given to the 'happiness of the child,' . . . the child's general well-being" (p. 26). Safety and social concerns, including the avoidance of "rowdy, rough children, bad language" (p. 39), were more important than strictly academic considerations. In a related study, Raab and Adler (1987) reported that 85% of placement requests in the Scottish cities of Dundee and Edinburgh were to adjacent schools within relatively homogeneous sections of each city, although there was a slight tendency to transfer from areas with a high level of social deprivation to areas that were less deprived. The 15% of all moves that were to nonadjacent schools were almost entirely from working-class to middle-class areas.

Slaughter and Schneider (1986) focused on parents' broad educational goals rather than on the specific criteria used in particular decisions. Based on interviews with 74 black and 57 nonblack (mostly white) middle- and upper income families whose children attended racially integrated private schools in Chicago, they identified six response patterns, which they labeled as follows: (a) authoritative, (b) deliberate, (c) humanistic, (d) moral, (e) practical, and (f) traditional. These response patterns varied in the degree of emphasis placed on the child's present experiences as compared to future success; on the relative importance of the child's cognitive, social, emotional, and spiritual development; and on the respective roles of the school, the teacher, and the parents in promoting the child's development. Although these response patterns reflect a variety of specific conceptions of educational excellence, all reflect parental concerns that are relatively holistic, rather than focused solely on the teaching and learning of cognitive knowledge and skills.

These studies by Maddaus, Petch, Raab and Adler, and Slaughter and Schneider provide evidence of what Cremin (1976) referred to as the "configuration of education." Clerico (1983) applied this concept to explain why conservative (fundamentalist) Protestant families enroll their children in Christian schools. Such schools, he suggests, complement the influences of the family, church, and friendship network. Coleman (1981; Coleman & Hoffer, 1987; Coleman, Hoffer, & Kilgore, 1982) expressed much the same idea in his conception of "functional communities" or "communities of interest," citing Catholic schools as his primary example. For some families, the neighborhood and neighborhood schools (which may be either public or private) are parts of a mutually reinforcing "configuration of education" or "functional community." Bronfenbrenner's (1979) theory of the ecology of human development is yet another conceptual scheme that emphasizes the social context of education and child rearing. He describes formal and informal settings linked together by shared values and by contacts between children and adults moving among these settings, and argues that such social linkages can support children as learners. Thus, parents may have good reasons, including educationally valid reasons, for basing their enrollment decisions on cohesive neighborhoods.

In the Alum Rock voucher demonstration, parents may have believed that they had enough program options (in the form of minischools) available within their own neighborhood school. On the other hand, there were significant differences in parental education and ethnicity among school attendance areas. Indeed, Alum Rock residents clearly distinguished between "hill" and "flatland" areas of the district, with hill areas having a higher percentage of high school graduates and a lower percentage of minority residents. In the 2nd and 3rd years of the demonstration, most of the expansion occurred through addition of schools in areas of the district with the lowest parental education and the highest minority populations (Bridge & Blackman, 1978; Weiler, 1974). One may infer that the importance of location was due at least in part to awareness of these social differences.

A critical issue for policymakers is how many parents would take advantage of which types of enrollment options, if they became available. Bridge and Blackman (1978) note that,

In theory, parents can exert some control over their children's schooling by: (a) moving the family residence to a preferred attendance area (lying about one's address will accomplish the same thing); (b) requesting an interschool transfer; (c) asking for a particular teacher, classroom or program, assuming that the school has more than one class at each grade level; (d) going outside the public school system to private schools, if any are available; or (e) keeping the child out of school altogether. (p. 8)

As was noted, only about 20% of Alum Rock parents sought interschool transfers, and Bridge and Blackman conclude that parents rarely pursue any of the alternatives listed "unless their neighborhood public schools are very bad" (p. 8). However, as already noted, flaws in the research design leave this conclusion open to question.

The issue of location, combining as it does parents' child-rearing goals and residential choices with parents' choice of school, is a key to understanding the extent to which parents will actively consider choices among schools, given increased opportunities to do so. Use of currently available opportunities, primarily residential or private school choice, may suggest a predisposition to use whatever options may be available at some future time. On the other hand, those parents who are able to achieve their goals with the options currently available may have no inclination to take advantage of new options and may in fact resist efforts to provide new options to other parents.

Several studies have attempted to determine how many parents would take advantage of various enrollment options if they were made available. Recent Gallup polls (Elam, 1984; Gallup, 1986; Gallup & Clark, 1987) suggest that significant numbers of parents might transfer their children to other schools if allowed to do so. In response to questions about parents' rights to choose the public schools their children would attend, 68% of all public school parents in 1986 and 76% in 1987 favored having such a choice, but only 24% (1986) indicated they would actually choose a different school if such a choice were available.

Gallup also reports that about half of all public school parents—45% in 1982 and 49% in 1986—say they would send their children to private (including church-related) schools if they could afford to do so, but only about half of those parents interested in private schools would make the switch if offered a $600 voucher. (This was asked in 1986, when the Reagan compensatory voucher proposal was under consideration by Congress.) A majority of public school parents (51% to 41%, with 8% having no opinion) favored a voucher system in the 1986 poll, although 54% oppose tax assistance to church-related schools.

Williams et al. (1983) found that the propensity to switch to a private school heavily depended on cost, with 23.5% of public school parents saying they would switch if given a $250 tax credit, 32.0% switching with a $500 credit, and 44.6% switching with a full tuition subsidy.

Darling-Hammond and Kirby, however, found that 23% of the public school parents they interviewed in Minnesota said they were "very likely" or "somewhat likely" to switch to private schools if given a tax deduction (not a credit) of $500 per elementary school child or $700 per secondary school child. In fact, deductions in these amounts had existed for 20 years, leading the researchers to conclude that "they were either unaware of the deduction or ill informed about how it operates" (p. 11). Furthermore, 98% of the private school parents contacted said they would have sent their children to private school even without the deduction, and only 10% said it was very important, in contrast to the 40% who said that free bus transportation to private schools was very important.

Interpreting the effect of tax credit based on information on tax deductions is difficult, in part because the actual value of a deduction is so much less than its face value. (A $500 deduction is worth between $50 and $80 in Minnesota, depending on one's tax bracket.) But the lack of information about or lack of understanding of a long-standing practice suggests the need for caution in interpreting hypothetical options. The most reliable way to test parents' preferences regarding private schools would be to conduct a demonstration such as the Nixon administration originally intended using vouchers.

FAMILY BACKGROUND DIFFERENCES
AND THE QUESTION OF EQUITY

In the debate over parental choice, one of the major points of dispute has centered on whether poorly educated and low-income parents (who are also disproportionately members of minority groups) would be sufficiently aware of possible options, able to gather and evaluate information about those options, and able to use opportunities for choice to benefit their children. Opponents of expanding parents' choice of school have expressed concern that relatively well educated and affluent parents would be better positioned to use whatever options were available to get their children into the "better" schools, leaving most children from poor families behind in schools that would find it increasingly difficult to meet their needs. Proponents of choice, on the other hand, argue that poor and minority families have the greatest need for improved schools and thus would benefit most from choice.

Two studies (Gallup, 1986; Williams et al., 1983) have found that minority group members and people living in central cities with populations over 50,000 are more receptive to vouchers and tuition tax credits respectively than are white parents and parents living in communities of fewer than 50,000. Williams et al. also report that the lower the family income and the lower the parents' education level, the more receptive parents are to tuition tax credits. Gallup, however, reports that people with incomes of $40,000 or more are more receptive to vouchers than are those with lower incomes. Gallup also found that high school graduates were most likely to favor vouchers, college graduates were slightly less likely, and those who did not go beyond grade school were least likely to favor them. The apparent discrepancies could be attributed to the fact that while Williams et al. surveyed parents only, the subgroup data reported by Gallup are for all adults surveyed whether or not they had children in school. Thus, the low level of support for vouchers among Gallup interviewees who had not gone beyond grade school could be attributed to older people generally having lower levels of education; persons 50 and older (presumably mostly without children in school) were strongly opposed to vouchers.

Williams et al. (1983) and Darling-Hammond and Kirby (1985) found that consideration of public schools in residential choice increased significantly with parental education and income. Wimpelberg (1982) reported the same result for parental education, but did not collect data on family income. Williams et al. reported that the frequency of consideration of public schools in residential choice is higher among white families (56.2%) and Hispanic families (54.1%) than among black families (33.1%). These findings suggest that inequities in access to housing based on income and race may be significant in parental choice under existing conditions.

Perhaps as a consequence of the greater opportunities that affluent, well-educated, and non-black families have to consider public schools in residential choice, or because of voluntary school desegregation programs, the data on consideration of other schools at the time of enrollment has a different pattern. Williams et al. reports that black parents are most likely to consider other schools (25.9%), followed by Hispanic parents (22.5%), and white parents (18.0%). Both Williams et al. (1983) and Darling-Hammond and Kirby (1985) report relatively high frequencies of consideration of other schools at the time of enrollment by parents with some college education in the income range between $15,000 and $25,000. In Williams et al.'s study, the lowest frequencies were for parents with postgraduate education and incomes over $50,000, parents who were most likely to have already achieved their school enrollment objectives through residential or private school choice.

The most critical question in this regard is whether there are racial/ ethnic or socioeconomic status differences in the propensity to pursue enrollment options *within the same attendance area*. Maddaus (1988a) found that 93% of the 67 elementary school-aged children he identified in two lower middle-income neighborhoods had been enrolled in schools other than the neighborhood public school, compared to 38% of the 71 children in a low-income neighborhood in the same public school attendance area, and 37% of the 89 children in middle- and upper middle-income neighborhoods of two adjacent attendance areas. He argues that the parents in the lower middle-income neighborhoods (typically high school graduates with family incomes of about $20,000 in 1984) viewed the neighborhood public school to which their children were assigned in negative terms, whereas better educated and more affluent parents whose children were assigned to other schools nearby viewed their neighborhood public schools more favorably. On the other hand, these lower middle-income parents had more information about and greater access to other schools than did the low-income parents whose children were assigned to the same school, as well as greater confidence in their abilities to make such decisions on behalf of their children.

Researchers at Alum Rock found persistent differences in information levels based on socioeconomic status and race/ethnicity, which decreased but did not completely disappear during the 5 years of the voucher demonstration there. Weiler (1974) concluded at the end of the 1st year of the study that

Anglos and blacks were somewhat better informed about the demonstration than were Mexican-Americans, particularly those Mexican-Americans interviewed in Spanish. Better educated and wealthier parents were a little more likely to know about vouchers. (p. xix)

A similar pattern emerged with regard to sources of information. Bridge and Blackman (1978) noted that information levels increased over time, as long as the rules governing the demonstration remained constant.

Differences in ability to gain information about schools related to socioeconomic status could have significant equity effects. Several studies (Gallup & Elam, 1988; Maddaus, 1988a; Powell, 1980; Skehan, 1985) reported that parents rely most heavily on informal (verbal) sources of information (e.g., their own children, other children, other parents, school board, and faculty members) about schools and child-care arrangements. Skehan (1985) found that dissatisfied parents rely more heavily on friends, neighbors, and other children than do satisfied parents. Powell (1980) noted that Detroit parents searching for child care turn to formal sources only when informal sources have been exhausted without yielding the desired results.

Other studies have noted that middle-income parents are better able to use social networks to gain information about schools than are low-income parents. Nault and Uchitelle (1982) found there was less awareness of choice among families in which the father had not attended college, although only 8 of the 48 families studied fell in this category, and these few might have been socially isolated in a highly educated community. Cochran and Henderson (1985) demonstrated that families in low-income neighborhoods tend to be more isolated and have fewer sources of information on child rearing than do families in more affluent neighborhoods. Maddaus (1988b) reported that families in middle-income neighborhoods described by most residents as "close-knit" were more likely than families in the low-income neighborhood he studied to have gained school-related information from neighbors. He argues that there are both time and financial costs involved in gathering information, and that families make that investment only when they have the necessary resources and see the likelihood of a return. Gerritz (1988) found that single-parent families and families with more than one child are "time poor," and therefore more likely to enroll their children in neighborhood public schools, even if the schools are of poor quality, than are two-parent families and families with only one child. Single-parent families and families with several children are also likely to have fewer financial resources.

Some studies also suggest that middle-income parents have greater access to formal (written) sources of information than do low-income parents. The lower information levels of low-income parents at Alum Rock were attributed in part to the use of written materials to convey the rules of the demonstration there. The Gallup poll (Gallup & Elam, 1988) found that private school parents, unlike public school parents, relied most heavily on the newspapers for information about schools, perhaps reflecting their generally higher educational levels. Parents who have access to a combination of both informal and formal sources have an advantage over those whose sources are more limited. Major changes in enrollment practices, such as the Alum Rock voucher demonstration, invalidate previous knowledge held by participants in informal social networks and require that parents make greater use of formal sources, at least temporarily.

Differences in family background also may be related to different criteria in school selection. Bridge and Blackman suggest that the parents they studied conceived of the available minischool programs as falling into one of two categories: "hard" alternatives, which are highly structured and emphasize "the basics"; and "soft" alternatives, which are more loosely structured and place greater emphasis on other subjects. They relate these distinctions to research by Kohn (1969), who theorized that parents seek success for their children based on the requirements of the occupations in which they themselves are engaged. Thus, middle-income parents would be expected to choose programs that emphasize independence and creativity, whereas working-class parents would prefer programs stressing obedience and respect for authority. Thus, given such contrasting options, parents might make choices that would result in socially homogeneous student groups. Bridge and Blackman report some tendency in this direction based on data from Alum Rock and from a schools-within-schools program in Mamaroneck, New York, an upper middle-class suburban community. Clerico (1983) note that conservative Protestants prefer traditional classrooms based on their religious beliefs, but apparently unrelated to parental occupation. Nault and Uchitelle (1982) note that parents prefer schools that operate in ways consistent with their own child-rearing beliefs and practices, but they offer no explanation regarding the sources of such beliefs.

Equally important to the problem of equity is the question of the extent to which relatively advantaged or white families use choice opportunities to increase or reduce contact between their own children and children from less advantaged or nonwhite families. Nault and Uchitelle (1982) report that 86% of the parents they interviewed "wanted a school where the children would be exposed to children of different ethnic and racial backgrounds" (p. 90), whereas less than a third wanted a school where "the children's backgrounds were similar to our own" (p. 90). Forty-four percent of the parents stated that they had chosen the community in which they lived because they wanted to live in an integrated community. And "two-thirds of the white parents chose the school in which their children would encounter fewer schoolmates of their own race" (p. 91), as did nearly all of the black parents.

Other studies, however, demonstrate little or no commitment on the part of white, middle-income parents to choose racially or socioeconomically integrated schools. Gratiot (1980) attempted to study social status (prestige) as an explanation for choice of private schools in a California school district with a combined black and Mexican-American population of less than 1%. She found that private school parents were less likely to agree that there were prestige differences among schools than public school parents, that parents whose children attended schools identified by other parents as having high prestige were less likely to identify those schools in that way, and that of those parents who said their children attended high prestige schools, all but one spontaneously added that that had not influenced their enrollment decisions.

Williams et al. (1983) reports that "mix of student backgrounds" ranked 9th out of a list of 11 factors for public school parents who considered other schools and all private school parents. Darling-Hammond and Kirby (1985) report that "socio-economic background of students" and "desegregation policy/student body composition" also ranked near the bottom of their lists of very important factors for parents choosing both public and private schools. For both studies, it is unclear whether the parents who chose these items were positively or negatively disposed toward schools with students of different backgrounds. Furthermore, the low response rate on these items may simply have reflected the fact that both studies included suburban and rural areas where student body composition and desegregation policy were not perceived to be pressing issues.

Slaughter and Schneider (1986), in their study of parents whose children attend racially integrated private schools in Chicago, found that black parents emphasize the relationship between educational quality and social diversity in schools more than white parents do. This finding is all the more significant because the white parents in this study were those whose children were perceived by their teachers to be most friendly toward their black classmates.

Maddaus (1988a) found that only 2 of the 39 white families he interviewed preferred integrated schools, and only 1 of the 2 actually chose an integrated school. Furthermore, most of the parents interviewed showed little awareness of the city's two magnet schools. On the other hand, most of these parents enrolled their children in public schools, all of which were integrated, even when some of these parents could have afforded to send them to nearly all-white private schools. Virtually all of these families made some reference to black students, integration, or busing, usually in neutral or guardedly negative terms, but other factors (e.g., academic quality, cost) prevailed in their enrollment decisions. Most parents preferred schools in which students and their parents, as well as staff, shared the values they wanted their children to accept, as opposed to schools with greater diversity of values. Several middle-income parents suggested that behavior and values were related more closely to income than to race. These parents expressed the same concerns about the behavior of low-income white children that they did about low-income black children, although racial balance considerations excluded low-income white children from schools in middle-income white neighborhoods, while allowing low-income black children to attend. Black families were conspicuously absent from all but the lowest income neighborhood in this study, and the parents interviewed made very few references to any kind of personal contact with blacks.

Rossell (1985) notes that "in desegregation plans with mandatory assignment, on average, 50 percent of the whites assigned to schools formerly above 90 percent black do not show up" (p. 9). Magnet school programs have been cited as a successful approach to promoting racial integration of schools, but Rossell notes that school districts often have to go to considerable lengths to attract enough white students, such as providing extra programs, visible white staff members, and limits on black enrollment. The success of magnet schools may be inversely related to the size of the cities attempting to use them.

Perhaps the clearest demonstration of the lack of interest among white, middle-income parents in integrated schooling is the "donut effect" in many metropolitan areas, where predominantly white suburbs surround predominantly minority inner cities. Weiler (1974) notes that efforts were made to interest nearby districts, which were predominantly white, in joining the Alum Rock district, with its 70% minority population, in the voucher demonstration, but these efforts were unsuccessful. Voluntary interdistrict transfer arrangements have been established in just a handful of metropolitan areas, including Boston, Massachusetts, Hartford, Connecticut, Rochester, New York, and Milwaukee, Wisconsin (Dougherty, 1982; Hentschke & Lowe, 1983; Kemper, 1989).

In summary, only the Nault and Uchitelle study provides evidence that significant numbers of white parents prefer racially integrated schools, and none of the studies reviewed suggest that middle-income parents prefer socioeconomic diversity. Although these studies do not demonstrate the validity of Coleman's (Coleman, Kelley, & Moore, 1975) "white flight" (or perhaps equally to the point "middle-class flight") conclusion, neither do they demonstrate a widespread commitment to social diversity. At best, most studies suggest that under normal circumstances some white, middle-income parents can be enticed to send their children to school with minority children from low-income families if enough incentives in the form of special programs can be provided, whereas others can be persuaded to accept minority students into schools in white neighborhoods so long as the character of the school is not perceived to change as a result.

Thus the question of equity has two sides: the ability of low-income (disproportionately minority) parents to gather information about schools and make choices that will benefit their children, and the willingness of middle-income (disproportionately white) parents to be attracted to schools in poor and minority neighborhoods or to accept the choices of poor and minority parents if such choices would result in their own children attending schools with greater diversity in student body composition.

CONCLUSIONS

Although conservatives and liberals alike have advocated parental choice of public schools as a means of promoting excellence while ensuring equity, this review of research findings suggests problems with both objectives.

The potential contribution to educational excellence of parental choice among public schools may be limited in at least two major ways. First, many parents have already made their choices among public schools through their decisions about residential location, and thus are unlikely to choose again by other means that require transporting their children significant distances. Furthermore, many parents, especially at the elementary level, have a more holistic view of "good schools" than appears to be held by policymakers. This view encompasses moral, social, emotional, and cognitive dimensions of education, which is seen as an aspect of child rearing. If this reading of parental goals is correct, parental choice may have more to contribute to the war on drugs than to the pursuit of global economic competitiveness.

With respect to equity, this review also identifies two major limiting factors. Ever since Alum Rock, researchers and policy analysts have noted that low-income families may be less able to make informed decisions than are middle-income families, at least until procedures become well established and effectively communicated through both formal and informal channels. But even assuming that low-income families could become well informed, this review suggests that many middle-income families may be reluctant to make choices themselves or to accept the choices of low-income parents if the effect of such choices is to markedly increase the social diversity of school populations and to change the perceived character of schools. Some middle-income parents may be receptive to incentives in the form of special programs, but their numbers may be too small to allow a major shift of low-income students from low-quality schools.

The research on parental choice of school in relation to excellence and equity is thus far suggestive rather than conclusive. More research is needed to further test the conclusions presented here regarding location and diversity. Research studies so far have used national samples or focused on urban areas, neglecting suburban and rural communities. The traditional practice of town tuitioning in northern New England offers an excellent opportunity to explore what parental choice could mean for the third of this nation's population that is rural. New state policies in Minnesota and several other states offer expanded opportunities for researchers.

Among research issues related to parents that still need to be addressed are the following:

1. What are the differences between those parents in a given school attendance area who enroll their children in the neighborhood public school and those parents in the same area who enroll their children elsewhere?

2. Under what conditions will parents in suburban areas agree to participate voluntarily in urban-suburban interdistrict transfer programs (or housing integration)?

3. What do parents in rural areas think about the trade-offs between small, community-based schools and larger schools with more curricular and extracurricular options?

4. What do parents mean by academic quality (i.e., what distinguishes a "good" school or "good" teacher)?

5. How much information do parents have about the new assessment examinations that have been adopted in many states, and does this information have any effect on their choices of schools?

6. What are the critical factors in decisions between public and private schools, and what changes would result in transfers from one sector to the other?

7. What do parents think and what do they do about school choices that are uncertain due to racial balance limits or selective admissions procedures?

8. How much do parents discuss choice of school with their children, and how much are those children actually involved in the decisions and how are they influenced by the process?

9. Do parents perceive that making a choice among schools has any effect on themselves personally, in terms of empowerment for their child-rearing responsibilities?

10. As parents become more familiar with a parental choice program over time, do they change the way they think and act with respect to it?

Parental choice of school is a complex issue, and this review has necessarily been limited in scope. After briefly highlighting the history of policy initiatives promoting parental choice, I have focused on what parents think and do. Further reviews and research are needed in the following areas: (a) analysis of program characteristics (e.g., extent of selectivity of admissions policies, availability of transportation, racial balance, and other restrictions on choice); (b) what policymakers, administrators, and teachers think and do; and (c) program impacts on excellence, equity, and empowerment.

It is hoped that existing research is but a beginning in our efforts to understand the educational and social implications of this major policy initiative.

REFERENCES

Bennett, W. J. (1985, November 13). *Statement by William J. Bennett, United States Secretary of Education, on The Equity and Choice Act of 1985 (TEACH)* [press release]. Washington, DC: U.S. Department of Education.

Blank, R. K., Dentler, R. A., Baltzell, D. C., & Chabotar, K. (1983, September). *Survey of magnet schools analyzing a model for quality integrated education: Executive summary* (Report No. 300-81-0420). Washington, DC: U.S. Department of Education. (ERIC Document Reproduction Service No. ED 236 304)

Braddock, J. H. (1981, November). Quality and equality: Compatible or incompatible goals. *Phi Delta Kappan, 63*(3), 156.

Bradley, A. (1989, April 5). Tax credits are too expensive, Bush asserts. *Education Week,* pp. 1, 17.

Bridge, R. G. (1978, May). Information imperfections: The Achilles' heel of entitlement plans. *School Review, 86*(3), 504–529.

Bridge, R. G., & Blackman, J. (1978, April). *A study of alternatives in American education, Vol. 4: Family choice in schooling* (Report No. R-2170/4-NIE). Santa Monica, CA: Rand.

Bronfenbrenner, U. (1979). *The ecology of human development: Experiments by nature and design.* Cambridge, MA: Harvard University Press.

Bush, G. H. W. (1989, January 18). "Perhaps the single most promising" reform idea [speech at the White House Workshop on Choice in Education]. *Education Week,* p. 24.

Catterall, J. S. (1982). The politics of education vouchers. *Dissertation Abstracts International, 43,* 1041-A. (University Microfilms No. 8220436)

Catterall, J. S. (1983). *Tuition tax credits: Fact and fiction.* Bloomington, IN: Phi Delta Kappa Educational Foundation.

Center for the Study of Public Policy. (1970, December). *Education vouchers: A report on financing elementary education grants to parents* (OEO grant CG8542). Cambridge, MA: Author.

Clerico, D. R. (1983). Searching for peace of mind: Parents' rationales for enrolling their children in a Christian school. *Dissertation Abstracts International, 43*, 2163-A. (University Microfilms No. 8228974)

Cochran, M., & Henderson, C. (1985, February). *Family matters: Evaluation of the parental empowerment program* (NIE Contract No. 400-76-0150). Ithaca, NY: Cornell University.

Coleman, J. S. (1981, November). Quality and equality in American education: Public and Catholic schools. *Phi Delta Kappan, 63*(3), 159–164.

Coleman, J. S., & Hoffer, T. (1987). *Public and private high schools: The impact of communities.* New York, NY: Basic Books.

Coleman, J. S., Hoffer, T., & Kilgore, S. (1982). *High school achievement: Public, Catholic, and private schools compared.* New York: Basic Books.

Coleman, J. S., Kelley, S. D., & Moore, J. A. (1975). *Trends in school segregation, 1968–75.* Washington, DC: Urban Institute.

Convey, J. J. (1986, April). *Parental choice of Catholic schools as a function of religion, race, and family income.* Paper presented at the annual meeting of the American Educational Research Association, San Francisco, CA. (ERIC Document Reproduction Service No. ED 269 542)

Coons, J. E., & Sugarman, S. D. (1978). *Education by choice: The case for family control.* Berkeley, CA: University of California Press.

Council of Chief State School Officers. (1987). *Education in the states: Vol. 1; State education indicators.* Washington, DC: Author.

Cremin, L. A. (1976). *Public education.* New York: Basic Books.

Darling-Hammond, L., & Kirby, S. N. (1985, December). *Tuition tax deductions and parent school choice: A case study of Minnesota* (Report No. R-3294-NIE). Santa Monica, CA: Rand. (ERIC Document Reproduction Service No. ED 273 047)

Donaldson, G. A., Jr. (1977). *Education vouchers in New Hampshire: An attempt at free market educational reform* (NIE Contract No. B2C-5331). Newton, MA: C. M. Leinwand Associates.

Dougherty, P. (1982, November 17). New state role called essential to urban-suburban integration. *Education Week*, p. 6.

Elam, S. M. (1984). *The Phi Delta Kappa Gallup polls of attitudes toward education, 1969–1984: A topical summary.* Bloomington, IN: Phi Delta Kappa.

Fantini, M. (1973). *Public schools of choice.* New York: Simon & Schuster.

Friedman, M. (1962). *Capitalism and freedom.* Chicago: University of Chicago Press.

Friedman, M. (1973, September 23). The voucher idea: Selling schooling like groceries. *New York Times Magazine*, pp. 22–23, 65, 67, 69–72.

Friedman, M., & Friedman, R. (1980). *Free to choose.* New York: Avon Books.

Gallup, A. M. (1986, September). The 18th annual Gallup poll of the public's attitudes toward public schools. *Phi Delta Kappan, 68*(1), 43–59.

Gallup, A. M., & Clark, D. L. (1987, September). The 19th annual Gallup poll of the public's attitudes toward the public schools. *Phi Delta Kappan, 69*(1), 17–29.

Gallup, A. M., & Elam, S. M. (1988, September). The 20th annual Gallup poll of the public's attitudes toward the public schools. *Phi Delta Kappan, 70*(1), 33–46.

Gerritz, W. H. (1988, April). Family preferences for K-twelve education: An explanatory model. *Dissertation Abstracts International, 48,* 2497-A. (University Microfilms No. 8726213)

Goldberg, K. (1988, May 18). Vermont's "tuitioning" is nation's oldest brand of choice. *Education Week,* p. 9.

Gratiot, M. H. (1980). Why parents choose nonpublic schools: Comparative attitudes and characteristics of public and private school consumers. *Dissertation Abstracts International, 40,* 4825-A. (University Microfilms No. 8006315)

Greeley, A. M., & Rossi, P. H. (1966). *The education of Catholic Americans.* Chicago: Aldine.

Green, T. (1988, February). The economy of virtue and the primacy of prudence. *American Journal of Education, 96*(2), 127–142.

Hentschke, G. C., & Lowe, W. T. (1983, January). *Toward increased voluntary interdistrict integration in New York State.* Rochester, NY: University of Rochester.

Kemper, S. (1989, April). This man believes he can save our schools. *New England Monthly,* pp. 42–45.

Kohn, M. L. (1969). *Class and conformity: A study in values.* Homewood, IL: Dorsey Press.

Kraushaar, O. F. (1972). *American nonpublic schools: Patterns of diversity.* Baltimore, MD: Johns Hopkins University Press.

Lines, P., & McGuire, K. (1984, February). *Education reform and education choice: Conflict and accommodation* (Contract No. NIE-P-83-0054). Denver, CO: Education Commission of the States. (ERIC Document Reproduction Service No. ED 253 960)

Maddaus, J. (1987, April). *Residential mobility and school enrollment.* Paper presented at the annual meeting of the New England Educational Research Organization, Stratton Mountain, VT.

Maddaus, J. (1988a, September). Families, neighborhoods and schools: Parental perspectives and actions regarding choice in elementary school enrollment. *Dissertation Abstracts International, 49,* 477-A. (University Microfilms No. 8806952)

Maddaus, J. (1988b, April). *Parental choice and quality education.* Paper presented at the annual meeting of the New England Educational Research Organization, Rockport, ME.

Maddaus, J. (1988c, November). *Parents' perceptions of the moral environment in choosing their children's elementary schools.* Paper presented at the annual meeting of the Association for Moral Education, Pittsburgh, PA.

Massachusetts Department of Education Office of Educational Equity. (1986, January). *Family choice and public schools: A report to the State Board of Education.* Quincy, MA: Author.

Massachusetts Department of Education Office of Educational Equity. (1988a, September). *Background papers on parent choice among public schools* (revised). Quincy, MA: Author.

Massachusetts Department of Education Office of Educational Equity. (1988b, October). *Why parents in five nations choose schools.* Quincy, MA: Author.

McCarthy, M. M. (1983). Tuition tax credits and the first amendment. *Issues in Education, 1*(2 & 3), 88–106.

McMillan, C. B. (1980). *Magnet schools: An approach to voluntary desegregation.* Bloomington, IN: Phi Delta Kappa Educational Foundation.

Murnane, R. J. (1984, March). *Family choice in public education: Possibilities and limitations* (Contract No. NIE-P-83-0065). Cambridge, MA: Harvard University. (ERIC Document Reproduction Service No. ED 253 961)

National Governors' Association. (1986). *Time for results: The governors' 1991 report on education.* Washington, DC: Author.

Nault, R. L., & Uchitelle, S. (1982). School choice in the public sector: A case study of parental decision-making. In M. E. Manley-Casimir (Ed.), *Family choice in schooling: Issues and dilemmas* (pp. 85–98). Lexington, MA: D. C. Heath.

Nelson, K. O. (1988, November). Reasons given by Anglo/Hispanic parents/guardians for choosing a Catholic high school in the Southwestern United States. *Dissertation Abstracts International, 49,* 1049-A. (University Microfilms No. 8814262)

Pear, R. (1985, November 14). Reagan proposes vouchers to give poor a choice of schools. *New York Times,* p. A20.

Petch, A. (1986, March). Parental choice at entry to primary school. *Research Papers in Education, 1*(1), 26–47.

Powell, D. R. (1980, June). *Finding child care: A study of parents' search processes* (Ford Foundation Grant No. 780-0372). Detroit, MI: Merrill-Palmer Institute.

Raab, G. M., & Adler, M. (1987, October). A tale of two cities: The impact of parental choice on admissions to primary school in Edinburgh and Dundee. *Research Papers in Education, 2*(3), 157–176.

Raywid, M. A. (1982). *The current status of schools of choice in public education* (NIE Contract No. G-80-0194). Hempstead, NY: Project on Alternatives in Education.

Raywid, M. A. (1984, February). *Family choice arrangements in public schools: A review of the literature* (NIE Contract No. NIE-P-83-0047). Hempstead, NY: Center for the Study of Educational Alternatives.

Raywid, M. A. (1987, June). Public choice, yes; Vouchers, no! *Phi Delta Kappan, 68*(10), 762–769.

Reagan, R. (1985, March 6). [Excerpts from address to the National Association of Independent Schools, February 28, 1985]. *Education Week,* p. 30.

Rossell, C. H. (1985, April). What is attractive about magnet schools? *Urban Education, 20*(1), 7–22.

Shanker, A. (1989, February 22). Choice plan can bolster public schools, but it's no education cure-all. *Education Week* (Convention Supplement), p. 10.

Skehan, J. (1985, April). *Where do citizens get most of their information about schools: An analysis.* Paper presented at the annual meeting of the New England Educational Research Association, Rockport, ME.

Slaughter, D. T., & Schneider, B. L. (1986). *Newcomers: Blacks in private schools* (Grant No. NIE-G-82-0040). Evanston, IL: Northwestern University. (ERIC Document Reproduction Service No. ED 274 768)

Smith, V., Barr, R., & Burke, D. (1976). *Alternatives in education.* Bloomington, IN: Phi Delta Kappa Educational Foundation.

Snider, W. (1987, June 24). The call to choice: Competition in the educational marketplace (A special report). *Education Week,* pp. C1–C24.

Snider, W. (1988, May 18). School choice: New, more efficient "sorting machine"? *Education Week,* pp. 1, 8.

Snider, W. (1989a, March 15). In nation's first open-enrollment state, the action begins. *Education Week,* p. 18.

Snider, W. (1989b, March 15). Iowa, Arkansas enact "choice"; Proposals gain in other states. *Education Week,* pp. 1, 19.

Snider, W. (1989c, January 18). Parley on "choice," final budget mark transition. *Education Week,* pp. 1, 24.

Weiler, D. (1974, June). *A public school voucher demonstration: The first year at Alum Rock* (Report No. R-1495-NIE). Santa Monica, CA: Rand.

Williams, M. F., Hancher, K. S., & Hutner, A. (1983, December). *Parents and school choice: A household survey.* Washington, DC: U.S. Department of Education. (ERIC Document Reproduction Service No. ED 240 739)

Wimpelberg, R. E. (1982, March). *Parents and sex equity in elementary schools: Parental preferences, choice and influence as they relate to the schooling of boys and girls.* Paper presented at the annual meeting of the American Educational Research Association, Chicago, IL.

Chapter 6

The Mentor Phenomenon and the Social Organization of Teaching

JUDITH WARREN LITTLE
University of California, Berkeley

Policymakers and educational leaders have thrust *mentoring* into the vocabulary of school reform as part of a mission to reward and retain capable teachers while obligating those teachers, implicitly or explicitly, to contribute to the improvement of schools and the quality of the teacher work force. For much of the past decade, the term *mentor* has been prominently associated with proposed shifts in teachers' professional relationships and with altered teacher roles in schools and school districts. Mentoring is a principal component of state-initiated teacher incentive programs (Hart, 1989; Neufeld, 1986; Wagner, 1985), university-based teacher preparation programs (Huling-Austin, 1988), and local programs of teacher induction and professional development (Stoddart, 1989).

Proponents of mentoring argue its merits on the basis of a "mutual benefits" model (Zey, 1984). By this argument, investing some teachers with the special titles, resources, and obligations of mentorship will more readily assure various individual and institutional benefits. The mentors themselves will receive public acknowledgement of their accumulated knowledge, skill, and judgment. Novice teachers will receive support that mediates the difficulties of the first years of teaching. Career opportunities in the occupation will be enriched. And schools, restructured to accommodate new teacher leadership roles, will expand their capacity to serve students and to adapt to societal demands.

Rhetoric and action have nonetheless outpaced both conceptual development and empirical warrant. Indeed, a certain "manic optimism" prevails (Elmore, 1989). Relative to the amount of pragmatic activity,

My thanks to Ann Weaver Hart, who served as advisory editor on this chapter, to Nathalie Gehrke and Mark Smylie for their comments and advice, and to Susan Sather for her assistance in searching the literature.

however, the volume of empirical inquiry is small. In a comprehensive review published in 1983, Merriam found scant material on mentoring in academic settings and made virtually no mention of mentoring for purposes of teacher induction, professional development, or career advancement among public school teachers (see also Galvez-Hjornevik, 1986). That is, as recently as 1983 there was no distinct line of research on mentoring in education—and certainly none on mentoring in K-12 teaching. Nonetheless, the scale of policy interest and practical experimentation since 1983 suggests a natural opportunity of considerable magnitude to examine the nature and consequences of these specialized teacher leadership roles. This review offers the beginnings of a rather substantial research agenda.

In this essay I examine mentorship as a structural and cultural feature of schools and the teaching occupation. The focus is the organizational and occupational significance of mentoring among practicing teachers, with emphasis on issues related to school organization, occupational socialization, and the structure of the teaching career. I begin with a conundrum: How to account for the rapidly escalating popularity of mentoring in an occupation that provides few precedents for formal and legitimate leadership by teachers on matters of professional practice.

Curiosity about the origins of mentoring among teachers stems in part from the cultural legacy of the mentor-protégé relationship. In the classical tale from which the term is derived, the departing Odysseus entrusts Mentor with the care and guidance of his son Telemachus. The relationship required of Mentor a full measure of wisdom, integrity, and personal investment. It required that Telemachus, as protégé, honor the differences in maturity and circumstance that separated them. The relationship between mentor and protégé was profoundly personal and mutually respectful, even though it was essentially asymmetrical. It exacted high demands and yielded substantial rewards.

The contemporary treatment of mentor-protégé relations is substantially more narrow. Clawson (1980) traces its transformation to the rise of apprenticeships, when a "more practical, less comprehensive concept of mentors" emerged, linking mentors primarily with career and less broadly with adult maturation (p. 146; but see Kram, 1983; Levinson, Darrow, Klein, Levinson, & McKee, 1978). In the mentor programs that have swept education, the demands on the mentor's competence, character, and commitment are often muted, reduced to formal eligibility criteria and specific job descriptions. Clawson argues, however, that comprehensiveness and mutuality remain the essence of the role. Like other theorists, Clawson confers mentor status only on those persons who fulfill several potential roles (see also Anderson & Shannon, 1988; Schein, 1978; Zey, 1984). Mentors worthy of the name serve as teacher, sponsor, role model, confidant, and more. First-person accounts detail the way in which mentorships unfold, touching persons' lives as well as their work and achieving their effects out of the reciprocal regard in which mentors and protégés hold one another (Parkay, 1988).

Even narrowed to occupational socialization, then, the concept of mentorship promises a great deal. To dignify teachers' responsibilities with the title of "mentor" is to signify inescapably the mentor's special capacities and to invoke a special relation between the mentor and other teachers. In Gehrke's (1988b) analysis, the mentor-protégé relation is best interpreted from the perspective of a gift-exchange economy that is fundamentally incompatible with narrowly defined, utilitarian interactions (a market economy). By this view, mentorship is most appropriately understood "within a system of gift exchange where costs cannot be calculated; where labor is not measured by hours at a specified rate but by an interior clock; and where worth is judged by the individual in terms of its personal effect, and by the group in terms of its support of unity" (p. 193).

Some critics voice skepticism about legislative or bureaucratic actions bent on converting the fundamentally personal, informal, and intense relations of mentoring to formal arrangements (Clawson, 1980; Gehrke, 1988a, 1988b; Kram, 1986; Zey, 1984). The broader cultural legacy of mentoring presents a model of human relationship that does not lend itself well to policy intervention. Common to instances of "significant mentorship" (Hardcastle, 1988) are a breadth, mutuality, and informality difficult to achieve within the confines of bureaucratic arrangements (see Clawson, 1980; Schein, 1978). Heavily standardized and bureaucratic environments, according to Zey (1984), do not support mentoring well. Other critics, alert to the particular history and circumstances of teaching, argue that mentor roles are also largely incompatible with prevailing values, norms, and structures of the occupation (Smylie, 1989; see also Griffin, 1985). Formal initiatives to develop and support mentor roles are thus in some respects an odd enterprise. To resolve the riddle of how formal mentoring has come to pass in education requires in part that we understand what transpires when fundamentally personal relations become the object of formal organization. Also, it requires that we attend to the apparent disjuncture between the egalitarian and individualistic traditions of teaching and the special status implied by the title of mentor.

These puzzles occupy a large proportion of the research on mentoring. In the first and largest section of this paper, therefore, I rely on implementation studies that chronicle the emergence of the mentor role and the attempted reconciliation of present purposes with inherited traditions. In the remaining sections I employ the major implementation dilemmas to interpret the practice of mentoring from the perspective of its two most commonly stated purposes: teacher induction and career enhancement.

These sections are organized respectively by two aspects of the mentor phenomenon that are prominent in literature spanning education, business, and other professions: (a) conceptions oriented to *helping,* with emphasis on emotional support, skill development, and work performance, and (b) conceptions oriented to *advancement,* with emphasis on enhanced career opportunity and reward.

THE EMERGENCE OF FORMAL MENTOR ROLES

In principle, mentor roles satisfy three related policy problems. Mentoring responds first to problems in the occupational induction of teachers. Experienced teachers acknowledged for their own record of classroom accomplishment are invited to pass their knowledge on to novices. Second, "the mantle of mentorship" (Lemberger, 1989) purportedly creates an incentive for teacher retention and commitment by conferring public recognition and reward on the most accomplished teachers. Last, the concentration of discretionary resources on mentors signals a shifting strategy for local professional development and program innovation; districts employ mentors as staff development and curriculum specialists in pursuit of broad school or district priorities. In all of these policy rationales, the implicit logic is that the concentration of resources on a relatively small proportion of teachers will yield benefits for the larger teacher population and for the institutions that employ them.

Implementation studies have clustered around the major local and state initiatives that exemplify these three policy interests. The various initiatives are similar in their origins, tending to arise as policy-level responses to work force and workplace issues. They are alike, too, in devoting substantial institutional resources to an enterprise by which teachers themselves bolster the capacities and commitments of the teacher work force. The initiatives nonetheless vary in the focus and clarity of the purposes and strategies they pursue, in the degree to which the intended roles and functions depart from traditions of autonomy and equal status among teachers, and thus in the burden of change they present. The various implementation studies reflect these differences as well.

Three examples illustrate the initiatives on which research has focused and the directions researchers have pursued. In California's Mentor Teacher Program, legislators placed reward and recognition for experienced teachers foremost. The emphasis on career incentives for individual teachers is reflected in the flow of dollars: Two thirds of the program's resources go directly into the hands of the mentor teachers in the form of moderately large stipends ($4,000 per year). Although the legislators explicitly anticipated that mentors would in turn contribute to teacher induction, professional development, and leadership in curriculum and instructional improvement, districts were granted a wide range of latitude to shape a program responsive both to local interests and local constraints (Wagner, 1985). Far West Laboratory for Educational Research and Development undertook nine case studies and a statewide survey as part of a 2-year investigation of the first stages of program implementation. Case studies supplied the main insights (Bird, St. Clair, Shulman, & Little, 1984; Hanson, Shulman, & Bird, 1985; Shulman, Hanson, & King, 1985), which in turn were tested against a broader array of policies and practices in a survey sample of 291 districts (Bird, 1986; Bird & Alspaugh, 1986).

In Connecticut, mentor roles were introduced as an essential feature of the state's new procedures for teacher certification and induction. These purposes were primary, career incentives were secondary (Allen & Pecheone, 1989). Mentors are expected to help prepare beginning teachers to satisfy the state's criteria for certification in 15 competency areas. In this regard, the Connecticut program is similar to others in which mentors' work is linked closely to local or state evaluation standards (Huffman & Leak, 1986; Stoddart, 1989). The Connecticut State Department of Education has supported program histories and program evaluations of the Connecticut Beginning Educator Support and Training (BEST) program since its inception in 1985-86 (Allen, 1989; Allen & Pecheone, 1989; Martin, 1987; Neufeld, 1986). Conceptually, the state's initiative is premised on a "screens and magnets" strategy (Sykes, 1983). Each of the studies, therefore, traces the development of the mentor role as part of a system in which more stringent assessment of teaching (better screening) is backed by more rigorous and frequent support of teachers (more compelling magnets). The various studies follow district-level pilot programs through a steady expansion in number from 5 to 25 and through the less steady, sometimes turbulent, search for shared goals and workable strategies. In the most recent phase, evaluations of pilot efforts in 25 of the state's 166 districts concentrate on the short-term effects associated with certain instrumental aspects of program implementation, especially the effort to achieve a subject-grade level match between mentors and new teachers (Allen & Pecheone, 1989).

In still other sites, career incentive programs (Hart, 1989; Hart & Murphy, 1989b; Smylie & Denny, 1989) or school improvement consortia (Wasley, 1989) have promoted specialized leadership positions that bear a close resemblance to mentor roles, though their titles differ. Rarely do the evolving roles entail formal authority for personnel or program matters, although they do engage some teachers in the supervision, assistance, and instruction of others. These experiments most closely approximate the "school restructuring" applications of mentorship, linked not to specific provisions for teacher certification or induction but to broadly stated aspirations for teacher leadership and career enhancement. Local career ladder experiments in Utah, also spurred by the screens and magnets logic, have been the site of investigations into school-level definitions of leadership roles, with special emphasis on the fit between teacher leadership and school goals (Hart & Murphy, 1989b) and on the "role politics" surrounding development of teacher leader and teacher specialist positions (Hart, 1989). A similar inquiry has followed a local career enhancement venture in which teacher leadership positions were introduced through a side letter agreement to a locally negotiated teacher contract (Smylie & Denny, 1989).

Enriched by advances in the study of innovations (McLaughlin, 1987) and by theories of work redesign (Hackman & Oldham, 1980; Nicholson, 1984), implementation studies have charted the progress of mentor initiatives by closely attending to local contexts and organizational dynamics. All the implementation studies incorporate in-depth interviews; each adds, to varying degrees, other elements of a case study approach. Interviews with district administrators establish the place of the mentor phenomenon in relation to other district priorities, goals, and history. District-level coordinators, principals, and mentors themselves link the program to local school and district history, and particularly to similar leadership roles that had been well or poorly accepted by teachers in the past. Union representatives and district administrators fill in the details of local negotiation over the form and content of mentors' work and the conditions of their selection. Mentors evaluate the arrangements made to prepare them for their new roles and to support them in their work. The mentors and the principals and teachers with whom they work describe and assess the actual work they have done in their capacity as mentor, and the time and other resources available to do it. Principals weigh the advantages and disadvantages of the arrangement from the perspective of the individual school and describe their own influence (or lack of it) in shaping the mentors' general role or specific responsibilities.

These studies have in common that they construct the implementation problem not only as the pursuit of broad policy goals and the implementation of a discrete program, but also as the redefinition of institutional roles, professional relationships, and the work of teaching. In some respects, those who would implement mentor roles are confronted with a two-part challenge: to introduce classroom teachers to a role with which they are unfamiliar; and to introduce the role itself to an institution and occupation in which it has few precedents (Bird & Little, 1985; Little, 1988; Smylie & Denny, 1989). Consistent with this perspective, Hart (1989) cast her study of school-level teacher leader and teacher specialist positions in Utah as a case in role innovation and work redesign. The "substantial discretion" attached to new teacher leader positions led Smylie and Denny (1989) to frame their own study around questions of role definition and role evolution. Similar issues surrounding role definition guided the earliest inquiries into the Connecticut pilot programs (Neufeld, 1986), and persistent issues of role ambiguity and role conflict surface in more recent work (Allen, 1989). Far West Laboratory described its comprehensive study of the California Mentor Teacher Program this way:

> The [mentor program] may be described as an effort to retain skillful teachers and to improve teaching by promoting direct, rigorous, and consequential activities and relationships between mentors and other teachers. The [studies] asked whether and how district efforts to implement the mentor program promoted those activities and relations. (Shulman et al., 1985, p. 2)

Bowing to Conservative Precedent

A single dominant theme emerges from the implementation studies: Mentor initiatives encounter consistent pressure to accommodate the individualistic and egalitarian traditions of teaching and to discount the status distinctions implied by the mentor title. At the school level, we find few cases in which the mentor role signals a reorganization of authority relations or an increase in the school's collective influence on practices of teaching (for one example of such a case, see Hart, 1989).

Certain conditions of implementation constrain or enable local actors, moving them toward a more ambitious or a less ambitious conception of the mentor role. Among them are the pace at which implementation proceeds, the sheer opportunity for work that is described as "mentoring," and the precedents that shape expectations for mentors' performance. On the whole, these conditions have favored narrow definitions of the mentor role and conservative solutions to implementation problems.

Pace of Implementation

Mentor programs have proliferated rapidly over the past decade. The magnitude of change implied by the mentor title invites a pace that is slow enough to achieve properly "integrative agreements" (Pruitt & Carnevale, 1982), but brisk enough to sustain momentum. The persistence of problems related to role definition in the Connecticut sites suggests that a slow pace alone (3 years of "pilot" activity) does not ensure that proponents of the innovation will grapple successfully with established practice (Allen & Pecheone, 1989; Martin, 1987). A rapid pace, however, coupled with high public visibility, almost certainly guarantees that districts will settle on conservative solutions to the predictable problems that arise when a proposed innovation runs counter to established norms and structures.

California's Mentor Teacher Program illustrates the problems associated with rapid starts and a fast pace in the early stages of a complex innovation. Pressed to move quickly following passage of the state's omnibus reform bill, teachers and administrators in many California districts achieved the fit between policy intent and local context that Berman and McLaughlin (1978) describe as "mutual adaptation" by compromising certain principal (but controversial) tenets of the legislative intent underlying mentorships. California launched a precipitous schedule of implementation in its first stages, urging districts to adopt the program in the closing months of the 1983-84 school year (Bird, 1986). Although participation in the California program was voluntary and although local districts retained substantial discretion in deciding a conception of the mentor role, the scale of the funding propelled districts to accept the program. By 1986-87, the budget supporting the mentor program constituted more than one half of the state's categorical staff development funding (Little et al., 1987). Districts' access to state-controlled funding for professional development resources was thus directly linked to participation in the mentor program. Meanwhile, a schedule of implementation linked to the state's fiscal year pressed districts to decide quickly what form the local program would assume. The result was a pervasive effort to define the mentor role within the boundaries of familiar roles and functions. Based on nine case studies and a survey of 291 districts, Bird (1986) concludes that "a good deal was lost, and little or nothing gained, by haste in implementing the mentor program" (p. 7). California's experience is mirrored elsewhere in the implementation studies. Hart and Murphy (1989b), too, attribute conservative program designs in Utah to the press of time in the early stages of implementation: "Because the time left by the state . . . between planning and implementation was limited, job descriptions often were modeled after preexisting special projects and unrecognizable from conventional practice" (p. 15). In Connecticut, where the state's teacher certification law introduces a relatively standardized conception of the mentor role, a 3-year sequence of pilot efforts has not relieved the state of many of the same implementation problems faced in sites with less well-bounded purposes and fewer program specifications. Externally established goals, even when broadly accepted in principle, do not appear to overcome the hold exerted by long-standing and taken-for-granted ways of working. The slower pace in the Connecticut sites, however, may have helped to forestall the kinds of agreements that compromise key principles and thereby contribute to a pattern of "vanishing effects" (Malen & Hart, 1987).

Rapid starts place a premium on reducing the tangle of competing preferences and countervailing practices. Smooth starts achieved through large-scale compromise bode ill for long-term success. Integrative agreements, according to some theorists, require both tolerance for conflict and sufficient opportunity for conflict resolution (Pruitt & Carnevale,

1982). Case studies of innovation in 12 school districts led Huberman and Miles (1984) to conclude that

smooth early use was a bad sign. Smoothly implementing sites seemed to get that way by reducing the initial scale of the project and by lowering the gradient of actual practice change. This "downsizing" got rid of most headaches during the initial implementation but also threw away most of the potential rewards; the project often turned into a modest, sometimes trivial, enterprise. (p. 273)

Broadly conceived policy initiatives, introduced rapidly in the spirit of reform, hold out mentor roles as one element in a new conception of teachers' professional relations. But mentor initiatives constitute a direct and substantial challenge to some of the most powerfully established norms of teaching and to established authority relations in schools. On that basis alone, argue Malen and Hart (1987), such initiatives are especially susceptible to the problem of vanishing effects. The problem is exacerbated when the pace of implementation outstrips the human and material resources available to manage the change.

Opportunity

The fit between the rhetoric and the reality of mentoring is in large part a function of opportunity. The implementation studies cast the question of opportunity in two ways. They first confront the question, To whom do the opportunities or obligations of mentorship fall? The formal designation of "mentors" then gives rise to the second question: When and how do mentors conduct their work?

The formalization of mentor roles brings with it institutional control over selection, or the systematic structuring of teachers' opportunity to assume professional leadership. Issues surrounding the criteria and process for selection have consumed a large share of the political and material resources devoted to implementation, and have occupied a central place in research. In one recent assessment of the prospects for teacher leadership, Little (1988) observed that

the most volatile issue in formal teacher leadership initiatives has been teacher selection. . . . The selection of leaders has been cast both as a technical problem (what are the acceptable criteria for performance?) and as a political problem (who will teachers accept as leaders, if anyone?). (pp. 100–101)

Little concludes that the selection problem is an artifact of isolated work in schools, a problem that achieves its present magnitude only because many teachers have no sensible grounds on which to grant or deny someone the right to lead them. Bird and Alspaugh (1986) observe, "On what basis do persons who work mostly in isolation accept a decision that some of them are better prepared for leadership than others?" (pp. 53–54). Acceptable selection criteria and processes comprise a large share of teachers' overall judgments about mentor programs, and a large portion of their complaints when things seem to go wrong. In interview data assembled from teachers in one career ladder site, "discontent and eroded commitment to the district emerged . . . when teachers questioned the quality of selection and discrimination associated with the new roles" (Hart & Murphy, 1989b, p. 23). Selection criteria, processes, and outcomes formed three of the eight criteria that Ruskus (1988) invited teachers and mentors to use in judging the overall effectiveness of California's mentor initiative in five districts. Across districts, the perceived validity of selection "was the most important determinant of perceived program effectiveness" (p. 199). The district with the highest rating on selection (and also the highest program effectiveness rating) employed a two-stage selection process in which extensive paper screening and principals' ratings were followed by interviews and observations of the highest ranking candidates. In that district, an objective rating form based on stated criteria resulted in the selection of one third of the applicants. By contrast, a district with consistently low ratings on selection (and the lowest rating on effectiveness) employed a more cursory review procedure, conducted interviews with all candidates but no observations, and was criticized by some teachers as relying on "subjective feelings" rather than "real evidence" (pp. 202–203).

To what extent do the formal selection processes—which may include formal applications, peer and supervisor recommendations, interviews, observations, simulations, or portfolios—capture the prospective mentor's persona among colleagues, or reflect teachers' expectations of a mentor's efforts? Teachers' complaints, recorded anecdotally through case study accounts, suggest that a selection process centered on a small sample of teacher's present work may be inadequate to assure the breadth and depth of teacher experience and knowledge that may be an essential prerequisite to leadership on matters of professional practice. Available case studies provide few examples of selection processes in which multiple lines of evidence (Peterson, 1984) are assembled persuasively. In most of the sites described by the implementation studies, teachers' eligibility for leadership positions was thought to be satisfied principally on the basis of short-term classroom observations or testimony by peers and administrators. Few assessed the particular combination of classroom-based expertise and collegial involvements that presage success in the mentor role. Teachers in one case study proposed that selection criteria balancing teachers' classroom expertise and their ability to work with colleagues would be "more in keeping with the meaning of a 'mentor'" (Shulman et al., 1985, p. 14).

Selection issues occupy a central place in the implementation panoply; the resolution of those issues affects opportunity by affecting individuals' access to the position and others' disposition toward them. Nonetheless, the obligations of mentorship are satisfied and its benefits assured only in the actual exercise of the role. Teachers judge mentors by the expertise that they demonstrate and by the effort they expend after being selected. Crucial to teachers' acceptance of the role of mentor, then, is their ability to confirm the worth of individual mentors in actual performance.

Despite the scrutiny given to the process by which teachers are selected to be mentors, a still greater burden of proof rests on the mentor who, once selected, must now actually mentor. Here the issue is the congruence among formal selection mechanisms, the actual demands of performance, and the informal regard of colleagues. Selection turns out to be less an event than a continuing process by which mentors earn their titles on the job. Through myriad daily encounters, and through subtle and not-so-subtle gestures, teachers affirm or reject the mentors' acclaimed status (Bird, 1986; Hart & Murphy, 1989b). On the basis of vignettes of teacher and mentor interactions (Allen, 1989; Shulman & Colbert, 1987), one can conclude that the closer the mentor comes to exerting influence on other teachers' work, the more stringent become the demands on the mentor's competence and character.

A teacher is selected as a mentor principally on the basis of accomplishments with children; the teacher is subsequently accepted as a mentor on the basis of accomplishments with fellow teachers and administrators. The demands on mentors' expertise are frequently far greater than a prospective mentor might anticipate on the basis of selection criteria alone. Admittedly, mentors appear more sanguine about the effectiveness of their work than are the teachers they purportedly serve. Teachers are less inclined to judge the mentors' efforts to be sufficiently influential. Teachers in five California districts consistently rated mentors' effectiveness in less glowing terms than did the participating mentors (Ruskus, 1988). In each of three areas of interaction (effectiveness with new teachers, with experienced teachers, and in facilitating communication) teachers' mean ratings of effectiveness were significantly below those of mentors themselves (p. 156). Teachers were also less willing to attribute impact on student progress or teacher retention to the efforts made by mentors; again, the mean ratings on the cross-district sample of teachers and mentors differed significantly. This finding parallels results of a case study of school-level instructional support teams in which team members rated their direct contacts with teachers as more frequent and more potent than did the teachers (Little & Long, 1985). One explanation accounts plausibly for these comparable patterns in the two studies. From the mentors' point of view, even a few direct consultations or classroom visits constitute a high level of activity in an overcrowded schedule. From the perspective of teachers at large, most of whom have not been touched directly by the mentors' activities, the work is less visible and less visibly consequential. Allowing for very real differences in effort and capacity among mentors, the fact remains that teachers' perceptions of their effort and effectiveness are largely contingent on their opportunity to acquire direct evidence of their work. When asked, teachers discriminate finely between those in leadership positions who do much and those who do little, those whose work makes a solid contribution and those whose work is "trite" or "frivolous" (Hart & Murphy, 1989b). Ruskus collects, but does not report, data that would permit her to distinguish effectiveness ratings given by teachers who were directly involved with mentors from those ratings based on less immediate contact. Such measures of mentors' effectiveness, sensitive to variations in direct involvement between mentors and teachers, will provide a more credible base than we have now for explaining teachers' acceptance of the mentor role and for determining the nature and extent of mentors' influence on teachers.

Concern for the performance aspect of the selection and subsequent acceptance of mentors has led states and districts to supply mentors with skill training or peer support groups (Bird & Little, 1985;Kent, 1985; King, 1988). By such training, mentors are sometimes helped to make explicit and accessible their own knowledge of curriculum, instruction, and classroom management. Often, however, they are asked to adopt concepts and terminology derived from classroom research (Kent, 1985) or from state and local teacher evaluation guidelines (Allen & Pecheone, 1989; Huffman & Leak, 1986). Communication skills, consultation strategies, and classroom observation techniques also form a large share of most training agendas (see, e.g., Brzoska, Jones, Mahaffy, Miller, & Mychals, 1987; Little & Nelson, 1989; State of Connecticut Department of Education, 1988). Indeed, even a cursory review of such guides leads one to conclude that the process of mentoring takes considerable precedence over its substance; training activities are heavily weighted toward ensuring smooth interpersonal relations between mentors and teachers or administrators.

Specialized training for mentors has become an increasingly common and prominent component of role development (e.g., Thies-Sprinthall, 1986). The earliest program ventures sparked widespread dispute about the need for organized training and support. Opponents of such training made the case that the very selection of teachers as mentors was intended to signal a high level of professional capacity, whereas advocates of training underscored the unfamiliar demands of mentoring for which the classroom provided little or no preparation (Bird & Little, 1985). In the first 2 years of California's state-supported program, nearly 40% of participating districts allocated no resources at all for postselection support of mentors; many others relied on occasional workshops sponsored by county offices of education or on other out-of-district opportunities (Bird & Alspaugh, 1986).

Structured training and support appears more likely where mentoring is linked to a single state or district policy goal, as in Connecticut's use of mentors for teacher certification (Allen & Pecheone, 1989), Los Angeles Unified School District's assignment of mentors to new teachers (Little & Nelson, 1989), and Toledo's involvement of experienced teachers in the evaluation and tenure of new teachers (Stoddart, 1989). At the school level, organized training and support are more likely where administrators and teachers have forged a clear link between the mentor role and school-level goals. In these instances, clearly defined policy purposes surrounding the mentor role increase the availability of training, but also dictate its content. By contrast, teachers are more likely to assume new leadership roles without benefit of formal training and support where those roles remain personalized, entrepreneurial, and less clearly connected to institutional priorities (Hart, 1989; Smylie & Denny, 1989).

Training is typically a post hoc accommodation, following the award of mentor status. Only rarely does selection to mentor roles require that the teacher first acquire experience in other mentor-like capacities, such as serving as a supervisor of student teachers. Nor do selection processes typically assess prospective mentors' disposition toward sharing ideas and materials, assisting others, or taking initiative with regard to professional practice (Allen, 1989; Smylie, 1989). These characteristic omissions from mentor selection routines may prove consequential, bearing in unanticipated ways on mentors' own perceptions of their role and on the expectations that others hold out for it.

Despite the apparent range in availability and content of mentor training, there are virtually no studies that trace the contributions made by postselection training to the subsequent performance of the mentors, or to their success in relationships with teachers or administrators. No studies compare mentors who receive training with those who are left to their own resources. Nor have there been any attempts to assess the relative leverage to be gained by investing institutional resources in postselection training versus various forms of preselection preparation of individuals, groups, or organizations.

The performance imperatives of mentorship render the second aspect of opportunity crucial: when and how mentors do their work. This performance aspect of opportunity is fundamentally an issue of time, the most highly valued and closely protected of teachers' resources. Those who control mentor programs, whether teachers or administrators, signal the importance they attribute to mentor roles by the amount of time they allocate for mentors' work, by policies that govern when the work of mentoring can be done, and by the formal and informal expectations that define what work counts as mentoring. Thus, some districts reserve mentoring for time outside the school day, whereas others argue that the benefits of mentoring require teacher-to-teacher consultation embedded in the daily work of teaching. Some districts or schools insist that mentoring entails direct one-to-one work with individual teachers, in and out of the classroom; other sites are broadly permissive about the nature of the mentor's activities.

The time mentors spend tends to be treated as a proxy for their effort and effectiveness. Teachers judge the worth of mentors in part by the amount of time they visibly devote to the work of mentoring. Visibility is a crucial component of the time equation. When mentors do the work of mentoring directly with teachers (or in their immediate presence), they enable teachers to judge the quantity and quality of their contributions. According to Hart and Murphy (1989b), "visibility of the work played a key role in teacher assessments of the worth of the program" (p. 27). Visibility is diminished when mentors' work is reserved to time outside the instructional day, to settings outside the mentors' own school, or to tasks far removed from the classroom (Bird, 1986). For example, the most prominent object of mentors' attention during the first 2 years of California's Mentor Teacher Program was curriculum. Mentors in many districts worked on individual curriculum projects, largely out of sight of their colleagues. Judging by district coordinators' estimates of mentors' time (Bird & Alspaugh, 1986), mentors on average spent more than 60% of their time doing something other than working with fellow teachers. On the basis of mentors' own accounts, this estimate may be conservative. Fewer than one in five of the districts surveyed required that mentors consult with or assist other teachers. The California experience is not unique. The 13 teacher leaders whose work was detailed by Smylie and Denny (1989) exemplify the discrepancy between aspirations and actual performance. "Although virtually all the leaders reported that they had interacted with and assisted other teachers, none of these activities was ranked among those consuming most of the leaders' time. The leaders have, therefore, spent most of their [time] engaged in activities that seem at variance with their primary conceptualizations of their roles. As one commented, 'There is much involvement at the district level. However, I need to do more at the building level, more one-to-one conversations with teachers' " (p. 8).

A permissive stance toward the actual substance of mentors' work has enabled districts and schools to secure short-run agreements to implement a mentor program. Except in Connecticut, where mentoring is linked to certification (Allen & Pecheone, 1989), teachers have successfully sought assurances that teachers' essential autonomy would not be jeopardized by mentors' intrusions into their classrooms. Such a permissive stance, however, tends to produce a low rate of direct teacher-to-teacher involvement of the very sort needed to convince teachers that mentors are fulfilling their obligations (Bird, 1986; Huffman & Leak, 1986; Little, Galagaran, & O'Neal, 1984). Mentors respond by seeking ways to showcase their work to teachers. Sometimes they succeed in broadening their base of support; in other instances, their efforts to publicize their activities only intensify teachers' opposition. Hart and Murphy (1989a) note that "praise was profuse" when teacher leaders tied their work clearly and productively to improvements in teaching and learning, but that complaints were equally profuse when leaders wasted teacher time in superficial activities inappropriately matched to teachers' interests or sophistication, or devoted their energies to short-term projects of dubious value. Teachers with strong academic records and high performance ratings had the highest aspirations for what might be accomplished through teacher leadership positions, and were the most critical of shortcomings produced by program compromises. These teachers were most' approving of long-range assignments that "gave teachers the power to function by marshalling the talents of other teachers to achieve learning by groups of students," while they "ridiculed short term, limited assignments" (p. 20). One teacher was "scathing in her criticism of trite, unnecessary tasks disconnected from outcomes" (p. 21). Visibility alone, it appears, is not sufficient to win teachers' endorsements.

Whatever the benefits that follow when mentors engage in "close-to-the-classroom" consultation or other involvements with teachers, the attendant compromises are not lost on the mentors or others with whom they work. In the name of school improvement or career enhancement, mentorship programs add to the burdens of the school-site faculty by removing capable teachers from the classroom. Time spent by a mentor in the classroom of a beginning teacher, for example, is time lost to the mentor's own classroom. Teachers routinely devote less time to mentoring during the school day than they are allotted by program resources (Allen & Pecheone, 1989; see also the data on underuse of allocated release time as a component of school improvement programs in Berman & Gjelten, 1984). Release time budgets intended as a support for the program may turn out to be a burden for mentors. Release time that draws teachers away from primary classroom responsibilities underscores, perhaps ironically, the marginal status of mentoring activity by placing teachers' work with fellow teachers in competition with the fundamental work of the classroom. To fulfill the obligations of mentoring, mentors risk compromising other valued institutional goals and increasing the strain on themselves as individuals. In one program evaluation, the shortage of qualified substitutes, the additional planning time required to prepare for substitutes, and the loss in instructional time and quality all led teachers to assess release time as an "impractical" form of support for the program (Allen & Pecheone, 1989). By contrast, they would have welcomed regularly scheduled contact time during the salaried workday. In sum, the structure of time and task constrains or enables mentors' work with teachers.

Precedents

Leadership by teachers is not entirely without precedent. Available models for leadership roles range from department- or grade-level head to committee chair to specialized staff development and curriculum development roles. On the whole, however, teachers have few models for an assertive conception of the mentor role, models that legitimate the kinds of relationships implied by the term. Despite certain long-standing precedents for formal leadership positions (Wasley, 1989), roles specifically dedicated to interpersonal guidance on matters of professional practice continue to represent a substantial departure from organizational and occupational tradition. Furthermore, districts or states rarely consider whether newly proposed roles are compatible with or in conflict with existing leadership opportunities (Hart & Murphy, 1989b).

Few of the available implementation studies explicitly confront local leadership precedents and their significance for newly introduced roles. In six of Far West Laboratory's nine case study districts, respondents described other roles with mentor-like features. In one district, demonstration teachers and resource teachers were admired for their assistance to new teachers and their contributions to curriculum (Shulman et al., 1985). These models of teacher-to-teacher exchange disposed teachers favorably toward the idea of mentorship. In another district, a troublesome precedent was created in the form of remediation teachers who had been widely viewed by teachers as servants of administration; support for the mentor role was less readily secured (Hanson et al., 1985).

The various implementation studies all highlight the ways in which mentoring is a departure from business as usual. Mentor roles turn out to be an innovation of considerable complexity. Unlike new curricula or pedagogical methods, this innovation is not subject to individual adoption at the level of the classroom; rather, it is a social relation that requires joint action and joint acceptance. The "smallest unit" on which the fate of implementation rests (McLaughlin, 1987, p. 174) is thus not the individual teacher but the mentor-protégé pair. To stress the image of the mentor-protégé pair is not to overlook the fact that many designated mentors or leaders work alone (e.g., to develop curriculum) or work with groups of teachers in workshop-type settings. It is, rather, to underscore the fact that the term mentor inevitably implies the existence of a protégé whether that protégé is a specific individual (e.g., a 1st year teacher), or a diffuse body of teachers (e.g., potential users of the mentor's curriculum ideas). The success of mentorship thus rests in part on the protégés' willingness to be mentored, whether directly or indirectly. Individuals' capacities, beliefs, and incentives do not account satisfactorily for local success. The skills and intentions of mentors are insufficient to sustain their interactions with teachers, which are approved or condemned within larger circles of peers. Mentoring is irretrievably a social and organizational phenomenon, and as such its utility as an organizational resource and a career incentive is shaped by social interaction.

Nicholson's (1984) theory of work role transitions helps to highlight some of the disjunctures between the demands of mentoring and the likely perspectives and experiences of prospective mentors. The ordinary stress associated with role transitions is intensified when new roles present radically different requirements from persons' experience, and thus exert new demands on personal knowledge, skill, judgment, confidence, and initiative. The particular adjustment that individuals make to their new roles can be traced, according to Nicholson, to their assessment of the differences or similarities in work demands, the dispositions they have acquired through past socialization, and the arrangements that now govern their work in a new position. However, Nicholson's analysis stops short of anticipating certain fundamental conditions that bear on the specific case of mentoring among teachers. First is the degree of clarity and normative agreement that provide meaning to a role and direction for its performance. Although differentiating positions on the basis of the discretion they permit, Nicholson appears to assume that persons make a transition to an established role with reasonably well-defined (even if broad) normative boundaries. The more ambiguous the role, the fewer are the grounds to which the individual can turn to judge his or her own capacity to succeed in the role or by which he or she can interpret feedback on performance (Dubinsky & Yammarino, 1984). Mentor roles are markedly ambiguous. Throughout the implementation literature, observers record the uncertainties of mentors, administrators, and teachers regarding the central purposes of mentorship and the specific behavior in which mentors should or might engage. Hart (1989) tells of the teacher leader who punctuated an interview with a poignant question: "What should we be doing?" (p. 26). The 13 teacher leaders interviewed by Smylie and Denny (1989) voiced similar concerns; although the new leaders were relatively secure in their own knowledge and in their aspirations, "they were much less certain about whether their fellow teachers understood their leadership roles and what those teachers and their principals expected of them in those roles" (p.

8). In the early stages of Connecticut's experimental programs, teachers designated as "assessors" received more support from teachers than those designated "mentors," despite the apparently disadvantageous connotations attached to the former title. Neufeld (1986) attributes this unanticipated development to the clear purpose, predictable behavior, and structured relationships associated with the assessor role, and the comparatively high level of ambiguity surrounding the mentor role.

The uncertainties of purpose or practice that individual mentors experience often go unrelieved by organizational intervention or support. Ambiguity and conflict surrounding role definition have been greatest where mentor roles remain unlinked to any larger picture, where norms are unfavorable to professional growth or career mobility, and where teachers have been left to "invent their roles as they went along" (Hart, 1989, p. 24). Roles appear to develop most fully where teachers and administrators establish the teacher leader's intended contribution to widely shared goals, then exploit resources eclectically and opportunistically in support of the leader's activities. But in the local career enhancement project examined by Smylie and Denny (1989), "the district decided intentionally to leave open the specific roles and responsibilities associated with these positions. It was the responsibility of the teachers who would assume these positions to develop them" (p. 4). In the absence of organizational purpose and sanction, mentors' individual and idiosyncratic efforts to fulfill their perceived obligations may only heighten their vulnerability. In the career ladder sites studied by Hart and Murphy (1989b), teachers successfully developed leadership positions only in those schools where the role was given institutional purpose and structure.

In the absence of organizational sanction, mentors must rely on personal resources to penetrate long-standing protections surrounding teacher autonomy. The actions that may be required to give meaning to the term mentor are precisely those proscribed by the dominant traditions of noninterference in teaching. Within the confines of the classroom, teachers recognize and defend a wide range of practice as falling legitimately within the bounds of teaching; the role of mentor has no such accepted heritage of wide, diverse, observable practice as its warrant. In most schools, teachers enjoy wide latitude to construct their relations with students and to make their curricular and instructional choices in accordance with personal preference; they enjoy correspondingly less latitude to comment on or attempt influence over other teachers' classroom work. The teaching role is most problematic, most narrowly defined, and most constrained precisely in the area (collegial involvement and influence) where the mentor role places its greatest demands.

Mentoring is, on its face, at odds with the prevailing organizational and occupational traditions in teaching. Bird and Alspaugh (1986) describe "the mentors' dilemma" as the tension between the leadership expectations implicit in the title of mentor and the inherited traditions of autonomy and equality: "the scarcity of traditions, organizational arrangements, and norms of interaction that would allow or enable mentors to do enough, with enough other teachers, to earn their extra pay and resources" (pp. 3–4). Mentors or teacher leaders are at substantial risk of defining their positions in ways that spark the resentment of teachers. Ironically, teachers may move from classroom teacher, with substantial discretion over the manner of their work, to a mentorship that finds them exercising less discretion and accommodating more constraints. In this instance, then, role ambiguity promises something more than personal disappointments or organizational incoherence. It lays the ground for active conflict among teachers, or between teachers and other constituent groups. Such conflict, in turn, has its own consequences. Teachers who have served as mentors or teacher leaders decline to do so again; the intended career incentive is diluted both for them and for the colleagues who have witnessed their defeat (Hart, 1989). Faced with mounting dissent, the institution makes moves to render the role harmless—and thus useless (Bird, 1986). The prospect of increased organizational capacity is weakened. The standard of mutual benefit is compromised.

Finally, theories of role transition tend to assume that persons make a transition from one role to another—from teacher to principal, for example. Even theories that account for newly created and individually wrought "idiosyncratic roles" assume that one enters fully into the new role (Miner, 1987). The rise of formal mentoring constitutes a radically different case, one in which the conditions for role conflict and role overload (Biddle, 1979) are likely consequences. In most instances, teachers retain the identities, obligations, perspectives, and affiliations of the classroom teacher while adding on, usually temporarily, the perspectives and perquisites of leadership. The ambiguities surrounding mentorship are compounded as teachers attempt to satisfy two sets of role demands that are not always compatible. Provisions for rotating the opportunities for leadership among a large pool of teachers place a premium on preserving one's identity as a classroom teacher and one's social standing with peers. For individual teachers, mentorships represent not permanent positions but short-term opportunities that one teacher likened to a short stepladder: "you step on and you step off" (Hart & Murphy, 1989b, p. 27). Smylie and Denny (1989) conclude that the teacher leaders are

in a precarious and ambiguous position with respect to violations of professional norms. They are well aware of this position but seem to want it both ways. That is, they seem to want the additional responsibility and recognition associated with their leadership positions but at the same time they wish to retain their status in the collegium. (p. 15)

In sum, conservative patterns of policy implementation underscore the conundrum that prefaced this review: How might we account for the emergence of a formal role that both sustains the essential character of the mentor-protégé relation and that successfully overcomes or displaces countervailing norms of privacy and equal status? In attempting to account fully for the prevailing configurations of mentoring, researchers have given special attention to two problems associated with specialized teacher leadership roles: the problem of expertise in teaching, and the problem of expert status among teachers.

The Problem of Expertise in Teaching

A recurrent paradox can be expressed this way: mentors' claims to professional expertise are both demanded by the role and denied by history and circumstance. Implicit in the title of mentor, advisor, consulting teacher, or master teacher is the presumption of wisdom—accumulated knowledge that can serve as the basis of sensitive observation, astute commentary, sound advice, and constructive leadership. Demonstrated knowledge and skill are the essential ground on which the role and title of mentor are founded. In the district survey completed by Far West Laboratory (Bird & Alspaugh, 1986), district coordinators rated subject matter and pedagogical knowledge as the two most essential qualifications for mentoring. Implementation of mentor initiatives is confounded by two issues related to expertise in teaching: debate over the existence of an agreed-upon body of knowledge to guide practice; and the accessibility of teachers' knowledge, in both technical and social-organizational senses.

What Mentors Know

What is the nature of knowledge to which a mentor might lay claim—knowledge that could serve as the basis of a relationship with teachers? Critics have argued that the low level of agreed-upon expertise in teaching simultaneously increases the stress on practitioners, constrains help giving, and leads teachers to discount criticism or advice (Edgar & Warren, 1969; Glidewell, Tucker, Todt, & Cox, 1983). In the past decade, however, two developments have altered the view of available expertise in ways that now inform the mentor initiatives. First, districts have incorporated into staff development and teacher evaluation a body of presumably codifiable knowledge arising from more than a decade of classroom research (Brophy & Good, 1986). This line of classroom research has supplied much of the expected language and content for mentors' work. Second, teachers' own practical knowledge has been granted more attention and greater deference (Buchmann, 1986; Elbaz, 1983; Pinnegar, 1987; Yinger, 1987). Studies of teacher thinking, planning, and situated decision making (Clark & Peterson, 1986) have helped to replace a "dim view of teacher knowledge" (Feiman-Nemser & Floden, 1986, p. 512) with a more respectful view. This line of research may go far to bolster public faith that some teachers, at least, command the sort of expert grasp of teaching that warrants mentor status.

The claims that underlie mentors' legitimacy rest both on the availability of an externally validated knowledge base and on the credibility of a recognizably knowledgeable work force. In practice, externally derived research knowledge and teachers' own experiential knowledge have often been accorded different weight. Where districts closely structure the mentor-protégé relation and where that relation is tightly coupled to personnel decisions, externally determined priorities and terminology are likely to override mentors' individual preferences and practices. In formal job descriptions and in the content of training, research-based content appears to dominate experience-based wisdom. Grounded largely in classroom research on discrete instructional or classroom management practices, the practice of mentoring in such sites has come to reflect a skill orientation toward teaching and teachers that mirrors its present dominance in professional development and teacher evaluation more generally. By this view, the primary purpose of mentoring is to produce skilled performance. The task of the protégé is first to elicit or recognize the mentor's skill and then to emulate it. This is an orientation reinforced where mentoring is joined with certification and evaluation (Allen & Pecheone, 1989).

The skill-oriented conceptions of teaching and mentoring are less clearly evident in cases where the mentor role is more loosely and permissively conceived. In open-ended and voluntary consultations among teachers or in the completion of special projects, mentors find more latitude to exploit their own knowledge and inclinations. Whatever other difficulties such a stance may engender (e.g., problems of role definition or problems of substantive merit in the work mentors elect to do), it appears to elicit more readily the form of teacher knowledge represented in studies of teacher thinking and teacher planning (Clark & Peterson, 1986) or in conceptions of teaching as structured improvisation (Yinger, 1987). In these broader conceptions of teachers' knowledge, discrete skill is embedded in metacognitive patterns that enable teachers to make sense of their work. What teachers know is manifest in their situated judgments and in the interpretations they construct. In Kennedy's (1987) analysis of professional expertise, persons require both technique and a grasp of its underlying rationale as the basis on which to innovate or to exercise judgment. The importance of being able to capture the intentionality of teachers' performance, and not merely to label and reproduce observable behavior, argues for a particular kind of relation between mentor and protégé. Returning to Gehrke's (1988b) critique: The gift of the mentor is not narrowly conceived technique, but "a new and whole way of seeing things" (p. 192).

Access to Mentors' Knowledge

Proponents of mentoring take for granted that properly selected mentors will be a source of expert knowledge to others. Access to mentors' knowledge, however, is arguably problematic. Can mentors express what they know in a manner accessible to others; will they have sufficient opportunity to do so; and if they can, will they feel obligated to do so? Matters of opportunity have been treated elsewhere in this essay. At issue here are mentors' ability to articulate their own expert knowledge and the incentives or disincentives that surround claims to expertise.

Access to mentors' knowledge is in part a function of the technical capacity to make explicit certain underlying principles of practice (Kennedy, 1987). One consequence of the persistent privacy of the classroom is that teachers rarely have occasion to talk to fellow teachers in detail about their work. Even more rarely are they called on to talk about or display their work for purposes of helping others succeed in teaching. Teachers come to experience their work—and to describe it—as intuitive, done without much conscious framing or reflection (Buchmann, 1986). To use one's own expert knowledge in the day-by-day, moment-by-moment enactments of teaching is a different matter, intellectually and interpersonally, from articulating that knowledge for the benefit of another's understanding and practice (Yinger, 1987). Although we have some examples of how mentors imagine such talk, based on their spoken responses to simulated requests or problems posed to them by beginning teachers (Parker, 1989), it seems probable that simulated responses overestimate mentors' willingness to propose straightforward diagnoses and to offer direct advice. Further, we have no way of knowing from these one-way simulations how beginning teachers would interpret the responses mentors give; can beginning teachers detect the knowledge that informs mentors' comments? In studies of preservice teachers, McAlpine, Brown, McIntyre, and Haggar (1988) discover with what difficulty experienced teachers express what they know, and with what difficulty novice teachers learn to elicit and comprehend that knowledge. One study of video-taped interaction between teacher advisors and experienced teachers provides some evidence that genuine interest and good intentions do not stop participants from talking past one another (Little et al., 1984). Advisors, employing a language derived from classroom research ("objectives," "transfer," "wait time"), analyzed lessons. Teachers, employing a different language, analyzed the ebb and flow of a classroom. Like the teachers described by Pinnegar (1987), they examined when and why they knew students were "with me," or what they did to "pull them in" if they were not. Examples of naturally occurring exchanges between mentors and teachers, now absent from the published literature, might enable us to ground global assessments of perceived effectiveness in concrete instances of communication about teaching.

Accessibility is only partly a matter of one's ability and opportunity to articulate one's principles and practices. It is also shaped by the incentives or disincentives that prompt mentors to extend their expertise to others or to withhold it. In their study of professional support among teachers, Glidewell et al. (1983) found that the relation between stress (need for help) and actual help seeking was mediated by the degree of teachers' commitment to established occupational norms of autonomy and equality. Based on Glidewell et al., we would expect that mentoring relations would be most likely to bear fruit where commitments to individual autonomy were weak and where countervailing norms of collegiality prevailed (see also Rosenholtz, 1989). Throughout the case literature, we find instances in which mentors express humility about their own expertise, fearing collegial censure (Little et al., 1984). The rewards are tenuous indeed. Neither in formal evaluation schemes nor in the informal reward structure of schools are teachers celebrated for contributing to the success of other teachers, nor penalized for failing to do so. In fact, the reward structure may operate to accentuate the norm of privacy and to promote hoarding of insights, methods, and materials. Revealing the "hidden cost of sharing expertise," Allen (1989) describes a "mentor as miser" syndrome that prevails when mentors' knowledge comprises a private store of ideas and materials that form the base of professional standing and sense of self.

The Problem of Expert Status Among Teachers

Publicly acknowledged and rewarded differences in expertise run counter to inherited traditions in teaching (Feiman-Nemser & Floden, 1986; Smylie & Denny, 1989). Within the culture of teachers, informal acknowledgements are common, but formal expert status is suspect. Thus, mentors discount their special expertise as a basis of their professional relations with teachers. The problem of expertise is at the heart of the pervasive ambivalence about mentoring and the source of what Bird (1986) characterizes as the mentors' dilemma: "The instrumental status differences that the Mentor Program calls for are virtually without precedent in teaching's egalitarian and individualistic tradition" (Bird & Alspaugh, 1986, p. 3).

Mentor roles achieve special significance (and are rendered specially problematic) in an occupation that is constrained by norms of equal status and autonomy, is flat in its career profile, and in which an agreed-upon body of professional knowledge and practice is absent. Occupational traditions are mirrored in organizational realities; schools rarely structure the work of teaching to promote the kind of mutual interdependence favorable to mentoring (Little, 1988). Smylie (1989) hypothesizes that mentor or master teacher initiatives are less likely to win teachers' support than are other forms of collegial exchange (e.g., peer support groups) because the former are largely incongruent with the dominant social contexts of teaching and the psychological dispositions of teachers. Relying on theoretical advances in the study of cooperation and helping behavior, and particularly on the contributions of Deutsch (1982), Smylie posits that teaching favors collegial learning arrangements that are cooperative rather than competitive, that assume equality of power and influence among all members of the group, that stress socioemotional support over task orientation, and in which social interaction is governed not by bureaucratic rules but by tacitly held norms. Smylie concludes,

Master teacher programs induce formal status differentiation among teachers. They place teachers in superordinate and subordinate roles and suggest nonreciprocal relationships among teachers. The relationship between master teachers and other teachers may be governed by rules and expectations developed outside the relationship and may be geared more toward task performance and accomplishment than socioemotional support. In addition, they may contain a competitive element in that the extrinsic rewards associated with attaining master teacher status are likely to be dependent upon the perpetuation of status differences. (p. 11)

The history of implementation is in part the history of accommodating the tensions surrounding leadership in teaching by teachers. Presumably, there are two responses to the conflict between norms of equal status and the implications of the mentor role. In one response, districts could work to justify legitimate differences based on demonstrated differences in knowledge, skill, and commitment (Bird & Little, 1985). In one of the two case study sites described by Hart (1989), this appears to have been the strategy. The modal response, however, has been to diminish the status implications of the title and the other resources attached to the role. Despite some prominent exceptions in the case literature, the main trends show efforts to accommodate rather than alter the egalitarian and individualistic traditions that inhibit the development of mentor roles.

The main tendency in formalized mentor programs has been to diminish the status differences implied by the title of mentor rather than to justify those differences or to create the conditions consistent with their existence. Status-reduction strategies may enable schools and districts to secure short-term support and to neutralize resistance in the early stages of a program. The nine case studies assembled by Far West Laboratory (Bird et al., 1984) and the five career ladder districts examined by Hart and Murphy (1989b) show the diverse means employed by districts to reduce the status significance of formal teacher leadership positions. In negotiation with teachers' associations, districts broadened the range of mentors' tasks but reduced their demands on special expertise, making the tasks more like familiar sorts of "extra work for extra pay." They enlarged access to a wider pool of teachers by modifying selection criteria and providing for frequent rotation of opportunities to apply. In doing so, they obscured the place that special expertise occupies in leadership and established the presumption that the earned right to lead was widely, if not uniformly, distributed among the teaching force.

Tensions surrounding mentors' expert status are also alleviated by organizing the work of mentoring at a distance from the classroom. The norm of noninterference is honored in part by the generally permissive orientation toward mentors' direct involvement with teachers; mentors work with individual teachers "by request." In large measure, mentor programs have achieved constituent support not by pursuing the classic dimensions of close interpersonal exchange and consultation associated with mentoring, but by evolving a generalized service role in support of staff development and curriculum development (Little et al., 1987). Districts have absorbed the mentor role into a general pattern of specialist positions that provide out-of-classroom opportunities for individual teachers and expand the district's capacity to pursue district goals. Among the sources of influence on mentors' plans in California districts, district priorities ranked highest; although there are wide within-district and between-district variations, many mentors worked throughout the district with greater consistency than in their own schools, and worked with their own faculties as a group less often than with groups assembled for districtwide workshops (Bird & Alspaugh, 1986).

Finally, the implications of the mentor title are softened by focusing the work of mentors in domains where status differences are genuinely more acceptable, as in support for first year teachers, teachers new to a district, teachers confronted with new instructional assignments, or teachers engaged in innovation. Of these, mentoring for purposes of teacher induction is the dominant case.

THE DOMINANT CASE: MENTORING IN SUPPORT
OF TEACHER INDUCTION

Intended improvements in teacher induction have supplied the dominant rationale for the proliferation of mentor roles and thus the main setting for empirical research. Fully two thirds of the published references to mentoring in the 1980s concentrate on mentoring as a principal component of induction programs (Gray & Gray, 1985; Huling-Austin, 1988; Stoddart, 1989). Implicitly, the main benefits of a mentor-protégé relationship are achieved within the first years of teaching, culminating in the certification decision in some states or in the tenure decision in local districts. In this sense, the dominant functions of mentoring in education parallel some of the recent formalized mentoring arrangements in business, industry, or government by concentrating on organizational entry (Zey, 1984).

The introduction of organizationally sponsored mentoring assumes particular significance against the backdrop of research on conditions of teachers' entry into teaching. Although some accounts of teacher careers distinguish between relatively easy and relatively painful beginnings (Huberman, 1986), observers spanning at least a century have highlighted the "reality shock" that commonly follows when novice teachers abruptly and without assistance assume full-scale and full-time responsibilities for teaching (Lacey, 1977; Lortie, 1975; Veenman, 1984; Zeichner & Gore, in press). Such conditions, say critics, drive capable people out of teaching. For those who remain, these same conditions place a premium on tricks of the trade that enable teachers to survive but that also retard their development of more principled understanding of teaching, their capacity for critical analysis or "expertise as deliberate action" (Kennedy, 1987, p. 148; see also Carter, 1988; Nemser, 1983). Once in command of a rudimentary set of knowledge and skill, teachers (like other beginning professionals) may engage in behavior that is self-validating and may discount criticism from others (Bucher & Stelling, 1977; Feiman-Nemser & Buchmann, 1986). Worse, such conditions may both produce and perpetuate marginal performance in the classroom and tenuous commitment to teaching (Bridges, 1986).

Under the terms of reform initiatives in the early and mid-1980s, teacher induction has been the object of efforts to expand support for new teachers while also tightening scrutiny of their performance. Mentorship occupies center stage in the design of such efforts. Its proponents anticipate that by direct assistance and personal involvement with new teachers, mentors will relieve some of the stress associated with the intellectual, social, and emotional demands of first year teaching. The test of mentor roles lies in mentors' ability to alleviate the shock of entry into teaching, hasten the pace of learning to teach, model favorable professional relations among teachers, and reinforce teachers' loyalty to the profession.

To what extent do such formalized arrangements simply extend naturally occurring helping relationships between experienced and novice teachers? At issue here are relationships of a magnitude and intensity adequate to ensure not only the comfort and self-confidence of beginning teachers, but also their professional competence and commitment. Little (1987) proposes,

A distinction is in order between the social support that puts newcomers at ease and the professional support that advances one's knowledge and practice of teaching. . . . Without diminishing the import of moral support and emotional solidarity, the central issue here is one of professional relations that go well beyond the usual "buddy" arrangement. (p. 498)

Despite the widely recognized maxim that teachers invite others to "ask if you need help," it appears that veteran teachers rarely engage in relations with beginning teachers that would warrant the designation of mentorship. To the extent that beginning teachers receive the kind of close attention that accords with the image of mentoring, it commonly derives from sources other than their peers. Even teachers who claim to have had a mentor typically found their support outside the teaching ranks; only 3 of 41 teachers interviewed by Gehrke and Kay (1984) identified other teachers among the significant mentors in their lives. These findings are consonant with other portrayals of informal induction (Lortie, 1975). As one might predict on the basis of generalized professional norms and the structural conditions of the work and workplace, informal mentoring of beginning teachers by experienced teachers is a low-incidence phenomenon. There are wide individual variations, though some schools more than others display norms supportive of intense and consequential support (Little, 1987; Meister, 1987).

Surveys centered specifically on mentoring relations may overestimate the importance of mentoring to teachers' careers as they are presently constituted. In the survey conducted by Gehrke and Kay (1984), many teachers claimed to have had a mentor, but relatively few of these relations approached the level of involvement that Clawson (1980) and other theorists would count as a genuine mentor-protégé relation. Despite the vivid portraits of the positive role models whom teachers later emulated or the negative ones whom they denigrated, rarely do we encounter tributes to a mentor in teachers' first-hand accounts of choosing to teach and developing one's teaching over time (Elbaz, 1983; Macrorie, 1984; Mead, 1989; Measor, 1985; Nias, 1989). Mentorship, it appears, is not firmly rooted in the informal conventions by which neophytes are brought into teaching. Policymakers, administrators, and academics have promoted formally assigned mentorships on the grounds that they both expand support and help to justify more stringent evaluation, thereby improving the prospects for a strong teacher work force. Looking to the traditions of teaching and preferences of teachers, however, formal mentorship may constitute a case of "contrived collegiality" in pursuit of institutional purposes to which teachers may or may not subscribe (Hargreaves & Dawe, 1989). Nonetheless, formal mentoring is on the rise, justified principally as a remedy for inadequate induction support and organized primarily in terms of expanded reserves of help.

Mentoring as Help-Giving

Because formal induction practices are dominated by a conception of mentoring as help or assistance, they are usefully interpreted in light of advances in the study of helping behavior. Studies that highlight the help giving aspect of mentoring range from program evaluations that assess the perceived utility of mentor assistance (Huffman & Leak, 1986) to microinteractional studies that probe the interpersonal dynamics of mentor-protégé interactions (Allen, 1989; Shulman, 1987). Virtually none of these studies, however, has been informed explicitly by the kinds of theoretical constructs that have shaped social-psychological investigations of helping behavior during the past decade.

The antecedents, character, and consequences of help all are rendered problematic by recent research; neither the nature of help nor its virtue remains taken for granted. Gergen and Gergen (1983) underscore the social construction of helping, maintaining that instances of help assume meaning only in the context of an interpretive system. In examples that range from a bystander's gesture of aid to a victim of trouble to large-scale interactions between Third World countries and aid-donating agencies, researchers find that both the definition of help and persons' attitudes toward it are conditioned on a complex host of individual and social circumstances (Fisher, Nadler, & Whitcher-Alagna, 1983; Gergen & Gergen, 1983; Gross & McMullen, 1982). This literature begins to account for the occasions on which help is sought or not, offered or withheld, accepted or rejected.

The program implementation literature highlights the dilemmas of the teacher turned mentor, and the conditions surrounding emergence of a mentor role. The induction literature, by contrast, focuses more closely on the teacher as the potential beneficiary of mentorship. By turning attention to the recipient of help, recent research questions long-standing assumptions about receptivity to and gratitude for aid. The choices that persons make to solicit aid or to accept assistance when it is offered are determined in large part by their assessment of its psychological and social costs: the costs to their sense of competence and their status with important others, and the obligations they incur by accepting proffered resources (Gross & McMullen, 1982).

Fisher et al. (1983) employ four theoretical models to explain persons' probable resistance to or acceptance of aid. Equity theories, together with related reciprocity and indebtedness models, start with the premise that persons seek parity in their interpersonal relations. To the degree that persons find themselves indebted in ways they cannot repay, or believe themselves to be implicitly derogated by their participation in a helping relationship, they can be expected to resist help (see also Greenberg &

Westcott, 1983). In business and industry, the success of informal mentorships rests largely on the mutual benefits they demonstrate. The assistance and sponsorship provided by the mentor is compensated as the protégé is delegated a larger share of the work, contributing to the mentor's own productivity and career prospects (Zey, 1984). Reciprocity is achieved. By this argument, mentorships among teachers can be expected to thrive to the extent that the participants detect some measure of mutual gain in the exchange of ideas, materials, methods, and labor.

A second and complementary theoretical perspective suggests that persons are reluctant to seek help when they believe that doing so will unduly restrict their own freedom to act. Reactance theory applies most clearly where seeking help entails restrictions on physical movement (e.g., hospitalization) but a broader interpretation is possible. This generalized psychological disposition toward freedom of choice may be accentuated in the context of teaching and other professionalized occupations, where professional norms favor autonomy. Based on reactance theory, then, we can expect help to be welcomed to the extent that it expands a beginning teacher's range of curricular or instructional options and sense of efficacy. To the extent that mentors are seen as agents of control who curtail curricular and instructional choice, however, help will be resisted. In one example, beginning teachers objected to teacher leaders' implications that they were only "really teaching" when they employed narrowly defined "principles of effective instruction" or clearly observable "elements of an effective lesson plan" (Hart, 1988, pp. 10–11).

Attribution theories rely on persons' own interpretations of the conditions and consequences of help to account for the incidence of help seeking. The complexities and subtleties of attribution theory cannot be represented adequately here, but certain main theoretical premises appear to have particular import for the success of mentoring in teacher induction. First, teachers are more likely to believe help is legitimate when they can attribute the need for help to the complexities of the task and the situation (external attribution) rather than to the limitations of their own competence (internal attribution). Formal teacher induction programs may induce receptivity to help by declaring publicly that the first years of teaching are especially demanding, regardless of individual skills and talents. Second, there is evidence that help is more often and more favorably accepted when it is offered than when it must be requested. The very act of requesting assistance may prompt internal attributions of failure (see also Gross, Wallston, & Piliavin, 1979). The prevailing norm of noninterference in teaching takes the form of an informal rule that one offers advice only when asked. Such an axiom may inadvertently depress help seeking.

In the fourth formulation developed by Fisher et al., the relationship between the situational conditions that create a need for help and persons' actual responses to aid are ultimately mediated by potential threats to self-esteem, social identity, and relations with others. To the degree that seeking or accepting help represents a threat to self-esteem, these theorists argue, persons will persist in attempts at self-help. To the extent that threats to self-esteem and social standing can be avoided (or advantage gained) persons will seek help from others. Combining this view with the other relevant theoretical frames, we can anticipate that threats to teachers' self-esteem are alleviated when the helping relation with mentors stems from legitimately difficult circumstances rather than from personal inadequacy, when it permits or even requires a degree of reciprocity, when it adequately preserves the teacher's freedom to act, and when it demonstrably contributes to the teacher's success and satisfaction.

Teacher induction programs that are founded on the utility of help confront both the general cultural ambivalence about help seeking and specific occupational prohibitions surrounding interference in teaching. Independent of their individual capacities and dispositions, teachers' attitudes toward mentoring are affected by general occupational images associated with professional autonomy and by local norms governing aid and assistance (Rosenholtz, 1989). Applying the broad social-psychological perspective associated with research on helping, Glidewell et al. (1983) examined the incidence of help among teachers. The central premise of their work is that stress-producing conditions can be expected to stimulate help seeking. In teaching and in other service professions, they argue, stress is exacerbated by lack of experience, lack of available expertise, ambiguity surrounding goal attainment, and departures from an optimal client load. These are factors that to varying degrees affect teachers in general, and that plausibly affect beginning teachers most. All other factors being equal, one might expect beginning teachers to be avid seekers of professional support or eager recipients of the support offered by others. But all other factors are not equal. In particular, Glidewell et al. demonstrate that the relationship between stress and help seeking is modified by teachers' commitments to traditional norms of autonomy and equal status. The norm of autonomy not only establishes a right to independent practice, but also obligates practitioners to take care of their own problems; the norm of status equality constrains practitioners to reject implications of status difference. Where these traditional norms have been weakened or displaced by norms of collegial support, teachers openly request and offer help, and the predicted relationship between stress and help seeking is sustained. Under such circumstances, competence-based differences in status appear to be acceptable (see also Smith & Sandler, 1974). Responsibility for the successful induction of beginning teachers or other newcomers is widely diffused. One of the five case study schools described in Meister's (1987) review of school-based induction programs exemplifies this situation. Where the traditional norms hold sway, however, teachers find covert ways to relieve stress without exposing their difficulties. Overt requests for assistance are rare. Through "experience-swapping" they garner information, advice, and sympathy indirectly. Discussions of teaching acquire a piecemeal character, of doubtful depth and consequence.

The relations between social-psychological conditions and personal reactions are intensified where the tasks requiring help are crucial. The more central the focus of help to one's professional identity (classroom instruction, in the case of teachers), the more salient become the conditions that support or threaten one's sense of self. Where competence in teaching is judged by individual prowess in the classroom, help seeking may be suppressed as teachers attempt to hide errors and publicize successes (McLaughlin & Pfeifer, 1988). Teachers' participation in mentoring may be affected directly by the external pressure to perform, and the consequences associated with failure. This is a prospect so far unexamined in the educational mentoring literature, although it has its parallels in business and industry (Zey, 1984): Genuine mentoring is more widespread under conditions of high interdependence, where each person bears the consequences of others' success or failure.

In sum, recent advances in research on helping force us to examine more closely the taken-for-granted assumptions that undergird formal mentor programs. The character and consequences of mentors' relationships with beginning teachers are productively placed in a broader social-psychological perspective, and formal mentor programs considered in the wider context of socialization into teaching.

Mentoring in the Context of Teacher Socialization

Studies of discrete induction activities form the largest single body of research explicitly centered on mentoring practices and relations. Precisely because of its association with specific initiatives, however, this research tends to display a narrowly programmatic conception of induction. It is virtually devoid of reference, for example, to the large and rich sociological and anthropological literature on induction into groups, societies, and occupations (Schlechty, 1985). Studies of teacher socialization help to locate mentoring roles and practices in the larger context of occupational and organizational induction. Although recent reviews of the teacher socialization literature give little or no explicit attention to the term mentoring, they do account for the role colleagues play in shaping teachers' perspectives and practices (Zeichner & Gore, in press). Individual studies examine the power of fellow teachers as positive or negative role models (Measor, 1985; Mead, 1989) and the norms governing advice giving among teachers that are central to mentoring (Glidewell et al., 1983; Little et al., 1984).

A socialization perspective makes central the web of professional relations and institutional purposes in which the mentor-teacher relationship resides. It permits us to trace the character and consequences of mentoring not only to the psychological dispositions and technical capacities of individuals, but also to the social context that enables or constrains such relationships (Smylie, 1989). It entertains a larger definition of the teacher's role, encompassing the teacher in the classroom, as a member of a faculty, and as participant in a wider professional community (Little, 1987). To sort out the relative contributions made by mentors to beginning teachers' success and satisfaction in teaching will require studies that encompass valued outcomes that range from a basic command of pedagogical technique to a capacity and inclination for well-informed innovation.

The broad socialization consequences of mentoring are masked by research designs that remain conceptually undeveloped and methodologically narrow. To date, we remain unable to assess the claims that have been made about the influence of mentoring on teachers' classroom performance, their long-term development, or their career commitment. Most accounts are based on post hoc questionnaires (Huffman & Leak, 1986) or on interviews with mentors and teachers (Allen, 1989); there are no published accounts of observed mentoring in action, even though some study designs provide for observation of selected activities (Wasley, 1989). Most studies concentrate only on direct participants in induction programs. In the absence of a comparison group of unmentored teachers it is difficult to determine what, if anything, mentors contributed to the possible differences between painful and easy beginnings, as Huberman (1986) characterizes them. Analyses fail to distinguish various dimensions of involvement and impact, relying instead on global judgments of utility and anecdotal accounts of the content of interactions. Aggregate analyses of beginning teachers, mentors, or even mentor-teacher pairs obscure consequential aspects of the specific school context in which mentoring is attempted. Post hoc, global assessments of a mentor's usefulness (Huffman & Leak, 1986) or official records of mentors' activities (Odell, 1986) would be profitably supplemented by detailed histories of mentors' interactions with beginning teachers. Such studies might productively combine elements of the structured field experiment, ethnography, and biography.

Program evaluations and case studies have only just begun to fill out a detailed picture of the actual work of mentors with beginning teachers. Despite theoretical and methodological limitations, certain themes emerge. In the early stages of mentoring, consultation on curriculum and instruction takes second place to information or coaching about the system at large (Odell, 1986; Stoddart, 1989). Newcomers, whether new to teaching or new only to the local system, expect mentors to help them make sense of the institution's formal and informal requirements and resources (Odell, 1986). Activities oriented toward emotional support constitute a small percentage of officially recorded support activities, but loom large in importance to beginning teachers (Allen & Pecheone, 1989; Huling-Austin, 1988). It seems likely that beginning teachers will judge even activities intended for other purposes in accordance with their effect on personal confidence and security.

The emphasis on comfort and harmonious relations between mentor and teacher may preclude productive confrontation with important but difficult matters of practice (Hollingsworth, 1989). In this, mentoring in support of beginning teachers differs from the informal mentoring that grooms selected individuals for leadership positions either in business (Zey, 1984) or in educational administration (Baltzell & Dentler, 1982). In these instances, the mentor's and protégé's career interests are closely linked. The prospects that they will rise or fall together help to drive an emphasis on competence. It is through close attention to practice that mentors become assured that their judgment (in recruiting the protégé) has been validated and that protégés acquire personal confidence in their professional competence. To uncover the complex connections between small practices and larger schema that advance understanding of teaching would seem to require both shared curiosity and joint scrutiny of practice. The relation between mentorship and "eased beginnings" ceases to seem self-evident. One might imagine, for example, that the presence of a mentor makes the first year of teaching more strenuous in the short run, even while promising substantial reward in the longer term. However, available accounts of mentoring suggest that mentors and beginning teachers spend too little time in one another's company, and too little of that time on actual classroom work, to achieve such understanding.

Even linked to formal induction programs, mentoring remains a relatively low-incidence phenomenon; beginning teachers typically report sparing contact with their mentors (Allen & Pecheone, 1989). The dilemma is exacerbated when mentors and beginning teachers work at a distance, assigned to different schools, grade levels, or subjects, or committed to different beliefs about teaching and learning (Shulman & Colbert, 1987). This has been the impetus for districts to attempt subject and grade-level matches in pairing mentors with beginning teachers. Presumably, such matches permit the mentor to establish a persuasive set of credentials, both formal and experiential, and to supply a substantively rich base for advice, assistance, and consultation. When asked, teachers claim to prefer a relationship with mentors whose present assignment or teaching history is close to their own (Huffman & Leak, 1986). However, interviews with teachers and mentors who have been matched on the basis of grade level and subject present a less clear picture (Allen & Pecheone, 1989). In districts where the mentor relation remains ambiguous, where norms of noninterference constrain mentors from posing tough questions about practice, and where mentoring takes place largely outside the classroom, there is little apparent return from an investment in subject and level matches. The attempt in teacher induction to achieve matchmaking through formal assignment appears to fail at least as often as it succeeds. It founders on its inability to produce genuine interdependence where it does not exist in the larger system, and by its inattention to local professional norms. It suffers, too, from uncertainty about how to reconcile the instrumental dimensions of the match (teaching assignment) with the inescapable social and emotional dimensions of personal interactions. In these respects, the experience in education parallels that of formal mentoring programs in business and government (Kram, 1986). Further, individual assignments have the effect of overemphasizing mentors' individual responsibilities for the success of beginning teachers, and masking the larger socialization context in which those teachers work. None of the available studies, however, has examined systematically the relationships among the amount of interaction, the character of the mentoring relationship, and the consequences for beginning teachers' performance and attitude. Such an analysis might address the policy problem posed by Huling-Austin (1988)—how much support is enough, or too much.

The litanies of trouble surrounding the first years of teaching have been chronicled persuasively (Veenman, 1984). Coupled with the burgeoning research on the subtleties and complexities of expert classroom teaching (Berliner & Carter, 1986; Doyle, 1979; Jackson, 1968, 1986; Yinger, 1987), they suggest some of the reasons why mentoring might be judged personally and organizationally productive. Mentor roles have emerged as the favored strategic option in larger policy initiatives surrounding teacher induction at the local and state levels, taking precedence over other alternatives that might include reduced work load, peer group support, and formally structured staff development. The very prominence of mentor roles signals a characteristic policy stance. The disadvantages associated with an abrupt entry into teaching are to be relieved not by altering the student load that novice teachers confront, or by slowing the pace at which they assume the full tasks of teaching, but by increasing their access to pedagogical expertise, organizational savvy, and socioemotional support.

In principle, mentoring seems a sensible response to the present inadequacies of teacher induction. Problems of expert status are in some measure relieved by legitimate differences of perspective and experience that mentors bring to a relationship with beginning teachers. The recurrent problems of the first year teacher are reasonably well addressed by the cumulative research on effective classroom management and instruction. Formal induction projects present naturally occurring experiments, most of which use mentor roles as one of several elements in a larger configuration of support. Such roles have been credited with having greater effect on beginning teachers than other program elements (Huling-Austin, 1988), although we have only weak evidence on which to sustain claims for the special salience of mentoring. On the whole, program evaluations treat mentoring as a self-contained intervention (e.g., Huffman & Leak, 1986). To date, there is no published research designed to examine mentoring as one of several policy alternatives, or to test its relative power when other features of the setting are favorable or unfavorable. The occasional assistance typically available as part of a formal mentoring arrangement, for example, is unlikely to compensate for problems of teacher misassignment or other forms of work overload. Given the structural and cultural constraints on mentoring, its salience is likely to depend on the degree to which it is congruent with other forms of support in the lives of beginning teachers. Discrete program evaluations and narrowly conceived policy studies have done little to inform the larger picture, addressing fundamental questions about the place of mentoring in the improvement of teaching or the strengthening of the teacher work force. Mentoring in education has derived its main justification from inadequacies in the induction of teachers. The rationales remain to be tested, but the opportunities to do so are plentiful. Such tests will be most persuasive if they are informed by recent advances in the study of helping and by a broad perspective on socialization into teaching.

MENTORING OPPORTUNITIES AND TEACHERS' CAREER ENHANCEMENT

A major impetus for the development of mentor roles and other teacher leadership opportunities rests with the public interest in a teacher work force that is competent, committed to teaching, and reasonably stable (Sykes, 1983). Mentorships are promoted on the grounds that such professional opportunities outside the classroom will help sustain the engagement and commitment of experienced teachers inside the classroom (Wagner, 1985). Less directly, the availability of mentorships and other specialized teacher leadership roles is expected to hold out an image of a more attractive career to those entering teaching.

Advancement Versus Retention

Case studies in business and in education provide an instructive contrast between conventional patterns of informal mentoring associated with career advancement and the emerging patterns of formal mentoring associated primarily with organizational entry or with institutional concerns for adequate levels of performance. In business and industry, informal mentoring has been the central element in a "system of professional patronage and sponsorship" (Shapiro, Haseltine, & Rowe, 1978, p. 55) devoted to long-term career development for a relatively small proportion of organizational newcomers (see also Kanter, 1977; Roche, 1979; Zey, 1984). In effect, mentors "oversee a career" for persons targeted for management positions (Zey, p. 7).

Mentorship survives, according to Zey (1984), on the basis of mutual benefits derived by the protégé, the mentor, and the organization at large. When the relationship is successful, the mentor boosts his or her own productivity through association with a capable protégé. The mentor's work load is eased, or time is freed to take on more ambitious projects, as some share of the work is gradually assumed by the protégé. By intensive collaboration with the protégé, and by having to make his or her own knowledge clear, the mentor spawns new ideas and new methods at a higher rate. In the words of one corporate mentor: "Two cannot only work better than one; they can often work better than two" (p. 81). The mentor-protégé relation "expands areas of permissible inquiry" by making it acceptable to ask naive questions (p. 18). The mentor both develops and demonstrates the protégé's knowledge and skill not by instruction or help but by orchestrating opportunity and by joint involvement in work. As the protégé wins the favorable attention of others in the organization, the mentor's reputation as a "promoter of good people" grows, and the mentor's own career prospects are enhanced. The protégé's path through the promotional ranks is cleared. Opportunities to demonstrate competence and initiative are made more readily available, and are more shrewdly constructed by the mentor to highlight the protégé's special talents. The organization, too, reaps certain benefits. Mentorship accelerates the pace at which newcomers acquire the technical, social, and political knowledge needed to succeed. Widespread mentoring helps to retain entrepreneurial individuals who might otherwise leave by assuring them adequate advancement opportunity and recognition, and by building personal as well as organizational loyalties within the corporation. A system of mentoring assures management succession and continuity. Together, these mutual benefits to mentor, protégé, and organization sustain the practice of mentoring; the supports for mentoring are weakened where the benefit to any of the three is uncertain. Both for individuals and for the larger organization, however, these are benefits that take time to mature.

The purposes and practices of informal mentoring in business have no readily apparent counterpart in mentoring among teachers, although they do have clear parallels in the practices by which classroom teachers are informally groomed for positions as administrators or specialists (Baltzell & Dentler, 1982). Retention, not advancement, is the stated institutional aim of formal mentoring among teachers. This concern with retention shapes the conception of mutual benefit that underlies mentor programs. By granting experienced teachers the status and responsibilities of mentorship, districts expect those teachers to experience a renewal of their enthusiasm for teaching. Prospects for career advancement are not considered central, though some mentors do in fact move on to administrative positions (Ruskus, 1988). By asking mentors to devote their talents and energy to the support of beginning teachers, the district anticipates a lower turnover rate and more appropriate tenure decisions. For beginning teachers, the benefit is in relief of the stress of first year teaching and in enhanced prospects for job security (tenure). For the experienced teachers with whom mentors work, the benefit resides in an expanded pool of ideas, methods, and materials, or sometimes in relief from negative evaluations. For the mentor, the expected benefits begin with the status associated with the title, compensation, and other resources it brings. Mentors in education, as in business (Zey, 1984), celebrate the way in which their own performance and learning expands as they attempt to review and reveal what they know to others. In education, mentorship increases the mentors' own access to still other professional development opportunities. Mentors in California districts, for example, were more likely than other experienced teachers to have observed in others' classrooms, and to believe that their own teaching had improved as a result (Little et al., 1987). Ultimately, the benefits must extend to the psychic rewards that accompany a close and productive relationship with other adults, paralleling the intrinsic satisfactions of the classroom. For the organization, successful mentoring increases the return on investment in selecting and hiring, and permits public assurance regarding pretenure screening and the overall quality of the teacher work force.

Mentoring in K-12 teaching thus neither promises nor is premised upon an advancement incentive, but rather on other dimensions of work that contribute to career satisfaction. In teachers' conception of career, an emphasis on the quality of professional experience outweighs opportunities for promotion (Bennet, 1985; McLaughlin & Yee, 1988; Yee, 1986). Recent developments in the organizational theory literature offer an alternative orientation toward career, one that takes its point of departure from the work itself and the social identities of the persons who do it. By this conception, teachers are considered members of an "occupational community" who

weave their perspectives on work from the existing social, moral, physical , and intellectual character of the work itself. Individual assessments of work and career are cast in terms of one's getting better (or worse) at what one does, getting support (or interference) from others, exerting more (or less) influence over the nature of one's work, and so on. (Van Maanen & Barley, 1984, p. 289)

This perspective on career suggests a broadened treatment of retention, one which encompasses not merely teachers' decisions to leave teaching or remain in the classroom but rather a wider view of sustained (or diminished) engagement in teaching. Teachers may stay in teaching or leave it; they may leave temporarily and then return; they may reinforce their enthusiasms for the classroom or steadily withdraw their labor over time, effectively retiring on the job. Hart and Murphy (1989a), following Bluedorn's (1982) model of job turnover, propose a view of retention that encompasses not only decisions to leave teaching or remain, but a wider spectrum of attitudes, decisions, and choices regarding commitment. A similarly broad perspective underlies Ruskus's (1988) analysis of teachers' orientations toward their work. Ruskus distinguishes among teachers who have actually left education or who voice intent to leave ("attriters"), those who leave the classroom for other positions in education ("climbers"), those who are simply putting in time ("lifers"), and those whose enthusiasm and commitment remain high ("stars"). By applying a broadened conception of retention, researchers are able to explore the career consequences of teacher leadership in ways that are tapped inadequately by concrete decision points alone. In principle, the models that reflect such expanded perspectives retain greater sensitivity to the actual patterns of occupational participation that teachers exhibit. At present, however, there are no studies that compare retention of mentors or other program participants to system rates describing the retention or attrition of classroom teachers. These include rates for denial of tenure, involuntary layoff, voluntary attrition, promotion, dismissal, or retirement. Nor are there studies that locate mentorship in the ebb and flow of a teacher's subjective career (Huberman, 1989).

Although actual data on retention of mentors are meager, the evolving conceptual framework holds considerable promise. It entails a shift from a linear, sequential conception of career to one shaped around the experience of teachers in teaching. It holds out a view of retention that extends beyond decisions to leave or stay, encompassing the range of attitudes and actions that make up commitment to teaching. Finally, it places the individual in an institutional and social context in which other factors (layoffs, family obligations) may determine direct participation in the teacher work force.

Power of the Career Incentive in Mentoring

The development and support of formal mentor roles is a substantial policy investment. In California, for example, the budget devoted to the mentor program represents the largest single share of the state's categorical staff development funding (Little et al., 1987). Its justification rests in large part on whether teachers find the role attractive. What do we know about the actual appeal of the mentor role, or about its power to secure or increase teachers' enthusiasm for teaching?

The rhetorical literature is replete with proposals to policymakers and administrators for the timely development of teacher leadership roles, and with relatively sanguine assurances of their appeal to experienced teachers (Carnegie Forum on Education and the Economy, 1986). The research literature suggests a more lively interplay of support and opposition among teachers themselves. It has not escaped the notice of teachers' organizations that the impetus behind teacher leadership positions and programs rests outside the teaching ranks (see, e.g., Cooper, 1988). Some critics argue that the expansion of teachers' opportunities for collaborative work has been matched by a commensurate increase in external control over the substance of teachers' work. Hargreaves (1989) asserts that "teachers are being urged and sometimes required to collaborate more, just at the point when there is less for them to collaborate about" (p. 29). But such commentaries fail to account for the fact that some teachers have in fact been actively involved in shaping such roles and have been eager to apply for them. So the question remains, for whom is the role an incentive?

Like most incentives, the opportunity to become a mentor is attractive to some and not others. Unlike other incentives, however, the success of mentoring (and thus the fulfilled promise of the incentive) depends on the direct participation or tacit acceptance of mentors by other teachers. The title of mentor, as Bird and Little (1985) have observed, "name[s] half of a relation" (p. 3). Thus, the nature and extent of its appeal to teachers is of special import. As part of their broader investigation of career ladder plans in Utah school districts, Hart and Murphy (1989a) assessed new teachers' support for leadership positions held by more experienced teachers. The new teachers, all with 5 or fewer years of teaching experience, were ranked on the basis of grade point average (academic record) and principal ratings (current performance) to form three groups of varying promise in teaching. In all but 2 of the 20 cases selected for intensive interview, the ratings of academic preparation and current teaching performance coincided. The highest ranking teachers offered the greatest support for differentiated roles, but also held out the most demanding standards for them: clear links between the tasks of leadership and the core functions of teaching and learning, stable and clearly differentiated opportunities (not short-term, marginal projects), and mechanisms for monitoring effort and impact. By contrast, low-ranking teachers were most likely to oppose or be indifferent toward the new roles, or to base their interest primarily on salary or on increases in teachers' power in governance and personnel matters. To construct the role in ways that catered to the concerns of the low-performing teachers might broaden the overall base of support in the short run, but almost certainly would result in losing the longer term participation and endorsement of precisely the target group of greatest interest to policymakers—the capable young teachers with high initial levels of enthusiasm and commitment. This evidence provides some grounds for advocating a more assertive definition of mentor roles. Missing from the equation so far, however, are the comparable orientations of high-performing and low-performing teachers at more advanced career stages.

Individuals' career histories and career aspirations may influence their decisions to pursue or avoid mentor positions. Research on teachers' careers has gradually abandoned its nearly exclusive attention to the first years of teaching and has begun to sketch the outlines of certain modal career cycles. The results have special significance for the study of formally devised career incentives, and particularly for incentives that carry with them certain professional obligations. The 160 Swiss secondary teachers in Huberman's (1989) 4-year study of teacher careers experience periods of engagement and disengagement, confidence and self-doubt, experimentation and retrenchment. These are patterns that change with time and circumstance. What teachers consider an incentive seems likely to vary with these fluctuations in experience and enthusiasm. Of particular interest here are those teachers in mid-career (7–18 years experience), whom Huberman characterizes as entering a period of experimentation and activism; such teachers may constitute the most receptive and appropriate pool of applicants for mentor positions. On the other hand, Huberman highlights that same period as one in which as many as 40% of teachers are specially prone to the kind of mid-career crisis that may prompt them to abandon the classroom. Would assuming a mentor role relieve such a crisis, or only exacerbate it? Ruskus (1988) distinguishes among mentors on the basis of their present orientation toward career. Among 12 mentors, only 4 professed to be firmly committed teachers. For 3, the mentor role served as one step along an intended path to administration. Of the remaining 5, 1 left teaching during the period of the study, and the remaining 4 expressed either intent to leave or a tenuous commitment to teaching. This profile of a small mentor population belies the assumption that mentors are drawn exclusively from a pool of professionally ambitious and entrepreneurial teachers. Ruskus does not explicitly analyze the effect of mentorship on the enthusiasm, indifference, or alienation that mentors express toward teaching. Her implicit conclusion is that assuming a mentor role reinforces commitments where they exist, but does not moderate career disappointments or dissuade teachers from leaving. Other case examples lend credence to this interpretation.

When career histories are joined by other aspects of teachers' life history and local context, accounting for the differential appeal of the mentor role becomes yet more complex. Because much of the work of mentoring is added on to the school day, teachers' interest in becoming a mentor may be contingent on the number and intensity of other obligations, both in and out of school. Family obligations or community involvements compete with school demands. Even within the school, active participation in student activities, curriculum committees, or other out-of-classroom activity limits the availability of some of the most energetic teachers. For teachers who find themselves already stretched thin, preferred incentives are likely to be those that ease the burden. Embedded in the anecdotes collected in the implementation literature are alternative scenarios—preferences for increases in base compensation, more generous allotments of in-school preparation time, fewer course preparations. Asked if the mentor opportunity would hold him in teaching, one teacher responded, "I hope so. I can't guarantee it, though. It doesn't solve most of my personal concerns about being a teacher such as low public esteem, low salary. . . . It doesn't do anything to solve these problems" (Hanson et al., 1985, p. 28).

Just as teachers' present circumstances and future aspirations shape their response to the mentor role, so past disappointments may color their view. Teachers who have been thwarted in more conventional career pursuits may avoid any situations that require teachers to compete for career rewards on the basis of performance; it seems unlikely that "the embittered Mr. Pickwick," having failed to secure the administrative post he desired, would find mentorship an attractive prospect (Beynon, 1985).

Whatever the factors that enter into teachers' initial response to mentoring as a career incentive, the eventual power of the role lies in the experience it offers to the mentors themselves. Where mentors fail to reap personal and professional benefits from their work (Zey, 1984), or where the risks associated with mentoring outweigh the rewards (Yoder, Adams, Grove, & Priest, 1985), mentoring is inhibited. On the basis of present research, the benefits seem far from certain and the risks substantial. Some anecdotal accounts, to be sure, support proponents' claims. The vignettes constructed by Hanson et al. (1985) from interviews of mentor-teacher pairs are one example. In these vignettes, mentors detail the intrinsic rewards associated with their new role. Of 11 mentors, 8 stressed the satisfactions associated with helping others. Two of the 8 argued that the formal mentor role created a legitimate mechanism for sharing ideas and materials, and 2 others took pleasure in receiving compensation for work they had previously volunteered. Others derived intellectual stimulation from their new association with other mentors or teachers and from their expanded participation in conferences and workshops. Only 2 presented the mentor position as part of a clearly defined agenda for career advancement into the ranks of administration. One acknowledges,

I need the experience because I want to be an administrator. Basically I'm building a resume. . . . The money is nice but it's not my real incentive. I am not just a teacher who is going to stay a teacher. I have aspirations. (p. 32)

But the benefits are by no means self-evident or uniformly accessible. Teachers who report having been mentored informally by peers found it hard to imagine what benefit the mentors derived from the experience (Gehrke & Kay, 1984). Although initially honored by their selection, mentors in formal programs subsequently experience considerable ambivalence, uncertain whether the mentor designation is a blessing or a burden (Allen, 1989; Hart, 1989; Shulman & Colbert, 1987). There is widespread evidence that teachers may experience an unwelcome transition from successful classroom teacher to failed mentor. Some of the basic conditions surrounding the role also undermine it. The time demands alone energize some, but exhaust many others (Hart, 1988). Problems of role stress—ambiguity, conflict, and overload—take their toll on teachers' commitment and performance. Mentors may be subjected to the disdain and censure of colleagues, and find themselves for the first time having to account publicly for their performance (Bird, 1986; Hart, 1989). The relation between formal mentors and individual teachers tends to be a short-term affair, offering scant opportunity for the essential features of the relation to mature (Gray & Gray, 1985). And teachers' own tenure in positions of mentorship itself is typically limited to a period ranging from a few months to 3 years. The shorter the period, the more deleterious the effects on mentors' own classroom performance and the fewer the achievements in which they might take pride.

The power of the mentor role to serve as a career retention incentive is further enhanced or diluted by the immediate contexts in which mentors attempt their work. The power of context is glimpsed in small vignettes of mentors' work (Allen 1989; Shulman & Colbert, 1987), but is analyzed more thoroughly in full-scale case studies informed by theoretical perspectives on work redesign and role innovation (Hart, 1989; Hart & Murphy, 1989b). The case studies generated in the wake of the Utah career ladder experiment, although not focused specifically on mentor roles, examine a set of circumstances that closely parallel the implementation of mentor initiatives in other locales. Cross-site analyses illuminate some of the structural and cultural features that can be expected to distinguish a professionally rewarding mentor experience from one that produces only anxiety and frustration. Two schools studied in depth by Hart (1989) were in many respects comparable environments for classroom teaching, with similar student populations, faculty composition, and material resources. They were, however, radically different environments for the introduction of new teacher roles and altered professional relationships. In one school, where norms favored mutual support and problem solving, teacher leaders joined other teachers and the principal to fashion their new roles in the service of widely shared school goals. Leadership tasks were linked demonstrably to improvements in teaching and learning, and communication about both efforts and progress was frequent and public. A second school left its newly assigned teacher leaders to invent their own roles in relation to a faculty whose members jealously guarded their professional prerogatives. Teacher leaders in both schools suffered a certain degree of personal role conflict and overload, but only in the latter school was personal struggle to learn a new role compounded by stresses generated by faculty opposition, faculty pressure to account for their actions, and persistent ambiguity regarding the main purposes guiding their work. The Utah findings are echoed in other studies. Three teacher leaders who were interviewed and observed in their capacities as leaders (Wasley, 1989) "all mentioned that their greatest challenge was to break into the school culture" (p. 7). Although only one of the three leadership cases approximates in purpose and practice the role of a mentor, Wasley concludes, "These cases suggest that each teacher leadership position is firmly rooted in its own context and that context is critically important to the success of the role" (p. 27).

Finally, the incentive power of a new role is compromised to the extent that its present legitimacy and future stability are in doubt. Teachers experience the relative stability or instability of the incentive in two ways: continuity in an individual's access to the role, and the continued existence of the formal role within the system at large (Hart, 1988). From an individual perspective, mentor roles constitute a small opportunity base—a scarce resource. California's Mentor Teacher Program, for example, funds a maximum of 5% of a district's teachers as mentors (Wagner, 1985). Only a relatively small percentage of teachers can occupy the roles at any one time, thus putting pressure on the system for short-term rotation of opportunities to expand the direct benefit to the largest possible pool of teachers. For the individual teacher, however, the power of the incentive is plausibly linked to one's prospects for getting it, and one's ability to remain in the position long enough to derive both its intrinsic and extrinsic rewards (and to offset the strains associated with learning a new role). Hart (1988) reports the shifting of views when one teacher who had argued previously for frequent rotation of opportunity began to see the merit of longer assignments: "all the training and the work the teacher leaders have been through would be lost if we turn it over so quickly. . . . We need more stability in the position" (p. 24). Another protests, "A career ladder's not a ladder if you fall off it automatically every year" (p. 24). Most of the mentors interviewed by Hanson et al. (1985) asserted their intent to remain in teaching regardless of their future success in competing for mentorships, but there were exceptions. One teacher specifies clearly that he "will stay in the profession as long as he is mentor" (p. 46). In both studies, for at least some teachers, the association between leadership opportunities and long-term career commitments was tied closely to issues of individual access. Individual interests are thus in tension with system imperatives.

As a career incentive, then, mentor roles appear to have differential appeal among individuals, differential power to affect retention compared to other incentives, and differential significance under varying contextual conditions. Furthermore, the power of the incentive can be expected to wax and wane as individual circumstances evolve, as the configuration of other incentives and disincentives shifts, and as elements of context yield greater or lesser support for mentors' work.

CONCLUSION

Mentoring among teachers in American schools has been spurred by public and professional debate over the quality of the work force, the vigor of the teaching occupation, and the conditions of improvement in schools. The proliferation of mentor programs results not from a groundswell of teacher interest, but is largely a product of policy interests and institutional concerns. Increased public attention to certification, tenure decisions, and teacher evaluation has driven the development of formal mentor roles. Much of the research, in turn, has taken the form of policy studies or program evaluations conducted in sites and settings shaped by formal intervention. In local schools, mentors fulfill three basic functions: They are guides to beginning teachers during a period of induction; they form a local cadre of staff developers or teacher consultants; and they lead or support program and curriculum development ventures. Of these, teacher induction programs provide the main setting in which the promise of mentoring has been tested. In all of them, however, the logic of help giving dominates. It is in this regard, primarily, that mentoring among teachers departs from traditions of informal mentoring in business and industry, where career advancement is the driving force and the main source of rewards for both mentor and protégé.

On the whole, research has been slow to pursue some of the larger questions implicit in the choice of mentoring as a favored policy option for supplying career retention incentives to experienced teachers and for expanding professional support in schools. There are few comprehensive studies, well informed by theory and designed to examine in depth the context, content, and consequences of mentoring. But the themes that run through smaller studies prove remarkably consistent. From a range of discrete investigations, we can piece together a picture of the emergence of formal mentor roles through the implementation of local and state-sponsored programs. We can begin to test the instrumental power of mentoring to relieve the reality shock associated with teacher induction or to stimulate innovations in curriculum and instruction. We also can begin to assess the incentive power of the role by finding whom it attracts, and why, and what rewards they find in the role over time.

Attempts to introduce mentoring relations into the formal structures of schools and districts display a marked conservatism. Formal programs reflect persistent pressures to narrow the definitions of the mentor role, accommodating (and thus helping to preserve) traditional norms of privacy and equal status. In the face of uncertainty, districts and schools have sought bureaucratic solutions to problems of professional relationship, employing job descriptions, selection criteria, and the regulation of opportunity to diminish problematic implications of the mentors' greater expertise, maturity, and status. From many of the case study scenarios, one is left with the sense that the problems surrounding the emergence of mentor roles are conceived as problems of a program to be marketed rather than as problems of a culture to be built.

The conservative tenor of implementation is reinforced where the purposes of mentoring remain ambiguous, where compromises are made with regard to selection, and where mentors' opportunities to earn teachers' respect are diminished by constraints on time and visibility. Mentors are inhibited further in their claims to special expertise and special status—claims that are inescapably implied by their title—by the relative scarcity of favorable precedents for leadership on matters of professional practice. In their efforts to fulfill their obligations, mentors encounter both general cultural ambivalence about help giving and specific occupational prohibitions regarding interference in others' work. In effect, they must engage in a precarious form of improvisation, writing the script and performing the play at one and the same time for an audience whose sympathy is far from certain. There is a certain poignancy in the portraits of mentors' work.

Formally structured mentoring among teachers, by comparison to the images evoked in the tale of Mentor and Telemachus (or other famous mentors and protégés), tends to be a narrowly conceived affair with narrowly utilitarian purposes. The features of mutuality and comprehensiveness, distinguishing marks of genuine mentor relations, are hard to detect. Pieced together, mentors' and teachers' accounts add up to a picture of a formal role much diminished in substance and stature from the one reflected in our broad cultural images. The relations between mentors and teachers, on the whole, stress matters of comfort over issues of competence. They provide socioemotional support but appear to exert little influence on teachers' thinking or performance. Teachers are more likely to credit mentors with providing moral support or enlarging a pool of material resources than with exerting direct influence on their curriculum priorities or instructional methods. In the end, these relations appear less mutually respectful than simply mutually reticent. The blatant disparity between the promise of the title and the patterns of practice led a teacher in one study to lament (even while crediting a mentor's assistance), "Where is the real mentoring?!" (Hanson et al., 1985, p. 27).

Though there are some significant exceptions in the case literature, mentors more often are constrained than enabled by the organizational circumstances in which they work. Some of these circumstances lend themselves to policymaking and bureaucratic control; others do not, and are more properly the object of leadership than rule making. To the extent that ambitious, assertive conceptions of the mentor role have been legitimated and defended, however, mentors appear more likely to engage in the kinds of relations and activities that one might, by common sense, associate with mentoring. Where more limited conceptions prevail, the activities and relations approximate familiar constructions of extra work for extra pay.

The promise of the mentor role rests in its ability to attract those teachers whose professional record is highly regarded and who thus are able to secure the admiration and acceptance of other teachers. The power of the mentor role to serve as an incentive to career retention and enhanced commitment has received far less attention in the research literature than its more instrumental aspects, despite the prominent attention to career incentives in the policy rhetoric. The major gains have been conceptual rather than empirical. Theorists have recast retention to include not only concrete decision points or events (to leave or to stay), but a long-term set of attitudes and actions by which commitment is enhanced, sustained, or eroded. Students of teachers' lives and careers show how the concern with retention might be located in a still broader conception of teachers' careers. And theories of work redesign and role innovation place questions of career incentive in the context of the relation between individual and institution.

The empirical gains are fewer. Anecdotal evidence, threaded through the case studies, suggests some preliminary, highly tentative, conclusions. The attractiveness of the role and thus the incentive to compete for it in the first place appears to be a function of both individual career orientation and organizational context. The effect of the incentive is bolstered to the extent that teachers are able to match their images of the role with the opportunities they actually encounter and the responses they meet from teachers and administrators. It is diminished, predictably, when the stresses of the new role outweigh its rewards—a not uncommon development, it appears. Although cast as a career incentive for experienced teachers and a resource for schools, mentorships turn out to place individuals in a personally and organizationally precarious position. The mutual benefits standard is met only with considerable difficulty.

The research on mentoring reflects its pragmatic origins. Policy interests and programmatic considerations have dominated; simple restatements of policy rationales have generally substituted for more clearly articulated and robust theoretical perspectives. A more rigorous theoretical base is clearly available. Implementation studies have employed theories of work redesign and role innovation to account for the emergence of mentor roles and for the particular form they have assumed. Similarly, research on the contributions of mentoring to teacher induction will be enriched by advances in research on help giving or by theoretical perspectives on socialization into occupations, organizations, and groups. To grasp the significance of mentor roles as career incentives will require that we locate mentoring opportunities within a broader perspective on teachers' lives and careers.

Added theoretical rigor brings certain methodological demands. The characteristic limitations that Speizer (1981) associates with studies of mentoring in business and the professions apply equally in education. Among the characteristic limitations are small sample sizes, an overreliance on retrospective accounts, the absence of control or comparison groups, and the scarcity of longitudinal designs. Although many of the available studies of mentoring in education employ multiple sites, the number of sites generally remains small, and there is little evidence of systematic variation in those contextual features most likely to affect outcomes. Relatively few have been fully conceived and analyzed as comparative cases adequate to the underlying questions of theory, policy, and practice. There are virtually no structured studies that compare formal mentor arrangements with the conditions, contexts, dynamics, and consequences of naturally occurring mentor relations. Nor are there studies that compare mentoring to other policy alternatives in teacher induction or in the domain of career incentives. Most studies are cross-sectional, concentrated on the early stages of program implementation and role developments. Many of the crucial questions surrounding the emergence of the mentor role, its nature, and consequences, cannot be addressed without longitudinal designs that distinguish between short-term and long-term effects on individuals and institutions.

The characteristic limitations of small samples (an inevitability in the study of teacher leadership positions) might be compensated more persuasively by other aspects of research design. Sampling and selection strategies, for example, only rarely account for the web of social and professional relations in which mentors attempt their work. Designs that sample mentor-teacher pairs offer greater power, though sometimes they are weakened by a selection bias introduced when mentors control the selection of teachers to be interviewed. When this occurs, the sample is disproportionately composed of successful pairs. Other anecdotal and survey evidence suggests that the experience reported by such pairs is not typical. The problems of a small sample are compounded further by limitations on sources and types of data. Although the pool of case materials has grown steadily, permitting a more systematic examination of the actual circumstances and practices of mentoring, the available evidence often lacks credibility. Most studies rely heavily on in-depth interviews that reveal mentors' perceptions, but also are constrained by mentors' perspectives and experiences. The perspectives of teachers at large, teacher protégés in particular, or administrators are represented more sparingly. Observations of mentors' work are rare in study designs, and rarer still in published reports. Nonetheless, the sheer scale of practical experimentation with mentor roles suggests that methodological remedies, like theoretical sophistication, are well within reach.

This review has been constructed not only to assess and organize the available research, but also to shape an agenda for subsequent research and professional debate. Debates over the meaning of mentorship in education derive in part from a Western cultural legacy in which the name of Mentor signifies wisdom, maturity, and a personal investment in the capacities and fortunes of the protégé. And, on a more contemporary front, they derive from an implicit comparison to perceived parallels in business and industry, where mentorship is first and foremost a form of sponsorship, a mechanism by which promising candidates are groomed for the ranks of management. The specific meaning of mentoring among American elementary and secondary teachers has only begun to emerge from a handful of comprehensive implementation studies and from a larger array of small-scale program descriptions and program evaluations.

This review began with a conundrum: how to account for the rapidly escalating popularity of mentoring in an occupation that provides few precedents for formal and legitimate leadership by teachers on matters of professional practice. In many respects, the puzzle remains to be solved.

Woven throughout quite diverse inquiries is a persistent ambiguity about the meaning of the very term of mentor, and a certain skepticism that mentor relationships at their richest could be achieved by formal arrangement. Yet the twin aims of formal mentor programs—to reward and inspire experienced teachers, while tapping their accumulated wisdom in the service of teachers and schools—contain the elements necessary to satisfy the criterion of mutual benefit that sustain practices of mentoring elsewhere. That standard of mutual benefit seems a worthy point of departure for research and for practice.

REFERENCES

Allen, J. R. (1989). *Mentors as misers: The hidden cost of sharing expertise.* Paper presented at the annual meeting of the American Educational Research Association, San Francisco.

Allen, J. R., & Pecheone, R. (1989). *Making mentoring matter: An evaluation of Connecticut's support program for beginning teachers.* Paper presented at the annual meeting of the American Educational Research Association, San Francisco.

Anderson, E. M., & Shannon, A. L. (1988). Toward a conceptualization of mentoring. *Journal of Teacher Education, 34*(1), 38–42.

Baltzell, D. C., & Dentler, R. A. (1982). *Local variations in the selection of school principals.* Paper presented at the annual meeting of the American Educational Research Association, New York City.

Bennet, C. (1985). Paints, pots, or promotion? Art teachers' attitudes toward their careers. In S. J. Ball & I. F. Goodson (Eds.), *Teachers' lives and careers* (pp. 120–137). London: Falmer Press.

Berliner, D. C., & Carter, K. J. (1986). *Differences in processing classroom information by expert and novice teachers.* Paper presented at the meeting of the International Study Association on Teacher Thinking, Leuven, Belgium.

Berman, P., & Gjelten, T. (1984). *Improving school improvement: A policy evaluation of the California School Improvement Program* (Vol. 2). Berkeley, CA: Berman, Weiler Associates.

Berman, P., & McLaughlin, M. W. (1978). *Federal programs supporting educational change, Volume 8: Implementing and sustaining innovations.* Santa Monica, CA: Rand Corporation.

Beynon, J. (1985). Institutional change and career histories in a comprehensive school. In S. J. Ball & I. F. Goodson (Eds.), *Teachers' lives and careers* (pp. 158–179). London: Falmer Press.

Biddle, B. (1979). *Role theory: Expectations, identities, and behaviors.* New York: Academic Press.

Bird, T. (1986). *The mentors' dilemma.* San Francisco: Far West Laboratory for Educational Research and Development.

Bird, T., & Alspaugh, D. (1986). *1985 survey of district coordinators for the California Mentor Teacher Program.* San Francisco: Far West Laboratory for Educational Research and Development.

Bird, T., & Little, J. W. (1985). *From teacher to leader.* San Francisco: Far West Laboratory for Educational Research and Development.

Bird, T., St. Clair, G., Shulman, J., & Little, J. W. (1984). *Expanded teacher roles: Mentors and masters.* (Interim report to the National Institute of Education,

Contract No. 400–83–0003). San Francisco: Far West Laboratory for Educational Research and Development.

Bluedorn, A. C. (1982). The theories of turnover: Causes, effects, and meaning. In S. Bacharach (Ed.), *Research in the sociology of organizations* (Vol. 1, pp. 75–128). Greenwich, CT: JAI Press.

Bridges, E. (1986). *The incompetent teacher.* London: Falmer Press.

Brophy, J. E., & Good, T. L. (1986). Teacher behavior and student achievement. In M. C. Wittrock (Ed.), *Handbook of research on teaching* (3rd ed., pp. 328–375). New York: Macmillan.

Brzoska, T., Jones, J., Mahaffy, J., Miller, J. K., & Mychals, J. (1987). *Mentor teacher handbook.* Portland, OR: Northwest Regional Educational Laboratory.

Bucher, R., & Stelling, J. G. (1977). *Becoming professional.* Beverly Hills, CA: Sage Publications.

Buchmann, M. (1986). Teaching knowledge: The lights that teachers live by. In J. Lowyck (Ed.), *Teacher thinking and professional action: Proceedings of the third International Study Association on Teacher Thinking conference* (pp. 2–16). Leuven, Belgium: University of Leuven.

Carnegie Forum on Education and the Economy. (1986). *A nation prepared: Teachers for the 21st century.* New York: Carnegie Corporation.

Carter, K. (1988). Using cases to frame mentor-novice conversations about teaching. *Theory Into Practice, 27*(3), 214–222.

Clark, C., & Peterson, P. (1986). Teachers' thought processes. In M. Wittrock (Ed.), *Handbook of research on teaching* (3rd ed., pp. 255–296). New York: Macmillan.

Clawson, J. G. (1980). Mentoring in managerial careers. In C. B. Derr (Ed.), *Work, family and the career* (pp. 144–165). New York: Praeger.

Cooper, M. (1988). Whose culture is it, anyway? In A. Lieberman (Ed.), *Building the professional culture of schools* (pp. 45–54). New York: Teachers College Press.

Darling-Hammond, L. (1988). Policy and professionalism. In A. Lieberman (Ed.), *Building the professional culture of schools* (pp. 55–77). New York: Teachers College Press.

Deutsch, M. (1982). Interdependence and psychological orientation. In V. J. Derlega & J. Grzelak (Eds.), *Cooperation and helping behavior: Theories and research.* New York: Academic Press.

Doyle, W. (1979). Classroom effects. *Theory Into Practice, 18,* 138–144.

Dubinsky, A. J., & Yammarino, F. J. (1984). Differential impact of role conflict and ambiguity on selected correlates. *Psychological Reports, 55,* 699–707.

Edgar, D. E., & Warren, R. L. (1969). Power and autonomy in teacher socialization. *Sociology of Education, 42*(1), 386–399.

Elbaz, F. (1983). *Teacher thinking: A study of practical knowledge.* London: Croom Helm.

Elmore, R. (1989). *Issues of policy and practice in mentor programs.* Paper presented at the annual meeting of the American Educational Research Association, San Francisco.

Feiman-Nemser, S., & Buchmann, M. (1986). Knowing, thinking, and doing in learning to teach: A research framework and some initial results. In J. Lowyck (Ed.), *Teacher thinking and professional action: Proceedings of the third International Study Association on Teacher Thinking conference* (pp. 602–627). Leuven, Belgium: University of Leuven.

Feiman-Nemser, S., & Floden, R. (1986). The cultures of teaching. In M. Wittrock

(Ed.), *Handbook of research on teaching* (3rd ed., pp. 505–526). New York: Macmillan.

Fisher, J. D., Nadler, A., & Whitcher-Alagna, S. (1983). Four conceptualizations of reactions to aid. In J. D. Fisher, A. Nadler, & B. DePaulo (Eds.), *New directions in helping* (vol.1, pp. 51–84). New York: Academic Press.

Galvez-Hjornevik, C. (1986). Mentoring among teachers: A review of the literature. *Journal of Teacher Education, 37*(1), 6–11.

Gehrke, N. J. (1988a). On preserving the essence of mentoring as one form of teacher leadership. *Journal of Teacher Education, 39*(1), 43–45.

Gehrke, N. J. (1988b). Toward a definition of mentoring. *Theory Into Practice, 27*(3), 190–194.

Gehrke, N. J., & Kay, R. S. (1984). The socialization of beginning teachers through mentor-protégé relationships. *Journal of Teacher Education, 35*(3), 21–24.

Gergen, K. J., & Gergen, M. M. (1983). The social construction of helping relationships. In J. D. Fisher, A. Nadler, & B. DePaulo (Eds.), *New directions in helping* (Vol. 1, pp. 143–163). New York: Academic Press.

Glidewell, J. C., Tucker, S., Todt, M., & Cox, S. (1983). Professional support systems: The teaching profession. In A. Nadler, J. Fisher, & B. DePaulo (Eds.), *New directions in helping* (Vol. 3, pp. 189–212). New York: Academic Press.

Gray, W. A., & Gray, M. M. (1985). Synthesis of research on mentoring beginning teachers. *Educational Leadership, 43*(3), 37–43.

Greenberg, M. S., & Westcott, D. R. (1983). Indebtedness as a mediator of reactions to aid. In J. D. Fisher, A. Nadler, & B. DePaulo (Eds.), *New directions in helping* (Vol. 1, pp. 86–112). New York: Academic Press.

Griffin, G. A. (1985). The school as a workplace and the master teacher concept. *Elementary School Journal, 86*(1), 1–16.

Gross, A. E., & McMullen, P. (1982). The help-seeking process. In V. J. Derlega & J. Grzelak (Eds.), *Cooperation and helping behavior: Theories and research.* New York: Academic Press.

Gross, A. E., Wallston, B. S., & Piliavin, I. (1979). Reactance, attribution, equity, and the help recipient. *Journal of Applied Social Psychology, 9,* 297–313.

Hackman, J. R., & Oldham, G. R. (1980). *Work redesign.* Reading, M A: Addison-Wesley.

Hanson, S., Shulman, J., & Bird, T. (1985). *California Mentor Teacher Program case study: Implementation in the Orchard Unified School District, 1984-1985.* San Francisco: Far West Laboratory for Educational Research and Development.

Hardcastle, B. (1988). Spiritual connections: Protégés' reflections on significant mentorships. *Theory Into Practice, 27*(3), 201–208.

Hargreaves, A. (1989). *Teachers' development and teachers' work: Issues of time and control.* Paper presented at the annual meeting of the American Educational Research Association, San Francisco.

Hargreaves, A., & Dawe, R. (1989). *Coaching as unreflective practice: Contrived collegiality or collaborative culture?* Paper presented at the annual meeting of the American Educational Research Association, San Francisco.

Hart, A. W. (1988). *Work restructuring effects on teacher career plans.* Paper presented at the annual meeting of the Northern Rocky Mountain Educational Research Association, Jackson Hole, WY.

Hart, A. W. (1989). *Role politics and the redesign of teachers' work.* Salt Lake City: University of Utah, Department of Educational Administration.

Hart, A. W., & Murphy, M. J. (1989a). *New teachers' responses to redesigned teacher work.* Paper presented at the annual meeting of the American Educational Research Association, San Francisco.

Hart, A. W., & Murphy, M. J. (1989b). *Work design where it happens: Five comparative cases of schools.* Paper presented at the annual meeting of the American Educational Research Association, San Francisco.

Hollingsworth, S. (1989, forthcoming). Prior beliefs and cognitive change in learning to teach. *American Educational Research Journal.*

Huberman, A. M. (1986). *Some relationships between teachers' career trajectories and school improvement.* Paper presented at the annual meeting of the American Educational Research Association, San Francisco.

Huberman, A. M. (1989). The professional life cycle of teachers. *Teachers College Record, 91*(1), 31–57.

Huberman, A. M., & Miles, M. B. (1984). *Innovation up close.* New York: Plenum Press.

Huffman, J., & Leak, S. (1986). Beginning teachers' perceptions of mentors. *Journal of Teacher Education, 37*(1), 22–25.

Huling-Austin, L. (1988). *A synthesis of research on teacher induction programs and practices.* Paper presented at the annual meeting of the American Educational Research Association, New Orleans.

Jackson, P. (1968). *Life in classrooms.* New York: Holt, Rinehart and Winston.

Jackson, P. (1986). *The practice of teaching.* New York: Teachers College Press.

Kanter, R. M. (1977). *Men and women of the corporation.* New York: Basic Books.

Kennedy, M. (1987). Inexact sciences: Professional education and the development of expertise. In E. Z. Rothkopf (Ed.), *Review of research in education* (Vol. 14, pp. 133–167.) Washington, DC: American Educational Research Association.

Kent, K. M. (1985). *Development and implementation of a program for training mentor teachers.* Unpublished doctoral dissertation, Nova University.

King, R. M. (1988). *A study of shared instructional leadership by mentor teachers in Southern California.* Unpublished doctoral dissertation, University of San Diego.

Kram, K. E. (1983). Phases of the mentor relationship. *Academy of Management Journal, 26*(4), 608–625.

Kram, K. E. (1986). Mentoring in the workplace. In D. T. Hall & Associates (Eds.), *Career development in organizations* (pp. 160–201). San Francisco: Jossey-Bass.

Lacey, C. (1977). *The socialization of teachers.* London: Methuen.

Lemberger, D. (1989). *The mantle of the mentor.* Unpublished paper, University of California, Berkeley.

Levinson, D., Darrow, C., Klein, E., Levinson, M. H., & McKee, B. (1978). *The seasons of a man's life.* New York: Ballentine.

Little, J. W. (1987). Teachers as colleagues. In V. Richardson-Koehler (Ed.), *Educator's handbook: A research perspective* (pp. 491–518). New York: Longman.

Little, J. W. (1988). Assessing the prospects for teacher leadership. In A. Lieberman (Ed.), *Building a professional culture in schools* (pp. 78–106). New York: Teachers College Press.

Little, J. W., Galagaran, P., & O'Neal, R. (1984). *Professional development roles and relationships: Principles and skills of advising* (Report to the National Institute of Education). San Francisco: Far West Laboratory for Educational Research and Development.

Little, J. W., Gerritz, W. H., Stern, D. S., Guthrie, J. W., Kirst, M. W., & Marsh, D. D. (1987). *Staff development in California: Public and personal investment, program patterns, and policy choices* (Report to the California Postsecondary Education Commission). San Francisco: Far West Laboratory for Educational Research and Development.

Little, J. W., & Long, C. (1985). *Cases in emerging leadership by teachers: The school-level instructional support team* (Report to the National Institute of Education). San Francisco: Far West Laboratory.

Little, J. W., & Nelson L. (Eds.). (1989). *Preparing mentors for work with beginning teachers. Program guide for mentor training.* San Francisco: Far West Laboratory for Educational Research and Development and Los Angeles Unified School District. Denver: ERIC Clearinghouse.

Lortie, D. (1975). *Schoolteacher.* Chicago: University of Chicago Press.

Macrorie, K. (1984). *Twenty teachers.* New York: Oxford University Press.

Malen, B., & Hart, A. W. (1987). Career ladder reform: A multi-level analysis of initial efforts. *Educational Evaluation and Policy Analysis, 9*(1), 9–23.

Martin, P. (1987). *Beginning educator support and training program: Study year evaluation.* Hartford, CT: Connecticut State Department of Education, Office of Research and Evaluation.

McAlpine, A., Brown, S., McIntyre, D., & Haggar, H. (1988). *Student teachers learning from experienced teachers, SCRE project report.* Edinburgh: Scottish Council for Research in Education (SCRE).

McLaughlin, M. W. (1987). Learning from experience: Lessons from policy implementation. *Educational Evaluation and Policy Analysis, 9*(2), 171–178.

McLaughlin, M. W., & Pfeifer, R. S. (1988). *Teacher evaluation: Improvement, accountability, and effective learning.* New York: Teachers College Press.

McLaughlin, M. W., & Yee, S. M. (1988). School as a place to have a career. In A. Lieberman (Ed.), *Building a professional culture in schools* (pp. 23–44). New York: Teachers College Press.

Mead, J. (1989). *Looking at old photographs: Who do teachers choose as models and why?* Paper presented at the annual meeting of the American Educational Research Association, San Francisco.

Measor, L. (1985). Critical incidents in the classroom: Identities, choices, and careers. In S. Ball & I. Goodson (Eds.), *Teachers' lives and careers* (pp. 61–77). London: Falmer Press.

Meister, G. (1987). *Current practices in new teacher development in Maryland.* Philadelphia, PA: Research for Better Schools.

Merriam, S. (1983). Mentors and protégés: A critical review of the literature. *Adult Education Quarterly, 33*(3), 161–173.

Miner, A. S. (1987). Idiosyncratic jobs in formalized organizations. *Administrative Science Quarterly, 32,* 327–351.

Nemser, S. (1983). Learning to teach. In L. S. Shulman & G. Sykes (Eds.), *Handbook of teaching and policy* (pp. 150–170). White Plains, NY: Longman.

Neufeld, B. (1986). *The Beginning Teacher Support and Assessment Program evaluation report.* Cambridge, MA: Education Matters.

Nias, J. (1989). *Primary teachers talking.* London: Routledge.

Nicholson, N. (1984). A theory of work role transitions. *Administrative Science Quarterly, 29,* 172–191.

Odell, S. J. (1986). Induction support of new teachers: A functional approach. *Journal of Teacher Education, 37*(1) 26–29.

Parkay, F. W. (1988). Reflections of a protégé. *Theory Into Practice, 27*(3), 195–200.

Parker, M. (1989). *Teaching teachers about teaching: Mentors talk about their work.* Paper presented at the annual meeting of the American Educational Research Association, San Francisco.

Peterson, K. (1984). Methodological problems in teacher evaluation. *Journal of Research and Development in Education, 17*(4), 62–70.

Pinnegar, S. (1987). *Learning the language of practice from practicing teachers: An exploration of the term "with me."* Paper presented at the annual meeting of the American Educational Research Association, New Orleans.

Pruitt, D. G., & Carnevale, P. J. D. (1982). The development of integrative agreements. In V. J. Derlega & J. Grzelak (Eds.), *Cooperation and helping behavior: Theories and research.* New York: Academic Press.

Roche, G. R. (1979). Much ado about mentors. *Harvard Business Review, 57*(1), 14–28.

Rosenholtz, S. J. (1989). *Teachers' workplace.* New York: Longman.

Ruskus, J. A. (1988). *A multi-site evaluation of the California Mentor Teacher Program.* Unpublished doctoral dissertation, University of California, Los Angeles.

Schein, E. (1978). *Career dynamics.* Reading, MA: Addison-Wesley.

Schlechty, P. C. (1985). A framework for evaluating induction into teaching. *Journal of Teacher Education, 36*(1), 37–41.

Shapiro, E. C., Haseltine, F. P., & Rowe, M. P. (1978). Moving up: Role models, mentors, and the "patron system." *Sloan Management Review, 19*(3), 51–58.

Shulman, J. H. (1987). *Expert witnesses: Mentor teachers and their colleagues.* Paper presented at the annual meeting of the American Educational Research Association, Washington, DC.

Shulman, J. H., & Colbert, J. A. (Eds.). (1987). *The mentor teacher casebook.* San Francisco: Far West Laboratory for Educational Research and Development.

Shulman, J., Hanson, S., & King, R. (1985). *California Mentor Teacher Program case study: Implementation in the Waverly Unified School District, 1984-1985.* San Francisco: Far West Laboratory for Educational Research and Development.

Smith, K. E., & Sandler, H. M. (1974). Bases of status in four elementary school faculties. *American Educational Research Journal, 2,* 317–331.

Smylie, M. (1989). *Teachers' collegial learning: Social and psychological dimensions of helping relationships.* Paper presented at the annual meeting of the American Educational Research Association, San Francisco.

Smylie, M., & Denny, J. (1989). *Teacher leadership: Tensions and ambiguities in organizational perspective.* Paper presented at the annual meeting of the American Educational Research Association, San Francisco.

Speizer, J. J. (1981). Role models, mentors, and sponsors: The elusive concepts. *Signs: Journal of Women in Culture and Society, 6*(4), 692–712.

State of Connecticut Department of Education. (1988). *A core training manual for the preparation of cooperating teachers and mentor teachers.* Hartford: Author.

Stoddart, T. (1989). *Structuring the mentoring relationship: A question of goals.* Paper presented at the annual meeting of the American Educational Research Association, San Francisco.

Sykes, G. (1983). Public policy and the problem of teacher quality: The need for screens and magnets. In L. S. Shulman & G. Sykes (Eds.), *Handbook of teaching and policy* (pp. 97–125). New York: Longman.

Thies-Sprinthall, L. (1986). A collaborative approach for mentor training: A working model. *Journal of Teacher Education, 37*(6), 13–20.

Van Maanen, J., & Barley, S. R. (1984). Occupational communities: Culture and control in organizations. *Research in Organizational Behavior, 6,* 287–365.

Veenman, S. (1984). Perceived problems of beginning teachers. *Review of Educational Research, 54*(2), 143–178.

Wagner, L. A. (1985). Ambiguities and possibilities in California's Mentor Teacher Program. *Educational Leadership, 43*(3), 23–29.

Wasley, P. A. (1989). *Lead teachers and teachers who lead: Reform rhetoric and real practice.* Paper presented at the annual meeting of the American Educational Research Association, San Francisco.

Yee, S. M. (1986). *Teaching as a career: Promotion versus development.* Stanford, CA: Stanford University School of Education.

Yinger, R. (1987). *By the seat of your pants: An inquiry into improvisation and teaching.* Paper presented at the annual meeting of the American Educational Research Association, Washington, DC.

Yoder, J. D., Adams, J., Grove, S., & Priest, R. F. (1985). To teach is to learn: Overcoming tokenism with mentors. *Psychology of Women Quarterly, 9*(1), 119–131.

Zeichner, K., & Gore, J. (in press). Teacher socialization. In W. R. Houston, M. Haberman, & J. Sikula (Eds.), *Handbook of research on teacher education* (chap. 19). New York: Macmillan.

Zey, Michael G. (1984). *The mentor connection.* Homewood, IL: Dow Jones-Irwin.

Chapter 7

Commitment and Control: Alternative Strategies for the Organizational Design of Schools

BRIAN ROWAN
Michigan State University

This paper describes two strategies for the organizational design of schools and demonstrates how these strategies reflect current themes in the school improvement literature. The paper is based on the increasingly common observation that two "waves" of inconsistent and potentially incompatible reform initiatives occurred during the 1980s (Bacharach, Bauer, & Shedd, 1988; Kirst, 1988; Passow, 1989). In a first wave of reform, many large urban districts and several state legislatures responded to the problem of low achievement in schools by increasing bureaucratic controls over curriculum and teaching (Furhman, Clune, & Elmore, 1988; Rowan, Edelstein, & Leal, 1983). However, a reaction to this approach formed when it was argued that bureaucratic controls over schools are incompatible with the professional autonomy of teachers and potentially damaging to teacher morale (Darling-Hammond & Wise, 1985; Rosenholtz, 1987). Thus, many observers now see the formation of a second wave of school reform, one that advocates a decrease in bureaucratic controls in education and the creation of working conditions in schools that enhance the commitment and expertise of teachers.

These observations pose a challenge to research on school organization. Throughout most of the 1970s, organization theorists described schools as loosely coupled systems that lacked both tight bureaucratic controls over teaching and the kinds of organizational supports that encourage professionalized teaching (Lortie, 1975; March & Olsen, 1976; Meyer & Rowan, 1978; Weick, 1976). This literature constituted a major theoretical advance, both in organization theory generally and in research on schools, but recent trends in school reform suggest that a continued fascination with loose coupling may be outdated. The educational reforms of the 1980s are designed to strengthen the weak bureaucratic and professional controls that led organization theorists to label schools as loosely coupled systems, and new models of schools as organizations are needed to guide and assess these reform initiatives.

The new reforms in education also pose a challenge to research on school effectiveness. This research has been mired for several years in debates about the characteristics of instructionally effective schools and as a result has never fully explained how the organizational design of schools affects teaching and learning in classrooms (Rowan, Bossert, & Dwyer, 1983). Yet just such an analysis is needed if researchers are to evaluate newly implemented and newly proposed reforms. There is a need, for example, to understand how bureaucratic controls over schooling affect the work of teachers and whether these effects lead to changes in student outcomes. Correspondingly, there is a need to understand how organizational structures that support complex forms of professional decision-making in classrooms affect the work of teachers and how these structures can improve student outcomes.

This paper addresses these issues by developing two models of school organization. The models, referred to as the *control* and *commitment* strategies for organization design, rely on different organization design features and attempt to affect different school processes to achieve school effectiveness. The control strategy involves the development of an elaborate system of input, behavior, and output controls designed to regulate classroom teaching and standardize student opportunities for learning, and the expected result is an increase in student achievement. The commitment strategy, by contrast, rejects bureaucratic controls as a mode of school improvement and instead seeks to develop innovative working arrangements that support teachers' decision-making and increase teachers' engagement in the tasks of teaching. The assumption of this approach is that collaborative and participative management practices will unleash the energy and expertise of committed teachers and thereby lead to improved student learning.

In this paper, these models will be used as a lens through which to review recent research on schools. Critical questions for this review include the extent to which these two models can be implemented in practice and whether, when implemented, they have the predicted effects on teaching and learning in classrooms. This review is then used to generate questions for future research on school organization and effectiveness.

BACKGROUND

Since Bidwell's (1965) seminal analysis of the school as a formal organization, organizational studies in education have continually noted the relative absence of coordination and control over classroom instruction in schools (Lortie, 1975; March & Olsen, 1976; Meyer & Rowan, 1977; Weick, 1976). Public schools and school systems, it seems, are large bureaucracies without strict bureaucratic controls and highly professional organizations that lack collegial forms of collaboration and control. These characteristics of schools not only have frustrated educational reformers for decades, but also have constituted a major puzzle for organization theorists.

Bidwell (1965) was the first to suggest an explanation for loose structuring in schools, and his analysis has been extended by others, including Weick (1976) and Meyer and Rowan (1978). According to these theorists, schools contain a "weak" technology of instruction. In this line of argument, the goals of classroom instruction are seen as variable and uncertain, and the cause-and-effect relationships linking teacher activities to student achievement are considered to be poorly understood. In loose coupling theory, this uncertainty is seen as a threat to the institutionalized legitimacy of schools; school personnel are hypothesized to avoid potential embarrassments that might arise from this uncertain technical core by developing what Meyer and Rowan (1978) called the "logic of confidence," a set of face-saving norms that allow schools to appear rational but which avoid any substantive inspection of this assumption. Thus, in loose coupling theory, the uncertain and poorly understood technology of instruction is seen to result in a lack of either bureaucratic or professional controls over classroom instruction.

Throughout the 1970s and early 1980s, policy analysts and organization theorists argued that the loosely coupled control system of schools needed reform. In part, these early reform arguments were motivated by new developments in research on teaching and by emerging research on school effectiveness. Together, these lines of research encouraged many reformers to develop a highly rationalized view of teaching and of school management (e.g., Murphy, Hallinger, & Mesa, 1985). Research on effective schools encouraged the notion that the goals of schooling could be clearly framed and measured in terms of basic skills outcomes (e.g., Edmonds, 1979), and research on teaching led to the view that a routine set of behaviors, typically identified as "direct instruction" (e.g., Rosenshine, 1983), could achieve these goals with high certainty. The problem of school reform became managing this highly rationalized technology by implementing tightened controls over teaching, controls that ensured that teachers taught toward prescribed goals using prescribed techniques.

As this view of effective schooling was disseminated, school districts and state legislatures across the country began to develop a host of bureaucratic controls over teaching (Furhman et al., 1988; Rowan, Edelstein, & Leal, 1983). For example, the emphasis on basic skills achievement in the effective schools literature led to the implementation of a strategy called "curriculum alignment." In this managerial strategy, standardized textbooks were used as input controls to constrain teachers' decisions about instructional content, and norm- or criterion-referenced tests were used as output controls to assess student achievement. Often, these input and output controls were reinforced by the implementation of more stringent behavior controls. For example, in the early 1980s, districts began to provide in-service workshops based on the early process-product research on teaching and to train principals in methods of instructional supervision. In many districts, the goal was to develop more uniform approaches to teaching and to tighten supervisory practices (Rowan et al., 1983). More recently, these trends have been reinforced by state-level policies that tighten curricular controls and set standards of evaluation for teachers (Furhman et al., 1988).

These early reforms also encouraged formalized procedures for coordinating instructional programs in schools. For example, grade-level objectives (and sometimes pacing guidelines) are used to standardize instruction across classrooms at the same grade level, and competency tests are used to assure that students have mastered appropriate basic skills objectives before moving to the next step in a sequentially organized curriculum. Finally, a movement is currently under way to make remedial instruction more "congruent" with regular classroom instruction by using the same instructional objectives and strategies in both special and regular classrooms (Johnston, Allington, & Afflerbach, 1985).

It is interesting that this trend in school improvement is consistent with much thinking in organization theory. Organization theorists have long held that routine technologies—those with clear goals and certain means—are best managed by implementing what Burns and Stalker (1961) called a "mechanistic" management structure (e. g., Perrow, 1967). In this approach to organization design, centralized decision making and standardized working procedures promote efficiency by focusing workers' efforts on achieving clearly defined goals and by minimizing workers' deviation from the prescribed means of achieving these goals. Thus, it should come as little surprise that educational managers and policymakers who were willing to assume that classroom instruction could be routinized were also willing to implement input, output, and behavior controls in schools. In fact, from the standpoint of organization design theory, this strategy made sense.

In the mid-1980s, however, researchers began to question this strategy for school reform. In part, this occurred as research on teaching turned away from the study of routine teacher behaviors and began to focus on the study of teachers as active decision makers working in complex classroom environments. What has emerged from this more recent line of research is a view of instruction not as a set of routine behaviors that can be scripted and implemented uniformly in classrooms, but rather a view of teaching as a nonroutine technology that relies on teacher judgment and expertise for its success (Berliner, 1986; Brophy & Evertson, 1976; Shulman, 1987).

Although this emerging view of teaching is similar in some respects to the earlier view described in loose coupling theory, there are important differences. Loose coupling theorists assumed that educational goals are vague, whereas current research on teaching holds that teaching goals are reasonably clear, but dynamic and multiple. Moreover, the loose coupling view, which developed largely in isolation from research on teacher effectiveness, assumed weak empirical connections between teaching activities and student outcomes. However, the view being developed in recent research on teaching assumes that empirical connections between various teaching strategies and student outcomes are both demonstrable through research and known to expert or master teachers. Thus, whereas loose coupling theorists stressed a lack of rationality in teaching, current views argue that the work of teachers is complex and nonroutine, but still subject to rational understanding (e. g., Shulman, 1987).

This revised view of teaching has important implications for the organizational design of schools. Organization theorists predict that when technologies are complex and not routine, organizational effectiveness is enhanced by developing what Burns and Stalker (1961) called "organic" forms of management. Nonroutine technologies require workers to engage in frequent searches for solutions to complex technical problems (Perrow, 1967), and as workers require more technical information to solve these problems, hierarchical and standardized approaches to work become inefficient. As a result, organizations develop lateral patterns of communication. Network structures replace hierarchical structures of management, and technical work comes to be guided by information and advice received from colleagues rather than by centralized and standardized task instructions. In this situation, a system of ad hoc centers of authority and communication emerges, with those possessing relevant information and expertise assuming leadership no matter what their formal position of authority (Burns & Stalker, 1961).

Themes consistent with this approach can be found in the literature on "restructured" schools and in recent discussions of teacher professionalism (Carnegie Task Force on Teaching as a Profession, 1986; Lieberman, 1988; National Governors' Association, 1986; Tucker, 1988). For example, one common theme is the call to replace hierarchical structures with network structures of decision making in schools. In this approach, teachers would assume expanded authority in schools, collegial patterns of interaction would be nurtured so that information and advice about teaching could be shared more frequently, and teamwork would be used as an integrative device for the school. In this setting, school leadership would be more widely exercised, with teachers emerging as leaders along-side the principal, and with information and advice supplanting formal rules and procedures in instructional decision making and evaluation.

COMMITMENT AND CONTROL AS ALTERNATIVE STRATEGIES OF ORGANIZATION DESIGN

This brief review of trends in the school improvement literature suggests that two very different theories of school effectiveness have emerged in education over the last decade. One theory holds that teaching is a routine technology and that a control-based strategy of organization design can enhance school effectiveness. The strategy associated with this approach involves the development of a standardized system of input, behavior, and output controls that constrain teachers' methods and content decisions, thereby controlling student access to academic content and assuring student exposure to a standardized quality of instruction.

This approach is consistent with the mechanistic forms of management that have dominated industrial organization for the past century. As such, much is known about the advantages and disadvantages of this approach. Clearly, at the turn of the century, mechanistic approaches to management increased industrial productivity. But organization theorists have also noted that this management strategy limits workers' commitment to the firm. In fact, as Burns and Stalker (1961) noted, worker commitment in mechanistic management systems is crucially dependent on loyalty to superiors. In education, this pattern of limited commitment is well known. Collective bargaining agreements often define the parameters of teacher commitment in schools (Mitchell, Kerchner, Erck, & Pryor, 1981), and teachers' commitment to school improvement often depends on the instructional and managerial leadership of school principals (Leithwood & Montgomery, 1982).

However, an alternative approach to school design has begun to emerge. This approach is grounded in a view of teaching as a complex and nonroutine technology; it assumes that organic patterns of school management that rely on network structures of coordination and control and the expansion of teacher authority can enhance teachers' commitment and improve instruction (Rosenholtz, 1987). In short, this approach relies on teachers' expertise and problem solving, rather than elaborate control systems, for the improvement of teaching.

Less is known about this approach to organization design, although it appears to be consistent with what Walton (1980) called the work "restructuring" movement in business and industry. Research on this approach in industry has suggested for some time that employee commitment and motivation can be increased when workers and managers have more authority, variety, and collegiality in their work (Porter, Lawler, &

Hackman, 1975; Turner & Lawrence, 1964). But more important, there is reason to believe that the basis of employee commitment also changes under organic management. As Burns and Stalker (1961) point out, "the emptying out of significance from the hierarchic command system [in organizations] . . . is countered by the development of shared beliefs about the values and goals of the concern" (p. 121). Thus, if this pattern of management were implemented in schools, we would expect "cultural" controls to replace formal controls and teachers to base their commitment to work on personal identification with the school mission rather than loyalty to superiors.

The interesting question about both these organization design strategies is whether they can be observed in practice, and whether, when implemented, they have the expected effects. To answer this question, I turn now to a review of recent research on school organization. The review is necessarily selective, concentrating on studies relevant to the control and commitment strategies of school reform.

THE CONTROL STRATEGY IN PRACTICE

The review begins with a discussion of the control strategy, with particular emphasis on the development of controls over curriculum and teaching in schools. Basic questions include whether the control strategy works as intended and whether the critics' fears about these practices are justified. Have increased bureaucratic controls succeeded in routinizing the core technology of schools, as the model supposes? Does the strategy produce the desired results? And, what are the effects of this strategy on teachers' morale and commitment?

Curriculum Alignment

I turn first to a discussion of curriculum alignment: the system of controls over curriculum goals, instructional materials, and student testing. I will review research on the various forms by which these controls are exercised in states and districts and consider the effects on teaching practices and teacher commitment that result from different types of controls.

A useful starting point is Goodlad's (1984) study of schools. Although research on loose coupling found that curricular controls in schools were weak (e. g., Meyer & Rowan, 1978), Goodlad's study demonstrated that by the 1980s, curriculum controls varied greatly, across both states and school districts. In fact, Goodlad found that tight curriculum controls had evolved in several states and districts, as demonstrated by the presence of subject-specific curriculum guides intended for use in classrooms. Nevertheless, Goodlad (1984) concluded that "teachers in our sample viewed [these] state and local curriculum guides as of little or moderate usefulness in guiding their teaching" (p. 49).

Floden et al. (1988) offer one explanation for teachers' indifference to these curriculum guides. In a study of districts in five states with various curriculum policies, they found that most districts had numerous policies about curriculum, texts, and testing. In fact, in three of the five states, more than 90% of the districts had districtwide curriculum objectives, and in the other two states 70% had districtwide objectives. Districtwide output controls also were evident. In four of the five states, more than 90% of the districts had districtwide testing programs, and one state had extensive, mandatory state testing. Finally, across all five states, 70% of the districts surveyed mandated texts, and 55% mandated timelines for covering district curricula. Thus, input controls and pacing guidelines were also prevalent.

Despite this, Floden et al. (1988) did not find a pattern of policy implementation consistent with a curriculum alignment strategy. In fact, they concluded that "districts tend to make unconnected decisions [about curriculum, texts, and testing] that do not lead to any clear pattern of curriculum policies" (p. 104). Moreover, there was little evidence that curriculum policies were reinforced by other controls, as shown by the finding that teachers were neither rewarded for following district rules about texts, objectives, or testing, nor punished for ignoring them.

The two studies just discussed suggest few effects of curriculum controls on teaching. However, these studies were undertaken before the state reforms of the early 1980s. Since that time, state reforms have begun to tighten controls over curriculum. For example, Furhman et al. (1988) noted that 43 states have increased high school graduation requirements in the past few years, and Airasian (1987) found that as of 1984, 29 states require students to take a competency or proficiency test at particular points in their student career, 15 states require mastery or exit tests as criteria for promotion, and 8 states tie grade-to-grade promotion to pupils' performance on standardized tests. The question is whether these forms of control affect teaching practices and teacher commitment.

Preliminary evidence suggests that state controls over curriculum are affecting school processes. For example, Clune, White, and Patterson (1988) studied the implementation of increased high school graduation requirements in 4 states, 13 districts, and 19 high schools. Before these requirements were implemented, 4 of the 13 districts in this study already had graduation requirements that exceeded the new state requirements, yet Clune found that new math or science courses were added in 12 of the 13 districts studied and in 17 of the 19 high schools. On average, it was estimated that 27% of the students took an extra math class as a result of these changes and 34% took an additional science class. Critics have charged that these new courses are likely to be "watered down" versions of academic classes, and although Clune (1988) found evidence of this, interviews conducted as part of the study suggested that state and district curriculum regulations prevented this from occurring in most schools.

Clune (1988) did not examine the effects of changed graduation requirements on student achievement in his study, so they must be inferred from other research. Studies that show a relationship between content covered and student achievement (Carter, 1984; Cooley & Leinhardt, 1980) predict that students who enroll in more science and math classes will learn more of the content taught in these classes. However, a careful study by Alexander and Pallas (1984) showed that completion of the kind of high school coursework mandated in recent reform proposals improved the achievement of students on average but had little effect on the achievement of students with low grade-point averages. Thus, further research is needed to ascertain the effects of increased student standards on student achievement. (For a more detailed review of this issue, see McDill, Natriello, & Pallas, 1985.)

An alternative form of state curricular control is found in state-level competency tests for students. Recent research suggests that these controls also can have important effects on school processes. For example, Rosenholtz (1987) investigated this issue through interviews with a stratified random sample of 73 elementary teachers in Tennessee during the first year of statewide minimum competency testing, and found that virtually all teachers interviewed altered the content of their instruction to conform to the content of the tests. Moreover, three fourths of the teachers complained of burdens stemming from the need to acquire materials to teach state-mandated skills and from the paperwork that accompanied the 20 to 30 tests given to each student each year. However, the study supported only in part the assumption that this form of curriculum control negatively affected the level of teacher commitment. Only 25% of the teachers interviewed thought their professional autonomy was compromised by these tests, and only about 20% thought they or others were contemplating leaving teaching because of these tests. Still, fewer than 25% of the teachers thought these tests were helpful.

An alternative form of curricular control results from output controls in education, for example, the use of test scores for school accountability. There is reason to believe that this pressure can increase the impact of local testing programs on teacher practices. For example, Darling-Hammond and Wise (1985) interviewed 43 teachers randomly selected from three large school districts in three Middle Atlantic states about their attitudes toward districtwide testing practices. They found that 95% of the teachers reported that the use of standardized tests in schools was altering their curriculum emphases, the amount of time spent teaching students how to take tests and specifically preparing them for tests, and creating pressures on teachers.

Even more pervasive effects of curriculum policies are found in schools implementing a more rigorous form of the control-based strategy. Increasingly, schools are implementing instructional management systems that tie student matriculation through a tightly sequenced series of behavioral objectives to mastery testing. Darling-Hammond and Wise (1985) called this form of curriculum control "competency-based education," and they found that this type of instructional management produced the strongest negative reactions of any curriculum policy discussed with teachers. Teachers reported that this instructional procedure affected pacing and content decisions and that it was excessively rigid.

Bullough, Gitlin, and Goldstein (1984) illustrate more clearly the effects of this kind of instructional system. They studied six schools in which the dominant curricular form was a set of predetermined behavioral objectives with pre- and post-tests determining student progress. The contribution of this study is its critical analysis of how a rationalized technology of teaching shaped teachers' thinking about instruction. In contrast to the study by Darling-Hammond and Wise (1985), this study found that teachers accepted the predetermined curriculum as legitimate and useful and even believed that they had a measure of autonomy within its tightly structured framework. However, one teacher narrowly defined autonomy and creativity as the freedom to "use a different worksheet or create a worksheet of my own, as long as it meets the objective" (Bullough et al., 1984, p. 349).

As Bullough et al. examined teachers' discussion of their work within this highly rationalized context, they concluded that teachers developed a "technocratic mindedness" in which they gave little thought to educational goals and instead fixed attention on the means to achieving goals. But even thinking about means was limited. Few teachers rejected the preestablished sequence of teaching and testing called for in this instructional program. Moreover, the technocratic view led teachers to define student needs in terms of test results rather than in holistic terms. Student needs were perceived to be met by directly teaching to the content of the tests. Also, public inspection of test results encouraged a rapid pace of work and competitiveness among teachers, and teachers came to value techniques that could accomplish an instructional objective in a minimum amount of time.

An interesting finding of this study was that teachers appeared to derive feelings of efficacy and security in this system. This may be due to the fact that the National Diffusion Network certified the instructional management system used in five of the schools as instructionally effective. In fact, many teachers praised its effect on student outcomes and motivation and enjoyed the sense of certainty they derived from using it. But Bullough et al. (1984) report that this certainty was accompanied by a particular conception of the task of teaching, a tendency to think of students as "products possessing a set of known and measurable qualities that teachers are to enhance" (p. 355). Thus, this highly rationalized form of instructional management apparently succeeded in routinizing the core technology of the schools. Teachers' conceptions of goals and means were narrowed, and teachers developed a sense of certainty about student outcomes (cf. Natriello, 1984, for a similar finding about teachers' routine conception of task).

To assess whether highly rationalized forms of instructional management affect student outcomes, one must rely on evidence other than that just reviewed. Much research supports the assumption that rationalized teaching approaches can positively affect student achievement, at least as measured on most tests of basic skills. For example, research on mastery learning (Block & Burns, 1976) suggests that using formative tests within a sequenced instructional program can improve student achievement, and Cohen's (1987) discussion of "instructional alignment" demonstrates that careful attention to the match between instructional tasks and the tasks presented to students on tests markedly improves their scores. All of this suggests the wisdom of teachers' adaptations to rationalized instructional management systems. When teachers are evaluated on the basis of student test performance, and when work systems encourage rapid pacing, teachers appear to have discovered the benefits of frequent testing and instructional alignment.

A criticism of these tightly structured instructional management systems, however, is that they encourage a technocratic mindedness in which the goals of instruction remain unquestioned and attention focuses on means. This can create problems when the tests and curriculum hierarchies that drive instruction focus exclusively on basic skills. As Darling-Hammond and Wise (1985) note, recent analyses of trends in test results show rising scores in basic skills areas but declining scores in writing, science, mathematical problem solving, and analytical reading. They suggest that teachers' adaptations to outcome-based controls that rely heavily on existing standardized achievement tests for accountability may be the source of this trend.

Behavior Controls

In addition to curriculum alignment, a mechanistic design strategy often includes an emphasis on increased behavior controls. Typically, these controls designed to standardize teaching practices take the form of in-service training programs in "effective" teaching practices and increased evaluation of teachers. The studies reviewed in this section suggest that states and local districts are increasingly implementing these kinds of controls.

At the state level, there appears to be a growing recognition that behavior controls represent a useful supplement to curriculum controls. As an example, Furhman et al. (1988) studied the implementation of education reforms in six states. In two of these states, a pattern of policy-making consistent with an overall control strategy was evident. In Georgia, the legislature recently enacted the Quality Basic Education Act, which not only strengthens various forms of curriculum control, but also mandates the evaluation of new and veteran teachers. In California, a similar strategy is evolving. Recent initiatives not only include more controls in the areas of curriculum and testing, but also more funding for statewide staff development programs for teachers, leadership training for principals, and a mentor teacher program. Thus, states are combining behavior controls with other forms of control in a pattern that resembles the mechanistic strategy of organization design.

One form of state-level behavior controls is embedded in career ladder programs. Although these programs are often seen as a means of enhancing the professional status of teachers, a critical and controversial component of first-round career ladder programs is the evaluation of teachers. Furhman et al. (1988) and Rosenholtz (1987) demonstrate that the career ladder programs in Florida and Tennessee created much discontent among teachers, in large part because teachers viewed the evaluation procedures used to place them at various positions on the career ladder as unfair and unreliable. Rosenholtz (1987), for example, interviewed a stratified random sample of 73 elementary school teachers in Tennessee after the first year of implementation of a career ladder program. She found that nearly two thirds of the teachers challenged the fairness and legitimacy of the evaluation procedures used in the program; only about one third thought the state's method of evaluation was appropriate, useful, or objective; and 82% thought mediocre teachers could be promoted to the two highest levels of the ladder under the current circumstances.

Furhman et al. (1988) suggest that locally developed career ladder programs may work better than centrally administered ones, in part because many of the political problems that arise from defining the nature of good teaching and allocating rewards can be handled more sensitively at the local level. This appears to be true in states that have taken a decentralized approach to career ladder programs. Still, local evaluation practices remain troubling.

As an example, Wise, Darling-Hammond, McLaughlin, and Bernstein (1985) studied teacher evaluation practices in 32 districts with reputedly well-developed evaluation systems and found that before putting new practices in place, teacher evaluation in these districts was given little time or attention. In fact, complaints that the old system was too formal, subjective, inconsistent, and ineffective—the same complaints raised against career ladder systems—motivated reform of local evaluation practices. Other studies confirm widespread dissatisfaction with evaluation procedures. Between 1981 and 1984, for example, data from the High School and Beyond study show that about 53% of the high schools in the United States changed their teacher evaluation practices (U. S. Department of Education, 1988).

Even in the new evaluation systems studied by Wise et al. (1985), there were obvious weaknesses. For example, few districts evaluated tenured teachers frequently, a finding confirmed by data from the High School and Beyond study showing that 76% of high school teachers in the United States are observed by a supervisor only once or twice a year (U. S. Department of Education, 1988). In addition, most of the 32 districts in Wise et al.'s study did not integrate teacher evaluation and other control systems. Thus, districts did not use conformity to curriculum guides as a criterion of evaluation (cf. Floden et al., 1988), and they made few systematic attempts to connect teacher evaluation to other types of behavior control, such as in-service education. In fact, Wise et al. concluded that teacher evaluation was largely independent of other control systems in the districts they studied.

Nevertheless, Wise et al. (1985) did find several districts with exemplary evaluation practices. These districts overcame complaints about evaluation, and teachers believed they benefited from the evaluation system. In these exemplary systems, teachers viewed evaluations as fair, reliable, and valid. This resulted from the use of a few highly trained evaluators, frequent observations, and a focus on minimum, rather than advanced, standards of teaching proficiency. Under these conditions, teacher apathy and resistance to evaluation decreased, teacher-administrator communication improved, and teacher awareness of school instructional goals and of alternative classroom practices increased.

These findings are consistent with work by Dornbusch and Scott (1975). These researchers found that teachers are more satisfied when evaluation is more frequent and when they perceive evaluation standards as fair. This work was confirmed by Natriello and Dornbusch (1980-1981), who found that teacher satisfaction with evaluation was greater when evaluation standards were uniform and shared, when observation and feedback were frequent, and when teachers believed they had input into setting criteria. Natriello (1984) also demonstrated that evaluation practices affected teachers' perceptions of what he called "leverage," that is, teachers' sense that increased effort would lead to greater effectiveness. The more frequent the evaluations, the more leverage teachers believed they had.

The review thus far suggests that evaluation systems can affect teaching practices under certain conditions, but that these conditions are not generally met in most districts. As a result, there appears to be widespread discontent with local evaluation practices, and perhaps because of this, many districts are turning to an alternative form of behavior control to change teaching practices: in-service training of teaching practices that have come to be known as "direct instruction" (Rosenshine, 1983). Although scholars have recently argued that this research is simply the first stage in the development of a better understanding of effective teaching practices (e. g., Berliner, 1986), school systems throughout the country have seized upon this research to implement staff development programs. Among the most popular of these is the Instructional Theory into Practice program developed by Madeline Hunter (1983), but other programs exist as well (e. g., Good & Grouws, 1979).

A research base is beginning to accumulate about the conditions under which these kinds of programs lead to the desired changes in teachers' classroom practices. For example, some researchers have attempted to establish the minimum conditions needed to successfully implement a staff development program based on direct instruction (for a review, see Coladarci & Gage, 1984). This line of work is important given the minimal time and resources devoted to staff development in the typical district. For example, data collected in 1984 as part of the High School and Beyond study showed that 78% of the high school teachers in the United States spent fewer than 3 half-days per year in in-service programs held for the whole school, and 74% spent fewer than 3 half-days per year in in-service programs held for smaller groups (U. S. Department of Education, 1988).

Coladarci and Gage (1984) examined whether changes in teachers' classroom teaching could result simply from mailing packets of information about direct instruction practices to teachers rather than engaging teachers more intensively with staff developers. Their review of research and field test, however, failed to confirm the efficacy of this approach. Instead, they suggested that two kinds of face-to-face interactions among teachers and staff developers are needed to change teacher behavior: initial meetings between teachers and staff developers to transmit information about new teaching practices and to encourage commitment to implementation, and extensive observation of teachers.

Sparks (1986) conducted a similar study that examined the relationship between staff development activities and 19 junior high school teachers' performance in classrooms. The teachers received training in direct instruction practices under three conditions: (a) participation in five workshops; (b) the workshops plus peer observation; and (c) the workshops plus coaching by a trainer. In this study, the sample as a whole improved significantly in implementing direct instruction practices, with the peer observation condition appearing to produce the most change in teaching behavior. Sparks explained these results by arguing that the peer observation group had the most intensive involvement in the program.

A problem with the studies by Colardarci and Gage (1984) and Sparks (1986) is that they only evaluated teacher activities during and shortly after participation in staff development activities. As a result, they provide little evidence of the potential for lasting change in teacher behavior. However, Stallings and Krasavage (1986) provide evidence on this point. Their 4-year study examined the implementation of a staff development program designed to improve student engagement rates and achievement in reading and math. The program provided teachers with 3 years of training in classroom management and the Hunter model of teaching, and each teacher received intensive coaching after each session.

Briefly, Stallings and Krasavage (1986) found steady increases in desired teacher behaviors during the 3-year training; they also found that student-engaged rates and achievement increased during the 2nd and 3rd years of the program. However, in the 4th year of the project, after the training and coaching activities were substantially reduced, there were decreases in teacher implementation of targeted practices, student-engaged rates, and student achievement.

The study reached other informative conclusions. First, as Robbins (1986) notes, the project developers thought that the coaching provided by developers could be replaced by peer observation and principal supervision and that these substitutes would maintain desired teaching behaviors. But these substitutes for coaching did not occur frequently and did not have the desired effect. Nevertheless, Robbins argued that there were lasting consequences from the program. Teachers became more collegial and supportive of experimentation, thought differently about teaching and learning, and began to influence working conditions that affected their classrooms. Thus, although specific teaching behaviors were not sustained, organizational changes occurred.

Summary

Taken as a whole, research indicates that few districts are currently implementing the control-based strategy of school improvement in an all-encompassing way. For example, there appear to be few attempts to tie curriculum policies together (Floden et al., 1988) or to link these to behavior controls (Wise et al., 1985). Moreover, even various types of behavior controls, such as teacher training and evaluation practices, appear to be unrelated in most districts (Wise et al., 1985).

Rowan (1986) proposed an explanation for the partial and inconsistent implementation of mechanistic models of control. In a survey of school districts engaged in implementing various control systems, he found that school districts had limited resources to engage in school improvement. As a result, school systems usually concentrated on a change in only one aspect of their overall control system, for example, curricular controls, testing programs, evaluation procedures, or staff development. Moreover, districts usually spent 3 to 5 years revising these control strategies. Under these conditions, the implementation of a comprehensive system of input, behavior, and output controls might take 15 or 20 years, as districts worked first on one dimension of control, and then another, until an entire control system was developed. Because few districts have stable leadership over this long a period, and because innovations in schools occur in fads, the chance for an integrated system of input, behavior, and output controls to emerge in school districts seems small.

The studies reviewed here also suggest the conditions under which a strategy of increased controls over teaching can affect teachers' conceptions of task, teacher behavior, and student opportunities for learning. Apparently, intensive controls have the most effects, as the studies by Bullough et al. (1984), Natriello (1984) and Robbins (1986) demonstrate. Competency-based instructional programs, frequent evaluations, and intensive staff development efforts can affect the way teachers think and talk about teaching and can lead teachers to have routine conceptions of their tasks. The studies by Clune (1988), Bullough et al. (1984) and Stallings and Krasavage (1986) also demonstrate that intensive applications of the control strategy can affect students' exposure to content and engagement in tasks. Thus, when intensive control systems are implemented at the school level, there is evidence that they work as intended. The systems increase the alignment between instruction and test content, the pace of instruction, student on-task behavior, and improve test results.

The data only partly confirm the notion that intensive controls over teaching damage teacher commitment in the school setting. In fact, competency-based instructional management and intensive evaluation appear to increase teachers' perceptions of efficacy, while intensive forms of staff training enhance feelings of cohesiveness. Apparently, it is inconsistent and weak applications of a control strategy that are damaging to teacher commitment, as the studies of evaluation practices by Rosenholtz (1987) and Wise et al. (1985) demonstrate. Moreover, claims that teachers react negatively to increased controls over teaching are only partly confirmed by this review. The interviews with teachers conducted by Rosenholtz (1987) and Darling-Hammond and Wise (1985), in fact, show mixed reactions to these developments, with only some teachers expressing dissatisfaction with mechanistic controls.

THE COMMITMENT STRATEGY

Evidence on the implementation of a commitment strategy of school design is less systematic than evidence on the control strategy, in part because the logic of this approach is just now beginning to emerge in education circles. However, research is now being conducted on various elements of this approach, and it is this research that is reviewed here. In particular, this section reviews recent research on teacher participation in decision making; on attempts to redesign teacher roles in ways that facilitate the development of network structures to support teacher decision making; on attempts to promote teacher collaboration and teaming; and on patterns of school organization that rely on communal rather than hierarchical forms of organization to achieve organizational integration. Each of these strands of research sheds light on how an organic approach to school management can be implemented and on its potential effects on teachers and students.

Teacher Participation in Decision Making

One aspect of a commitment approach is the attempt to increase teacher participation in school decision making. This strategy is based on the assumption that the hierarchical organization of schools deprives teachers of important opportunities for decision making, and that this, in turn, not only leads to dissatisfaction among teachers, but also deprives the organization of a valuable source of technical expertise. Thus, school reformers are currently arguing for increased levels of teacher participation in school decisions under the assumption that this will enhance both teacher commitment and school quality (e. g., Conley, Schmidle, & Shedd, 1988).

Data from a survey of teachers and administrators undertaken in 1984 as part of the High School and Beyond study (U. S. Department of Education, 1988) provide a useful starting point for a discussion of teacher participation in decision making, at least in U. S. high schools. These data indicate that decisions on classroom practices in American high schools are already highly decentralized, but that decisions over other issues, especially budgeting and hiring practices, are highly centralized. For example, teachers were asked to rate the amount of control they had over various aspects of the school on a scale of 1 to 6, with 6 indicating total control. The percentage of teachers rating as 5 or 6 was 92% for control over teaching techniques, 72% for the content and skills taught in a class, 88% for the amount of homework assigned to students, 68% for disciplining students, and 65% for control over textbooks and materials. On other aspects of school decision making, however, teachers have less control. When principals were asked to rate the amount of influence teachers had on school decisions on a scale of 1 to 6, with 6 indicating a great deal of influence, the percentage of principals checking the two highest categories of influence was 11% for teacher influence in the allocation of funds, 7% for hiring new full-time teachers, and 6% for dismissing or transferring teachers. Central administrators controlled these aspects of decision making (U. S. Department of Education, 1988).

In a recent survey of 1,789 National Education Association (NEA) members, Bacharach, Bauer, and Shedd (1986) found that teachers desired greater participation in school decision making. For example, the percentage of teachers wanting more participation was 73% for decisions about expenditure priorities, 70% for budget development, and 65% for staff hiring. A large majority of teachers in this study also wanted more participation in staff development decisions (70%), evaluation practices (63%), and decisions about grading and grouping practices (55%). As these authors report, the survey "demonstrate[s] convincingly that most teachers think they should have considerably more opportunity to be involved in decision making" (Bacharach et al., 1986, p. 251).

The review thus far indicates that centralized decision making is common in certain areas, particularly in the dispursement of funds and staff hiring, and that teachers desire more participation in these decision areas. As a result, much attention has been given recently to "site-based" management, a management strategy that attempts to increase school autonomy in decision making. Clune and White (1988) recently reviewed the literature on this management strategy and noted several common themes. First, most discussions of site-based management advocate decentralization of district decision making in three areas: budgeting, curriculum, and staffing. In addition, almost all discussions advocate the establishment of a school council to assist school principals in policy development and policy-setting activities. However, as Clune and White (1988) note, this literature is "not the product of systematic empirical investigation but rather represents the experience of [program] advocates or program officers" (p. 9).

Clune and White (1988) used snowball sampling to locate 31 school districts in 17 states and one Canadian province that were implementing this innovation, and they conducted short telephone interviews with respondents in each of these districts. The study found a variety of patterns of implementation in the 31 districts. For example, districts varied in the extent to which they decentralized decisions about curriculum, staffing, and budgeting, with several districts decentralizing in all three areas, some in the areas of budgeting and staffing only, some in the area of budgeting only, and some making only a philosophical commitment to decentralization that did not include formal arrangements for implementation. The study also found that although nearly every district had a school management council, the composition and selection of council members varied from district to district. Given this variation in the amount and type of decentralized decision making across programs, it should come as little surprise that the activities of councils also varied greatly.

The implementation of site-based management required some adjustments in the roles of education personnel, although this was true more often for administrators than teachers. Most respondents, in fact, thought that the principal's response to the innovation was critical to successful implementation. Teachers' roles changed little, except that they were now accorded more opportunity to participate in policy formation. Most respondents believed that this opportunity improved teacher-principal communication and staff morale. However, some respondents noted that site-based management did little to change the patterns of leadership within the school, because those who had always been influential were appointed to school councils.

These observations are supported by a detailed case study of school site councils undertaken in Salt Lake City and reported by Malen and Ogawa (1988). This study included careful interviews and observations in six schools in a district with a long tradition of "shared governance" and substantial experience in the implementation of school site councils. The study found that although these councils had broad jurisdiction and formal policymaking authority, and despite the fact that the program included specific training provisions intended to support a redistribution of decision-making authority, the councils did little to alter the influence relationships typically found in schools. The researchers explained these findings by reference to various normative agreements and role orientations among participants that discouraged conflict and disruption of normal patterns of professional relationships among principals, teachers, and parents. The result was that a decision-making body with broad formal powers in fact became what the researchers called an "auxiliary" decision-making unit, one that operated to maintain rather than alter traditional relationships in the schools.

Despite these findings, there is reason to believe that strategies designed to alter decision-making practices in schools are worth pursuing. In fact, research generally supports the wisdom of including teachers in decision making, especially when such participation leads to increased influence over school policies. For example, Newman, Rutter, and Smith (1985) used data from the High School and Beyond study to measure teacher influence in decision making in several areas, including curriculum, staffing, and budgeting. They found that a principal's leadership and responsiveness affected the amount of influence teachers had in school decisions, and that schools with higher teacher influence had better staff morale, teacher efficacy, and sense of community. This is consistent with a great deal of previous research showing that as organizational climates in schools become more open and participative, teacher satisfaction increases (Miskel & Ogawa, 1988). Moreover, Anderson (1982, p. 400) reports studies in which teacher participation in decision making was found to be associated with higher student achievement.

Network Structures of Professional Control

A second component of the commitment approach consists of calls to create a career ladder with "lead" or "mentor" teacher positions in it. Indeed, in many reform proposals (e. g., Carnegie Task Force, 1986), this design change is seen as essential in developing networks of professional control in schools. Currently, however, practitioners are struggling to provide a definition and rationale for these programs. In many states, these programs are essential elements in a control-based strategy of school improvement that attempts to closely evaluate teacher performance and tie evaluations to merit pay. But this emphasis, as we have seen, has been controversial. Thus, an alternative rationale for career ladders is that this innovation can be used as part of a commitment strategy that allows teachers to act as mentors and support one another outside the system of hierarchical and bureaucratic controls in education. Moreover, it is hoped that teachers who assume lead or mentor positions will benefit from the enriched nature of their work and thus be more committed to teaching as a profession (Schlechty, 1989).

Some observers have noted that opportunities for teachers to participate in this kind of organizational arrangement already exist in schools. For example, a recent study by Hatfield, Blackman, Claypool, and Mester (1985) demonstrated that in many districts, teachers already perform many of the tasks called for in career ladder proposals. In a survey of 81 school districts in Michigan, these researchers identified many organizational positions that the authors called "extended" roles. Among these were grade-level chair, department head, coordinator, consultant, staff developer, teacher trainer, committee chair, and master teacher. The researchers also surveyed 120 teachers holding these kinds of positions. The results showed that 63% of the individuals occupying extended roles received additional compensation, and that a majority reported receiving strong support in various forms from district and school administrators. Most reported that a major function of their extended role was to interact with peers, but only 29% believed they had adequate time to perform this task. Still, 90% derived satisfaction from their role, 96% thought they were successful, and 82% thought the role was an important part of their career advancement.

Hart (1985, 1987) studied the implementation of a career ladder in a medium-sized district in Utah. In an initial study, she conducted 27 interviews with teachers, principals, and the superintendent of the district. Teacher leaders, selected through careful evaluation, constituted 10% of the district teaching force. An additional 40% were teacher specialists. Teacher leaders most often worked full time at the school level, whereas teacher specialists assumed limited duties outside the classroom. The implementation of this new program was consistent with the principles of organic management. Teachers were given much authority to formulate and implement the initiative, and the program stressed collegiality. Under these conditions, Hart (1985) reported that both probationary and experienced teachers began to request assistance from teacher leaders, faculty interaction and cohesiveness increased, and faculty meetings became arenas for important decision making.

In a second study, Hart (1987) surveyed 389 teachers in the district. She found that teachers defined the role of teacher leader in terms of acting as mentors to other teachers, fostering curriculum development and instructional improvement, and participating in broader school improvement and management activities. Teachers had different reactions to this initiative. Teachers most involved in the initiative—probationary teachers and teacher leaders—reported the most favorable reactions to the efforts of teacher leaders. The results also indicated that teachers assessed the impact of the innovation on schools differently, with elementary teachers reporting more favorable impact than secondary teachers. Attitudes toward the peer supervision component of the program were mixed, although teacher leaders (who did the supervision) appeared less satisfied with this aspect of the program than did other teachers. However, on the whole, teacher leaders saw the initiative as leading to career growth.

In summary, it appears that participation of teachers in extended roles fosters high levels of commitment and satisfaction, whether this participation occurs from the normal trend toward differentiated staffing that accompanies educational bureaucratization or results from the implementation of a career ladder program. Extended roles apparently foster opportunities for career growth and for variety and authority in work, especially when compared to the usual role played by teachers. All of this suggests to many observers (e. g, Hart, 1987; Rosenholtz, 1987) that theories of job design developed in the literature on business management hold true in educational organizations. In this literature, jobs that provide workers with enhanced opportunities for authority, variety, autonomy, and collegiality have been found to affect worker commitment (Porter, Lawler, & Hackman, 1975; Turner & Lawrence, 1965; Walton, 1980). Unfortunately, in a recent review of research on job satisfaction and motivation in education, Miskel and Ogawa (1988) found no studies explicitly designed to test theories of job design in school settings.

The data also indicate that much remains to be learned about how the jobs of teachers can be redesigned and the effects of these new designs on teacher commitment and productivity. The career ladder initiatives described here did little to fundamentally alter the role of classroom teachers. Instead they simply provided lead teachers a chance to move out of the role of classroom teacher and to work at the school level assisting other teachers and acting as quasi-administrators. This is different from typical job design arrangements in business or industry, where workers still perform the same production task, but do so by performing a greater variety of tasks and by receiving more autonomy and participation in decision making about how the task is done.

Moreover, as Schlecthy (1989) notes, the creation of new roles for teachers within a career ladder is problematic. Few career ladder programs have given attention to how the distribution of opportunities for these new types of jobs among faculty can be accommodated to changing age distributions in the teaching force. Obviously, financial conditions may prevent districts from promoting all teachers to the top of the career ladder, and thus problems of distributive justice in the allocation of lead teacher spots may occur when many teachers have seniority and are eligible for promotion. One solution may be the rotation of qualified teachers through lead positions, as was done in the schools Hart (1987) studied. But this raises other questions. For example, Schlecthy (1989) cautions that the long-term effects of extended roles on teachers have yet to be observed. If career ladder programs are seen as career enrichment programs rather than job enrichment programs, then the long-term effects of these programs on teacher attitudes and organizational commitment require much more investigation.

Collegiality Among Teachers

A related theme in the school improvement literature is the call to increase collegiality and collaboration among teachers. The goal of this reform is to break down patterns of teacher isolation stemming from the "cellular" form of organization in schools (Lortie, 1975; Pellegrin, 1976). From the standpoint of organic management, the cellular arrangement of schools and the associated pattern of teacher isolation are problematic, because they force teachers to depend on their own resources to resolve instructional, curricular, and management problems that arise during the planning and conduct of instruction. The commitment approach sees benefits to the development of collegial working arrangements among teachers. Consistent with the literature on organic management, school reformers assume that collaborative arrangements will enhance teachers' capacity for learning and problem solving, build solidarity and cohesiveness within the school, and satisfy teachers' needs for affiliation.

A recent study by Zahorik (1987) provides useful information about the amount and nature of collegial interaction among teachers in schools. Zahorik interviewed 52 teachers in six elementary schools and found that teachers spent an average of about 63 minutes a day at various times and places in the school conversing with other teachers. On average, about 65% of this time, or 40 minutes per day, was spent in conversations related to teaching, learning, or other education-related matters. Teachers in this study estimated that they initiated giving help to other teachers about 10 times a week and received help from other teachers about 8 times a week. The most frequent exchanges took place among teachers at the same grade level. All 52 of the teachers rated exchanges with school colleagues as a major source of help, compared with 18%, 20%, and 41% who viewed professional literature, in-service, and university courses, respectively, as helpful. Consistent with other research, it was also found that teachers in schools with team arrangements gave more help than teachers in schools with traditional arrangements (cf. Cohen, 1986).

Zahorik (1987) also studied the content of help teachers gave one another. Using teacher estimates, he concluded that about 70% of help received concerned materials, discipline, classroom learning activities, and the learning problems of individual students. Problems of teacher behavior—how to apply specific teaching techniques—and problems related to goals and objectives, student evaluation, and room organization were much less frequent. Teachers reasoned that they talked less about these issues because they already knew much about these subjects and because teacher behavior is personal, private, idiosyncratic, and intuitive. Few thought that time and opportunity prevent exchanges of information about teaching behaviors.

Zahorik's (1987) study demonstrates two conditions that affect the development of collegiality among teachers: school organization and faculty norms of privacy. With respect to the first theme, Zahorik's work is consistent with earlier studies. For example, research at Stanford University in the early 1970s studied the effects of organizational arrangements on teacher collaboration and collegiality in elementary schools. In one study, Meyer, Cohen, Brunetti, Molnar, and Leuders-Salmon (1971) found that teachers in open space classrooms exerted more influence on each other than did teachers in more conventional teaching arrangements. This reciprocal influence was even greater among teachers who were also members of teams. In another study, the Stanford group used regression analyses to demonstrate that collaborative arrangements among teachers were more likely when teachers used a complex instructional technology that involved the use of differentiated reading materials and multiple reading groups (Cohen, Deal, Meyer, & Scott, 1979). Thus, this study confirms a major assertion of the organic approach to management: Teachers who operate more complex forms of instructional technology are more likely to look to colleagues for support and information.

Zahorik's (1987) study also confirms the importance of faculty norms in promoting collegiality. For example, Little's (1982) study of six schools that varied in the success of staff development and student achievement located four practices that characterized the more successful schools: teachers engaged in frequent talk about teaching; teachers were observed and critiqued; teachers designed and planned teaching materials together; and teachers taught other teachers in various ways. Little explained the development of these practices by reference to the development of norms of collegiality and continuous improvement among the faculty at the successful schools. Thus, these schools, which had intensive forms of collaboration and collegiality, differed from those studied by Zahorik in that teachers sought to improve their teaching rather than being satisfied with it; in addition, these teachers had managed to overcome the norms of privacy noted by Zahorik.

Still, the general effects of collaboration on teacher commitment and teaching practices have proven difficult to establish. For example, a study by Miskel, McDonald, and Bloom (1983) of approximately 1,500 teachers in 89 elementary and secondary schools in Kansas used survey data to test relationships among variables measuring work system interdependence (e. g., joint planning, use of materials, etc.), teacher-teacher communication, and variables measuring teacher commitment, in this case teacher perceptions of organizational effectiveness and job satisfaction. The analysis showed positive correlations among these variables, but a multiple regression analysis failed to confirm the hypothesis that work system interdependence and communication positively affected teacher job satisfaction or perceived effectiveness. Instead a measure of teacher isolation was found to have positive and significant effects on these commitment outcomes, suggesting that teachers who work alone, rather than with others, experience more positive commitment outcomes.

The effects of teacher collegiality on classroom instruction are also difficult to establish. Zahorik (1987, p. 394) concluded that teachers in the schools he studied showed higher levels of collegiality than is generally thought to be the case in schools, but that the information shared among colleagues in these schools was "shallow" and thus unlikely to lead to profound change in teaching practices. Similarly, the Stanford studies found limited effects of collaboration on classroom practices. Although complex instructional arrangements led to increased teacher communication and made team teaching arrangements more likely, participation in team arrangements did not lead to the kind of complex teaching arrangements that were being supported by state policies in these schools (Cohen et al., 1979).

The failure of these studies to find effects of collegiality on teacher practices and commitment may be due to the fact that collegiality in these schools was too weak to produce the expected effects. For example, in the study by Miskel et al. (1983), variation in measures of work system interdependence and teacher communication were restricted to the lower end of the range of possible scores. The same could be true of the studies by Zahorik (1987) and Cohen et al. (1979), neither of which noted a general pattern of intensive and sustained collaboration. However, when an intensive pattern is present, expected effects have been found. For example, Intili (1977), using data from the Stanford studies, found that when teacher participation in teaming arrangements was intensive and sustained, decision making by teachers became more reflective. And Bird and Little's (1985) case study of a junior high school found two departments that worked closely over a 5-year period to enrich classroom environments and improve student achievement. In these departments, teachers argued that collaboration produced more good ideas about methods, materials, and organization than could have been produced alone.

Thus, various factors appear to condition the effects of collegiality. Simple attempts at promoting collegiality that allocate small amounts of time and result in limited contact do not appear to have great effects on teacher commitment or teaching practice. Instead, the development of a faculty culture that reinforces the norm of continuous improvement and sustains intensive collegial relations over prolonged periods appears to be required if collegial relationships are to improve teaching activities and enhance teacher commitment.

The Development of Community in Schools

A final theme in the commitment approach relates to Burns and Stalker's (1961) insight that in organic management, formal authority structures become less important in directing work, and informal norms or cultural controls guide work and sustain workers' commitment. In part, this entails the development of shared values that unify members of different subunits and orient them to a common purpose. This theme is also found in much of the writing on effective schools (e. g., Purkey & Smith, 1983; Rutter, Maughan, Mortimore, Ouston, & Smith, 1979), and although somewhat underemphasized in writings on the second wave of educational reform, it is also critical to the commitment approach to organization design (Rosenholtz, 1985). Here, I refer to this process as the development of community within schools.

Understanding of this issue has been greatly enriched by a recent study by Bryk and Driscoll (1988). These researchers used data from the High School and Beyond study to develop an index of community in high schools and to test the effects of community on a variety of teacher and student outcomes. The importance of the study lies in its attention not only to the integration of teachers into the life of the school community, but also in its attention to the integration of students into school life. Thus, schools that form tight communities

attend to the needs of students for affiliation and . . . provide a rich spectrum of adult roles [that] can have positive effects on the ways both students and teachers view their work. Adults engage students personally and challenge them to engage in the life of the school. (Bryk & Driscoll, 1988, p. 3)

In the view of these authors, school communities have three core features: a shared value system, a common agenda of activities, and collegial relations among adults coupled with a "diffuse" teacher role. The shared system of values in the school is carefully nurtured by faculty culture, and provides a set of expectations that can motivate and guide the behavior of both students and faculty (cf. Metz, 1986). A common agenda of activities serves to unite school members both physically and spiritually, thus providing faculty and students alike with a base of common experiences. Finally, teachers in communal schools develop a strong sense of collegiality and engage in a diffuse role that brings them into frequent contact with other faculty and with students in settings other than the classroom.

Based on these ideas, Bryk and Driscoll (1988) developed an index of communal organization in high schools and demonstrated the powerful effects of this pattern of organization on teacher and student outcomes. In data from this study, schools that scored high on an index of communal organization showed higher teacher efficacy and satisfaction, higher staff morale, higher teacher enjoyment of work, and lower teacher absenteeism. Students in schools with a higher score on the communal organization index were more interested in academics, were absent from school less often, cut class less often, and were more orderly. Finally, student dropout rates were lower in these schools, and student achievement in math (the only achievement outcome considered) was higher.

There are two cautions about these results. First, the values in a communal organization are important to achieving the results found in the Bryk and Driscoll (1988) study. Obviously, much research supports the notion that high expectations for students is a critical part of the value system of any school. However, other value systems, although commonly shared, may not be as powerful in improving student performance. For example, Swidler's (1979) case studies of alternative schools describes the development of a shared value system that encouraged students in one school to think of themselves as "bad," and she ably describes the debilitating effects of this shared culture on student academic performance.

Second, Swidler (1979) found that in the schools she studied, the role of teachers may have been overextended. In these alternative schools, which she labeled "schools without authority," the lack of hierarchical structure forced teachers to rely on personal bonds with students to maintain order and motivate learning. What Swidler found in this setting was that those teachers who were most successful in this context also were the most likely to be worn out by the experience and to leave teaching. Thus, Swidler's case studies usefully demonstrate the limits of communal organization. The efficacy of this form of organization depends critically on the shared value system of the school and on the extent to which personal bonds are reinforced by the traditional hierarchy of schools.

An important question concerns the extent to which public schools can achieve this communal form of organization. For example, Bryk and Driscoll (1988) found that Catholic and other private schools show more evidence of communal organization than public schools. In addition, their study found that communal forms of organization are more likely to be present in smaller schools, in schools that were ethnically homogeneous, and in schools that can control student entry and exit. To the extent that these conditions are lacking in many public schools, it should be more difficult for these schools to achieve communal organization. The creation of magnet schools may help ease these tensions within the public school system (e. g., Metz, 1986). In addition, a study by Fuller and Izu (1986) suggests that dependence on a single source for school funding, rather than dependence on a host of local, state, and federal funding sources, increases values consensus within schools. Thus, a tendency for states to increase their percentage of school funding at the expense of federal and local sources could promote communal organization.

Summary

Use of the commitment approach to school improvement is similar in two respects to use of the control strategy. First, evidence indicates that the commitment strategy is inconsistently and partially implemented in schools. In part, this stems from the newness of the approach, which leads to a lack of clear design principles. This lack of clarity is evident in Clune and White's (1988) study of site-based management, where patterns of implementation varied widely. But it is also evident in the implementation of career ladders, where research shows that this innovation has been seized upon by advocates of both the control and the commitment strategies of school improvement. More important, we know little about how the various elements of a commitment strategy can be combined. The work of Bryk and Driscoll (1988) suggests that when various elements of the commitment strategy are combined into a single index of school organization, the effects on teacher commitment and student achievement are powerful, but more studies are needed to examine the effects of simultaneously combining various forms of site-based management, job enrichment schemes, and patterns of collegiality in schools.

Second, the commitment strategy, like the control strategy, appears to work best when it is applied intensively. This is best illustrated in the case of collegiality, where only the most intensive forms of collegial support and interaction appeared to produce effects on the type of activities and decision making undertaken by teachers. At the same time, there appear to be important limits to the intensive application of the commitment strategy, particularly when it seeks to institutionalize communal forms of organization. Swidler's (1979) study suggests that too much extension of the teacher role, particularly toward the establishment of personal relationships with students, can create "burnout" among the most committed teachers. This is consistent with the literature on job design in business and industry, which cautions against making jobs too demanding on employees (Porter et al., 1975). An important theme for future research should be to assess whether a point of diminishing returns is reached in which efforts to build teacher commitment instead increase teacher fatigue.

In addition, the question of whether a commitment strategy leads to improved schools deserves more thorough analysis. The studies reviewed here demonstrate rather persuasively that teachers' commitment to schooling can be affected by increasing their influence in school decisions, by raising levels of collegiality, and by extending their roles. What is less clear is the extent to which any of these design strategies affect the quality of teaching and increase student achievement. What is largely missing from the literature on teacher commitment are the kinds of studies by those interested in the implementation of staff development programs in direct instruction. Although it makes sense to assume that teachers who bring more energy to the classroom and feel more efficacious in it will perform better, direct evidence on how collegiality and increased participation affect teaching practices is weak. A study by Ashton and Webb (1986), which attempted to trace the complex pattern of causal relationships leading through school organization to teachers' feelings of efficacy and then to the effects of teacher efficacy on teaching behaviors and student achievement, is useful. But this study demonstrated only inconsistent effects of teacher efficacy on teaching behavior and student achievement (Chap. 5). More research, using an expanded set of commitment variables, is needed to address the consequences of a commitment strategy for teaching and learning.

CONCLUSION: TOWARD A THEORY OF
ORGANIZATIONAL DESIGN IN SCHOOLS

The evidence reviewed here suggests that both the commitment and control strategies can lead to improved student outcomes, but that neither approach is consistently implemented in most schools. This should not come as a surprise, because the approaches developed here are abstract models. Although it would be interesting and informative to investigate the validity of these models as taxonomies of organizations, decades of organization research suggest that there is little reason to expect ideal types based in theory to be observed in pure form in practice (e. g., Pugh, Hinings, & Hickson, 1969). As in other complex organizations, traditions of practice, environmental pressures, and community settings hinder the development of preferred or consistent design strategies in schools.

As a result, it seems more appropriate for future research to advance from a stage in which school organization and effectiveness are discussed in terms of abstract models or taxonomies to a stage in which researchers investigate subsidiary issues that would inform the development of organization design principles for schools. To summarize the results of this literature review and extend the ideas in it, I conclude with a discussion of four such issues that can be used to guide future research.

The Nature of Teaching as an Organizational Technology

The discussion in this paper began with the assumption that different conceptions of teaching lead to different patterns of organizing. An immediate implication of this observation is that the nature of teaching is not fixed and immutable but rather varies across organizational settings. Indeed, the research reviewed here confirms this assumption. In some settings, for example competency-based instructional programs, there was evidence that teachers viewed their tasks as routine (Bullough et al., 1984), whereas in other settings, for example the complex and individualized classrooms studied by the Stanford group (Cohen et al., 1979), teachers apparently were confronted with complex decisions that required support and interaction with colleagues.

Few discussions of teaching recognize this variability or consider how task conceptions are embedded in the social organization of schools. This is especially true of the literature on teaching as a profession, where it is assumed that practitioners always view teaching as a complex and nonroutine task. But it is time to move beyond this decontextualized view of teaching and to begin to formulate hypotheses about the conditions within classrooms that make the task of teaching more or less complex.

A useful starting point is the work of the Stanford group, in which the materials used in classrooms (i. e., the number of different reading texts) and the grouping patterns in classrooms (i. e., the number of different reading groups in operation) combined to affect the complexity of teacher decision making. This insight connects the work on teachers as decision makers to the work of Barr and Dreeben (1983) and others who have studied the social organization of learning in classrooms. What is needed are studies that test the assumption that materials and grouping practices in classrooms affect teachers' perceptions of the complexity of teaching tasks, and research that attempts to discover how other contextual features (e. g., the types of students served in classrooms, the subject matter taught, or the grade level of instruction) affect teachers' conceptions of task.

The Relationship of Teaching Tasks to Design Features

There is also a need to examine the relationship between the nature of teaching tasks and organization design features in schools. Here again the work of the Stanford group (Cohen et al., 1979) is pioneering. This research found that the organization of classrooms into a complex technical form led to the development of organic forms of management. But more studies are needed to confirm these results. In addition, theorists often argue that technical forms and management forms must be matched for an organization to be effective. This kind of thinking leads to the prediction that schools in which classrooms require complex teacher decision making but that lack organic patterns of management will be less effective than similar schools that have organic management. This kind of theorizing requires complex research designs that go beyond a simple analysis of relationships between types of teacher decision making and patterns of school management to consider the interaction of teacher decision making, organization form, and school effectiveness. In organization theory, pioneering work of this sort was done in the 1960s by Woodward (1965). However, similar theories have yet to be tested in educational organizations.

It is interesting that the assertion that organizations adapt their management form to the type of technology they operate may explain why some forms of organic management are unstable in schools. To the extent that teachers conceive of their tasks as routine, as the evidence collected by Bullough et al. (1984) suggests they can, organization theory suggests little rationale for collegiality or other intensive forms of decision support. Perhaps this explains the inherent instability of collegial groups and teams noted by the Stanford group (Cohen et al., 1979). It also suggests that organic forms of management may not enhance instructional effectiveness across all conditions of classroom organization. In fact, when the technology of instruction is routinized, as it is in many behavioristic instructional systems that have tightly specified curriculum hierarchies and tie student progress to testing, a mechanistic and control-oriented strategy may be appropriate and lead to increased instructional effectiveness.

The hypothesis also suggests that organizational arrangements that are control based are not well-suited to the management of schools that require teachers to make complex decisions about instruction. In fact, it makes sense to assume that when teachers view their teaching tasks as complex and nonroutine, they would also report that control-based strategies of organization design were ineffective. Thus, just as organic designs may be inappropriate and unstable in some circumstances, mechanistic approaches to school design can be expected to be ineffective and to promote teacher resistance under certain circumstances.

The Relationship of Organization Design to Classroom Outcomes

Still a third line of research is needed to clarify the relationships between characteristics of school organization, teacher commitment, and classroom outcomes. Research on the effects of organization structure on teacher commitment variables is widely scattered, as the review indicates, and much of the recent dialogue about the negative effects of bureaucratic controls in schools and the positive effects of organic designs is based on impressionistic evidence or research using simple methodological designs. More careful studies, based on explicit theoretical conceptions, are needed. For example, it would seem useful to attempt to replicate studies found in the job design literature or to explicitly test other theories of job motivation in educational settings.

This involves two problems. First, there is a need to conceptualize the organizational structure of schools and to explore how the jobs of teachers can be enriched. For example, common and standardized questionnaires about job characteristics from the job design literature (see, e.g., Miner, 1980, chap. 9) could be used to measure aspects of job autonomy, responsibility, and variety, and to assess the extent to which various alternative structural designs in schools increase or decrease these characteristics in the roles performed by teachers and students. Also, there is a need to ascertain the extent to which job characteristics and other school design features affect commitment outcomes such as teacher efficacy, satisfaction, engagement, and sense of cohesiveness.

Second, especially critical for commitment theorists, is the need to examine how increases in worker commitment affect those teacher and student behaviors in classrooms that in turn affect student outcomes. Ashton and Webb (1986) have done pioneering work in this area, but it is limited to teacher efficacy. The problem for future researchers will be to specify observable teacher and student behaviors or mental schema that produce improved teacher and student performance to see if these are systematically affected by levels of teacher commitment. As a start, it is reasonable to begin with teacher and student behaviors discussed in process-product research on teaching, because this conceptual model at least provides a set of variables related to increased basic skills performance. More work will have to wait for new conceptions of teaching and learning.

There is also a need for further work on the effects of bureaucratic control strategies on teaching and learning. Although much research supports the assumption that strategies of curriculum alignment, competency-based instructional management, and intensive in-service programs on direct instruction affect teacher and student behaviors associated with increased basic skills achievement, more research is needed to examine whether these behavioristic and control-oriented strategies can equally affect higher order thinking and problem solving among students.

Conditions for Successful Implementation

Researchers should adopt an "open systems" perspective on organizational design and study how the successful implementation of a design strategy is constrained by several factors. One of these factors is the set of dependency relationships schools have with agencies in their environment. The research by Fuller and Izu (1986), for example, demonstrates that the presence of multiple sources of funding in many schools prevents the formation of a unified value system, an important element of organic management. Moreover, the active regulation of states, especially those operating with a control strategy for school improvement, will affect the ability of local schools to develop organizational designs of their own choosing. More research on how environmental conditions and policy decisions affect organization designs is needed, as is more research on how schools can free themselves of environmental constraints in order to pursue their own design strategies. Here, research comparing magnet or private schools, which are free of some constraints, with other public schools might prove useful.

Finally, theories of school design need to consider how design variables interact with the personal characteristics of teachers to produce commitment outcomes. For example, Walton's (1980) studies of "high commitment" work systems in industrial settings suggest that a commitment strategy of organization design not only enhances worker commitment, but also depends critically on high worker commitment for its success. A related point is found in research on job design, which shows that not all workers prefer to work in enriched jobs (Miner, 1980). As a result, successful work restructuring efforts in industry have necessarily been accompanied by intensive recruitment efforts that carefully screen employees (Walton, 1980).

Those who advocate the simultaneous restructuring of schools and professionalization of teaching have not fully appreciated these findings. Although many are aware that failure to implement a commitment strategy of organization design can discourage professionalized teachers, few have given attention to the idea that the success of the commitment strategy depends on recruiting particular kinds of teachers and on experienced teachers' reactions. Based on research in business and industry, and on the findings of research reported here, not all of today's teaching force should be expected to react uniformly and favorably to a commitment strategy. Thus, research that identifies the characteristics of teachers who thrive in organic settings would be useful, not only to bring educational studies in line with more general theories of organizational behavior, but also to guide future recruitment efforts in the teaching profession.

Conclusion

The research reviewed here establishes a new and complex agenda for future research on school organization and effectiveness. This agenda arises from consideration of organization design strategies being advocated in the educational policy environment. If researchers are to provide information relevant to practice, it follows that they need to design research capable of evaluating these new design strategies. The research reviewed here and the discussion of needed future research suggest a host of issues that need to be examined in this new agenda and provide a conceptual framework for developing theories of organizational design for schools.

REFERENCES

Airasian, P. W. (1987). State mandated testing and educational reform: Context and consequences. *American Journal of Education, 95,* 393–412.

Alexander, K. L., & Pallas, A. M. (1984). Curriculum reform and school performance: An evaluation of the "New Basics." *American Journal of Education, 92,* 391–420.

Anderson, C. S. (1982). The search for school climate: A review of the research. *Review of Educational Research, 52,* 368–420.

Ashton, P. T., & Webb, R. B. (1986). *Making a difference: Teachers' sense of efficacy and student achievement.* New York: Longman.

Bacharach, S. B., Bauer, S., & Shedd, J. B. (1986). The work environment and school reform. *Teachers College Record, 88,* 241–256.

Barr, R., & Dreeben, R. (1983). *How schools work.* Chicago: University of Chicago Press.

Berliner, D. C. (1986). In search of the expert pedagogue. *Educational Researcher, 15,* 5–13.

Bidwell, C. (1965). The school as a formal organization. In J. G. March (Ed.), *Handbook of organizations.* Chicago: Rand McNally.

Bird, T., & Little, J. W. (1985). *Instructional leadership in eight secondary schools.* Boulder: Center for Action Research.

Block, J. H. & Burns, R. B. (1976). Mastery learning. In L. S. Shulman (Ed.), *Review of research in education* (chap. 1). Itasca, IL: Peacock.

Brophy, J. E., & Evertson, C. (1976). *Learning from teaching: A developmental perspective.* Boston: Allyn and Bacon.

Bryk, A. S., & Driscoll, M. E. (1988). *An empirical investigation of the school as community.* Chicago: University of Chicago, Department of Education.

Bullough, R. V., Gitlin, A. D., & Goldstein, S. L. (1984). Ideology, teacher role, and resistance. *Teachers College Record, 86,* 339–358.

Burns, T., & Stalker, G. M. (1961). *The management of innovation.* London: Tavistock.

Carnegie Task Force on Teaching as a Profession (1986). *A nation prepared: Teachers for the 21st century.* New York: Carnegie Forum on Education and the Economy.

Carter, L. F. (1984). The sustaining effects study of compensatory education. *Educational Researcher, 13,* 4–13.

Clune, W., & White, P. A. (1988). *School-based management: Institutional variation, implementation, and issues for further research.* Madison, WI: Center for Policy Research in Education.

Clune, W., with White, P., & Patterson, J. (1988). *The implementation and effects of high school graduation requirements: First steps toward curricular reform.* Madison, WI: Center for Policy Research in Education.

Cohen, E. G. (1986). On the sociology of the classroom. In J. Hannaway & M. Lockheed (Eds.), *The contributions of the social sciences to educational policy and practice: 1965–1985* (pp. 127–162). Berkeley: McCutchan.

Cohen, E. G., Deal, T. E., Meyer, J. W., & Scott, W. R. (1979). Technology and teaming in the elementary school. *Sociology of Education, 52,* 20–33.

Cohen, S. A. (1987). Instructional alignment. Searching for a magic bullet. *Educational Researcher, 16,* 16–20.

Coladarci, T., & Gage, N. L. (1984). Effects of a minimal intervention on teacher behavior and student achievement. *American Educational Research Journal, 21,* 539–556.

Conley, S. C., Schmidle, T., & Shedd, J. B. (1988). Teacher participation in the management of school systems. *Teachers College Record, 90,* 259–280.

Cooley, W. W., & Leinhardt, G. (1980). The instructional dimensions study. *Educational Evaluation and Policy Analysis, 2,* 7–26.

Darling-Hammond, L., & Wise, A. E. (1985). Beyond standardization: State standards and school improvement. *Elementary School Journal, 85,* 315–335.

Dornbusch, S. M., & Scott, W. R. (1975). *Evaluation and the exercise of authority.* San Francisco: Jossey Bass.

Edmonds, R. (1979). Some schools work and more can. *Social Policy, 9,* 28–32.

Floden, R. E., Porter, A. C., Alford, L. E., Freeman, D. J., Irwin, S., Schmidt, W. H., & Schwille, J.R. (1988). Instructional leadership at the district level: A closer look at autonomy and control. *Educational Administration Quarterly, 24,* 96–124.

Fuller, B., & Izu, J. A. (1986). Explaining school cohesion: What shapes the organizational beliefs of teachers? *American Journal of Education, 94,* 501–535.

Furhman, S., Clune, W. H., & Elmore, R. F. (1988). Research on education reform: Lessons on the implementation of policy. *Teachers College Record, 90,* 237–257.

Good, T., & Grouws, D. (1979). The Missouri Mathematics Effectiveness Project: An experimental study in fourth-grade mathematics classrooms. *Journal of Educational Psychology, 71,* 335–362.

Goodlad, J. I. (1984). *A place called school: Prospects for the future.* New York: McGraw-Hill.

Hart, A. W. (1985). *Formal teacher supervision by teachers in a career ladder.* Paper presented at the American Educational Research Association, Chicago.

Hart, A. W. (1987). A career ladder's effect on teacher career and work attitudes. *American Educational Research Journal, 24,* 479–504.

Hatfield, R. C., Blackman, C. A., Claypool, C., & Mester, F. (1985). *Extended professional roles of teacher leaders in the public schools.* East Lansing, MI: Michigan State University, Department of Teacher Education.

Hunter, M. (1983). *Mastery teaching.* El Segundo, CA: TIP Publications.

Intili, J. (1977). Structural conditions in a school that promote reflective decision-making. *Dissertation Abstracts International, 38.*

Johnston, P., Allington, R., & Afflerbach, P. (1985). The congruence of classroom and remedial instruction. *Elementary School Journal, 85,* 465–477.

Kirst, M. W. (1988). Recent state education reform in the United States: Looking backward and forward. *Educational Administration Quarterly, 24,* 319–328.

Leithwood, K. A., & Montgomery, D. J. (1982). The role of the elementary school principal in program improvement. *Review of Educational Research, 52,* 309–339.

Lieberman, A. (1988, February). Expanding the school leadership team. *Educational Leadership, 45,* 4–8.

Little, J. W. (1982). Norms of collegiality and experimentation: Workplace conditions of school success. *American Educational Research Journal, 19,* 325–340.

Lortie, D. (1975). *Schoolteacher.* Chicago: University of Chicago Press.

Malen, B., & Ogawa, R. T. (1988). Professional-patron influence on site-based governance councils: A confounding case study. *Educational Evaluation and Policy Analysis, 10,* 251–270.

March, J. G., & Olsen, J. P. (1976). *Ambiguity and choice in organizations.* Bergen, Norway: Universitetforlaget.

McDill, E. L., Natriello, G., & Pallas, A. M. (1985). Raising standards and retaining students: The impact of the reform recommendations on potential dropouts. *Review of Educational Research, 55,* 415–435.

Metz, M. H. (1986). *Different by design: The context and characteristics of three magnet schools.* New York: Routledge & Kegan Paul.

Meyer, J. W., & Rowan, B. (1977). Institutionalized organizations: Formal structure as myth and ceremony. *American Journal of Sociology, 83,* 340–363.

Meyer, J. W., & Rowan, B. (1978). The structure of educational organizations. In M. W. Meyer and Associates, *Environments and organizations.* San Francisco: Jossey Bass.

Miner, J. B. (1980). *Theories of organizational behavior.* Hinsdale, IL: Dryden Press.

Miskel, C., McDonald, D., & Bloom, S. (1983). Structural and expectancy linkages within schools and organizational effectiveness. *Educational Administration Quarterly, 19,* 49–82.

Miskel, C., & Ogawa, R. (1988). Work motivation, job satisfaction, and climate. In N. Boyan (Ed.), *Handbook of educational administration* (pp. 279–304). New York: Longman.

Mitchell, D. E., Kerchner, C. T., Erck, W., & Pryor, G. (1981). The impact of collective bargaining on school management and policy. *American Journal of Education, 89,* 147–188.

Murphy, J., Hallinger, P., & Mesa, R. P. (1985). School effectiveness: Checking progress and assumptions and developing a role for the state and federal government. *Teachers College Record, 86,* 615–641.

National Governors' Association. (1986). *Time for results.* Washington, DC: Author.

Natriello, G. (1984). Teachers' perceptions of the frequency of evaluations and assessments of their effort and effectiveness. *American Educational Research Journal, 21,* 579–604.

Natriello, G., & Dornbusch, S. M. (1980–1981). Pitfalls in the evaluation of teachers by principals. *Administrator's Notebook, 29,* 1–4.

Newman, F. M., Rutter, R. A., & Smith, M. S. (1985). *Exploratory analysis of high school teacher climate.* Madison, WI: Wisconsin Center for Education Research.

Passow, A. H. (1989). Present and future directions in school reform. In T. G. Sergiovanni & J. H. Moore (Eds.), *Schooling for tomorrow: Directing reforms to issues that count* (pp. 13–39). Boston: Allyn and Bacon.

Pellegrin, R. J. (1976). Schools as work settings. In R. Dubin (Ed.), *Handbook of work, organizations, and society.* Skokie, IL: Rand McNally.

Perrow, C. (1967). A framework for the comparative analysis of organizations. *American Sociological Review, 32,* 194–208.

Porter, L. W., Lawler, E. E., & Hackman, J. R. (1975). *Behavior in organizations.* New York: McGraw-Hill.

Pugh, D., Hinings, C. R., & Hickson, D. J. (1969). An empirical taxonomy of structures of work organizations. *Administrative Science Quarterly, 14,* 115–126.

Purkey, S. C., & Smith, M. S. (1983). Effective schools: A review. *Elementary School Journal, 83,* 427–452.

Robbins, P. (1986). The Napa-Vacaville Follow-Through Project: Qualitative outcomes, related procedures, and implications for practice. *Elementary School Journal, 87,* 139–151.

Rosenholtz, S. J. (1985). Effective schools: Interpreting the evidence. *American Journal of Education, 93,* 352–388.

Rosenholtz, S. J. (1987). Education reform strategies: Will they increase teacher commitment? *American Journal of Education, 95,* 534–562.

Rosenshine, B. (1983). Teaching functions in instructional programs. *Elementary School Journal, 83,* 335–352.

Rowan, B. (1986). *Rationality and reality in instructional management: Results from a survey of school districts in the Far West.* Paper presented at the annual meeting of the American Educational Research Association, San Francisco, CA.

Rowan, B., Bossert, S. T., & Dwyer, D. C. (1983). Effective schools: A cautionary note. *Educational Researcher, 12,* 24–31.

Rowan, B., Edelstein, R., & Leal, A. (1983). *Pathways to excellence: What school districts are doing to improve instruction.* San Francisco: Far West Laboratory for Educational Research and Development.

Rutter, M., Maughan, B., Mortimore, P., Ouston, J., & Smith, A. (1979). *Fifteen thousand hours: Secondary schools and their effects on children.* Cambridge, MA: Harvard University Press.

Schlechty, P. C. (1989). Career ladders: A good idea going awry. In T. J.

Sergiovanni & J. H. Moore (Eds.), *Schooling for tomorrow: Directing reforms at issues that count*. Boston: Allyn and Bacon.

Shulman, L. S. (1987). Knowledge and teaching. *Harvard Educational Review, 57,* 1–22.

Sparks, G. M. (1986). The effectiveness of alternative training activities in changing teaching practices. *American Educational Research Journal, 23,* 217–226.

Stallings, J., & Krasavage, E. (1986). Program implementation and student achievement in a four-year Madeline Hunter Follow-Through Project. *Elementary School Journal, 86,* 117–138.

Swidler, A. (1979). *Organization without authority: Dilemmas of social control in free schools*. Cambridge, MA: Harvard University Press.

Tucker, M. S. (1988, February). Peter Drucker, knowledge work, and the structure of schools. *Educational Leadership, 45,* 44–47.

Turner, A. N., & Lawrence, P. R. (1964). *Industrial jobs and the worker*. Boston: Harvard University.

U.S. Department of Education. (1988). *High school and beyond administrator teacher survey (1984): Data file users manual*. Washington, DC: U.S. Department of Education.

Walton, R. E. (1980). Establishing and maintaining high commitment work systems. In J. R. Kimberly, R. H. Miles, and Associates, *The organization life cycle*. San Francisco: Jossey Bass.

Weick, K. E. (1976). Educational organizations as loosely coupled systems. *Administrative Science Quarterly, 21,* 1–19.

Wise, A. E., Darling-Hammond, L., McLaughlin, M., & Bernstein, H. T. (1985). Teacher evaluation: A study of effective practices. *Elementary School Journal, 86,* 61–121.

Woodward, J. (1965). *Industrial organization: Theory and practice*. London: Oxford University Press.

Zahorik, J. A. (1987). Teachers' collegial interactions: An exploratory study. *Elementary School Journal, 87,* 385–396.

IV.
EDUCATION IN THE PROFESSIONS

Chapter 8

Feminist Critiques in the Professions

NEL NODDINGS
Stanford University

There is a lot of talk these days about the professionalization of teaching. To understand feminist criticism of the professionalization movement, it is helpful to know something about the impact of feminism on other professions. It is also important to recognize that feminism is not a unitary movement. There are several ways to categorize feminists and feminist theory (see Offen, 1988), and critiques depend, at least in part, on the perspectives taken.

Two systems of categorization will be useful in this review. Offen (1988) distinguishes between *individualist* and *relational* feminism. Individualist feminism has often been associated with *liberal* feminism—a program that aims mainly at securing for women rights and privileges equal to those of men. However, the individualist form of argument can be found in political orientations other than liberalism. Primarily, individualist arguments aim at a gender-free ideal and emphasize abstract concepts of individual rights (Offen, 1988, p. 136). In contrast, relational feminism often advocates gender sensitivity and emphasizes experience, needs, and responsibility. Both kinds of argument will show up in the review of feminist critiques.

Kristeva (1982) has identified three attitudes or generations of feminism. (These need not be thought of as historical, although they can be identified in history; an individual woman or group can represent in life or thought any one of the generations.) In the first generation, women seek equality with men; this is the typical liberal position. In the second, they embrace their own special qualities and reject uncritical assimilation into the male world; the emphasis here is on moving the best female qualities into the public world. In the third, women critique what they sought

My thanks to Courtney Cazden and Madeleine Grumet for helpful comments on the first draft of this chapter.

393

and accomplished in the first two phases and seek solutions that arise out of a careful synthesis of old and new questions. Critiques typical of each generation have emerged in the professions.

In this review, I will look at law, nursing, education (at the university level), and school teaching. Law is chosen as a paradigmatic profession that has a growing feminist component. Nursing is chosen for its parallels to school teaching. Critiques in both professions are useful in analyzing the professionalization of teaching. In all of these critiques we will find a deep distrust of professionalism as it currently appears and considerable ambivalence about women's participation in professions. One theme was set by Virginia Woolf in 1938 (1938/1966); she asked

Do we wish to join that procession, or don't we? On what terms shall we join the procession? Above all, where is it leading us, the procession of educated men? . . . What is this "civilization"? What are these ceremonies and why should we take part in them? What are these professions and why should we make money out of them? Where in short is it leading us, the procession of the sons of educated men? (pp. 62–63)

D. Smith (1987) expresses well reasons for distrust and ambivalence in her critique of contemporary sociology. She says, "The organization of professional knowledge is more than a guarantee of standards, more than a monopoly of knowledge and skill, it is a monopolization of control within a dominant class" (p. 217). This concern will be heard throughout the critiques that follow. It is part of a larger concern to transform professional life in light of values and attitudes traditionally associated with women.

LAW

In 1960, only 3% of lawyers were women (Rhode, 1988), and it was not until 1972 that all accredited law schools admitted women. By the mid-1980s, women made up 14% of practicing lawyers, although fewer than 5% of the partners in the largest firms were women, and female lawyers earned an average of 40% less than male lawyers (Rhode, 1988). These figures reveal both dramatic progress and the need for more to be done.

As more women have become lawyers and law professors, the practice and theory of law have become targets for transformation. Topics of interest to women have become important areas of discourse and litigation. New critiques of legal theory and the language of legal discourse have emerged. A different attitude toward the profession and professionalization has been articulated. Legal education has been criticized scathingly, and a feminist pedagogy is developing.

Challenges to Legal Theory

Feminist criticism in legal theory is an amalgam of feminism and a movement in law known as critical legal studies (CLS). Feminists who went to law school were often attracted to CLS (Menkel-Meadow, 1988) but soon found that women's issues demanded a different focus and that the feminist desire for transformation had a different origin. Whereas CLS concentrated on the inherent inadequacy of theories of rights and other conceptual issues, feminists wanted to focus on the condition of women under the law. Feminist critique, says Menkel-Meadow, "originates not only in conceptual constructs but in experience—in *being* dominated, not just thinking about domination" (p. 61).

CLS theorists (Gordon, 1982; Schlegel, 1984) anticipated a clash over the role of rights in promoting better conditions for oppressed groups, and the tension between activism (which almost demands the use of rights language to achieve its ends) and transformational theory remains high. This tension runs though all of feminism and is central to debate in both the disciplines and the professions. On the one hand, many feminists agree with CLS theorists that there is something fundamentally wrong with the language of rights and justice (DuBois, Dunlap, Gilligan, MacKinnon & Menkel-Meadow, 1985; Gilligan, 1982; Noddings, 1984; Olsen, 1984); on the other hand, feminist legal theorists and practitioners must use existing law to remedy the wrongs currently suffered by women. (For some insight on this issue and for a historical and personal account of the development of "feminist jurisprudence," see Menkel-Meadow, 1988.)

The debate over rights is part of a larger controversy in contemporary feminism. Feminists in the 19th century disagreed on matters of egalitarianism. Elizabeth Cady Stanton, for example, took a strong egalitarian position, insisting that women should have the vote and that divorce law should be reformed (P. Smith, 1970). Her argument (see DuBois, Dunlap, et al., 1985, p. 65) was that women and men are basically the same and that the rights of men obviously should be conferred on women. Catherine Beecher (1871) and Nette Brown (see DuBois, Dunlap, et al., 1985; P. Smith, 1970), however, argued that women are importantly different from men and that their welfare requires a different education and different position in public life. These arguments illustrate the difference between individualist and relational feminism, and they also point up the possibility of women living in the same historical time but in two different feminist generations or attitudes. The arguments between Stanton and Beecher and Brown were forerunners of the current sameness-difference debate that MacKinnon (1987) finds so unproductive. Whichever way one cuts it, MacKinnon insists, women get the short end of things. If they are the same as men, then they are inferior men (Nette Brown also argued this); but if they are different, they are different from men, so man is still the standard.

The paradox inherent in the sameness-difference approach illustrates the depth and extent of domination in our social structures. Just as men have dominated, and still dominate, women, so the wealthy and better educated dominate the poor and less educated. Hierarchical structures serve the continuance of domination, and thus hierarchy has become a target of feminist reform efforts. Indeed, questions about the prevalent use of hierarchies and challenges to their legitimacy mark every form of feminism (see Offen, 1988, p. 152). I will say more about such questions and challenges when I discuss legal education, other professions, and a feminist critique of teacher professionalization, where objections to hierarchy are highlighted.

Arguments about language appear in feminist legal theory as they do in feminist theory in general. Spender (1980) and Daly (1973, 1978, 1984) have argued that men have seized and kept the power of naming for themselves. The result has been that women are held to a male standard, encounter difficulty in articulating their own experience, and are simply left out of descriptions (and prescriptions) purporting to be universal. Bender (1988) discusses the "reasonable person" standard in tort law as an example of male naming and the implicit male norm underlying it. Noting that the standard was originally stated in terms of a "reasonable man," she suggests that the change in words from "man" to "person" does not eliminate sexism in the concept. If the generic use of "man" failed to capture universal experience, so does "person" when the entire body of legal thought surrounding the notion of a "reasonable person" has grown out of male experience and has been articulated by male theorists. Female experience simply disappears.

Arguing that verbal substitutions designed to eliminate sexism often perpetuate or embed it, Bender seeks an alternative that challenges the underlying model. She asks, "Should our standard of care focus on 'reason and caution' or something else?" (p. 22). Bender and several other feminist legal theorists (Frug, 1979, 1985; Minow, 1987; Rhode, 1988; Scales, 1986) suggest that *care* in the sense of concern and responsiveness should play a greater role in both law and professional education. Care as caution and prudence is typically a male orientation; care as concern and responsiveness traditionally has been associated with females. Challenges that attack fundamental notions such as the reasonable person standard clearly threaten the foundations of traditional legal theory.

In its current emphasis on care and response, feminist legal theory has been influenced by the work of Gilligan (1982). This influence can be traced to at least two interests that Gilligan and legal theorists hold in common: abortion and moral theory. Feminist legal theorists have been deeply involved in issues of special concern to women—abortion, child care, pornography, rape, sexual harassment, domestic violence, equity in the workplace (see MacKinnon, 1987)—and they have been concerned about the moral foundations of law.

Common interests led to a symposium (sponsored as the 1984 James McCormick Mitchell Lecture at the law school of the State University of New York, Buffalo) in which Gilligan, DuBois (a historian), and several legal theorists discussed feminism, moral values, and law. In this conversation it became clear that the renewed emphasis on relational feminism holds considerable attraction for feminist legal theorists. Menkel-Meadow, referring to Gilligan's (1982) description of Amy and Jake's moral thinking, asks, "What would the legal system look like if Amy had devised it, either alone or with Jake's help?" (DuBois, Dunlap, et al., 1985, p. 53). Menkel-Meadow's question echoes a basic theme of contemporary feminist legal theory.

Although the Mitchell Lecture symposium reveals interest in and respect for relational feminism, it also contains the concern expressed repeatedly by MacKinnon. This concern centers on the origin and nature of the "different voice" described by Gilligan. MacKinnon traces the different voice (if one exists) to oppression and subservience and fears that whatever good it has to express will be denigrated by its very difference, that is, by its association with females (DuBois, Dunlap, et al., 1985, pp. 74–75). She would prefer to argue for the values Gilligan locates in female discourse without ascribing them to women. There seems to be an inconsistency, however, in MacKinnon's agreeing with Gilligan that the values described in *A Different Voice* are positive but at the same time insisting that women do not know what their values really are because they have not been allowed to articulate them. MacKinnon's focus is on power and its redistribution. Many other feminist legal theorists want to be sure that the values traditionally associated with women are not lost as power is distributed more equally.

Some legal theorists concerned about women's issues retain the language of rights but introduce a relational emphasis. Goldstein (1988), in his analysis of abortion, argues that abandoning the language of rights would place women at great risk in a system of law in which "the discourse of rights dominates to the exclusion of all else" (p. 33). He prefers to work within the standard discourse but to define a notion of *relational* rights. From his relational perspective, the fetus must be considered part of a dyad, and the quality of the relation is paramount in deciding whether an abortion should be performed. Goldstein's argument is an attempt to incorporate the relational perspective of care and responsibility into the traditional discourse of rights, caution, and prudence. He argues that government must respect relational rights and "dyadic autonomy." In supporting Roe v. Wade, Goldstein stresses that "mother-love" is so fundamental to child welfare that women must be entrusted with the right to choose for the dyad. He claims, "The dyadic approach has the advantage of not requiring a radical and general reevaluation of the language of rights and individualism in all spheres in order to apply to procreation" (p. 92), but whether such an approach will satisfy those who see fundamental flaws in the discourse of rights or an irrevocable connection between rights and individualism remains to be seen.

Discussion of abortion is part of a larger concentration on issues of particular importance to women. Dunlap (in DuBois, Dunlap, et al., 1985) organizes these issues into four clusters: physical health, money, violence-empowerment, and creativity. Women in law are concerned with all of these clusters, and the categories are not discrete. Matters of money affect matters of health, and violence is clearly related to all three other categories. Underlying concern in all four clusters is a basic moral theme: "The idea that harm and pain and hurt that are gender-correlated must end, must be prevented, must be remedied" (Dunlap, in DuBois, Dunlap, et al., 1985, p. 15). At bottom, the feminist movement in law is concerned with a sweeping reevaluation of moral theory and its connection to law.

Legal Education

Like women educators in other professions, female law professors have to decide between assimilation and transformation (or alteration). Clearly seeing some benefit in the latter, Rhode (1988) says,

Concerns about care, context, cooperation, and relationships historically associated with women have been undervalued in professional cultures, and changes in that value structure need to begin in professional school and continue in professional organizations. (pp. 1205–1206)

The changes implied by a focus on the concerns listed by Rhode involve form, content, and pedagogy, and most feminists seek practical steps to advance their program. CLS theorists have led an attack on hierarchy that some feminist critics see as impractical. Kennedy (1983), for example, has recommended revolutionary changes in law school: dismantling the system of elite and lower echelon schools, rotating professors among schools, providing equal pay for all employees. Although feminist critics often sympathize with Kennedy's critique of hierarchy (Hantzis, 1988; Menkel-Meadow, 1988), they note that his proposals have not been enacted and that some of his recommendations and comments are themselves elitist. Hantzis points out that Kennedy relies almost solely on "an objective and exhaustive intellectual stance." His ideal law student is "elitist and male." (*Literally*, Hantzis says in a footnote, "When Kennedy speaks of the liberal idealist and Marxist students, the pronouns are female. With the 'exceptional' student, however, the pronouns are male" [p. 160].)

Feminist legal theorists want both to use the system for the betterment of women and to transform it for the benefit of everyone, and this ambiguous attitude shows up in their project to build a feminist pedagogy. As part of their practical program they attack particular features of hierarchy—for example, those that grow out of false dichotomies such as rational-emotional, analytical-intuitive, impartial-partial, hard-soft. These dichotomies are used to associate males with preferred qualities and females with inferior qualities (Menkel-Meadow, 1988; Olsen, 1984). Exposure of the faults of hierarchy is part of feminist pedagogy, but preparation for law is still preparation for hierarchy.

Feminists are particularly concerned with the gender hierarchy, and feminist legal theorists are working to expose patriarchal assumptions built into supposedly neutral law (Rifkin, 1980). This effort involves an emphasis on topics of particular interest to women: abortion, marital abuse, property rights, rape. As Menkel-Meadow, MacKinnon, and others have pointed out, rape laws are notorious examples of the interests and power of patriarchy. According to these laws, rape occurs only on penetration. (The terror and pain a woman experiences are unimportant compared with the spoiling of property.) Further, even the possibility of rape as a legal verdict has depended on the victim's status. (A wife could not be raped, for example, because her body belonged to her husband; similarly, a woman of ill repute could not be raped, because her way of life gave tacit consent to such behavior.) These laws are gradually changing under the concerted attack of feminist legal theorists (see MacKinnon, 1987), but progress has been slow.

In addition to a new emphasis on topics of importance to women and attention to the moral foundations of law, feminist theorists urge reform in pedagogy. Theorists interested in humanistic perspectives on legal education and professionalism have similar concerns (Dvorkin, Himmelstein, & Lesnick, 1981). Indeed, many of the topics the humanists write about are central in feminist thinking: the need to maintain a personal identity while building a professional one, the importance of reciprocity in the professional/client relationship, the place of moral values in the practice of law.

Neither group has made revolutionary suggestions for classroom reform, although feminists have given more direct attention to the problem. Dvorkin et al. (1981) did not intend "to describe a humanistic legal education or to articulate the concrete changes that would be necessary to bring this perspective into the classroom" (p. 3). Rather, they tried to set a direction for the study of humanistic education and its bearing on law. As educators they face the same problems that theorists in professional education have encountered whenever attempts have been made to reform education from a humanistic perspective: a glutted curriculum with no apparent expendables; an entrenched ideology; a rigid structure of classes and credits; an archaic system of admission, prerequisites, and standardized testing that reaches into early elementary school; and a repugnant mode of evaluation that withstands almost any amount of tinkering and minor change.

On one level, humanism and feminism have much in common; on another, the gulf between them is enormous. As Rich (1979) points out, *humanism* is a word that has long been associated with and representative of masculine domination. A humanistic or liberal education has meant education for hierarchy, preparation for a man-centered professional world in which only a few are free to pursue self-fulfillment. The university, Rich says, is "above all a hierarchy" (p. 136), and questions raised much earlier by Virginia Woolf (1938/1966) are still pertinent today.

Feminist legal educators, therefore, draw on theories of feminist pedagogy rather than those of CLS or humanistic theories. (Examples often mentioned include Belenky, Clinchy, Goldberger, & Tarule, 1986; Bunch & Pollack, 1983; Culley & Portuges, 1985; Klein, 1987; Piercy, 1982; Rich, 1979.) Feminist pedagogy involves a shift from teacher to students as the center of attention; openness and dialogue; student-to-student talk; increased participation of students in the choice of questions, topics, and projects; more opportunities for direct contact in the field; variable modes of evaluation; more generous and direct help in learning; and a reluctance to grade on the basis of "natural" talent or test scores. Feminist law professors have begun to examine some of these issues with respect to law classrooms (Hantzis, 1988; Jaff, 1986; Pickard, 1983; Wildman, 1988).

Having convicted humanism of hypocrisy, feminists nevertheless espouse many humanistic goals for the professions and education, but they reject the tradition and its entrenchment in exclusivity and hierarchy. Theoretically, a reconciliation between humanists and feminists might be powerful, but such a pact could also be "tragic and dangerous," as Rich suggests. Many feminist legal theorists agree with Rich when she concludes, "Feminism is a criticism and subversion of *all* patriarchal thought and institutions—not merely those currently seen as reactionary and tyrannical" (p. 134). At some point reconciliation will be a goal, but it may have to be an outcome of reform, not a move contributing to reform.

Summary

Feminist thinking is clearly having an impact on legal theory. In a recent article in the *New York Times* (Lewin, 1988), Geoffrey Stone, Dean of Law at the University of Chicago, calls it "the most interesting intellectual movement in law in quite some time," and Stephen Gillers, New York University School of Law, says, "It's a reconstruction of legal theory. Ultimately, we're going to feel it through an avalanche of a thousand little decisions." It is pressing for a closer connection among law, justice, and care, for changes in tort law, for a framework that encompasses women's experience.

The impact on practice is not so great. MacKinnon (1987) documents the gains and losses women have incurred as a result of changes brought about by feminist legal maneuvers. Despite legislation ensuring equal pay, women still earn far less than men doing the same jobs. Changes in rape law have been made, but the rape rate is up, and the conviction rate is not. In part because of reforms feminists wanted, more women are now losing custody of their children. MacKinnon cites the laws on sexual harassment, domestic battery, and marital rape as a few exceptions to an otherwise bleak picture. Even the right to abortion remains tenuous and could be lost. (For a full account of these ups and downs, see MacKinnon, 1987.)

Finally, the impact on legal education seems so far to be minimal. The odd parody of Socratic teaching (the model is Professor Kingsfield) continues (Hantzis, 1988; Menkel-Meadow, 1988; Wildman, 1988), abated here and there by humanist or feminist teachers. Concern with ethics and moral theory may be increasing. Perhaps the most promising sign is that feminist legal theorists are well informed in feminist theory and that coalitions are forming across disciplines and professions. Feminists are exploring ways in which to redesign the classroom according to feminist vision. All feminist educators, not just feminist legal professors, face similar problems in redesigning professional preparation and redefining what it means to be a professional.

NURSING

In contrast to law, nursing has long been a woman's occupation. Women have not had the problem of breaking into a man's profession to become nurses, although in this country, at least, women of color have experienced difficulty becoming nurses (Reverby, 1987). A major problem for nurses has been, and still is, a collective one: how to get full professional recognition for nursing in the array of otherwise male-dominated professions. A second important problem is that of defining the profession according to its own internal standards when the "true" professions expect and press for a different kind of definition. Proposed solutions to these two great problems are often at odds with each other.

Nineteenth century conceptions of professionalism emphasized a dimension of altruism and service. Indeed commitment to service lay at the heart of professionalism, and even today professions espouse formally a dedication to their clients (Greenwood, 1957; Larson, 1977). But this century has seen a shift to power and privilege as the earmarks of professionalism (Larson, 1977). With the pursuit of power and prestige, professions have taken on characteristics inimical to service: hierarchies of power; less and less direct contact between professional and client; highly specialized languages; great monetary expenditures required in preparatory education; an increase in internal talk as contrasted to interaction with the larger community; and an overall exclusivity marked by racism, sexism, and classism (Sykes, 1987).

Nurses rarely have shown interest in becoming this sort of profession despite considerable pressure to do so. Today nursing theorists, influenced by feminism and the intrinsic demands of nursing, are involved in sophisticated projects to define nursing and nurse education in a way that maintains human caring as their central mission. Can a feisty "semiprofession" (Etzioni, 1969) define itself in a way that rejects major features of existing professions and still become a profession? This is the conflict nurses face.

Nursing and Feminist Theory

Nursing theory today is frankly influenced by feminist theory (see *Caring and Nursing: Explorations in the Feminist Perspectives,* 1988). Central to its development is the concept of human caring (Gaut, 1979; Leininger, 1984; Watson, 1979, 1985). Although caring construed as a set of activities has always been a defining feature of nursing (Reverby, 1987), the new wave of theory on caring draws directly on feminist analyses in psychology (Gilligan, 1982), philosophy (Grimshaw, 1986; Vetterling-Braggin, Elliston, & English, 1977), ethics (Hoagland, 1987; Noddings, 1984), political theory (Eisenstein, 1979; Ferguson, 1984; French, 1985; Jaggar, 1983), and theology (Daly, 1973, 1978; Ruether, 1983b). In introducing the Conference on Caring and Nursing (1988), Gaut called on the conferees as women and nurses to build not only a new profession but a new world.

Nurse theorists like Watson, Gaut, and Leininger emphasize the importance of relatedness and responsiveness in caring. Watson (1985) states as a basic assumption for the science of caring in nursing that "caring can be effectively demonstrated and practiced only interpersonally" (p. 8). This assumption contrasts sharply with the medical model's assumption that caring can be accomplished through technical means (see Watson, 1985).

Nurse theorists do not reject the medical model in its entirety; they endorse technical competence and the use of medical technology. But they strongly deny the completeness of the medical model and its centrality to nursing. For nurses, patients must be persons, and the nurse must attend to personal, emotional, and even spiritual needs as they are revealed in their interactions with patients.

Emphasis on the interpersonal nature of caring has sometimes led nurses into direct conflict with the medical establishment. Whereas nurses insist that they, as professionals, must spend more time with their patients to manage all aspects of their treatment and recovery, the American Medical Association (AMA) is pressing for a new hierarchy of medical technologists, each of whom will spend correspondingly less time with individual patients and attend to increasingly specialized tasks (Associated Press, 1988). Occasionally, exceptions to this trend are approved by the medical establishment, and nurses become part of care management teams in which they exercise considerable autonomy in patient care (Millenson, 1988). Although nurses express great satisfaction with such systems, planners admit that the systems are time consuming to implement. A tension remains between the medical model with its emphasis on curing and efficiency and the nursing model with its emphasis on caring and interpersonal effectiveness (MacPherson, 1983; J. Thompson, 1987).

The relationship between nursing and feminism has long been paradoxical, and the paradox highlights conflicts within feminist theory. Just as feminists have been torn between individualist and relational modes, nurses have faced the dilemma of exalting "the womanly character and service ethic of nursing while insisting on the right to act in their own self-interest" (Reverby, 1987, p. 121). Since the 1880s, when nursing leadership made its first organized attempt to gain control of the profession, this dilemma has plagued nursing.

Just as feminist theorists have sometimes rejected liberal or individualist feminism, nurses have often rejected it, and there is evidence that nursing's widespread avoidance of feminism is really a rejection of individualist positions (K. Miller, 1988). The paradox is foreshadowed in the life of Florence Nightingale. Today, Nightingale might be attracted to relational feminism. Her emphasis on caring and promoting the general welfare are central to the new wave of feminism. If she fell short, it would be in forgetting that feminists—*any* feminists—must give special attention to the status and condition of women. Here Nightingale's actual record is ambiguous, but she certainly failed to meet the (liberal) feminist standards of her own time. She had no great interest in women's suffrage or oppression (Welch, 1988). But Nightingale did hold strong convictions about women's capacities for thought and professional activity (Nightingale, 1859/1969; Yaros, 1988), and her writing on these topics echoes the accepted line in individualist feminism. A problem here is that we find this sort of thinking—that women have the same abilities as men and can succeed in the public world if they really try—in antifeminism as well as feminism. (Decter, 1983, is an example.) A feminist has to address the problem of women's oppression.

Another aspect of the historical conflict can be found in contemporary nursing theory and relational feminism. Although there is an obvious congruence between nursing's model of human caring and ethics of care in feminist theory, some nursing theorists (and some feminist theorists, too) worry about the renewed emphasis on service and caring. To emphasize caring is to invite further oppression and exploitation (Hoagland, 1987; Houston & Diller, 1987). Nurses work hard, and some of their work strongly resembles traditional women's work. Webster (1988) speaks of "the burden of caring as a palpable creeping exhaustion" (p. 199) and describes caring taken to extremes as a form of codependency. She also comments that "our ambivalence about caring is paralleled by our ambivalence about motherhood" (p. 195), but she points out (in agreement with Mitchell & Oakley, 1986) that this ambivalence may be healthier than a premature and perhaps misleading clarity.

It may be that feminist nurses, like feminist lawyers, are entering Kristeva's (1982) "third generation" of feminism, in which feminists sort through the goals and values of each preceding generation and construct a vigorous, new synthesis free from the earlier tests of orthodoxy. Affirmation of caring challenges the first generation; doubts about caring and self-sacrifice challenge the second generation. Perhaps a reaffirmation of caring in a context that promotes self-care will characterize the third. But, again, even this characterization fails to capture the vigorous diversity in contemporary feminist thought.

Like feminists in law, nurse feminists are concerned not only with theory but with the day-to-day problems of women, particularly women's health and exploitation. In an important sense, problems of caring are problems for women. About 75% of this country's care givers are women (Sommers & Shields, 1987), and many middle-aged and older women live in poverty as a direct result of the demands of care giving. This is an enormous and still growing problem, and it is one that requires public action. At the same time, it requires a dedication to the loving care of individuals that characterizes nursing at its best and that is described by current feminist theories of caring (Waerness, 1984).

Most care giving today is unpaid. If women were paid for their hours of care giving, the national bill for a year's care would run to around $10 billion (Ward, 1988). Because 97% of nurses are women, the unpaid care giving of their sisters heightens the conflict over caring. On the one hand, caring is central to nursing, and nurse theorists are developing models of professional nursing built on concepts of caring. On the other hand, caring has long been associated with unskilled "woman's work," and any profession that embraces it is automatically devalued (Finch & Groves, 1983).

Nurses are further distressed by their own role in modern medicine. As patients are no longer cared for in institutions, and out-patient clinics have grown up, more and more care must be done at home—by women (Glazer, 1984, 1988). Nurses, therefore, agonize over the burdens that are shifted onto other women. Here, again, the link between nursing and feminism is strong and obvious.

Feminist nursing theorists are also unhappy with the epistemic model that underlies medicine. Disavowing Cartesian dualisms, many now describe a concept of health that is "qualitative, idiosyncratic, and contextual" (S. Smith, 1988, p. 355). Feminists and feminist nurses not only want primary control of their own bodies (Daly, 1978), but they also seek epistemologies, metaphysics, and ethics that recognize the embodied nature of human existence (Belenky et al., 1986; Scheman, 1983; J. Smith, 1981; Watson, 1985; Zegans, 1987). In their emphasis on relatedness, fluid boundaries, and connection, nurse theorists are working toward a feminist theory of health (Frye, 1983; S. Smith, 1988).

Nursing Education

Conflict between the models of caring and medical science extends into nursing education. Here, too, technical models have been valued more highly than caring, and nurse educators have followed the trend set in other professions to require more years of training and to equate technical competence with nursing itself (Reverby, 1987). But changes are appearing. Papers have recently been presented on caring in nursing education (Sheston, 1988) and caring for nurses (Brockman, 1988; Keen, 1988). Watson's (1979, 1985) texts are frankly metaphysical and humanistic and draw important distinctions between medical science and the human caring central to nursing.

Nurse educators are also showing interest in feminist epistemologies and ways of knowing (Belenky et al., 1986; Harding & Hintikka, 1983). Blending recent feminist ideas with work on ways of knowing in nursing (Carper, 1978), Jacobs and Chinn (see K. Miller, 1988) have presented a model of nursing knowledge that draws on feminism, humanism, and nursing experience. Knowlden (1988), building on the work of Gilligan and Belenky et al., has presented research that describes nurse caring as constructed knowledge.

There is also considerable interest in qualitative studies both in research (Chaska, 1978; Leininger, 1985) and teaching (Crowley, 1988). In the latter, feminist nurse educators are looking carefully at case studies in nurse training to expose incidents of male domination (Roberts, 1983; Thompson, 1987; Yarling & McElmurray, 1986) and to encourage nurses to develop their own ethical ideals (Crowley, 1988).

In developing material for discussion of medical and nursing ethics, nurse educators are drawing on the work of feminist philosophers and ethicists (Hoagland, 1987; Houston & Diller, 1987; Noddings, 1984). Much of this work reflects the double concern about caring and the continued oppression of women, nurses in particular (Pence, 1987; Pitts, 1985; Veatch & Fry, 1987). Pitts (1985) and Yarling and McElmurray (1986) analyze a covert curriculum that socializes nurses to subordinate themselves and their ethical commitments to the authority of physicians. Taught formally to be patient advocates, nurses learn informally to remain silent even when physicians abuse patients (Crowley, 1988).

Summary

Nurse theorists have taken a courageous stand in affirming caring as the central concept in nursing. Drawing on their own experience, the history of nursing, humanist ideas in ethics and aesthetics, and feminist theory, they are beginning to build a coherent theory of nursing that is not subordinate to medical science. It is too early to predict whether nursing as a profession will survive the conflict it has joined, but its struggle is inspiring to all feminists engaged in the examination of professionalism.

Like legal theorists, nurses have also begun to think about feminist pedagogy. So far, pedagogies for nursing have concentrated on breaking free of oppression and remaining dedicated to human caring. Current interest in feminist epistemologies may eventually lead to full-blown feminist pedagogies, but at this time neither lawyers nor nurses have produced mature theories of teaching and learning.

EDUCATION

There are several reasons why one might predict considerable feminist influence on education at the university level. First, given the pronounced need for well-developed feminist pedagogies, one might expect a surge of interest in the teacher education community. Second, education is a blatantly hierarchical profession; professors of education are still mostly male, school administrators are overwhelmingly male, and school teachers are mostly female. This situation should invite feminist criticism. Third, education draws on literature from the disciplines and the professions, and both have been affected to some degree by feminism. (On the disciplines see DuBois, Kelly, Kennedy, Korsmeyer, & Robinson, 1985; Spender, 1981.)

Despite powerful reasons for predicting feminist influence, one's expectations are only partly met. Educationists have long been concerned with gender (Tyack & Hansot, 1988), but few have been interested in feminist theory. In contrast to law and nursing, writers in education draw relatively less often on the rich and growing body of feminist literature. A special issue of *Educational Researcher* (June/July 1986) was devoted to "The New Scholarship on Women," but even here few of the writers cited the feminist literature so familiar to theorists in other fields. There are important contributions to feminist theory in education and some writers do build on existing feminist theory, but so far this writing has had little impact on the mainstream of educational thought. The most prominent feminist influence is largely from individualist, first generation, perspectives. Feminist work in education is divided mainly into first and second generation thinking, and so far the two have not engaged in productive dialogue to construct what Kristeva calls third generation thought.

Education and Feminist Theory

The subject of sex differences, says Chipman (1988), has been "far too sexy a topic." Educational researchers and policymakers have concentrated on gender differences for over a century, and most of the differences uncovered have been small or unimportant. Yet such differences continue to intrigue professional educators, and some even make front page newspaper stories (Benbow & Stanley, 1980). Some studies explain patterns of differences in terms of biological factors (Maccoby & Jacklin, 1974), and others trace differences and difficulties to school factors (Frazier & Sadker, 1973; Sexton, 1969). Hochschild (1973) raised questions about the usefulness of research on gender differences in academic achievement 16 years ago, but the research goes on (Eccles, 1984, 1986a, 1986b; Hyde & Linn, 1986; Linn & Peterson, 1985). As Chipman (1988) comments, "Small average sex differences are important because ... Why?" (p. 49) Such criticism may now begin to push researchers into asking more useful questions.

In addition to the empirical study of sex differences in academic aptitudes and achievement, educators have long expressed normative views on the education of women. Some 19th century writers advocated a special form of academic education for women that would prepare them for their work as wives and mothers (Beecher, 1842/1977; Willard, 1819/1918); others declared that women could profit from studying whatever men studied (Nightingale, 1859/1969; Wollstonecraft, 1792/1975); and still others argued that women should not be exposed to male-style academic study because such study would shrivel their ovaries (Clarke, 1873).

This last illustrates a highly misogynist line of debate that followed

Darwin's *Origin of the Species* (1859/1964) and *Descent of Man* (1871). In Europe Paul Mobius (1908), a pathologist, declared women to be spiritually inferior, childlike, and incapable of reasoned thought. Forced to engage in intellectual activity, they would be incapacitated for breeding and turn into "useless hybrids." This kind of thinking was by no means rare; Mobius had considerable influence on other thinkers, including Freud (see Dijkstra, 1986). Misogynist thought built on Darwinian theory to suggest that evolution increases the intellectual gap between men and women (Weininger, 1903/1975). Indeed, such notions have been so persistent that Hubbard (1979), a contemporary feminist biologist, felt compelled to ask, "Have only men evolved?" and to expose the long history of sexism in science.

Educationists have been slow to recommend the incorporation of such material into either the school or university curriculum even though females might profit from an understanding of the forces that have kept them out of science, mathematics, and the professions. Feminist criticism suggests that an inclusion of misogynist material is vital for several reasons: First, it is part of history (Burstyn, 1986); second, to promote real change, it is necessary to show that male ideological bias has been pervasive and affects every facet of intellectual and political life (Ruether, 1983a); and, third, as Hubbard (1979) has pointed out and Chipman (1988) suggests, this line of thinking underlies the fascination with sex differences alluded to earlier. Following MacKinnon (1987), feminist critics object that a concentration on differences is unlikely to promote the cause of women.

In addition to the dominant educational research on sex and gender differences, there is a body of material generated by Marxist and critical theories (see, e.g., Apple, 1979, 1982, 1986; Bowles & Gintis, 1976; Carnoy & Levin, 1985; Giroux, 1983). This material concentrates mainly on the economic oppression of racism and classism and the role schools play in reproducing (and to a degree, resisting) that oppression. Some feminists argue that these writers tend to sustain "the very terms and prejudices of the system that they [attempt] to criticize" (Grumet, 1988, p. xiv). O'Brien (1981) has argued that Marxist and critical theorists fail to recognize the hard work of women in care-giving tasks as labor worthy of analysis, and I (Noddings, 1989b) have argued that these analyses entirely overlook the attitudes of love and care that are characteristic of many activities performed by women.

Another obvious difficulty with Marxist and critical theorists' analysis is that the peculiar features of women's oppression are lost in the focus on economic oppression. Not all women are economically oppressed, but all women have suffered patriarchal oppression. Feminists are understandably skeptical about assurances that race, class, and gender can all be studied effectively together simply because they are all forms of oppression. Just as feminist legal theorists had to break away from CLS (Menkel-Meadow, 1988) to focus on the experience of women, so feminist theorists in education feel the need to draw more heavily on feminist theory and the life experience of women. A main objection of feminist criticism in this area is the scarcity of feminist literature cited by Marxist/critical theorists. In an overview of a volume on class, race, and gender (Weis, 1988), for example, McCarthy and Apple (1988) include 100 reference notes; only 4 cite feminist sources.

Closely related to the objections to critical theory is a complaint against all forms of educational theory that retain man (white, middle class, liberally educated man) as the standard against whom all others are evaluated. In a series of important essays, Martin (1981, 1982a, 1982b, 1984, 1985, 1987b) argues that the school curriculum has been constructed around the public and productive interests of males. The experience of women in raising children, maintaining homes, caring for the ill and aged is entirely omitted from the disciplines traditionally constituting a liberal education. Martin advocates a "new ideal" of the educated person, one that will "bring women into educational thought" (1984). Grumet (1988), too, has argued for a curriculum that includes the experience of women and for autobiographical methods in both research and teaching. Another eloquent voice in this line of argument is that of Thompson (1985, 1986a, 1986b, 1986c), who recommends that the attitudes, skills, and interests of home economics be made more available to both girls and boys in the curriculum. Tetrault (1986b) has explored the place of women in the history curriculum and has also recommended a gender-balanced education (1986a). I, too, have explored what the curriculum might look like if the experience of women were its foundation (1987, 1989a, 1989b). These are all relational arguments that show considerable respect for second generation feminist thinking.

Although feminist arguments for radical changes in the curriculum have so far had little impact on mainstream curriculum theorists, feminist theories have generated lively discussion in the areas of ethics and moral education. The Kohlberg-Gilligan debate on moral reasoning has been central here and has spilled over into similar controversy on interpersonal understanding (see Gilligan, 1982; Lyons, 1983).

The feminist contribution to ethics and moral education is clearly relational; it rejects the traditional image of a lone moral agent struggling to sort principles and commit himself to a logically justifiable course of action. It concentrates on needs rather than rights (Gilligan, 1982; Noddings, 1984), dialogue among moral agents rather than the internal debate of a single moral agent (Haan, 1978; Lyons, 1983), the strength of maternal thinking (Noddings, 1989a; Ruddick, 1980), and the relationship between feminist thought and peace education (Boulding, 1981; Brock-Utne, 1985; Martin, 1984; Reardon, 1985; Ruddick, 1989). The debate has included philosophers as well as psychologists, sociologists, and educationists. (For an excellent review and critique of the material on ethics and moral education, which is much too extensive to summarize here, see Sichel, 1988; for one on feminism and peace studies, see Brock-Utne, 1985.)

Possibly the best known research on women in education appears in a line of thought that is largely individualist. This is the first generation mode of "the new scholarship on women" (Biklen & Shakeshaft, 1985). In the introduction to this section, I noted that this research may be criticized for its neglect of feminist theory and its impact on the disciplines, but it may still be categorized properly as feminist research. Edson (1988) comments on the view that feminist scholarship must proceed from a "recognizable feminist analytical perspective on the oppression and liberation of woman" (Dubois, Kelly, et al., 1985, p. 7) and admits that, from this perspective, her own work—and, by implication, most of the new scholarship on women that appears regularly in educational research—is not "feminist" (p. 5). But she offers an alternative clearly acceptable to first generation feminists when she notes that feminist scholarship addresses the experience of women in public life and includes a commitment to the betterment of women.

Edson's study of women in school administration and those by Schmuck (1975; 1987) and Shakeshaft (1985) document the difficulties women experience in trying to enter educational administration. In reading this work, one is struck by the persistent male domination of a profession that is largely female and by the sometimes blatant expressions of prejudice that women still encounter. One is also dismayed by the separation of female administrative aspirants from feminist thought. Their formal education has not included the rich bodies of thought on relational feminism or even that on women's history. The understanding of these hard-pressed women, revealed again and again (see Edson, 1988), is that each must prove herself to be equal to or better than male competitors. Although they see inequities clearly, they rarely express the idea that there is something fundamentally wrong with the entire structure of schooling. Their feminism, when it is confessed at all, is individualist.

Educational research is ripe for third generation thought. Both relational and individualist arguments contribute to the understanding of women's condition and to recommendations for change. Just as feminist legal theorists recognize that a choice must be made between assimilation and transformation, feminists in education need to define and debate the choice in education.

Education and Feminist Pedagogy

Like legal theorists, feminists in education have been torn between assimilation and transformation. Much effort has gone into securing equal opportunities for women within the standard mode of schooling (see Klein, 1985). Feminists have advocated an end to sex stereotyping in textbooks, greater funding for women's athletics, and more attention to female students in mathematics and science classes. They have also worked for an increase in the number of female school administrators. As in law, however, the outcomes have been mixed. Title IX, designed to protect equal opportunities for females in education, has been largely ignored (Tyack & Hansot, 1988). Women administrators are still scarce, particularly at the level of high school principal and superintendent (Edson, 1988). Changes in school textbooks have occurred, but these usually involve the inclusion of females in male activities. Males are rarely portrayed in female activities, and when they are, protests sometimes arise (Tyson-Bernstein, 1988; Vitz, 1986).

None of these efforts, important as they are, do much to develop a distinctly feminist pedagogy. Miller (1987) calls for teaching and learning that are "collaborative, cooperative, and interactive" (p. 52), and many feminist educators (e.g., Schuster, 1987) mention the ground-breaking work of Belenky, Clinchy, Goldberger, and Tarule in *Women's Ways of Knowing* (1986). Occasionally, we hear reports of feminist seminars in teacher education (Tetrault, 1987).

There are signs that a genuine feminist pedagogy is incubating. If there are not as many feminist courses and seminars in professional education as we would wish, there is at least a great deal of material to be discussed in them. The work of Grumet (1987a, 1987c, 1988) suggests powerful uses for autobiography in both teaching and research. Similarly, Pagano (1988) uses students' personal accounts as case study material in a teacher education curriculum. This work bears striking similarities to the feminist pedagogy developing in nursing.

Summary

There is considerable feminist activity in professional education. Most of it has been, and still is, motivated by what Kristeva calls first generation thinking. It is largely in the individualist mode and relies on mainstream educational theory. As in law, the results have been mixed. Pushing for equality, women have sometimes lost ground.

In addition to the politically important first generation work, a theoretically important body of material is growing out of second generation thought. This work relies mainly on relational arguments and draws heavily on feminist theory. In its tone, direction, and heritage it closely resembles the work of feminist legal theorists. Its potential is enormous, but it is too early to predict whether that potential will be realized.

It seems fair to say, however, that the greatest promise for fulfillment lies in a dialogue not yet realized—a productive conversation between first and second generation feminist thinkers. When that occurs, feminist educators will have some influence on both the disciplines and the professions through profound changes in curriculum and classroom practice.

SCHOOL TEACHING

It is hard to separate discussion of school teaching from that of professional education because the latter clearly has so much theoretical influence on the former; that is, much of what is written about school teaching comes from university educationists. In this section, I will confine discussion to recent proposals for the professionalization of school teaching and to feminist critiques of these proposals.

Given the earlier analysis of critiques in law, nursing, and professional education, several parallels and contrasts are evident. First, although there are feminist critiques in professional education that closely resemble those in legal theory, the dominant critiques of school teaching as a profession almost ignore the concerns of women. Second, the centrality of care giving, especially in elementary education, has long presented a conflict with the professionalization of teaching just as it has in nursing. Third, recent reform advocates' (Holmes Group, 1986) enthusiastic endorsement of liberal education, hierarchy, and increased control of accreditation should induce lively feminist objections of the sort already suggested by Virginia Woolf and Adrienne Rich.

The Professionalization of School Teaching

In the wake of renewed concerns about the quality of American education (National Commission on Excellence in Education, 1983), a movement has been initiated to professionalize teaching (Carnegie Task Force on Teaching as a Profession, 1986; Holmes Group, 1986). Early, critical reactions to this movement included doubts about the connection between professionalization and desirable effects for students. The question, still vitally important, was this: How is professionalization an answer to the problem of improving education for school children? This challenge did not come mainly from feminists (although it could have), and it is important to recognize that professionalization has been criticized by theorists other than feminists, just as legal theory has its critics in CLS as well as in feminist theory.

The main features of the Carnegie and Holmes reports are strikingly similar. Both recommend the establishment of standards controlled by the profession, an emphasis on graduate level professional training, and the creation of advanced positions in teaching (Sykes, 1987). The first recommendation has already been initiated in establishment of a National Board of Professional Teaching Standards, and work is under way on the development of prototypes for teacher assessment (Shulman, 1987). Reaction to this work raises serious questions concerning what teaching is about and the qualities that teachers must display to be considered good teachers (Wirsing, 1987). It also suggests concerns about the composition of the profession that will supposedly control its own standards (Freedman, 1988).

The Holmes Group's recommendation that the undergraduate education major be abolished is especially interesting. The recommendation is rationalized as a necessary part of professionalization (professional education in all respected professions is *graduate* education), even though present evidence suggests that elementary school teaching (for which teachers are usually prepared at the undergraduate level) is somewhat better than teaching in secondary schools, which in general requires graduate-level preparation. The Holmes writers admit that most observers evaluate teaching in elementary schools as "more lively, imaginative, and considerate of students" (Holmes Group, 1986, p. 16) than that observed in high schools, but they suggest that weaknesses at both levels can be remedied by strengthening the liberal arts component of undergraduate education and locating most professional education at the graduate level. This decision to brush aside the judgment of "most observers" underscores the cogency of the question cited at the outset: What *is* the connection between professionalization and better education for school children?

The third recommendation of the Carnegie and Holmes reports involves the establishment of career ladders or positions of advancement within teaching. Without such positions, it is argued, teachers who want to advance must leave the classroom for administration. With advanced levels of teaching responsibility, teachers can have real careers in teaching. The Holmes Group suggests a three-tiered system: novices or instructors (who will work under close supervision of professional teachers and can be licensed for no more than 5 years); professional teachers (who will hold master's degrees in teaching and will have passed various examinations in addition to those required for initial licensing as instructors); and career professionals (who will have fulfilled still more requirements and whose responsibilities will shift from direct contact with students to supervision, curriculum development, and other professional tasks). This recommendation, which introduces a new and rigidly defined hierarchy into teaching, raises a host of actual and possible objections from feminists.

Feminist Critiques

As in legal theory, there are several perspectives from which education and schooling are criticized. The dominant critiques of school teaching, however, are not feminist critiques; they are largely traditional in the sense that they place great faith in educational research and in a standard sociological description of professions. They might also be described as masculine insofar as they fail entirely to take account of feminine experience. Both the Carnegie and Holmes reports and most of the criticism leveled at them fall into this traditional masculinist category.

Criticism of the Holmes Group's recommendations has been plentiful. An entire issue of the *Teachers College Record* (Spring 1987) was devoted to such criticism. Although several writers criticized the Holmes prescription for hierarchy (see, e.g., Conley & Bacharach; Darling-Hammond; Feinberg; Raywid), none of these critiques is explicitly feminist. The only feminist critique (Martin, 1987a) concentrates on the important issue of rethinking liberal education.

However, in the same issue of the *Record,* Traver (1987) takes a feminist perspective in his review of the third *Handbook of Research on Teaching.* He finds the voices of both teachers and women strangely missing from the *Handbook*'s more than 1,000 pages. His observation underscores the contention I made earlier that feminist theory, despite its impressive growth, has not yet greatly influenced mainstream educational thought. Traver calls for attention to this body of literature and also to autobiographical method, which is eminently compatible with feminist methods (see Biklen, 1983; Elbaz, 1983; Grumet, 1988; Spencer, 1986).

Similarly, again in the same issue, Grumet (1987b) draws attention to the "excessively empirical" nature of many reviews of feminist scholarship in education. Such reviews promote an illusion of scholarly feminist activity in education when, in fact, much of the most exciting work in feminist theory has not been included in educational debate. Grumet points out that this empirical emphasis leads to a devaluation of significant work in philosophy, literature, and psychoanalysis.

The dominant critiques of professionalization, like those of education in general, leave the basic structures intact. A main complaint against the dominant critiques is that they ignore women's experience. They take for granted that people enter professions with an eye toward advancement in a hierarchy and power over others. Although neither the Holmes nor Carnegie groups can be accused of accepting the old stereotypes of women as passive, lacking drive, uninterested in intellectual work, and lukewarm in professional commitment (see Biklen, 1987), they do accept the masculine stereotypical notions of professional life. Hence, with no attention to the ways in which women work and divide their commitments, these critiques of a profession that has long been occupied by women (Freedman, 1988) are invitations to assimilate or get out.

There is considerable evidence that women teachers *are* deeply committed to their work with students (Biklen, 1987; Boston Women's Teachers' Group, 1983; Edson, 1988; Gilligan, 1982). Further, they do not see a sharp separation between their work as homemakers and teachers. They accept responsibility for the growth of others and derive deep satisfaction from their nurturing roles. The picture of deeply committed nurturers is very different from the earlier stereotype that was used as an excuse for women's absence in administrative positions. But it is still a picture that produces conflict in teachers as it does in nurses.

The centrality of caring in teaching and nursing has contributed to the devaluation of both occupations (Freedman, 1988). But whereas nursing is attempting to hold its ground through the development of sophisticated models of human caring, teaching is giving way to the domination of scientific methods and a medical model of professionalization. If this domination is allowed to continue, women may indeed be "weeded out of woman's true profession" (Freedman, 1988).

One difficulty seems to be that, aside from the writers mentioned, the powerful feminist critiques in education have not yet been focused on the professionalization of school teachers. The conflict is understandable. On the one hand, women teachers want to be professionals—that is, they want to be recognized as committed, effective teachers (Biklen, 1987)— but, on the other hand, they recognize that someone must do the care giving in this society, and they feel considerable anger when they are pressed to give up what they regard as central to their work. Their fear is that, in the new move to professionalization, teachers who move farther from actual contact with children will be regarded and rewarded as "more professional" than those who work directly with children. This is a potentially devastating criticism of the new recommendations.

Feminist critics evince great concern for children. It is not clear to them that the professionalization of teaching will benefit children. Their agenda would require beginning with families and children (Biklen, 1983; Grumet, 1988; Spencer, 1986). They might ask, How can teaching be restructured so that teachers who are parents can combine the two roles more effectively? Can we provide educational forms of child care on school campuses? Can we arrange for flexible teaching schedules and partnerships that will allow men and women who wish to spend more time parenting to do so without losing professional status and opportunities? Can we provide more time for teachers to be with their students, to develop caring relationships, and make shared decisions with them? (Noddings, 1988). These questions represent a different perspective on teaching and on life than those raised by advocates of professionalization.

Summary

School teaching, like nursing, suffers from a conflict between two models of professionalism. The model of human caring now under development as a theory of nursing is similar to the model of commitment to children embraced by many school teachers. From this perspective, a "professional" is a good, caring teacher. But teachers are now hard pressed to join the ranks of "true professionals," and this seems to involve a different form of commitment—one that requires more hours on the job site, more years of study, a visible drive to advance in a hierarchy, and some detachment from direct contact with students.

Feminist theory and criticism are growing in education as they are in legal theory, but first generation thought still dominates educational perspectives on women. Most of the work cited in mainstream literature accepts, implicitly or explicitly, the idea of assimilation: Women are just like men; they can and should be equally represented in all the fields men have dominated until now.

A new generation of feminists in law, nursing, and education urges both women and men to place a higher value on the activities traditionally called "women's work." They call for appreciative reflection on the qualities historically associated with women. These feminists want transformation, not assimilation, and they argue strongly that the welfare of women, men, and children alike depends on the choices we make now.

REFERENCES

Apple, M. W. (1979). *Ideology and curriculum.* Boston: Routledge & Kegan Paul.

Apple, M. W. (1982). *Education and power.* Boston: Routledge & Kegan Paul.

Apple, M. W. (1986). *Teachers and texts: A political economy of class and gender relations in education.* Boston: Routledge & Kegan Paul.

Associated Press. (1988, June 30). Nurses are upset with AMA. *Peninsula Times Tribune,* p. A-11.

Beecher, C. (1871). *Woman suffrage and woman's profession.* Hartford: Brown & Gross.

Beecher, C. (1977). *A treatise on domestic economy.* New York: Schocken Books. (Original work published 1842)

Belenky, M. F., Clinchy, B. M., Goldberger, N. R., & Tarule, J. M. (1986). *Women's ways of knowing.* New York: Basic Books.

Benbow, C. P., & Stanley, J. C. (1980). Sex differences in mathematical ability: Fact or artifact? *Science, 210,* 1262–1264.

Bender, L. (1988). A lawyer's primer on feminist theory and tort. *Journal of Legal Education, 38*(1&2), 3–38.

Biklen, S. K. (1983). *Teaching as an occupation for women: A case study of an elementary school.* Syracuse: Education Designs Group.

Biklen, S. K. (1987). Women in American elementary school teaching: A case study. In P. A. Schmuck (Ed.), *Women educators: Employees of schools in Western countries* (pp. 223–242). Albany: State University of New York Press.

Biklen, S. K., & Shakeshaft, C. (1985). The new scholarship on women. In S. S.

Klein (Ed.), *Handbook for achieving sex equity through education* (pp. 44–52). Baltimore: Johns Hopkins University Press.

Boston Women's Teachers' Group (S. Freedman, J. Jackson, & C. Boles). (1983). Teaching: An imperilled "profession." In L. S. Shulman & G. Sykes (Eds.), *Handbook of teaching and policy* (pp. 261–299). New York: Longman.

Boulding, E. (1981). Perspectives of women researchers on disarmament, national security and world order. *Women's Studies International Quarterly, 4*(1), 27–41.

Bowles, S., & Gintis, H. (1976). *Schooling in capitalist America.* New York: Basic Books.

Brockman, D. S. (1988, May). *Nurturing the human spirit in the work place: Caring for the nurse.* Paper presented at the Tenth National Research Care Conference, Boca Raton, FL.

Brock-Utne, B. (1985). *Educating for peace: A feminist perspective.* New York & Oxford: Pergamon Press.

Bunch, C., & Pollack, S. (Eds.). (1983). *Learning our way: Essays in feminist education.* Trumansburg, NY: Crossing Press.

Burstyn, J. N. (1986). Integrating the new scholarship on women into required courses in schools of education: The case of history. *Educational Researcher, 15*(6), 11–13.

Caring and nursing: Explorations in the feminist perspectives. (1988, June). Presentations at a conference sponsored by Doctoral Student Group and Center for Human Caring, Denver.

Carnegie Task Force on Teaching as a Profession. (1986). *A nation prepared.* New York: Carnegie Forum on Education and the Economy.

Carnoy, M., & Levin, H. (1985). *Schooling and work in the democratic state.* Stanford, CA: Stanford University Press.

Carper, B. (1978). Fundamental patterns of knowing in nursing. *Advances in Nursing Science, 1*(1), 13–23.

Chaska, N. (Ed.). (1978). *The nursing profession: Views through the mist.* New York: McGraw-Hill.

Chipman, S. F. (1988). Far too sexy a topic [Review of J. S. Hyde & M. C. Linn (Eds.), *The psychology of gender*]. *Educational Researcher, 17*(3), 46–49.

Clarke, E. H. (1873). *Sex in education.* Boston: Osgood.

Conley, S. C., & Bacharach, S. B. (1987). The Holmes Group report: Standards, hierarchies, and management. *Teachers College Record, 88*(3), 340–347.

Crowley, M. (1988). Feminist pedagogy: Nurturing the ethical ideal. In *Caring and nursing: explorations in the feminist perspectives* (pp. 300–317). Presentations at a conference sponsored by Doctoral Student Group and Center for Human Caring, Denver.

Culley, M., & Portuges, C. (Eds.) (1985). *Gendered subjects: The dynamics of feminist teaching.* Boston: Routledge & Kegan Paul.

Daly, M. (1973). *Beyond God the father.* Boston: Beacon Press.

Daly, M. (1978). *Gyn/ecology: The metaethics of radical feminism.* Boston: Beacon Press.

Daly, M. (1984). *Pure lust.* Boston: Beacon Press.

Darling-Hammond, L. (1987). Schools for tomorrow's teachers. *Teachers College Record, 88*(3), 354–358.

Darwin, C. (1871). *The descent of man.* London: J. Murray.

Darwin, C. (1964). *The origin of the species.* Cambridge, MA: Harvard University Press. (Original work published 1859)

Decter, M. (1983). The liberated woman. In M. B. Mahowald (Ed.), *Philosophy of woman* (pp. 34–41). Indianapolis: Hackett.

Dijkstra, B. (1986). *Idols of perversity.* New York & Oxford: Oxford University Press.

DuBois, E. C., Dunlap, M. C., Gilligan, C. J., MacKinnon, C. A., & Menkel-Meadow, C. J. (1985). Feminist discourse, moral values, and the law—a conversation. *Buffalo Law Review, 34*(1), 11–87.

DuBois, E. C., Kelly, G. P., Kennedy, E. L., Korsmeyer, C. W., & Robinson, L. S. (1985). *Feminist scholarship: Kindling in the groves of academe.* Urbana and Chicago: University of Illinois Press.

Dvorkin, E., Himmelstein, J., & Lesnick, H. (Eds.). (1981). *Becoming a lawyer: A humanistic perspective on legal education and professionalism.* St. Paul, MN: West.

Eccles, J. (1984). Sex differences in mathematics participation. In M. Steinkamp & M. Maehr (Eds.), *Women in science* (pp. 93–137). Greenwich, CT: JAI Press.

Eccles, J. S. (1986a). Gender-roles and women's achievement. *Educational Researcher, 15*(6), 15–19.

Eccles, J. (1986b, April). *Sex differences in achievement.* Paper presented at the annual meeting of the American Educational Research Association, San Francisco.

Edson, S. K. (1988). *Pushing the limits: The female administrative aspirant.* Albany: State University of New York Press.

Eisenstein, Z. (Ed.). (1979). *Capitalist patriarchy and the case for socialist feminism.* New York: Monthly Review Press.

Elbaz, F. (1983). *Teacher thinking: A study of practical knowledge.* New York: Nichols.

Etzioni, A. (Ed.). (1969). *The semi-professions and their organization: Teachers, nurses, and social workers.* New York: Free Press.

Feinberg, W. (1987). The Holmes Group report and the professionalization of teaching. *Teachers College Record, 88*(3), 366–377.

Ferguson, K. (1984). *The feminist case against bureaucracy.* Philadelphia: Temple University Press.

Finch, J., & Groves, D. (Eds.). (1983). *Labour of love: Women, work, and caring.* Boston: Routledge & Kegan Paul.

Frazier, N., & Sadker, M. (1973). *Sexism in school and society.* New York: Harper & Row.

Freedman, S. (1988, May). *Weeding woman out of "woman's true profession"—A critical look at professionalizing teaching.* Paper presented at the annual meeting of Professors of Curriculum, Boston.

French, M. (1985). *Beyond power.* New York: Summit Books.

Frug, M. J. (1979). Securing job equality for women: Labor market hostility to working mothers. *Boston University Law Review, 59,* 55–103.

Frug, M. J. (1985). Re-reading contracts: A feminist analysis of a contracts casebook. *American University Law Review, 34,* 1065–1140.

Frye, M. (1983). *The politics of reality: Essays in feminist theory.* Trumansburg, NY: Crossing Press.

Gaut, D. (1979). *An application of the Kerr-Soltis model to the concept of caring in nursing education.* Unpublished doctoral dissertation, University of Washington.

Gilligan, C. J. (1982). *In a different voice.* Cambridge: Harvard University Press.

Giroux, H. (1983). *Theory and resistance in education: A pedagogy for the opposition.* South Hadley, MA: Bergin & Garvey.

Glazer, N. (1984). Servants to capital: Unpaid domestic labor and paid work. *Review of Radical Political Economics, 16*(1), 61–87.

Glazer, N. (1988). Overlooked, overworked: Women's unpaid and paid work in the health services "cost crisis." *International Journal of Health Services, 18*(1), 119–137.

Goldstein, R. D. (1988). *Mother-love and abortion.* Berkeley and Los Angeles: University of California Press.

Gordon, R. (1982). New developments in legal theory. In D. Kairys (Ed.), *The politics of law: A progressive critique.* New York: Pantheon Books.

Greenwood, E. (1957). Attributes of a profession. *Social Work, 2,* 45–55.

Grimshaw, J. (1986). *Philosophy and feminist thinking.* Minneapolis: University of Minnesota Press.

Grumet, M. R. (1987a). The politics of personal knowledge. *Curriculum Inquiry, 17*(3), 319–329.

Grumet, M. R. (1987b). [Review of E. C. DuBois, G. P. Kelly, E. L. Kennedy, C. W. Korsmeyer, & L. S. Robinson, *Feminist scholarship: Kindling in the groves of academe.* Champaign: University of Illinois Press.] *Teachers College Record, 88*(3), 474–478.

Grumet, M. R. (1987c). Women and teaching: Homeless at home. *Teacher Education Quarterly, 14*(2), 39–46.

Grumet, M. R. (1988). *Bitter milk.* Amherst: University of Massachusetts Press.

Haan, N. (1978). Two moralities in action contexts: Relationship to thought, ego regulation, and development. *Journal of Personality and Social Psychology, 36,* 286–305.

Hantzis, C. W. (1988). Kingsfield and Kennedy: Reappraising the male models of law school teaching. *Journal of Legal Education, 38*(1&2), 155–164.

Harding, S., & Hintikka, M. B. (Eds.). (1983). *Discovering reality: Feminist perspectives on epistemology, metaphysics, methodology, and philosophy of science.* Dordrecht, Holland: D. Reidel.

Hoagland, S. (1987). Moral agency under oppression: Beyond praise and blame. *Trivia, 10,* 24–40.

Hochschild, A. (1973). A review of sex role research. In J. Huber (Ed.), *Changing women in a changing society* (pp. 249–267). Chicago: University of Chicago Press.

Holmes Group. (1986). *Tomorrow's teachers.* East Lansing, MI: Author.

Houston, B., & Diller, A. (1987). Trusting ourselves to care. *Resources for Feminist Research, 16*(3), 35–38.

Hubbard, R. (1979). Have only men evolved? In R. Hubbard, M. Henifen, & B. Fried (Eds.), *Biological woman: The convenient myth* (pp. 17–46). Cambridge, MA: Schenkman.

Hyde, J. S., & Linn, M. C. (Eds.). (1986). *The psychology of gender: Advances through meta-analysis.* Baltimore: Johns Hopkins University Press.

Jaff, J. (1986). Frame-shifting: An empowering methodology for teaching and learning legal reasoning. *Journal of Legal Education, 36,* 249–267.

Jaggar, A. M. (1983). *Feminist politics and human nature.* Totowa, NJ: Rowman & Allanheld.

Keen, P. (1988). Caring for each other. In *Caring and nursing: explorations in the feminist perspectives* (pp. 272–299). Presentations at a conference sponsored by Doctoral Student Group and Center for Human Caring, Denver.

Kennedy, D. (1983). *Legal education and the reproduction of hierarchy—A polemic against the system.* Cambridge, MA: Harvard University Press.

Klein, R. (1987). The dynamics of the women's studies classroom: A review essay of the teaching practice of women's studies in higher education. *Women's Studies International Forum, 10,* 187–206.

Klein S. S. (Ed.). (1985). *Handbook for achieving sex equity through education.* Baltimore and London: Johns Hopkins University Press.

Knowlden, V. (1988). Nurse caring as constructed knowledge. In *Caring and nursing: Explorations in the feminist perspectives* (pp. 319–339). Presentations at a conference sponsored by Doctoral Student Group and Center for Human Caring, Denver.

Kristeva, J. (1982). Women's time. In N. O. Keohane, M. Z. Rosaldo, & B. C. Gelpi (Eds.), *Feminist theory: A critique of ideology* (pp. 31–54). Chicago: University of Chicago Press.

Larson, M. S. (1977). *The rise of professionalism.* Berkeley: University of California Press.

Leininger, M. (1984). Care: The essence of nursing and health. In M. Leininger (Ed.), *Care: The essence of nursing and health* (pp. 3–15). Thorofare, NJ: Slack.

Leininger, M. (Ed.). (1985). *Qualitative research methods in nursing.* New York: Grune & Stratton.

Lewin, T. (1988, September 30). For feminist scholars, second thoughts on law and order. *New York Times,* p. B-1.

Linn, M. C., & Peterson, A. C. (1985). Emergence and characterization of sex differences in spatial ability: A meta-analysis. *Child Development, 56,* 1479–1498.

Lyons, N. P. (1983). Two perspectives: On self, relationships and morality. *Harvard Educational Review, 53,* 125–145.

Maccoby, E. E., & Jacklin, C. N. (1974). *The psychology of sex differences.* Stanford, CA: Stanford University Press.

MacKinnon, C. A. (1987). *Feminism unmodified.* Cambridge, MA: Harvard University Press.

MacPherson, K. I. (1983, January). Feminist methods: A new paradigm for nursing research. *Advances in Nursing Science, 5*(2), 17–25.

Martin, J. R. (1981). Sophie and Emile: A case study of sex bias in the history of educational thought. *Harvard Educational Review, 51,* 357–372.

Martin, J. R. (1982a). Excluding women from the educational realm. *Harvard Educational Review, 52*(2), 133–148.

Martin, J. R. (1982b). Two dogmas of curriculum. *Synthese, 51,* 5–20.

Martin, J. R. (1984). Bringing women into educational thought. *Educational Theory, 34*(4), 341–354.

Martin, J. R. (1985). *Reclaiming a conversation.* New York and London: Yale University Press.

Martin, J. R. (1987a). Reforming teacher education, rethinking liberal education. *Teachers College Record, 88,* 406–410.

Martin, J. R. (1987b). Transforming moral education. *Journal of Moral Education, 16*(3), 204–213.

McCarthy, C., & Apple, M. W. (1988). Race, class, and gender in American educational research: Toward a nonsynchronous parallelist position. In L. Weis (Ed.), *Class, race, and gender in American education* (pp. 9–39). Albany: State University of New York Press.

Menkel-Meadow, C. J. (1988). Feminist legal theory, critical legal studies, and legal education or "The fem-crits go to law school." *Journal of Legal Education, 38*(1&2), 61–86.

Millenson, M. L. (1988, July 24). Nurses prescribe doses of TLC. *Chicago Tribune,* p. 4.

Miller, J. L. (1987). Women as teachers/researchers: Gaining a sense of ourselves. *Teacher Education Quarterly, 14*(2), 52–58.

Miller, K. L. (1988). A study of nursing's feminist ideology. In *Caring and nursing: Explorations in the feminist perspectives* (pp. 57–77). Presentations at a conference sponsored by Doctoral Student Group and Center for Human Caring, Denver.

Minow, M. (1987). Supreme court foreward: Justice engendered. *Harvard Law Review, 101,* 10–95.

Mitchell, J., & Oakley, A. (1986). *What is feminism: A reexamination.* New York: Pantheon.

Mobius, P. (1908). *Ueber den physiologischen schwachsinn des weibes.* Halle: Carl Marholm.

National Commission on Excellence in Education. (1983). *A nation at risk.* Washington, DC: U.S. Government Printing Office.

Nightingale, F. (1969). *Notes on nursing: What it is, and what it is not.* New York: Dover. (Original work published 1859)

Noddings, N. (1984). *Caring: A feminine approach to ethics and moral education.* Berkeley and Los Angeles: University of California Press.

Noddings, N. (1987). Do we really want to produce good people? *Journal of Moral Education, 16*(3), 177–188.

Noddings, N. (1988). An ethic of caring and its implications for instructional arrangements. *American Journal of Education, 96*(2), 215–230.

Noddings, N. (1989a). Shaping an acceptable child. In A. Garrod (Ed.), *Learning for a lifetime: Moral education in perspective and practice.* Dartmouth: University Press of New England.

Noddings, N. (1989b). *Women and evil.* Berkeley and Los Angeles: University of California Press.

O'Brien, M. (1981). *The politics of reproduction.* Boston: Routledge & Kegan Paul.

Offen, K. (1988). Defining feminism: A comparative historical approach. *Signs, 14*(1), 119–157.

Olsen, F. (1984). Statutory rape: A feminist critique of rights analysis. *Texas Law Review, 63,* 387–432.

Pagano, J. (1988). The claim of philia. In W. F. Pinar (Ed.), *Curriculum theory discourses* (pp. 514–530). Scottsdale, AZ: Gorsuch Skarisbrick.

Pence, T. (1987). Approaches to nursing ethics. *Philosophy in Context: An Examination of Applied Philosophy, 17,* 7–16.

Pickard, T. (1983). Experience as teacher: Discovering the politics of law teaching. *University of Toronto Law Journal, 33,* 279–314.

Piercy, M. (1982). Unlearning not to speak. In M. Piercy (Ed.), *Circles in the water.* New York: Knopf.

Pitts, T. (1985). The covert curriculum. *Nursing Outlook, 33*(1), 37–39, 42.

Raywid, M. A. (1987). Tomorrow's teachers and today's schools. *Teachers College Record, 88*(3), 411–418.

Reardon, B. A. (1985). *Sexism and the war system.* New York: Teachers College Press.

Reverby, S. (1987). *Ordered to care.* Cambridge, England: Cambridge University Press.

Rhode, D. L. (1988). Perspectives on professional women. *Stanford Law Review, 40*(5), 1163–1207.

Rich, A. (1979). *On lies, secrets, and silence.* New York & London: W. W. Norton.

Rifkin, J. (1980). Toward a theory of law and patriarchy. *Harvard Women's Law Journal, 3,* 83–95.

Roberts, S. J. (1983). Oppressed group behavior: Implications for nursing. *Advances in Nursing Science, 5*(4), 21–31.

Ruddick, S. (1980). Maternal thinking. *Feminist Studies, 6*(2), 342–367.

Ruddick, S. (1989). *Maternal thinking: Towards a politics of peace.* Boston: Beacon Press.

Ruether, R. R. (1983a). The feminist critique in religious studies. In E. Langland & W. Gove (Eds.), *A feminist perspective in the academy* (pp. 52–66). Chicago: University of Chicago Press.

Ruether, R. R. (1983b). *Sexism and God-talk.* Boston: Beacon Press.

Scales, A. (1986). The emergence of a feminist jurisprudence: An essay. *Yale Law Journal, 95,* 1373–1403.

Scheman, N. (1983). Individualism and the objects of psychology. In S. Harding & M. B. Hintikka (Eds.), *Discovering reality: Feminist perspectives on epistemology, metaphysics, methodology and philosophy of science* (pp. 225–244). Dordrecht, Holland: D. Reidel.

Schlegel, J. (1984). Notes toward an intimate, opinionated, and affectionate history of the Conference on Legal Studies. *Stanford Law Review, 36,* 391–411.

Schmuck, P. A. (1975). *Sex differentials in public school administration.* Arlington, VA: National Council of Women in Educational Administration.

Schmuck, P. A. (Ed.). (1987). *Women educators: Employees of schools in Western countries.* Albany: State University of New York Press.

Schuster, D. T. (1987). Adult development and learning: New lessons for teacher education. *Teacher Education Quarterly, 14*(2), 68–76.

Sexton, P. C. (1969). *The feminized male: Classrooms, white collars, and the decline of manliness.* New York: Random House.

Shakeshaft, C. (1985). Strategies for overcoming the barriers to women in educational administration. In S. S. Klein (Ed.), *Handbook for achieving sex equity through education* (pp. 124–144). Baltimore: Johns Hopkins University Press.

Sheston, M. L. (1988, May). *Caring in nursing education: The development of a construct.* Paper presented at the Tenth National Research Care Conference, Boca Raton, FL.

Shulman, L. S. (1987, September). Assessment for teaching: An initiative for the profession. *Phi Delta Kappan, 69*(1), 38–44.

Sichel, B. A. (1988). *Moral education.* Philadelphia: Temple University Press.

Smith, D. E. (1987). *The everyday world as problematic: A feminist sociology.* Boston: Northeastern University Press.

Smith, J. (1981). The idea of health: A philosophic inquiry. *Advances in Nursing Science, 3*(3), 43–50.

Smith, P. (1970). *Daughters of the promised land.* Boston and Toronto: Little, Brown.

Smith, S. K. (1988). A feminist analysis of constructs of health. In *Caring and nursing: Explorations in the feminist perspectives* (pp. 341–362). Presentations at a conference sponsored by Doctoral Student Group and Center for Human Caring, Denver.

Sommers, T., & Shields, L. (1987). *Women take care.* Gainesville, FL: Triad.

Spencer, D. A. (1986). *Contemporary women teachers: Balancing school and home.* New York: Longman.

Spender, D. (1980). *Man made language.* London: Routledge & Kegan Paul.

Spender, D. (1981). *Men's studies modified: The impact of feminism on the academic disciplines.* Oxford: Pergamon Press.

Sykes, G. (1987, April). *Teaching and professionalism: A cautionary perspective.* Paper presented at Michigan State University.

Teachers College Record. (1987). *88*(3).

Tetrault, M. K. (1986a). The journey from male-defined to gender-balanced education. *Theory into Practice, 25,* 227–234.

Tetrault, M. K. (1986b). Thinking about women: The case of United States history textbooks. *The History Teacher, 19,* 211–262.

Tetrault, M. K. (1987). The scholarship on women in teacher education: A case study of Lewis and Clark College. *Teacher Education Quarterly, 14*(2), 77–83.

Thompson, J. L. (1987). Critical scholarship: The critique of domination in nursing. *Advances in Nursing Science, 10,* 27–38.

Thompson, P. J. (1985, June). *Clio's stepdaughters: Reclaiming our heritage.* Paper presented at the annual meeting of the American Home Economics Association, Philadelphia.

Thompson, P. J. (1986a). Beyond gender: Equity issues in home economics education. *Theory into Practice, 25,* 276–283.

Thompson, P. J. (1986b). Hestian hermeneutics. In L. Peterat (Ed.), *The conversation and company of educated women: A colloquy on home economics education* (pp. 79–87). Urbana-Champaign: University of Illinois.

Thompson, P. J. (1986c). Home economics and the Hestian mode. *Illinois Teacher of Home Economics, 29*(3), 87–91.

Traver, R. (1987). Autobiography, feminism, and the study of teaching [Review of M. C. Wittrock (Ed.), *Handbook of research on teaching* (3rd ed.)] *Teachers College Record 88*(3), 443–452.

Tyack, D., & Hansot, E. (1988). Silence and policy talk: Historical puzzles about gender and education. *Educational Researcher, 17*(3), 33–41.

Tyson-Bernstein, H. (1988). *A conspiracy of good intentions: America's textbook fiasco.* Washington, DC: Council for Basic Education.

Veatch, R. M., & Fry, S. T. (1987). *Case studies in nursing ethics.* London: J. B. Lippincott.

Vetterling-Braggin, M., Elliston, F., & English, J. (Eds.). (1977). *Feminism and philosophy.* Boston: Little, Brown.

Vitz, P. E. (1986). Religion and traditional values in public school textbooks. *The Public Interest, 84,* 88–89.

Waerness, K. (1984). The rationality of caring. *Economic and Industrial Democracy, 5*(2), 185–212.

Ward, D. (1988). Gender and cost in caring. In *Caring and nursing: Explorations in the feminist perspectives* (pp. 156–165). Presentations at a conference sponsored by Doctoral Student Group and Center for Human Caring, Denver.

Watson, J. (1979). *Nursing: The philosophy and science of caring.* Boston: Little, Brown.

Watson, J. (1985). *Nursing: Human science and human care.* Norwalk, CT: Appleton-Century-Crofts.

Webster, D. (1988). Mental health: the politics of self-care. In *Caring and nursing: Explorations in the feminist perspectives* (pp. 182–211). Presentations at a conference sponsored by Doctoral Student Group and Center for Human Caring, Denver.

Weininger, O. (1975). *Sex and character.* New York: AMS Press. (Original work published 1903)

Weis, L. (Ed.). (1988). *Class, race, and gender in American education.* Albany: State University of New York Press.

Wildman, S. M. (1988). The question of silence: Techniques to ensure full class participation. *Journal of Legal Education, 38*(1&2), 147–154.

Willard, E. (1918). *A plan for improving female education.* Middlebury, VT: Middlebury College. (Original work published 1819)

Wirsing, M. E. (1987). Holmes and Carnegie: The myth of bold new reform. *Teacher Education Quarterly, 14*(1), 40–51.

Welch, M. (1988). The context of nursing and feminism in nineteenth century England. In *Caring and nursing: Explorations in the feminist perspectives* (pp. 95–109). Presentations at a conference sponsored by Doctoral Student Group and Center for Human Caring, Denver.

Wollstonecraft, M. (1975). *A vindication of the rights of woman.* New York: W. W. Norton. (Original work published 1792)

Woolf, V. (1966). *Three guineas.* New York: Harcourt Brace. (Original work published 1938)

Yarling, R. R., & McElmurray, B. J. (1986). The moral foundation of nursing. *Advances in Nursing Science, 8*(2), 63–75.

Yaros, P. S. (1988). The feminist movement and the science and profession of nursing: Analogies and paradoxes. In *Caring and nursing: Explorations in the feminist perspectives* (pp. 111–121). Presentations at a conference sponsored by Doctoral Student Group and Center for Human Caring, Denver.

Zegans, L. S. (1987). The embodied self: Personal integration in health and illness. *Advances in Nursing Science, 4,* 29–45.